# SOCIOLOGY

THE DISCIPLINE AND ITS DIMENSIONS

# SOCIOLOGY

## THE DISCIPLINE AND ITS DIMENSIONS

An Introductory Sociology
*for*
All India Civil Service Examinees,
Undergraduate Students, General Readers

Parimal B. Kar

*To be had of*

New Central Book Agency (P) Ltd

LONDON
HYDERABAD ERNAKULAM BHUBANESWAR
NEW DELHI KOLKATA PUNE GUWAHATI

**NCBA**

REGD OFFICE
8/1 Chintamoni Das Lane, Kolkata 700 009, India
email: ncbapvtltd@eth.net

OVERSEAS
NCBA (UK) Ltd, 149 Park Avenue North, Northampton, NN3 2HY, UK
email: ncbauk@yahoo.com

EXPORT
NCBA Exports Pvt. Ltd, 212 Shahpur Jat, New Delhi 110 049
email: ncbaexports@ncbapvtltd.com

BRANCHES

2/27 Ansari Road, 1st Floor
Daryaganj, **New Delhi** 110 002
email: ncbadel@ncbapvtltd.com

House No. 3-1-315, 1st Floor
Nimboliadda, Kachiguda, **Hyderabad** 500 027
email: ncbahydb@ncbapvtltd.com

Shop Nos. 3 & 4, Vinayak Towers
681/B Budhwar Peth, Appa Balwant Chowk
**Pune** 411 002
email: ncbapune@ncbapvtltd.com

GSS Shopping Complex, 1st Floor
Opposite College Post Office, Convent Road
**Ernakulam** 682 035
0484-4021054/53

Shop No. 15, Bharati Towers, Ground Floor
Forest Park
**Bhubaneswar** 751 001
email: ncbabub@ncbapvtltd.com

Radhamayee Complex (Second Floor)
Opp. SBI, Panbazar, Jaswanta Road
**Guwahati** 781 001
email: ncbaguwahati@ncbapvtltd.com

**SOCIOLOGY** • Parimal B. Kar



Second Edition: July 1990
Reprinted: January 2005
Reprinted: March 2009
Reprinted: March 2012
Reprinted: January 2017

PUBLISHER
Central Educational Enterprises (P) Ltd
54B Patuatola Lane, Kolkata 700 009

TYPESETTER
New Central Book Agency (P) Ltd
8/1 Chintamoni Das Lane, Kolkata 700 009

PRINTER
New Central Book Agency (P) Ltd
Web-Offset Division, Dhulagarh, Sankrail, Howrah

COVER DESIGNER
Siddhartha Kar

PROJECT TEAM
Joydeep Ghosh and Prabhat Jas

ISBN: 978 81 7381 156 2

Price ₹ 285.00

# PREFACE TO THE SECOND EDITION

The first edition of the book was exhausted within a fairly brief period of time. For unavoidable reasons, the book has been out of print for over a year now.

In the second edition, a new chapter of 'Race' has been added. Besides, new sections on the following subjects have been included. 1. State of Socialisation (Ch. V). 2. Regionalism in India (Ch.VI). 3. A note on sanskritization (Ch. X). 4. Caste among the non-Hindus (Ch. X). 5. Inter relationship ofinstitutions (Ch. XIV). 6. Kinship in Indian culture (Ch. XVI). 7. A detailed analysis of jajmani system (Ch. XVII). 8. Proudhon on property (Ch. XVII). 9. Contribution of Montesquieu and Tocqueville to political sociology (Ch. XVII). 10. Religion and Morality (Ch. XX). 11. Alternative theories of the rise of capitalism (Ch. XXII). 12. The concept of Westernization (Ch. XXII).

I hope the new edition will be found useful by those for whom the book has been written.

I should like to thank Sri Jogendra Nath Sen for the interest and care he has taken in the publication of the second edition.

*49/1, Gurupada Haldar Road,*
*Calcutta 700 026*

PARIMAL B. KAR

## Author

Sri Parimal B. Kar joined Scottish Church College as a Lecturer in Economics and Political Science in 1949 and a year later he moved to Asutosh College, Calcutta.

For over ten years, Sri Kar was actively involved as a volunteer in community development work. In 1956 he underwent Village Apprenticeship Training organised jointly by the Ford Foundation, Calcutta University and the Development Department, Government of West Bengal. As a part of this training, he had first-hand experience of working with Village Level Workers (VLWs) in diverse fields. Many of his articles on Work Camps and Fundamental Education were published by the Co-ordination Committee for International Voluntary Work Camps, UNESCO, Paris. The pilot project on Youth and Social Service which he organised on behalf of Asutosh College was recognised in 1957 as one of the five UNESCO Associated Youth Enterprises in S. E. Asia. He chaired the working group on 'Education of youth for social and international responsibility' at the 11th UNESCO Conference of Organisers of International Voluntary Work Camps, held in New Delhi in 1958.

He has travelled extensively in India and abroad. He participated in an international seminar in 1958 in Thailand on 'The role of youth in a changing society', organised by the American Friends' Service Committee in collaboration with the Thai Ministry of Education and UNESCO. In 1960 he went to the U.S.A. on a grant under the Educational Exchange Program of the Government of the U.S.A. During this trip he studied first-hand various social welfare agencies in that country, and took a course on Social Group Work at the School of Applied Social Sciences, Western Reserve University, Cleveland, U.S.A. He also studied first-hand youth services in England, France and West Germany.

His book entitled *An Outline of Sociology* was published in 1964. Another text book on sociology in Bengali entitled *Samajtattwa* was published in 1974 by the West Bengal State Book Board. The book has run into four editions so far. He has written two books for neo-literates one of which won from the Government of India a national award in 1979.

# PREFACE TO THE FIRST EDITION

This book is intended for the use of those who appear at the All-India Civil Service Examinations with Sociology as an optional paper as well as for undergraduate students and the general reader.

Alexander Pope wrote in the early eighteenth century : "The proper study of mankind is man." We know from our own experience that man is, by nature, a gregarious animal. And Fichte reminded us that "man becomes man only among men." This book is a systematic study of man in the company of men, of *Man in Society* from different aspects. By reflecting on the different patterns and textures of social relations, we can understand better our own behaviour and that of our fellows.

Sociology has a long past but comparatively a short history. The science of society is a relatively new discipline. In some ways, it is a composite of several older disciplines. A study of the science of society, therefore, requires exploration in very broad terms of these older fields of knowledge, such as economics, political science, history, geography, biology, etc., in order to form an idea of the various dimensions of the subject. An attempt has been made in this book to indicate these dimensions.

In this book I have tried to present, in broad terms, the views of eminent sociologists on various aspects of society. I have explained these theoretical concepts by illustrations drawn from the Indian scene. I have treated the subject in a way that might give the impression that there is a consensus among sociologists on all topics covered by this book. In fact, this is far from true. There are differences and disagreements among sociologists. There are problems which are yet to be resolved. I have, however, referred to a few controversial matters which concern sociologists and have briefly presented their varying perspectives without any attempt at bringing about a synthesis among these different points of view. The readers may arrive at their own conclusions after having considered the perspectives of different writers. If the readers are intellectually stimulated to do this exercise, the labour put in by the author would be amply compensated.

Discerning readers will not fail to notice that the topics covered by this book are arranged in a logical order. They are advised to think over this arrangement and to try to reflect on this logical order. That would enable them to have an insight into what may be called the social order.

My intellectual debt to the great masters of sociology is immense. I have acknowledged this debt in appropriate places in the book. Their influence upon my thinking is so deep and abiding that in a few places their phrases may have gone into the book without acknowledgment. For all such possible lapses, I offer my apologies. I missed acknowledging in the book my debt to Marion J. Levy, Jr., and Francesca M. Cancian on whose two articles on Functional Analysis in the International Encyclopaedia of the Social Sciences (Volumes 5 and 6) I relied heavily in writing the section on Structural-Functional Analysis.

My special gratitude goes to my wife without whose encouragement the book would never have been begun and without whose kindly insistence it would never have been finished. I offer my thanks to Prof. R. K. Ghosh, Head of the Department of Mathematics, St. Xavier's College, Calcutta, and Dean of Studies, Institute of Modern Management, Calcutta, for the kind interest he took in the publication of the book.

The cover design is by my nephew, Siddhartha Kar, whom I thank heartily for the nice job he has done.

I should also like to thank Sri Swadesh Sen for the care and interest he took in the expeditious publication of the book.

7A, Amrita Banerjee Road,
Calcutta 700 026

PARIMAL B. KAR

# CONTENTS

CONTENTS

# SOCIOLOGY
# THE DISCIPLINE AND ITS DIMENSIONS

## CHAPTER – ONE

## DEFINING SOCIOLOGY

### 1. THE STORY OF SOCIOLOGY

What is Sociology about ? What is the main object of sociological study ?

At first glance, the answer is simple. Sociology studies the behaviour of human beings in society. It may, however, be rightly pointed out that other social sciences, such as Political Science, Economics, History, etc., do the same. How is Sociology different from these disciplines ?

This point can be explained very simply with the help of the following illustration : "Eating a slice of buttered toast for breakfast can be analysed in terms of the nutritive value of the food consumed, the eating habits of individuals, the economics of the bread, dairy, and home-appliance industries, a conventional or customary dietary pattern, or even as a possible source of social friction because the wife does not make the toast dark enough to suit her husband's taste."[1] The key words in this statement — 'nutritive value', 'individual habits', 'economics of industries', 'conventional customary patterns' and 'social friction' — are drawn from the following disciplines : nutrition, psychology, economics, and sociology.

This illustration makes two things clear : (i) that it is always the *focus* of interest which distinguishes one social science from another, and (ii) that sociology is concerned with social relationships, with relationship of man to man, with human interactions. The life of man is many-sided. For instance, he is an economic man, a political being, a social man, or a man devoted mainly to religious pursuits. But whatever he does in these various capacities, *man relates himself to man.* Thus, "if two people meet in the market place, they are not just two 'economic men', but two human beings, and they enter into relationships that are not simply economic". Sociology studies this *social* aspect of man. Sociology differs from other social sciences in this particular respect. No other social science takes the study of social relationship as its central theme. The focus of interest of all other social sciences is different. Economics, for instance, is concerned with a man in his capacity as a manufacturer or a trader, a buyer or a seller, and the relationships he enters into in these capacities. Similarly, political science is concerned with a man in his capacity as a citizen, a voter, a candidate in an election for a political office, or a campaigner for a political cause.

Sociology does not, however, study everything that happens in society or under social conditions. For example, sociologists study religion only in so far as it affects social relationships, i.e., the relationship of man to man, of one group to another, or of one group to the whole society. They do not study religion as such, i.e., its theology, beliefs, rituals, etc. Likewise, sociologists are interested in political organisations or in economic institutions only in so far as they have a bearing on the social life of man. They will study, for example, economic division of labour only to the extent that it affects human relationships.

While dealing with the elements of 'human relationship' in diverse fields covered by various social sciences, sociology seeks to discover the interrelationships of human activities in these fields — familial, educational, economic, political or religious. The basic assumption on which the sociologists proceed is that what happens in any of these fields affects others. In other words, sociology is concerned with the 'whole' of human society, and not with the 'parts' which make up the 'whole'. Seen thus, sociology is not "the great residual category of the social sciences".

The purpose of sociological study is not, however, simply to describe social relationships, but also to analyse them and to discriminate between their specific forms, varieties and patterns. The sociologists are expected to look ahead and to suggest guideposts for social action in response to the changes which give rise to social problems.

In the 19th century a French philosopher named Auguste Comte (1798 - 1857) gave the name 'Sociology' to this new social science. 'Sociology' is composed of two words : *socius* meaning companion or associate, and *logos* meaning word. Thus, the term formed from these two words means talking about society, as Geology (*geos* meaning earth) means talking about the earth, Biology (*bios* meaning life) means talking about life and Anthropology (*anthropos* meaning man) means talking about man. *Socius* is a Latin word and *Logos* is a Greek word, and the name of our discipline is thus a hybrid offspring of two languages.

Since the dawn of civilization man has been concerned with his life among his associates. Both the problems and promises of common living excited him and agitated his restless and inquisitive mind. Various social sciences gradually evolved in response to the varied needs of common living. All such enquiries were once a part of philosophy. Philosophy embraced all fields in an undifferentiated and amorphous fashion. With the passage of time, however, one by one the various social sciences "cut the apron strings", as it were, and began to pursue separate and independent paths of their own. The name 'political philosophy' bears witness to this development. Political philosophers inquired into the evolution of the state, the growth and nature of state authority, the relationship between the citizens on the one hand and the state authority on the other and various other problems and concerns of a political nature. Likewise, economics, as a separate and independent social science, inquired into the problems concerning production and distribution of commodities as well as the larger questions of economic growth. In this manner, various other social sciences, such as anthropology, psychology or the science of the behaviour of men, gradually evolved. Sociology is the youngest of these social sciences. The evolution of this youngest social science is a fascinating story. Auguste Comte coined the term 'sociology' to designate this youngest social science during the first half of the eighteenth century. But we have to look back to the preceding one hundred years (1750 - 1850) in order to identify properly the forces which were primarily responsible for the growth of sociology as an independent discipline.

During the second half of the eighteenth century a few far-reaching changes had occurred in Western Europe. These changes agitated the minds of the people and made them keenly conscious of what had happened around them. To begin with, the industrial revolution of England was one such event of tremendous social significance. It not only revolutionised the method of production; it also brought about far-reaching social changes. For instance, industrial revolution brought in its wake labour-capital dispute, the problems of ensuring social and economic security to industrial workers, the problems of housing, the gradual disappearance of once peaceful and stable rural communities and increasing concentration of people in urban areas. All on a sudden the people were brought face to face with problems which they or their forefathers had never experienced before. These challenges stirred deeply the minds of men. And they began to ponder over ways of combating social evils which emerged as an off-shoot of industrial revolution. New philosophies were propagated and hotly debated. New ideals and ideologies were born. These captured the imagination of the people which provided a spur to social action. The cumulative effect of such stirrings in the minds of men found expression in the clarion call for liberty, equality and fraternity in the mouths of the votaries of the French Revolution. There was a radical transformation in the attitude of the people to the problems which beset them. For instance, poverty was once looked upon as a case of ill luck for an individual or a family for which there was no remedy except to pray for Divine grace. Sometimes poverty was looked upon as an act of individual failure and the responsibility for being poor rested squarely upon the concerned individual. But the industrial revolution shattered such ideas to pieces. The people could see before their eyes the increasing concentration of wealth on the one hand and increasing destitution of large sections of people on the other. They realised for the first time that poverty was basically a social evil to be combated as such. Social surveys were undertaken with a view to assessing the nature of the problem and exploring ways of meeting the same. The first step towards the scientific study of society was thus taken.

We may also note, in this connection, another equally important development which had taken place during this period. Since the second half of the seventeenth century European sailors travelled to far-off lands braving the high seas. They brought back to their native lands, in addition to merchandise, rich experiences of a varied nature. Through them the scholars as well as ordinary men and women became acquainted with the ways of behaviour of people in those strange and far-off places. Such exposure to alien cultures made them conscious of cultural differences among peoples. They began exploring the possible ways in which societies must have evolved from a barbaric stage to a comparatively more advanced stage in course of centuries. The study of history proceeded on new lines altogether. Whenever they failed to connect the missing links in their exposition of the evolution of societies, they relied on conjectures on the basis of their understanding of normal human behaviour. They asked themselves a simple question : how would a normal human being act or react under certain circumstances ? They prepared a connected story of social evolution on the basis of their perception of the normal behaviour of an individual or a group. This kind of Conjectural History paved the way towards the growth of sociological thinking on certain lines. In the first place, their conceptions of the evolution of society and of human progress deeply influenced sociological thinking in the years to come. This aspect will be exhaustively dealt with in a subsequent chapter. Secondly, the new approach to historical studies and investigations led people to look at society as a 'whole'. The idea steadily gained ground that the state and society were two distinct entities and that the latter embraced the whole life of man. This conception of society helped considerably towards the growth of sociological thinking. Thus, the conditions which gave rise to sociology as an independent discipline were both intellectual and social. These two were obviously interwoven, so that one could not be disentangled from the other. Morris Ginsberg has identified the chief intellectual antecedents of sociology thus : "Broadly it may be said that sociology has had a fourfold origin in political philosophy, the philosophy of history, biological theories of evolution, and the movements for social and political reforms which found it necessary to undertake surveys of social conditions".[2]

In addition to the European traditions of social and political philosophy, another important root of sociology has been the American traditions of social concern with pressing social problems, such as crime, slum life, divorce and the assimilation of immigrants. As a matter of fact, an interest in social welfare and social reform was mainly responsible for a rapid development of the discipline in the twentieth century.

## 2. TOWARD A DEFINITION OF THE SCOPE OF SOCIOLOGY

In the light of the brief survey of its origin, we may discuss some of the characteristics which sociology in its formative period assumed. In the first place, sociology was assumed to be encyclopaedic in scope. All types of social relationships were conceived to be the concerns of sociology. Secondly, the entire sociological approach was evolutionary in character. The two dominant influences in this regard were the philosophy of history and the biological theory of evolution. Thirdly, sociology was conceived to be a positive science. In the eighteenth century sociology was modelled on physics and in the nineteenth century on biology. The writings of Comte and Spencer illustrate the influences of these two natural sciences on sociological approaches. Fourthly, though sociology claimed to be a general science, it was particularly concerned with problems which disturbed society in the wake of sweeping changes brought about by industrial revolution. As Bottomore has pointed out, "it was above all a science of the new industrial society". Finally, in addition to its scientific character, sociology had also an ideological dimension. Various kinds of ideologies, both conservative and radical, crept into sociological discussions. Ideological debate is still continuing among present-day sociologists.

The delineation of sociology as encylopaedic in scope raised opposition from many quarters, particularly from those who were working in narrower and more specialised fields. It was argued that the definition of the scope of sociology as an all-embracing science of society did not permit subtle analysis in most cases. It was, therefore, held that sociology would forfeit its claim to be treated as a distinct social science.

In view of these criticisms, attempts were made to define the scope of sociology on two distinct lines. First, sociology was conceived to be a social science concerned with a specially defined field. It was held that rigorous analysis of chosen fields of social living would be more rewarding and purposeful. Second, sociology was viewed as a synthesis of all social sciences. That is, there should be an attempt not at absorbing but at co-ordinating other social sciences, such as political science, economics, social philosophy, etc.

Among those who conceived of sociology 'as a clearly defined specialism', particular mention may be made of Ferdinand Tönnies, Georg Simmel, Alfred Vierkandt and Leopold Von Wiese. Their work was analytical and conceptual in character.

Tönnies classified societies into two categories — namely, *Gemeinschaft* (or community) and *Gesellschaft* (or association) — on the basis of the degree of closeness or intimacy among the members of the society. His analysis of social bond followed this categorisation. Like Hobbes, Tönnies was also concerned with the problem of how order is maintained in society. His investigations into the nature of the tie which binds people to one another sprang from this basic concern about the problem of social order. "His was the first successful attempt in analytical sociology and it prepared the way for the development of the formalists to whom we now turn — Simmel, Vierkandt and von Wiese".[4]

According to Simmel, social interactions among people should be analysed and classified into various forms or types. The description of the forms of this interaction is the task of formal sociology. He explained his point of view with the help of an analogy. We express our thoughts through language. A grammarian is not concerned with the contents of the language, but with the structural forms of the language through which the contents come to life and become meaningful. Similarly, argued Simmel, social interactions assume various forms. But some forms of behaviour amongst the members of a society toward one another may be identified — such as, superiority and subordination, competition and co-operation, division of labour, etc. "However diverse the interests are that give rise to these sociations, the *forms* in which the interests are realised may yet be identical".[5] Simmel argued that we should abstract from human relationships those *forms* of interaction which are common to diverse situations. "It was a cardinal principle in Simmel's view of sociology that it should not be encyclopaedic, but rather be strictly limited in its scope. Hence, he defined it in terms of the study of the forms of interaction."[6]

Vierkandt took an even more restricted view of sociology than Simmel himself. He held that sociology should be concerned, not with actual societies, but with forces which knit the people together in a society. A particular society — say, an Indian society or a Chinese society — is of interest to sociologists only as illustrations of particular types of social relationships. What is of deeper interest to them is to try to understand and analyse the mental processes which shape particular types of social relationships. His purpose, according to Mitchell, was to arrive at basic elements of a social kind. He held that these are found in such social entities as liking, obeying, submitting, etc.[7]

Like Simmel, Dr. von Wiese tried to establish sociology as an independent science. According to him, there are two fundamental social processes in human society, namely, associative and dissociative. The examples of the former are contact, approach, adaptation, combination, and union, and those of the latter are competition, opposition, and conflict. There is yet a third category — a mixed form — sharing both associative and dissociative social processes. He applied this classification not only to groups and collectivities but also to individuals. Each of these social processes, in its turn, is sub-divided into many sub-classes which, in their totality, give about 650 forms of human relationship.[8]

The views of Analytical and Formalistic school, as presented above, have been subjected to various criticisms. In the first place, the Formalistic school has restricted the scope of sociology to abstract forms without reference to the concrete expressions of these forms of social relationship in actual social situations. It is held that such a study would prove to be absolutely barren. Thus, for example, a study of competition would be meaningless unless the actual social situation is considered. Economic competition does not mean the same thing as competition, say, in the field of art. Secondly, Sorokin has raised a more fundamental question. Is it not fallacious, he argued, "to isolate the 'social form' from its content ..... and then to state that social forms can remain identical while their members change" ?[9] He elaborated his point thus : "We may fill a glass with wine, water, or sugar without changing its form; but I cannot conceive of a social institution whose 'form' would not change when its members, for instance, Americans, were superseded by quite a new and heterogeneous people, e.g., by Chinese or Bushmen",[10] Thirdly, the analytical and formal sociology developed as a reaction to the 'encyclopaedic' character of sociology. But Sorokin rightly pointed out, is a worthwhile sociological analysis possible without borrowing or using data of biology, anthropology, history, psychology, political science, economics, and literature ? "In brief, 'the sin of encyclopedism' is as common within the formal sociology as within the 'non-formal' sociology it criticises".[11]

It follows, therefore, that the advocates of the analytical and formalistic school have failed to build sociology as an independent and autonomous discipline. The "pretension of formal sociology to play the same role for other social sciences which is played by mathematics or physical mechanics in regard to other physical and technical sciences" is not justified in any way.[12]

One must concede, however, that the analytical and formal school "has contributed something valuable to a definite part of sociology in *systematizing human relations and social processes.*"[13] Sorokin has underscored the value of the contribution of this school in this regard thus : "The multitude of concrete human relationships and the complexity of social processes make it necessary to classify them into a few large classes, with further sub-divisions, in this way preventing us from becoming lost in a wild forest of interrelations."[14].

There is yet another school of sociologists who are in favour of adopting a *synthetic* approach to sociology. They argue that the different parts as well as the various activities of society are inter-related and inter-dependent. The society is not certainly organic in nature. But it is also not entirely mechanical. There are certain ties, both psychological and social, which bind the people together in a society. Different social sciences concern themselves with different aspects of social living. For example, political science deals with political activities of social men, Economics with activities of a purely economic nature. All other social sciences likewise confine themselves to their respective fields. Since the society is an indivisible whole, one type of activity cannot be isolated from the rest. On the contrary, one type of activity will impinge on other fields of activity. There is, therefore, the need for a discipline which would focus attention on the 'whole' of society. "Its purpose then would be to discover how the institutions which make up a society are related to one another in different social systems".[15] Prominent among those who subscribe to this line of thinking are Emile Durkheim and Hobhouse.

Durkheim divides Sociology into three broad divisions, namely, Social Morphology, Social Physiology and General Sociology. Social Morphology is concerned with the nature and extent of influence exercised by such factors as geographical location, size and density of population, etc. on the organization of social life. Social physiology deals with the genesis and nature of various social institutions. Discussions on Social Physiology are so directed as to throw light on the social background of, say, religion, morals, law, economic institutions, etc. In General Sociology attempt is made to find out if there are links among various institutions which would be treated independently in Social Physiology, and in that event to discover general social laws.

Durkheim lays particular stress on this type of analysis. In his view, whatever happens in society has one or more social causes which he calls 'social facts'. For example, in his analysis of suicide he shows that suicide, though an individual act, may by ascribed to social causes.

Hobhouse represents the philosophical side of sociology, speculative and evolutionary. He conceives sociology as "a science which has the whole social life of man as its sphere". Its relation with the other social sciences is considered to be "one of mutual exchange and mutual stimulation". In his view there are some central conceptions that pervade the entire society and inform all its parts. It is possible to have a fuller comprehension of the whole from the study of the parts. General Sociology is thus a synthesis of the various social sciences. Such a synthesis does not, however, consist "in a mechanical juxtaposition" of the findings of various social sciences. Since central conceptions pervade the whole, including its parts, a mutual relationship of give-and-take exists between the whole and its parts. While studying the parts, a sociologist is to correlate the results of the study with an eye to the whole of society. The study of the parts then contributes to a fuller comprehension of the whole.

There is no conflict between an analytical study of the parts which make up the society and a synthetic approach to the study of the whole society. The parts of society are so closely interwoven that it is not possible to study a particular part in isolation from the rest. At the same time, the study of the whole society is not possible without studying the parts which make up the whole.

In the light of the above discussion, we may construct a general outline of the scope of sociology. In the first place, the analysis of various institutions, associations or social groups which are the outward expressions of social relationships of man, should be the concern of sociology. Secondly, the links among the different parts or elements of society should be unravelled and analysed. For example the way economic, political or legal institutions are interconnected, each having a bearing on the other, should be a matter of investigation in sociology. "The basic conception, or directing idea, of sociology is, therefore, that of *social structure* : the systematic interrelation of forms of behaviour or action in particular societies. From this follows the sociologist's interest in those aspects of social life which has previously been studied only in a desultory manner, or which had been the object of philosophical reflection rather than empirical inquiry : the family and kinship, religion and morals, social stratification, urban life."[16] Thirdly, sociology addresses itself to an analysis of the factors which contribute to social stability as well as to social dynamism. Every society exhibits these two characteristics. There is order in society; but it is not an unchanging order. Sociology seeks to identify, describe and explain the factors which contribute to or impede the continuity of social systems through time. Fourthly, it is the task of a sociologist not simply to identify, describe and explain the changing pattern of society but also to indicate the trend of the changing pattern and the aftermath of the changes overtaking the society. Though it is not within his legitimate domain for a sociologist to decide on matters of policy or to prescribe remedies for the resultant social problems, he makes available to the policy-maker the findings of his study which would be one among many other factors to be considered in social planning. Seen in this perspective, a sociologist is not an academic recluse, spinning speculative theories which may or may not be relevant to real life-situation.

## 3. SOCIOLOGY AND OTHER SOCIAL SCIENCES

The scope of sociology will be better understood in the light of its relationship with the other social sciences and with all other disciplines concerned with the social life of man. With this end in view, we may discuss its relationship with two important social sciences, Economics and Political Science, with two general sciences. Psychology and Social Anthropology, and, finally, with History and Philosophy.

### Economics and Sociology

Economics is primarily concerned with the production and distribution of goods and commodities which are scarce in supply. It is also concerned with the larger questions of economic growth and distributive justice, its principal aim being furtherance of economic well-being of the people.

For a long period, the economists attempted to develop the subject as an autonomous discipline. This is evident from the fact that most of the economic laws were subject to the proviso "other things remaining the same", that the concept of the "economic man" was visualised as some one who is governed in his economic pursuits solely by rational considerations of maximising productivity (or utility) and minimising cost (or disutility).

In course of time, however, it was widely appreciated that in real life situation, 'other things' do not remain the same. As a result, economic laws suffer distortion. Similarly, it was found that economic rationality is very much affected by non-economic considerations. For example, the forces of tradition, patriotism, altruism, kinship loyalty, to name only a few, affect very much the economic rationality of man. These limits, among many others, of 'pure' economics show that economics cannot be an entirely autonomous discipline. In this connection, reference may be made to very interesting findings of E.E. Hagen.[17] In course of his investigation into the cases that impede fast economic growth in Burma, Hagen noted that Burmese tradition and the type of education that an average Burmese receives since childhood do not encourage the growth of innovative personality which is the *sine qua non* of rapid economic advance. Hagen, though a professional economist, goes beyond economic theory and examines how people of various cultures behave and relates the same to the backgrounds in which they live. Similarly, Max Weber in course of his investigation into the causes of the rise of capitalism in the 18th century England showed how religious orientation of the people deeply influences their economic motives. Following the lead given by Max Weber many sociologists have sought to explain many aspects of economic behaviour which were previously neglected by professional economists. Moreover, sociologists have made significant contribution by analysing the structure of industrial society, the problems and promises of urbanisation, division of labour and occupational structure, property system, etc.

Sociology is also deeply influenced by Economics. "Thus economic phenomena are constantly determined by all kinds of social need and activity and in turn they are constantly re-determining, creating, shaping and transforming social need and activity of every kind".[18] This explains the fact that many sociologists have approached the study of society through economic institutions. In many sociological writings the pride of place is enjoyed by economic activities of man.

Recent literature in both the disciplines shows clearly that both economics and sociology are coming closer together. The *focus* of interest of each, however, remains different. Economics gains in depth as a result of sociological investigations into the economic behaviour of men. Likewise, Sociology, a comparatively younger entrant into the family of social sciences, gains considerably from the tools of analysis developed by Economics, comparatively a much older social science.

## Political Science and Sociology

State and Government and all the issues associated with these two — such as, nature of authority and power, ends of the state, forms of government, grounds for political obligations, etc. — constitute the concern of political science. Obviously, political science confines its study to the political motivations and political activities of men. Sociology, on the other hand, has a much wider view and embraces the totality of life of man in society. Political Science sought to carve out its distinct field of study by concentrating on the formal political structure. The study of the state meant analysis of articles of constitutions, legislations passed by governments, and the institutions for which the Constitution made provision.

After the end of the Second World War, the study of political science underwent a radical change. Doubts were expressed about the usefulness of such an approach on the ground that too little attention was given to the context within which institutions and constitutions operate. It was argued that political institutions reflect something more substantial, viz., the structure of behaviour of men in a variety of fields, social, political and economic. Political institutions are, therefore, likely to be affected by changes in the structure of behaviour. It is pointed out that the danger for the student of politics who concerns himself mainly with institutions or constitutions lies in the fact that where political institutions might be outmoded because of changes in the behaviour structure of the people or where political institutions might be set up without sufficient regard for the social or political processes of a society, he might be studying, as it were, the shadow rather than the substance of politics.[19]

The development of behaviourism in political science has been largely an outcome of sociological influence. The objects of research in political science during the last two decades have been largely sociological in kind — namely, political parties and pressure groups, the role of elites in the political process, bureaucracy, relation between class, caste and politics, etc. As a matter of fact, it is often difficult to distinguish political science from political sociology. As in Economics, so also in the case of Political Science, one can clearly perceive a distinct tendency towards coming closer together of Political Science and Sociology. Nevertheless, the main *focus* of interest of Political Science remains essentially political in orientation while that of Sociology is distinctly social.

## Psychology and Sociology

The question concerning determining the relation of psychology and sociology has evoked, among sociologists, a great deal of controversy. The controversy centres around two extreme views expressed by John Stuart Mill and Emile Durkheim. According to Mill, human mind is active behind all that he does. It is, therefore, necessary to analyse his mental processes in order to understand meaningfully his overt actions and social relationships into which he enters. "Human beings in society have no properties but those which are derived from, and may be resolved into, the laws of the nature of individual man."[20] In his view, a general science of society cannot be logically developed without taking into account "the laws of the nature of individual man". Durkheim, on the other hand, dismisses psychological explanations of social behaviour as having no basis at all. In his analysis of the prevalence of variations in suicide rates among different sections of the population, he distinguishes between an individual act and the social forces determining the same. He admits that given certain circumstances a man with a psychological predisposition to suicide is more likely to kill himself. But Durkheim insists that the force which determines the suicide is not psychological but social. He thus makes a distinction between the phenomena studied by psychology and those studied by sociology. Sociology is to study the *social facts*. The explanation of social facts can only be found in terms of other facts, not in terms of psychological facts. Durkheim goes further to say that "whenever a social phenomenon is directly explained by a psychological phenomenon, one can be sure the explanation is invalid."[21]

These two extreme views have their partisans among sociologists even today. But most of the sociologists are in favour of adopting positions which range between these two extremes. According to some (Morris Ginsberg, for example) there are behaviour patterns which are amenable to psychological analysis and there are some which are not. The latter may be explained in terms of sociological laws alone. There are, again, some sociologists (Max Weber, for example) who argue that even where strictly sociological explanation of behaviour patterns is possible, it is desirable to probe the mental processes in order to get a better insight into the causes of social action. Those who share this view hold that psychological and sociological explanations complement each other. Though the controversy about the relation of these two disciplines is not yet settled, there is a growing awareness about the complementary roles of the two. Nevertheless, the distinctive focus of each discipline should not be ignored. Psychology is interested mainly in the individual, in his qualities of mind and temperament, in his nervous system, in his hopes and fears, and in the order and disorder of his mind. The primary interest of sociology, on the other hand, is not the individual or his personality or his behaviour. The society in which the individual lives and the persisting interaction that takes place within a group or between groups constitute the basic concerns of sociology. These differences in approach will be evident from the fact that the psychological explanation of war is completely at variance with the sociological explanation.

There was a time when affinity between sociology and social psychology used to be emphasised, and the latter was looked upon as a bridge between psychology and sociology. Social psychology is that branch of general psychology which "deals with the psychological aspects of social life". The specific field of study of social psychology is the "interplay between individual character and social structure". Though it maintains, like psychology, a primary interest in the individual, social psychology "concerns itself with the way in which the individual behaves in his social groups, how he behaves collectively with other individuals, and how his personality is a function both of his basic physiological and temperamental equipment and of the social and cultural influences to which he is exposed"[22]. Thus, while social psychology is concerned with group orientation of the individual, sociology is interested in "the groups themselves and the larger social structures within which both individual and group processes occur".[23] Apart from these differences in approach, the method of investigation of social psychology is different from that of sociology. Like general psychology, social psychology also emphasises quantitative studies, statistical analysis and experiments to the neglect of the social milieu in which investigations are carried out.

Though the focus of interest of psychology, social psychology and sociology remains distinct, it is not always easy to draw the line of separation. One discipline overlaps into the other, often making the boundary lines indistinguishable.

### Social Anthropology and Sociology

The two disciplines originate from two different sources. Sociology has grown out of philosophy of history. European traditions of social and political philosophy and social survey. Another root of sociology has been the American traditions of social concern with pressing social problems. Social Anthropology, on the other hand, has developed out of physical Anthropology. Subsequently, it drew sustenance and strength from biology.

Anthropology literally means the science of man. Its subjectmatter is very wide and diverse. Archaeology is its concern; so also is linguistics. It also studies the physical characteristics of man classified in various groups. These studies are carried out by a separate branch of anthropology called Physical Anthropology. Anthropology is also concerned with the culture and social life of man. The branch of anthropology which does this is known as Cultural or Social Anthropology. It appears, therefore, that anthropology, particularly social anthropology, covers more or less the same ground as is done by sociology. This statement is, however, subject to qualifications. In the first place, anthropology in all its branches has been concerned all throughout with the study of pre-literate, aboriginal people who had little or no contact with the civilised society. Sociology, on the contrary, concerns itself with societies which are literate, advanced and exposed to all kinds of civilizational influences. Secondly, since the pre-literate, aboriginal societies were small, both in terms of number and in terms of distribution over space, the social anthropologists were concerned with the "whole" of society, and not with any particular aspect of it. Social anthropologists like Radcliffe-Brown, Malinowski and a host of other scholars, including Margaret Mead, studied primitive 'cultures' in all their aspects — religion and magic, morals and social norms, sex and play, economic pursuits like hunting, fishing and gardening. In view of the complex and large societies sociologists are concerned with, it is not possible for them to investigate the "whole" of society. They choose particular fields of study and relate their findings with those of other sociologists. The perspective of a sociologist is thus entirely different from that of a social anthropologist. Thirdly, the methods of investigation in social anthropology and sociology vary for obvious reasons. Field work and close observation of 'cultures' under study are considered to be indispensable for anthropological investigations. A social anthropologist lives among the people he studies, sharing their lives, learning and speaking their language and observing societies as "functioning wholes". A sociologist, for obvious reasons, cannot adopt this line of study. He depends largely on questionnaire, and occasionally conducts interviews with a selected group of his unit of study. A sociologist observes from outside; an anthropologist observes from inside. The former is a non-participant observer, the latter a participant observer.

With the virtual disappearance of primitive pre-literate societies, thanks to media of mass communication and easy and quick means of transportation, the social anthropologists have been undertaking, of late, studies of particular aspects of present-day modern societies. They have also been adapting their style of investigation to the requirements of their study. Both sociologists and anthropologists are found to adopt the same or nearly similar objects for their investigations. For instance, the Indian caste system has been investigated equally competently both by anthropologists and sociologists. Often it is difficult to distinguish an anthropological study from a sociological one. If this trend continues, the distinction between the two disciplines might get obliterated in course of time in future.

**History and Sociology**

There are three dimensions of historical studies : First, the narrative aspect. A historian tells "the thing as it happened." Second, the investigative and interpretative aspect. A historian is not only a story-teller; he is also an investigator and interpreter. Historians speak of "cause" in history or of "explanation" or "interpretation" or of the "logic" of the situation or of "the inner logic of events". Third, historian's record is a guide to the understanding of the present and the future. "Good historians", says E.H. Carr, "whether they think about it or not, have the future in their bones. Besides the question 'Why ?' the historian also asks the question 'Whither ?'

It will be seen from the following discussion that historical studies are considerably enriched by sociological studies in all these three dimensions. In his role as a story-teller, a historian faces a difficulty inasmuch as an event includes the feelings and the spirit of the participants and the onlookers. Indeed, these non-factual ingredients are often the most significant in any historical recital. The dictum 'history is the biography of great men' was a reputable dictum at the beginning of this century. Individuals were looked upon as decisive factors in history. Under the impact of sociological studies, however, the action of social forces rather than the behaviour of individuals has become the object of historians' enquiry. A historian is thus able to tell his story in a more convincing way. But the debate as to whether the object of the historians' enquiry is the behaviour of individuals or the action of social forces has not yet died down. There are historians who are sorry for the "mass murder of historical characters" by treating them as "puppets of social and economic forces". In his book 'What is history ?' E.H. Carr, however, observes that the exaggerated importance that is given to the role of 'great men' in history "does not fit the more complex society of our times" and that "the birth in the nineteenth century of the new science of Sociology was a response to this growing complexity".

The close relation of sociology and history may also be discussed with reference to the interpretation of a unique historical event, e.g., the industrial revolution in the eighteenth century England by Max Weber. The event becomes meaningful when it is looked at from a sociological point of view. As a matter of fact, "the debate about the origins of modern capitalism which began with Max Weber's revision of the Marxist account has been continued by historians and sociologists from Tawney upto the present time". Max Weber's analysis of the origin of capitalism holds lessons for the historian in assessing the prospective trend of events. It is often said that "history is an explanation of how we come to be doing what we usually do." We are interested in what had occurred in the past chiefly because we want to understand what is occurring today. And we want this chiefly because we want to influence what will occur in future. As in the case of Weber's analysis of the origin of capitalism, historian draws upon sociology not simply to understand the past and the present but also to show how to change the present into a better future. In much contemporary historiography and sociology the same basic framework of reference is employed, specially where economic and social history are concerned.[24]

Sociology has also to draw heavily on history to get a wider perspective, i.e., a historian's vision. At present, sociology faces two opposite dangers — the danger of becoming ultra-theoretical and the danger of becoming ultra-empirical. The first is the danger of losing itself in abstract and meaningless generalisations about society in general. Society with a capital 'S' is as misleading a fallacy as History with a capital 'H'. This danger is brought nearer by those who assign to sociology the exclusive task of generalising from the unique events recorded by history. It has even been suggested by some that sociology is distinguished from history by having "laws". The second danger is of a sociology "split into a series of discrete technical problems of social re-adjustment." Sociology is concerned with historical societies, every one of which is unique and moulded by specific historical antecedents and conditions. But to attempt to avoid generalisation and interpretation by confining oneself to so-called 'technical' problems of enumeration and analysis is merely to become the unconscious advocate of a static society. Sociology, if it is to become a fruitful field of study, must , like history, concern itself with the relation between the unique and the general. That is, sociology must become dynamic — a study not of society at rest (because no such society exists) but of social change and development.

We may, therefore, conclude by saying that the more sociological history becomes, and the more historical sociology becomes, the better for both the disciplines. The frontier between the two should be kept wide open for two-way traffic.

**Philosophy and Sociology**

While tracing the roots of sociology in the second half of the 18th century and the first half of the 19th century, we noted that one such root was the then prevailing social and political philosophy in Europe. Sociology originated to explain the social crisis in Europe during that period and "to provide a social doctrine which would guide social policy." Sociology was thus conceived in philosophical terms. For a long period of time since then, sociological problems had been approached from a philosophical point of view. Thus, while analysing the direction of social change, many philosophical questions had been raised. Does social change connote social progress ? Do some basic values or over-riding principles envelop the entire society ? In course of time, however, sociology ceased to raise such questions and there was a conscious attempt to develop sociology as a positive science, freed from all kinds of ideological trappings. Apparently, the contact between philosophy and sociology was snapped. But this absence or loss of contact was more apparent than real. There are some areas where the two disciplines overlap.

In the first place, sociology is concerned with the behaviour of men in society. Since such behaviour is deeply influenced, among others, by the value-orientation of the people, a sociologist has to reckon with values while analysing social behaviour. He does not, of course, deal with values in the way a philosopher does. He treats values as "social facts", as something given, and analyses their impact on the social behaviour of men.

A sociologist has, however, to keep himself abreast of the philosophical basis of values. In the absence of such acquaintance, he would not be able to assess properly the world-view, hopes, aspirations and dreams of the people. If, for example, a sociologist is not broadly familar with the philosophical basis of Indian culture, he would signally fail to interpret and analyse Indian society. Only by some training in social philosophy can a sociologist get an insight into the working of mind of the people and into their attitudes rooted in tradition.

Secondly, it is argued that sociological discourses sometimes lead to philosophical thought. While treating religion, Durkheim, for example, discusses first the social influences upon the categories of thought and proceeds to epistemological discussion — "a conception of social milieu as the determining cause of social facts".[25] Durkheim expresses his views thus : "I believe that sociology, more than any other science, has a contribution to make to the renewal of philosophical questions ..... sociological reflection is bound to prolong itself by a natural progress in the form of philosophical reflection".[26] That sociological reflection may eventually lead to philosophical reflection may be indicated with reference to a very simple example. It is the duty of every social being to abide by the norms prescribed by society in the interest of social stability. But a question may legitimately be raised : what should an individual do if he cannot persuade himself to conform to certain socially prescribed norms and he adduces very convincing arguments for not doing so ? Should he follow his conscience and choose to go alone and expose himself to social strictures ? In such an event, what amount of relaxation can be made by society ? How will problems of this nature be resolved ? These questions have stirred the minds of men in the past and will continue to do so in the years to come. Various schools of philosophical thinking have arisen centering around these questions. Posterity has found that Socrates was right in the type of views he held and propagated and that his contemporaries were clearly in the wrong. But Socrates had to pay the penalty for being a non-conformist. Socrates was not alone. Every age has produced non-conformists who were penalised for expressing their honest convictions that were not in conformity with prevailing socially accepted norms. Such cases raise questions which are the concerns of both sociologists and philosophers.

## 4. INTERNAL LOGICAL CHARACTERISTICS OF SOCIOLOGY

In the preceding section we discussed, as it were, the outer limits of sociology. We tried to have a very general conception about the areas where sociology and other disciplines concerned with the life of man in society overlap and about the areas where sociology diverges from them. In this section we propose to look at the subject from within : its structure, its approach, its nature as well as its characteristics.

To begin with, sociology has developed as a value-free discipline. It is concerned with what is, not with what ought to be. The values which a society upholds and which influence the social behaviour of men are accepted by sociologists as 'facts' and analysed objectively. They do not analyse values themselves. It is thus not a normative discipline like Ethics or Religion. Further, the sociologists simply indicate the directions towards which the society is moving and refrain from expressing views on the directions in which society should go. In this respect it is to be distinguished from Social and Political Philosophy.

Secondly, Sociology is an empirical discipline. It is guided by rational considerations in its analysis of social phenomena, and not in terms of ideology.

Thirdly, Sociology has developed as an abstract discipline like Physics, Chemistry or Mathematics, and not as an applied science like Engineering or Computer Science. A sociologist analyses society from different angles and acquires knowledge about society and patterns of social interactions. A physicist or a mathematician does not build bridges. An engineer, however, utilises the knowledge of Physics or Mathematics in building bridges. In the same manner, it is for administrators and social workers to utilise the fund of knowledge acquired by sociologists in the field of social planning.

Fourthly, Sociology is a general and not a special social science. It is concerned with human relationships and patterns of social interactions in general, and not any particular aspects of the same. An economist confines his attention to interactions in the economic sphere only. Likewise, a political scientist is primarily concerned only with interactions in the political field. A sociologist, however, focuses his attention on human or social relationships which are common to all these specialised fields.

Sociology is thus an objective, a pure, an abstract, an empirical and a general social science.

Two questions, however, remain to be explored further. To what extent can sociology fulfil the criterion of objectivity ? In what sense is sociology treated as a science ? The examination of these questions may be taken up together in the following section.

## 5. THE PROBLEM OF OBJECTIVITY

We noted in the above section that the guiding principles of sociology are objectivity and ethical neutrality. According to this yardstick, the sociologists are to approach the problems of, say, social change dispassionately without bringing to bear upon their discussion ethical considerations. Even an emotive theme like family disorganization should not excite the feelings of a sociologist in any manner. His personal likes or dislikes should not be allowed to influence his judgment. The principles of objectivity and ethical neutrality were the outcome of positivism and evolutionism of the eighteenth and nineteenth centuries which influenced sociological thinking during its formative stages. Comte, for example, was very much influenced by the method of investigation of Physics, and he laid down, as a sociological rule, the need for establishing causal relations between social phenomena through direct, empirical observation of these phenomena. Likewise, Spencer approached Sociology strictly on the lines of the theory of organic evolution. In his view also direct, empirical observation of social phenomena was the appropriate sociological method. Subjective perceptions of what is good or bad, desirable or undesirable, have therefore no place in sociological analysis.

Ideally speaking, this approach is commendable. In actual practice, however, it may not be easy to follow strictly this ideal. To begin with, sociology is not an exact science like physics or chemistry. The subject matter of the physical sciences is external to the investigator. He can afford to be neutral and unbiased in his approach. It has been very aptly said that : "The stars have no sentiments, the atoms no anxieties that have to be taken into account, observation is objective with little effort on the part of the scientist to make it so."[27] Those who are concerned with the social universe are thus at a disadvantage in comparison with those who are concerned with the physical universe. In the former case, the investigators and researchers are themselves immersed, as it were, in the objects of their study. They are, so to say, participant-observers. Their own emotions and sentiments, human as they are, cannot fail to sway their judgment this way or that. There is a second reason for their failure to be truly objective in their approach. Like all others, sociologists live in a normative society. Since their childhood, they have been exposed to the values which the society upholds, to the ways of behaviour which the society considers to be appropriate. They assimilate most of these values and ways of behaviour and follow them almost unconsciously all throughout their lives. Apart from human qualities of passion, sentiments, emotions and attachments, their thinking processes are conditioned by the society in which they are born and brought up. Is it not too much to expect that they will be able to dislodge these completely from their minds after having imbibed all these since early childhood ? A sociologist can, therefore, never be objective to the same extent and in the same manner as a natural scientist can. The sociological ideals of objectivity and ethical neutrality should be understood, subject to these qualifications.

It is necessary to point out, however, that there is disagreement among sociologists about the methodological norm of objectivity and ethical neutrality. There are sociologists who are prompted by the zeal of social reformers and argue that sociological investigations should be directed towards social reform and adoption of ameliorative measures. In their view sociologists cannot, and should not, sit in 'ivory tower' in utter disregard of what they consider to be undesirable and detrimental to the larger interests of society. The debate is still continuing among sociologists about the goal of sociological investigation. "It is desirable to recognise, however, that social action and sociological enquiry are two different enterprises. One can indulge in both, but not at the same time. Social and political action require commitment, but scholarship requires detachment."[28]

Because of its avowed methodological norm of objectivity and ethical neutrality, sociology is sometimes given the label of 'science' ranking it with physical sciences. This is obviously wrong. Sociology is not an exact science. The objects of its investigation very often defy exact, or even nearly exact, measurement. Quantification is not possible in cases where human emotions or sentiments are involved. Human responses to the same stimulus vary from person to person, from group to group, and also over time. Generalisation in such cases will naturally be approximate. Conclusions may have to be hedged in by a number of qualifications. The errors which creep into the generalised conclusions because of the nature of variables one deals with in social science cannot always be identified and their effects measured. In physical sciences, on the other hand, the variables one has to consider in observations and experiments can be limited and controlled. The errors which enter into measurement because of the nature of variables are fairly known. Their effects can also be measured. The result may be subtracted from the total score. Unlike social sciences, finding in physical sciences is thus more or less exact, the margin of error being reduced to the minimum. The label of 'science' cannot, therefore, be tagged on to sociology.

If, however, we mean by 'science' an attitude of mind, an attitude or approach distinguished by objectivity, rationality, and readiness to subject every hypothesis to rigorous test, then sociological investigations partake of the nature of scientific investigation. A sociologist tries his utmost to be as objective as is humanly possible for a member of society. He refuses to accept any statement or hypothesis unless he finds convincing evidence to corroborate the same. He examines all social phenomena rationally and logically and tries to find causal explanation for the same. Sociology may be described as a 'science' in so far as it follows scientific methodology and tries to exclude all subjective perceptions which are not supported by evidence.

## 6. THE METHODOLOGICAL ISSUE REGARDING THE USE OF LANGUAGE IN SOCIOLOGY

In physical as well as in social universe, we observe a bewildering variety of 'things' and bewildering variety of relationships among those 'things'. Mere observation of these 'realities' does not give us any coherent image of the nature and relationships of what we observe. Every discipline, therefore, selects particular attributes from a complex reality according to its own focus of interest and groups them under different names in order to discern similarities and differences. These groups bearing different names are called concepts. A concept is a logical ordering device in the midst of bewildering variety. The reality becomes meaningful to us only through concepts. To name is to know is an ancient maxim. "If we accept the distinction between matters of fact and matters of relation, then knowledge, as a combination of the two, depends on the correct sequence between factual order and logical order. For experience, the factual order is primary; for meaning, the logical order. Mind knows nature by finding some language in which to express an underlying pattern. Knowledge, thus, is a function of the categories we use to establish relationships, just as perception, as in art, is a function of the conventions we have accepted in order to see things 'correctly'."[29]

The physical and natural sciences generally borrow words from Greek and Latin in order to name the concepts. The language in which the concepts in these disciplines are used is thus very specific and carries only *one* meaning. There is little or no scope for ambiguity or confusion. Sociology has, however, used words from everyday use and ascribed specific technical meanings to these in order to describe concepts. The words like 'culture', 'society', 'community', 'status', 'role','association', etc. stand for certain concepts in sociology which differ in meaning from what is conveyed in everyday use of these words. For example, the word 'culture' in everyday use means something refined, something cultivated and matters of mind and spirit as distinguished from gross material things. A 'cultured' man stands for some one who is refined in his tastes, urbane and polished in manners, and appreciative of fine arts like painting, music, dance, etc. In sociology, however, the word 'culture' has a wider meaning and implies a way of life, embracing all aspects of social life. Similarly, many words of everyday use are used in sociology to convey some technical meaning different from what it means in general use. There is, therefore, some scope for confusion among those who are initiated into sociology for the first time. The meanings of such words used in a technical sense in sociology will be discussed in course of our discussion in the following pages. This is an important point which should be borne in mind by an introductory student of sociology. The problem of language is, unfortunately, further complicated by the fact that the sociologists themselves do not always use the same words in the same technical senses. "Sociologists earnestly desire a well-ordered, systematic set of concepts, and have made much progress toward that end. But the goal is not yet achieved."[30]

## NOTES

1. Ely Chinoy : *The Sociological Perspective*, Random House, New York, 1954, Page 5.
2. Morris Ginsberg : *Reason and Unreason in Society* (1947), p.2. Quoted by Bottomore in his book *'Sociology'* (1971), p.16.
3. T.B. Bottomore : *Sociology* (1971), p.20.
4. G. Duncan Mitchell : *A Hundred Years of Sociology* (1968), p.106.
5. *ibid*, p.107.
6. *ibid*, p.110.
7. *ibid*, p.111.
8. Sorokin : *Contemporary Sociological Theories* (1928), p.495.
9. *ibid*, p.499.
10. *ibid*, p.500.
11. *ibid*, p.503.
12. *ibid*, p.503.
13. *ibid*, p.506.
14. *ibid*, p.506.
15. Alex Inkeles : *What is Sociology* ? Prentice-Hall of India, Edition (1964). p.14.
16. T.B. Bottomore : *Sociology (1971)*, p.25.
17. E.E. Hagen : *On the Theory of Social Change : How economic growth begins* (1962).
18. Mac Iver : *Community : A Sociological Study*, p.50.
19. Robert A. Dahl and Deane E. Neubauer : *Readings in Modern Political Analysis*, (Prentice-Hall, Inc. Englewood Cliffs, 1968).
20. J.S.Mill : *System of Logic*, Book VI, Ch.7. Quoted by Bottomore in his book *'Sociology'* (1971), p.67.
21. E.Durkheim : *The Rules of Sociological Method*, Ch.5.
22. R. Bierstedt : *The Social Order*. Tata McGraw-Hill Publishing Co. Ltd. (1970), p.9.
23. *ibid*, p.9.
24. Bottomore : *Sociology*, p.76.
25. Raymond Aron : *Main Currents in Sociological Thought*, Vol.2, (Penguin Books) 1982, p.78.
26. Quoted by Bottomore in his book *'Sociology'*. p.79.
27. R. Bierstedt : *Social Order*, p.21.
28. R. Bierstedt : *ibid*, p.28.
29. Daniel Bell : *The Coming of Post-industrial society*.
30. R. Bierstedt : *Social Order*. p.26.

# CHAPTER-TWO

## SOCIOLOGICAL METHODS

We have seen that there are disagreements among sociologists about the scope and proper study of sociology. Similar disagreements also exist among them about the proper method of pursuing sociological studies and investigations. Such disagreements are due, in part, to their varying sociological perspectives.

### 1. HISTORICAL OR EVOLUTIONARY APPROACH

Early sociologists were concerned with a description of the main trends in the evolution of humanity as a whole. Their thinking was dominated by a conception of man and society progressing through definite steps of evolution, marking successive stages of greater and still greater complexity to some final stage of perfection. This kind of thinking on evolutionary lines is represented by a number of theories. All these theories are based on the assumption that man's social development requires that at every stage social forces play their roles according to 'natural law' to be succeeded by a different stage and the process goes on till the stage of perfection is reached. Biological theory of evolution is often invoked in support of this line of thinking. Examples are Comte's law of the three stages, the Marxist theory of a movement from a classless society through various forms of class differentiation to a classless society again, Hobhouse's effort at correlating social development with mental development as well as many other theories of social evolution, Durkheim's theory of a historical trend, or evolution, from a low to a high degree of specialisation giving rise to the distinction between two main types of society — one marked by what he called 'mechanical solidarity' and the other by 'organic solidarity'. Ferdinand Tönnies also harped on the evolutionary theme when he distinguished between *gemeinschaft* and *gesellschaft,* the community-type of society gradually evolving into a corporate or associational type of society. It is interesting to note that some social scientists have used the evolutionary concept of society in support of their respective social or political philosophies. For example, William Graham Sumner, who is known as a 'Social Darwinist', argued against social reform and all attempts at social change on the ground that such efforts were against the law of nature and that social evolution must be allowed to run its natural course. "That is why", he said, "it is the greatest folly of which a man can be capable, to sit down with a slate and pencil to plan out a new social world."[1]

Such pre-occupations with social evolution do no longer concern the sociologists of this century. There are various reasons for this. A mass of evidence has been collected to show that human societies do not pass through a fixed and limited number of stages in a given sequence. Moreover, the conditions in the twentieth century do not inspire the confidence that the contemporary society is the highest stage of man's social life. Nor is there any indication that man's social life is progressively improving to reach a still higher or better stage.

Though the evolutionary model has been, for all practical purposes, abandoned, by presentday sociologists, we should not ignore the achievements of thinkers who belonged to this school. To begin with, the early evolutionists "classified in illuminating ways a mass of ethnographic and historical materials, and outlined possible typologies of human society"[2] Secondly, they "made important contributions to our knowledge of social changes".[3] In the light of their discussions, we are able to identify the factors which bring about changes in social structure and lay down, instead of a general theory of social evolution, conditions which tend to produce changes in particular areas of social life. The works of Max Weber are examples of this type of formulation. He did not formulate a grand theory of the whole course of social evolution like many evolutionary thinkers mentioned earlier in this section. His study of the origins of capitalism relating religion to economic pursuits and that of the development of modern bureaucracies are typical examples of his distinctive historical approach.

## 2. THE COMPARATIVE APPROACH

The point of view of those who are in favour of pursuing the comparative approach has been very succinctly expressed by Durkheim. It is argued that in natural sciences checking and cross-checking of data are possible through various kinds of experiments. In social sciences, however, such experiments cannot be undertaken in order to establish causal relationships with regard to social phenomena. We are, therefore, obliged, says Drukheim, "to use the method of indirect experiment" which is another name for comparative method. "In essentials this method is an application of a general rule of inductive logic : to vary the circumstances of a phenomenon with the object of eliminating variable and inessential factors, and so arriving at what is essential and constant. What is peculiar to the method is the use of data derived from different regions or different times."[4] Doubts may be raised as to whether precise causal connections may at all be established in social sciences. Even then, it is doubtless true that illuminating light may be shed through the method of comparison which enables us to explain the nature of social phenomena. Some examples will be in order. By comparing the differences in the rates of suicide committed by people in different groups within the same society, Durkheim tried to find out the *social* factor which was mainly responsible for the differential rates. Thus, he presented statistical evidence to show that there is a higher suicide rate among married people without children then among those who are married and have children. He also concluded on the basis of statistical evidence that suicide rate generally rose in times of severe economic depression as compared to that in times of economic stability. Cross-cultural studies are also undertaken in order to get new insights into social phenomena. Max Weber, for example, studied the religion of India and China in the light of the teachings of Calvinism, which, in his view, instilled among the faithful the virtues of work ethics and 'worldly-asceticism', and tried to seek an explanation as to why the 'East remained an enchanted garden'. With an improvement in the means of communication and transportation, first-hand cross-cultural sociological studies have increased in number in recent years, resulting in wealth of information which augurs well for broadening the base of sociological researches in future. Commenting on the importance of comparative studies in respect of complex social formations or institutions, Ginsberg observes that "as soon as sociology passes from the descriptive to the analytic level, the comparative method is essential alike for genetic connexions and for establishing any other mode of causal relationship."[5] By way of illustrating how genetic connections are established by comparative studies, Ginsberg says that "if we wish to know the conditions under which slavery, or serfdom, or any other forms of economic organization arises, it is necessary to study their history in different societies."[6] Again, by way of illustrating how comparative studies are helpful in establishing various kinds of causal relationships, Ginsberg observes : "The problem of the extent to which a phenomenon like the rise of nationalism is conditioned by the need for economic or political unification, by the growth of the middle classes, or by war, or the problem of the limits set to national assimilation by racial heterogeneity or differences in religion, obviously requires wide comparative study for its solution".[7]

There are, however, some difficulties in pursuing the comparative method. To begin with, Radcliffe Brown pointed out that "the comparative method alone gives you nothing. Nothing will grow out of the ground unless you put seeds into it. The comparative method is one way of testing hypothesis."[8] The difficulty of using the comparative method arises out of the absence of a well-formulated hypothesis. In its absence the entire exercise may be futile. Secondly, difficulty may also arise in connection with definition of the unit of comparison. Thus, it is a formidable task to compare whole societies with one another. As a way out of this difficulty, the procedure which is often used is to compare specific social institutions in two or more societies. It is argued that the conclusions arrived at on the basis of such comparative studies of specific institutions are of little significance. An institution, it is pointed out, is an integral part of the whole society and, as such, one cannot understand or appreciate the value or usefulness of the institution when it is detached from the context of the whole society. Such studies, thus, become much too mechanical. These are real difficulties of which one should be aware at the time of undertaking cross-cultural studies. Such awareness coupled with taking of abundant precaution, as the circumstances require, would considerably minimise the extent of distortions which might creep into cross-cultural studies of institutions.

## 3. STRUCTURAL-FUNCTIONALIST APPROACH

Social thinkers of all ages have dwelt on analogies between society and living organisms. The unity of a living organism prompted them to look for factors which kept the society together. They asked themselves two basic questions : (i) How is social life maintained over time in spite of the fact that membership of society changes completely from generation to generation ? (ii) How is the unity of social life maintained ? Answers to these two basic questions were sought in the linked concepts of "structure" and "function" which appeared in the writings of Spencer and Durkheim and figured prominently in those of social anthropologists, Malinowski and Radcliffe-Brown. The analysis of society in terms of the concepts of "structure" and "function also appears quite prominently in the writings of Talcott Parsons and Robert Merton. As a matter of fact, for the past few decades functional analysis has been a major approach to understand and explain the nature and organisation of society. The term "functional analysis" or "structural-functionalism" has, however, been applied to a great variety of approaches which share one common element or feature, namely, relating one part of a society or social system to another part or to some aspect of the whole. Now-a-days the functionalist approach is generally known as the structural-functional school of sociology.

Let us see how structural-functionalist theorists answer the two basic questions raised in the preceding paragraph. To the basic question as to how the social life is maintained despite a complete turnover in its membership in every generation, they answer that each society develops structures which are found appropriate for meeting the demands of social life. A change in the membership of society does not necessarily or automatically bring about a change in the social structures which are either pre-conditions or consequences of organised social life. To the second basic question as to how is the unity of social life maintained, the structural-functionalist writers offer the explanation that the different structures of society are integrated and co-ordinated so as to preserve the unity of society as a complete system like that of a living organism. In other words, the structural-functionalist theory takes a total view of society and does not take up for analysis any institution or structure in isolation from other institutions or structures. The explanations offered to these two basic questions bring out the essence of structural-functionalist approach.

Alex Inkeles has analysed very precisely and pointedly the differences in approach between the evolutionary and functionalist writers. "The evolutionary and functional views are not opposed to each other, but their interests and emphases are different. The evolutionary perspective is similar to Comte's idea of "social dynamics", whereas the structural-functional approach is a contemporary relative of his "social statics". The evolutionist is concerned with the classification of societies according to an established evolutionary scale. Time, stages of development, and change are, therefore, central to his interest. The structural-functional approach involves a more limited time perspective. It stops the motions of the system at a fixed point of time in order to understand how, at that moment, it works as a system. When considering a particular institution, those guided by the evolutionary perspective try to understand how the evolutionary stage of the society as a whole shapes the form of the institution. The structural-functionalists will emphasise more how the institution contributed to keeping the society in operation".[9]

The structural-functionalist approach has been criticised on the ground that it is a static theory and ignores the forces and processes of social change, and that it is essentially conservative in nature. The theory is also criticised on the ground that it does not take into account social tensions and conflict situations which occur not infrequently in social life. These criticisms will be taken care of in a subsequent chapter devoted to a detailed discussion on this topic.

## 4. SOCIAL FACT APPROACH

This approach was advocated by Durkheim with an eye to the scientific study of society. He was convinced that as long as the subjective world, i.e., the world of ideas, beliefs and values, remained outside the objective world, its scientific investigation would be impossible. But how could this be achieved ? This was to be achieved through, what he regarded as the most fundamental of his *Rules of Sociological Method*, the principle that all social phenomena were to be considered as 'things', distributed along a continuum running from the spatial structure of society at one end to its rules, beliefs and emotions at the other end. His intention was thus to indicate that these various phenomena "are not merely plastic creations of the will of the observer, but share the properties of physical objects in the sense that they exist independently of his observation of them. He cannot, therefore, discover their characteristics by *a priori* reasoning or by introspective examinations of his own consciousness". This did not mean, however, a denial of any meaning they might have for individuals. An individual may cherish a particular faith and seek solace in that faith. But its scientific investigation required that it be regarded as external to man and treated objectively like any other social phenomena. These various social phenomena, including beliefs, values, attitudes, etc., were characterised by him as 'social facts' to which he attributed two characteristics : (i) the attribute of exteriority in the sense that 'social facts' were to be regarded as external to man; (ii) the attribute of constraint in the sense that these stood over the individual in some compelling way — such as, law, customs, and the whole range of moral obligations which exercise constraint upon him. In short, Durkheim's conception of sociology as an autonomous science of society required him : (i) to 'bring the ideal into the sphere of nature', in the methodological sense of adopting the same attitude towards both social and natural phenomena which, he believed, would guarantee sociology's status as a science; (ii) to 'remove nature from the sphere of the ideal', in the theoretical sense of explaining society in purely social terms which, he believed, would guarantee the autonomy of sociology.'[10]

Durkheim emphasised the close kinship among all the highly diverse social facts. He felt that each social fact must be related "to a particular social milieu, to a definite type of society". To do otherwise, he cautioned, is to leave social facts — the facts of religion, law, moral ideas, and economics — "suspended in the void". It is impossible, he contended, to understand the nature and significance of these social facts" unless they are seen in their relations to each other and the collective milieu in the midst of which they develop and whose expression they are."[11]

Durkheim's most fundamental principle with regard to his approach to the study of society was, thus, "the objective reality of social facts". Some criticisms have been raised against this approach. To begin with, by terming the existing factual order "objective" and "real", those tendencies at work which tend to negate the existing order are obscured and, even when perceived, are defined as unreal.[12] Secondly, doubts are raised as to whether objective and scientific analysis of social facts is at all possible. Facts do not speak for themselves nor do they present themselves before us for observation and experiment. Some theory or hypothesis (however tentative it might be) directs our attention and accordingly we observe 'facts' or 'things'. We tend to observe what we intend to observe and we fail to observe what we are not inclined to observe. Again, we tend to invest meaning in what we observe in terms of a theory or hypothesis. Interpretation is never objective, as is claimed, with regard to matters relating to man and his social universe. Subjective bias and prejudice imperceptively and without our knowing it influence our interpretation. Thirdly, social facts are supposed to exercise external coercion upon individuals. But the fact that individuals are able to change social facts is not at all considered. Zeitlin has, therefore, observed that : "In place of 'society' as a concept referring to the interactions and interrelationships of individuals, we are given a reified conception of society as a real, living entity — a *thing.*"[13]

The limitations of the approach to sociological study in terms of 'social facts' arise from the extreme position taken by Durkheim with regard to the nature and properties of social facts. In the instant case, in his anxiety to exclude two potentially competing forms of explanation of social life — viz., *naturalism* and *psychologism* — and also in his eagerness to establish sociology on a scientific basis, Durkheim took up an extreme position that "society is ever-already present',[14] that social phenomena have to be explained only in terms of other social phenomena, and that this was the proper concern of the new science of Sociology — an object which belonged to sociology alone.

## 5. SOCIAL ACTION APPROACH

The concept of social action has been claimed by some sociologists as a key concept in sociology. An individual has different statuses in society — a husband, a father, a neighbour, a teacher and many such statuses — and his roles or patterns of behaviour vary in terms of these different statuses. Social interaction is, therefore, essentially status interaction. Analysis of social phenomena in terms of status and role becomes much too mechanical unless we take into account his state of mind, his perceptions, his emotions and his choices. Social relationships, which constitute the essence of society, acquire a meaningful pattern when we try to seek an answer to the question : *Why* do people behave as they actually do in certain circumstances ? This is true of all branches of social science. For example, analysis of the processes of democratic government becomes truly meaningful when we take into account the voting behaviour of the people — that is, when we seek an answer to the question as to why people vote in the manner as they actually do. "The sociologist more than any other social scientist must necessarily give attention to the behaviour of the person, because he is interested in the nature of social action as such and hence he is interested in human motivation at its deepest level".[15] It is, therefore, worthwhile attempting to develop a general theory of social action.

Action takes place in a situation which has a number of components or aspects. It includes the *actor* (i.e. the person on whose behaviour we are for the present focussing our attention) and an *objective situation* which may be social (other individual actors or groups) or non-social (physical environment). Analysis of action is an examination of how the actor reacts to the objective situation as he finds it.

An actor reacts to the situation with an eye to the attainment of some goal. All action is, therefore, goal-oriented or motivational. What are the motives which generally prompt a man to act ? The views of Max Weber and Talcott Parsons may be considered in this connection.

Max Weber classifies types of action under four categories. First, rational action in relation to a goal. The actor conceives his goal clearly and adopts means with a view to attaining it. Thus, the action of the engineer who is engaged in building a bridge in terms of a clear-cut blue-print employing all his resources and technical skill comes under this category. Secondly, affective or emotional action. This refers to the emotional reaction of an actor to his objective situation. The case of a mother who feels disturbed and slaps her child comes under this category. Thirdly, traditional action. Such action is dictated by customs or beliefs which have become habitual and second nature, as it were, of the actor. Observance of folkways comes under this category. Fourthly, rational action in relational to a value. The action of the brave captain who goes down with his sinking ship comes under this category. The captain chooses to die simply because he considers it dishonourable not to do so.

According to Talcott Parsons, there are three aspects of this process of motivation : these are cognitive, cathectic and evaluative. These correspond respectively to knowledge about goal-attainment, sentiments and morals. An actor may cognise the situation when he strives to attain a goal. That is, he must have idea or information about the methods or ways which are relevant to goal-attainment. An actor may be cathecting towards them. That is, he must have some feelings about the objective situation in relation to his needs. He may be evaluating the situation, considering it in the light of his value-judgment, such as his ideas of what he should do.

All these elements or aspects of motivation become or are made social through the process of interaction. Interaction takes place when any one actor ("ego") considers the actions of another actor ("alter"). If the interaction between "ego" and "alter" is regular, then certain mutual expectations will arise. Eash party tries to predict what the other will do and each modifies his conduct somewhat in order to meet the expectations of the other. The pattern of mutual expectations which gradually emerges through regular interactions becomes a set of norms. Both "ego" and "alter" accept these norms as binding upon themselves. These norms define their mutual rights and obligations. What the "ego" does in relation to the "alter" or what the "alter" does in relation to the "ego" broadly conform to the normative pattern.

Parsons goes further in linking the nature of social action to the characteristic features of different types of social systems. He does this by referring to the different types of action that are possible. These are known as ***pattern variables.*** He formulates four key variable properties of action patterns. Each such action pattern is presented as a binary choice that arises in every social relationship. The first two choices (noted below), viz. (i) and (ii), relate to ego's orientation to others — i.e. what ego expects from his relationships to others. The last two choices, viz. (iii) and (iv), relate to the way alters (individuals or status groups) are defined by the ego — i.e. the type or nature of relationships which the ego maintains with the alters. The four pattern variables are :

(i) Affectivity vs. Neutrality.

Whether ego has emotional attachment to alter in the sense that he seeks or expects mental satisfaction from his relationship with the alter or whether ego is emotionally neutral towards alter in the sense that he neither seeks nor expects any gratification from his relationship with the alter. For example, the relationship of ego with his friend belongs to the first category and his relationship with a stranger or with one who is only his acquaintance belongs to the second category.

(ii) Diffuseness vs. Specificity.

Whether ego seeks or expects a broad range of satisfying relationships with alter or whether ego seeks a narrower and much more specific satisfaction from his relationship with alter. Two cases might be cited to illustrate these two kinds of relationships. Relationship among friends belongs to the first category because friends do not seek a specific kind of satisfaction from their mutual relationship. The pattern of obligation is not defined. A friend is expected to do whatever he can for his friend, if asked. The roles of husband in relation to his wife or of wife in relation to her husband, of mother or father in relation to their children come under this category. On the contrary, the relationship of a patient to his doctor is based on the fulfilment of a very specific need. The role of landlord toward his tenant or the role of a teacher toward his pupils are examples of relatively specific roles.

(iii) Particularism vs. Universalism.

Whether ego defines alter in terms of a very special kind of relationship they have or in terms of alter's membership of a broader class or status group. By way of illustration of the first category we may refer to the very special kind of relationship that exists among friends or among kins. The role of father or son is particularistic. When, however, ego defines his relationship with alter in terms of the consideration that the latter is a male or a female or a fellow citizen, we have the example of the second category. "The role of a judge in court is universalistic. A judge is supposed to to take decisions, not on the basis of the social position of the persons before the bench, but on the basis of strictly impersonal criteria of justice".[16] In other words, we manifest 'particularism' when we give special consideration to people because of their particular relationship to us. We manifest 'universalism' when we treat more or less alike all who come before us in a given status-position.

(iv) Ascription vs. Achievement (later generalised by Parsons to Qualities vs. Performance).

Whether ego defines alter in terms of criteria which have nothing to do with the latter's achievements or performance or whether ego defines alter solely in terms of the latter's performance or achievement. Relationship of ego to alter based on consideration of age, race, sex or caste group illustrates the former and relationship based on 'merit norms the latter. "If my treatment of you is mainly on the basis of what you are in yourself, in contrast to what you have done, I stress *quality* over *performance*".[17]

The significance of this scheme of pattern variables lies in the fact that content analysis of both personal relationships and societal types can be made in terms of this scheme.

The first terms in the four pattern variables — viz., affectivity, diffuseness, particularism and ascription — bring out the broad norms of relationships among friends. By contrast, the second terms in the four variables — viz., neutrality, specificity, universalism and achievement (or performance) — bring out the broad norms of secondary relationships — say, between a doctor or a lawyer and his client. A doctor or a lawyer is expected to be neutral, specific, universalistic and performance-oriented towards his clients.

In *The Social System* (Chapter V) Parsons uses the pattern variables in order to bring out the characteristic features of two types of societies, viz., traditional and modern. At one extreme, traditional societies exhibit "particularistic-ascriptive" characteristics where the emphasis is on kinship relations, and most important activities — such as, work, education, leisure pursuits, religious practices, etc. — are carried out by members of the family or by relatives. The relations among kinsmen reflect not simply the dominant particularistic-ascriptive values of the society, but are also likely to be "affective" and "diffuse". In passing, we may note a very significant observation of Parsons. Since "merit norms" or achievement values are superseded in traditional societies by more dominant values of ascription, particularism and affectivity, the possibilities for economic, political and other forms of socio-cultural development are very much restricted in such societies. Modernisation of these societies can, therefore, begin only after appropriate values conducive to socio-economic development have developed as a dominant force.

In contrast, value priorities are reversed in the more modernised societies. As rationalisation gradually pervades such a society, the universalistic-achievement values begin to dominate the entire social fabric. Relationships among people tend to be impersonal and characterised by qualities of 'neutrality' and 'specifity'. It is thus obvious that all the first terms in the four variables define the characteristic features of a traditional society while all the second terms those of a modern society.

Conceptually, pattern-variable scheme is one of the main innovations of Talcott Parsons. The idea underlying the scheme has been widely accepted and used. He re-defined in terms of theories of action the contrasts between traditional and modern societies which were found in earlier theories of Comte (the law of the three stages). Ferdinand Tönnies (transition from Gemeinschaft to Gesellschaft). Max Weber (transition from traditional to rational-legal basis of authority), and Durkheim (transition from mechanical solidarity to organic solidarity).

## 6. VERSTEHEN APPROACH

*Verstehen* method refers to the study of social action "by interpreting the motivational processes of the actors in their situational, historic, or symbolic contexts. It means, essentially, putting oneself, in imagination, in the place of the other and, through intuition, coming to understand his action".[18]

*Verstehen* method was developed by scholars belonging to Historicist School in Germany. In order to bring out the significance of this method, the contrast between the Positivist School and the Historicist School should be discussed. Positivism in Western Europe sought an approach to social life closely modelled on natural science. Acting units were individuals since no physical links existed among groups of individuals after birth. All subjective properties, definable by their meanings to various actors or culture groups, were virtually excluded. In the extreme (radical positivism) this was a bio-social view of men as organisms adapting to environments like any animals. This view was epitomised by Darwin, behaviourist psychology, and instinct theories. In contrast, idealist approaches stressed precisely the subjective, symbolic qualities of men that set them apart from other species. In contrast to the physical systems treated by Positivist Science, the Historicists called attention to the "ideal reality" of cultures whose comprehension required Verstehen method. Historicists challenged the uncritical rationalism of positivism and stressed the unique integrity of each total cultural system.

It is suggested that some special method or approach, denied to students of the natural universe, has been conferred upon those who enquire into the social universe. Two characteristic features of the social universe are emphasised in this connection : (i) that men have a special kind of knowledge about themselves, and (ii) that we have a knowledge of human nature which is different from our knowledge of the nature of the physical world. The advocates of *Verstehen* method argue that this method is particularly useful in acquiring an "insight" or "understanding" into matters relating to human relationships.

The advocates of *Verstehen* method, however, failed to specify in detail the operations to be performed in using the method. Theodore Abel tried to specify the operations involved with the help of illustrations. For example, if statistical technique discloses a high correlation between crop yields and marriage rates, we say we 'understand' the relationship because we have a behaviour maxim or guiding principle which tells us that when people feel prosperous they are more willing to make commitments than when they do not. The 'understanding' is the process of connecting the observation with the maxim or general principle. In other words, *Verstehen* brings to awareness and makes explicit the maxim that intervenes between our perceptions of stimulus and response. This is specially necessary when the observed behaviour is neither routine nor commonplace and when the connections are other than those we would expect.

The steps involved in following the Verstehen approach are, therefore, three : (i) internalising the stimulus, (ii) internalising the response, and (iii) applying behaviour maxims. The techniques by which we do this are not, however, specified. These are matters of sympathetic imagination and of introducing our own personal experience into the situation. This happens generally in the imputation of motives. The source of behaviour maxims is not in science but in personal experience. Thus, the pursuit of *Verstehen* approach is the application of personal experience to observed behaviour.

Theodore Abel has referred to certain limitations of *Verstehen* as a method of enquiry. In the first place, personal experience is variable and its quality depends upon the introspective capacity of the interpreter. Secondly, this method simply suggests connections, but is unable to verify them. Thirdly, the suggested connection is only a possibility. We need to utilise the more positivistic methods of experiment and comparison in order to determine the probability.

Having made these criticisms, Abel concludes that *Verstehen* cannot serve as a method of scientific analysis and cannot add to our store of knowledge. Nevertheless, he concedes that *Verstehen* is the chief source of hypothesis, and, as such, it has an important role "as an indispensable instrument in the study of social phenomena".[19]

## 7. STATISTICAL OR MATHEMATICAL APPROACH

Sociological study is a study of human relations. The model for such a study is this. The investigator begins with a hypothesis. From this he draws various inferences and these, in turn, are subjected to empirical test which confirms or refutes the hypothesis.

Generally, one arrives at a hypothesis on the basis of simple observation of the social phenomena, attempting to perceive with *insight* the casual relations between various aspects of the social phenomena. According to Professor W. Waller,[20] in the social sciences we may obtain insight in three distinct ways :

1. By direct study of human behaviour.
2. By studying certain symbols abstracted from reality — these symbols are ususally numerical.
3. Through sympathetic penetration.

The first method is simple. In studying any set of social phenomena directly, we pass them before our eyes in an attempt to discover recurrent patterns. These recurrent patterns gradually crystallise into concepts. When sociologists study the customs or institutions of a community, they generally follow this method.

The second method is that of the study of symbols derived from social phenomena. The quantitative symbols furnished by statisticians and reports about a social phenomenon furnished by others come under this category. The statistical method remains immensely important in any method of social study. This is due to a variety of reasons : (i) The best use of statistics is for the study of various kinds of mass phenomena. In certain classes of phenomena, the important facts are numerical relations. Sometimes social facts are so widespread that they cannot be directly studied. But they must be converted into figures and studied in this symbolic form with a view to obtaining insight. (ii) Statistics may give added objectivity to social investigations by substituting the study of quantitative symbols for the direct study of social phenomena. Social phenomena are sometimes so charged with emotion that even the most impartial observer may well doubt whether he has interpreted them without bias. (iii) Another use of statistics is in determining the relative numerical importance of known causal factors. It is, for example, a generally accepted fact that people who have deep emotional attachments to their village do not generally develop into committed factory workers. If we want to know *how many* such people have developed this state of mind, we are required to take the help of statistics. (iv) The role of statistics is often that of making more exact something that is already known.

The third method of obtaining insight is through introspection or sympathetic penetration. The behaviourist who tries to study human relations directly cannot dispense with sympathetic insight. The statistician must also draw more or less upon sympathetic insight for interpretation of his phenomena. When we observe something directly or through language or mathematic symbols, there starts certain mental processes in ourselves. Waller has very well said that "the mind of man is a tiny pencil of light exploring the illimitable dark".

While pointing out the limitations of statistics, W. F. Ogburn observed : "The increasing usefulness of statistics has brought its devotees. But devotion is unreasoning, and loyalties are more appropriate to group action than to clear thinking. Schools of thought based on loyalty to authority or emotional attachments should be more frequent among scholars and artists than among scientists. For these reasons a discussion of some of the limitations of statistics seems appropriate".[21]

To begin with, the language of statistics is a very serious limitation. Figures do not necessarily convey meaning as clearly as does the language. The process of deriving knowledge from statistical figures and tables is one of explanation and interpretation in the same way as one gets the meaning of a political cartoon in a newspaper. The second limitation of statistics arises from the fact that it does not guarantee a reliable composite picture. Statistical information is generally collected in respect of a single phenomenon or a series of them. These studies may be exact. But in order to get a composite picture of the whole, various statistical data have to be selected and given varying emphasis. Bias in selecting data and emphasising some data more than others may distort the composite picture, even when each element of the composite is scientifically accurate. For instance, a conservative and a radical may visit Soviet Russia at the same time and collect the same or similar data and use the same for writing books so different that the time and place might not be recognisable as the same. Thirdly, statistics may prove to be a hindrance in studying certain social phenomena. If, for instance, we want to draw a well-balanced picture of family as an institution on the basis of quantitative or factual records, our study would inevitably be one-sided. This is because of the fact that we may not have adequate records on certain aspects of the family. Fourthly, too much reliance on statistical measurement is criticised on the ground that it often "becomes emptied of meaning". Sorokin, for instance, expressed concern about the loss of meaning which results when the sociologist relies more on "statistical manipulation of data" and does not directly experience the social situations under study. "Only through direct empathy can one grasp the essential nature and difference between a criminal gang and a fighting battalion, between a harmonious and a broken family".[22]

## 8. COMPOSITE APPROACH, RESEARCH DESIGN AND RELATED MATTERS :

A contrast is made between the 'holistic' approach and the 'compositive' in the study of society.[23] In the former, societies are supposed to be studied as wholes. In the latter, societies are studied in terms of parts or elements which constitute the society. It is obviously impossible for sociologists to study modern societies as 'wholes'. Study of parts or elements of society is undertaken now-a-days in terms of a research design.

A research design is the logical and systematic planning of piece of study or research. The plan is initially vague and tentative. It undergoes gradual changes as the investigator gains new perspectives and insights in the course of his investigations. In drawing up the study plan he is required to take certain decisions with regard to : (i) *what* the study is about and the types of data that are needed; (ii) *why* the study is being made; (iii) *where* the required data can be found; (iv) *where,* or *in what areas* the study will be carried on; (v) *what periods of time* will be covered by the study; (vi) *how much material* or how many cases will be required for the study; (vii) *what* would be *the bases of selection of the data;* (viii) *what techniques* of gathering data will be adopted.

A study or research design includes at least the following component parts which are interdependent and not mutually exclusive :

(i) **Sources of information to be tapped**

The sources an investigator should tap vary with his interests and the type of his study. Sources are generally of two kinds : documentary sources and field sources.

The documentary sources of information are those which are avilable from published and unpublished documents, letters, etc. The documentary sources may be classified further into two sources : primary and secondary. The Census Report, for instance, is a primary source of information. The research papers or articles based on Census Report are examples of secondary sources of information. One has to be very careful in handling secondary sources. Sometimes secondary sources of information may have to be checked and verified with reference to primary sources.

The field sources of information are those which are collected directly from persons who are in a position to shed light or supply information on the subject or subjects under study by virtue of their intimate and long experience about men and affairs that are relevant to the study. When field sources of information are tapped, care must be taken to check information supplied by a person with reference to what is supplied by another. This is a safeguard against the study being distorted by unreliable information.

(ii) **Nature of study**

Study of a social phenomenon may take the following forms : a statistical study, a case study, a comparative study or some combination of these and other types. The choice of the nature of study depends on the subject to be investigated. The nature of study appropriate for investigating a small group may be unsuitable for investigating a phenomenon which demands consideration of a large number of cases spread over a wide area.

(iii) **Objectives of research studies**

Objectives of research studies depend upon the goal to be attained. There may be various types of goals : to gather descriptive data, to seek explanatory data, to collect and analyse data which may be of use in deducing a theoretical construct, or to gather data for the purpose of enunciating a suitable social policy or evolving guidelines for social planning.

(iv) **Socio-cultural context of study**

Study of a social phenomenon requires observation of the physical environment as well as the cultural milieu. No man or group of men lives in a vacuum. To understand as to why a group of men in a certain community broadly conform to the prevailing norms or deviate from these, one has to take into account the socio-cultural factors which mould the personality-patterns of these people.

(v) **Dimensions of study and sampling procedures**

Decision on how many cases are to be considered for a particular study depends on three factors : (i) the requirements of study, (ii) the availability of resources and (iii) the availability of time to the investigator.

In certain cases the dimensions of study may be so large as to require sampling of data. In such cases precaution should be taken to ensure that the sample is unbiased and that the sample is large enough to produce reliable results.

### (iv) Delimitation and formulation of a problem

It has been well said that "a problem well-formulated is a problem half-solved". Logical formulation of a problem is the first initial step. The next important step is to delimit the scope of enquiry so as to place the object of study in sharp focus and facilitate completion of the study within the limitations of time and resource. The third important step is to follow systematic procedure and to be discriminatory in the use of data. One may have a vague idea of the object of study when he works out the preliminaries. The successive stages of research and accumulation of data tend to clarify it. Adherence to systematic procedure tends to validate it. Intensive study and painstaking pursuit of procedure are required throughout the scientific voyage.

## Data Collection

Data from primary sources may be collected by observation, personal interview, conference, correspondence, questionnaire and other devices. Of these, observation, interview and questionnaire are very important methods for collecting data. A somewhat detailed discussion of these three devices is given below.

## Field Observation

For the purpose of studying social phenomena, observation means something more than "seeing". It is purposive observation. The first step in the study of social phenomena is to formulate a hypothesis on the basis of stray information or experience gained from mere "seeing". The next step is for the investigator to look closely in the light of the formulated hypothesis at the phenomena under study and test the correctness or otherwise of the hypothesis. If the hypothesis is found to be wrong, the investigator has to formulate another hypothesis and proceed to test the newly formulated hypothesis through intensive observation. In order to avoid confusion and bring to bear upon the study a sharp focus, the investigator should avoid all peripheral issues which, he thinks, will not be meaningful in terms of testing the hypothesis.

Field observation may be controlled and non-controlled in their participant and non-participant aspects. It should, however, be noted that whenever controlled study of a social phenomenon is undertaken, it actually ceases to be observation as such and data collection and data processing become important tools of analysis in such cases.

### Non-controlled and non-participant observation

Non-controlled and non-participant observation is actually a study of a particular social phenomenon from "outside". It may take the form of scattered and occasional visits, and casual observation of the object of study. In the nature of things, such investigations suffer from some inherent weaknesses. The investigator should, therefore, take particular care to avoid distortions creeping into the study. To begin with, while describing the social situation under study, the investigator should scrupulously avoid making subjective generalisations which, on the face of it, are his 'impressions'. Thus, while describing a slum situation, the investigator should not make a statement which runs as follows : "The slum has the appearance of a dull, drab and cheerless place." Such impressionistic statements run the risk of being tinged by subjective bias. To that extent the study is not without blemish. Secondly, 'impressions' gained from casual observation should be properly checked with all the relevant information the investigator has in his possession. The perspective gained from one angle may differ from the perspective gained from another angle. Thirdly, there is a common tendency among us all to read the minds and attitudes of other people in terms of our own values. The investigator should be aware of this danger also.

Nothwithstanding these limitations, non-controlled non-participant observation may throw light on the hitherto unknown aspects of the life of a people, paving the way for a more systematic and in-depth study.

**Non-controlled participant observation**

According to this method, the investigator participates in the life of the community under study and observes first-hand the way the people live, move, think and act. The degree and period of participation may vary with the nature of study undertaken by the investigator. This method was followed by social anthropologists like Malinowski, Radcliffe-Brown, Margaret Mead and others.

Non-controlled participant observation is advocated on the ground that one gets a spontaneous and un-posed picture of the life and activities of the people. It is easier to get answers to the question : ***Why*** do people behave or act the way they do ? Aspects of behaviour which may appear puzzling to an outsider may become meaningful to those who get an opportunity to observe life at close range in all its completeness and naturalness.

The success of this method, however, depends largely upon the "insight" of the observer. It has been very well said : "The mind of man is a tiny pencil of light exploring the illimitable dark". The advance of any branch of knowledge, including science, depends upon the insight of the inquirer. A participant observer has to look at events and social phenomena and think about them all the time until these become luminous and arrange themselves into causal configurations.

Participant observation may, however, be subject to serious error because of the bias and predilections of the observer creeping into the interpretations of the observed phenomena. This is a real danger. Bertrand Russell pointed out that even students of natural science are not immune to the influences of the personal factor. He said : "The manner in which animals learn has been much studied in recent years, with a great deal of patient observation and experimentation..... One may say broadly that all the animals that have been carefully observed have behaved so as to confirm the philosophy in which the observer believed before his observations began. Nay, more, they have all displayed the national characteristics of the observer."[24] If individual passions and prejudices influence so deeply studies of the animal world, how can we rule out completely the influence exercised by such personal factors of the investigator when he is engaged in the study of human behaviour ? This calls for special training of the investigator in order that he may, as far as possible, keep his investigations objective. Margaret Mead spoke of the need for the training of social investigators so that they may "form an estimate of their own strengths and weaknesses as observers". Such training, she claimed, would minimise errors of observation and would further sensitize the observer to the problems of others and create sympathetic insight. The training would, therefore, facilitate, at least to some degree, the understanding of people's behaviour in a certain set of circumstances and in a certain cultural context. In fact, there is no substitute for disciplined imagination.

**Personal Interview**

Interviewing, as the term implies, is an interactional process. When we say so, we do not confine ourselves simply to conversations between the interviewer and the informant. The reaction of a respondent can be obtained not only from his verbal expressions, but also from the way he expresses himself — his intonation, modulation of his voice, expression of his face, his glances and gestures, his pauses in the course of his discussion, etc. Verbal words of the informant may apparently convey one *meaning*, while the *point* that he wants to make may have to be gleaned from the way the words are uttered or the way the sentences are couched. While listening, the interviewer has to consider two contents of a communication : *meaning* and *point.* Meaning is something abstract and depersonalised. When we know the language, we know only the *meaning* of a communication, but not the *point. Point* is something very personal. The following example will bring out the distinction between *meaning* and *point.* The husband puts to his wife the suggestion that Mr.X may be invited to dinner. In reply, the wife says : Well (a pause), if you are so keen, you may do so. The words expressed by the wife give the *meaning* that she has no objection to Mr.X being invited. But what is the *point* she makes ? The pause and the phrase "if you are so keen" indicate that she does not wholeheartedly approve of the proposal. This is the *point* she makes. Besides, the behaviour of the informant — a blush, nervous laugh, sudden pallor, undue embarrassment — may provide very significant data for the interviewer.

Personal interview is not an independent and separate tool in social exploration. It is supplementary to other techniques. As a matter of fact, personal interview, when combined with other techniques, yields the best results. There are certain advantages to be gained from personal interview technique. First, flexibility is a great strength of the interview method. If required, a question may be re-phrased. If the answer is vague, it may be checked with reference to answers to other questions. In fact, a skilled interviewer may be able to gather more information than is possible to collect through other tools of investigation. Secondly, personal interview affords an opportunity to probe the depths of feeling of the interviewees — their truimphs and disappointments, their hopes and fears, their joys and sorrows, their aspirations and uncertainties. These constitute the elements of human personality. No other technique can compete with personal interview in entering the innermost recesses of the mind of an interviewee.

The limitations of interview, even when it is used as a supplementary technique, should be kept in view. To begin with, reference has already been made about the possibility of the findings being vitiated by the subjective bias of the interviewers. Sometimes guesses, impressions and unwarranted interpretations may creep into the analysis of the materials collected in the course of interview. Secondly, the informants are sometimes found to modify facts consciously and present them during interview. Thirdly, the interviewees may suffer from faulty memory, faulty perception, lack of ability to articulate adequately. Given these limitations, they may fail, even with the best of intention, to give a fairly accurate account of the events they are asked to relate. It is also found that they remember recent events much better than events which they experienced much earlier. Likewise, some events register themselves on their memories more strongly than other contemporary events. Also painful and embarrassing experiences are either forgotten or consciously ignored. Mental retention being thus a highly selective process, the materials supplied by the informants may not always be reliable. Fourthly, not much research has yet been done in the field of interviewing technique. As a result, interviewing is even now largely an art rather than a science. Specific guidelines for the interviewer have not been evolved on an exhaustive scale, so as to minimise the play of subjective factors. Finally, the structured interview (i.e. when the interviewer meets the respondent with a set of questions seeking his response) does not yield reliable results. The content of response is severely restricted with the result that the full meaning of the response may not be revealed. Thus, to a question as to whether the respondent visits art exhibitions or a place of worship more or less regularly, he may reply in the affirmative, stressing further that he rarely fails to do so. Will it be proper to conclude on the basis of this response that he is a great lover of art or an ardent devotee ? The fact might be that he is prompted to visit these places for reasons other than those which immediately appear to us to be plausible. There is hardly any scope in a structured interview to unfold the layers of inner mental processes.

Many of the aforesaid limitations may, however, be considerably overcome by a perceptive and imaginative investigator. The limitations relate basically to the limited ability of the investigator to be sufficiently sensitive and aware of the broader context in which the meanings of responses are to be sought, and not to the interview technique as such.

## Questionnaires

Questionnaires are now widely used in collecting data, particularly when data are to be collected from a large number of people who are scattered over a wide area. Questionnaires are generally mailed out to informants asking then to fill in the questionnaires in the light of instructions specified in a covering letter. Questionnaires are used both as independent and separate method of collecting data and as supplementary device to check data gathered through observation and personal interview. This device is eminently suitable for quantitative measurement of a large mass of collected data.

Questionnaires may be of two types : the structured and the unstructured. Structured questionnaires are those which are prepared in advance, keeping in view the requirements of the study design. The questions are very definite and precise and are so set as to check information supplied in response to one question with that supplied in response to one or more questions. Such cross-checking tends to make the answers more reliable. Structured questionnaires may be of two types : open-end and closed-form questionnaires. Open-end questions give an opportunity to informants to express themselves spontaneously on certain issues. They are not inhibited in their responses in the sense that they are not required to keep themselves confined to a rigid framework. Open-end questions are very useful for two purposes : first, to make intensive study of a limited number of cases; secondly, to make preliminary exploration of a field of enquiry which may be followed up on the basis of preliminary exploration. The drawbacks of open-end questions arise out of the fact that many answers may be found to be irrelevant for purposes of enquiry and some answers may lack focus and hence may not be amenable to categorisation. The closed-form questions are generally used when categorised information is required for a particular study.

Unstructural questionnaires are generally known as interview guides. When an investigator interviews people, he is free to arrange the previously formulated questions according as the situation demands. If he feels that answer to a set question seems evasive or not sufficiently revealing, he may ask a fresh question in order to make the previous answer more meaningful. It is obvious that unstructured questionnaire is highly flexible and may be profitably used to reveal the mind of the informant. The disadvantage of unstructured questionnaire is that a mass of non-comparable data may be collected which may defy all attempts at categorisation and scientific analysis.[25]

## NOTES

1. Quoted from W.G. Summer by Alex Inkeles in his book : *What is Sociology* ? (Prentice-Hall publication, 1965), p.30.
2. Bottomore : *Sociology* (1971), p.53-54.
3. *ibid,* p.54.
4. Ginsberg : *Essays in Sociology and Social Philosophy*. Penguin Books, 1968. p.50.
5. *ibid,* p.51.
6. *ibid,* p.51.
7. *ibid,* p.51.
8. Quoted by Bottomore, *op. cit,* p.55.
9. Alex Inkeles, *What is Sociology* ?, page 35.
10. Derek Gregory : *Ideology, Science and Human Geography*, Hutchison of London, 1978, p.88.
11. Durkheim : "Sociology" in Wolff (ed.), *Emile Durkheim*, Quoted by Alex Inkeles in *What is Sociology* ? p.6.
12. Irving M. Zeitlin : *Ideology and the Development of Sociological Theory*, (Prentice-Hall) 1969, p.268.
13. *ibid,* p.268.
14. Derek Gregory : *op. cit,* p.88.
15. K. Davis : *Human Society*, Macmillan Internation Edition, 1970, p.121.
16. Harry M. Johnson : *Sociology*, Allied Publishers, 1966, p.138.
17. Alex Inkeles : *What is Sociology* ? p.74.
18. *ibid,* p.6.
19. Article on Theodore Abel by Robert Bierstedt, International Encyclopaedia of Social Sciences, Vol.18, pages 3-4.
20. Article on *Insight and Scientific Method*, published in the *American Journal of Sociology*, XL (1934-35), reproduced in *Reading in Sociology*, edited by A.M. Lee, Barnes and Noble, 1951, p.19.
21. W.F. Ogburn : Article on Limitations of Statistics, published in *The American Journal of Sociology*, XL (1934-35), reproduced in Readings in Sociology, ed. by A.M. Lee.
22. Sorokin : *Fads and Foibles in Modern Sociology and Related Sciences*, 1956, p.160, Quoted by Alex Inkeles in *What is Sociology* ? p.96.
23. Morris Ginsberg : *Essays in Sociology and Social Philosophy*, p.59.
24. Bertrand Russell : *Philosophy*, W.W. Norton & Co., 1927, pp. 29-30.
25. The ideas contained in the section on Research Design and the methods of collecting data are derived with suitable modifications from *Scientific Social Surveys and Research* by Pauline V. Young, Prentice-Hall (India), 1979.

# CHAPTER – THREE

## NATURAL ENVIRONMENT AND SOCIETY

Man is born on earth. He lives on earth. He builds his culture and society on earth. It can, therefore, be expected that the environment around him – the flaura and fauna, the mountains and rivers, the plains, moulds, deserts, etc. – would deeply affect the way he lives, thinks and acts. Even the sun, the moon and the stars deeply affect him. We cannot, therefore, study society without taking into account the natural environment, including the geographic factor. There is, however, disagreement about the extent of influence exercised by such factors. One philosopher said that "geography is a most enlightening science. In describing the habitat of man it largely explains his history".[1] Another philosopher said with impatience : "Do not speak to me of geographical determinants. Where the Greeks once lived the Turks live now. That settles the question."[2] These two statements are obviously contradictory. Both cannot be right or wrong at the same time. It is, therefore, our task to make a balanced assessment of the influence of natural environment on human society. We may, in the interest of clarity, divide our study into two parts : the study of geographic factor and the study of ecological factor.

### 1. GEOGRAPHIC FACTOR

Sorokin defined geographical environment thus : "..... by this concept we mean all cosmic conditions and phenomena which exist independent of man's activity, which are not created by man, and which change and vary through their own spontaneity, independent of man's existence and activity. In other words, if we take the total environment of a man or that of a social group, and subtract from it all environmental agencies directly or indirectly created or changed through man's existence and activity, we will have left approximately what is known as geographical environment".[3] An analysis of Sorokin's definition reveals that all the natural phenomena that we see and experience around us may be listed as geographic factors. These factors include motions of the earth, the velocity of its revolution and rotation, earth's proximity to the sun, the chemical composition of its crust, the nature of the atmosphere enveloping it, the distribution of its land and water masses, the size and location of its continents, the seasonal changes, the amount of rainfall, the clouds that float in the sky, the rivers that flow down to the sea, etc. However long the list may be made, the constituents of geographic factor will not be exhausted. For analysing the impact of geography on society and culture, we may, therefore, classify these elements into four broad categories : (i) the motions of the earth; (ii) the distribution of land mass and water mass; (iii) climate, and (iv) natural resources. We may take up *ad seriatim* these four factors and try to ascertain the influence exercised by these factors on society.

**Motions of the earth**

Our behaviour-patterns, daily work-schedules as well as festivals and ceremonies are deeply affected by the motions of the earth. Rotation of the earth on its axis gives us day and night. The division of twenty-four hours into day and night determine largely *when* a work is to be done or *how* it is to be done. In a rural society where electrical light is virtually absent. there is a clear-cut division of *what* work is to be done during sun-lit hours and *what* work may be reserved for hours after sun-set. The work-schedule of a ruralite clearly demonstrates this aspect. Hours of meditation or deep contemplation are, for obvious reasons, reserved for hours before sunrise and hours after sunset. The presence of adequate artificial light in modern societies, particularly in urban areas, has radically altered this kind of work-schedule. Even then, in major areas of life the distinction between day-time activity and night-time activity still remains. The revolution of the earth around the sun produces seasonal changes. Changes in season have a profound influence upon man. His thinking as well as the nature of his activities undergo changes according as there are alterations in seasons. Different kinds of festivals are associated with different seasons.

**Distribution of land mass and water mass**

The arrangement of land and water masses has a profound influence upon the life of man. The way of life of those who live in high mountains differs markedly from that of those who live near the sea. The differences are exhibited in their food habits, dresses, occupations and even in the festivals they observe. For example, the people who live in the Himalayas have a worshipful attitude towards high peaks near their places of residence which inspire their awe and wonder. Again, those who live near the sea worship the sea which holds for them both terror and hope, problems and promises.

**Climate**

Climate is an important factor in the life of man. This will be evident from the contrasting activities of those who experience harsh cold climate for the major part of the year and of those who experience pleasant warm climate for the best part of the year. The influence of climate is also seen in the types of dress worn by men and women in warmer and cooler regions. Huntington was of opinion that 'physical strength, mental activity, and health are correlated with variations in temperature and humidity'.[4] Many more examples may be cited to establish correlation between climate and various aspects of the lives of men. That climate exercises some influence is an undeniable fact.

**Natural resources**

Availability or non-availability of natural resources are important factors to be reckoned with in assessing the probable quality of life of a group of people. Bearing in mind the exceptions, it will not be far off the mark to say that the greater the availability of natural resources, the greater is the probability of that society becoming more affluent and vice versa. Not simply the quality of life, even the nature of life of the society largely depends on the type of natural resources which the society can make use of. Thus, a group of people endowed with abundant supply of agricultural resources would, in all probability, develop into an agrarian society. On the contrary, those having abundant supply of industrial raw materials, such as iron ore, coal or petroleum, would have the resource-base for launching on its career as an industrial society.

**Conclusion**

Obviously, geography, climate and natural resource have a very close and deep bearing on the life of man. One important qualification should, however, be added to this generalised statement. Geographical factor, climatic factor and resource factor are only *limiting* factors, and not *determining* factors. Now, man has obtained mastery over nature. Technological revolution in the field of transportation has virtually eliminated distances and brought nearer peoples living thousands of miles away from one another. If the people of a particular society are creative, innovative and energetic, they may, with effort and imagination, surmount the disadvantages in terms of geography, climate and natural resource. Japan, for example, is not endowed with natural resources which conventionally form the basis of an industrial society. Yet Japan has emerged as a leading industrialised nation in the world. There are countries in the Third World which are very rich in resources but very poor in terms of exploitation of those resources to their advantage. It follows, therefore, that whatever importance the geographic, the climatic and the resource factors have, these are relatively minor in comparison with many other social factors which have a deep bearing on the activities of men. Broadly speaking, these factors may, at best, limit the directions that social development is likely to take, but can, under no circumstances, determine decisively the infinite details of these societies. These factors, according to Professor Toynbee, may be regarded as challenges to which adequate response must be given by people of a society. A strong challenge often provokes a highly creative response and, as a result, life becomes enriched in terms of variety and fullness. But, according to Professor Toynbee, sometimes there comes a point where the severity of challenge is no longer stimulating but overwhelming. The society as a whole may not be able to rise to the occasion and resist the tide. The identity of the society may in that event get completely lost and submerged by the overwhelming factor. Did not the Mohenjodaro civilisation disappear because of its inability to meet the challenge which simply overwhelmed it ? These are, of course, extreme cases. Under normal circumstances, the reciprocal relationship of social and natural factors should be recognised. Bierstedt emphasised this reciprocal relationship thus : "Nature is vast and man is puny, but this, of all comparisons, is the least significant. Every item of culture that man devises or invents is a new sentence in his declaration of independence from nature, and although his independence can never be complete, it is immeasurably greater than that enjoyed by any other animal. It enables him to assert his own dominion over the earth that sustains him and gives him life."[5] He, therefore, concludes the discussion thus : "Geography, in short, governs the possible, not the actual. History is not a simple function of habitat, nor culture of climate; neither mistral nor monsoon determines morality, nor soil society."[6]

## 2. ECOLOGICAL FACTOR

We often hear now-a-days a recurrent complaint that man has destroyed nature, that man has polluted his environment, that man has disturbed the ecological balance, and that, as a result, he has created conditions that are far from being conducive to a clean and healthy life. The complaint deserves careful study.

Social or human ecology borrowed its conceptual framework and much of its method from plant and animal ecology. In the biological science, the concept is concerned with the fact that "the structure and behaviour of organisms are significantly affected by their living together with other organisms of the same and other species and by their habitat."[7] Human or social ecology proceeds on the assumption that men are also animals, and as such "they exhibit the effects of physical aggregation and of their habitat."[8] In other words, human ecology is the study of groups in relation to their environment. This is not altogether a new branch of knowledge. Much of what is characterised today as social or human ecology had already been studied in a less systematic and scientific manner by geographers, historians and philosophers under the general theme of 'environmentalism'.

The importance of ecological balance may be studied with reference to the influence exercised by animals, insects and microbes upon human beings and their societies. "We prey upon some of them and they, of course, return the compliment. Nature exhibits an endless cycle of eating and being eaten, and from this process our own kind is not exempt".[9] Lions and tigers prey upon human beings, and we include in our dietary menu a variety of fish and meat. In the animal world, one is the food of the other. If, for some reason, a particular species becomes extinct, the lives of animals which preyed upon this particular species would be endangered. The importance of maintaining ecological balance is brought out dramatically by the relationship that Darwin and Huxley discovered between the number of old maids in a region's population and the abundance of its clover crop. "Old maids, it seems, have a propensity to keep cats. As the cats increase, the field mice decrease, because more of them are eaten by more cats. If the number of field mice decreases, the number of bumblebees increases, because the mice feed on bumblebee larvae. As bumblebees increase, so also does the clover, because the clover flower is pollinated primarily by bumblebees. In short, as the number of old maids increases, so also does the yield of clover. But this is only half the story. An increase in the clover yield contributes to the prosperity of farmers, induces them to marry, and thus reduces the number of old maids. This reduces the cats, increases the mice, reduces the bumblebees, and reduces the clover crop. In short, an increase in the clover crop ultimately causes its decrease. And similarly, an increase in the number of old maids ultimately brings about their decrease, which again results in increase and so on in a cycle revolving forever."[10]

Stories like these illustrate the important point that a balance has to be maintained between man and the animal world around him. There are, for instance, birds which are very useful in keeping the environment clean. The crows, vultures and some other birds are known as scavenger birds because they live on what man throws around him which tends to pollute the environment.

We may also think of the ecological relationship between human species and its food supply. It is common knowledge now that industrial pollutants tend to decrease the supply of fish in the rivers and vast masses of water into which these pollutants flow. The insecticides and pesticides which are generally used for controlling the diseases of plants have the same effect of reducing the supply of fish when these flow into rivers and tanks and pollute water. It is thus abundantly clear that alterations in the balance between men and other species may have serious social consequences.

But keeping in view the unique characteristics of man and the human community, we should distinguish human ecology from plant and animal ecology. Unlike plants and animals, human beings possess elaborate technology and culture; hence they can, in large measure, make their own environment. Moreover, in human groups we find the life of the individuals regulated by formal organisations and institutions. The influence of physical factors upon social life and psychological phenomena cannot, however, be altogether ignored. We may look upon them as conditioning factors that offer the possibilities and set the limits for social and psychological existence and development. As Wirth puts it : "they set the stage for man, the actor".[11]

## 3. GEOGRAPHICAL BACKGROUND OF INDIAN CULTURE

The essence of Indian Culture is found in the Rig-Vedic dictum : *Ekaṁ sad, viprā bahudhā vadanti.* That is, Truth is one; sages call it variously. According to Professor Nirmal Kumar Bose,[12] this unique aspect of Indian culture is, to a certain extent, to be ascribed to the geographical characteristics of the land. Her "vast dimensions, varied physical features, and variety of climate tended to effect different zones with different racial and linguistic peculiarities and different regional spirits".

At the same time, India "found it possible to follow a more or less sheltered course of cultural evolution" because of geographical characteristics of the land. India was "protected by the Himalayan mountain barriers which permitted only a trickle of the invaders or colonizers, necessitating the submergence of their advance parties in the local population in the absence of constant re-inforcements from the rear". There were also the high seas on the south which afforded similar protection. Her insularity made India develop into a distinctive cultural unit and saved her from "the fate that overtook the ancient civilizations of Egypt and Mesopotamia". The magic spell of her natural unity in the midst of diversity had its impact on her culture and on all those who came to India during different periods in the past, "welding them all into a vast synthesis wherein their essential elements have been preserved".

It is interesting to note that Panikkar, the noted historian, has drawn attention to the divisive influence of geographical factors on Indian culture. He referred to the peculiar character of the extension of land towards the south which "because of the change in climate following latitudinal differences, always creates problems of integration". According to him, "despite the unity of India based on Sanskrit language and culture and on Hindu religion and social institutions, geography is constantly trying to assert itself with the result that ethnically and linguistically Deccan and South India still continue to be separate from the North.

While referring to the influence exercised by geographical factors and climate on the character and mental make-up of people living in different geographical zones of India, Professor Bose observes : "In the fertile Gangā valley, which provided cheap livelihood without struggle, life of ease fostered intellectual pursuits and nature favoured philosophical speculation, resulting in the growth of art, literature, and philosophy. This environment, however, did not foster exact sciences. Those inhabiting the coastal regions became mariners and established trade relations with the world. The residents of different regions, e.g., the Punjabis, Rajputs, Sikhs, Marathas, Bengalis, Gurkhas, Telugus, Tamils and others, owe some of their peculiar physical and mental characteristics, in a large measure, to the geography of their regions".

## NOTES

1. Quoted by Bierstedt in his book *'Social Order'* page 34 from George Santayana, *The Life of Reason.*
2. Quotation from G.W.F. Hegel in Bierstedt's book *Social Order.*
3. Pitirim A. Sorokin : *Contemporary Sociological Theories.* Pages 101-102.
4. Bierstedt : *op. cit,* p.46.
5. *ibid,* p.62.
6. *ibid,* p.63.
7. An article on Human Ecology by Louis Wirth in The American Journal of Sociology. L (1944-45). Reproduced by A.M. Lee in his book *Readings in Sociology,* p.139.
8. *ibid,* p.139.
9. op cit p.85
10. op. cit. p.85
11. Louis Wirth, *Human Ecology,* an article reproduced in *Readings in Sociology,* edited by A.M. Lee, page 147.
12. N.K. Bose, *The Geographical Background of Indian Culture,* an article in *'The Cultural Heritage of India,* Vol.I, published by the Ramakrishna Mission Institute of Culture, Gol Park, Calcutta.

# CHAPTER – FOUR

## CULTURE

To any casual observer, human behaviour will reveal two characteristics : the first, that human beings are social animals, and not isolated creatures; the second, that the behaviour of human beings shows regular and recurrent patterns. Certain types of human action are frequently repeated. Thus, when we meet somebody, we generally greet him. The forms of greeting, however, vary among different groups of people. For instance, in India we greet by saying 'namaste' or 'namaskar', or we observe a form of salutation by joining the two palms together. The Western people, on the other hand, greet people by uttering standardised phrases, such as 'How do you do ?', 'Hallo', etc. or by shaking hands. That is, every group of human beings has its own standardised way of greeting. Similarly, we can think of innumerable instances of similarities in human behaviour. The existence of similarities does not, however, mean complete identity of behaviour. Each particular human group — for example, Chinese, Indians, Burmese, etc. — has its unique standardised pattern of behaviour.

These two aspects of human behaviour, i.e., the social character of human life and the existence of a standardised pattern of behaviour, are obviously the basis for the study of sociology. Sociologists have developed two concepts, *culture* and *society*, in order to account for and explain the regularities in human action and the fact of social life.

### 1. DEFINITION OF CULTURE

The sociological meaning of the term *culture* differs sharply from the ordinary and literary uses of the term. In conventional usage, the word *culture* is employed to designate only those particular traits and behaviour systems that are regarded as refinements, such as painting, music, poetry, philosophy, art galleries, etc. The adjective 'cultured' stands close to 'cultivated' or 'refined'. The sociological use of the term *culture* does not, of course, exclude music, painting, and art galleries; but it also includes football, cricket, beliefs, superstitions, practices, and even crimes. That is, it includes all activities that are characteristic of a given group of people. In sociological usage, *culture* refers to the totality of what is learned by individuals as members of society; it is a way of life, a mode of thinking, acting, and feeling. "A culture refers to the distinctive way of life of a group of people, their complete design for living".

The two essential points in regard to culture are emphasised in the definitions of Sir Edward Tylor and Robert Redfield. According to Tylor, "culture is that complex whole which includes knowledge, belief, art, morals, law, custom, and any other capabilities and habits acquired by man as a member of society." Redfield speaks of culture as "an organised body of conventional understandings manifest in art and artifact, which, persisting through tradition, characterises a human group". The phrases *'acquired by man'* and *'persisting through tradition'* throw into focus two important dimensions of culture. A human child, as he grows up, learns gradually from parents or from members of the group among whom he is born and among whom he lives. The fact of *learning* indicates that one cannot acquire culture in isolation from society. In other words, the concept of culture has a social context. Redfield's use of the phrase 'persisting through tradition' is a recognition of the important fact that what is learned in one generation is passed on to successive generations. This is a unique aspect of human culture. Acquisition of a particular way of life (i.e., culture) through tradition is possible simply because human beings possess the ability to learn from the group — an ability which the lower animals have in a very limited degree. We cannot explain the standardised patterns of human behaviour in terms of inherited instincts or natural tendencies. Most animals are equipped by heredity with special skills and instinctive knowledge which enable them to meet their basic needs and to adapt themselves to their environment. Consider, for instance, the habits of some species of fish to move out of sea to spawn in fresh water or the annual migration of birds in winter from cold climate to comparatively warmer areas. The patterns of behaviour are inherited which appear automatically at the appropriate time, and are not learned from other members of the species. Man, on the other hand, possesses little, if anything at all, of instinctive skills or knowledge which might enable him to survive singly or in groups. The reason for the survival of man lies in the fact that he has "the capacity to invent and learn language, which, in turn, enables himself to build a culture and to organise society" This art of symbolic communication enables man to transmit experiences gained in one generation to successive generations. No knowledge is lost. A human baby need not burn his finger to learn that one should not put one's finger into fire. He is forewarned by his elders. Because of his capacity to communicate symbolically, man has been able to develop various kinds of 'cultural aids' to fulfil his various needs. In order to ward off summer heat, a man need not, like an animal, keep himself submerged in water. Instead, he has devised electrical fans, coolers, etc., to relieve him from summer heat. It has been very well said that a man does not grow fir like animals in a cold climate; he makes a fir coat to keep himself warm. The behaviour of man is thus largely a product of *learning* (emphasised by Tylor) and *experience* (emphasised by Redfield). These characteristics of culture have led some writers to define culture 'as man's social heritage'.

The word *"super organic"* is used by some writers[1] to emphasise a certain degree of independence of culture from inorganic and organic elements. It is said that the inorganic phenomena are investigated by the physical sciences, the organic by the biological or "life" sciences, and the superorganic by the social sciences or the humanities. The term superorganic does not, however, indicate that it is, in any way, superior to the organic or the inorganic. The suggestion which is implicit in the word is that a phenomenon which is looked at from a physical or biological point of view is altogether a different phenomenon when looked at from a cultural point of view. For example, a banyan tree carries one meaning to a botanist who examines the tree objectively from a scientific point of view and finds out its characteristic features which distinguish it from other trees. The same banyan tree appears to be a different phenomenon altogether when looked at from a cultural point of view. To some, the tree is an object of worship. Some may emphasise its utilitarian aspects by referring to the fact that it provides the much-needed shade to those who take rest under its spreading branches. Similar is the case with organic objects. A cow, for example, is just an animal like many other animals to a biologist. From a cultural point of view, however, a cow is something more than an animal. It is, for instance, a sacred animal to a devout Hindu. The word "superorganic" therefore — if one refrains from attaching metaphysical connotations to it — fixes our attention upon the *social meaning* of physical objects and physiological acts and emphasises the fact that this *social meaning* may be relatively independent of physical and biological properties and characteristics. In this sense "the superorganic" becomes a useful synonym for 'culture'.[2]

We noted in the first paragraphs of this chapter that each particular human group has its own distinctive standardised pattern of behaviour. It is rooted in the traditions of the group and it is shared by all the members of the group. In other words, each group has a distinct *design for living.* The concept of culture as a distinct design for living is a useful tool for differentiating one society from another. Indian society, for instance, is to be distinguished from, say, Chinese society in terms of their respective designs for living.

The meaning of culture becomes clear when we take into account these four dimensions of the concept — that it is (i) learned behaviour, (ii) the social heritage, (iii) superorganic, and (iv) a design for living. Each one of the expressions is used to emphasise a slightly different aspect of a complex phenomenon. The first one suggests that culture is learned and taught and shared and can by no means be acquired by an individual in isolation from society. The second expression suggests the idea of 'inheritance', the idea that culture is handed down from generation to generation, and that something is added to and lost from that inheritance in each generation. The third expression suggests that culture varies in relative independence of physical constituents and biological components and has an independent meaning. The fourth expression suggests that culture varies from one society or group to another, that it varies in different places at the same time and in the same place at different times. Acquaintance with these four dimensions of culture is essential to an understanding of the basic concept.

## 2. CULTURAL SIMILARITY AND DIVERSITY

At a fairly high level of abstraction, there are substantial similarities in the patterns of culture found among different groups of men. That is, there are traits common to all cultures. This universal culture-pattern may be expressed in terms of the following : (i) All peoples have a family system. (ii) All have a language. (iii) All have developed some sort of a system relating to food, clothing, shelter, etc. (iv) Every social group has some kind of government and patterns of social control. (v) Property systems and inheritance rules are found in all lands. (vi) People in all groups worship a Higher Power. We may suggest in this way still other universal patterns of culture.

At a much lower level of abstraction, however, we find almost endless diversity in cultural patterns. Thus, Hindus refuse to eat beef, while the Christians and Muslims have no such taboo in respect of beef. What is quite normal and conventional among one group may be highly objectionable to another group. For example, the Andamanese do not whistle at night because they believe it will attract spirits; among non-Andamanese, say, among us, on the other hand, it is supposed to be one way to keep up one's spirits when walking past a graveyard at night. Even differences in attitudes and behaviour-patterns persist among groups within the same society — for instance, among rural folk and urbanites.

**Why cultural similarity**

Some writers have argued that the biological nature of man largely explains the existence of similarities in broad cultural patterns. We may consider here some biological facts : namely, the difference between the sexes; the long dependence of human infants upon others for survival; the organic drives generated by hunger, thirst, and sex; the processes of maturation and aging; and, finally, the fact of death.

These biological facts form the basis upon which many universal elements of culture are built — for example, the standards regulating the relations between sexes; the practices relating to child care and child rearing; the methods of cooking food; the practices relating to disposal of the dead.

**Why cultural diversity**

Biological factors cannot obviously explain adequately the growth of cultural patterns. There are many aspects of cultural life of a community which cannot be easily related to biological facts, such as bodily adornment, decorative art, dancing, hair styles, etc. These cannot be explained in terms of biological needs.

Some writers have tried to explain diversities in cultural patterns in terms of race, and some others have explained these differences in terms of geographical and climatic variation.

**Race and Culture**

Those who explain cultural diversities in terms of race assume that the external physical characteristics — such as, the shape of the head, colour of the hair, eyes and skin, height, body build, etc. — have a definite relationship to the kind of behaviour people will exhibit and the kind of culture they will possess. According to this view, the Negroes, Caucasians, and the Mongoloids are expected to possess different cultures by virtue of their different biological features.

This view is unacceptable for various reasons. To begin with, from the biological point of view, all races of men originate from the same trunk. This view has been upheld by the UNESCO Committee of Experts on Race Problems.[3] Secondly, most peoples have mixed racial ancestry. This makes the concept of race of dubious reliability for social science. Thirdly, the irrelevance of heredity to the kind of culture an individual acquires is confirmed by a number of studies that have been made in this field. The following report of an American brought up in a Chinese family illustrates this point. "A few years ago a young man of American parentage, who had been reared in a Chinese family from infancy on, paid his first visit to America. Reporters commented not only upon his apparently complete bewilderment in the American way of life, but also upon the fact that his walk, arm and hand movements, and facial expression were 'Chinese — not American' They insisted that one had to fix one's attention upon his blond hair and blue eyes to convince oneself that he was of white stock at all. Here the point is that an individual's acts and attitudes not only failed to resemble not only those of his own close relatives in this country but that they resembled those of all members of an alien physical group and contrasted with those of all members of his own physical group".[4] Fourthly, there is overwhelming evidence that similar cultures can be found among peoples with very different physical characteristics, that different cultures can be found among peoples with similar characteristics, and that culture may change quickly without any corresponding change in racial composition of the people.

**Culture and climatic and geographical factors**

The evidence which invalidates racial theory also refutes the theory of climatic and geographical determinism of culture. The same patterns of culture may prevail under widely different climatic and geographical conditions. For instance, European ways of life have been adopted by some sections of the population in almost all the countries outside Europe and America. The ways of life in big cities of the world exhibit broadly common features which cut across national frontiers. Likewise, different ways of life are found under similar climatic and geographical conditions. Dissimilarities of social practices among various groups of Indians illustrate this point.

We cannot, however, totally dismiss climatic or geographic facts from consideration. It is true, as is evident from the above discussion, that climate and geography cannot be regarded as *determinants* of culture. We should, however, look upon them as *problems* — extreme heat or cold, for example — which different groups of men may meet differently. Thus, a person can meet the problem of heat in tropical climates by taking to a loin cloth, or by sleeping through the hottest part of the day, or by using electric fans. The way a person meets such problems obviously affects other aspects of his life and thus marks a distinct way of life.

## 3. MATERIAL AND NON-MATERIAL ELEMENTS OF CULTURE

The full meaning and scope of culture is brought out by making a distinction between symbolic elements of culture and non-symbolic products of cultural behaviour. It is sometimes useful, for reasons discussed below, to bear in mind the distinction between a system of cultural behaviour and the products of these systems. These products may be both symbolic and non-symbolic. Symbolic traits constitute a large part of every culture. Every word in our language is a symbolic trait, and every idea or belief is a complex of such traits. It is through these traits that the experiences of mankind throughout the centuries can be stored in books and libraries where each generation may acquaint itself with valuable accounts of other people's trials and errors, their successes and failures.

In addition to the symbolic traits that constitute an important part of every culture, there are non-symbolic or material traits that are associated with behaviour systems. Examples of non-symbolic or physical traits of cultural behaviour are buildings, bridges, dams, books, etc.

The significance of non-symbolic cultural traits lies in the fact that they have an existence independent of the behaviour that produced them. Very often they survive long after the people who produced them have ceased to exist. For example, we can investigate the physical traits dug up in the ruins of ancient societies and can reconstruct the modes of life, i.e., the cultural behaviour, that are likely to have prevailed among those people.

We may discuss here a question relating to the criterion by which to judge whether a physical object is or is not cultural. Does an ordinary rock lying in a field or by a roadside come under the category of a cultural object ? Obviously, it does not, because such a rock is neither a part of a behaviour system nor a product of such a system. Man has nothing to do with its creation or location, and people react to it in the same way as they react to the millions of other objects called rocks. If, however, it is found on closer examination that the rock has a groove around its middle, indicating that it was once used as a man-made tool or weapon, it becomes a product of human behaviour. It seems fairly reasonable to conclude that the rock was once used in behaviour systems, such as fighting or the production of food. In other words, this particular rock has a meaning which rocks in general do not have. Similarly, an ordinary piece of ground becomes a cultural trait if its meaning is modified, as in the case of a holy place, a burial ground or a football ground, as a result of interhuman behaviour. We may conclude, therefore, that the *use* of an object, not its intrinsic character, determines whether it is to be regarded as a cultural trait.

The symbolic and non-symbolic products of cultural behaviour are integrated closely together and form part and parcel of a standardised pattern of behaviour, a consistent and systematic whole.

**Culture and Civilisation**

The distinction between material and non-material elements of culture is made the basis of a distinction between culture and civilisation by MacIver. Culture, it is held, "deals with interests and values conceived as ends." Civilisation, on the other hand, refers to "the whole mechanism and organisation which man has devised in his endeavour to control the conditions of his life." Since culture is concerned with end, it is internal and value-oriented. On the other hand, since civilisation is concerned only with means, it is external to man and utilitarian in character. "The civilisational means may be represented by a ship which can set sail to various ports. The port we sail to remains a cultural choice."[5]

The important differences between the characteristics of the two orders may be discussed from the following points of view :

*Civilisation has a definite standard of measurement, but not culture.* The apparatus of civilisation can be measured on the grounds of efficiency. Thus, we recognise the superiority of the tractor over the hand plough or of power loom over handloom. We have, however, no universal measuring rod by which to assess cultural achievements. These are judged by purely subjective criteria. Judgments vary in different ages and among different groups. Hence it is not easy "to study the changes in the ideas that cluster round the everyday life, the popular philosophies, the notions of authority, the doubts and the certitudes, the fears and the hopes of men."[6]

*The transmission of civilisation is easier than that of culture.* Since civilisation is something external to man, amenable to quantitative measurement, it is easily comprehended and communicated. We can use and enjoy without any special effort or even without any particular qualification on our part the greatest achievements of civilisation, such as the automobile, the radio, the refrigerator, the television, etc. But it requires a certain level of mental development, and sometimes appropriate temperament, to appreciate and assimilate the works of culture, such as the beauty of a painting or the moral fervour of philosophical discourse. "Culture is communicated only to the like-minded. No one without the quality of the artist can appreciate art, nor without the ear of the musician can one enjoy music."[7]

*The achievements of civilisation are marked by progressive improvement, but culture is subject to retrogression as well as to advance.* An achievement of civilisation becomes a permanent possession of mankind, and serves as a basis for further improvement. Thus, the aeroplanes of the thirties have been superseded and rendered obsolete by more efficient aeroplanes of today. Further, the achievements of civilisation tend to accumulate and, as a result, the areas of civilisation get widened. To bullock carts and horse-drawn carriages, for instance, are added the automobiles and aeroplanes of today. Hence, civilisation always marches in the same direction, "provided there is no catastrophic break of social continuity." We cannot, for obvious reasons, say the same thing of cultural works, "of our dreams and our sculptures, our conversation and our recreation". Can we say, for example, that the Bengali poetry of today is better or richer than that of the thirties or forties of this century simply because it has the benefit of the experience of about fifty years following the outstanding contributions of Tagore ? If we trace the course of any cultural pursuit, it will be clear beyond doubt that it has been subject to stagnation and retrogression during some period or periods of history. The past of a culture does not obviously assure its future.

*The expansion of a civilisation follows different principles from those which determine cultural development.* Being utilitarian in character, civilisational means spread quickly. If found to be efficient, an apparatus of civilisation is adopted by men wherever they have the means to acquire it. Thus, even a savage is ready to replace his bow and spear with the rifle. It is a simple matter of choice to adopt or discard a particular achievement of civilisation. But the transference of cultural elements from one area or community to another is not so easy. Culture is so closely interwoven into the fabric of life of a community that the people cannot freely abandon its culture and adopt another. Culture determines the quality of life of a people and gives it strength. Hence, even when one civilisation covers the globe, the cultural differences among different peoples will endure. In fact, people resist the advance of civilisation when such an advance affects, to their disadvantage, their cultural life. Hence, diffusion of culture is more slow and gradual than that of civilisation.

The differences in the processes of expansion of the two orders may be studied from another point of view. In the case of civilisation, transference or diffusion is limited to recent or contemporaneous contributions to the stock of civilisation. But "cultural elements may be adopted as readily from the past as from the present, from any epoch of the past no less than from the present hour .... Its range of selection runs from the newest culture-fashion to the myths that linger from the dawn of history".[8]

*These differences in the processes of advance of the two orders are important from the point of view of social change.* It may so happen that the advance of civilisation "outstrips the formation of those cultural attitudes necessary for its maintenance". Consider, for example, the functioning of democratic institutions in the newly-independent countries of Asia and Africa. Many of these countries adopted parliamentary democracy on the western model. But the functioning of parliamentary democracy in a large number of these countries has not been satisfactory because "the proper cultural preparation is lacking". Similarly, full benefits of industrialisation cannot be obtained unless appropriate work culture conducive to industrialisation is developed.[9]

*Culture and civilisation cannot, however, be treated in isolation.* Cultural pattern is responsive to changes in civilisation, and, at the same time, acts back on the latter so as to influence its character and direction. A seed needs proper soil and climate for its growth and fruition. Likewise, cultural interests of men thrive better in appropriate environment. To go back to the simile of MacIver and Page, the more efficient the ship, the greater is the number of ports that lie within the range of our choice.

The use or application of civilisational apparatus is, on the other hand, governed by cultural considerations. The industrial plant, for example, can turn out necessaries or luxuries, the comforts of life or the munitions of war. The use to which we put our industrial plant is largely a result of our cultural choice. That is, the set of priorities we keep before ourselves determines our choice.

Even the invention or development of technological device or similar other apparatus of civilisation is also governed by cultural choice. Basically, culture implies valuation. Every change in valuations of a group of people registers itself in institutional change. Thus, slavery was once considered to be natural. Gradually, however, these ideas changed in the course of centuries. These changes are reflected "in our regard for the individual, for the non-abstract, living human being". This change in attitude towards human personality provided undoubtedly a spur (strengthened, of course, by other motivations) to invention and extensive application of labour-saving devices and automation. The changes in the sphere of state-activities, similarly, owe their origin tc the changes in our concept of 'good life' which we expect the state to uphold and provide for its citizens.

## 4. THE CONTENT OF CULTURE

In the above section we have classified the content of culture into two large components : material culture and non-material culture. The concept of material culture is quite clear because it is tangible. The same cannot be said of non-material culture. If it is defined as a residual category in the sense that 'everything that is not material is non-material culture', some amount of vagueness is likely to enter into the definition. Non-material may include "items of several fundamentally different kinds". We defined culture as the complex whole that includes all that we think and do as well as all that we have. In other words, *thinking, doing* and *having* are the three components of culture. We may, therefore, adopt a three-fold classification of culture thus :

Culture

| (Thinking) | (Doing) | (Having) |
|---|---|---|
| Values, beliefs and ideologies | Norms | Material |

Material components of culture have been discussed in some detail in the foregoing section. Ideas and Norms constitute the elements of non-material culture. We may discuss these two elements, viz., values, beliefs and ideologies as well as norms, in some detail in the following sections.

### Values

One cannot meaningfully interpret many aspects of the culture of a group without a broad acquaintance with the 'values' and 'beliefs' of the group. 'Value' may be defined as a conception or standard by which feelings, ideas, actions, qualities, objects, persons, groups, goals, means, etc. are evaluated as desirable or undesirable, more meritorious or less, more correct or less. A social group is emotionally committed to the 'values' which prevail. 'Values' are seldom questioned. These are tacitly accepted. Such 'values' may grow out of deep philosophical reflection or out of practical experience and knowledge about the physical and social universe. When we speak of the spirit of Indian culture or the Indian way of life, we actually mean the values which permeate the Indian society and regulate the thinking and behaviour of Indians in general. 'Values' are generally arranged in a hierarchical order — some dominant some less dominant and still some others secondary.

### Beliefs

Unlike 'values' which are essentially social in nature, 'beliefs' are more personal. 'Beliefs' do not lay down, like 'values', any standard by which to judge anything as good or bad, appropriate or inappropriate, desirable or undesirable. 'Beliefs' are neither true nor false. The efficacy or validity of a 'belief' is not tested by knowledge or experience of the physical and social universe. Thus, the primitive people in all parts of the world 'believed' in the world of spirit and took various means to propitiate or control evil spirit. Many people in all parts of the world even today entertain such 'beliefs'. Even in advanced societies of today, 'beliefs' exist side by side with modern scientific knowledge. For example, a devout Hindu or a Moslem or a Christian says a silent prayer at the same time that he is taking a patient's temperature with a thermometer. It is wrong to assume that 'beliefs' are confined to religious sphere alone. In modern societies, economic, political and social 'beliefs' have assumed a tremendous importance. Some governments consider certain political or social ideas to be inimical to its security and spare no pains to suppress those ideas. Most often such perceptions are based on untested knowledge and are thus of the essence of 'beliefs'.

Because of its intimate relation to conduct, 'belief' has been of continuing interest to social philosophers and its psychological nature a frequent subject of study. It is generally recognised that to the extent that an idea fills the mind to the exclusion of possible alternatives we tend to hold it true. Thus, fixed ideas and inflexible 'beliefs' arise in a state of mental debility. Certain psychologists emphasise the active element of assent in the judgment that something is true. Some have stressed the purely voluntary character of this assent while others insist that when we truly believe, as when we truly love, we feel compelled to do so. The recognition that we have a choice means that another view is possible, and this is implicit doubt.

Whatever the psychological characteristics of belief, it is clear that its specific forms are largely *social* in origin. These are in many cases conditioned by our habitual emotional reactions with the result that through following a certain mode of life, one generally ends by sharing the beliefs of others who follow that mode.

'Beliefs' may be institutionalised. A dogma, for example, is a religious belief that members of a particular religious group 'must' accept. Similar is the case with a political dogma or creed which the members of the particular political party 'must not' challenge.

**Ideologies**

In addition to 'values and 'beliefs', there are other ideas which the members of a society are expected to believe and uphold not because these are true (the question of truth may be impossible to determine) but because these are considered right or good or proper in that society. As a matter of fact, there is, so to say, a moral obligation to believe and uphold those ideas if one wishes "to remain in good standing" in that society. These are the ideologies. Every society has its set of ideologies. For instance, those who share the contemporary culture of the Indian society also share the ideology "The truth shall prevail". It is accepted as a self-evident truth. No one needs to prove the validity of the motto. The possibility that falsehood may sometimes win over truth is not taken into account. Such considerations are irrelevant. The proposition that 'the truth shall prevail' is thus ideological rather than scientific. Some sort of sanctity is attached to these ideologies. Not that all those who accept this ideology act according to the standard implicit in the ideology. One may often say and do things bordering more on falsehood than on truth. Yet no one can openly advocate falsehood as a national motto. It is easier to indulge in falsehood than it is to advocate it. Similarly, a life of renunciation is accepted as an ideal by almost all sections of the Indian people. One who gives up all his earthly possessions and severs connections with his family and friends and takes to the life of a *'sanyasin'* or *'fakir'* is held as an ideal. But few mothers would encourage their sons to follow the ideal. On the contrary, in most cases they would be genuinely unhappy if their sons decide to follow the ideal. No effort will be spared to dissuade them from taking to the life of a *'sanyasin'* or *'fakir'*. Nevertheless, the life of renunciation is upheld as an ideal and one who practises the ideal is held in high esteem.

The following example may be cited to indicate the nature of ideology. In the late thirties, Bertrand Russell was appointed to the faculty of The City College of New York as a teacher in mathematical logic. The offer of appointment aroused very strong and bitter resentment. The ground on which the appointment was opposed was that in one of his works Russell had suggested that the taboo on adultery be reconsidered, and that such relaxation might contribute to the stability of marriage. The opposition was so violent and strong that ultimately the budgetary provision for his salary was withdrawn and the entire proposal was dropped. It is to be noted that Russell himself was not guilty of having committed adultery. He only expressed his personal views on social morals which offended the sensibilities of the people and challenged their ideological stance on adultery. It is also to be noted that his views on morals had nothing to do with his teaching mathematical logic. Apparently, it is easier to commit adultery than it is to advocate it openly. It is thus evident that all societies cherish some ideologies and these ideologies are an intimate and important part of their culture.[10]

**Utopian Structures**

Ideologies are defined by some sociologists as *'utopian structures'* which may be defined as those particular sets of normative patterns which, though not institutionalised, do require allegiance to them as institutionalised ideals. Allegiance to them as ideals is highly traditionalised in both conformity and sanction aspects. Thus, one does not in fact expect conformity to the principle of 'Love thy neighbour as thyself'. But its expression as an ideal is certainly institutionalised in some social contexts and its perpetuation is institutionalised.

**Norms**

We have seen that culture means the way of life of a people living in a particular society. It is the cementing bond which knits the people together. Through experience people in society have discovered what is right and proper and what is improper and wrong for a healthy social life. These standards of behaviour, called *norms,* are built into the cultural life of the people. When sociologists use the concept of norm, they refer not to ways of thinking but to ways of doing. Most of the things we do as members of society and most of the things we refrain from doing are cultural in character. A close analysis of cultural pattern reveals its prescriptive and proscriptive elements. It prescribes the way the people should behave. It also proscribes certain patterns of behaviour which the people should avoid. Culture is, therefore, essentially a bundle of do's and don'ts. And the society in which the people live is essentially a normative society.

These prescriptive and proscriptive elements of culture, however, differ in terms of the degree of pressure which the society brings to bear upon its members to conform to the norms. In some cases, the society exercises the utmost pressure to enforce conformity; in some cases the pressure is comparatively mild and in some cases the pressure is virtually non-existent. The norms are accordingly classified into *institutions, mores* and *folkways.* We take up these norms in a reverse order.

**Folkways**

The term 'folkways' was coined by William Graham Sumner, the Yale University sociologist.[11] Folkways are conventional practices which are accepted as appropriate but not insisted upon. All forms of social etiquette and models of social behaviour go by the name of 'folkways'. They may vary from society to society, and from time to time. The folkways generally relate to dress, polite behaviour or etiquette and convention. Thus, a Rajput, who does not wear a turban, is ignoring one of the folkways of the Rajput community. A Westerner, who refuses to wear a tie on formal occasions, is ignoring one of the folkways of the Western society. Similarly, ladies are expected to wear a particular type of dress when they attend a wedding reception and to dress differently when they attend a funeral. Society has also developed what is called etiquette or standard of polite behaviour in order to make social living smooth and pleasant. Thus, when a host, who invites people to a dinner on some occasion, asks his guests about the quality of food served, etiquette demands that the guests should speak well of the quality of cooking even though it may not really be so. Polite behaviour demands that one should not be truthful in such matters. There are also well-established conventions in every society which its members are expected to conform to. Thus, it is generally accepted as a sign of good behaviour that one should not ask a stranger or a chance acquaintance about the salary he draws. This is considered to be impolite and unconventional. Those persons who deviate from any of the aforesaid patterns of behaviour may be looked upon merely as eccentric or staunch individualists.

Folkways are norms to which we conform because it is customary to do so in our society. Conformity to the folkways is neither required by law nor enforced by any special agency of society. Folkways perform two important functions. First, folkways constitute an important part of the social structure and contribute to the order and stability of social relationships. Second, conformity to folkways gives a sense of security to the members of society.

**Convention**

Convention emphasises common agreement about a customary practice. It has many forms. Thus, in a social gathering we generally ignore aspects of a situation that are likely to cause bitterness or to produce difficulties. The relation between two gentlemen, for instance, may be far from cordial. But when they meet in a social gathering, they generally follow the convention not to bring out their conflict into the open lest that should spoil the congenial atmosphere of the gathering. Similarly, there is a tacit agreement not to ask a stranger or a chance acquaintance about his salary. The convention is thus a very useful code which "serves to maintain a superficial but often serviceable type of solidarity".

**Etiquette**

The term etiquette is used for certain customary practices in 'polite society' generally involving detailed formalities. For example, it is bad manners for a host to sit down before his guest takes his seat. Similarly, social etiquette demands that men should get up when a woman guest arrives. "In fact, every group that possesses a tradition of any length develops a protocol of regulations prescribing the norms of behaviour for certain events". Etiquette serves a social purpose because it prescribes the procedure for specific occasions or circumstances. Since it represents a code of manners of a group, etiquette distinguishes superficially a social class, and is sometimes made a criterion of one's right to belong to it.

**Mores**

The more binding folkways were characterised by Sumner as 'mores' (the plural form of the rarely used Latin word 'mos', pronounced mó-rez).[12] He defined the mores as "the popular usages and traditions, when they include a judgment that they are conducive to societal welfare, and when they exert a coercion on the individual to conform to them, although they are not co-ordinated by any authority ...." Mores are norms to which we conform because it is considered to be *morally* appropriate in our society. Mores differ from folkways in the sense that moral conduct differs from merely customary conduct. Our society requires us to conform to the mores without, however, having established a special agency to enforce conformity. Conformity to mores is enforced in various ways. Any failure to conform to the prevailing mores is followed by moral disapproval and frequently strong pressure from those who disapprove of such violation. Some examples would make the meaning clear. The man or woman who pushes to the head of the queue and tries to board a bus or tram out of turn is violating one of the mores of the society. It is more likely in such an event that he would not be allowed to board the bus by jumping the queue. The man who supports a wife and a mistress is regarded as having committed an immoral act. Hence, he is charged with violation of mores. Various kinds of social pressure in the form of satire, social boycott, etc. are brought to bear upon him to enforce conformity to mores.

As group standards and value judgments vary, so does the mores. Thus, one group condemns the re-marriage of widows on moral grounds whereas another group may not find anything morally wrong in re-marriage of widows and may actually commend it. Similarly, among Hindus in North India married women are obliged to cover their heads while among Hindus in South India only widows (and not all married women) are obliged to cover their heads.

The mores perform three important functions in social life. In the first place, since mores are strongly enforced by a group which constantly exerts pressure on every individual member, they determine much of our individual behaviour. Secondly, by conforming to the group mores, an individual identifies himself with the group. Such identification is obviously essential for satisfactory social living. Thirdly, the identification of individuals with the group serves to bring about and maintain group solidarity. A group striving for greater solidarity tries to strengthen the hold of its mores on the members.

The mores are usually agents of conservatism in social life. They represent a vast amount of past experience of the group which is "transformed and stereotyped into tradition". Naturally, therefore, members of a group look upon them as 'right' and 'proper'. They are also not inclined to pursue practices or methods which are not approved by the prevailing mores, sometimes out of fear and sometimes out of uncertainties inherent in untried means.

A word of caution about the distinction between folkways and mores. The distinction between the two is not rigid. What is considered to be mores today may be considered to be folkways in future and vice versa. It all depends upon the degree of importance attached by a society to certain norms.

**Customs**

Folkways and mores together constitute the customs of society. Just as an individual is habituated to do certain things during certain hours of the day, so also the members of a society *habitually* follow folkways and mores. These are social customs.

Individual acts, if repeated, become habits. Thus, when a person gets up early in the morning regularly, we call it his habit. "Habit means an acquired facility to act in a certain manner without resort to deliberation or thought". When we form a habit, it becomes easier for us to act in a certain way, and difficult to act in ways other than the one to which we are habituated. Habit-formation is a part of our learning process. Once a habit is formed, it becomes a part of our nature — a "second nature", as it is called.

Habit is useful to us in our day-to-day living. There are many acts which have to be repeated every day, such as brushing teeth and washing mouth in the morning, using soap at the time of taking bath, etc. Our lives would have been miserable if we had to think afresh each day of each step of these processes. It is undoubtedly a tremendous gain to be able to entrust these repetitive acts "to the semi-conscious operations of habit". We thereby gain time for more useful jobs. MacIver and Page have therefore observed : "Habit as the instrument of life economises energy, reduces drudgery and saves the needless expenditure of thought".[13]

But habit has another aspect also. Once habituated, we follow mechanically certain ways of doing things as a matter of routine. We do not generally think of alternative ways. Habit thus acts "as a conservative force in social life". Among 'barriers' to social change, the most important one is that presented by habit.

It is, however, wrong to assume from the aforesaid discussion that man is a slave to his habit, that habit is "some all-powerful master ruling us against our will". The actual choice from among a set of alternatives is made by a man who acts on his own. Once the decision has been made, "habits begin to confirm the choice, to counter its disadvantages and disappointments, to close the alternatives".[14]

When individual habits are repeated among masses of people, and when the repetition is frequent enough, they become customs. The distinction between habit and custom is not, however, merely a quantitative one. Custom is more than the habits of a group. It has a social quality, which is lacking in the case of habit. A habit concerns an individual who may form his habits in isolation from the society. A hermit, for example, may develop certain habits which do not concern the society at all. A custom, on the contrary, has behind it the sanction of society. It exists as a part of the social fabric. Ogburn and Nimkoff have therefore observed : "Customs are social habits and through repetition become the basis of an order of social behaviour".[15]

Though habit and custom are distinct, yet they are sometimes causally related in social life. Thus, "the customs of the group are translated through education ...... into the habits of each generation, and the habits thus formed perpetuate the customs."[16] Here customs precede and influence habits. But habits also precede and influence customs. "When personal habits are sufficiently similar, such as those induced by the discovery of new techniques, they are apt not only to modify old customs but also to stimulate new ones".[17] In urban areas, for instance, many people develop the habit of dining out in hotels and restaurants. When such a habit becomes fairly common among the members of a community, the custom of arranging receptions (say, in connection with marriage) in hotels, instead of at home, becomes increasingly popular. Similarly, many new habits induced by many new scientific devices and industrialisation in general "have undermined old customs and have helped to bring about others".

Custom has been the earliest means of social regulation. Where social organisation is simple, custom plays an important part. It is virtually the king. "With the weight of tradition behind it, custom ordains every occasion, assigns to each his rights and duties, adjusts the claims and interests of each to those of the rest".[18]

Custom has not grown in any community by a conscious effort, but "by an imperceptible process of growth as a reflex from the feelings of order, justice, and utility that existed in the minds of the people". It is obeyed for a variety of reasous. It is obeyed because of habit, of its social utility, and of the security which it provides. Thus, a community which is exposed to acts of aggression from without is likely to develop various customs which are conducive to the growth of militant outlook. At the time of the Moghuls, the Rajputs developed customs which had this very purpose in view.

But as social relations become complex, custom fails to provide with sufficient promptness the new rules for the regulation of new problems as they arise. There are several reasons as to why the rule of custom must be supplemented by some other social code. In the first place, custom lacks authoritative agency to enforce its decision in cases of dispute. Secondly, customs are effective in a simple society marked by face-to-face relationships. In such a society "no one escapes beyond the range of gossip, of group opinion and group control". Besides, seldom does any novel situation arise for which custom cannot provide. In a complex society, on the other hand, personal relationships are replaced by impersonal ones and old ways of life are replaced, partially or wholly, by new ways. It is, therefore, natural that the effectiveness of custom as an agency of social control diminishes in a complex society. Thirdly, a complex society consists of different groups having different customs. These differences in customs may arise from differences in the linguistic or religious or ethnic backgrounds of these groups. In such cases customary rules must be replaced by a code of conduct equally acceptable to all the groups.

**Traditions**

When customs operate for a fairly long period of time and acquire a strength because of their having continued for a long period, these are generally referred to as traditions of the society. Traditions may, therefore, be defined as customs of very long standing.

The term 'tradition' may also be defined as an institution whose perpetuation is institutionalised — that is, as a special form of institution. A tradition in this sense is a double institutionalisation : (i) the structure concerned is an institution, and (ii) the perpetuation of the structure is also an institution.

**Fashion**

We may introduce here the concept of fashion. It refers to changing customs which lack continuity and persistence and are expected to change rapidly, usually within limits set by the prevailing mores. Fashion does not affect basic values. It affects those aspects of life which are considered to be relatively of minor importance. For example, there is in every group a customary dress for men and women. But slight variations in such customary dress may become fashionable for some time. Hence, MacIver and Page have defined fashion as "the socially approved sequence of variation on a customary theme". As compared to fashion, custom is more enduring, more closely related to the life and temperament of the group, and more intimately wedded to tradition. Fashion, on the other hand, is concerned with the superficial aspects of life, and is definitely opposed to tradition. Some sociologists, therefore, define fashion as the "imitation of contemporaries", and contrast it with custom which is the "imitation of ancestors".

The meaning of fashion will be more adequately brought out when we contrast it with style. Style is more individualistic and personal, as is the case with an artist who follows a style of his own. When his style is followed more widely by others, then the element of fashion comes in. Similarly, a film actress may follow a particular hair style of her own. When this particular hair style becomes popular and is widely copied by others, it becomes a 'rage', a fashion with a group.

Though fashion is concerned with the superficial aspects of life, yet it satisfies some of the deeper urges of man. A hankering after novelty, a craving for distinction, and the need for conformity — these are the three demands of social men which are satisfied by fashion. The demand for novelty is not always consistent with the demand for conformity. A harmonisation between these logically opposite needs is brought about by fashion. Since fashion is concerned with the external and superfluous aspects of social life, it does not stand in the way of conformity. At the same time, the slight changes from the established practices in dress, hair styles or other forms of behaviour satisfy the craving for novelty. These minor changes "seem for the moment to give the victory to the individual".

In an open-class society marked by vertical mobility, external symbols are very important in determining the status of a person[19]. Since fashion generally radiates from "the prestige-owning groups" the people follow a fashion because it meets their desire to look respectable. Different types of fashion represent different "standards of income and of taste". So a person who is eager to show off his distinctions in these fields naturally adopts the prevalent fashionable practices.

Fashion has gained greater prominence in modern times than it ever did before. As soon as a new fashion is introduced, it extends over a very wide area, and affects people belonging to all classes. Fashions also change with greater frequency today than it ever did before. We may explain these developments with reference to the following factors : (i) Changes in class structure : Under the closed social system, status of a person depends on birth, land ownership or wealth. External symbols are not, therefore, very important in determining his status. Under the impact of technology and industrialisation, the closed social system is being replaced at a very rapid pace by an open class structure (even in developing countries) in which possession of external symbols adds to the status of a person. Naturally it becomes fashionable to imitate the ways of those who have prestige in that particular field. (ii) Increased prosperity and leisure : Almost all forms of fashion make a demand on one's purse and time. Previously, only a few could afford the necessary time and money to cultivate fashionable practices. But the application of technology has made available to a large number of people greater amount of prosperity and leisure. Hence, what was once a privilege of the few is now within reach of a large number of people. (iii) Easy means of communication : The spread of fashion in modern times is also the result of the enormous development of the means of communication which has practically annihilated distances. Different regions and communities have, consequently, lost their previous compactness and aloofness. "Contacts bring alien customs together and diminish the sanctity of many of the established ways". In these circumstances, custom and tradition naturally lose hold, and fashion gains ground. (iv) Modern industrial organisation and mass media of communication : Modern industrial organisation is associated with mass production of commodities. So sales agencies are "at work to stimulate the growth of fashion and above all to accelerate the change of fashion" in order to push the sale of particular products. When a new model or a new design of a product is brought out, the advertising agencies utilise the available mass media of communication to impress upon the people that a new fashion has arrived in the market and that people of good taste should have it. "Modern advertising shows more and more the tendency to praise less the quality of the goods which are advertised than *to suggest social image.* Modern research has proved that people buy not only to satisfy material needs but that *an act of social communication is linked with the purchase.* In this way people take part in the way of life and habits of a highly esteemed minority group"[20]. It is, therefore, no wonder that it becomes 'fashionable' at a particular time to buy a certain commodity or to see a particular film, or to wear a particular type of dress.

## Institution

There is no consistent integration among the various norms of society which we have discussed thus far. Obviously, it is not possible to bind the society with the help of folkways and mores which are not enforced very strongly. Nor are there specific agencies to enforce these norms. This gap is filled in by another type of norm called institution. The concept of institution suggests the idea of some sort of social control. It denotes "patterns of approved or sanctioned behaviour" of a group which has sometimes the backing of the law as well as the moral approval of the community.

For instance, marriage may be viewed as an institution which regulates the mating relationship between man and woman. This may be distinguished from courtship which is considered to be a custom which is not insisted upon before a couple decides to marry. But the society will not allow a man and a woman to live as husband and wife unless they are formally married according to socially approved practices. Complications arise with regard to a child born of a couple who were not married according to socially accepted practice. Such a child bears the stigma of an illegitimate off-spring affecting adversely his rights to property as well as his social standing.

One should bear in mind the distinction between the sociological meaning of the term 'institution' with its meaning in ordinary parlance. Anything that is *socially* established is called an institution in ordinary speech. Thus, by educational institution, we mean a school or college. In Sociology the term 'institution', like many other sociological concepts, carries a very specific meaning. According to sociologists, the institutions are developed with a view to fulfilling certain interests or special objectives. We may show the relation between social organisation (or association), institutions and special interests with reference to the following chart[21] :

| Association | Characteristic Institutions | Special Interests |
|---|---|---|
| The Family | Marriage, the home, inheritance | Sex, home parentage |
| The College | Lecture and Examination system, graduation | Learning, vocational preparation |
| The Business | Book-keeping system, Incorporation, Share capital | Profits |
| The Trade Union | Collective bargaining, strike, picketing | Job security, wage rates, conditions of work |
| The Church | Creed, Communion, forms of worship | Religious faith |
| The Political party | Party machine, political platform | Office, power, government policy |
| The State | Constitution, legal code, forms of government | General regulation of the social order. |

The aforesaid chart becomes meaningful when we are clear about the points of distinction between an association and an institution. An association is an organised group. It may be large or small. It is organised with some specific purpose or purposes in view. Since it is an organization, it has obviously some structure and some continuity. It has, in addition, an identity and a name. An institution, on the contrary, is not at all a group, whether organized or unorganized. "An institution is an *organised procedure* ..............., a formal, recognised, established and stabilised way of pursuing some activity in society. In succinct terms, then, *an association is an organized group; an institution is an organized procedure*"[22]. The distinction may be illustrated with reference to concrete cases. Two street urchins may be engaged in fighting, one trying to run the other down. In another case, in an organised show two boxers may be engaged in the same kind of activity with the similar objective of one knocking the other down. There is, however, an important difference between these two cases. In the former, the activity is unorganised and not related to any established and recognised procedure. In this sense, the activity (i.e. fighting between the urchins) is not institutionalised. In the second case the boxers are engaged in a fight strictly in terms of a rigorous set of norms. In this case, the boxing activity is institutionalised. Such organised procedure is an institution. We may think of another case. A child is taught at home by his father, mother, elder brothers or sisters. He may also be taught by his teachers in the school. Teaching at home is unorganised, and it does not follow any prescribed procedure. Teaching in the school is, however, very much formal and organised to the minutest details, starting from a prescribed daily time table to the holding of periodical and annual examinations. Here the teaching procedure is institutionalised. The school is an association and the procedure of teaching at school is an institution. Similarly, "the care and cure of the ill can be institutionalised in some societies, political leadership in others, and intercession with the gods in all". Thus, we have educational institution, political institution, educational institution or religious institution.

Two simple tests may be applied in order to dispel the confusion with regard to the distinction between these two phenomena, associations and institutions. The first is that an association has always a reference to a location. An institution, on the other hand, has no such reference. It is absurd to think of an institution having a locational dimension. Thus, a college or a university has a location, but, not teaching procedure or examination system or education. The second test is that one belongs to an association but not to an institution. We belong to a college or a university, but not certainly to the examination system. Likewise, we may belong to *a* family, but not to marriage or to *the* family conceived as a complex of various procedures regulating mutual relationship among members of the family and various functions like procreation and upbringing of children.

Similarly, *a* government is an association, government an institution. The Government of India, the Government of Maharastra or, for the matter of that, any government is an organised group and hence an association. "Government, on the other hand, as a regular and recognised way of governing — that is, of making political decisions, enacting and enforcing laws, and maintaining formal order in a society — is ..... an institution"[23].

We may now enquire in what respect an institution, which has been defined as an established procedure, differs from other social norms, particularly from folkways and mores. The latter are "sustained and sanctioned by unorganised groups within a society and by entire communities". We have already seen that there are no special agencies to enforce folkways and mores. Institutions, on the other hand, require specific associations to sustain them. Wherever there is an institution, there is also an association to sustain and enforce that particular institution. Thus, to impart elementary education to a child is a customary activity carried on by members of the family. But when we come to formal education, we have to think of schools and colleges in order that an elaborate procedure may be set up for the purpose of imparting teaching, "Institutions and associations are thus concomitant and correlative phenomena".[24] To cite another example, the customary greeting procedure, whether by joining the two palms together and saying 'namaste' or by shaking hands and saying 'hallo', is sanctioned and sustained by the unorganized community. A salute, on the other hand, is sustained and supported by the Army or the Police organization. The former is a folkway and the latter an institution.

**Law**

We have noted that in a complex society custom fails to regulate social life very effectively on certain occasions. There is, therefore, the need for a legal code as the regulator of social life. Laws deal with external conduct and are enforced by a system of compulsions. Law has been variously defined. According to the Analytical Theory, law is, in the last analysis, reducible to the commands of a determinate superior. The

Historical School of Jurisprudence objects to this view. According to this school, law is the product of different social forces. From this point of view, law may be defined as the totality of the historical, moral, religious, economic and ethical forces functioning within society. Woodrow Wilson, who sought to harmonise these two views, defined law as "that portion of the established thought and habit which has gained distinct and formal recognition in the shape of uniform rules backed by the authority and power of government". We may reduce from this definition certain essentials of law. These are : (i) the presence of a civic community; (ii) laws as reflecting the social conditions of that community; (iii) laws as a body of rules; (iv) laws as regulating the external conduct of man; and (v) laws as implying coercion, ***more physical than moral.***

From this point of view, non-legal norms of society may be distinguished from laws which are "***legally*** established norms which may or may not have the moral sanction, characteristic of the mores". Non-legal norms are also distinguishable from laws from another point of view. Non-legal norms, to use one of Sumner's expressions, are ***crescive.*** That is, they just grow. "A simple example can be found in the college classroom. Seats are normally unassigned and students sit where they like. After the first few meetings of the class, however, the students tend to occupy the same seats every day and may even develop a proprietory attitude toward them. Thus a seating pattern emerges that was wholly unplanned".[25] On the other hand, laws are ***enacted.*** They are enacted by legislatures, interpreted and applied by the courts, and enforced by the executive branch of the government.

The functions of law are broadly two in number. First, to maintain an order "within which men shall find security and the common conditions of opportunity". Second, to adjust and peacefully settle "those conflicts of interests between individuals or groups which they cannot settle for themselves or in the settlement of which they encroach on the interests of others".

It is, therefore, obvious that law is an instrument in the hands of the government to maintain law, order and security. The nature of this instrument also indicates its limitations. Law is primarily concerned with the external acts of men, and not with their motives, thoughts and attitudes. Its scope is thus much more restricted than that of ethics which control the totality of human life, both his thoughts and deeds. Law is virtually ineffective to produce any effect in those areas where emotions and sentiments are involved, as in the case of religion.

We noted that custom is inadequate to deal with problems of a relatively complex society. So also is law ineffective to "prescribe religions or other forms of belief". But the fact remains that both types of code are essential in social life. In important respects they are interdependent. It has been said that in the development of law, custom is the conservative element, and legislative enactment the radical. The chief function of custom is to maintain the status quo. But customs become sometimes inconsistent with the spirit of the time. In such cases legislative enactment should provide rules consistent with newer social needs.

Laws should not be invented, in the sense that they should not be far in advance of what is recognised as usual by the general conscientiousness of the people. A law remains a dead letter when it is far in advance of what is recognised by the people to be necessary and useful. Laws must, therefore, be supported by custom. Custom also supplements law and prepares the way for its development. Aristotle remarked that "a law derives all its strength from custom". The customary law in India and the Common Law of England are good illustrations of the notable part played by custom in the evolution of law. By way of emphasising the part played by custom in the development of law, MacIver says : "In the great book of law the State merely writes new sentences and here and there scratches out an old one. Much of the book was never written by the state at all".[26]

## 5. WHY DO WE CONFORM TO THE NORMS ?

Human groups are cultural groups, and are organised around norms or standards of conduct. A group, therefore, brings pressure upon those who deviate from these standards. Pressure is applied in three inter-related areas : the physical, the economic, and the socio-psychological.

Since man is a cultural animal, he communicates largely through symbols — such as language, for instance. Human group, therefore, mainly utilises the symbolic sanctions or socio-psychological means of exerting pressure. Thus, we apply the *praise* mechanism "as a device to elicit behaviour in accordance with the social norms". We also apply the *satire* mechanism to achieve the same object. That is, we ridicule the person or persons who deviate from the social norm or standard. In a small community, marked by intimate acquaintance among its members, *gossip* mechanism is very effective as a means "to prevent our deviations from convention from becoming too flagrant or too frequent".[27] When the symbolic or social-psychological sanctions fail, physical and economic sanctions are applied. Thus, a mother punishes her child when he misbehaves despite repeated warnings. The idea behind such corporal punishment is to inflict physical pain in order to bring pressure upon the deviationist to conform to the mores of the community. Economic sanctions are also applied in certain circumstances. When a father warns his son saying that unless he mends his ways, he will lose his pocket allowance, he is applying economic sanctions against his son in order to force him to conform to the ways of his choice. Economic rewards are awarded for good behaviour. Cases of monetary penalty and cash award are quite common in every society. Very often, these three types of sanction are combined in various ways.

Hope of reward and fear of punishment are not, however, the only reasons for our conformity to the norms of our society. There are other bases of conformity which we explore in the following paragraphs.

### Indoctrination

Among the processes and devices that tend to perpetuate the norms and bring about some sort of conformity among members of a group, socialisation or social indoctrination plays an important part. Social indoctrination refers to "the inculcation of modes of thought and patterns of belief" among its members from infancy onwards. This learning process is called socialisation by which the values of the group are incorporated into the personality of the growing child.

### Habituation

Closely related to this direct method of communication and instruction is habituation which may be described as "the process in which people unconsciously adapt their ways of thought to the social conditions under which they live". Once we get used to a particular way of life we look upon it "as both inevitable and good".

Thus, habituation and indoctrination work together towards the same goal, each strengthening and re-inforcing the other. Through these two devices, men develop loyalties and convictions in regard to group mores.

### Utility

In many social situations we recognise the rational efficacy of the norms to which we conform. "Thus, we stop at a red light and go on a green one, not only because we are indoctrinated and habituated to the practice, but because we recognize that this kind of regulation is useful to everyone, ourselves included".

**Group identification**

Sometimes we conform to the group norms not because we are indoctrinated or habituated to particular norms but simply because we identify ourselves with the group by doing what the group members do. No one likes to be singled out and identified as a non-conformist. Group identification gives us a feeling of security and helps to dispel a feeling of loneliness.

## 6. SUBSIDIARY CULTURE CONCEPTS

Sociologists have analysed 'culture' and 'cultural behaviour' in numerous ways and developed many concepts in order to bring out the varied facets of this important social phenomenon. These may be described as subsidiary culture concepts. Some of these are discussed below.

**Culture trait or culture item**

When we talk about a very small bit of culture, we use the terms 'trait' or 'item'. We may think of various types of culture traits. Thus, a spoon may be regarded as an item of material culture. The idea that 'cleanliness is next to godliness' may be looked upon as an item of ideational culture. To say 'namaste' or good morning to an acquaintance is an item of culture associated with behaviour or social norms.

**Culture Complex**

A culture complex is a functional combination of closely inter-related traits within a culture. That is, culture complex refers to a combination of culture items or culture traits. Thus, shoe making is a culture complex which is a product of combination of various culture traits, such as tanning of leather, use of appropriate needles and other implements, the art of sewing, etc. Likewise, cooking is a culture complex which consists of various culture items like the art of making fire, the use of spices in proper proportions, the making of utensils, the art of growing vegetables, etc.

**Culture pattern or Culture Configuration**

Just as item combines with item or trait with trait to form a culture complex, so also various culture complexes combine together to produce a culture pattern or culture configuration. Culture complexes of a group may be lumped into the following six categories : (i) economic, (ii) familial, (iii) educational, (iv) political, (v) religious, (vi) recreational. Culture complexes of these six basic types combine with one another in an almost infinite number of ways to create the general culture fabric of a society. When we speak of an agrarian society or a technological society, we actually refer to particular types of culture pattern characteristic of a particular society. When we speak of Indian culture or French culture we do so keeping in view the unique culture pattern or configuration which obtains in Indian society or French society.

**Sub-culture and Contra-culture**

Culture of a sub-group is called sub-culture. For example, Assamese or Maharastrian culture, though essentially a part of Indian culture, has some distinctive features of their own. Therefore, Assamese culture and Maharastrian culture may be characterised as sub-cultures.

In a highly stratified society, different social classes may develop distinctive cultural features of their own — say, in the matter of dress, etiquette, food habits and even intonation. Such social classes may be said to have developed sub-cultures.

When, however, differences of a sub-group are emphasised more than similarities, endangering the persistence of the culture of which it is an off-shoot, the particular sub-culture develops into what Yinger characterised as contra-culture.[28]

### Cultural alternatives

When we speak of culture as a cementing bond in society or as a normative pattern to which the members of society conform, we do not mean that culture is a mould which shapes all individuals alike. On the contrary, culture presents alternative lines of action or conduct for individuals in certain cases which are equally acceptable. Such alternative lines of action or conduct are called cultural alternatives. A discerning observer of cultural scene in contemporary India will confirm the existence of various forms of greeting which are equally accepted as 'proper'. "The point is that there are cultural alternatives as well as cultural specifications and not all cultural patterns are cultural imperatives".[29]

### Cultural universals

Those culture traits which are necessary to all members of the society and are followed by all of them are called cultural universals.

### Cultural specialities

Cultural specialities are elements of culture which are shared by some, but not all, groups within a society. For example, baby nursing is a female speciality not shared by men. Nearly every group in society — each age-group, sex group, occupational group, religious group — has certain traits not shared by other groups.

### Core Culture

That part of the total culture of a society which is shared by most members of the society is called core culture.

### Cultural diffusion

Cultural diffusion refers to a process by which culture traits and culture complexes spread from one society to another. Thanks to modern means of transportation and electronic communication, what is developed in one society is spread to other societies all over the world. This applies not simply to items of material culture but also to items of non-material culture. If there are no artificial restrictions like an embargo imposed by a government, political and religious ideas may spread like wild fire from one continent to another.

### Acculturation

The process of acquiring the item or items of culture of a society not one's own is called acculturation. When in Rome, we are advised to do as the Romans do. If one is in contact with another culture for a prolonged period of time, he is likely to acquire in course of time some elements of the culture with which he has been in contact. If, for example, an Indian, having lived in the U.S.A. for several years, acquires the American habit of taking dinner at 6 or 6.30 p.m., he may be said to have been acculturated to some elements of American culture.

### Cultural relativism/relativity

The principle of cultural relativism may be stated thus :

Standards are relative to the culture in which they appear. It is almost impossible to find absolute standards in human societies. In its simplest terms, cultural relativism means that actions that are moral in some societies are immoral in others, that propositions considered true in some are false in others, and that conduct that is approved and even prescribed in some is disapproved and even forbidden in others.

The principle of cultural relativity raises a question about the possibility of universal norms. Are there any actions that are acceptable alike in all societies or condemned alike in all ? Anthropologists and sociologists are not in complete agreement on this issue. We may think of some universal norms. But some exceptions readily come to mind. Thus, all cultures condemn pre-meditated murder. Exceptions are, however, made during war. Likewise, incest taboo is universally accepted as a proper code of conduct. But one will immediately recall that marriage between brothers and sisters was permissible among the members of the royal family in ancient Egypt.

A distinction may be made between a cultural absolute and a cultural universal. Some elements of culture may become universal without becoming absolute. For example, Western type of clothing may be universal, but can never be absolute in the sense that this kind of dress would be the only proper clothing to wear.

**Syncretism**

The process of re-interpretation with retention of original function is called syncretism. Religion provides many examples of syncretism. In parts of Catholic Negro America, African deities have become identified with Catholic saints.

**Cultural survival**

Sometimes culture traits, items or complexes survive in a society long after their original function has disappeared and sometimes even after the limited reason for their establishment has been forgotten. We observe today many customs and practices which were considered useful and meaningful by those among whom those customs and practices developed. Even though those customs do no longer carry any meaning to us, yet we follow them through sheer habit. These are called cultural survivals. A very interesting example may be cited. "The sleeves of men's jackets still have three or four buttons at or near the cuff, but these buttons serve no function whatever, except possibly a decorative only. According to one theory, Frederick the Great of Prussia introduced these buttons on uniforms in order to discourage his soldiers from indulging in the somewhat unaesthetic — to say nothing of unhygienic — practice of wiping their noses on their sleeves".[30]

**Culture conflict**

The term culture conflict is an ellipsis. That is, it is people who are in conflict with one another, not cultures. The reason which prompts people to fight with one another may sometimes have a cultural base. In such cases it is convenient to describe the conflict in terms of the concept of culture conflict. For example, the cow is a sacred animal and beef is a forbidden food in terms of Hindu culture. To a Moslem, on the other hand, the cow is like any other animal and there is no taboo against the eating of beef. When Hindus and Moslems live side by side and there is no attempt on either side to make suitable adjustments, their cultural attitude towards this animal alone may be, and have been in the past, perennial sources of conflict.

**Ethnocentrism**

Ethnocentrism is related to the principle of cultural relativism. We have a tendency to evaluate other cultures in terms of our own. That is, the ways of behaviour of people, who belong to a culture other than our own, are measured and evaluated in terms of the standards and norms with which we are familiar. History is replete with examples when people of one cultural group looked upon those who belonged to another cultural group as barbarians.

**Temporocentrism**

Bierstedt has defined temporocentrism as "the unexamined and largely unconscious acceptance of one's own century, one's own era, one's own lifetime, as the center of sociological significance, as the focus to which all other periods of historical time are related, and as the criterion by which they are judged".[31] We have a tendency to look upon the present as more important than the past, all the present practices as superior to those of the past.

## 7. DIFFERENTIAL NORMS AND CONFLICT SITUATIONS

We may discuss the following situations in order to indicate how differential and contradictory norms lead to conflict situations.

India is a pluralistic (multi-group) society. There are various groups which differ from one another in terms of language, religion, dress, food habits, race, etc. These differences are reflected in the norms. One does not conform to *all* lhe norms in a complex society, but to *most* of the norms prevalent in the larger society. In addition, one conforms to those norms which are specific to one's group. This consideration introduces a complicating factor in any treatment of the norms — viz., the existence of contradictory norms. Thus, Hindus may bring out a religious procession, accompanied by music. Moslems may object to the procession proceeding near their mosque on the ground that their religion forbids music being played near the mosque. There is thus a conflict situation being created by contradictory norms of the two communities.

We may conceive of another type of conflict situation arising out of contradictory norms. In a rapidly changing society, the norms of an older generation seldom coincide in all respects with those of the younger generation. This type of situation is generally characterised as generation gap.

Contradictory norms also arise because of the world having become smaller as a result of quicker means of transportation and communication. Thus, it is difficult to be an internationalist and a good patriot at the same time. Similarly, it is difficult to be a good citizen and a pacifist at the same time.

Two consequences of such contradictory norms may be noted. First, some sociologists believe that such conflict situations are largely responsible for the high incidence of mental diseases in modern societies. Second, differences in norms, particularly when these are contradictory, are barriers to understanding.

## 8. DEVIANCE

Man is a cultural being, and not an automaton. He does not, therefore, blindly conform to the socially approved norms of conduct. He may, and does occasionally, deviate from an accepted path. Some of these deviances are positively sanctioned, in the sense that these are rewarded. Some are negatively sanctioned, in the sense that these are punished. There are again some deviances which are not taken notice of and simply accepted. In sociology the term 'deviance' is reserved for "those situations in which behaviour is in a disapproved direction, and of a sufficient degree to exceed the tolerance limit of the community".

Deviance, it should be emphasised, is a relative term. There is no absolute way of defining a deviant act. Deviance is defined in relation to a particular standard or value-judgment. And standards or value-judgments do not remain fixed or constant over time. As such, deviance varies from time to time. Since value-judgments of one society vary from those of another, deviance also varies from one society to the other. What is deemed to be a deviant act in one society may not be so deemed in another society.

### Physiological and psychological theories

According to those who seek to explain deviance in physiological terms, particular individuals are more prone to deviant behaviour than others because of their genetic make-up. Are deviants born ? According to these thinkers, the answer is in the affirmative. Lombroso, an Italian criminologist, believed that heredity plays an important part in determining deviant behaviour.

Sociologists tend to dismiss physiological theories of deviance, arguing that values are learned rather than being genetically determined. "It is not yet possible to isolate a gene or a combination of genes and to show conclusively that they influence particular actions".

Psychological theories of deviance are broadly similar to those of physiological theories. It is assumed that deviants are abnormal among a group of normal population. Their abnormality explains their deviant conduct. Psychological theories, however, differ from physiological theories in that the deviant's abnormality is learned rather than genetically determined. They point to "abnormal experience rather than abnormal genes as the basis for deviance".

Sociologists tend to dismiss psychological theories as well, arguing that it is more worthwhile emphasising the social and cultural factors which produce a deviant mentality rather than probing the recesses of the mind. The latter exercise involves us in another difficulty. "There is little agreement among psychologists about what constitutes mental health and on how to measure personality characteristics".

**Functionalist (Durkheim's) approach to deviance**

A functionalist looks to the society as a whole, rather than to the individual. That is, it seeks to trace the source of deviance in the nature of society rather than in the physiological or psychological characteristics of an individual.

Interestingly enough, functionalists refer not only to the dysfunctional aspects of deviance but also to the functional aspects. They look upon deviance as a threat to social order and, as such, dysfunctional for society. Hence social control mechanisms are to be invoked in order to check deviance and preserve social order. They argue that deviance can also be functional inasmuch as "all social change begins with some form of deviance". If we are to ensure social change, some sort of flexibility has to be accepted. What is considered deviant today may become quite normal tomorrow. Just as a certain amount of change is healthy for society so that it may not stagnate and degenerate into a fossil, so also is deviance wholesome for society. Sometimes deviants break new ground and direct attention to changes which were long overdue. Emile Durkheim argues in The Rules of Sociological Method that "crime is an inevitable and normal aspect of social life", and that "it can also be functional". According to him, crime becomes dysfunctional only when "its rate is unusually high".

What is, then, the way out ? Should crime or other forms of deviance be simply tolerated ? Durkheim's answer is a firm 'No'. Punishment must be provided "to maintain the collective sentiments at their necessary level of strength". Without punishment, the collective sentiments would lose their force to control deviance and its rate would reach a point where it becomes dysfunctional. Durkheim is, therefore, of the view that a healthy society requires both deviance and punishment, disorder as well as order.

**Robert Merton on Deviance**

Merton accepts the viewpoint of the functionalist writers that all members of society share similar values. But in a class-ridden society, all people do not have the same opportunity of realising the shared values. By way of example, Merton referred to the American society in which one of the shared values is the end of achieving material success. Achievement of material gain is the hall-mark of a successful individual. But the society does not provide for or ensure equal opportunity to achieve material success. Those who occupy higher positions in the class hierarchy have greater opportunity to achieve material success than those who find themselves in the disadvantaged positions. Naturally, the end of achieving material success places pressure upon these people to use other than the socially approved means in pursuit of success. Merton, therefore, argues that there is a seeming contradiction between cultural goals and socially restricted access to these goals. The outcome is deviance of various sorts. In Merton's words, "the social and cultural structure generates pressure for socially deviant behaviour upon people variously located in that structure"

**Deviance and Marxian perspective**

The application of Marxian theory to the study of deviance became increasingly popular during the seventies of this century. It is argued by Marxist writers that power vests in the hands of those who own and control the means (or forces) of production, because economic power is an adjunct to political power. Those who are economically powerful are more likely to become politically powerful also. Naturally, the laws and many other social norms will reflect the interests of those who are at the helm of affairs. As such, the definition of deviance is also given by those who make the law in order to serve their own interest, and not necessarily the interest of those who do not belong to that charmed circle of economically privileged group. It is further argued that capitalist mode of production emphasises the maximisation of profits and accumulation of wealth. Narrow self-interest, rather than public weal, motivates primarily economic and secondarily all other types of behaviour. "Mutual aid and co-operation for the betterment of all are discouraged in favour of individual achievement at the expense of others. Competition breeds aggression, hostility, and particularly for the losers, frustration". The stage is thus set for deviant behaviour.

Many cross-cultural studies, i.e., studies involving socialist and capitalist societies, have been undertaken in order to establish that the socialist societies record a lower crime rate in comparison with capitalist societies. One such study, having its focus on American society, records as follows : "Most crimes in this country share a single important similarity — they represent rational responses to the competitiveness and inequality of life in capitalist societies". It is also pointed out that in capitalist societies white-collar crimes and deviant practices committed by individuals and groups belonging to the higher classes are neatly swept under the carpet and hidden from public view. Such selective application of the law gives the impression that criminals are mainly located among the working class. The fact,according to these writers, is that greed, self-interest and hostility, which are concomitants of a capitalist society, generate deviance of all kinds, including crime, at all levels of society.

In contrast to this picture, the socialist societies, in which the means of production are communally owned, it is claimed, record a much smaller number of all sorts of crime. The explanation is advanced that individual self-interest and greed are largely subordinated in socialist societies to considerations of social welfare and collective responsibility.

If the above analysis is correct, the solution to the problem of deviance lies on the road to socialism. It is held that such a conclusion is much too simplistic. The essence of the arguments of these writers is that "deviance can be ultimately accounted for in terms of the economic infra-structure". The argument is questionable. "There is ample evidence of crime and deviance in communist society ranging from petty theft to political and religious dissidence". Marxist writers fail to explain adequately the existence of cases of deviance in societies where the forces of production are communally owned. Nevertheless, the Marxist writers focus attention on aspects of society (that generate deviance) which were not sufficiently emphasised in other theories of deviance.

## FOOT NOTES TO CHAPTER – IV

1. The word 'superorganic' was introduced into sociological literature by Herbert Spencer and later emphasised again by A.L. Kroeber.
2. Bierstedt : *The Social Order,* p.129.
3. UNESCO *Courier,* July-August, 1950. Page 8
4. Kluckhohn, Clyde, and W.H. Kelly, *The Concept of Culture,* in *The Science of Man in the World Crisis.* Quoted by Ely Chinoy in his book, *Sociological Perspective,* page 14.
5. MacIver and Page, *Society,* page 581
6. *ibid,* page 586
7. *ibid,* page 501
8. *ibid,* page 502
9. For a detailed statement of this question, consult the section under Cultural Lag.
10. Bierstedt : *The Social Order,* pages 162-164
11. For a classical study of norms, consult Sumner's *Folkways : A Study of the Sociological Importance of Usage, Manners, Customs, Mores and Morals.*
12. The word *mores* is the Latin word for customs. In Sociology the word is used as a synonym of *'morals.* The word is also the Latin source of the word 'morals'.
13. MacIver and Page, *Society,* page 191
14. *ibid,* page 193
15. Ogburn and Nimkoff, *A Handbook of Sociology,* page 340
16. MacIver and Page, *Society,* page 196
17. *ibid,* page 196
18. B. Malinowski in *Crime and Custom in Savage Society,* quoted by MacIver and Page in their book, *Society,* page.176.
19. For a fuller explanation, consult the chapter on Social Stratification.
20. Bulletin of UNESCO Youth Institute, No.11, July, 1962, page 26
21. MacIver and Page, *Society,* page 18
22. Bierstedt, The *Social Order,* page 321
23. *ibid,* page.324
24. *ibid,* page 322
25. *ibid,* page 216
26. R.M. MacIver, *The Modern State,* page 478
27. MacIver and Page, *Society,* page 144
28. Yinger : *Contra-culture and Sub-culture,* American Sociological Review, 25 (October, 1960), pages 625-635. Referred to by Anderson and Parker in their book 'Society : Its Organisation and Operation', page 51
29. Bierstedt : *The Social Order,* page 194
30. *ibid,* page 169
31. *ibid,* page 177

# CHAPTER FIVE

# CULTURE AND SOCIALISATION

In the previous chapter we indicated that culture is transmitted from one generation to the other. The process by which it is done is known as socialisation. A new born individual, an unsocialised organism, is moulded by the society into a socialised individual. What is transmission of culture from the point of view of the society as a whole is socialisation from the point of view of the individual. The process of culture transmission is a fascinating story. We may briefly discuss the part played by various agencies in the socialisation process.

## The family

The family gets the baby first. Hence the process of socialisation begins in the family. A child is born with some basic abilities that are genetically transmitted through germ plasm. These abilities and capacities are shaped in ways determined by culture. The mother with whom the relation of the child is the most intimate plays a significant role in the process of moulding the child in the initial stages. Subsequently, father and older siblings transmit to the child many other values, knowledge and skill that children are expected to acquire in that particular society.

## The Peer Group

As the child grows older, his contemporaries begin to influence him. He spends most of his spare hours outside his work and study schedule with his peers in the playground and places outside his home. The attraction of peers is virtually irresistible to him. He learns from them and they also learn from him. With the passage of time, the peer group influence surpasses that of parents significantly. It is not surprising that teen age is the age of parent-child misunderstanding.

In the socialisation of the child, the members of the family, particularly those who exercise authority over him, and the members of his peer group exercise two different kinds of influence upon him. Both authoritarian relationships (typified by the former) and equalitarian relationships (typified by the latter) are equally significant to him. He acquires the virtues of respect, constraint and obedience from the first type of relationships, and the virtues of co-operation based on trust and mutual understanding from the second.

The importance of authoritarian element in the socialisation process may be explained thus. First, the pattern of behaviour expected of a child in a society does not usually or in all cases correspond to the innate inclinations of the child. On the contrary, on many occasions he is taught to act contrary to biological inclinations and follow the prescriptions as well as the proscriptions of society. Those who are mature and can command his respect and attention are obviously the proper persons to initiate the process of socialisation. Secondly, many cultural elements—both prescriptive and proscriptive—are not always amenable to reason. The child will naturally resent being asked to behave in a manner contrary to what his natural inclinations prompt him to do. In cases like this, the authority of those who are responsible for reproducing and maintaining a child are in a unique position to make him accept their instructions without questioning the logic and the necessity of the contents of those instructions. He has to accept these simply because his superiors lay them down for him.

The importance of equalitarian element in socialisation process rests on altogether different grounds There is free and spontaneous interaction, instead of coercion, among those who have equalitarian relationships. They view "the world through the same eyes," share the same subjective attitudes and, consequently, have perfect "understanding" of one another. This applies to age mates, sex mates and class mates. They learn from one another "small folkways, shades of meaning, fads and crazes, secret modes of gratification, and forbidden knowledge." Some such knowledge is "often socially useful and yet socially tabooed". Kingsley Davis has given the example of knowledge of sex which "is supposed to remain a closed book until marriage". If this were followed, the problems of maladjustment and aberration of many kinds would not have been infrequent. Fortunately, such knowledge is "transmitted as a part of the lore that passes from child to child".[1]

**The School**

When the child comes to the school, his formal indoctrination into the culture of the society begins. He is exposed to a wider background than hitherto known to him. He is formally introduced to the lore and the learning, the arts and the sciences, the values and the beliefs, the customs and taboos of the society from a wider circle, his teachers play a very significant role. The child may admire, respect and love some of his teachers. The impression which they make during this impressionable age lasts almost throughout his life.

**The books**

In literate societies another important agency of socialisation is the printed word in books and magazines. Our cultural world—experiences and knowledge, values and beliefs, superstitions and prejudices—is expressed in words. "Words rush at us in torrent and cascade; they leap into our vision as in newspaper, magazine and textbook...... The words are always written by someone and these people too—authors and editors and advertisers—join the teachers, the peers and the parents in the socialisation process".[2]

**The mass media**

Apart from newspapers which carry printed words, the two other mass media, viz., the radio and television, exercise tremendous influence in the socialisation process. They "assault our ears" and communicate directly their messages and these messages also "contain in capsule form the premises of our culture, its attitudes and ideologies". The role of television, in particular, is very significant. It communicates directly to both our ears and eyes and thus leaves a strong impression.

In individual cases, of course, the importance of these influences varies. Different people react to the same suggestion differently. Responses vary in terms of their natural predilections. "Some of us respect tradition; others fear the opinion of their peers; and still others prefer to listen to the 'thousand tongues' of conscience".[3] David Riesman has characterised the first group as 'tradition-directed', the second as 'other directed' and the third as 'inner-directed'.[4] While discussing the nature and impact of socialisation process, one cannot afford to ignore these innate characteristics of human nature.

**Socialisation and the self**

The 'self may be viewed from two angles : the self as subject and the self as object. The nature of the self, as seen by oneself from inside, is something which transcends all scientific investigations. It is a mystery which language fails to describe. Every person has a consciousness of self, Such consciousness finds expression in the use of the pronoun "I". This is the subjective self.

G.M. Mead pointed out that an essential characteristic of the self is its "reflexive character". By this he means that the self can be both subject and object to itself. Thus, when we say "the nature of the self", we reflect upon self and become selfconscious. We make self an object and when we do so the subjective self disappears.

In sociology we are concerned with the objective self. "The heart of socialisation", says Kingsley Davis, "is the emergence and gradual development of the self or ego. It is in terms of the self that personality takes shape and the mind comes to function".[5] The objective self, therefore, becomes an object of inquiry. Where does this self arise ? Are we born with it ? Is it something the individual brings with him as he confronts society ? Or, is it something that he receives from society as a gift of the confrontation ? In seeking an answer to these questions, we may explore the theories developed by Charles Horton Cooley, George Herbert Mead and Sigmund Freud. Though these three eminent scholars differ among themselves, yet all of them, having pursued the subject on the lines of their specialisation, come to the conclusion that the self is social and that self-consciousness arises only in and through interaction with others.

### C.H.Cooley

One of the earliest scholars to tackle this problem was C.H. Cooley. In his book, *Social Organisation*, he writes that "self and society are twin-born", that "we know one as immediately as we know the other", and further that "the notion of a separate and independent ego is an illusion". In other words, self-consciousness can arise only in society and it is inseparable from social consciousness. The self, in short, is social. In this connection, we may refer to Cooley's famous "looking glass" conception of the self. The basic idea of this conception is as follows : "The way we imagine ourselves to appear to another person is an essential element in our conception of ourselves. Thus, I am not what I think I am and I am not what you think I am. I am what I think you think I am".[6] To Cooley, the proof of this view may be found in our experience that "we are ashamed to seem evasive in the presence of a straight-forward man, cowardly in the presence of a brave one, gross in the presence of a refined one......"[7]. It follows, therefore, that we make a conscious attempt to show a different self in the presence of different social groups. Two corollaries follow from this inference : (i) that we are different in different groups, and (ii) that we depend upon the presence of other people and group for our conception of ourselves. Having made such a step-by-step analysis, Cooley concludes that the self is social and that it is not possible to develop self-consciousness in the absence of society.

### G.H. Mead

G.H. Mead (1863-1931), the philosopher and psychologist, agreed wholeheartedly with Cooley that it is absurd to look at the self or the mind from the viewpoint of an individual organism. Although it may have its focus in the organism, it is undoubtedly a social product and a social phenomenon. The chain of arguments which Mead advances in support of this conclusion and also in support of his theory of "Me" and "I" may be briefly summarised.

The self arises in interaction with the social and non-social environment. The social environment is particularly important. The following example may be cited. The baby cries and mother responds by giving milk or something good. If the mother continues to respond with care and love, the baby will eventually learn to distinguish between the state of affairs when the mother is present and the state of affairs when the mother is absent. The mother will be 'internalised' as an object. Primitive symbolic communication will be established. Thus, when the baby cries it will mean "I want mother". The mother's behaviour will convey to him the meaning that 'mother is pleased with me'. or that 'mother loves me'. Here we have the beginning of the consciousness of self. The formation of the self thus involves 'taking the role of other", seeing oneself, in imagination, as an object seen by someone else. The child, putting himself in the place of another, not only forms a concept of himself but also evaluates that concept and invests it with feeling and warmth.

Just as the child learns to develop an attitude towards objects in the environment, so he learns to take the same attitude toward himself that others take toward him. When the mother tells the child that he has done something good or bad, she is not only trying to teach the child what the words mean. She treats the child as an object toward which she takes a certain attitude and tries to get the child to do the same. He is encouraged *to take himself as an object*. He evaluates and controls himself the same way he evaluates and controls other object and he does so from the standpoint of someone else. In short, the child is taught to make appropriate responses to his own behaviour as well as to other objects in his environment. This process is characterised by Mead in terms of the 'I' and the 'Me'— the 'Me' being that group of organised attitudes to which the individual responds as an 'I'. He called the acting self the 'I'. The 'Me', on the other hand, is that part of the self which consists of the internalised attitudes of others.

The following illustration given by Mead will be instructive :

"Consider a politician or a statesman putting through some project in which he has the attitude of the community in himself. He knows how the community reacts to this proposal. He reacts to this expression of the community in his own experience—he feels with it. He has a set of organised attitudes which are those of the community. His own contribution, the 'I' in this case, is a project of re-organisation, a project which he brings forward to the community as it is reflected in himself. He himself changes, of course, in so far as he brings this project forward and makes it a political issue. There has now arisen a new social situation as a result of the project which he is presenting. The whole procedure takes place in his own experience as well as in the general experience of the community. He is successful to the degree that the final 'me' reflects the attitude of all the community".[8]

## Sigmund Freud

If Mead used two components of the 'self', 'I' and 'Me', Freud used three, the *id*, the *ego* and the *super ego*. The *id* represents our appetites, those inborn drives that prompt us to act, the impulse to do what we want to do. It seeks pleasure and avoids pain, reminiscent of the famous saying of Jeremy Bentham that "Nature has placed mankind under the governance of two sovereign masters, Pain and Pleasure".

We are not, however, permitted to do what we want to do. As social beings, we are obliged to adjust our desires and impulses, so that no social disharmony takes place. The second mechanism of the mind, the *ego*, helps us to do this. It mediates between the natural impulses of the *id* and the demands of the society in which we live . The *ego* thus acts as the manager of the self and facilitates the adjustment of the individual to society.

Apart from social restraint, there is another restraint upon the unfettered play of the impulses. This is the moral restraint. The third mechanism of the mind, the *super-ego* tells us what is morally right and what is morally wrong. It tells us what ought to be done and what ought to be avoided. The *super-ego* imposes the moral imperatives of society.

If we take the three components of mind together, it appears that the id and the *super-ego* stand in two opposite poles. Complications may develop as a result of such opposition. It is understandable that all our impulses cannot be satisfied in the social context. At the same time, all our impulses cannot be restrained either without doing harm to emotional stability of the individual. It is the task of the *ego*, the manager of the self, to act as an umpire in the perennial conflict between the in-born impulses and drives on the one hand and the 'thousand tongues' of conscience on the other.

The conflict, referred to above, is an internal conflict, the self in conflict with itself. Consciousness of 'self' arises out of this conflict. "It is in the repression of impulse that we become conscious of the fact that there is something else in the universe than ourselves, and it is this consciousness that gives us also the sense of self".[9]

We have considered the views of three scholars who belong to three distinct disciplines. In spite of their different intellectual orientations, however, they arrive at a conception of the 'self' that requires society.

**Stages of socialisation**

Socialisation is, in essence, nothing but learning to participate in social roles. The most important things to be internalised are the social roles themselves. But in order to be able to play one particular social role adequately, one must be familiar with the social roles of other persons in the same social system. In other words, a child need not only to learn the social roles he himself is expected to play but also the social roles of other persons with whom he will interact. It is particularly to be noted that internalisation of social roles that a child is required to play vis-a-vis social roles of other persons with whom he comes in contact and interacts is the same thing as the growth of personality. With growing years, a child internalises varied roles which he himself plays as also the roles of other persons. Obviously, at each stage of socialisation, the child internalises a *system of roles*, and not just one role.

We may discuss briefly four stages of socialisation :-

**The first stage or the oral stage**

In the womb the foetus is warm and comfortable. At birth, the baby faces his first crisis: he must breathe, he must exert himself to be fed, he is susceptible to cold,wet and other discomforts. He cries a good deal in order to attract attention. During the first stage of socialisation, he seeks to establish what is called *oral dependency*. By his cries he is able to build up fairly definite expectations about feeding time and also about his pressing needs for care. At this stage, the baby is not involved in the family as a whole. He is rather involved only in the sub-system consisting of him and his mother. If the father or anyone else in the family performs the role of the mother in caring for the baby no role differentiation is made. That person will also be performing the role of 'mother'. At this stage, the baby does not seem to internalise any role at all. He is so passive as compared to his mother that it is doubtful as to whether he internalises two roles at all. By the time *oral dependency* has been established, his own role and that of his mother are probably 'merged' together. This is the stage, according to Freud, of "primary identification."

**The second stage or the anal stage**

This stage probably begins soon after the first year and extends upto the third year. This period is called anal stage because toilet training is the main focus of attention of the socialising agent, particularly mother. During this stage, the child internalises two roles - his own and that of his mother.These two roles are now clearly separated.The child not only receives *care* , he also receives *love* and gives *love* in return. During this stage, the child is taught as to how to discriminate between 'correct' and 'incorrect' behaviour, first by advice and/or hints given by the mother and, secondly, by being rewarded or appreciated for correct performance and not rewarded or appreciated for incorrect behaviour.

**The third stage**

This stage extends from the fourth year to puberty, (i.e., age of 12 or 13).In the course of the third stage, the child becomes a member of the family as a whole. He identifies himself with the social role ascribed to him on the basis of his biological sex. Identification means either of two closely related things: (i) One identifies with a social *role* . That is, one not only internalises the role but adopts it as one's own. (ii) One identifies with a social *group* . That is, one internalises the role system of the group and considers oneself a member of it. Identification in the first sense links a boy with his father and brothers, but not with his mother. A girl, on the other hand, identifies with her mother and sisters, but not with her father. Identification in the second sense links a boy or a girl with the family, including both parents and all siblings. There are, thus, three kinds of identification: (i) With the father or mother, as the case may be (ii) With the siblings.(iii) With the family as a member.

**The fourth stage: Adolesence**

Adolescence, which begins roughly at puberty, is the age during which the young boy or girl has a tendency to get away from parental control. The "crisis" of this age arises from the fact that adolescents hanker after greater freedom while there is parental control over many activities in which he loves to have his own way.

The strain involved in transition during the adolescent period depends upon the cultural definition of adult roles. In some societies vital decisions concerning adolescents are taken by the parents or guardians. That makes transition easier. In India it is so. Thus, the choice of a marriage partner is made by elders within conventional rules. In some others, particularly in Western societies, adolescents are required to take important decisions more or less on their own. Obviously, in such cases transition is somewhat different and puts strain on them.

## NOTES

1. Kingsley Davis : *Human Society*, pages 217-218
2. Bierstedt : *The Social Order*, Pages 201 - 208
3. ibid page 202
4. David Riesman : *The Lonely Crowd*.
5. K. David : *Human Society*, page 208
6. Bierstedt : *The Social Order* , page 189
7. C.H. Cooley : *Human Nature and the Social Order* , page 184. Quoted by Bierstedt
8. G.H. Mead: *Mind as the Individual Importation of the Social Process* . This article has been incorporated in Readings in Sociology, edited by Alfred McClung Lee, page 86
9. Bierstedt : *The Social Order* , page 193

# CHAPTER SIX

# SOCIETY

## 1. DEFINING SOCIETY

The concept of society is given different meanings by different writers,. It is difficult to find a definition which will be universally accepted by all sociologists. It does not, of course, mean that society means different things to different men. It will be more appropriate to say that different sociologists look at society from different angles and emphasise one or two aspects more than others. This will be clear from the following definitions of society. Mac Iver has defined society thus : "Society is a system of usages and procedures, of authority and mutual aid, of many groupings and divisions, of controls of human behaviour and of liberties. This ever-changing, complex system we call society. It is the web of social relationships. And it is always changing".C. H. Cooley has given a broadly similar definition of society : "Society is a complex of forms or processes each of which is living and growing by interaction with the others, the whole being so unified that what takes place in one part affects all the rest". Looking at the society from a different angle, Ginsberg defines society as "a collection of individuals united by certain relations or modes of behaviour which mark them off from others who do not enter into these relations or who differ from them in behaviour". Giddings shares the viewpoint of Ginsberg and gives the following definition of society : "Society is the union itself, the organisation, the sum of formal relations in which associating individuals are bound together".

If we analyse these four definitions, it will appear that these fall under two types: (i) the functional definition which views society as a *process*, and (ii) the structural definition which views society as a *structure*. The definitions of Mac Iver and Cooley come under the first category while those of Ginsberg and Giddings under the second.

It should be noted, however, that there is really no conflict between the two views of society, viz, society viewed as social relationships or as a process and society viewed as a structure. As a matter of fact, these two views complement each other.

### Society viewed as social relationships

As social beings, men not only live together, but they also continually interact. Every man shapes his action and conduct in relation to the behaviour of others with whom he comes in contact. Such interaction may take various patterns. Thus, one's action may be modelled on the example of others, as in the case of a student imitating his teacher or of a child imitating his parents. Or, one's action may be influenced by considerations of what others might do, as in the case of a consumer buying, say, stocks of sugar on the anticipation that the traders would raise prices. Or, one's action might be oriented so as to bring out response from others, as in the case of a journalist or a writer exaggerating a particular event in order to focus public attention to a particular issue.

Interaction is not, however, one-sided. It is a two-way process. Thus, from one point of view, society is the "web of social relationships," as Mac Iver puts it, or "a complex of forms or processes each of which is living and growing by interaction with the others", as Cooley defines it. This social relationship or interaction is not something static; it is always changing. In the words of E. Chinoy, "interaction is a persisting process of action and interaction".

When we view society as social relationships, we should bear in mind two features, which characterise society : (i) *Mutual recognition.* That is, different members in a society recognise the presence of one another, and orient their behaviour one way or the other. In the case of physical relationship, such as the relationship between a typist and the type-writer, there is no such mutual recognition. The psychical condition, a characteristic feature of social relationship, is lacking here. (ii) The second feature is *a sense of belonging together or a consciousness of kind,* as Giddings puts it. If social relationships are marked merely by conflict or hostility, then the term society cannot be appropriately applied, as in the case of two armies engaged in conflict in the field of battle. A society consists of people who share attitudes, beliefs and ideals in common. There might, of course, be feuds and mutual hostility among members of a society. But these are, in the nature of things, transitory and occasional. In the words of Mac Iver : "Co-operation crossed by conflict marks society whereever it is revealed...".

## Society viewed as a structure

Those who view society as a structure conceive of society as a set of institutions that provide a framework for social life. According to this view, society is not merely a collection of institutions, but a complex structure of institutions relating to and impinging upon one another which, according to Ginsberg, "mark them off from others who do not enter into these relations or who differ from them in behaviour". The view of society as a structure may be illustrated with reference to the concepts of *status and role.*

If we look around us, we shall find a variety of norms or standards for behaviour. Relatively few of these standards apply universally to all people. Some apply to a group and some may apply to a single individual. Thus, every civilized society recognises that murder is a serious offence punishable under law. This is a universal norm. But if it is established that a man murdered the burglar in self-defence, he may escape punishment. Or, when a soldier kills people in the field of battle, he escapes legal action. These illustrations reveal that the question whether a social norm will apply to a particular person or not depends upon the position or status he occupies in society. The norm attaching to a particular status will be quite unacceptable for people belonging to another status. The combination of these norms is known as role, appropriate for a particular status. Status and role are thus two sides of a single coin. *Status is the position in relation to other positions. Role is the pattern of behaviour expected of persons who occupy a particular status.*

Status is thus only a social identification tag. A significantly large number of the social interactions between people in a complex society are *status interactions and not personal interactions.* Each of us has social relations with barbers, bus conductors, bus drivers and many other persons. It is interesting to recognise that we have social relations with many of these people without knowing their names or their antecedents except their status. When we board a bus, there are status interactions between passengers on the one hand and bus conductors on the other. There are hardly any personal interactions.

If we consider just a *point* of time, both status and role would appear to be static concepts. Status is fixed and unchanging. So also is role. Viewed in this context, the society is a structure.

If, however, we consider a *period* of time, both status and role would appear to be dynamic concepts. Status changes in relation to other statuses from time to time. There is a corresponding change in role also. The relation between teachers and students is not the same today as it was, say, fifty years ago. In terms of status and role, there has been a perceptible change. We may easily imagine that similar changes would take place in course of time in future. Sometimes new obligations and new responsibilities may be added to a status or old ones removed. If, for example, a new Act provides that the General Secretary of the students' union would be an *ex officio* member of the Governing Body of a College, the additional responsibility would alter both the status and role of the incumbent of this office. We may also conceive of two different incumbents of particular office (i.e., the status remaining the same) performing quite different roles (i.e., performing its functions in different fashions). In almost all areas two different incumbents of an office will approach their tasks in different ways. Two successive Principals of a College, for instance, may tackle the task of maintaining discipline in two different ways.

Viewed in the context of period of time, it would thus appear that society is a process and that social relationships are in a state of flux. If there is any equilibrium in society, it is a moving equilibrium.

The society is, thus, viewed both as a process and as a structure. It is, however, important to bear in mind that there is really no conflict between the two views of society. Those writers who look at society as social relationships have to consider institutions (i.e., the complex structure of status and role) in their analysis of society. Those who look at society as a structure must necessarily pay some attention to social relationships also which obviously change with the passage of time. The two views complement one another.

It may be noted in passing that it is not without reason that one who studies society must take into account these two views of society. As Mac Iver has said : "Society exists only as a time-sequence. It is a becoming, not a being; a process, not a product". This is the essence of society. If, however, we are to analyse society, distinguishing its different parts and studying inter-relationships among these parts, we have no other way but to conceive society as a structure. One cannot make such an analysis when the object of analysis is ever-changing and novel. A medical student studies a skeleton in order to gain knowledge about human anatomy. Likewise, analysis of society as a structure is a step towards understanding the essence of society.

## 2. ASCRIBED STATUS AND ACHIEVED STATUS

We have seen in the above section that we fill or occupy a status, and play or perform a role in terms of that status. But how do individuals occupy statuses ? There are two ways of doing so : by ascription and by achievement.

We may illustrate ascribed status with reference to the status based on sex, age, order of birth, biological relationship to others (such as, father, mother, brothers, sisters, etc.) and birth in a particular family. Sex status is obviously ascribed. One is born a male or a female. The difference in sex makes a lot of difference in the upbringing of the child inasmuch as a male child is expected by the society to perform a role different from that of a female child. Similarly, age status depends on factors about which we can do nothing, "beyond disguising our age by a few conceits and subterfuges". With the passage of years, one grows old and nothing can be done to check the process of aging. The order of birth is likewise ascribed. One is born the eldest child or the youngest child or a child between these two extremes. This is important from the point of view of society. For example, in societies where primogeniture prevails the eldest son inherits the property of his father. According to Hindu tradition, the eldest son enjoys a privilege to the exclusion of all his brothers of performing certain religious rites. Besides, in almost all societies the eldest or the youngest child has a special place in the family in terms of parental affection and indulgence. Similarly, being a brother or a sister is a kinship status and, like all other kinship statuses, is thrust upon the individual without having any choice in the matter. Birth in a particular family is similarly ascribed. One is born a Brahmin or a Sudra and one occupies a high or a low status in Hindu society accordingly. An individual may be extremely fortunate in being born in a family enjoying an honoured place in the society in terms of its scholarly attainments for two or three successive generations. The concerned individual naturally basks in the sunshine of family reputation and enjoys a prestigious status in the estimation of the society. An individual, on the other hand,may suffer in terms of social prestige because of his being born in a family having a bad reputation in the estimation of society.

If ascribed status implies membership of involuntary groups, achieved status means membership of voluntary groups. Thus, marital and parental statuses are achieved. One does not have to become a husband or a wife or a parent. Educational and occupational statuses are also achieved. One has to go through an educational process in order to become a graduate. Similarly, one becomes an engineer by acquiring the necessary qualifications.

### Sociological significance of the distinction

From sociological point of view, the distinction between ascribed and achieved statuses is significant. Usually, emphasis in a traditional society is more upon ascription than on achievement. An individual is evaluated mainly in terms of his kinship connections, caste and family tradition. Emphasis in a modern society, on the other hand, is more on achievement rather than on ascription. An individual is judged by what he is rather than by the group to which he belongs. We may note, in passing, a very significant comment of Talcott Parsons on the modernisation process in a traditional society. Since merit norms or achievement values are superseded in traditional societies by more dominant values of ascription, the possibilities for economic, political and other forms of socio-cultural development are very much restricted in such societies. Modernisation of these societies can begin only after appropriate cultural environment is created, so that achievement values emerge as a dominant force.

Another allied aspect of sociological importance is the fact that ascribed status influences, to a large extent, one's achievements in life. An individual might be born with in-born talents of a very high order. But if his ascribed status is such as to prevent him from utilising his talents fully, he may not succeed in bringing into full play his potentialities. For instance, a talented boy or girl, born in a poor Harijan family, may be deprived of an opportunity of completing even his primary education. On the other hand, a boy or girl of mediocre calibre may be so favourably circumstanced because of his birth as to be a successful man in life. It is, therefore, wrong to assume that ascription and achievement are two distinct categories altogether, having no relation with each other.

Kingsley Davis has added another dimension to the debate concerning ascription vs. achievement. In his view, the problem of a simple-stable society, with its emphasis on ascribed status and rigid institutional patterns, "is its lack of adaptability to changing conditions". He goes further to say that such societies "may pursue ancient custom to the point of ossification and disaster". The complex-unstable and specialised society, with its emphasis on achieved statuses and flexible institutional patterns, on the other hand, "runs the risk of uncontrolled individualism with consequent loss of social cohesion". He expresses the fear that "intense specialization leads to a failure of society's members to understand one another", and that, as a consequence thereof, "social order will disappear" in the absence of some sort of integrating force binding the members together. The danger inherent in a society in which achievement values emerge as a dominant force is indicated by Davis in unambiguous terms : "The more a society becomes dependent upon specialization and its statuses become accessible through individual achievement, the more tenuous becomes the integrating principle unless ( and this is the difficult part) the realm of sacred common values remains superior to the everyday world of competitive interest"[1].Thus, each kind of society—the simple-stable and the complex-unstable—has its peculiar problems.

Davis emphasises that both ascription and achievement are indispensable for the health of the society "in which ascribed status helps to provide the constancy, achieved status the change". The way the ascribed status helps to maintain the stability of society is described by him in these words. "To fix persons in statuses independently of their personal qualities requires a firm system of institutional controls. Ascribed statuses are generally broad ones in which the technical aspect is not complicated; the important things are sentiment, custom, and ritual rather than rational skill. To dispense with ascribed statuses altogether would knock a powerful prop from under the common values and ends which give society its cohesiveness, especially if these were further destroyed by scientific criticism and individualistic motivation"[2].

Davis argues that apart from societal integration, ascribed status also helps considerably in integrating individual personality. He says that there is every reason to believe that the "the individual could not stand the insecurity, conflict, and turmoil" which would follow in the wake of emergence of achievement value as a dominant force at the cost of ascription value. "The integration of the personality", says Davis, "reflects the integration of society, and a regime of pure competition would produce neither the one nor the other "[3]. He further asserts that status ascription should not be regarded "merely as an anachronism from a pre-democratic era", but rather as "a universal and systematic part of society on which the process of socialization and the maintenance of solidarity are both dependent"[4]. A society cannot avoid ascribing a status to the uninitiated child and thereby protecting him from competition at a very early age and creating conditions conducive to the transmission of the formal and informal aspects of societal culture. Ascription enables the child to be familiar with and get the advantages of authoritarian and equalitarian relationships. We have seen in the previous chapter that in the process of socialisation both the authoritarian and equalitarian relationships are equally important.

## 3. STATUS INTERACTIONS

We have seen that social interactions do not actually mean personal interactions but status interactions. When a prospective railway passenger stands on one side of the ticket counter to purchase tickets for his journey, he does not know personally the gentleman on the other side of the counter who is selling tickets. Nor does the gentleman on the other side know him personally. The only thing which they know about each other is that one is a railway employee and the other is a passenger. In this case the interaction takes place between a railway employee and a passenger and not between Mr. Singh, the employee, and Mr. Pandit, the passenger. Both are, so to say, faceless. Their respective roles are, however, known to each other. There is, therefore, smooth transaction of business. Or, take the case of a traffic police. He wears a particular type of dress which marks him off from others. His dress is something like an identification tag. People do not make any mistake in identifying him as a traffic police. They know the role that he is expected to play as a traffic police. His directions and orders, are, therefore, complied with by pedestrians and bus and car drivers. Here the status matters and not the individual who occupies the status. It is immaterial as to whether the man is tall or short, healthy or sickly, fair or brownish in complexion. All of us play various roles in terms of various statuses we occupy. Sociologists have studied the issues connected with role-playing from different angles. Accordingly, they have developed various concepts like *role-set, role-conflict,* role re-inforcement and *role-changing*.

## Role-set

It is an important aspect of organised social life that social positions (statuses) are related. Thus, a college professor interacts with his colleagues, with the members of the ministerial and lower subordinate staff of the college, with President and other members of the Governing Body of the college, with his students and sometimes with the guardians of his students. As a college professor, he interacts with these people and, may be, with many more. Sociologists have used the concept of role-set to include persons with whom the professor interacts in his capacity as a college professor. Thus the term role-set is used when a particular occupant of a particular position is taken as the point of reference to the total number of occupants of the correlative social positions with whom he must ordinarily interact.

All of us have multiple statuses, and for each status there is a corresponding role-set. A professor, for instance, has one role-set in his capacity as a professor. He may have another role-set in his capacity as a political activist, and yet another role-set in his capacity as an enthusiastic Secretary of a Football Club.

The role of an individual in relation to the various positions in his role-set involves somewhat different patterns of behaviour of each. At the same time, his own position is not perceived in the same way by the occupants of all the various positions in his role-set. Some of these persons may be his status-equals, some inferior and some superior. Thus, in our example, the status of a college professor is perceived differently according to the status and role of the beholder. It is instructive to consider some of the consequences of the fact that members of a role-set, occupying varying positions, may make conflicting demands and exert pressure in different ways. In our example, the college professor may be pressurised by his colleagues in the profession (say, the members of the College Teachers' Association) to join an agitation in the form of continuous cease-work for an indefinite period in support of their demand for redressal of certain long-standing grievances. He may also be pressurised by the college authority not to participate in an agitation designed towards dislocation of college academic schedule. The professor may be pressurised by his students also because of his possible failure to fulfil his role-obligations to his students in the event of his joining the agitation. He may be similarly pressurised by the guardians of his students.

What is the outcome of such conflicting pressures ? Some of the factors affecting the outcome of the struggle have been identified by R.K. Merton. These are mentioned below.

(i) **Insulation :** The norm which lays down that a person, whatever be his rank or profession, has a right to agitate in support of his demands for redress of legitimate grievances, has the function of insulating the professor (in our example) from interference by others with his right to agitate. He will meet all criticisms and resist all pressures pointing out that societal norms permit him to cease work in order to press his demands.

(ii) **Varying interest of the members of the role-set :** The various members of one's role-set usually have varying degrees of interest in one's activity. Other things being equal, those with less interest can be ignored. In our example, it is for the professor to judge the situation and decide whom to ignore.

(iii) **Power distribution :** The distribution of power in one's role-set is seldom equal. Very often, a person is allowed a certain degree of role autonomy by the fact that the members of his role-set neutralise one another to some extent. In our example, this particular factor does not appear to be quite relevant.

(iv) **Playing off one member against the other :** Another factor affecting the outcome of the struggle is the common strategy of making known to the various members of the role-set that conflict exists among them, and playing one member against another. In our example, the students might have some grievances against college authorities. This factor may be taken advantage of . They may agitate against college authorities, thereby making it difficult for the latter to take firm action against the college professor.

(v) **Power to withstand pressure on the strength of combination :** If a college professor is victimised or pressurised to his disadvantage by the authorities, he may, in combination with others of his status group, resist them and thereby seek to protect the interest of the professor against whom disciplinary action is contemplated.

In the context of the aforesaid factors, we cannot say, for certain, what the eventual outcome will be. It would be a gross error, however, to think, in general, that a college professor's conformity to the norms of his role depends simply upon the degree of autonomy he is able to keep in tact against his role-set. On the contrary, his conformity to his role obligations depends partly upon the pressures from his role-set.

It is to be particularly noted that the varying roles that a person performs by virtue of occupying a particular position and interacting with his role-set are technically not different roles. These are different 'faces', so to speak, of the same role.

The example of a college professor affords us an opportunity to call attention to an important distinction : the distinction between a *role* and the *role performance* of a particular occupant of that status. The *role* is much the same for all college professors at any given time, but the *achievement* of all the professors is, of course, not the same. Closely related to these facts is the distinction between the *prestige aspect of the college professor's status and the prestige of any particular professor*. The prestige of eminent professors like Dr. Radhakrishnan and Dr. Zakir Hussain may be cited as examples of the latter.

## Role Conflict

In role conflict, two groups are brought into a kind of relation with each other through the fact that the same person occupies a role in one of the groups which, to some extent, is incompatible with a role he occupies in the other. Let us take, for instance, the case of the General Secretary of the Students' Union of a college who becomes (as under

The Calcutta University Act, 1979) *ex officio* member of the Governing Body of the College. Suppose the Principal of the College reports to the Government Body the case of a student adopting unfair means and threatening the invigilators in the examination hall and recommends stringent disciplinary action against him. In the instant case, the General Secretary in his capacity as a representative of the students would obviously very much like to plead for condonation of the offence whereas as a member of the Governing Body it is not easy for him to ignore the serious nature of the offence and persuade the Governing Body to take a lenient view of the case.

## Re-inforcement of roles

If a person occupies two roles one of which re-inforces his motivation to conform to the role obligations of the other, we have the opposite of role conflict. One of the best examples of this in contemporary society is the mutual re-inforcement of occupational role and familial role, if both are occupied by an adult man. Indeed, most husbands and fathers cannot fulfil their obligations in the family unless they perform well in an occupational role outside the family. His satisfactory performance in the latter sphere will very likely open up for him prospect of a higher income which, in turn, will enable him to spend more on his family and fulfil his family obligations better. The obligation and wish to support a family are presumably strong incentives for a man to do well in his occupation. Some writers (for example, Talcott Parsons) therefore go so far as to say that having an occupational role is part of the role of husband-and-father.

One point needs, however, to be added , We should bear in mind that every role has more than one obligation. It is possible to fulfil one obligation—namely, supporting a family and providing wife and children good things of life— while neglecting other obligations, namely, giving time for one's wife and children. Any two roles occupied by the same person, although they may re-inforce each other, may also conflict in practice if he fails to allot his time and energy properly between them. Such failure is not, however, due to role conflict (because in the nature of things there is no *inherent* role conflict) but to *deviation in role performance*.

## Role changing

As people grow older, or win promotion, or move from one job to another, they may change many of the roles they play. Once a person changes from one role to another— from teacher to businessman, or from child to adult, or from legal practitioner to judge of a High Court—he must adjust to a new set of conditions. Besides, people expect him to behave differently.

As a striking example of role changing involving dramatic ceremony, we may consider the case of sacred thread ceremony(*upanayana ceremony)* which exists among Brahmins and Kshatriyas. When a boy reaches a certain age, he is given a sacred thread which he is required to wear all throughout the rest of his life as his caste identification mark. The elaborate ceremony in connection with the event, involving rituals and feast, dramatises the new role of the boy as a brahmin or a kshatriya. The ceremony is meant to impress upon relatives and friends that the boy has assumed a new role.

Such dramatizing of the change of roles is found in other spheres also in contemporary society. Kings are crowned, presidents are installed, ministers and judges are sworn before they assume their new roles. The ceremonies are always witnessed by others who, by their presence, recognise that the honoured individual has assumed a new role. If everyone refused to recognise him in any but his old role, he would be helpless to enforce his new duties. The very fact that everyone expects him to behave in an entirely new way makes it much easier for him to do so. That is why even the most unlikely people often grow to fit their new offices and roles. Marriage is another familiar role-changing ceremony. The solemn wedding ceremony and change of name, merry-making and the honeymoon away from friends and neighbours—all make it easier for the young couple to assume their new identities.

## 4. ALL-INCLUSIVE SOCIETY AND DIFFERENT GROUPINGS

We confined our attention so far to the all-inclusive society and ignored, for the sake of convenience, different groupings which may exist among the members of a society. These different groupings have been studied by sociologists from different points of view. One may get an in-depth view of society by having a look at these groupings. It is also to be noted that these groupings have changed in nature with the gradual transformation of agrarian society to industrial society.

### Gemeinschaft and Gesellschaft

According to Tönnies, since the second half of the 19th Century, society has been gradually moving from *gemeinschaft* to *gesellschaft,* i.e., from community to association. In other words, when industrialisation and urbanisation did not make much headway, life in society was largely communal in nature. But gradually, with the spread of industry and increasing urbanisation, life became largely associational in nature. "Gemeinschaft (community) is old ; Gesellschaft (society) is new as a name as well as a phenomenon .... Wherever urban culture blossoms and bears fruits, Gesellschaft appears as its indispensable organ. The rural people know little of it"[5].

**Gemeinschaft** or community is defined as "intimate, private, and exclusive living together" in a localised group most of whose members know one another and have a feeling of 'belonging' to one another. It is also implied that there is a powerful body of public opinion to which the behaviour of all its members is subject. One basic element of community is thus a sentiment of unity, a sense of pride among the people who constitute a community. Sociologists also add another dimension to the concept of community which, in their view, consists of a group of people who occupy a defined territory within which the group is assured of a self-sufficing life. That is, the territory must be such as to enable the people to pursue the total round of life, from their birth to their burial. A community has, thus, two attributes : (i) locality and (ii) community sentiment.

This view of community obviously embraces a very wide range of groups, starting from a neighbourhood or village to a metropolitan city. Sometimes a small community may be a part of a larger community. These small units of a larger community may still be called communities in so far as the people of these parts maintain distinctiveness of their own as compared to those of other parts and they spend all their lives within the bounds of the smaller community.

It should, however, be noted that with the passage of time the possibilities of self-sufficient life within the limits of small areas are increasingly being narrowed down. This is primarily for three reasons. To begin with, the advance of technology and expansion of consumer goods industries are responsible for introducing sophistication into the needs and demands of the people making it difficult for small communities to satisfy them. Secondly, improvement in transport and communication is responsible for making different areas inter-dependent. Thirdly, introduction of mechanical power and technology in the fields of manufacturing industries and agriculture, supplemented by improvements in transportation and communication, have led to modern urban society where many people live in cities, often with population numbered in millions. Small, self-sufficient communities are relevant only for primitive people whose needs are simple and demands few. For these reasons, the trend today is towards bigger communities.

As communities get larger and more complex, they tend to lose person-to-person contacts marked by intimacy and mutual dependence, and to become more impersonal. As a result, the individuals get considerable freedom from social control and the group-bonds get weaker. Large communities, however, have some advantages in comparison with small communities. Large communities make possible a multiplicity of social organisations with the consequent advantages of specialisation. These advantages are absent in small communities where everything is done through the community and the family.. For instance, larger communities can afford to have different types of clinics and hospitals which, with their improved techniques, nurse and heal better than families do. As civilised beings, writes MacIver, we need both large and small communities. "The great community brings us opportunity, stability, economy, the constant stimulus of a richer, more varied culture. But in the smaller community we find the nearer, more intimate satisfaction. The larger community provides peace and protection, patriotism and sometimes war, automobile and the radio. The smaller provides friends and friendship, gossip and face-to-face rivalry, local pride and abode. Both are essential to the full life process" [6]

We have noted above that the *size* of a community is an important determinant of its characteristics. There are, however, various other factors which introduce differences among communities. For instance, among a group of towns of the same size, some may be largely *industrial* with most of their populations employed in factories, some may be *agricultural* towns with most of their inhabitants dependent on trade with the surrounding farmers, one may be a *university town*, another a *health resort*. All these towns, for obvious reasons, reveal different characteristics of their own.

Besides, towns of the same size may be different according to the *religion* and culture of the regions in which towns are located. If there is a high degree of literacy and cultural development in the region, cultural life of the city will also be highly advanced. Likewise, the institutions of a town reflect the dominant religious activities of the people. For instance, towns like Varanasi, Vrindaban or Tirupati, which have grown around temples, reveal characteristics that are different from those of commerce cities like Calcutta, Madras or Bombay.

But the major differences among communities rest on whether they are *rural* or *urban*. The distinctive characteristics of these two kinds of communities are discussed in the last section of this chapter.

**Gesellschaft** or association is defined as 'public life', as something which is consciously and deliberately entered upon [7]. MacIver defined an association "as a group expressly organised for the pursuit of an interest or group of interests in common [8]" Examples are an athletic club, a dramatic society or an association for the pursuit of scientific investigations. These illustrations point to the fact that persons with similar interest form a group to pursue their common interest. Such a group is known as an association. Associations may, therefore, be viewed as special interest groups. Modern industrial societies of the West or the ways of life in mammoth cities like Calcutta or Bombay or Delhi are associational in character in which the hold of tradition and neighbourhood has largely broken down.

An association may be distinguished from a community from the following points of view. First, while an association is developed with a particular or special interest in view, a community is the total organisation of social life within an area. When, however, an association has plurality of ends, it approaches the concept of community. Secondly, in a community individuals are involved as complete or whole persons. For instance, when the residents of a village or a neighbourhood are engaged in some common action for improving the quality of community life, they are involved as whole persons who are known to one another, more or less, on a person-to-person basis. In an association, on the other hand, the members are not 'wholly' involved as individuals. They are rather involved as 'functionaries' for the satisfaction of specific and partial ends. Thirdly, a community is united by an accord of feeling or sentiment among individuals, whereas an association is united by a rational agreement of interest. Fourthly, association has no reference to geographical location, but "the residential tie to an area is one attribute that distinguishes a community from other social groups". Thus, Indian Science Congress is an association. A community may comprise a number of associations.

### Durkheim on organic solidarity and mechanical solidarity

The relationship between the inclusive society on the one hand and the social groupings on the other has been analysed from another angle. Traditional and pre-industrial societies, argued Durkheim, were bound together by a common world-view, a common belief system and a common way of thinking. There was not much differentiation. He characterised the links of unity among people in traditional societies as *mechanical solidarity*. Modern industrial societies, by contrast, are marked by specialisation, complementarity and interdependence. The ruling principle of industrial societies is 'structural differentiation'. The people in these societies are bound together by a set of relationships which are so interdependent that sub-groups assigned to specific functions cannot remove themselves without severe material dislocation to the community as a whole. The unity and cohesion among people can, thus, be explained only in terms of their interdependence. Durkheim characterised the cohesion among these people as *organic* solidarity.

"Durkheim explained the transformation from one to the other by a 'law of gravitation of the social world'. This law related the progressive division of labour to an increase in social interaction (which he called 'moral density'). But 'moral density can not grow unless material density grows at the same time', so that 'the number and rapidity of the means of communication and transportation' were 'a visible and measurable symbol' of changes in moral density and could take their place in the general formula. Durkheim then argued that as the contacts between traditional societies increased, so conflicts over the allocation of scarce resources between them became more likely, and they had to be resolved by a division of labour which transformed them into modern societies. 'Similar occupations located at different points are as competitive as they are alike', he wrote, 'provided the difficulty of communication does not restrict the circle of their action'. In this simple model of a competitive space-economy, therefore, social differentiation was literally an agreement to differ, produced by changes in the spatial structure of society. The consensus might well be facilitated by some kind of cultural reinforcement mechanism, indeed it generally was, but its *explanation* remained a basically morphological one"[9].

**Redfield's approach in terms of Little Community**

Redfield advocates the study of large all-inclusive society in terms of the study of little communities. He advances two arguments in favour of this approach. First, the little community "is a kind of human whole with which students of man have a great deal of experience"[10]. Secondly, "it is easier to develop a chain of thought in relation specially to villages and bands than to try to do so also in relation to personalities and civilizations and literatures"[11].Thirdly, "the small community has been the very predominant form of human living throughout the history of mankind ... One estimate is that today three-quarters of the human race still live in villages"[12].

Redfield defines the little community in terms of four characteristics :

(i) *Distinctiveness* - It is not difficult to identify 'where the community begins and where it ends'. (ii) *Smallness* - Being small, the little community 'is the unit of personal observation'. (iii) *Homogeneity* - 'Activities and states of mind are much alike of all persons in corresponding sex and age positions; and the career of one generation repeats that of the preceding'. (iv) *Self-sufficiency* - It 'provides for all or most of the activities and needs of the people in it. The little community is a cradle-to-the-grave arrangement'[13].

## 5. RURAL AND URBAN COMMUNITIES

We have already noted that the major differences among communities rest largely on whether they are *rural* or *urban* . Most of the world has been rural most of the time. Even today the percentage of the world's population that live in cities is indeed very small.

What are the characteristics of urban communities? In almost all the countries of the world, urban communities are distinguished from rural ones on the basis of population. Thus, communities containing population of 2000, 2500. 20,000, and of 30,000 are regarded as urban in France, the United States, Holland and Japan respectively. In Iceland the line is drawn at 300. The distinctions made on the basis of population make no meaning. The differences among towns of varying population are sometimes so great that they are really differences of kind, and not simply of degree. A municipal town containing, say, 20,000 population stands in sharp contrast to metropolitan cities like Delhi, Bombay or Calcutta, Sometimes urban and rural communities are distinguished in terms of geographical location. But it is difficult to tell where one ends and the other begins. "Scattered farmsteads pass imperceptibly into villages, and villages into towns". Rural areas also differ in many respects. For example, in the U.S.A. farmers generally live in the centre of their farm lands, and not in villages. The farmers in India, on the other hand, live in villages from which they go out to cultivate the field. Like cities, again, the size of villages also differs very widely. "The contrast between city and country, therefore, breaks down into a series of contrasts. We may think of a spectrum with the rural community standing at one extreme and the large-scale metropolis at the other"[14].

An urban area is defined in the Indian Census in terms of the following features. All areas under a Municipal Corporation or a Municipality or under a Notified Area Committee or under a Cantonment will be regarded as urban areas. Besides, those areas which will satisfy the following pre-conditions will also be considered to be urban. The pre-conditions are : (i) The density of population per square mile should not be less than 1000. (ii) The total population of the area should not be less than 5000. (iii) Of the total number of employed people, at least three-fourths must be employed in non-agricultural occupation. (iv) According to the State Census Commissioner the area must exhibit distinct urban features. Obviously, areas which do not satisfy these conditions are classed as rural.

The outstanding sociological characteristics that differentiate a rural community and an urban one are the modes of community life, habits and attitudes of the people, and not simply size and geographical location. The principal occupation of the people in rural areas all over the world is farming. And farming is not merely an economic activity, it is also a way of life. Whatever might be the differences in terms of race and climate, of location and of resources, there is a marked and general contrast in every country between the social life of the rural areas and that of urban areas.

A typical rural outlook is determined chiefly by three factors; (a) Predominance of primary, face-to-face relationships and contacts in rural ares. The ways of a ruralite are, therefore, fixed for him by society, usage and custom. Mention may be made, in this connection, of the relatively dominant role of the rural family. An urbanite,on the other hand, has an exactly opposite setting. He lives under conditions characterised by decline of primary, face-to face relationships and corresponding increase of secondary group ties., (b) His occupation, viz. farming, which, as we have already noted, broadly influences his attitude towards life, his philosophy, his thoughts and aspirations. There is little, if at all, variety in the occupational pattern of a ruralite. The towns and cities, in contrast, offer an almost limitless range of ways to make a living. It is, indeed, impossible to describe the diversity and the heterogeneity of occupational life in the city. The occupation of an urbanite keeps him aloof from nature. (c) Absence of keen competition among farmers tends to make them more conservative and tradition-bound. The living and working conditions of an urbanite are comparatively more competitive than is ever known to the farmer.

We should also take into account the homogeneity and heterogeneity of the environmental conditions of a ruralite and an urbanite respectively. "The countryside presents a sameness to those who dwell on the land. The city alters its attractions with every passing block. Soil and cement are two different environments, and of the two the cement has more shapes....(The countryman) responds more directly to the hours of daylight and the hours of night, and follows in greater harmony the progression of the seasons. The earth itself gives him a predominant mode of occupation and determines his time to work and his time to sleep. The country pursues his span of life in intimate relationship with the physical forces that made the day and the year, the weather and the wind. The city man, on the contrary, performs his tasks in independence of the wind's vicissitudes and the season's change"[15].

The differences in the physical base of social life in rural and urban communities bring about differences of socio-cultural and socio-psychological phenomena found in these communities. We may discuss some of these specific points of contrast.

### Socio-cultural contrasts between city and country

To begin with, a rural community is necessarily a little community. The smallness in size permits frequent face-to face contacts among the members of such a community. Each person knows "a great deal about his neighbours, their activities, preferences and attitudes". The social pressure is, therefore, very effective in enforcing conformity to group mores. In addition, the dominance of the family extends over very wide fields of individual life in rural areas—over marriage, mode of living, occupation, recreation, etc. The urban community, on the other hand, is a large community in which the dominance of the family and the intimate face-to-face relationships tend to be more and more dissolved. In this "impersonalised urban world", therefore, specialised agencies like police, courts, teacher and social workers take over the regulatory functions of the family and the neighbourhood.

Secondly, in the country, where farming is a dominant mode of occupation, a farmer cannot obviously be a specialist. He has to know how to cultivate different kinds of crops and to tend different kinds of animals, how to mend a fence and repair a plough, and to dig a well and repair his dwelling hut. He acquires skills of a more general and unspecialised kind. His work being unspecialised, the need for specialised organisation is virtually eliminated. A rural community cannot also afford to support too many specialised agencies or organisations."The few organisations most frequently found in a small community are the family and some religious organisation. These two organisations perform many functions other than procreation, child-bearing, and worship that in a large community would be found in single special purpose organisations, such as a factory or a sports club"[16]. In the city, on the contrary, each man is a specialist, performing day after day, and in all seasons, essentially the same job. Economic functions are taken away from the household and individual is thrown into associational relations determined by specific interests of work and temperament.

Thirdly, absence of variety of occupations in rural areas tends to narrow down the possibilities of horizontal mobility of a farmer from one occupation to the other. Nor does he have the scope, so long as he remains a farmer, of promotion or elevation up the social scale according to his ability and experience. The economic specialisation of the urban community is, on the other hand, "the source of social groupings, both vertical involving occupational divisions on the same social level, and horizontal", involving divisions of unequal social status.

Fourthly, in rural areas the family is relatively dominant, and consequently, the individual does not seem to count as a separate entity. As a matter of fact, the status of the individual depends largely upon the status of the family. Whatever might be his special talents and capabilities, he cannot outgrow his family. In other words, ascription, rather than achievement, is the ruling principle in the determination of the social status of an individual. In the city, on the other hand, the status of an individual depends largely upon his accomplishments, merits and capabilities. This is due to the fact that urban life is characterised by competition and mobility.

Finally, the comparative stability and serenity of rural life amidst natural surroundings is reflected in its cultural expression which "tends to retain a relatively simple form, as folklore, folk legends, folk songs, folk dances". On the other hand, the urban life is cut off from natural surroundings. Hence it lacks stability and serenity of rural life. Moreover, urban community is heterogeneous and changeful. The urbanite, therefore, wants among other things, novelty and excitement.

**Socio-psychological contrasts between city and country**

Differences in objective situations that obtain in the country and the city impress themselves on the mentality of the ruralite and the urbanite.

To begin with, agriculture is affected, to a large extent, by the forces of nature—such as rainfall, sunshine, drought and flood—which are beyond the control of farmers.

Naturally, they become fatalistic and superstitious. "He must come to terms with inscrutable powers, and the limits of his power make him susceptible to traditional beliefs". An urbanite, on the contrary, is not bound by any such shackles of tradition. He develops a more dynamic and positive approach towards life. Nothing seems to be beyond his powers. He develops the capacity of responding quickly to changing situations.

Secondly, community sentiment is less intense in the city than that in the country. MacIver and Page discuss this difference from three aspects : (i) *We-feeling* of the urbanite is less intense than that of the ruralite. This is due to the fact that many specialised associations compete with the community for the allegiance of an urbanite. For this reason, he fails to grow feeling of deep attachment and identification with the community. (ii) The *role-feeling* is similarly affected. In rural areas, everybody knows what others do or should do. Naturally, each one is conscious of his responsibility and of the role he must play. In the cities, such a feeling is altogether absent because of the complexities and vastness of the city. (iii) The *dependency-feeling* of the city-dweller is also comparatively less. Since he does not grow any community sentiment, and since he does not depend on the community for the satisfaction of his needs, it is easy for him, more than the countryman, to move from one community to the other.[17]

We have sketched above some of the principal sociological differences between the rural and urban ways of life. It is true that no sharp line can be drawn between them but it is nevertheless true that throughout history these two ways of life have exemplified two different cultures. Vast changes in the means of communication and transportation in recent decades have narrowed down considerably the disparities between them. But some differences will probably remain, giving one cast to rural life and another to urban. "In this respect we have to think of country and city, not in the geographic sense as two different places, but in the sociological sense as two different kinds of groupings and two different modes of life"[19].

## Urbanisation and urbanism

The words 'urbanisation' and urbanism' sometimes cause confusion. This is partly due to the conflicting senses in which the terms are interpreted in some of the books on urban sociology. It is best perhaps to refer to urbanisation as a *process* and urbanism as a *condition*.

"Urbanisation is the process in which rural areas become transformed into urban areas, the process in which the country becomes *citified*,, the process by which cities rise and grow"[19]. Hope Tisdale places emphasis upon the aspect of *concentration* and gives the following definition of urbanisation. "Urbanisation is a process of *population concentration*. It proceeds in two ways : the multiplication of points of concentration and the increase in size of individual concentrations. Urbanisation is a process of becoming. It implies a movement from a state of less concentration toward a state of more concentration"[20]. J. Clyde Mitchell refers to urbanisation "as being the process of becoming urban, moving to cities, and corresponding *changing of behaviour patterns*"[21]. It appears from these three definitions that urbanisation has three dimensions: (i) The process of the countryside gradually acquiring physical characteristics of urban areas. (ii) The process of population concentration. (iii) The process of changing of behaviour patterns.

Urbanism is more than a statistical concept. It cannot be correlated simply with the percentage of people in a country or state who live in cities. Urbanism refers to a 'way of life' thought to be specially characteristic of cities. A number of typical features have been identified as constituting urbanism. A representative list of these features includes the following : (a) A complex division of labour with a diversified occupational structure. (b) High territorial and social mobility. (c) Marked functional dependence of the population. (d) Substantial personal anonymity in inter-personal contacts. (c) Reliance on indirect modes of social control[22]. There are two criticisms against this view. In the first place, it is argued that such a conception does not limit phenomena to cities because these characteristics have spread or diffused from the city to the countryside, resulting in an urbanisation of formerly rural areas. Secondly, such a view intermixes characteristics of individual behaviour (for example, anonymity) with characteristics of organised social systems (for example, a complex division of labour and functional dependence). In spite of the difficulties hinted at in the aforesaid criticisms, there is no practical alternative but to accept broadly the representative list of features as constituting urbanism.

## 6. NATURE OF URBANISATION IN INDIA

India is not an exception to the world-wide trend of mass exodus of people from rural areas and their settlement in ruban centres. In India the rural-urban migration began during the thirties of the twentieth century. The pace of such migration increased manifold during the post-independence period. There is an increasing concentration of people in small, medium and large-sized towns, leading to a spatial expansion of the urban settlements. In addition, new towns centering around the setting up of new factories are coming up in increasing numbers.

Sociologists have explained the global trend towards rural-urban migration in different ways. The explanatory causes may be classed under two categories : the push factor and the pull factor. In some cases the situation in the countryside may be so inhospitable as to force people to leave their hearth and home. Sociologists characterise such factors as 'push' factors. The people living in the countryside may also be attracted by better opportunities of employment and good living (these may also be fancied rather than real) in urban areas and decide to move out. Sociologists characterise such factors as 'pull factors'. It is difficult to say for certain which of these factors plays a more decisive role in rural-urban migration. On the contrary, it is more probable that both the factors are responsible for influencing the decision of the people to migrate.

We may enumerate briefly the 'push' and 'pull' factors which are operative in the Indian situation. Among the 'push' factors the following are particularly important. To begin with, man-land ratio in the countryside has changed to the disadvantage of the farmers, so that the arable land available to them has diminished considerably. This has severely restricted the scope for expansion of employment opportunities and created scarcity in food supply. Secondly, the rate of increase of public investment in the countryside has not kept pace with the rate of increase of population. This has further aggravated the problem of food scarcity and restriction in employment opportunities. Thirdly, expansion of primary education in the countryside, paradoxically enough, has not produced, in many cases, the desired result of benefiting the community and the persons who are so educated. In traditional societies, including India, literacy is a status symbol. As such, to make a person literate has the effect of alienating him from his ancestral occupation, because literacy tends to give him the impression that manual work or farming operations are not proper calling of a literate person. They, therefore, migrate to urban areas in search of new 'pastures'. Fourthly, farming in India provides seasonal employment. Naturally, those who are engaged in farming are forced to move to urban areas in search of odd jobs when there is not enough work in the field. In course of time, some of them stay on in the periphery of towns and cities.

Among the 'pull' factors, mention may be made of the following. In the first place, the comparative affluence and the existence of varied and numerous employment opportunities in towns and cities attract large numbers of people from the countryside. Secondly, in the cities and towns there is heterogeneity, not simply in matters of employment, but also in patterns of recreation, in education, in modes of transportation, in styles of living and styles of thought as well as in kinds of stimulation. In contrast to life in the countryside which is dull, monotonous and uneventful, life in towns and cities attract people from the countryside. Thirdly, the partition of the country on the eve of India's independence led to a mass exodus of people from East Bengal and West Punjab. Millions of uprooted people without home and jobs, for obvious reasons, preferred to stay in towns and cities proper or in the peripheries in order to eke out a living. They had no other alternative. As a consequence, the concentration of population in cities and towns all over India, West Bengal and Punjab towns in particular, swelled all on a sudden. Fourthly, it is pointed out that in India "family and village ties are sufficiently strong to create an obligation upon the successful migrant to help sponsor new entrants to the city"[23]. The cumulative effect of this has been that "it (the upswing in urbanward migration) has now progressed to a point where the residents of almost every village have relatives or fellow villagers in at least one ( and possibly several) of the major cities"[24].

Western countries also experienced urbanisation as a sequel to expansion and diversification of industries. But urbanisation in these countries was entirely different in nature from that in India. As in India, people living in rural areas were attracted to cities and towns by the prospect of better employment opportunities and higher income. In most cases their dreams were fulfilled. They got jobs and were successful in increasing their income. Moreover, there were also opportunities of getting trained and acquiring necessary skills which helped them not only to make themselves employable but also to become competent and skilled factory hands. As a result, they could identify themselves completely with the urbanities and they no longer remained 'outsiders'.

In India the picture is just the opposite. The expectation with which the people flock in large numbers from rural areas to towns and cities remains unfulfilled in most of the cases. They fail to get jobs or to acquire the necessary skill to make themselves employable as factory hands. They are, thus, forced to live in urban slums or in slums adjoining city areas. Physically, they might be living in cities and towns. But they do not belong to cities and towns in the sense that they do not share in the lives of city people. They do not have the necessary income to participate in various urban activities—recreational, educational and civic. Their only goal is to earn some money and just stay alive. They have no means either to contribute to urban life or to benefit from urban amenities. Some sociologists have characterised such a situation as ***subsistence urbanisation.*** It is alarming to note that most of these people are unlikely to escape from the subsistence urbanization level of living even after a long period of stay in cities and towns. Commenting on this aspect of urbanisation. Gerald Breese makes some significant observations : "The grossly low level of subsistence urbanization may be so close to an agricultural subsistence level of living that the difference may be just one of locale. This plight may be even more intolerable when it is *daily compared with examples of the opposite extreme in level of living enjoyed by a lucky few* '[25]. (Italics ours). The frustration which may be engendered by this kind of experience leads to alcoholism, delinquency, anti-social activities of various kinds and sometimes angry protest movements. Gerald Breese, therefore, observes : "The prospects for the ordinary inhabitant of an urban area in a newly developing country is that things will be worse before they are better. A high degree of physical urbanization—in terms of *where* people live—is quite likely to be characterised by a low degree of social urbanization, in the sense of providing appropriate amenities for urban life"[26].

Thus, we see that the process of urbanisation in India is far removed in nature from the urbanisation process in Western societies. Daniel Lerner has gone so far as to say that the urbanisation that we see in India and in other developing nations of Asia and Africa "bears more resemblance to the mass migrations of human hordes driven by famine and pestilence in the centuries preceding the modern epoch"[27]. Joel M. Halpern has characterised the incorporation of very large number of rural people into towns and cities without their being absorbed into the urban ways of life as "peasantization of cities"[28]. The dilemma faced by developing nations, including India, is cited by Kingsley Davis thus: "If they do not substantially step up the exodus from rural areas, these areas will be swamped with underemployed farmers. If they do step up the exodus, the cities will grow at a disastrous rate"[29]. There is little doubt that the latter trend is increasing in India at an alarmingly fast rate.

## 7. THE REGION AND REGIONALISM

What is a region ? Lundberg defines region "as an area within which the people and the different constituent communities are conspicuously more inter-dependent than they are with people of other areas"[30]. A region usually combines rural and urban communities into one unit. These two types of communities tend to coalesce. Just as the city and country dwellers are being brought nearer to one another with improved means of communication and transport, the enviornments of the city and the country are tending to become common possession of all those who inhabit certain large areas. These areas, the home of city and country alike, are the regions.

The distinguishing characteristics of a region are the following. In the first place, each region is a locality having a "specific geographic character : common properties of soil, climate, vegetation, agriculture and technical exploitation". Secondly, a region, in so far as it has become an integrated area of social life, exhibits "a balance, a state of dynamic equilibrium, between its various parts". It means that technological or social changes introduced in any part of the region will, directly or indirectly, bring about changes in the entire region. It also means that a region must be large enough to encompass a variety of interest and activities, urban and rural as well as industrial and agricultural, to ensure balance, though not economic or political self-sufficiency. On the other hand, the region must be small enough "to keep these interests in focus and to make them a subject of direct collective concern". Finally, regions do not have sharply drawn boundaries. They merge into one another, forming inter-dependent units of the large community[31].

The community feeling within a region is called regionalism. It differs from sectionalism in that it implies an integral relationship with a larger whole while the latter emphasises separation and segregation from the larger whole.

### Regions in India

By way of illustration, we may consider some of the sub-areas in India other than those imposed by political divisions between states. Under the States Reorganization Act,

1956, India has been divided into five different zones : (i) *Northern Zone* which includes Jammu and Kashmir, Punjab, Haryana, Rajasthan, Uttar Pradesh and Delhi. (ii) *Western Zone* which includes Maharashtra and Gujarat. (iii) *Southern Zone* which includes Tamilnadu, Karnataka and Kerala, (iv) *Central Zone* which includes Andhra Pradesh and Madhya Pradesh (v) *Eastern Zone* which includes Assam, Behar, Orissa, West Bengal and other North Eastern States. These zones were created in order to facilitate discussion on economic and other matters of mutual interest. The creation of these zones is a recognition of the fact that in each zone there is a combination of physiographic, economic and cultural factors.

## Regionalism in India

In the Indian context, regionalism refers to assertion of distinct ethnic, linguistic or economic rights by various groups within the nation. Since regional consciousness is based on linguistic, economic, ethnic and cultural identities of the people living in a specific geographical area, we may speak in terms of economic regionalism, linguistic regionalism, political regionalism and even sub-regional movements (for instance, Gorkha movement in Darjeeling hill area or the Bodo Movement in Assam) within the general frame of regionalism. Regionalism, in the Indian context, is thus a multi-dimensional concept. This is because of the fact that the term 'region' refers not simply to a geographical territory, as is often assumed, but also to common characteristics of culture nurtured and nourished for a considerable period of time by the people of a geographical area. These cultural traits are contrasted with characteristic cultural features in other parts of the larger geographical entity.

A distinction may be made between two types of socio-cultural regions. One type includes regions marked out by observers and/or specialists on the basis of some defining features. The other type includes regions which the people in the concerned areas perceive and which may attract their loyalties, give them separate identification tags, as it were, and form the basis for joint action.

These two types are not, however, mutually exclusive categories. Nevertheless, it may be recognised that the regions marked out by analytic observers and/or specialists are not necessarily recognised by the people who reside within those areas. Thus, the five zones marked by the States Reorganization Act, 1956, are very useful taxonomic concepts for those concerned with economic planning. Taxonomic regions can reveal quite accurately a great deal of information which can be useful for economic and social planning as well as for a general understanding of distribution of socio-cultural zones and social processes. The nature of such regions depends on which traits are selected as significant and what purpose the formulation is intended to serve. But few, if any, residents of the respective zones, have any notion that they can be so classified. On the contrary, if a number of people strongly feel that they share a regional identity, that feeling, in itself, is a common feature. The analytical observers and specialists must take the perception of the people into account. Government authorities may denote a new political entity which may then become in terms of perception of the people within it an important region.

The geographic spread of a region varies according to the criteria and purposes selected by the researcher. For certain criteria and purposes the whole Indian sub-continent can be treated as one region, as Emeneau had done in respect of certain linguistic traits (Murray B. Emeneau : India as a linguistic area. Language 1956) and as Kroeber had done in regard to civilisation (A.L. Kroeber : Culture groupings in Asia. South Western Journal of Anthropology 1947). For other purposes a small tract like Coorg can validly be considered a separate region both by the observers and by the residents themselves. For instance,

Srinivas has pointed out that the people of Coorg can be classified as practising a special variety of Hinduism as contrasted with that practised in adjoining areas, described by him as " Peninsular Hinduism" which, in its turn, is a part of the vast region of "All India Hinduism". Even much smaller tracts and population can usefully be denoted as regions for certain purposes.

Since the seventies regionalism has developed as a major social and political force in the Indian sub-continent. The origin of regionalism may be explained in various ways and from different perspectives. Some of these may be discussed briefly.

To begin with, mention may be made of the creation of an independent nation in a pluralistic society within which sectional interests vigorously compete for shares of the nation's resources and for symbols of regional eminence. According to some analysts, in a vast and diversified polity like India, regionalism is a legitimate phenomenon. Assertion of regional rights is interpreted by some as an expression of the quest for a human identity. According to Rajni Kothari, "the way to deal with them lies not in dubbing them anti-national and crushing them with the use of state force but in respecting and recognising their underlying motives and aspirations and fit them into the larger framework of national unity."

Secondly, the growth in importance after independence of regional languages and in the number of people educated in those languages led to their enhanced self-identification with the language and the region of their domicile. The process began in the 19th century when local leaders deliberately propagated regional speech, literature and practices as ways of opposing the language and influence of the elite, mainly English-speaking elite.

The linguistic separation between regions is another element in sharpening loyalty to region.

The social force of linguistic identification, however, developed greatly after independence because of the following reasons : (a) Improvement in communication within the regions; (b) Propagation of regional language for educational, literary, religious and political purposes; (c) The need felt by local political leaders for supra-local alliances in order to swing political weight.

Thirdly, when people belonging to a particular ethnic group reside permanently within a specific geographic area, their ethnic feelings find expression in the form of increased regional loyalty. Many recent regional movements in India, such as movement for Gorkhaland in Darjeeling, Bodo movements in Assam, and Jharkhand movement in Bihar and West Bengal are basically movements for establishing ethnic identity. It may be pointed out that ethnicity is not peculiar to India. It is a world phenomenon. No large nation-state today is free from ethnic upsurges. Recent ethnic troubles between Azerbaizans and Armenians show that even a highly centralised Communist state is not free from ethnic clashes. It may further be pointed out that ethnicity is to be distinguished from racial identity. "Race tends to refer to the biological aspect of group difference, ethnic to a combination of the cultural aspect plus a putative biological element because of the assumption of common descent". (Nathan Glazer : An article entitled "Ethnicity— a world phenomenon", published in the Encounter. 1975).

## 8. TYPES OF SOCIETY

Each human group develops its own social and political structure in terms of its own culture and history. Three broad types of social structures may be distinguished. First,the tribal society represented by the social structures of African tribes. Second, the agrarian social structure represented by the traditional Indian society. Third, the industrial social structure represented by the industrially advanced countries of Western Europe and U.S.A. Sociologists also speak of yet another type, called Post-industrial Society, which is emerging out of the industrial society. We may note briefly the features of these types of societies.

### Tribal Society

The leaders of Indian tribes met at a conference in Shillong in 1962 and defined a tribe as " an indigenous homogeneous unit speaking a common language, claiming a common descent, living in a particular geographical area, backward in technology, pre-literate, loyally observing social and political customs based on kinship". This definition brings out broadly the features of a tribe.

The economic and social structure of a tribal society may be briefly described thus:

Hunting and food-gathering constitute the main occupation of a typical tribal community. There exists a simple division of labour based on age and sex. Private ownership of property is virtually non-exîstent, so also is exchange and credit. The patterns of economic activity are, thus, simple and undifferentiated which bear no comparison to the complex economic structure of the present-day industrial society.

The social structure is highly integrated and unified, class division of an industrial society is practically unknown. The interaction among the members of a tribal society follows the pattern of interaction among the members of a primary group. Secondary ties are non-existent. As such social control is exercised through folkways and similar other informal ways. Religion of the tribal people is expressed in terms of totemism, magic and fetishism.

### Agrarian Society

As the name suggests, the dominant occupation of the people in such a society is agriculture. Naturally, the domestication of plants and animals constitutes an important economic activity. There also exists, alongside agriculture, varied economic occupations, such as those of artisans, weavers, potters, blacksmiths, etc. A simple division of labour characterises such a society. There is practically no scope for complex division of labour which we find in an industrial society. There are varying patterns of land ownership. There are, in the first place, absentee landowners. They do not cultivate the land in their possession and let it out for sharecropping.These share-croppers cultivate the land on a crop-sharing basis. There are, secondly, supervisory farmers who own land but get their land cultivated by hired labourers who do not generally own any land themselves. Thirdly, there are small cultivator-owners who own and cultivate their small holdings.

The domestication of animals and the discovery of agriculture brought about a revolutionary change in the patterns of living in man's distant past. His food supply became more abundant, more predictable. Men no longer had to live in small and wandering groups, hunting, fishing, and gathering wild fruit in order to survive. Agriculture enabled them to settle in larger and more stable communities. There emerged, as a result, what is called village community. The social life of an agrarian society is, therefore, village-oriented. Physical mobility being virtually non-existent because of inadequate development of the means of transportation, primary group relationships prevail in an agrarian society. Social control is naturally exercised through informal means, such as folkways and mores. Family is a very important institution in an agrarian society, catering to the myriad needs of its members. The family serves practically as a miniature community. The patterns of living being, more or less, unchanging and the production-relations also being virtually stabilised, the social divisions into classes in such a society exhibit the features of a closed social structure. Agriculture is, to a large extent, affected by the elements of nature—flood and drought, for instance— which are beyond the control of farmers. The people, therefore, become fatalistic and superstitious and observe rituals and practices designed to influence the elements of nature. They turn to God either to *persuade* Him with their prayers or to *compel* Him to listen. These two elements are inextricably mixed in religions of agrarian society.

## Industrial Society

Pre-industrial society is dependent on raw labour power and the extraction of primary resources from nature. Industrial society, on the other hand, "is organised around the axis of production and machinery for the fabrication of goods. In its rhythm of life and organisation of work, industrial society is the defining feature of the social structure—i.e. the economy, the occupational system, and the stratification system—of modern Western society".[32]

The industrial society, which emerged in the wake of industrial revolution, is distinguished by a new economic order. The entire production is shifted away from the family and the household to the factory. Family is no longer a production unit, as in an agrarian setting. Moreover, machine technology, which is the basis of the new economic order, is the cause as well as the effect of a complex division of labour.

Another significant change in the economic field is the separation of ownership and control in industrial enterprises. At present, the large companies which dominate the major branches of industry are managed and directed by individuals who do not own them. The owners (i.e., those who purchased the equity shares are the thousands of small and medium share-holders who are primarily concerned with the profitability of the enterprise. A detailed discussion on the sociological significance of this development will be found in the chapter devoted to economic institutions of society (Chapter 17).

An industrial society is marked by disappearance of the neighbourhood and predominance of secondary relationships. Both in size and spatial distribution, population records an increase. Social mobility becomes easier and possible because of improved means of transportation. Social control is possible only through formal means, such as law and order machinery of the political authority. We have already noted elsewhere in this chapter that an industrial society is largely associational in nature. Numerous associations grow in order to take care of varied needs of the people—health care, education, recreation, etc. As a result, the family is divested of many of its functions and is no longer a miniature community catering to the myriad needs of its members. Moreover, physical mobility facilitates social mobility. No one seems destined as in an agrarian society, to be tied down to the class to which one is born, Merit norm, rather than ascription, becomes the dominant value. One can, therefore, improve one's social status by fulfilling the merit norms prescribed by society. In other words, open class structure replaces the closed class structure of an agrarian society. In addition, women are no longer tied down to their domestic chores from sunrise till sunset. Mechanical devices of various kinds free them from domestic drudgery and they can afford enough time to qualify and compete for jobs which were previously considered to be the exclusive domain of men. In an industrial society men and women compete on an equal footing in all spheres of life. Further, a far-reaching change in outlook is discernible. Fatalism and superstition of old days are replaced by a pragmatic and rational outlook. Attitude towards religion also undergoes a radical change. People are increasingly becoming aware of the fact that science may be able to explain eventually most human behaviour but can never tell them how they *should* behave. Science also does not tell them what goals they should try to achieve. Science is concerned with facts, not with the meaning of life. People in an industrial society are, however, deeply concerned with the meaning of life. Industrial society disturbs people economically, socially and even emotionally. Like the primitive people, they also need, in no small measure, a re-assurance in a world of neck to-neck competition and the co-existence of success and failure, of frustration and fulfilment. They, therefore, turn to religion as an emotional support in a disturbing environment, as an end in itself.

**Post-industrial society**

Daniel Bell coined the phrase *post-industrial society* some years ago to describe the new social structures evolving in modern industrially advanced societies, particularly in the U.S.A. since the second half of the twentieth century. The singular feature of the post-industrial society, according to Professor Bell, is an important new principle, *the codification of theoretical knowledge,* which now shapes innovation in science, technology and social policy. Post-industrial society is actually a "new *knowledge society* which is emerging out of the older corporate capitalism". Professor Bell says that the concept of the post-industrial society is a large generalisation. In order to make its meaning more easily understood, he specifies five dimensions or components of the term[33] :

1. **Economic sector : the change from a goods producing to a service economy.**

Bell explains the change thus: Many agrarian societies (India, for instance) have a high proportion of persons engaged in services of a personal sort (e.g. household servants) because labour is cheap and usually unemployed. In an industrial society different services tend to increase because of the need for auxiliary help for production, namely, transportation and distribution. In a post-industrial society, however, the emphasis is on a different kind of service. Personal services (retail stores, hair-cutting saloons, laundries, garages, etc,), business services (banking and finance, real estate, insurance), services related to transportation, communication and utilities are not distinctive features of this society. What is unique for post-industrial society are services related to health, education, research, and government. This category represents the expansion of a new intelligentsia in the universities, research organisations, professions and government.

2. **Occupational distribution : the pre-eminence of the professional and technical class.**

The post-industrial society is characterised by a change in occupational distributions—that is, not only *where* people work, but the *kind* of work they do. To a large extent, occupation is the most important determinant of class and stratification in the society.

Within industrial societies, the semi-skilled worker has been the single largest category in the labour force. In a post-industrial society the expansion of the service economy has naturally brought about a shift to white-collar occupations. By 1956 in the U.S.A. the number of white-collar workers, for the first time in the history of industrial civilization, out-numbered the blue-collar workers in the occupational structure. Since then, the ratio has been widening steadily. By 1970, the white-collar workers out-numbered the blue-collar by more than five to four .

The most startling change has been the growth of professional and technical employment—jobs that usually require some college education—at a rate twice that of the average. While the growth rate of the professional and technical class as a whole has been twice that of the average labour force, the growth rate of the scientists and engineers has been triple that of the working population.

**3. Axial principle : the centrality of theoretical knowledge as the source of innovation and of policy formulation for the society.**

Industrial society is concerned with the co-ordination of machines and men for the production of goods. Post-industrial society is organised around *knowledge* for the purpose of social control and the directing of innovation and change. This, in turn gives rise to new social relationships and new structures. Knowledge has, of course, been necessary in the functioning of any society. What is distinctive about the post-industrial society is the change in the *character of knowledge* itself. What has become crucially important for the organisation of decisions and the direction of change is the emphasis on *theoretical* knowledge, as opposed to empirical knowledge and the codification of knowledge into abstract systems of symbols that can be used to illuminate many and varied areas of experience. Every modern society now lives by innovation and social control of change, and tries to anticipate the future in order to plan ahead. The need for forecasting and planning makes theoretical knowledge so crucial.

**4. Future orientation : the control of technology and technological assessment.**

Modern industrial economies became possible when societies were able to create new institutional mechanisms to build up savings (through banks, insurance companies, equity capital through the stock market, and government levies, that is, borrowings and taxes), and to use this money for investment. The ability consistently to re-invest annually at least 10 per cent of GNP became the basis of what W. W. Rostow called the 'take-off stage for economic growth. But a modern society, in order to avoid stagnation or maturity has to open up new technological frontiers in order to maintain productivity and higher standards of living. Marx argued that a capitalist economy has to expand or die. Later Marxists, such as Lenin or Rosa Luxemburg, assumed that such expansion necessarily has to be geographical. Hence the theory of imperialism. But, contrary to these assumptions, the greater measure of expansion has been technological which prevented an industrial society from stagnation. Without new technology,how can growth be maintained ? The development of new forecasting and "mapping techniques" makes possible a novel phase in economic history—the conscious, planned advance of technological change, and hence the reduction of uncertainty about the economic future.

### 5. Decision-making : the creation of a new intellectual technology

Whitehead wrote : 'The greatest invention of the nineteenth century was the invention of the method of invention. A new method entered into life. In order to understand our epoch, we can neglect all the details of change, such as railways, telegraphs, radios, spinning machines, synthetic dyes. We must concentrate on the method itself; that is the real novelty, which has broken up the foundations of the old civilization"[34].

One can say in the same spirit that the methodological promise of the second half of the 20th century is the management of organized complexity (the complexity of large organizations and systems, the complexity of theory with a large number of variables), the identification and implementation of strategies for rational choice in games against nature and games between persons, and the development of a new intellectual technology which, by the end of the 20th century, many be as important in human affairs as machine technology has been for the past century and a half. What is distinctive about the new intellectual technology which, by the end of the 20th century, may be as important in human affairs as machine technology has been for the past century and a half. What is distinctive about the new intellectual technology is its effort to define rational action and to identify the means of achieving it. All situations involve constraints and contrasting alternatives. And all action takes place under conditions of certainty, risk or uncertainty. Certainty exists when the constraints are fixed and known. Risk means that a set of possible outcomes is known and the probabilities for each outcome can be stated. Uncertainty is the case when the set of possible outcomes can be stipulated,but the probabilities are completely unknown. Further, situations can be defined as 'games against nature' in which the constraints are environmental, or 'games between persons' in which each person's course of action is necessarily shaped by the reciprocal judgments of the others' intentions. In all these situations, the desirable action is a strategy that leads to the optimal or best solution, i.e. one which either maximises the outcome or tries to minimise the losses[35].

The professional and technical classes enjoy a pre-eminence in the social hierarchy of the post-industrial society. 'Knowledge' is the new principle of stratification in such a society.

## NOTES

1. Kingsled Davis : *Human-Society*, page 220
2. *ibid*, Pages 221-222
3. *ibid*, Page 222
4. *ibid*, page 222
5. Ferdinand Tönies : *Fundamental Concepts of Sociology (Gemeinschaft and Gesellschaft)*, translated and supplemented by Charles P. Loomis. American Book Co. N.Y. 1940 pages 37-39
6. MacIver and Page, *Society*, page 11
7. Bottomore, *Sociology*, page 100
8. *ibid*, page 12
9. Derek Gregory, *Ideology, Science and Human Geography*, page 85
10. Bottomore, *Sociology*, page 103
11. *ibid*, page 103
12. *ibid*, page 103
13. *ibid*, page 103
14. MacIver and Page, *Society*, page 312
15. Bierstedt, *The Social Order*, page 418

16. Ogburn and Nimkoff, *Handbook of Sociology*, page 276
17. MacIver and Page, *Society*, pages 327-328
18. Bierstedt, *The Social Order*, page 427
19. *ibid*, page 417
20. Hope Tisdale,*The Process of Urbanisation, Social Forces,* 20 March, 1942, Quoted by Schnore in *Sociology, An Introduction,* edited by N.J. Smelser, page 107
21. Gerald Breese, *Urbanisation in Newly Developing Countries*, page 3
22. Albert J.Reiss, Jr., *Urbanism,* in A Dictonary of the Social Sciences quoted by Schnore in *Sociology. An Introduction,* edited by N.J.Smelser, page 106
23. Donald G. Bogue and K.C.Zachariah,*"Urbanisation and Migration in India"*, in Roy Turner, ed., *India's Urban Future* (Berkeley & Los Angeles, California, University of California Press (1962), page 45. Quoted by Breese in his book entitled *'Urbanisation in Developing* Countries" pages 81-82
24. *ibid*, pages 81-82
25. Gerald Breese, *Urbanisation in Newly Developing Countries*, page 99
26. *ibid*, page 100
27. An article by Daniel Lerner entitled *The Transformation of Institutions* included in the book, The Transfer of Institutions, edited by William B. Hamilton. Pages 19-22
28. Joel M. Halpern, *The Changing Village Community*, Prentice-Hall, 1967, page 2
29. Kingsley Davis, *The Urbanization of the Human Population,* Scientific American (September,1965), page 51
30. Lundberg, *Sociology*, page 141
31. MacIver and Page, *Society*, page 343
32. Daniel Bell, *The Coming of Post-Industrial Society*, page X
33. *ibid*, pages 14-33
34. A. N. Whitehead, *Science and the Modern World* page 141. Quoted by Daniel Bell, page 28
35. The section on post-industrial society is a reproduction, with suitable modifications, of Professor Bell's treatment of the theme.

# CHAPTER SEVEN

# SOCIAL ORGANISATION

## 1. FORMAL ORGANISATION

In a society the activities that an individual undertakes fall under two broad categories : those which he himself *plans* and those which are *planned* for him by others. In both the cases the activities are goal-oriented in the sense that some special purpose is sought to be achieved. There is, however, a significant difference between the two. In the former, no formal authority is created. In the latter, a formal authority designed to achieve certain purposes is created. The social arrangement in which a group of people plans the activities which others are obliged to participate in is called a *formal organisation*. For instance, a school or a college is a formal organisation inasmuch as the teachers plan the activities of students in order to teach them. Similarly, all large-scale organisations are formal organisations.

A formal organisation is distinguished by two features : (i) the organisational pattern is clearly spelt out in a document which, generally, consists of two parts : the Memorandum of Association embodying the objectives and the Rules and Regulations embodying the rules of management. (ii) Once organised and formally registered under the law of the land, the formal organisation acquires a legal personality which can sue and be sued in the Court of Law. It can also survive beyond the lives of those who brought into being the formal organisation.

## 2. ELEMENTS OF FORMAL ORGANISATION

Three things are generally required in order to plan social activities systematically : (a) a *theory* of how the activities are to be planned in order to achieve the purpose or objective of the organisation; (b) *resources* which can be mobilised for the purpose; (c) creation of a clear-cut *authority* system to direct the activities in a planned manner so as to ensure the achievement of goal of the organisation.

### The theory

No formal organisation can succeed in the absence of a clearly defined set of ideas as to how the activities are to be carried out over a period of time, taking into account the possible changes in the variables in future and the steps to be taken to meet the situation arising out of changed circumstances. Such theorising is an indispensable step towards planning a large-scale formal organisation.

A theory consists of the following :

**(a) A technical-costs theory** : In order to ensure the success of a planned activity, there must be an informed awareness about the required technical resources and costs to be incurred for having those resources. For instance, in teaching the competence of teachers is a *sine qua non* for success. Hence the needed technical skill of a teacher has to be clearly determined and the cost that has to be incurred in order to enlist the services of a technically qualified teacher should also be ascertained beforehand.

**(b) A market theory :** A part of the planning process is not simply to ensure the high quality of a service, but also to be certain that the service in question has a demand. If, for instance, the best available teachers are recruited to teach a subject which fails to attract students, the entire enterprise falls through.

## Resources

All organisations need resources. Resources may be of various kinds. We may think of three kinds of resources - men, money and materials. Men who are involved in the activities of the organisation, directly or indirectly, are to give to the organisation time which they could utilise elsewhere. The organisation must, therefore, devise ways of utilising the services of the needed men who may be persuaded to give their time to the organisation rather than to other alternative uses. Similarly, financial resources which have many other alternative uses must be attracted to the organisation. Finance must be made available if the organisation is to function. Finally, no organisation can achieve anything in the absence of the needed materials. Materials may be a building or a shed, depending on the kind of use. Materials may also consist of tools, or libraries or means of transport or any other thing specially required for carrying out the activity. The point is that all these materials have alternative uses. Hence, the organisation must ensure that the materials are available to it and not diverted to alternative uses.

It is not enough to have men, money and material for the organisation. There are pulls from alternative uses which may attract these resources away from the organisation. Hence appropriate measures have to be devised so as to repel or neutralise such pulls. This must be an on-going process. Any slight slackening of efforts in this regard may lead to the loss of resources to the organisation.

There is also the problem of obsolescence, depreciation and physical wearing out of materials. These must be periodically replenished.

There is the further problem of putting the resources—men, money and materials—to the best use in order to derive the maximum advantages and minimise cost. The use of the resources should, therefore, "be scheduled, controlled, cost-accounted and directed". This requires a well-designed administrative structure.

Thus, the resources have to be *created* in the sense of making them available, *defended* in the sense of checking diversion to alternative uses, *replenished* in the sense of replacing old, worn-out materials by new and improved ones, *administered* in the sense of maximising benefit and minimising loss.

## The authority system

The optimum use of resources demands a well-knit administrative structure, providing for supervision, control and discipline. The essential elements of such a structure are the following :

(i) To fix *responsibility* for action taken or not taken is a very important task. It is also a very difficult task. Difficulty is all the greater when activities of the organisation involve delegation of authority on the one hand and taking of responsibility on the other. For instance, a teacher of a university or a college may be appointed to teach a particular subject on the assumption that he knows the subject and also the best way to put across to the students the essentials of the subject. After the responsibility to take care of the students is delegated to him and he undertakes the responsibility, weeks and months may pass without anyone cautioning him that his teaching leaves much to be desired. In the circumstances, will it be fair to make him wholly responsible for the distressing state of affairs ? In the interest of efficient and smooth functions of the organisation, the activities should be so organised as to assign specific responsibility for a specific job, so that no one may be in doubt as to where responsibility lies.

(ii) *Supervision* of activities is necessary in order to ensure that work progresses according to schedule. Supervision may be of two types : *statistical* and *visual* .

Statistical supervision refers to the method of supervising or assessing performance on the basis of the relevant statistical data. The grading of tests in an educational institution is a familiar example of this kind of supervision. A teacher does not keep a watch on his students to find out when, for how many hours and in what manner does the student study. His supervision work is confined to the 'grades' the student obtains. A similar device of measuring performance is also followed in factories in the form of statistical curves.

*Visual* supervision is nothing but our commonsense view of checking performance. In the nature of things, visual supervision is relevant for small-sized organisations and is completely unsuited to large-sized ones.

(iii) *Discipline* is necessary in every walk of life. An organisation which scores low in terms of discipline is more likely to fail in achieving its goal and vice versa. The success of an organisation to enforce discipline depends on two factors : (a) The degree to which the 'carrot' and the 'stick' (i.e., reward and punishment) are adequate enough to motivate the concerned people. (b) The degree to which these rewards and punishments are "related in a reliable and precise way to the actual level of performance".

There are, however, two difficulties in the way of enforcing discipline. In the first place, if there are stronger motivations in comparison with the system of rewards and punishments maintained by the organisation, the organisation may fail to enforce discipline as well as it should. In India, for instance, attachments to family ties are so strong that factory workers are in the habit of absenting themselves from factory duty and migrating to their villages on festive occasions or during particular seasons. Migratory labour, which is an anti-thesis of factory discipline, may be explained by the fact that attachment to one's kith and kin is a greater attraction than the reward offered by the organisation for regular attendance. Secondly, the problem of maintaining discipline arises when rewards are given to those who do not deserve them or when punishments are imposed upon some in the most unwarranted manner. These things weaken the morale of the members when they see " under the sun, that the race is not to the swift, nor the battle to the strong, neither yet bread to the wise, but time and chance happeneth to them all ". Justice is not easy to achieve either in a society or in an organisation.

## 3. TYPES OF ORGANISATIONS

Organisations differ from one another in terms of variation in their key elements - viz., theory, resource, and authority system. The classification of organisations on these lines would be extremely complex because combination of all the possible variations of key elements would defy all attempts at clear-cut classification.

We may, however, distinguish between four types of organisations which have dominated sociological thinking about organisations since the categories were developed by Max Weber in the first part of the twentieth century. These four types are (i) organisation under *charismatic leadership,* (ii) organisation under *feudal administration,* (iii) modern *bureaucracies* and (iv) *professional* type of organisation.

**First type : Charismatic leadership**

The underlying principle of such an organisation is the charisma of the boss of an organisation in the perception of those who serve there. Charismatic administration occurs whenever people in the organisation believe, in respect of the particular area of activity, that "history is the lengthened shadow of man". Such a faith in the leader develops when the leader is a man of genius and is credited with intelligence and wisdom far superior to those of others in the organisation. If, for instance, a reputed scientist heads an organisation in which all research activities are carried on in terms of his perception of what is to be done or what is good or bad for the organisation, the organisation may be said to be under a charismatic leadership. His perception alone counts, and nothing else.

**Second type : Feudal administration**

We may begin the discussion with reference to an exampie. Now-a-days the dealer for a company performs a number of functions for the company. He advertises the product to the community, renders the service provided for in the warranty, sometimes arranges financing the sale of the product, and does many other things. The manufacturer assumes that the dealer would do all these in his own interest (which eventually furthers the interest of the manufacturer himself) if the dealer is given complete control of an area for his operations. The dealer, on the other hand, has some obligations to the manufacturing company which gives him dealership right over a particular area. For instance, he is not allowed to sell a similar competitive product manufactured by another company. These rights and obligations are now-a-days written into a contract. Within the framework of the contract, the dealer enjoys a good measure of autonomy, with little or no interference from the manufacturing firm.

This kind of administration concerning the manufacturer and the dealer is characterised as *feudal* inasmuch as it broadly follows the traditional (not contractual) pattern of relationship which prevailed among fief-holders and lords during the Middle Ages. Under feudalism, vassals held lands from lords-superior on condition of military service.

**Third type : Bureaucratic system**

Bureaucratic organisation is basically a rule-centred organisation. Only the rules, laid down in black and white, count. All the values and principles of the organisation are embodied in these rules. The personnel of the organisation from the top officials to the lowest subordinates hold office under certain conditions for which they draw a salary. All of them have to go through some kind of an indoctrination process in order to familiarise themselves with those rules. The rules may be concerned with company policies, political ideologies or religious dogmas, depending on the nature of activity of the company. Another unique feature of this kind of organisation is that bureaucrats are organised on a hierarchical basis.

**Fourth type : Professional type of organisation**

When the organisational activity is determined in terms of specialised knowledge of the trained members of the organisation rather than by a charismatic leader, or by tradition, or by bureaucrats, we get a professional type of organisation. The distinguishing mark of this kind of organisation is that there is a wide delegation of responsibility to people who are assigned the job after their competence has been certified by a group of peers. Universities and hospitals are typical examples of this type of organisation. After the competence of teachers and doctors is assessed, they are entrusted with a responsibility which is defined by the incumbents themselves. They enjoy a large measure of autonomy. It is assumed that they would make full use of their competence in their respective fields. The top echelon of authority - the Vice-Chancellor or the Principal of a Medical College - would not interfere with the job of a teacher in his class room or laboratory. One reason, of course, is that it is not possible for anyone of them (if they do not belong to the discipline) to judge the competence of bio-physicists, political scientists, economists, etc. Consequently, extreme decentralisation of responsibility to men chosen for their competence is a distinctive feature of professional organisations.

## 4. EFFECTS OF ORGANISATIONS ON DAILY LIFE

We noted in the previous chapter that life in the present-day society has become largely associational in nature. Various organisations cater to the variety of needs of people. In fact, hardly any aspect of social life, particularly in urban areas, is left which is free from organisational planning. Even recreation has developed into a large industry. Theatre and movie houses, travel agents, tourist guides, hotel complexes and many more institutions and agencies comprise parts of a major recreational industry. Works of art are not patronised today by individual connoisseurs of art but by highly organised museums. Likewise, a net-work of libraries meet the need for reading materials of a large number of people. These examples are illustrative of the trend which Kenneth Boulding has characterised as 'Organisational Revolution'. The terms 'organisational man' or 'management man' are increasingly becoming popular and are widely being used. This is a development which affects social and individual life in various ways. We may note some of the consequences.

To begin with, planning, if properly done, reduces wastage and increases efficiency. Social purposes are, therefore, more efficiently achieved in societies in which activities are very extensively planned.

Secondly, a man's waking hours are sharply divided between *work* (that is, activities which are *planned* for him by others) and *leisure* (that is, leisure-time activities which he himself plans and decides). Moreover, in terms of time allotted for these two categories of activities, work dominates over leisure. This means that a man's waking hours are devoted mostly to activities that are decided and planned by others. It is particularly so in big cities and metropolitan areas where people have to negotiate long distances to go to their work places. As a consequence, they have less time available to them to follow their creative pursuits.

Thirdly, occupations multiply as the number of specialised organisations increases and as the creation of sub-organisations within organisations progresses. As a result, people become specialised in particular activities. Multiplication of occupations also leads to the growth of variety of economic-interest groups that we find in modern society.

Fourthly, in a society where social activities are largely planned and organised, a man interacts with a large number of people with whom he has no emotional attachment. The quality of emotional and spontaneous relationship which generally prevails among friends and relatives is lacking in such interactions. This feature has been characterised by Talcott Parsons as *affective neutrality*. Relationship is, on the other hand, largely functional. Thus, the two residents of a particular locality may meet and establish social relationships as, say, members of the local School Board. They do not establish any relationship between whole personalities in all areas of life, as in friendly or kin relationships. This characteristic of social relations is called "functional specificity".

## 5. INFORMAL ORGANISATION : EMERGENCE OF INFORMAL STRUCTURES WITHIN A FORMAL ORGANISATION

Informal relationships grow even in a highly integrated formal organisation. Various reasons are responsible for this. In the first place, the members of a formal organisation are also members of a variety of other groups. If these other groups have a fairly strong in-group feeling, their members are likely to carry over their attitudes and relationships into the formal organisation. Secondly, sometimes the attitudes which are prevalent in the wider society are reflected in a bureaucratic organisation. For instance, informal groups on caste, ethnic or clanish lines may develop.

Such informal groups may be utilised for the furtherance of the goals of the formal organisation. Sometimes such groups may also prove to be dysfunctional in so far as they impede the attainment of the goals of the formal organisation.

The activities of some of these informal groups may be of 'deviant' nature, as judged from the point of view of formal organisations. The following example may be cited. Since bank employees in general, and some employees of a particular section in particular, are aware of share market fluctuations, they may form a group in order to earn extra money by engaging themselves in share market speculations.

An important point may be noted here. Such 'deviant' conduct is sometimes known to the authorities of the formal organisation and connived at by them. This is so because of the assumption that such 'deviant' conduct may not be dysfunctional for the formal organisation and that, in any case, it would often be foolhardy for higher officials to attempt to suppress them.

Under certain conditions, the formal set-up of a formal organisation may be replaced by an informal one. For example, the chairman of a formal organisation, who is on the verge of retirement, may pass on many of his responsibilities to the person next to him. Such a devolution of authority is obviously informal and not consistent with the rules of the organisation. This kind of arrangement may be characterised as 'latent' in the sense that the new line of authority is not made 'explicit' to all the personnel in the organisation. Just as there may be 'latent' functions, so also there may be 'latent' structures.

## 6. MODES OF PARTICIPATION : DEMOCRATIC AND AUTHORITARIAN FORMS

Some organisations encourage their members to participate in decision-making while others restrict this privilege. Parent-Teacher Association belongs to the first category. N.C.C. or Boy Scouts belong to the second.

The considerations which are taken into account in determining the mode of participation of members are the following :

(i) If a group meets occasionally mainly for purposes of deliberation and discussion, democratic forms are appropriate. If, however, a group is engaged in activities of a long-term nature, it usually adopts authoritarian style of functioning. The reasons are obvious. Such a group must have specific goals to achieve. This objective can be attained only when a hierarchical structure is organised in which a few persons are assigned the responsibility of taking decision and making all others comply with their directions. All large-sized organisations, with small variations, follow this pattern.

(ii) Democratic style of functioning does not generally obtain in organisations in which participation is involuntary or in which participation is compensated fully either in monetary terms or in terms of service. In such cases, democratic set-up is not obviously required either to induce or to sustain participation.

(iii) Democratic forms are considered to be appropriate in those cases in which high levels of loyalty and zeal are required or in which the members of the organisation are expected to take risks.

(iv) The principle of democratic participation of the employees and workers may be introduced in a formal organisation like a factory, in which authoritarian controls predominate, in order to maintain high morale.

### Some general observations on democratic vs. authoritarian forms of participation.

Some general observations are called for in order to bring out the complex nature of the issues involved.

To begin with, the term 'authoritarian' should be interpreted in proper context. Thus, authoritarian forms, when limited to specific activities and controlled by law and custom, do not necessarily challenge the cultural ideals of a democratic society. For example, there is authoritarian administration within most of the governmental agencies. But the head of the agency is invariably responsible to people at the top who are themselves responsible, directly or indirectly, to the legislature.

A second point to be borne in mind is that all organisations, which are controlled from the top, are not necessarily authoritarian. There are organisations which permit considerable decision-making by committees, wide autonomy for subordinate officials and encourage initiative from below. Such organisations are definitely democratic in spirit and, to some extent, in form, even though final responsibility and authority remain at the top.

Thirdly, it is worth noting that, in actual practice, no neat division into democratic and authoritarian types is possible. Both forms generally co-exist side by side in many large organisations. In some areas of decision-making and functioning, the pattern may be authoritarian, and in some other areas it may be democratic.

Finally, it is interesting to note that the style of functioning of a particular top executive may give a totally wrong impression about the character of the organisation. Thus, an executive may be temperamentally unfit to carry his subordinates with him and may unnecessarily estrange them by his authoritarian behaviour. Such behaviour may be associated with an authoritarian organisation. But the two should not be confused. There may be in that very organisation another executive of the same rank who is tolerant and understanding in his outlook and in his dealings with his subordinates.

## 7. VOLUNTARY ASSOCIATION

Definitions of the term 'voluntary association', as it apples to organisations in modern societies, differ widely. Generally, a voluntary association is defined as an organised group of persons, having the following attributes : (i) The membership of a voluntary association is neither obligatory nor acquired by birth. (ii) A voluntary association exists independently of the state. (iii) These organisations have little capacity to discipline the participants. The members participate in various activities voluntarily. (iv) The basic structure of a voluntary association is formed by groupings with *different levels of activity*. The core or centre of the group consists of highly active people - say, an executive committee or a paid staff. These highly active people are sufficiently committed to the group so that, within certain limits, their activities can be systematically planned for the achievement of the goals of the group.

The binding force which keeps a voluntary association together is conversation and publicity of the issues and activities that the group is concerned with. The activists in the organisation must take special care to ensure that the activities and 'achievements' of the organisation are publicised, thereby enlisting public support and enthusiasm. The activists must also 'talk to people and invite their suggestions or proposals for improving the quality of the 'activity' of the association. The success of a voluntary association thus depends largely on the ability of the activists to publicise and create enthusiasm among the members of the public to get interested in the activities of the association. The fundamental dynamics of voluntary associations, therefore, revolve around variables and concepts which play a very small part, if at all, in formal organisations which depend more on resource, force, support of law and well-knit rational planning designed to achieve goals.[1]

---

1 Ideas and concepts which appear in this chapter are mainly derived from an article entitled 'Formal organisation' written by Arthur L. Stinchcombe included in 'Sociology'— An Introduction edited by Smelser.

# CHAPTER EIGHT

# SOCIAL GROUPS

## 1. WHY SHOULD WE STUDY GROUPS ?

Sociological study of groups is largely a twentieth century phenomenon. During the nineteenth century and the first two decades of the twentieth century sociologists were mostly pre-occupied with major trends in societal evolution. Tönnies, Durkheim, Marx, Max Weber and others tried to identify and explain the major historical trends, particularly the impact of industrial revolution on society. There was, of course, recognition in the writings of a few sociologists about the importance of group ties, C.H. Cooley, for instance, indicated the value of primary group relationship to an individual. However, the fact theat individual behaviour is as much a *group* phenomenon as an *individual* one was being emphasised from the early twenties. Since then, this particular aspect has been studied by social scientists from different perspectives according to their respective orientations, such as sociologists, psychologists, psychiatrists and even physicians. As a result, there is now a voluminous literature dealing with social groups.

A study of small groups acquires importance in view of the following considerations. To begin with, social groups, however small in size, deeply affect the society. History is replete with cases which indicate that the decisions of small groups have a critical effect upon the larger society. Revolutionary movements in all countries and at all times were invariably initiated by small groups. Secondly, no man is an isolated island. The isolated individual who lives all by himself is either a philosopher's fiction or an abnormal being. In other words, man is a social animal. The sociable nature of man is to be found in the groups which he forms. Human life is essentially group life. The study of groups is, therefore, of crucial significance in understanding the behaviour of men and women. Any casual observer of human begins will confirm that a group exercises considerable influence on its members, particularly when they are young. Moreover, group is a medium through which "we learn culture, we use culture, and change culture". Thirdly, "small groups are a special case of the more general type of system, the social system. Not only are they micro-systems, they are essentially microcosms of larger societies .... Through careful examination of these micro-systems, theoretical models can be constructed and then applied to less accessible societies for further test and modification. Small-group research is thus a means of developing effective ways of thinking about social systems in general ". The fourth reason for studying small groups is social-psychological. "Because social pressures and pressures from the individual meet in the small group, it is a convenient context in which to observe and to experiment on the inter-play among these pressures. Scientific investigation may lead to general laws about how individuals cope with social realities".

## 2. WHAT IS A SOCIAL GROUP ?

Bottomore defines a social group "as an aggregate of individuals in which (i) definite relations exist between the individuals comprising it, and (ii) each individual is conscious of the group itself and its symbols".[3] In other words, a social group has an organisational aspect (rules, rituals, structure, etc.) and a psychological aspect (consciousness of the members). Thus, a social group is a collection of a number of persons linked together in a system of social relationships with one another. According to MacIver and Page, "social relationships involve some degree of reciprocity between those related, some measure of mutual awareness as reflected in the attitudes of the members of the group". That is, the members interact with one another according to the norms or standards accepted by the group.

**Nature of social groups**

The *nature* of social groups will be clear if we make a distinction among the following kinds of groups :

| Types of Groups | Consciousness of kind | Social interaction | Social organisation |
|---|---|---|---|
| Statistical | No | No | No |
| Societal | Yes | No | No |
| Social | Yes | Yes | No |
| Associational | Yes | Yes | Yes |

Statistical groups are formed by sociologists and statisticians, not by the members themselves. These groups are groups for the purpose of research investigations. Thus, sociologists and statisticians may classify children in terms of age (say, children between the age- group 1—5 years, 5 years 1 month —10 years, etc.). These are statistical groups which are significant in so far as these are useful for purposes of investigation into some social phenomenon.

Societal groups differ from statistical groups in one very important characteristic, viz. consciousness of kind. Societal groups include all ethnic groups, all regional groups, all national or state groups, and all occupational groups. Examples are groups of males, females, elderly people, Maharastrians, Tamilians, Bengalees, Assamese, plumbers, etc.

Social groups are characterised by social contact and communication as well as social interaction and social intercourse. Social groups can be of many kinds — friendship or acquaintance groups, neighbourhood groups, play groups and many others.

A social group, as defined above, is also characterised by some as *quasi-group* or a *potential group* because it lacks structure or organisation and whose members may be unaware, or less aware, of the existence of the grouping.

Within an organised group there may exist a number of potential or quasi-groups. These groups serve very useful purposes. "Potential groups are a great source of flexibility and stability. They exert influence at all times because actual groups fear them. It is especially important that they can be activated in support of the rules of fair play ..... We shall not appreciate the full importance of potential group unless we realise that their influence is felt within every actual group. Then we must realise that they cut across many social groups, thus being great latent sources of power ..... In short, 'potential groups' are a form of social control latent in every group and in the society as a whole. They remind us of the great importance of the press and other channels by which publicity is given to people's action"[4]

An *associational group,* or, more simply, an association, is an organised group. It satisfies the criteria of social groups and has, in addition, a formal structure or an organisation. Thus, the All-India Railway Workers' Union is an associational group inasmuch as its members are united together by a similarity of interests. They are expected to behave in a particular way and conform to or abide by the obligations imposed by the group. Similarly, teachers of secondary schools, say, of Delhi or Bombay do not form a social group (in the strict sense of the term) simply because they have similar characteristics or identical interests. But as soon as they form an Association of Teachers, they form a social group.

## 3. CLASSIFICATION OF SOCIAL GROUPS

The variety and diversity of human groups defy all attempts at categorisation. Groups can be considered in terms of their major interests — as in the case of religious groups, political groups, etc — and, then, these may further be sub-divided on the basis of sects, cults, etc. in the case of religious groups or on the basis of pressure groups, interest groups, etc. in the case of political groups. Groups may be considered in terms of their organisational structure as well. Thus, we speak of democratic group, totalitarian group, etc. Groups may also be considered in terms of the socio-economic class to which the members may belong — as in the case of industrial groups, agrarian groups, etc. In this way innumerable illustrations may be given in order to show that any conceivable criterion may be made the basis of classification of groups. It is, therefore, not possible to consider all types of groups. We shall, therefore, consider only those social groups which are regarded as the most general and most widely acceptable.

We may first take up the classification given by Cooley, Angell and Carr[5] who arranged, in order of increasing size and decreasing intimacy, social groups into four general classes :

(i) *Intimate pair-groups,* such as mother and child, husband and wife, lover and sweetheart. They characterised such groups as *sub-primary groups.*

(ii) *Primary groups* characterised by (a) face-to-face association, (b) small numbers, (c) unspecialised purpose, (d) comparative intimacy, and (e) relative permanence. The home, the spontaneous play group and the neighbour are typical examples.

(iii) *Quasi-primary groups* : These are organised face-to-face intimate groups, limited in some degree by special purpose and by the fact of organisation. Boy Scout troops, College Unions. Luncheon Clubs, etc. are examples. They have many of the characteristics of primary groups and may, in fact, perform many of the functions of primary groups. Yet organisation and the limitations of special purpose give them some of the characteristics of secondary groups.

(iv) *Secondary Groups* : These are groups wholly lacking in intimacy of association and usually in most of the other primary and quasi-primary characteristics. Associations, Corporations are among the examples.

**The definition and nature of primary group**

The concept of the primary group was introduced by C.H. Cooley. By primary groups he meant the intimate, personal, 'face-to-face' groups. For example, our companions and comrades, the members of our family and our daily associates may come under this category. *The expression 'face-to-face' should be interpreted figuratively, not literally.* It is possible to have face-to-face relations with people who are not members of our primary groups. Likewise, it is possible that we may not have face-to-face relations with those who are members of our primary groups. For example, we may have face-to-face relations with our barbers or laundrymen. There may not, however, be intimacy or primary-group relations with them, even though we see them face to face. On the other hand, we may correspond regularly with our close friends whom we may not have seen for many years. *It is the degree of intimacy, or social distance, rather than physical distance that determines the primary group.* Relationships among primary group members are based on personal intimacy, and not on contractual obligations. These relationships are often long-lasting.

These intimate and closely-knit groups are primary in different senses. First, face-to-face group is the nucleus of all social organisations — "it is the unit cell of the social structure", as MacIver and Page have described it. It can be found in all societies. Secondly, an intimate group provides the most significant social and psychological experience for its members. Thus, the primary group in the form of the family helps a child to acquire within the confines of a small group his personality as well as "his earliest and completest sense of social unity". It is through such groups that we, as play mates and friends, give expression to our social impulses.

These primary groups can be characterised as *informal*. These informal relationships emerge from frequent interaction among members who come together freely and spontaneously, as is illustrated by the play group, the study group or a group of friends. Though the members of these groups may not develop any formal organisation, they assign, more or less spontaneously, different statuses and roles for each of them. When a group of children regularly play together or when a group of friends frequently meet, they grow a sense of common identity, and share common values and obligations, though they may not be aware of these things. The primary groups emerge whenever and wherever a group of people meet more or less regularly and interact with one another.

It will, however, be wrong to assume that primary groups are found only in social groups of the nature of the family, the play group, the group of friends, etc. They appear even in the midst of very highly organised and complex groups : in college dormitories, in factories and offices, in the army and in prisons. We find in these groups both a formal blue-print arrangement and informal face-to-face groupings. In a college hostel, for instance, there are formal rules and regulations that guide the conduct and mutual relationships among the boarders. But there emerges a number of friendship groups or interest groups which have the qualities of both spontaneity and intimacy. The boarders derive psychological satisfaction in and through such informal groupings. The presence of such informal groups in factories influences, to a considerable extent, the morale of the workers, their productive efficiency and industrial relations in general. This explains the growth and development of the field of 'industrial sociology'. Those who have done research on inter-personal relationships in the army, the prisons, the office or the factory have discovered the existence of primary groupings in these formal establishments also.

**Importance of primary group**

Primary group relationships are equally important to both the young and the adult. A child, for instance, experiences social living for the first time in and through the family and the peer group. These groups are characterised by intimacy and spontaneity and, as such, the child learns many things concerning social life—the basic values, the prescriptive and proscriptive aspects of social norms—almost effortlessly from these groups. Since relationships in such groups are marked by love, affection and mutual trust and understanding, communication from the one to the other is easy. In course of time, a child integrates the values and ideals of society in his personality. In the absence of primary group relationships at an early age, indoctrination into the ethos of society would have been a very difficult process.

Secondly, primary group relationships are equally important for the adults. This aspect was discovered accidentally. During and immediately after the Second World War the number of mental patients in the U.S.A. far outnumbered the availability of psychiatrists in that country. In the circumstances, the patients could not be attended to singly. The only alternative left was to keep a group of patients under one psychiatrist. The outcome of this arrangement was unexpected. The patients responded to treatment much more quickly and much better than they used to be treated singly under a psychiatrist. Such miraculous improvement was attributed to the fact that the primary group relationships which developed among patients in course of their treatment provided the required psychological support and confidence. This discovery led to a new line of treatment called *'primary group therapy'* in general hospitals also. The results of this experiment have been equally encouraging. Being encouraged by such success, some of the Western countries introduced the 'group approach' in reforming and rehabilitating the convicts housed in prisons. In the U.S.A. this group approach is being widely used in tackling cases of juvenile delinquency. A new line of professional approach called *'Social Group Work'* has consequently emerged in social work field. The importance of primary groups in tackling cases of mental, physical and social illness cannot, therefore, be over-emphasised.

Thirdly, research investigations have revealed that the task of maintaining discipline, punctuality and morale among workers in large establishments yields better results if one proceeds through numerous primary groups which develop spontaneously among them. The techhiques of primary group approach in these fields constitute the subject matter of a new branch of sociology called Industrial Sociology.

It will be appropriate to refer to a paradox. On the one hand, we are increasingly becoming aware of the important role that primary groups play in the complex society of ours. There is, on the other hand, disappearance at a pretty fast rate of the conditions that are favourable for the growth of primary groups. The improved transportation has increased the pace and range of physical mobility. As a consequence, neighbourhood is fast disappearing. The bonds of intimacy among neighbours and kins are, naturally, getting weakened in the changed circumstances. Moreover, life has become complex and the needs of people varied and multifarious. Different types of associations, therefore, needs must grow in order to cater to the myriad demands of people. In other words, life tends to become more associational and increasingly less communal in nature.

## The definition and nature of secondary group

In the changed circumstances, we develop, in contrast to the intimacy and spontaneity of primary groups, formal organisations described as *secondary groups* (this term was not introduced by Cooley) in which the individuals have functionally defined roles as members of the group. Personal intimacy and face-to-face relationships are altogether absent in these secondary groups. We may consider, for instance, the case of 'big' colleges in which the student population is so large that teacher-student relationships are not based on personal acquaintance, but on specialised group roles. Students are, in most cases, known to teachers by their roll numbers, and teachers are generally known to students by their initials.

Today an increasing number of our relationships are secondary. One reason is that our contacts have grown in number and variety as a result of improvements in means of communication and transport. We may find another reason in the complexities of modern social life which require accomplishments of a large number of tasks through formal, bureaucratised, large-scale organisations, as in the case of wide-spread network of health services. Many other essential services are provided by similar largescale organisations. All these have naturally led us to develop a number of secondary ties.

The decline of the primary group and the corresponding increase of secondary groups have one very immediate consequence. Because of the nature of secondary groups we are now associating more as mere functionaries and less as whole persons. In primary groups people meet as persons with no limitations of artificiality, special purpose, and the like. In secondary groups, on the other hand, they are functioning units in an organisation, or mere acquaintances at best. Secondary groups may, therefore, be called partial associations. This means that under such conditions associating persons "present only special facets of themselves to one another". They do not meet as whole persons, as in primary groups. In big colleges, students listen to formal lectures from professors, and they have no conception of what the individual professors are like as persons than the professors have of what the individual students are like as persons. Similarly, as consumers we buy our household necessities from individuals who leave their impact upon us merely as functionaries, never as whole personalities.

## Secondary group contrasted with primary group

The secondary group can be contrasted with the primary group from the following points of view : (i) The secondary groups are relatively bigger in size as compared to the primary groups. (ii) Relationships among members in secondary groups tend to be formal and impersonal, while relationships among members in primary groups are characterised by spontaneity and personal intimacy. In other words, we have personal relations with members of the primary group and status relations with members of the secondary group. (iii) Since secondary groups are organised for the pursuit of specific interests members come together for limited purposes and leave the group as soon as the purposes are fulfilled. Thus, a student leaves his educational institution as soon as his objective of getting a degree or a diploma is achieved. In most cases the relationship between a student and his teachers is snapped as soon as he goes out of the institution. This illustrates the fact that secondary groups are transitory in character; they do not last very long. On the contrary, the primary groups, since emotional attachments characterise the relationships among members, are often long-lasting. (iv) The secondary group relations are devoid of sentiment characteristic of primary group relations. The secondary relationships are instrumental in accomplishing certain specific tasks. In this sense, they may be regarded as functional in character. The primary relationships, on the other hand, go beyond the fulfilment of certain functions. They establish intimate person-to-person contacts which are, psychologically speaking, more satisfying to the members than secondary relationships.

It may be noted that this distinction between primary and secondary group, between primary group relations and secondary group relations has been used by many sociologists to describe the total character of a society, although they do so under different labels. For instance, if in Cooley we have primary and secondary, in Tönnies we have 'Gemeinschaft' and 'Gesellschaft', in Durkheim 'mechanical solidarity' and 'organic solidarity', in Sorokin 'familistic' relations and 'contractual' relations. Talcott Parsons elaborated this basic distinction in terms of 'pattern variables'.

## In-group and Out-group

The groups with which an individual identifies himself completely are his in-groups. He has feelings of attachment, sympathy and affection towards the members of these groups. He uses the word 'we' with reference to these groups. Family is a familiar example of in-group for most of the individuals.

An out-group, on the other hand, is defined by an individual with reference to his ingroup. He uses the word 'they' or 'other' with reference to his out-groups. The relationship of an individual to his out-group is marked by a sense of remoteness or detachment and sometimes even of hostility.

It is obvious that in-groups and out-group are not actual groups except in so far as people create them in their use of the pronouns 'we' and 'they' and develop a kind of attitude towards these groups. The distinction is nevertheless an important formal distinction because it enables us to construct two significant sociological principles.

The first of these principles is that in-group members tend to stereotype those who are in the out-group. Thus, the north Indians have stereotypes of those who live in the south. As a matter of fact, those who live south of the Vindhyas are lumped together by many northerners and given a stereotype, ignoring completely that those who live south of the Vindhyas are dissimilar in many respects, in terms of dress, food, language, etc. The southerners likewise have their own stereotypes of the northerners which do not take into account the variations among northerners. The significant thing is that such stereotypes are usually formed by considering only what appears to the members of the in-group the least respectable traits to be found in the character of the members of the out-group. Another significant thing is that "we tend to react to in-group members as individuals, to those in the out-group as members of a class or category. We tend to notice the differences between those who are in our in-groups and to notice only the similarities of those in the out-group".[6] The people of each linguistic state in India have a tendency to form stereotypes of the people of other linguistic states. A Punjabi, for instance, has a stereotype or a generalised perception of what a Bengalee stands for and how he behaves, completely ignoring the fact that all Bengalees do not fit in with that stereotype. Those Punjabis who have lived with Bengalee families for a fairly long period of time know from their experience that all Bengalees are not similar and that stereotypes are based on wrong perceptions. In fact, *social distance* encourages such categorization and discourages individual differentiation. Knowledge of this principle helps considerably to reduce the unfortunate effects of such categorization into stereotypes and to demolish the barriers that obstruct the easy communication and intercourse between people and people.

The second principle that is deduced from the in-group—out-group distinction is that any threat—real or imaginary—from an out-group tends to bind the members of the in-group against the members of the out-group. This may be illustrated with reference to our experience in family situations. Mencius, the Chinese sage, said many years ago : "Brothers who may quarrel within the walls of their home, will bind themselves together to drive away any intruder". Likewise, when any criticism emanates from the members of the in-group, it is not only tolerated but its assessment is sought to be made in a cool and dispassionate manner. When, however, similar criticism comes from the members of the out-group it is resented and hotly contested, sometimes in an unjustified manner. This is an important principle which should be kept in view while offering any suggestions for reform or improvement of a condition which concerns the members of an out-group.

## Reference group

The concept of reference group was first developed by Hayman. Subsequently, Turner, R.K. Merton and Sheriff elaborated it further.

The concept of reference group, as originally developed, may be explained thus : In some situations we conform not to the norms of the groups to which we actually belong but rather to those of the groups to which we should like to belong, those with which we would like to be identified. A reference group may not be an actual group. It may even be an imaginary one. Any group is a reference group for some one if his conception of it, which may or may not be realistic, is part of his frame of reference for assessment of himself or of his situation. Thus, an individual who is anxious to move up the social ladder usually has tendency to conform to the norms of etiquette and speech of a higher social class than his own because he seeks identification with this class. By way of illustration, we may refer to the concept of 'sanskritisation' enunciated by Srinivas. "Sanskritisation is the process by which a 'low' Hindu caste, or tribal or other group, changes its customs, ritual, ideology, and way of life in the direction of a high, and frequently, twice-born caste. Generally such changes are followed by a claim to a higher position in the caste hierarchy than that traditionally conceded to the claimant caste by the local community. The claim is usually made over a period of time, in fact, a generation or two, before the 'arrival' is conceded".[7]

The concept of reference group is sometimes given a wider meaning in that it calls attention to the fact that groups to which one does not belong and cannot belong or with which one does not want to identify also serve as reference groups.

For members of a particular group, another group is a reference group if any of the following circumstances prevail :

(1) When members of the first group aspire to membership in the second group, the second group serves as the reference group of the first.

(2) When members of the first group strive to be *like* the members of the second group in some respect, the second group serves as the reference group of the first. It is to be noted here that the first group wants to be *like* the second group simply because the first group cannot secure the membership of the second group. For example, the non-Brahmins in some parts of India have a tendency to emulate the ways of behaviour of the Brahmins (compare the concept of sanskritisation) in order to acquire the prestige of the Brahmins.

(3) When the members of the first group derive some satisfaction from being unlike the members of the second group in some respect, and even strive to maintain the difference between themselves and the members of the second group, the latter group is the reference group of of the first. For example in the U.S.A. the whites strive to remain unlike the Negroes. The satisfaction of some white Americans in just being 'white' is possible only with reference to the 'non-white' group. Further, the status of being a 'white' is not simply a matter of possessing 'white' skin. It also involves, in terms of prestige, superiority in ranking and enjoyment of privileges.It is, therefore, not unlikely that the 'whites' could lose their superior status without losing their white skin. The whiles, therefore, strive to distinguish themselves from Negroes by retaining privileges.

(4) When, without necessarily striving to be like or unlike or to belong to the second group, the members of the first group appraise their own group or themselves by using the second group or its members as a standard for comparison, the second group becomes the reference group of the first.For example, in some situations the non-teaching employees of colleges are found to assess their own performance or record of attendance with reference to those of the teachers.

## Voluntary groups and involuntary groups

The distinction between voluntary and involuntary groups corresponds exactly with that made between achieved and ascribed statuses. There are some groups we join on our own. These are voluntary groups of which we choose to become members.For example, one becomes a member of a literary group, not because one has to but because one decides to seek the membership of the group to pursue one's literary interests. There are, however, some groups of which we are members because we have to. We have no choice in the matter.These are involuntary groups. One becomes, for instance, a member of a caste group simply because he is born into that particular caste. Similarly, one is a Tamilian. a Gujarati, an Assamese or a Bengalee because one is born of parents who belong to that particular linguistic group.

## Large group and small group

Groups may also be classified on the basis of the number of members composing the group.A large groups is obviously a group comprising a large number of members and small group a group of limited number of members.

Strictly on the basis of the strength of membership, a group is generally classfied into categories. The first is called a *dyad* or a group consisting of a pair- mother and child, a married couple, a partnership of two, etc. A *dyad* grows around mutual love and similarity of interests or predilections of the pair, and hence it may break up as soon as the motive force bringing the pair together disappears. The second is called a *triad* or a group comprising three persons. The signnificance of a *triad* is brought out by Simmel thus: "in groups of three, the third person may act as a mediator, as a holder of the balance of power, or as a divider who creates conflicts that destroy any sense of unity between any two of the persons". The third is a group comprising more than three persons. This kind of group is further sub-divided into large and small depending on the number of persons who comprise the group.

## Patterned and non-patterned group

There are groups which are organised on a hierarchical principle.Thus when a football team participates in a competition, the team consists of, besides the players themselves, a team manager, a coach and a captain chosen from among the players,All of them are assigned very specific roles and the relationship among them is also governed by specific norms. Such a group is called a patterned group. There are numerous groups of this category in every society. A group which is designed to achieve some goal needs must be patterned.

There are, again, some groups which are organised informally, the members having no specific role obligations.On the contrary, they enjoy a considerable amount of freedom within the confines of a very broad framework. There is generally no hierarchy.Such a group is called an informal or a non-patterned group. This type of group allows a considerable amount of flexibility to its members and, as such, is most suited in situations which call for creativity, and innovaiton from its members.

## NOTES

1. Theodore M. Mills, *The Sociology of Small Groups*, page 3
2. *ibid*, page 2
3. Bottomore, *Sociology*, page 99
4. Harry M. Johnson, *Sociology*, Pages 387-388
5. C.H. Cooley, R.C. Angell and L.J. Catt, *Introductory Sociology*
6. Bierstedt, *Social Order*, page 291
7. M.N. Srinivas, *Social Change in Modern India* , page 6

# CHAPTER NINE

# COLLECTIVE BEHAVIOUR

## 1. NATURE OF COLLECTIVE BEHAVIOUR

The gregarious instinct of men brings them closer together, and they form various types of groups, such as community, association, class, ethnic group, etc. These groups are, however, of a somewhat permanent nature. In these cases, group ways are institutionalised, and become a part of the permanent social structure. Besides these institutionalised ways of life, men also manifest feelings and ways of behaviour which are of a temporary character. They form themselves into groups which are ephemeral and do not hold the interest of the members for long. Examples of these temporary groupings are the crowd, the public, the mob and the audience. Before we take up these particular forms of collective behaviour, we may discuss, in general, the nature of collective behaviour and the causes which are responsible for the same.

Collective behaviour generally centres around a phenomenon which is essentially ephemeral in nature. If, for instance, there is a street accident, a number of people would at once be attracted to the place where the accident had occurred. Their patterns of behaviour on such an occasion may vary. Some may proceed to assault physically the persons responsible for the accident. Some may remain silent spectators. Those who proceed to assault exhibit all the characteristics of collective behaviour. That is, they behave in a way different from the way they would behave under normal conditions. Their patterns of behaviour do not conform to the ways of behaviour prescribed by the norms of society.

The second characteristic of collective behaviour is that those who are attracted by an accident or event do so haphazardly without any prior planning. Nor do they know one another. All of them remain virtually anonymous. Anonymity encourages them to behave recklessly and irresponsibly.

The third characteristic of collective behaviour is that it is a passing phase. As soon as the focus of interest which attracts individuals is removed, they disperse.

The fourth characteristic of collective behaviour is that it is unpredictable. People may react to the same or similar stimulus differently. When people go to see, say, a football match, some may shout and yell at some stage of the game, some may dance, some may pelt stones at the players and some may hurl filthy and abusive language at the umpires.

It is to be noted that, however unpredictable the nature of collective behaviour may be, it has some relationship with the broad cultural pattern of the community. For instance, an excited crowd in England indulges more in physical assault and battery than in destruction of property. In France, on the other hand, an excited crowd indulges less in physical violence and more in destruction of property. The differences in the collective behaviour of the people in the two countries have to be sought in the different value-orientations of the two cultures. The teachings of Catholic religion not to do physical harm to anyone as well as the prevalence of stringent laws against physical violence since the days of the French Revolution have created, in course of time, a climate of opinion against physical violence.

In England, on the other hand, the people have been long accustomed to looking upon public property as sacrosanct and inviolable.

**Under what circumstances does collective behaviour appear ?**

Collective behaviour apparently differs from the patterns of behaviour prescribed by the norms of society. It is, therefore, necessary to identify the circumstances which encourage people to act contrary to social norms.

To begin with, when the normal social life is disrupted for some reason, some people may get bewildered as to how to meet the changed situation. Some may react in fear and some others in anger. In either case, the pattern of behaviour influenced by such attitudes is likely to be at variance with the normal behavioural pattern of the community. If, for instance, there is a sudden outbreak of ethnic, racial or communal violence, the affected people cannot obviously behave normally. Fear, anger and a determination to take revenge may, in combination, produce a state of mind which is inimical to observance of social norms. They behave in the most irrational and irresponsible manner and throw to the winds, for the time being, the inhibitions which were built into the cultural fabric of the community over a long period of time extending over two, three or several generations. Similar behavioural pattern is displayed in cases of natural catastrophe when people have a feeling of having lost their moorings.

Second, sometimes elements of collective behaviour are built into the cultural life of the community deliberately in order to remove monotony from everyday life. For instance, social norms allow people to deviate, within limits, from normal pattern of behaviour and indulge in revelry — a kind of behaviour which is frowned upon and even castigated at other times. This type of institutionalised deviation is sometimes explained in terms of what may be called a safety valve theory. People, in general, have many submerged cravings and desires which, if not fulfilled, may create emotional disturbance to individuals and tend to disturb social order. The society, therefore, provides an opportunity to people to release their pent-up feelings and emotions by following behaviour of a deviant nature on some particular occasions. For instance, during 'holi' young men and women are allowed to indulge in revelry and gaiety. Similar indulgence is allowed on many festive occasions, such as marriage, by allowing both men and women, young and old, to behave in a manner not considered proper at other times.

Thirdly, loss of faith in the uprightness of law-enforcing agencies also creates conditions which favour the growth of collective behaviour. For instance, if the impression gains ground among a section of population that the police sets at liberty the people apprehended for anti-social acts for some consideration, there would obviously grow a tendency among these people to take the law into their own hands and beat the alleged culprits mercilessly instead of handing him over to the police, contrary to canons of equity and established social norms.

Fourthly, if the social order is not based on justice and fairplay, the people would naturally feel frustrated. Following frustration, discontent would grow. In the initial stages frustration and discontent may be diffused and unorganised. But gradually frustration starts the process of circular response among people and feeling of discontent and frustration get crystallised and take the form of a purposive movement designed to disturb the social order. Collective behaviour is thus the off-shoot of an inequitable social order.

## 2. CROWD

The most pronounced expression of collective behaviour is found in the crowd. Mac Iver and Page defined a crowd "as a physically compact aggregation of human beings brought into direct, temporary, and unorganised contact with one another". What distinguishes a crowd from other forms of collective behaviour is not the physical proximity of its members, "specially in a society like ours with instruments of mass communication like the newspaper and the radio'. A story published in a newspaper may start a wave of panic among a group of people who may manifest all the characteristics of crowd behaviour. Some of these characteristics may be briefly noted.

To begin with, the essence of crowd behaviour is the *highly emotional responses* of individuals when they are released from the restraints that usually inhibit extreme behaviour. Secondly, *numbers* are necessary to make a crowd. A chance meeting of friends or acquaintances on the street after a long interval may make them talk and behave in a highly emotional manner. But it is not a crowd because numbers are so small as to give such meetings the character of face-to-face groups. Thirdly, in a crowd numbers are *randomly* "thrown together in physical proximity". There is no set purpose or pre-planning which precedes the formation of a crowd. In this respect, "the crowd differs from such groups as the assembly, public meeting, reception, and so on, where the participants fall into a pre-determined order and are arranged according to some principle of selection".

When a College Athletic Club wins a trophy, say, in a football match, the students celebrate the event by dancing, singing, raising slogans, or even by looting the pavement shops. They exhibit, in other words, all the characteristics of crowd behaviour. On the other hand, when the students walk orderly in a procession in order to register their protest against anything which they consider to be undesirable, they cease to be a crowd.

### The bases of crowd behaviour

Crowd behaviour is characterised by "highly emotional responses of individuals when they are released from the restraints that usually inhibit extreme behaviour". In a crowd individuals do things which they would never do singly or under normal circumstances. Everyday social controls may break down, and the crowd may throw away the standards and habits of conduct "which the education and discipline of civilised life have built up in its members". What releases these customary restraints and leads to crowd behaviour ?

Crowd mentality is characterised by intensified feeling and heightened suggestibility. That is, once a crowd is assembled, the individuals get so excited that each member responds uncritically to the stimuli provided by the other members. Because of intensified feeling characteristic of a crowd, there occurs in the members of a crowd "a partial dissociation of consciousness". For the time being, they lose their critical judgement and accept unreservedly whatever suggestions come to them. When we are critical about a matter, we subject every suggestion to close scrutiny in the light of our experience and judgement. For reasons discussed below, the members of the crowd, however, lose this critical judgement temporarily.

(i) *The admired leader* : When a suggestion comes from one whom the crowd respects and admires, it hardly exercises its critical judgement and tends to accept the suggestions as truth. A clever and popular leader can easily convince the over suggestible crowd that its interests are in danger and that the real solution lies in the leader's suggestions.

(ii) *Numbers :* The *numbers* in a crowd tend to impart to the members a sense of security characteristic of an anonymous group. There is, consequently, a "loss of the sense of responsibility, the breakdown of inhibitions, experienced by its individual constituents". This factor explains the fact that a member of a crowd does things which he would never do under normal conditions. A student of a college, for instance, does not normally dance in streets nor does he loot pavement shops; but in a victory celebration, following a match, he does. As long as he is in a crowd, he tends to throw to the winds his sense of individual responsibility. As MacIver and Page put it : "Deviational behaviour is momentarily supported by the numbers of the crowd, providing the individual a short-lived social sanction for the acts forbidden in everyday life".[1]

(iii) *Interstimulation and crowd rhythm :* Crowd rhythm makes for greater suggestibility in crowds. A rally cry or a form of applause serves to bring down the barriers between individuals and forge links of solidarity among them. Gradually, they develop similar mood and "exhibit simultaneous and rhythmic gestures'. At this stage, "each individual seems to function as an amplifier of a mood, of a feeling, or merely of a verbal expression". Every individual, therefore, stimulates the other. As a consequence, excitement grows, and with it the suggestibility of each individual. Skilled politicians and party manipulators use various techniques with a view to producing crowd rhythm and winning crowds to their purposes.

## Crowd behaviour and culture

Crowd behaviour differs from one society to the other in terms of differing cultural standards and values. To illustrate this point, Ogburn and Nimkoff refer to two interesting contrasts presented by rioting mobs in France and England. Assault and battery are much more common in English-speaking countries than in France where rioters wreak their vengeance on property rather than on persons. The conduct of the English crowds may be explained by the fact that the English people have developed in the course of centuries a respect for public property. On the other hand, the Catholic religion, with its emphasis on the security of human life, and the stringent French laws against assault (which go back to the days after the Revolution) explain comparatively little loss of life in French riot that involves huge damage to property. It is evident, therefore, that culture affects crowd behaviour. Long-established cultural tradition determines the outward expression of 'mob-feeling'.

Education has also a bearing on crowd behaviour. The spread of education among people tends to protect them against over-suggestibility. They become less credulous, and more critical. Education lessens the chances that "a person will behave irrationally or irresponsibly in certain situations". It also lessens the chances of inter-stimulation and "crowd contagion". Hence educational system in every civilised country has developed various devices to teach individuals to protect themselves from reacting instantly and automatically to suggestion, such as the debate, the public forum, and the scientific method. "In a debate the suggestions released by one side are challenged by the counter-suggestions of the other side. The open forum provides even more protection against the dangers of suggestibility, because the participants are encouraged to ask questions and to cross-examine the spokesmen for particular points of view. Science and scientific method furnish the greatest protection against emotional and irrational conduct. Suggestions are not enough; science demands evidence.[2]

Apart from these cultural or educational media, another protection against ' crowd contagion' is to avoid crowds, the anonymity provided by urban living conditions enables people to keep themselves isolated without attracting much attention. Even neighbours may be strangers to one another in cities. But such an anonymous life is not possible in less urbanised communities in which neighbours are intimately acquainted with one another. There is thus a possibility that the position that a city-dweller takes may be influenced more by his conviction than by his consideration for the feelings and opinions of others, as is the case of a person who lives in a small rural community. Ogburn and Nimkoff, therefore, conclude that "in a city, public opinion can be more objective and rational than it is in a folk society.[3]

**Types of crowd**

Crowd is classified by sociologists into various types, depending on the perspective from which they look at the crowd phenomenon. Some emphasise the way a crowd is formed, some emphasise the purpose which distinguishes one crowd from another, and some others emphasise the behaviour-pattern of a crowd. In the light of their discussions we may distinguish between four types of crowd.

(i) *The like-interest or casual crowd.* In a like-interest or casual crowd, "there is a common external *focus* of interest but not a common interest". Thus when a crowd gathers to watch a street accident or a fire, the individuals who compose the crowd seek merely to satisfy their curiosity. Sometimes such a crowd may gather out of sheer panic. These crowds have no other object to fulfil. Sometimes such a crowd is also characterised as a *spectator crowd.*

(ii) *The common-interest or action crowd.* A common-interest or action crowd is brought together by some common purpose. The crowd that participates in a popular celebration, in a spontaneous outburst of group joy or hatred, or in a strike demonstration, falls under this category. The common purpose which brings such a crowd together may either be expressly defined, as in the case of a revolutionary crowd which has a specific goal to achieve; or, the purpose may not be very sharply defined, as in the case of a crowd that gathers to celebrate, say, the Republic Day. In most cases the fulfilment of individual self-interest is the basis of this kind of crowd behaviour. Thus, when the depositors of a particular Bank get scared, for some reason or the other, that the Bank would, in all probability, fail to honour its commitments to its depositors in near future, the latter would rush to the Bank to withdraw their deposits. They exhibit in their conduct all the characteristics of crowd behaviour. Though each depositor has his own personal interest to fuilfil, they rally together in order to serve which they consider to be their common interest. Barriers between individual subscribers are broken, and each stimulates the other. As a consequence, suggestibility of each individual grows.

(iii) *Expressive crowd.* Sometimes a group of people exhibit in their conduct all the attributes of crowd behaviour in order to express their feelings of joy or sorrow. Thus, the supporters of, say, a victorious football team express their joy by singing and dancing on the streets and shouting various kinds of slogans. On some occasions, such expressions of joy take ugly forms. They not only shout, sing and dance, but they also tease the passers-by and even go so far as to loot the pavement shops. The expressions of grief and sorrow over some tragic accident or event also exhibit the characteristics of crowd behaviour.

(iv) *Conventionalised crowd.* Which discussing the features and origin of collective behaviour, we noted that sometimes people are allowed, on certain specific occasions, to be non-conformist in respect of certain social norms in order to give release to pent-up feelings and emotions. For instance, while celebrating 'holi', holi-revellers exhibit, in their conduct, some of the characteristics of crowd behaviour. Crowds of this type are known as conventionalised crowd.

## 3. MOB

A crowd is transformed into a mob when the people concerned become disorderly. The situation may be such as to make the people highly excited. The admired leader may deliberately incite people by giving inflammatory speeches. His attempt at exciting people will be successful if, in particular, the people have been nursing grievances against an agency or a group for a long period of time. It will, however, be wrong to assume that only a crowd exhibits mob behaviour. Even a stable group, such as the army or the police or the factory workers, may, all on a sudden, become disorderly in their conduct.

In terms of the nature of conduct, mobs are generally classified into two categories : the first. the *purposive and active mob :* the second, the *confused and random mob*. These two types of mobs may be explained with reference to an example. If, for instance, a revolutionary leader forcibly takes control of the Legislative Chamber, there might follow two different types of outcome. If the large majority of the legislators are in sympathy with ideals and action-programmes of the revolutionary leader, they may indulge in revolutionary activities under his direction. Such a group may be called a *purposive and active mob*. If, on the other hand, a sizeable number of legislators are opposed to the ideals and activities of the revolutionary leader, they may get confused and act in a disorderly manner. This group may be called a confused and random mob.

We should bear in mind that a mob easily grows in an environment in which conflicting interests, ideals or norms exist side by side. If, for instance, two separate groups of people with distinct life-styles, customs and traditions live in geographically contiguous areas, they may develop relationship of enmity. On some flimsy ground they may, therefore, become highly excited and hurl filthy abuses at one another and indulge in disorderly conduct.

## 4. AUDIENCE

When a group of people meet at a particular place at a particular time with a specific object, it is known as an audience. Those who go to the playground to see a cricket match or those who go to a public hall to listen to a lecture come under this category. But those who witness a match or lisen to a lecturer on the television screen at home do not form an audience. The first characteristic of an audience is that people assemble at a particular place *with some common or similar interest in view.* The second characteristic of an audience is that they are expected to *conform to the universally accepted code of conduct.* For instance, it is an accepted code that a speaker should not be interrupted or asked a question while he is speaking. Likewise, it is an accepted norm that one should not applaud in the midst of a symphony orchestra. But one is expected to applaud at the end of each 'number'. On the other hand, it is an accepted code that spectators can yell and shout while a football match is being played. Thus, codes of conduct vary with different audiences. The principle which determines broadly such codes is that the audience should not be allowed to do things or act in a manner prejudicial to the goal or purpose for which the audience is assembled. The same principle dictates that people are expected not to engage in conversation while a drama is being played on the stage.

Kimball Young has classified audience into three distinct categories. The first type is called *information-seeking audience.* Those who assemble in order to seek information or knowledge fall under this category. The second type is called *recreation-seeking audience*. Those who go to the play ground to watch a game or to the movie house to see a film come under this category. The third type is called *conversional audience*. There may be two types of conversional audience. These may be explained with reference to examples. There may be some people who entertain certain beliefs or values, but who entertain, at the same time, some doubts about them. In such cases, the concerned persons may attend meetings and discussion groups in order to dispel doubts and seek re-inforcement and support in favour of values and beliefs which they cherish. There may be another type of conversional audience. Religious discourses and meetings organised by political parties are designed to propagate certain ideas and ideologies. There may be people who attend such discourses and meetings in order to familiarise themselves with the ideas which are sought to be propagated through such discourses and meetings. Such people may be called conversional audience.

## 5. PUBLICS

"When the interest of a group of individuals in a social issue or set of social values is more abiding and more rational than it is in a crowd, we call the group a public". Since publics are interest groups, we may think of different kinds of publics. Thus, a newspaper seeks to cater to the different types of publics by dividing the paper into different sections, such as film, theatre or entertainment section, sports section, youth section, etc. One important characteristic of public is that though its members share common interest, they do not necessarily have a common approach or a common viewpoint. For instance, those who are interested in the cinema may have different ideas about the qualities of a good cinema or the meaning of good acting. It follows, therefore, that public is characterised by discussions and controversies, and hence by the formation of public opinion. Since public opinion is processed through discussion and controversy, it is generally free from the emotional overtones characteristic of crowd mentality.

When the members of the public take a stand on some specific social issues, we call it public opinion. The concept of public opinion is relevant particularly in a society that is characterised by complex rapid changes. In a static primitive society no new issue obviously arises. Hence, all these issues can be easily met by the prevailing folkways. There is not much discussion or controversy about what ought or ought not to be done. In a complex rapidly changing society, on the other hand, there is scope for controversies and differences of opinion. Hence, "the issues that beset publics under conditions of rapid change may be numerous and acute".

A study in contrast between a crowd and a public will bring out clearly the characteristics of the latter. In the first place, a crowd implies an assemblage of people. A group of people becomes transformed into a crowd only when they are assembled and exhibit as a result of close contact other features of crowd behaviour. A public, on the other hand, does not imply that its members needs must assemble. They may remain scattered all throughout the country. The communication among them may be established, though indirectly, through the mass media, such as newspapers, radio and television. The views of the public also find expression through these mass media. Secondly, since a crowd is formed through direct contact among people, a crowd is necessarily less numerous than a public whose members may be scattered over a wider area. Thirdly, numbers and spatial distribution of the members of the public protect them from being highly suggestible and emotional. In the case of a crowd, the excitement of one individual affects others around him. In a public, for obvious reasons, such inter-stimulation does not exist. Each individual member of a public takes his decision on his own in terms of his predilections, interests and judgment.

A question may be raised here. If the members of the public take decisions independently, then how does a public opinion grow ? It is true that the members of the public lie scattered with no direct means of communication among them all. There is, however, a common culture which links them together and moulds their processes of thinking and doing along certain set broad lines. No individual member of the public can ignore this cultural influence. In the circumstances, the opinions that the members of the public arrive at have some common elements on basic issues even though substantial differences on matters of details may exist. It will, therefore, not be an exaggeration to suggest that public opinion can never grow among people in the absence of a cultural unity.

**Propaganda and Public**

While drawing a comparison with the crowd, some people suggest that, unlike a crowd, the public is guided by intelligence and reason. This is probably not always true. It is undeniable that the members of the public cannot escape the influence of tradition which deeply affects both their intelligence and reason. Moreover, public opinion does not necessarily grow on the basis of evidence alone. Subjective perceptions give shape to public opinion to a large extent. It is, therefore, not proper to consider public opinion as objective. In this connection, we may refer to the part played by the highly sophisticated techniques of publicity, advertising and propaganda, in particular, in moulding public opinion. Through graphic symbols, music, gestures, and combinations of words the propagandist makes impressions upon masses of people. These impressions are sometimes vivid. They are frequently charged with emotion. They may be wholly or partially true, confusing or false. Nevertheless, people are powerfully influenced in their judgement by the impressions made by the glittering and attractive symbols presented by the propagandist. Propaganda is made under cover so that the members of the public fail to discriminate between fact and merely imagined ideas.

We have seen that public is characterised by discussions and controversies, and that rationality, rather than emotion, guides the conduct of the members of the public. But propaganda may stir up the emotion of the public on a particular issue, and it may abandon processes of rational thinking and discussion, and may give way to emotion. When this happens, it ceases to be a public and becomes a crowd.

C. Wright Mills in his book *The Power Elite* has expressed the apprehension that our lives in present-day society are so deeply influenced by carefully orchestrated propaganda that the society of publics is gradually being transformed into a mass society. He noted the following indications of mass society which are increasingly becoming evident. (i) There is a tendency among people to accept uncritically the views which are expressed or conveyed through mass media. These are not usually subjected to critical scrutiny. (ii) The mass media in present-day society are so organised today that it is not possible for anybody, either individually or collectively, to challenge effectively any information or fact conveyed by the mass media. (iii) The concerned authorities at different levels are in a position to manipulate facts and mould the views of the people in the way they like. No informed public opinion can grow in such a miasma of distortions. Commenting on this aspect, Mac Iver and Page observe : "Propaganda and demagoguery were hardly new in the days of ancient Greece and Rome. But today, with the great increase in the range of communications and in the size of audiences, and with the constant improvement of the techniques of persuasion, the latter have become an instrument of social control of unprecedented possibilities".[4] They therefore, conclude by emphassing " the need for that social education which guards us against the most expert of 'practitioners of propaganda' ... and which permits us to exercise to the utmost our individual discernment".[5]

## NOTES

1. Mac Iver and Page, *Society*, Pages 427
2. Ogburn and Nimkoff, *A Handbook of Sociology*, Page 157
3. *ibid*, Page 157
4. Mac Iver and Page, *Society*, Page 436
5. *ibid*. Page 436

# CHAPTER TEN

# SOCIAL STRATIFICATION

## 1. SOCIAL DIFFERENTIATION AND INEQUALITY

'All men are created equal' — this is the refrain in the declarations of all ideologues, past and present. But the fact is that inequalities are inherent in the nature of human beings. Apart from the natural differences, human beings are also differentiated according to socially approved criteria based on either natural differences like sex and age or social differences like kinship, occupation, etc. Social differentiation on the above lines leads to a social situation in which socially differentiated men are treated as socially unequal from the point of view of enjoyment of social rewards, such as wealth, income, status, power, etc. These may be taken as evidences of social inequality.

In sociological analysis, we are to "shift our attention from inequalities inherent in the nature of human beings to those inherent in their conditions of existence"[1]. It is undeniable that at birth men are endowed with unequal qualities, both physical and mental. Investigations into these questions are the concerns of biologists, and not of sociologists. Sociologists take these inherent inequalities as given. They are rather concerned with social conditions which give rise to various forms and kinds of inequality. Social differentiation is one such form. Thus, human beings in all climes and ages have been differentiated in terms of sex. Men and women are assigned different statuses and roles. Not only are their activities differentiated; but these activities are also differently evaluated. Similar social differentiation is made in terms of age. The young and old are different in terms of activities they are expected to engage in. They are also different in terms of social prestige which is associated with each. Likewise, kinship usage, which regulates behaviour among kins, introduces differentiation. Some of the rules of comportment or manners may be considered in this connection. Thus *deference* usages are a ritual expression of social inequality. According to this usage, a lower-status person gives deference to a higher-status person. Another widely accepted basis of social differentiation is occupation, such as a group of engineers, of doctors, or of teachers. These occupational divisions make up what is called *vertical* divisions of the community.

## 2. SOCIAL STRATIFICATION

In addition to the aforesaid phenomena of social inequality, there is another type of social inequality which is sociologically more important. These are *horizontal* divisions of society into various social strata, each stratum marked by socially recognised upper or lower status, more or less, on a permanent basis. The people who belong to each such stratum constitute a social class. Morris Ginsberg defines social classes "as portions of the community, or collections of individuals, standing to each other in the relation of equality, and marked off from other portions by accepted or sanctioned standards of inferiority and superiority"[2]. The society in which divisions into such social classes exists is known as a stratified society. According to MacIver and Page, social stratification implies three features ; (i) a hierarchy of status groups; (ii) the recognition of the superior-inferior stratification; and (iii) some degree of permanence of the structure.

"Borrowed by analogy from the earth sciences, the term 'social stratification' has come into general sociological use only since about 1940, although the matters to which it refers have been discussed under the heading 'social class' for a very long time. However, in contrast to its earth-science usage the sociological usage of the concept of stratification often includes, implicitly or explicitly, some evaluation of the higher and lower layers, which are judged to be better or worse according to a scale of values"[3].

For a more comprehensive understanding of the nature of social stratification, we may note that the social positions assigned to the various social strata are unequal with regard to property, power, social evaluation and psychic gratification. 'Property' refers to the rights one enjoys over goods and services. Thus, one's income or income-yielding wealth may be considered to be his property. 'Power' refers to one's ability to fulfil one's needs or meet one's demands. Obviously, 'power' is inextricably mixed up with property. Greater amount of property means greater power, and less amount of property means less power. 'Social evaluation' means the prestige or honour that a person enjoys in the estimation of the society by virtue of his belonging to a particular social stratum. 'Social evaluation' thus means that people belonging to a particular stratum may enjoy greater prestige and honour in comparison with people belonging to another stratum. 'Psychic gratification' (applicable to people belonging to higher social classes) refers to the satisfaction or pleasure that a person has on account of his possession of power, prestige or property.

## Characteristics of social stratification

The following characteristics of social stratification may be noted.[4]

The first characteristic is that it is *social* in nature. The *social* aspect of stratification may be explained with reference to the following. (a) To say that stratification is social is to emphasise the obvious that one is not talking about biologically caused inequalities. (b) The distribution of rewards is governed exclusively by social norms or conventions which may prevail in a society. (c) The term 'social' implies the continuity of these norms effected mainly by socialisation. The division of society into hierarchical status groups is not simply a one-generation affair; it continues from generation to generation. This can be explained, in part, by the processes of socialisation in terms of which every child is indoctrinated with the values of the class and such values become, in course of time, a part and parcel of his personality structure. (b) Stratification is dynamic in nature, mainly due to dynamic social forces. Since socialisation is not always perfect and since conformity is not uniform, and further since the values which the society upholds do not remain the same over time, the structure and nature of stratification prevalent in a society always undergo changes. (e) Social stratification is closely connected with other social institutions. It is affected by and, at the same time, has effects upon such matters as marriage, religion, education, economic structure, political system, etc.

The second characteristic of social stratification is its *antiquity*. There has not been any society in the past in which social stratification, in some form or other, was not found, not excluding the small wandering bands that characterised society in the earliest days of man. "In such primitive conditions, both age and sex in combination with physical strength must have been important criteria of stratification"[5].

The third characteristic of social stratification is its *ubiquity*. Social stratification is not only an antiquated institution. It is also very much in existence amongst us even today in all parts of the world. Various forms of protest movements against existing inequality that disturb the peace and tranquallity of all societies around the globe confirm the existence of stratification, including socialist countries and non-literate societies of today. Some form of socially structured and sanctioned inequality of power, property, and prestige is a universeal phenomenon.

The fourth characteristic feature of social *stratification* is its *social concomitants* which may be expressed in terms of (a) *life chances* and (b) *life styles.*

## Life chances

What is the meaning of the term 'life-chance' ? "The significance of a class system is that it greatly affects the social rewards of people. The members of a particular class have more or less the same 'life-chances', that is, the same probability of securing the good things of life ......"[6]. Gerth and Mills are of the view that life-chances include "everything from the chance to stay alive during the first year after birth to the chance to view fine arts, the chance to remain healthy and grow tall, and if sick to get well again quickly, the chance to avoid becoming a juvenile delinquent — and very crucially, the chance to complete an intermediary or higher educational grade"[7]. If we analyse the above description of life-chance, as suggested by Gerth and Mills, it will be apparent that life-chances are mutually determining, that one life-chance can determine another and vice versa. Thus, if a man is accidentally born into a wealthy family, he can afford to seek education in institutions of renown which, in turn, helps him get a highsalaried appointment. This, again, affords him an opportunity to get good food, to stay healthy and, in case of illness, to get best available treatment. He can afford to have exposure to many good things of life — art, music, dance, drama, etc. If, on the other hand, he is born into a family which does not open up these opportunities easily, he is naturally condemned to a lower rung of social fabric. A point should, however, be made here. It is difficult to say which factor is basic and which is not. It may be wealth in one case in determining life-chance and, in another case, it may be education. The fact remains that social stratification determines life-chances of individuals.

## Life style

What is the meaning of the term life-style ? The term has been variously defined. Broadly, the term denotes a style of life which is distinctive of a particular social status. These distinctive features may be in terms of places of residence (residential areas in every community have gradations of prestige-ranking), in terms of types of homes (in a factory-town, for example, a particular type of residential building is meant for people belonging to a particular income-bracket), in terms of schooling (people who have had their schooling and the schooling of their children in, say, La Martiniere, Doon School or some such public school, generally have a higher prestige-ranking than those who were educated in vernacular medium schools), in terms of dress, etc. Present-day media advertisement for a particular dress material may display it with the caption : This particular dress is meant for a man of culture. You are a man of culture. And so you must have it. Because of this kind of 'hidden persuasion', dress occupies a very high place in one's life-style in modern society.

Life style may be viewed as a *sub-culture* "which distinguishes one stratum from another within the framework of a commonly shared over-all culture. Such distinctive patterns will be found most likely in those societies with a high degree of concern for status-honor, where individual behaviour is always shaped by a concern for whether it is appropriate for membership in a particular socio-economic level. The pressures to adopt appropriate styles may be sufficiently subtle so that an individual is unaware of the extent to which he orients his choices to considerations of status"[8].

**Some dimensions of social stratification**

Social stratification is multi-dimensional. It is the case not only in present-day complex societies but it is so in other types of societies and in other historical periods as well. We have seen that in a stratified society, social positions are evaluated according to a scale of values. Among the various criteria of evaluation that appear to be related to class status in our complex society, we may briefly discuss the following. The list below is not necessarily exhaustive. Only the most important of these criteria or dimensions have been included. The order in which the list has been drawn up does not mean any order of relative importance. In theory, each is as important as every other. In any concrete social situation, however, one may be more important in the determination of behaviour than another.

(a) **Wealth, property or income.** Wealth is important not only in itself but for what it enables its owners to do. Wealth multiplies his living choices, his life chances, and his opportunities.

In addition. wealth, property or high income serve as symbols of success in a society in which material success is upheld as a worthwhile achievement.

An additional observation needs to be made here. Wealth itself may in some case be less important than the *manner* in which it was acquired. Is the money 'old' and 'dignified' or 'new' and 'ostentatious' ? Sometimes inherited wealth confers a higher prestige than earned wealth.

Further, different *ways* of earning it are subject to varying evaluations. Honest enterprises are obviously rated high in comparison with criminal enterprises. Sometimes manufacturers have an edge over traders in terms of enjoyment of social esteem. This brings us close to the occupational criterion.

It is obvious, therefore, that wealth or income is not a simple criterion, but rather a relatively complicated one. If we use it as a single criterion of class, ignoring all these considerations, the chances are that we shall arrive at erroneous inferences.

(b) **Family or kinship.** Class status, in general, is a family rather than an individual phenomenon. It also comes to be a hereditary one. That is, class status, once attained, tends to endure through several generations. When class endogamy (i.e. marriage within the class) is encouraged and customarily practised, class status can be perpetuated over relatively long periods.

(c) **Location of residence.** There is always an ecological correlate of class status. In the U.S.A., for example, areas of residence are demarcated, more or less, on class lines. Consequently, as a person moves up the social ladder, he changes his residence and chooses the area which is appropriate for people of his class. So when one knows the address of a person, one knows at once the status of the person concerned. The fact that a person lives in a locality, considered respectable in public estimation, adds to his standing in society. In the absence of other criteria, sheer location of residence can sometimes serve as an index of class position.

(d) **Duration of residence.** No one can expect to achieve the highest class status automatically by acquiring substantial 'property' and establishing residence in the 'best' locality unless he is also a member of an 'old' family.

(e) **Occupation.** Evaluations of occupational statuses vary widely from society to society and from time to time in the same society. In India, for instance, white collar occupations usually obtain a higher evaluation in comparison with bluecollar occupations. In different societies and in different historical periods, the relative amount of prestige which attaches to a particular productive role or occupation may vary. "This variability is a result of the fact that the same necessary function in a social system — for example, the military function and roles — may be somewhat differently valued according to the different sets of values that prevail in different social systems and at different times"[9]. The differential evaluation of occupational statuses offers a number of clues to the ideologies that prevail in different cultures.

(f) **Education and knowledge.** In all societies learning, whether sacred or secular, distinguishes those who have it from those who do not. This is true for three reasons. (i) Its acquisition requires effort. (ii) Its possession permits the performance of tasks that would otherwise be impossible. (iii) The amount of knowledge that individuals acquire, either formally through education, or informally, affects the way they behave.

It may be noted that this dimension of stratification produces effects independently of the other dimensions, and that possession of education and knowledge may help one to acquire control over other dimensions of stratification.

## Correlations among rankings

All of these criteria tend to make up what we have already noted a distinct *life style* or manner of living. There is one almost infallible symptom of a shared life style that enables persons otherwise unknown to one another to recognise that they belong essentially to the same class. This system has to do with the culture of eating, and might therefore be called the alimentary index. Some call it *commensalism,* that is, sharing a common table. The question of who eats with whom will almost invariably disclose the strata of a society. This is to be found not only in a caste-ridden society like ours, but also in all other stratified societies.

## Status consistency and status inconsistency

Individuals or groups in a society are ranked along several dimensions of social stratification. It is understandable that rankings along several dimensions of social stratification may all be highly correlated with one another (i.e., all high, all medium or all low in rank) or much less highly correlated (some high, some medium, and some low in rank). The former is called an example of *status consistency.* That is, the concerned individuals or groups satisfactorily fulfil the requirements of all the criteria which are taken into account in determining social status. The latter is an example of *status inconsistency,* because according to some criteria one may have a high status, according to some a medium status, and according to some others a low status. A few simple examples will be illuminating. If, for example, a high caste Brahmin marries a girl belonging to a comparatively lower caste, a status inconsistency is the probable outcome. Likewise, the marriage of the daughter of the *nouveaux riches* to men of distinguished lineage may give rise to the problem of status inconsistency. The position of the many high-caste Brahmin priests with low occupational prestige is another phenomenon of this nature.

A series of analyses and research studies have been undertaken to investigate social stratification in these-terms. It has been found that status inconsistency results in types of behaviour different from those caused by status consistency. It has also been found that each specific pattern of inconsistency has its own specific consequences. It has also been found that various kinds of status inconsistency may last long enough and that there is no universal tendency toward status consistency, that is, toward highly positive correlation among the individual's several rankings.

## 3. VARIATIONS IN STRATIFICATION STRUCTURES

Stratification structures vary (a) in terms of *degrees of flexibility* of the structure and (b) in terms of *form.*

### Open class structure and closed class structure

Some systems of stratification exhibit high flexibility in the sense that one can move up or down from one status to another on fulfilling or failing to fulfil the criteria which mark a particular status-position in a society. Thus, if wealth is accepted in a society as the distinguishing mark of a higher social class, one who acquires it gets elevated in social standing and one who, for some reason, loses property or wealth loses his social standing as well. This type of stratification is called *open class structure*.

The type of stratification which does not permit such mobility from one status position to another, either up or down, is known as *closed class structure*. The Indian caste system exemplifies this type.

It may be noted, however, that no society is hundred per cent 'open' or hundred per cent 'closed'. These are the two poles and in between there are various types, each type marked by various degrees of flexibility. The Indian caste system, for instance, has about 5,000 sub-castes.

### Forms of stratification structures

Stratification structures may take various forms of which four are typical : (a) Slavery; (b) Estates; (c) Caste; and (d) Class.

### Slavery

Slavery is an age-old institution. It prevailed in its extreme form in ancient Greece and Rome and in the southern states of the U.S.A. in the eighteenth century and continued till the third quarter of the nineteenth century. In its modified form, slavery existed in almost all parts of the world. The features of slavery in its extreme form are the following. First, slave belongs to his master to whom he is subjected in all respects. The master possesses him in the same manner and to the same extent that he possesses his household goods — furniture, utensils, etc. Second, the question of enjoyment of political rights by slaves does not naturally arise. Third, socially he is despised. Fourth, '*begar* ' or compulsory labour is a *must* for a slave. The master can make him work for as many hours as he wants and in as arduous works as he chooses. This is the motive force which sustains the institution. The basis of slavery is economic.

The decline of slavery may be attributed to two causes. To begin with, there has been in all periods of history a conflict between the conception of slave as an object or property and the conception of slave as a human being with inherent emotions, feelings and potentials for growth of personality. In ancient Greece, the Sophists denounced the institution of slavery as barbaric and unnatural. The voice of protest against the inequities of the institution have been raised in all subsequent periods in all parts of the world. Second, the inefficiency of slave labour also accounts for its steady decline and ultimate disappearance.

## Estates

The people of a feudal society were divided into three groups : (i) The *First Estate* which consisted of the clergy. (ii) The *Second Estate* which consisted of the aristocracy. (iii) The Third Estate which consisted of the common people.

The feudal estates of Mediaeval Europe had three important characteristics. In the first place, the estates were legally defined - each estate having a status in the sense of a complex of rights and duties, of privileges and obligations. Secondly, the estates represented a broad division of labour. "The nobility were ordained to defend all, the clergy to pray for all, and the commons to provide food for all'. Thirdly, the feudal estates were political groups. It should be noted that classical feudalism consisted of only two estates, the clergy and the nobility. These two groups possessed political power. The serfs, in this sense, did not constitute an estate.

"The decline of European feudalism after the twelfth century is associated with the rise of a third estate, not of the serfs or villeins, but of the burghers, who behaved for a long period as a distinctive group *within* the feudal system before they transformed or overthrew it"[10].

## Caste

The caste system, in cruel or mild form, has always existed, and is still existing, in every civilised country in the world. That the line of demarcation between different employments or grades of work, "almost equivalent to an hereditary distinction of caste", was known in the 19th century England was admitted by J.S. Mill.[11]

We have also on record the interesting views of Plato on hereditary divisions of society. In *The Republic* (III. 415) Plato addresses the Athenian Citizens with the following words : "You are brothers, yet God has framed you differently. Some of you have the power of command, and in the composition of these he has mingled gold, wherefor they have also the greatest honour; others he has made of silver, to be auxiliaries; others again who are to be husbandmen and craftsmen he has composed of brass and iron; and *the species will be generally preserved in the children* ...... And God proclaims as a first principle to the rulers, and above all else, that there is nothing which they should so anxiously guard, or of which they are to be such good guardians, as of the race". In this famous parable of the metals we have in a nutshell the Indian caste system. Regarding the professions of the caste, Plato says that the husbandmen should always remain a husbandman, a soldier always a soldier, etc. (III. 397 D). But he does not say that in every caste the son should practise his father's profession as is implied in the caste rules of India.

The special features of the Indian caste system, which distinguishes the Indian variety from other similar systems of social stratification, consists in this hereditary principle. It is the existence of this principle alone that justifies translating *varnadharma* as caste-system instead of class-system. But the traces of this hereditary principle grow fainter as we look back further and further into *Rigvedic* and Indo-Iranian times.

**Historical background of Indian caste system**

By the end of the *Rigvedic* period, the division of society into the four classes - the priest (Brahmana), warrior (Kshatriya), peasant (Vaisya), and serf (Sudra) - was regarded "as fundamental, primeval, and divinely ordained". These divisions have survived to the present day. The Sanskrit word used for them, *'Varna'*, means 'colour', and itself indicates, according to Basham, "their origin in the development of old tribal class structure in contact with people of different complexion and alien culture"[12]. In his opinion, the four varnas of India developed out of very early Aryan class divisions, for some class stratification existed in many Into-European communities. If mutual exclusiveness be the chief criterion of caste, then the early Vedic period had only two castes : the *Arya* and the *Dasa* or *Sudra*. But the Aryans were divided into three classes. The main body of the Aryan community was composed of the *vis,* ruled by a small number of petty princes *(Rajanya* or *Kshatriya),* who had certain priestly families (Brahmins) as their spiritual advisers. This three-fold division of the Aryan is of hoary antiquity, going back at least to the Indo-Iranian era[13], for the Arthravan (priest) and the Rathaestar (charioteer), mentioned in the *Avesta,* are evidently the Iranian counterparts of the Vedic Brahman and Rajanya, and the *Vastrya* (tiller) and the *Huitay* (artisan), mentioned in the *Avesta,* may well correspond to the Vedic Vis. Both the Rig Vedic Aryans and the Iranians of the age of the Gathas were, therefore, distinctly class-conscious, as is inevitable in every society that has left behind the state of primitive savagery. But there is nothing to show that the Gathic Iranians or the Rig Vedic Aryans were already divided into castes[14].

The subsequent development of the three primitive classes of the Aryan community was not the same in Iran and India. In Iran the Aryans met no aboriginal population utterly different from them and conspicuously marked by dark skin colour, and, therefore, the primitive classes there developed along normal lines as in every country of the world.

In India, however, it was far otherwise. Here the Aryans met a dark aboriginal population perhaps superior to them in civilisation (as suggested by the ruins of Mohenjo-Daro and Harappa) whom they, for that very reason, learnt to fear and hate immensely. The primitive class-consciousness of the invading Aryans could not but grow sharper in these circumstances. Basham explains this development in these words : "In India class stratification grew more rigid when, in the Vedic period, a situation arose rather like that prevailing in South Africa today, with a dominant fair minority striving to maintain its purity and its supremacy over a darker majority"[15]. In course of time, tribal class-divisions hardened, and "the dark-skinned aboriginal found a place only in the basement of the Aryan social structure, as a serf with few rights and many disabilities"[16].

**Varnasrama-dharma**

It is now agreed on all hands that the social divisions in India were not hereditary in the beginning, and that they were only functional divisions. The phrase *varnasrama-dharma* is interpreted to mean that Dharma is not the same for all. There is, indeed, a common Dharma, a general norm of conduct, which all must follow equally, but there is also a dharma appropriate to each class and to each stage in the life of the individual. The dharma of men of high birth is not that of humbler folk, and the dharma of the student is not that of the old man. Basham, therefore, remarks that "this thorough-going recognition that men are not the same, and that there is a hierarchy of class, each with its separate duties and distinctive ways of life, is one of the most striking features of ancient Indian sociology"[17].

The underlying strength of the Indian caste system which sustained it for thousands of years is to be sought in the security and protection it assured to the lowest of the low. There was, no doubt, some inequity and exploitation in the system. Those who belonged to the upper strata did not hesitate to take advantage of their position and to enjoy privileges at the cost of those who were below in the social hierarchy. It is amazing that in spite of such exploitation, there has been no caste war on a widespread scale, as is to be expected in such situations. Some people have tried to explain this by pointing out that the Brahmins cleverly related the social system to religion and succeeded, to a large extent, in building up a superstitious regard for this social institution. The views of Dr. B. K. Ghosh may be quoted in this connection : "In India there was not even a derelict state to enforce the caste-laws. Rather the caste-laws were enforced on the state in India by the Brahmanical theocracy. So the Brahmins have always ruled supreme in matters of caste, and they did not abuse their powers the less because they were Brahmins. But even in the process of abusing their powers the Brahmins built up round the prostrate body of decadent Hinduism an effective armour of social sanction which enemies superior in military prowess and political acumen have not been able to completely destroy in spite of continuous assault for more than a thousand years"[18].

It is difficult to accept in its entirety the explanation of Dr. Ghosh. Is it possible to sustain an institution based on exploitation for thousands of years simply by building up a religious armour around the institution ? As already indicated in the foregoing paragraph, the source of strength of the system lay probably in the fact that caste laws afforded economic security to the bulk of the population. The vulnerable section was protected from cut-throat competition by specifying clearly the activities appropriate to each class and forbidding other classes from interfering in domains not reserved for them. Hindu social structure was built on the principle that in the interest of society all functionaries—viz., the potters, blacksmiths, barbers, washermen, brahmins, etc.—were obliged to confine their activities to their respective fields and contribute their mite to the all-round well-being of the society. If all of them contributed to the furtherance of societal interest, the society also would, in its turn, protect all, even the humbler folk, from unhealthy competition of people more able and far more resourceful. The people were enjoined to abide by the dictum: Follow the calling assigned to you, come what may. It is dangerous to stray away from one's assigned vocation and take to a course not one's own. That is, each individual was asked to follow the *dharma* appropriate to his class, and not to tread on others' domains. Originally, the *dharma* of each class must have been related to the inherent propensities and abilities of men, the underlying assumption being that men are not always the same. Caste rules did for the weaker sections of the population what trade and craft guilds did for their counterparts in Europe. The assurance that no one, whatever be his physical and mental deficiencies, would be forced to destitution contributed, in a large measure, to the stability and continuity of the system over thousands of years.

In this connection, reference to Durkheim's discussion on alientation and stratification and his emphasis on a stable society as a pre-requisite for an integrated personality will be in order. "The absence of an established harmony of means and ends, far from producing freedom, produces, according to Durkhem, resentment and apathy—the war of each against all. Durkheim's theory therefore leads to the ironic conclusion that people should feel freest in a closed, integrated system in which *they have little choice of occupation or opportunity for social mobility,* while in an open,universalistic system they should feel coerced, dehumanised, estranged. In the latter case it follows that they will also experience a need to, in Erich Fromm's words, 'escape from freedom'. Society's emphasis on success thus becomes the principal source of alienation."

In course of time, however, the privileged class, as is expected, developed vested interest and the principle of not denying to Caesar what belonged to Caesar was given up. The appeal was always made to the ancient authorities. Little attempt was, however, made to interpret their truths in terms of changing conditions. As an inevitable consequence of all this, the creative and spiritual forces weakened and only the shell of what used to be so full of life and meaning remained. They clung stubbornly to forms and shells and rags of the past and missed nine-tenths of its nobler meaning. The static repetition of the forms and caste rules accompanied by "feebleness of the creative intuition" made the system immobile and completely incongruous with the moving times. Inequities and injustices multiplied. The deserving were denied their dues on grounds of their low caste and the most undeserving got more than their deserts by virtue of their belonging to the charmed circle of the high caste. The faith which sustained the system for thousands of years gradually lost its hold. Even its economic *raison d'etre* was not there. It was now left to the more powerful force like industrialisation and science to strike it hard and destroy its economic base.

**Characteristic features of Indian caste system**

As indicated in the foregoing paragraphs, the Indian caste system underwent radical transformation in course of time. As it is today, the Indian caste system exhibits the following characteristics : (i) Birth determines the caste of an individual. (ii) Merits or achievement do not enable one to elevate oneself from a lower caste to a higher caste. On the contrary, any failure to conform to caste norms may lead to the degradation of a person from a higher caste to a lower caste. (iii) Caste system is endogamous. That is, the members of a caste marry within the caste group. Marriage outside one's caste is forbidden. (iv) Caste exclusiveness is not confined to marriage alone, but embraces almost all areas of social life, particularly in the matter of food. Food cooked and served by members belonging to a lower caste are generally not taken by those belonging to a higher caste. (v) Generally, caste distinctions are displayed in surnames, so that the caste of a person can be immediately known from his surname. When you meet a person bearing the surname 'Pandit' or 'Acharya' or 'Bhattacharya', you know at once that he is a Brahmin. Surname serves as a caste identification mark.

The aforesaid characteristics may be regarded as the marks of the caste system in general. This is not to suggest that the pattern is uniform in all parts of the country. Actually, there are variations, though minor, among different sections of the Hindu society and in different regions. Why or how these variations occur may be discussed with reference to certain examples.

To begin with, one of the axial principles of the caste system is the maintenance of *purity* in daily living. Different kinds of standards are set for assessment of purity. Thus, among some groups particular occupations are considered to be *impure* and hence unbecoming of high caste people to follow. Similarly, some occupations are rated to be pure and appropriate for these people. Judged by this standard, some people may lose their status because of their taking to a calling considered inappropriate for people of higher caste. Likewise, there is a tendency among those who are low in the caste hierarchy to avoid taking up occupations considered low in social estimation. In general, white-collar jobs are rated higher in terms of social esteem in comparison with blue-collar jobs. Once the idea of 'purity' is accepted as a standard of evaluation, numerous sub-castes emerge because the yardsick is entirely subjective. And mind knows no limits in determining what is pure and what is impure. As Milton said, mind is its own place; it can make a heaven of hell and hell of heaven.

Besides occupation, the idea of purity affects kitchen also—the type of food to be taken, the manner of cooking food, the caste of the people who cook the food and such other considerations that vary from place to place and group to group. Some high caste people do not hesitate to eat uncooked food served by low caste persons while they refuse to accept cooked food from these very people. Innumerable subcastes have grown around this yardstick. Vegetarian food is considered traditionally a 'pure' food while non-vegetarian food is considered to be 'impure'. There is naturally a tendency among those who occupy a low place in the social hierarchy to shun non-vegetarian food and to seek to elevate their social status by taking 'pure' vegetarian food, by following a calling considered 'pure' and by observing rituals and other ways of life that are appropriate for high caste people. Professor M . N. Srinivas has termed this tendency among low caste people to upgrade themselves as *sanskritisation.* He gives the following definition of sanskritisation : "Sanskritisation is the process by which a 'low' Hindu caste, or tribal or other group, changes its customs, ritual, ideology, and way of life in the direction of a high, and frequently twice-born, caste. Generally such changes are followed by a claim to a higher position in the caste hierarchy than that traditionally conceded to the claimant caste by the local community. The claim is usually made over a period of time, in fact, a generation or two, before the 'arrival' is conceded"[20].

These illustrations indicate that the system of caste has never been absolutely static. This point has to be taken into account for a proper appreciation of the nature of the caste structure as it exists today. Another factor which contributed, in no small measure, to the dynamism of the caste structure is land ownership. The so-called 'low' caste people improved their social position considerably by owning land. The observations of Professor Srinivas are very pertinent in this regard : "The power and prestige which land-owning castes command affect their relations with all castes, including those ritually higher. This is true of parts of the Punjab where the land-owning Jats look upon the Brahmins as their servants, and of Madhopur village in eastern Uttar Pradesh where formerly the dominant Thakurs refused cooked food from all Brahmins except their gurus or religious teachers"[21].

The first social anthropologist to draw attention to the association between caste and land-ownership was F. G. Bailey who conducted field studies in Orissa in the early fifties. Bailey found that land came to the market and the same changed hands from Brahmins, the traditional land-owners, to non-Brahmins who did not own any land in the past. Another revealing fact which he recorded was that the Kshatriyas who were the traditional land-owning class till the end of the nineteenth century owned only 28 per cent of it when Bailey made his study[22].

It should, however, be noted that though the high caste people may experience a fall in secular rank, their ritual rank does no necessarily suffer a corresponding fall. The observations of Beidelman will be in order in this connection : "At the risk of inconsistency I must emphasise that there are many areas in which ritual seems to operate independently of economic determinants. In Senapur and Rampur the Brahmins were not the powerful or economically superior caste, but were subordinate to the Jats and Thakurs. But by consensus the village would probably agree that these same Brahmins are ritually supreme"[23].

Inter-caste marriage also served to soften the rigours of caste rigidity in some cases. Caste is, no doubt endogamous. But throughout historical periods inter-caste marriage took place, resulting in upgradation or degradation in status of families. "The giving of girls in marriage to boys from a higher caste or higher section of the same caste added to the prestige of the wife-giving lineage and caste. In some cases it also enabled the lower group to claim, eventually, equality with the higher group"[24].

Professor Srinivas has referred to the "fluidity" of the political system in pre-British India as an important source of caste mobility. Some sections took advantage of political instability and attempted to wrest political power which was an avenue, among others, to upward social mobility. Such an attempt could, however, be made by a group on fulfilment of three pre-conditions : "a martial tradition, numerical strength, and preferably also ownership of a large quantity of arable land". After having captured political power, it had to "sanskritise its ritual and style of life and lay claim to being Kshatriya". In order to strengthen its claim further, it has to "patronize (or even create) Brahmins who would minister to it on ritual occasions, and produce an appropriate myth supporting the group's claim to Kshatriya status"[25]. In course of time the claim of the group was established and accepted by the community. This adds another dimension to the dynamism of the system.

On a close scrutiny of the prevalent caste divisions, one would fail to find a rational principle underlying the existing caste differentiation. There are groups whose traditional occupations can by no means be characterised as 'impure' and yet those groups were assigned a lower social status in comparison with groups whose traditional occupations were decidedly of a lower order. One explanation for such irrational assignment of caste ranking is that those who were at the helm of political affairs at the time may have been displeased with a particular section for not being sufficiently loyal to it and out of spite may have assigned to it a comparatively lower caste ranking.

Till the early period of the British rule there have been many such cases of caste mobility. But the system itself continued, more or less undisturbed. The establishment of British rule on a firm footing, however, brought about a radical change in so far as the caste system was concerned. Westernisation, which followed the British rule, was, in the words of Professor Srinivas, "a fundamental process, and not something superfical and external". It was a process which struck at the economic base of the caste system by introducing market economy as well as technology in the method of production. Westernisation also brought about a radical change in the outlook of the people. The inequities of the caste were brought home to the elitist sections of the population by their exposure to Western education and Western ways of life. Through them it percolated to the lower strata. Consequently, the caste lost its economic rationale and its ideological base— the twin forces which sustained the system through centuries. The present day method of production in factories made it virtually impossible for high caste people to maintain their aloofness from those who belonged to comparatively lower caste. They not only worked together in close contact but also took their tiffin and lunches in the factory canteens which were not organised on caste lines. The experiences of the work place were carried over to their families and wider social relationships. While commenting on this aspect, Morgan and Ward make the following observations : "But we should stress that social experiences that members undergo within organisations feed back into their life outside, into primary groups such as the family, and into their general relationships in the community and elsewhere ....... that while we all belong to families, most people in developed societies spend most of their time within the framework of one organisation or another. Unlike the simpler societies, kinship by no means constitutes the dominant mechanism in social life"[26].

Another aspect of Westernisation, viz. urbanisation, also contributed substantially to the weakening of the traditional caste base. "Urban life sets up its own pressures, and a man's daily routine, his place of residence, the times of his meals, are influenced more by his job than by caste and religion"[27].

Finally, the Constitution of India has prohibited untouchability and declared illegal all practices relating to untouchability in public places.

The cumulative effect of the operation of forces listed above has been the weakening of the caste structure on the social plane. In most parts of India, particularly in urban and semi-urban areas, the importance of caste has declined as a social force. Rural areas are also catching up reasonably fast.

It is a paradox that while caste is fast losing its ground on the social plane, it is gaining a fresh lease of life in the political life of the community. Caste considerations influence political activity at every stage from the panchayat right up to Parliament. While the caste is breaking down in social or cultural fields, conflicts between castes are being intensified by party politics, linguistic and regional rivalries, and other current developments.[28] A careful study of elections in India offers undoubted evidence that the tactics of the political parties and the general nature of election compaigns are accentuating, rather than diminishing, caste differences and prejudices. A great deal of attention is given to caste considerations by Indian politicians, irrespective of whether they belong to the right or to the left, in spite of their professions to the contrary. If, for example, a particular caste-group happens to be of a sizeable number in a constituency, the political parties involved in the contest generally set up candidates belonging to that caste. Selig Harrison, reflecting on the role of caste in Indian politics, observes : "Political competition in a representative system was bound to give casteism 'a new lease of life', as Vinoba Bhave put it if only because the single-member constituency inherently favours — barring gerrymandering — any social group in any country which happens to live in close proximity in a particular locality .... The most perplexing election surprises become crystal-clear when the caste factors in a constituency come to light"[29].

## Class

There is a vast literature on the definition of *class*, or *social class*. A distinction is sometimes made between the two terms. *Class* is defined in terms of objective criteria such as economic power, while *social class* is defined in terms of subjective criteria, such as class consciousness. The general tendency, however, is to use these two terms as synonymous.

### Marxian approach to stratification

The term *social class* is used in different ways by different writers. It would be difficult to incorporate in a single definition all the elements which appear in these different versions. For an understanding of the origin and nature of social class, it is worthwhile considering the views of Karl Marx, Max Weber, and functionalist writers.

Marx is considered to be the 'Copernican' hero in the history of the evolution of social stratification theory. He emphasised the basic importance, as a criterion of stratification, of the individual or the group in the economic structure. The emphasis contributed toward all subsequent stratification theory. He made *class* the central aspect of his analysis of society. Though most sociologists in subsequent years have disagreed with many, if not most of Marx's assumptions about the subject, many of the non-Marxist or anti-Marxist ideas on the subject have been developed by way of reaction to the original formulations of Marx.

Marxist sociology starts from the premise that the primary function of social organization is the statisfaction of basic human needs—food, clothing, and shelter. Hence the productive system is the nucleus around which other elements of society are organised.

Marxist definition of class arises from his assumption of the primacy of production. A class is constituted by any aggregate of persons who play the same part in the production mechanism. In *Capital* Marx outlined three main classes who are differentiated according to relations to the means of production : (i) *Capitalists* or owners of the means of production receiving profit; (ii) *workers* or all those who are employed by others and receive wages; (iii) *landowners* who receive rent. Marx considered landowners different from capitalists and as survivors of feudalism. He recognised that there is differentiation within each of these basic categories. For example, he looked upon petty bourgeoisie as a transitional class who, by the pressure of economic forces in a capitalist society, would eventually bifurcate, one going down and joining the ranks of the proletariat and the other going up to join the ranks of capitalists. Marx, however, dramatised the antagonism between classes by referring to two extreme cases—the bourgeoisie and the proletariat or those who own the means of production and those who do not.

Thus, Marx distinguished classes in objective terms; that is, in terms of their position in the productive system. But his primary interest was in understanding the emergence of class consciousness among the depressed strata, so that it could serve as a basis for conflict with the dominant class.

Marx. therefore, distinguished between what he called a *class in itself* (the German *an sich)* and a *class for itself* (the German *für sich* ). The former refers to a situation in which the class members do not understand their class position, the numerous constraints they work under, or their 'true class interests'. When the workers fight for higher wages only, they may be said to be imbued with trade union consciousness, and not class consciousness. In such a situation, the workers may be engaged in intra-class competition and rivalry. These workers constitute a *class in itself* or a class *an sich.* They cannot wage a class struggle with the bourgeoisie. On the other hand, the class *für sich* or the *class for itself* is a self-conscious class, a large proportion of whose members consciously identify with the class and think in terms of waging a struggle as a class with the dominant class. According to Marx, only when *für sich* attitudes develop does the class struggle really emerge

Marx was of the view that class consciousness does not develop automatically. On the contrary, only through purposive effort does class consciousness grow. The Communist Party was assigned by him the responsibility of developing *für sich* attitudes among the proletariat. While discussing the preparatory stages of class struggle in Communist Manifesto, Marx outlined the role of the Communist Party in these words : "The Communists fight for the attainment of immediate aims, for the enforcement of the momentary interests of working class; but in the movement of the present, they also represent and take care of the future of the movement ..... But they never cease, for a single instant, to instil into the working class the clearest possible recognition of the hostile antagonism between bourgeoisie and proletariat ...... "Seen in this perspective, Marx does not appear to be a determinist.

Marx, therefore, looked at class both objectively and subjectively. Fulfilment of objective conditions alone does not entitle a group to be treated as a class. Only when the group develops *für sich* attitude or class consciousness), (which is to be distinguished from trade union consciousness), does it become truly a class. Thus, Marx based his definition of class on two criteria : (i) the economic status and (ii) class consciousness among those who belong to the same or similar economic status.

Marxian conception of social stratification has been subjected to several criticisms. It is pointed out, in the first place, that this concept does not take account of different types of differentiation which exist in present-day complex societies. These differences are far greater in number that those Marx had experienced or visualised. "For example, the analysis of social stratification needs to take into account such differences as those between owing and managing business roles, between business and professional occupational roles, and between skilled and unskilled labour roles"[30]. Secondly, Marxian concept of stratification ignores a variety of other social-structural factors that are of the greatest importance in analysis of stratification, viz., lineage and kinship affiliations in almost all societies and ethnic affiliations in societies which are ethnically differentiated. In U.S.A., for example, the coloured people constitute a class in an ethnically stratified society not so much in terms of their economic status but in terms of their bearing a visible ethnic identification tag. Thirdly, while Marx placed almost exclusive emphasis on economic factors as determinants of social class, Max Weber suggested that "economic interest should be seen as a special case of the larger category of 'values' which included many things that are neither economic nor interests in the ordinary sense of the term. For Weber, the Marxist model, although a source of fruitful hypotheses, was too simple to handle the complexity of stratification. He, therefore, sought to differentiate among the various sources of hierarchical differentiation and potential cleavage"[31].

### Weberian approach to stratification

Max Weber's approach to stratification was based on two Marxian approaches. In the first place, Weber began with the situation that Marx identified—namely, that social stratification is an organised manifestation of unequal power in society. Secondly, although this generalisation is universal, he, like Marx, focussed on industrial societies and capitalism in particular for analysis of social stratification.

Weber confined his analysis to institutionalised power—that is, to power that can be exerted in a legitimate and regular manner. This eliminates from the discussion any illegal force, such as a criminal action and piracy or any abuse of power through extra-legal means.

For analytical purposes, Weber separates institutionalised power into three spheres of activity—economic, social and political. Within these three spheres, power is expressed in terms of class, status and party respectively. He then analysed the characteristics of power in each of these spheres by way of describing the system of stratification. It should, however, he noted that the aforesaid classification given by Weber is not a static classification, each sphere completely demarcated from the other two. On the contrary, he considered the interactions and tensions among those spheres.

**Economic sphere :** In Weber's analysis, all people with similar economic interests and with similar economic power belonged to the same class. The definition comes very close to that of Marx, *but not in all respects.* Max Weber meant by economic factor not simply the relations of production, but also the relations that develop in the market place. He thus expanded Marx's conception, so that stratification consisted of more than two antagonistic economic classes. He further showed, as will be evident from the following paragraphs in this section, that economic antagonisms among classes need not be fatal for one particular class, in contrast to the view of Marx.

Max Weber did not accept the Marxian concept of two classes divided into those people who owned the means of production and those who did not. Instead, he analysed in economic terms the means by which economic power could be gained. For instance, ownership of the means of production can result in monopoly or control over the sale of economic goods as well as their manufacture. This kind of ownership thus becomes a kind of economic power. Ownership can also lead to the accumulation of property. Further, ownership can also mean the ability to take advantage of education in order to enhance one's economic and social standing. Weber was of the view that each of these aspects could, ideally, be ranked in terms of the power that each conferred, and that the class structure of a society could be determined.

Weber was more pessimistic than Marx concerning the probability of a proletarian triumph over the bourgeoisie. Marx assumed that the arena of the market place could produce the necessary consensus, consciousness and organisation for a social movement. Weber, on the other hand, contended that it could not, because the market produced temporary alliances that were dissolved once the immediate economic gain was attained. Classes could find a basis for common action; but that basis could not be simply economic. Weber was of the view that Marx's error lay in his assumption that economic forces would, more or less automatically, be translated into social forces.

**Social sphere :** The second sphere of power is social. Weber used the term *status* to mark off different strata in this sphere. All persons who enjoy in society's estimation similar honour or prestige and who follow similar life style generally belong to the same status group. Status is thus judged by standards that are accepted in the community. While class is a form of impersonal economic placement, status is tied to personal evaluations. In addition to life style and patterns of taste and consumption, levels of education, kinship and occupation are also used as bases for evaluating the status of persons in the society. There is generally a correlation of these various types of ranking in order to ascertain the resultant status of the individual. Weber had thus, in contrast to Marx, a multi-dimensional approach to stratification.

It may justifiably be argued that part of the status evaluation depends upon economic criteria. Maintenance of life style obviously depends upon money. There are, however, advantages in keeping class and status distinct, since the distinction between them can be illuminating. For example, the *noveau riche* are those who have become wealthy only recently, but whose aspirations for high status are not immediately realised. On the other hand, there are the high status elite who may lack money or economic power, as in the case of faded aristocrats or high caste Brahmins with very low incomes. In other words, the two dimensions of class (measured in economic terms alone) and status really measure different facets of stratification.

**Political sphere :** Political power was the last of the three dimensions that Weber identified. He developed this aspect of stratified power least, and he treated it mainly as a residual category. This is so because political power may reflect social and economic power. In fact, there is a clear tendency for individuals to convert their power in one sphere into commensurate power in other spheres. Thus, men of wealth seek status and political power. Those in high status positions seek to exert political influence. Politicians too are interested in status and economic power.

There are, however, advantages in having an analytical separation of these three spheres. As an illustration, we may consider a case where the three spheres exist in tension. During the period of early capitalism, each of the three power spheres was located in a separate sector of the population. The descendants of the earlier feudal aristocracy managed to maintain their status power. In a society in transition when all other traditions were pushed aside, the traditional status appeared to remain, more or less, undisturbed. Economic power was concentrated in the new bourgeosie who had acquired, in Marxian terms, ownership of the new means of production. Political power was, however, less localised and more dispersed, being shared between the older aristocracy and the new claimants to power. As capitalism developed, the separation of these three spheres of power created tensions. For instance, business could not be conducted independently of government which became a major factor in the economic sphere. Therefore, the economic elites had to work more closely with the political elites. Moreover, there was a tendency among individuals to translate their position in one power hierarchy to a comparable position in another power hierarchy. Thus, the economic and political elites sought to realise a comparable standing in the status hierarchy. In this way, a trend was established toward a merger of the three elite groups.

**Marxian social class and Weberian social status**

The basis of social class is indisputably economic. They are characteristic groups of the industrial societies which have developed since the seventeenth century. Difficulties arise, however, when an attempt is made "to specify the number of social classes or to define their membership precisely"[32]. Nevertheless, most sociologists recognise the existence of an upper class (who own or control the major portion of the resources of a society), a working class (who are industrial wage-earners engaged in blue-collar occupations) and a middle class (who are a residual category engaged mostly in white-collar occupations and liberal professions like medicine and law). In the Third World countries, a fourth class, viz. the peasantry, can be identified who differ in attitudes and ways of behaviour from industrial workers.

In industrial societies today, the social classes cannot be distinguished on economic grounds alone. The picture of social stratification is complicated, as pointed out by Bottomore, by the existence of *status groups* alongside social classes. We have already seen that status groups are differentiated, among other things, by the 'life-styles' of the people who compose these groups, while social classes are differentiated in terms of their relation to the production and acquisition of goods.

The difficulty in drawing up a coherent picture of social stratification in Western industrial societies arises from the fact that in these societies there has been "a real abatement, though by no means a disappearance, of class differences and class conflicts"[33]. Since industrialisation substantially improved the economic condition of the working class, the sharp distinction between the 'Haves' and 'Have-nots' have lost its focus in Western societies in the sense that the 'Have-nots' have access to many good things of life which were denied to them during pre-industrialisation period, namely, good food, decent dress, opportunities for school and higher education, facilities of medical care, etc. In this context, the distinctions among social classes rest primarily on 'life-styles' of people defined in terms of several criteria which are deemd by the society to be symbols of honour and prestige. These social classes may better be called status groups. Stratification based on prestige and honour affect the class system, as Marx conceived it, in two important ways : (i) "by interposing between the two major classes a range of status groups which bridge the gulf between the extreme positions in the class structure", and (ii) "by suggesting an entirely different conception of the social hierarchy as a whole, according to which it appears as a continuum of more or less clearly defined status positions, determined by a variety of factors and not simply by property ownership, which is incompatible with the formation of massive social classes and with the existence of a fundamental conflict between classes"[34]. The characteristic features of these status groups is that the relations between these are those of *competition* and *emulation,* and not of conflict, as suggested by Karl Marx. While outlining the trend in Western societies on the above lines, Bottomore observes as follows : "Thus in place of classes pursuing their economic interests at the expense of the community, the democratic societies are moving towards a system of groups which are less exclusive, less clearly defined, less widely separated in social level, and not pursuing with the same tenacity their narrow group interests"[35].

## Functionalist approach to stratification

Although the ideas of Marx and Weber are the most fruitful sources of theory on social stratification, much of contemporary sociology emphasises the functionalist approach to the subject. This approach is associated with the names of Emile Durkheim, Kingsley Davis, Talcott Parsons, and Robert K. Merton.

Functionalists point to the complex nature of modern society and to the highly differentiated system of roles which must be performed. A society must, therefore, distribute its population in different positions of the social structure and motivate them to perform different roles. The problem of motivation must be solved at two levels : first, to induce individuals to fill certain positions and, second, to induce them, once they fill those positions, to perform satisfactorily the duties attached to those positions.

The problem of motivation arises because of two reasons. First, the duties attached to various positions are not all equally pleasant or equally hazardous, or equally important to the life of the community. If all the duties were similar in terms of these criteria, it would hardly make any difference as to who filled which position. But actually all duties are not equally important or equally pleasant. Naturally, it matters very much as to who gets into which positions. Second, the vast variety of positions that must be filled differ in their requirement for skill, education, intelligence, commitment to work, and the like.

Functionalist writers argue that in an unstratified society—that is, one in which rewards are relatively equal for all tasks—those positions which involve hard and strenuous labour, greater anxiety, postponement of gratification and the like—will not be filled by people who are most competent for the jobs. "The stratification system is perceived, therefore, as a motivation system; it is society's mechanism for encouraging the most able people to perform the most demanding roles in order to have the society operate efficiently"[36]. In other words, the system of stratification solves the problems of *motivation* and *placement.*

Kingsley Davis points out that society has, at its disposal, three kinds of rewards to motivate individuals and place them at appropriate places.[37] These are : (i) economic incentives—the things that contribute to sustenance and comfort; (ii) aesthetic incentives—the things that contribute to humour and diversion; (iii) symbolic incentives—the things that contribute to self-respect and ego expansion. These rewards are usually 'built into' the positions. Since the rewards and perquisites are unequal, the society needs must be stratified, because that is precisely what stratification means.

We have so far discussed the need for hierarchical differentiation. But we have yet to explain how men evaluate different individuals in the stratification system. Talcott Parsons has pointed to three sets of criteria which are used as a basis of ranking. These are *possessions* (those attributes which people own); *qualities* (belonging to individuals, including ascribed statuses, such as race, sex, lineage or a specific ability); and *performance* (i.e. judgements about achievements). According to Parsons, societies vary considerably in the degree to which their central value system emphasises possessions, qualities or performance in locating people in the social hierarchy. He points out that, ideally speaking, a feudal social system stresses ascribed qualities, a capitalist society emphasises possessions and a pure communist system would assign prestige according to performance. Parsons points out that no actual society approximates to these three ideal-type models. On the contrary, each society has included elements of all three. Societies vary in terms of variations in the emphasis placed on these three elements.

The functionalist writers have undoubtedly shed light on a very important aspect of social stratification. But we cannot explain all kinds of stratification in terms of their theories. To begin with, the stratification that emerges out of the relationship between the victor and the vanquished cannot obviously be explained in functional terms. In all historical periods and in all countries the victors have deprived the vanquished from all the good things of life and pushed them down to the basement of society. Secondly, the stratification that results from racial or ethnic differences cannot also be explained by functionalist theories. Can the discriminatory treatment meted out to the Negro in various walks of life be explained in functional terms ? Their deprivations and comparatively low social status are to be attributed mainly to their colour and not necessarily to their lack of ability or skill. We have already seen that when the Aryans met the aboriginal population on coming to India who were in many ways different from them and conspicuously marked by dark skin colour, they were given a place in the basement of the Aryan social structure as a serf with few rights and many disabilities. Functional explanation is obviously irrelevant in such cases. Thirdly, in many countries land ownership has been the basis of social stratification, particularly in agrarian societies. European feudalism was based, among other things, on land ownership. Similar was the case in respect of social stratification in Middle East—particularly Lebanon, Syria and Egypt—in which stratification was based for several centuries on land ownership. Such social divisions had obviously nothing to do with role allocations in terms of social requirements. Fourthly, both Marx and Max Weber emphasised the role and importance of economic forces in the emergence and maintenance of a stratified society. Though Marx and Weber differed in details, both of them identified stratification as a manifestation of unequal power. And unequal power may be attributed, in many cases, to unequal distribution of economic resources among different sections. Though there are limitations to economic interpretation of social stratification, it throws into sharp focus an aspect of society which has been neglected in functional explanation.

The observations of Bottomore on the difference in approach of the Marxist and the functionalist theories with regard to social stratification are very illuminating. Bottomore observes as follows : "Whereas the Marxist theory unmistakably reflects the character of social and political conflicts in nineteenth century Europe, the functionalist theory reflects equally clearly the social situation in the U.S.A., where neither a working class political movement nor a working class ideology has ever become established, and where the social hierarchy has been conceived very largely as a system of loosely organised status groups, membership of which is related to individual abilities. The Marxist theory emphasises conflict between large and stable groups, with strong community sentiments, while the functionalist theory emphasises the integrating function of social stratification based upon individual merit and reward. The latter theory has many points of resemblance with Durkheim's theory of the division of labour .... Neither of these two theories has the universality which it claims. An adequate theory would have to take more serious account of the variety of stratification systems, would regard social stratification as a derivative institution most closely linked with property and the division of labour, but also with war and religion, and would deal systematically with the connections between social stratification, political institutions and cultural phenomena"[38].

## 4. SOCIAL MOBILITY

The basic question concerning stratification is : How much opportunity is there to move from one position to another in society ? The study of such movement is the study of social mobility.

### Horizontal and vertical social mobility

The movement can obviously occur in any of three directions : from lower to higher, from higher to lower, or between two positions at the same level. The first two types of movement are known as vertical mobility and the third one as horizontal mobility. In other words, when a person changes his status by moving from one position to another, the movement is called vertical mobility. Vertical mobility may be either upward or downward, depending on whether one enhances one's social status or loses it. On the other hand, when a person moves from one position to another and does not change his status in any way, the movement is known as horizontal mobility.

In a perfectly open society in which vertical mobility is unrestricted, the chance of every individual to choose and secure the position most suitable for him is equal, limited only by his suitability and preference for the position. It is to be particularly noted that suitability for a particular position (or task) depends entirely on native talent and that ascriptive statuses, such as lineage, ethnic membership, father's position, etc., would not in any way impede the free flow of persons into positions most suitable for them.

By contrast, in a totally closed society, in which possibilities of upward vertical mobility are absent, the individuals are assigned positions at birth. Once such positions are assigned, they cannot advance and improve their social status in any way.

It may be noted that no society ever existed, or does exist today, in which either social mobility is totally unrestricted or possibilities of social advance are completely closed. These are two polar extremes and all societies actually fall between these extremes.

Vertical mobility is particularly significant in social life. In the first place, vertical mobility is consistent with democratic ideals of society. 'Equal opportunity for all' is an important democratic principle, and this is exactly what is implied in vertical mobility. Secondly, absence of vertical mobility impedes the free flow of talents into positions in which such talents are needed most. In cases such as these, the society loses. Moreover, absence of mobility creates conditions in which potentialities of individuals are not realised in full and put into use. It is not obviously possible for anyone to realise his latent talents in a vacuum. Such talents get atrophied in the absence of opportunities for using these talents.

## Causes of vertical mobility

We have already noted that vertical mobility is present, in some form or other, in all societies. From that point of view, it is an inherent trait of all stratified societies. Why is it so ? Obviously, there are some inherent causes. Some of these causes are noted below :

(i) In societies where some upper positions are filled for a definite period, it follows that on the expiry of the term, the previous incumbents have to be replaced. Hence the inevitability of new persons being elevated to high positions. If the incumbents are chosen from all the strata of society, there is a possibility of the vertical current circulating from the bottom to the top.

(ii) There are certain criteria for evaluating people in different strata. Those who belong to the lower strata will obviously try to acquire or emulate the ways of life, manners and life-styles of those who belong to the upper strata. In course of time, the people belonging to the lower strata would be able to qualify for membership of the upper strata. Reference may be made, in this connection, to 'sanskritization'.

(iii) In many societies vertical mobility is caused by an insufficient self-perpetuation of the upper strata. Through a low birth rate within the upper layers, a 'social vacuum' may be created which can only be filled by persons recruited from the lower layers.

(iv) A general cause of vertical mobility is the unfitness of many individuals to perform the proper functions of their social stratum. This may be caused by (a) the dissimilarity of parents and children in terms of capacity and (b)) the profound change which many persons undergo in the course of their lives.

It is obvious that a fairly high degree of correspondence between the social positions of the members and their ability to perform the proper functions of their strata is a pre-requisite for the continued existence of the group. When the discrepancy becomes too great, the people who fail to come up to the standard have to yield place to others. For instance, a man of ability—dynamic, intelligent and resourceful—may have built up a business empire in his life time. If his son does not possess the qualities to perform his tasks enjoined by his position, be cannot obviously stay there. Nature abhors vacuum. As such, he will be replaced by more capable persons from below.

Sometimes persons undergo a profound change in the course of their lifetime owing to physical or mental sickness, accidents, and such other causes. They may lose their ability, because of these changes, to perform properly their functions. Hence, the need arises for replacing such persons with different ones.

(v) Another cause of vertical mobility is an incessant change in the environment, particularly in the socio-cultural environment—of groups and their members. Changes in the socio-cultural environment create, almost without cessation, favourable conditions for some members and unfavourable conditions for others, leading respectively to promotion and demotion. As Sorokin has pointed out : "A whimsical change in public taste makes millionaires out of Sinatras and beggars out of many 'old-fashioned' singers"[39]. Likewise, rich deposits of oil, iron ore, etc. among a population that is aware of their industrial and economic uses serve to enrich the owners of such land and elevate them in social hierarchy.

In view of the aforesaid possibilities, it is fair to conclude that the dynamism of socio-cultural life alone is sufficient to produce an incessant stream of vertical mobility within any group. The main cause of vertical mobility is inherent in the socio-cultural groups themselves. Factors external to the group may re-inforce or hinder it, but they are merely secondary.

**Inter-generational and intra-generational mobility**

Social mobility is a complex phenomenon. It has many facets. In addition to the three types of mobility—termed as upward, downward, and horizontal—it may also be looked at with reference to *time.* We may think of two kinds of mobility in terms of dimension of time. First, changes in status can occur from one generation to another. This is called *inter-generational mobility.* Thus, the son may go up or down the social ladder by taking up an occupation which ranks higher or lower in social evaluation in comparison with that of his father. Second, changes in social status can occur within one generation. This is known as *intra-generational* or *career mobility.* This happens when a family may experience rise or fall in social status within one generation.

## 5. STRATIFICATION IN SOCIALIST SOCIETIES

It is argued by some that social stratification is a phenomenon peculiar to capitalist societies alone, and that society is not stratified in socialist countries in which the means of production are communally owned or controlled. The basic assumption of such an assertion is that communal ownership of the forces of production paves the way toward an egalitarian society. Classes based on relations of production would disappear, because all would share the same relationship to the forces of production, viz., that of ownership. The experiences of East European countries and of U.S.S.R. may be cited in order to test the validity of the assertion. It may, however, be pointed out that no two socialist countries are alike in all respects. The discussions that will follow in the following paragraphs will, therefore, be on a very broad and general level.

It is pointed by those who oppose the contention that socialist societies are not stratified that East European societies have not been able to abolish social stratification altogether. The following social strata have been identified in socialist societies of Eastern Europe and U.S.S.R.[40].

1. White-collar intelligentsia (holding professional, managerial, and administrative positions).
2. Skilled manual workers.
3. Lower white-collar workers
4. Unskilled manual workers.

It is pointed out that the differences in income earned by these groups are quite significant, even though the differences are not as great as in capitalist societies. In terms of occupational prestige, the top administrators, managers and professionals occupy the highest positions with manual workers forming the base of the prestige hierarchy. It is further pointed out that there is a fairly close correlation between levels of income, levels of skill and expertise, as well as prestige ranking. This is broadly similar to what obtains in the Western societies[41].

According to Wlodzimierz Wesolowski, the Polish sociologist, the stratification in socialist societies is basically different from that obtaining in capitalist countries. To begin with, the sources of inter-class conflict have disappeared with the elimination of class distinctions in the Marxian sense. Secondly, there is consequently no possibility of one class exploiting the rest of the population. Thirdly, income differentials are determined and hence justified by the principle 'to each according to his work'. Fourthly, one's income or reward is not only linked to the volume of work but also to its quality. That is, income is "a function of the level of skill and education necessary for carrying out a given job"[42].

Wesolowski justifies power differentials in socialist societies on the ground that social life in large and complex societies would be impossible without some form of power hierarchy —that is, hierarchical differentiation into positions of command and of subordination. He further points out that power is utilised in the larger interest of the society and not in furtherance of the interest of those occupying positions of command.

Altogether a different picture is presented by a Yugoslavian writer, Milovan Djilas.[43] He is of opinion that power is being misused in socialist societies in the interest of those who exercise power. A new class has, in his opinion, placed itself in the positions of bourgeoisie in the Western societies. This new class consists of what he characterises as 'political bureaucrats' many of whom are highly placed office-bearers of the Communist Party. Djials further argues that these political bureaucrats take important decisions on production schedule and patterns of distribution in such a manner that they may be benefited. As a consequence, large income differentials separate these classes from other sections of society. Income differentials are reflected in the 'life styles' of the new class of political bureaucrats. Djilas also points out that in a sense this new class is more exploitative than the bourgeoisie because it exercises and enjoys almost unlimited power. The observations of Bottomore on this point are very illuminating. "Contrary to the orthodox Marxist view, popular control may well be greater in some of the capitalist countries, where independent trade unions can bring pressure to bear upon managements, and where the competition among political groups prevents the emergence of a single, omnipotent elite"[44].

There is, however, one important difference between the bourgeoisie in the West and the new class of political bureaucrats in socialist countries. In the West, property can be passed on from father to son. There is, therefore, a tendency for wealth to accumulate in a few hands. Newly earned income is added to the inherited wealth. In the words of Hugh Dalton, dead hand is allowed to propel the boat of the present generation. In socialist societies, no such inheritance of property is legally permissible. Secondly, the new class is apparently more 'open' than the bourgeoisie. "A Hungarian study conducted in 1963 showed that nearly 77 p.c. of managerial, professional and administrative posts were filled by individuals from manual and peasant families. In Yugoslavia, the 1960 census indicated that nearly 62 p.c. of managerial and administrative positions were filled by individuals with manual backgrounds ....."[45].

It is, however, pointed out that the upward mobility in these countries is partly due to the fact that because of technological break-through, there has been a very rapid expansion of these occupations. It is difficult to say what would happen when expansion of avenues in these occupations would gradually slow down. Another factor to be taken into account is that the rate of downward mobility in these societies is low which suggests that "the offspring of privileged status groups can usually bank on reproducing their parents' status".

A number of American sociologists have come forward with a new theory which they call 'convergence theory'. Clark Kerr is one of the main proponents of this theory. The views of this school may be summarised as follows. Technology has its own demand. It calls for the same occupational structure, the same accent on specialisation and technical skill and expertise, as well as the same need for 'incentive' as a spur to creativity and additional effort. Similar technology is being introduced in both capitalist and socialist societies. It can, therefore, be expected that the demands of technology will be met similarly in these two types of societies. As a result, the stratification systems in these societies will be increasingly the same or similar. This is the essence of the convergence theory.

One of the main defects of the convergence theory is that it ignores or under-emphasises the basic differences in the social systems of the capitalist and socialist societies. Communal ownership of the means of production and private ownership of the same are not just aspects of two different economic systems. They also indicate,among others, far-reaching differences in the stratification structure. Thus, income differentials in socialist societies are considerably lower than those in capitalist societies. The distinction between white-collar and brown-collar jobs is much less pronounced in socialist sooieties in comparison with capitalist societies. These and many other differences distinguish the stratification structures in these two systems. It is not possible, given the present state of affairs in the East and the West, to hazard the prediction that the stratification structures would eventually converge in future.

## 6. A NOTE ON SANSKRITIZATION

As already noted in an earlier section of this chapter, orginally Hindusm was, in essence, a way of life. There was a clear recognition "that men are not the same, and that there is a hierarchy of class, each with its separate duties and distinctive ways of life". There was a general norm of conduct, called *Dharma,* for all. But there was also a norm of conduct or *dharma* appropriate to each class. The norm of conduct or *dharma* of men of high birth was not that of men of comparatively humbler rank. In course of time, this kind of division became very rigid and mobility from one class to another, particularly upward vertical mobility, was completely closed. The four-fold class division was transformed into division on caste lines.

One of the axial principles of the caste system is the maintenance of purity in daily living. Different kinds of standards are set for determination of purity. Prominent among these standards are occupation and food. Some occupations are rated to be pure and hence considered to be appropriate for people of upper caste. Some occupations are considered to be impure and hence inappropriate for upper caste people and appropriate for people belonging to comparatively lower caste. Similarly, the idea of purity affects kitchin also —the type of food to be taken, the manner of cooking food, the caste of the people who cook and serve food, etc. There are very elaborate rules governing caste rules regarding food, and these rules vary from place to place and from group to group. Innumerable sub-castes have grown around this yardstick.

There is naturally a tendency among those who occupy a low place in the social hierarchy to shun those kinds of food which are considered to be impure and to take to 'pure' food in order to elevate their social status. They are also anxious to elevate their social status by observing rituals and other ways of life that are appropriate for high caste people. Professor M.N.Srinivas has termed this tendency among low caste people to upgrade themselves as *sanskritization*. He gives the following definition of sanskritization : "Sanskritization is the process by which a 'low' Hindu caste, or tribal or other group, changes its customs, ritual, and way of life in the direction of a high, and frequently twice-born, caste. Generally such changes are followed by a claim to a higher position in the caste hierarchy than that traditionally conceded to a claimant caste by the local community. The claim is usually made over a period of time, in fact, a generation or two, before the 'arrival' is conceded"[46].

Srinivas, however, points out that "there has been not one model of sanskritization but three or four, and during the early period of Indian history there was some rivalry between the different models"[47]. That is, apart from Brahminical model there were other models, such as, Kshatriya, Vaishya and Sudra.

Srinivas also points out the role of the dominant castes in setting the model for the majority of people living in rural areas including, occasionally, Brahmins[48]. "The mediation of the various models of sanskritization through the locally dominant caste stresses the importance of the latter in the process of cultural transmission. Thus if the locally dominant caste is Brahmin or Lingayat, it will tend to transmit a Brahminical model of sanskritization, whereas if it is Rajput or Bania, it will transmit Kshatriya or /Vaishya models. Of course, each locally dominant caste has its own conception of Brahmin, Kashtriya or Vaishya models"[49].

If the locally dominant caste belongs to the lower stratum of caste hierarchy, the upper caste people may try to conform to or abide by the ways of living of the former. While referring to this aspect, Srinivas observes as follows : "The representatives of the Great Tradition may succumb to the Little Traditions, and this seems to have happened occasionally"[50]. (A note on Great Tradition and Little Tradition : In his book *Peasant Society and Culture,* Redfield postulates that civilisations, as distinguished from primitive societies and cultures, are made up of distinct but inter-related parts or levels that have special contents and styles associated with them. In its simplest form, Redfield identifies a *great tradition,* embodying the thought,values, customs and world-view of the reflective few in society. The great tradition is associated with specialists in the maintenance and development of the tradition, the literati, the priests and ritual specialists, the cultural consumers of the cities, the royal courts, and the ritual centres. The little *traditions* are found among the unreflective masses, the illiterate, the uneducated, the unreflective).

While emphasising the role of centres of pilgrimage and monasteries as sources of sanskritization, Srinivas observes as follows : "Each pilgrimage centre had its own hinterland ....... a pilgrim centre as well as a monastery managed to influence the way of life of everyone in its hinterland. When section of a dominant caste came under the influence of a centre or monastery, Sanskritization spread vertically to non-dominant castes in the area and horizontally to members living elsewhere. Such spreading has been greatly facilitated in recent years by a variety of forces, technological, institutional and ideological"[51].

While referring to the possibility of upper class people conforming to the ways of living of tribals, Srinivas observes as follows : "S.L. Kalia has described the process of 'tribalization' occurring in Janusar-Bawar in U.P. and in the Bastar region of M.P., according to which high-caste Hindus temporarily resident among tribal people take over the latter's mores, ritual and beliefs which are in many respects antithetical to their own"[52].

Srinivas also characterises conformity to Western ways of living as sanskritization. Thus, he observes : "Westernization, like sanskritization, is a blanket term : it includes Western education as well as the adoption of Western ways of life and outlook ...... westernization helps to spread Sanskritization through the products of its technology—news papers, radio and films"[53].

In order to bring out the implications of sanskritization vis-a-vis the social structure, he observes as follows : "Mobility associated with sanskritization results only in *positional* changes in the system and does not lead to any *structural* change"[54].

Some observations on the concept of sanskritization, as developed by Srinivas, will be in order.

In the first place, the term 'sanskritization' is likely to convey a wrong impression inasmuch as there are no Sanskritic rituals. Sanskrit is simply a language and does not imply a way of life or a set of rituals. There are rituals assoiated with Brahmins, Kshatriyas or Vaishyas. When upper caste people conform to or accept the ways of living of comparatively low caste people, the process is also characterised as 'sanskritization'. Srinivas himself says : "The agents of socialization were (and are) not always Brahmins"[55]. In this context the use of the term 'sanskritization' is misleading.

Secondly, the process of change, which Srinivas sought to explain in terms of 'sanskritization', can be adequently explained in terms of 'reference group' concept, without the complexities created by the use of the term 'sanskritization'. Srinivas himself is conscious of this when he observes : "The usefulness of sanskritization as a tool in the analysis of Indian society is greatly limited by the complexity of the concept as well as its looseness"[56].

Thirdly, the complexity of the concept becomes apparent when his concept of sanskritization also subsumes what he characterises as 'westernization'. The close association of Indians with the British for over a century and a half created in the former "certain value preferences" for "western technology, institutions, ideology and values". Thus, the process termed as *westernisation* is not very different from that termed as *sanskritisation*. He attempts to draw a line of separation between the two concepts thus : "sanskritization occurs generally as part of the process of the upward movement of castes while Westernization has no such association"[57]. But when westernization is looked upon by the people as a symbol of a higher social status, some people would naturally take to western ways of life as part of the process of moving up in the social hierarchy. This process may also be characterised as sanskritization when he says : "This adoption of the symbols of higher status has been called Sanskritization"[58].

## 7. CASTE AMONG THE NON-HINDUS

Four religions—namely, Islam, Christianity, Zoroastrianism and Judaism — were brought into India and, in course of time, became established here. There is no firm historical evidence to explain their introduction in this country. Probably the merchants had been mainly instrumental, in the initial stages, in carving out a popular base, however limited, for these religions. Of these four religions, Zoroastrianism and Judaism are confined to relatively small, localised groups. Islam and Christianity were, however, more widely accepted, largely because rulers of these religions conquered large territories and a large number of Hindus became converts to these religions.

``Converts lacked any new social base to go with their new scripture and had little alternative but to continue in the pervasive caste system"[59]. Therefore, Muslims and Christians are found to ``participate in their local social orders as jati groups." Typical jati affiliations of Muslims and Christians are discussed in the following sections.

**Caste among Indian Muslims**

Ghans Ansari drew up a sketch of Muslim social organisation in the state of Uttar Pradesh thus[60] :U.P. Muslims group their jatis in several blocs, not unlike the varna categories. A major distinction is between the *Ashraf,* the "honourable", and the *Ajlaf,* the ``commoner."

The former are supposed to be descendants of distinguished foreign, non-Indian, ancestors. Traditionally, they are landowners, civic and religious leaders. They are also generally more wealthy and ``more purely Islamic" among the Muslims of their locality. According to Ghans Ansari, there are four classes of Ashraf in U.P. Those who belong to the highest class are called *Sayyad.* They claim their ancestry from the daughter of the Prophet and her husband, the fourth Caliph of Islam. "Sayyads are further divided into some twenty sections; endogamy is common within each section but is not mandatory". Next to Sayyads are the *Shaikh.* They claim to have descended from Arab ancestors who were among the first followers of the Prophet. Marriage may be contracted between *Sayyads* and *Shaikhs.* There are two other ``classes", viz. the *Mughals* and *Pathans.* They are supposed to have descended from Mongol and Aghani conquerous. The *Sayyads* and *Shaikhs* rarely enter into matrimonial relationships with these two ``classes."

Those Muslims who are engaged in scavenging, sweeping and other menial tasks rank very low in the social hierarchy. ``In Uttar Pradesh they are commonly descended from converts who retained their former jati name, occupation, poverty, and disabilities. Muslims of higher status do not ordinarily take food from them. Sometimes they are not allowed to worship inside the village mosque but must stand and pray outside. They are treated in much the same way as their Hindu counterparts[61]. There is, however, one very important difference. A ``high Muslim may choose to take food from them or worship with them without incurring the kind of penalties that a high-ranking Hindu might suffer for such transgression"[62].

The middle ranks among Muslims of U.P. include Muslim Rajputs and the *clean occupational castes.* The social distance between them and the highest Muslims may be explained with reference to the following illustrations. Zarina Ahmad [63] reports that in the villages she studied no member of an Ashraf group will marry a non-Ashraf or even take food with one. Ghans Ansari reports that Muslims of the Shi'ah sect are stricter about food than are Sunnis. Shi'as are supposed to refuse prepared food from any non-Muslims but Sunnis will take such food from `Clean Hindu Castes'. Mandelbaum refers to an incident from a village of Lucknow district. The incident illustrates Muslim sensitivity to rank. One of the guests at a wedding in an Ashraf family was a woman of the *manihar,* bangle-seller jati, who had just returned to the village after a long absence. Her husband had prospered; she wore expensive cloths, and, not being recognised as she came in, she was seated at a table with Ashraf ladies. In the middle of the meal, one of the Ashraf women recognized her; the other women at once stood up and refused to sit at the same table with the *manihar* woman. It caused a lot of embarrassment, but the *manihar* lady had to sit and eat on the floor." Evidently, these Muslim ladies were reacting exactly in the way high caste Hindu ladies would do in similar circumstances.

Even in Pakistan villages, traditional social groupings continue. Zekiye Eglar[64] reports the following with reference to a Punjabi Muslim village in Pakistan : ``A child learns the caste it belongs to from the time it begins to speak and tells it when he gives his personal name. Very early, the child also learns that it can marry only within its own caste.' Inayat Ullah reports the following about another Punjabi village of Gujranwala District, Pakistan : ``The first question to be asked from a visitor is about his caste, as this information decides whether he is to be given a cot to sit on or is to seat himself on the ground; and whether a special meal is to be cooked for him, or whether ordinary food would be sufficient."

The *Moplah* (Māppilla) Muslims of Kerala are also divided into castes. The *Thangals,* who claim descent from the Prophet's daughter, Fatima, are at the top. The *Arabs,* who are descendants of immigrants from Arabia, come next. The Pusālars said to be recent converts from the fisherman caste, occupy the third position. The *Ossans,* who are barbers by occupation, are at the bottom.

## Caste among Indian Christians

Indian christians were, by and large, converts. Even after conversion to Christianity, ``functioning *jatis* of converts did take form and were articulated into their local social hierarchies." As a consequence, caste divisions occur among Indian Christians, both Catholic and Protestant. For example, the Syrian Christians of Kerala, the earliest converts to Christianity in India, claim to have been recruited originally from Nambutri Brahmins and Nayars and, as such, they claim superior ranking among Christians. This is, more or less, true of all converts throughout India. Caste restrictions are rigidly observed among the christians of the West Coast. Thus, a Catholic Brahmin from Maḥáráshtra would marry none other than a Catholic Brahmin. The example of Nadar converts in Madras is very interesting. Though the Christian missionarics urged them to become one united body in the fellowship of Christianity, it was not possible for Nadars to do so. They faced a dilemma. They were in need of belonging somewhere socially and culturally. They could not establish social and cultural contacts with Europeans for obvious reasons. They could not also do so either with those converts who had traditionally enjoyed higher social status than the Nadars nor with those converts who were traditionally below them in social ranking. They had, therefore, no other alternative but to form a new jati after conversion. "The new jati became almost as rigorous and endogamous unit as their original jati. The Christian Nadars have much the same marriage preferences and affinal relations as do the Hindu Nadars; they use similar kinship terms and roles; they observe similar practices of ritual seclusion and purification"[65].

It should, however, be noted that conversion weakens pollution ideas. Social life among Christian converts is more free than among Hindus.

## Caste Among Sikhs

Equality is a basic tenet of Sikhism. But this has not prevented the emergence of castes among Sikhs. They are broadly divided into Sardārs and Mazhaḇis. The former consists of high castes and the latter of sweepers. The Sardārs include jāt and Kamboh (land-owners), Tarkhān (carpenter), Kumhār (potter), Mehra (water-carrier), and Cimba (washerman). The first two castes regard themselves as superior to others. The Mazhabis were converted to Sikhism from a low caste and much later than the higher caste groups. In some parts of Punjab there exist the Sānsi (shepherd) who were farmerly included among the "Criminal Tribes". Sānsi converts of Sikhism rank even lower than Mazhabis.[66]

## Caste Among Jews

The ancient Indian settlements of Jews are in Cochin and in Maharashtra. Although both settlements were numerically small, they were divided into jatis.

The Cochin jews are divided into two jatis, viz.. the White jews and the Black jews. Their relations are like those of a higher and a lower jati elsewhere in the region. The White jews would not intermarry or interdine with the Black jews. They would not even count a Black jew as one of the *minyam,* the minimum number of ten required for congregational worship. A traveller's report of 1570 gives the first mention of their social organization consisting of "a sephardi community and other congregations of the black jews". The sephardic families were descendants of immigrants from Europe. North Africa and the Middle East. They came after the Portuguese opened the sea route from Europe to India in the early sixteenth century. The descendants of these sephardic families came to be çalled White jews. The White Jews were generally lighter in skin colour than the Black Jews, though some of the White jews were as dark as any of the Black jews.

A third jati arose from converts made by the White jews from among their servants. They were called by the Hebrew term *meshuhararim* and referred to as Brown jews in English.

The other ancient settlement of jews in India is in the Marathi-speaking rigion. These jews are known now by the Hebrew term, Bene Israel, sons of Israel. Prior to the eighteenth century they did not know Hebrew and apparently had no knowledge of or contacts with other jewish groups. They lived in some Konkani villages as oil-pressers. This was not considered to be a prestigious occupation and for that reason they did not rank high in their villages.

Like oil-pressers in other regions, they attempted to improve their social status by such reforms as purifying their diet and prohibiting the re-marriage of widows.

After Cochin jews established contact with them in the eighteenth century and after they came to know of other foreign jews in Bombay city in the nineteenth century, they were exposed for the first time to Judaic scriptural law and other aspects of Judaism. They immediately took to it but did not relinquish their jati divisions.

Like the Cochin Jews, but independently of them, the Bene Israel were separated into two jatis—the higher jati being called the *Gora,* i.e. the fair ones, and the lower jati the *Kala,* the dark ones. There was no inter-dining or inter-marriage between the two groups. They, however, worshipped in the same synagogue. The *Gora* jews claimed purer Jewish ancestry while the *Kala* jews were considered to be of mixed origins.

Most of the Bene Israel now live in Bombay city. Quite a large number have migrated to Israel. The barriers between the two jatis are far less rigid in the city than they had been in the Konkan villages.[67]

These Jewish jatis provide further examples of the gravitational attraction of the Indian caste system. There is nothing unusual about it. Such influence is exerted by the social order of the dominant group on the smaller and culturally different groups of people in all places and at all times

## NOTES

1. Andre Beteille, *Inequality and Social Change,* page 2
2. Morris Ginsberg, *Sociology,* page 159
3. Article by Bernard Barter in *International Encyclopaedia of the Social Sciences,* volume 15
4. Melvin M. Tumin, *Social Stratification,* pages 14-18
5. *ibid,* page 16
6. Ogburn and Nimkoff, *A Handbook of Sociology,* page 350
7. Gerth and Mills, *Character and Social Structure,* quoted by Tumin in *Social Stratification,* Page 56
8. Tumin, *Social Stratification,* pages 66-67
9. Article by Bernard Barber in *International Encyclopaedia of the Social Sciences,* volume 15.
10. Bottomore, *Sociology,* page 187
11. Quoted in *Cambridge History of India,* Vol. I, page 280
12. Basham, *The Wonder That Was India,* page 35
13. Dr. B.K. Ghosh, *Hindu Ideal of Life,* page 49
14. V.M. Apte, a *Bulletin of the Deccan College Research Institute,* Vol. II, pages 34-49. Quoted by Dr. B.K. Ghosh in his book, *Hindu Ideal of LIfe.*
15. Basham, *The Wonder That Was India,* page 138
16. *ibid* page 138
17. *ibid,* page 138
18. Dr. B.K. Ghosh *Hindu Ideal of Life* (Manu Extension Lectures), pages 67-68
19. An article on *Social Class* by S.M. Lipset in *International Encyclopaedia* of the *Social Sciences,* volume 15.
20. M.N. Srinivas, *Social change in Modern India,* page 6
21. *ibid,* page 13
22. F.G. Bailey, *Caste and the Economic Frontier, 1957,* Quoted by Andre Béteille in his book, *Inequality and Social Change.*
23. Beidelman, A *Comparative Analysis of the Jajmani System,* pages 18-19. Quoted by Srinivas in his book, *Social Change in Modern India.*
24. M.N. Srinivas, *Social Change in Modern India,* page 30
25. *ibid,* page 32
26. A quotation from an article on Work, Industry and Organisations by D.H.I. Morgan and Robin Ward in Peter Worseley's book *Introducing Sociology*
27. Srinivas, *Social Change in Modern India,* page 123
28. Palmer, *The Indian Political system,* page 17
29. Selig Harrison, *The Most dangerous decades,* page 109. Quoted by Palmer in his book. *The Indian Political system*
30. An article by Bernard Barber in *The International Encyclopaedia of the Social Sciences,* Vol.15
31. An article on *Social Class* by Seymour M. Lipset in *The International Encyclopaedia of the Social Sciences.* Vol. 15
32. Bottomore, *Sociology,* page 194
33. *ibid,* page 196
34. *ibid,* pages 196-197
35. *Bottomore, Classes in Modern Society.* Quoted by the author in his book, *Sociology,* 190-191
36. An article on *Social Class* by Lipset in *The International Encyclopaedia of the Social Sciences,* Vol.15
37. Kingsley Davis, *Human Society.* page 367
38. Bottomore, *Sociology,* page 202
39. A.M. Lee (Ed.) : *Readings in Sociology,* 1959. Article entitled *General Causes of Vertical Mobility* by Sorokin.
40. Haralambos, *Sociology—Themes and Perspectives,* 1980, page 91.

41. *Ibid,* page 92
42. *ibid,* page 92
43. *ibid,* page 92
44. Bottomore, *Sociology,* page 143
45. Haralambos, *Sociology,* page 93
46. Srinivas op. cit page 6
47. Srinivas op. cit page 23
48. Srinivas op. cit page 21
49. Srinivas op. cit page 14
50. Srinivas op. cit page 20
51. Srinivas op. cit page 23
52. Srinivas op. cit page 19
53. Srinivas, *India-Social Structure*, Publications Division, Govt. of India, page 77
54. Srinivas op. cit page 7
55. Srinivas *Caste in Modern India and other essays,* page 114
56. *ibid,* page 44
57. Srinivas *India-Social Structure,* page 77
58. *ibid,* page 77
59. D.G.Mandelbaum : *Society in India,* page 545
60. Ghaus Ansari : *Muslim Caste in U.P. a study of culture contact.* The Eastern Anthropologist. Special Number. Referred to by Mandelbaum in his book, pages 549-550
61. Mandelbaum : *op. cit,* page 550
62. *ibid,* page 550
63. *Muslim caste in Uttar Pradesh.* The Economic Weekly, 14, 1962, Referred to by Mandelbaum, page 550
64. Zekiye Eglar : *A Punjabi Village in Pakistan.* Columbia University Press, New York. 1960. Referred to by Mandelbaum, page 551
65. Mandulbaum, *op. cit,* page 568
66. M.N.Srinivas : *India-Social Structure,* Publications Division,Govt. of India, 1969, page 7
67. Mandelbaum, *op. cit,* page 562

# CHAPTER ELEVEN

# SOCIETY AND PERSONALITY

The gregarious instinct of man finds expression in the society which he forms. The society also, on its part, prepares him through process of socialisation as its 'fit' member. It is, therefore, not proper to think of one without the other. The two are, indeed, inextricably mixed.

Among Western political scientists, two different views prevailed regarding the mutual relationship between the society on the one hand, and the individual on the other. One was the theory of social contract and the other organic or organismic theory. According to the former, men used to live orginally in a state of nature. In course of time, however, the state of nature failed to meet their needs for reasons variously explained by the various advocates of the theory. Subsequently, therefore, they set up a civil society on the basis of a contract. This theory has practically no sociological significance inasmuch as there is no recognition in the theory of the sociable traits of human beings. The organic theory draws an analogy between the human body on the one hand and the state on the other, and compares the cells of an organic body with the individuals who compose the society. The advocates of the theory go so far as to suggest that individuals are dependent on the state to the same extent and in the same manner as the cells are dependent on an organic body. They, therefore, conclude that it is impossible for individuals to lead a meaningful life outside the state. This theory also has no sociological significance for two reasons: first, no distinction is drawn between state and society; second, the separate entity of individual personality is neglected in the theory.

Sociological discussions on the relationship between personality and society have centered around two issues: (i) the role of culture in moulding personality, and (ii) the relative importance of heredity and environment on personality development. We shall discuss these two issues in the following pages.

## 1. WHAT IS PERSONALITY ?

According to Kimball Young, "personality is a ..... patterned body of habits, traits, attitudes and ideas of an individual, as these are organised externally into roles and statuses, and as they relate internally to motivation, goals and various aspects of selfhood". By personality we, therefore, mean " the integration of the social-psychological behaviour of the human being, represented by habits of action and feeling, attitudes and opinions"[1]. It may be noted that this behaviour contrasts with physiological behaviour, although the two are related.

It may further be noted that personality, as defined above, is developed in social situations and is expressed in interaction with other people. In the chapter entitled 'Socialisation and the Self', we have seen that consciousness of 'self emerges only in social situations. This aspect was discussed at length from the points of view of Cooley, Mead and Freud.

In order to bring out the various dimensions of personality, we may consider the views of two psychologists, viz. Allport and Watson. Allport defined personality thus :

"Personality is the dynamic organisation within the individual of those psychological systems which determine his unique adjustments to his environment"[2]. Watson gave the following definition of personality: "Our personality is..... the result of what we start with and what we have lived through. It is the 'reaction mass' as a whole"[3]. An analysis of these two definitions would bring out the characteristic features of personality.

To begin with, self-consciousness is one of the most important characteristics of personality. Whenever an individual becomes conscious of his 'self' he is said to be endowed with a personality. We do not ascribe personality to a child. The reason is simple. There is no integration in the thinking, reflection and the behaviour pattern of a child. Such integration takes place only in the case of an adult individual. Animals lack personality, while men possess personality. This is one of the distinctions between men and animals

The second characteristic of personality is that it is 'social' in origin. It has been established beyond all controversy that no individual can develop his personality if he is denied the company of men since birth all throughout the impressionable years of his life. "In 1938, a girl about six years of age called Anna was found by social workers in an attic-like room in her grand-father's house where she had been kept since she was five and one-half months old. Her clothing and bedding were filthy. She was unable to walk, talk, or use gestures. She could not feed herself when food was placed before her. She was emaciated and under -nourished, with skeleton-like legs and bloated abdomen. She had been fed virtually nothing but cow's milk by her mother, who was a moron. Anna was an illegitimate child and was presumably isolated because her grand-father, a widowed farmer, in whose house the mother lived was hostile and opposed to having the child in the house. The mother, we were told, was engaged in heavy work on the farm and had little time for Anna. After she was found by the social worker, Anna was removed to a country home where she stayed about a year and half, and where she learned to walk, feed herself, and understand simple commands, but not to talk. Finally, she was moved to a private home for retarded children, where she lived for three years until her death from haemorrhagic jaundicing in 1942. Before her death, Anna could bead strings, identify a few colours, build with blocks. She was clean about her clothing, habitually washed her hands and brushed her teeth, and walked well . She had a pleasant disposition and tried to help other children. She talked mainly in phrases" [4]. This example brings home to us nost dramatically the consequences of extreme social isolation of a child. For this reason, Fichte observed : "Man becomes man only among men".

The third characteristic of personality is that its nature cannot be properly understood without reference to the goal or goals that the individual concerned keeps before him. Apart from simple biological needs, man has also various kinds of needs derived from social living itself. Pursuit of goals designed to meet these needs affects personality. A man having one kind of goal is likely to behave differently from a man having a different kind of goal.

The fourth characteristic of personality is that it is an integrated whole in which the biological, psychological and social elements are all integrated into a complex whole. All these elements cannot be separated from the individuality of man. During the early years of childhood, one is guided by various biological and psychological drives such as hunger, emotion, etc. With the passage of time, the judgment begins to play its part and an integration is sought to be established among various elements. The greater the integration among these various elements, the greater is the chance that an integrated personality would grow.

**Role of culture in the development of personality**

According to some sociologists, the development of personality and the acquisition of culture are not different processes, but one and the same learning process. The studies carried out in 1937 by Linton, the social anthropologist, and Kardinar, the psychoanalyst, demonstrate that each culture tends to create and is supported by a "basic personality type". In their view, the basic personality type found among most of the members of a particular society is the result of the culturally similar early childhood experiences, and not of instincts or inherent 'drives'.The child is not born in a vacuum but in a cultural context which affects his mental make-up, habits and attitudes. A given cultural environment sets off its participant members from others operating under different cultural environments.

The following illustrations may be cited in support of the above thesis. Culture consists of both material and non-material elements. According to Ogburn, both of these elements have a bearing on personality. By way of illustrating the influence of material elements of culture, he referred to the influence of plumbing on the formation of habits and attitudes favourable to cleanliness and to the relation of clocks to punctuality. Ogburn says that the American Indians who had no clocks or watches in their culture had little notion of keeping appointments on an exact time. According to him, the difference in the personality of an American Indian from that of a white American in the matter of punctuality may be traced to differences in the material elements of their culture (in the instant case, the possession of watches or clocks or their absence in their respective cultures). Likewise, some cultures greatly value cleanliness, as is clear from the saying: "cleanliness is next to godliness", The trait of cleanliness is greatly encouraged by the technology of plumbing and other cultural aids that are found with it.

Language affords an instructive example with regard to the connection between the non-material or abstract elements of culture and personality.Since language is the medium through which an individual obtains his knowledge about the basic premises and various facets of the "culture" of his community, it may be regarded as the principal agency for moulding his personality. This is evident from the fact that people who cannot speak generally exhibit warped personality.

It is evident from the aforesaid examples that culture has a very close bearing on the development of personality. Ideas, values, and behaviour patterns of an individual are largely the outcome of cultural conditioning.

It should not, however, be concluded that culture is a massive die that shapes uniformly all those who come under it with an identical pattern. Within the same culture, personality traits differ— some more aggressive and some less, some more submissive and some less, some more sensitive and some not so sensitive, and so on. In fact, culture is only one among many determinants of personality.

In fact, neither psychology, with its emphasis upon individual differences, nor sociology, with its emphasis upon cultural similarities, can by itself give an adequate account of personality. It would be better to regard personality also as a bio-social phenomenon.

Two facts about the confrontation of the individual and his culture should, however, be stressed. First, it is a two-way process. Ernest van den Haag has very poetically expressed it thus: "One lives in the tension between society and solitude". Second, the process is a continuous one, not something that begins in infancy and ends at adulthood. Ruth Benedict in her book, The Patterns of Culture, emphasises these aspects thus:".... no anthropologist with a background of experience of other cultures has ever believed that individuals were automatons, mechanically carrying out the decrees of their civilisation. No culture yet observed has been able to eradicate the difference in the temperaments of the persons who compose it. It is always a give and take. The problem of the individual is not clarified by stressing the antagonism between culture and the individual, but by stressing their mutual reinforcement. This rapport is so close that it is not possible to discuss patterns of culture without considering specifically their relation to individual psychology".

## 2. MEANING OF HEREDITY

Every act of generation in nature is the transmission by the parents to their offspring of certain characteristics, biological, psychological and physical. The complex of the characteristics thus transmitted is known by the name of heredity.

It would be illuminating from the point of view of the exploration of the meaning of heredity to consider if there is any such things"as inheritance of physically acquired characteristics".Valuable research has been conducted about the question of acquired characteristics, physical and moral. These research studies have established that physically acquired characteristics are not physically inherited. Thus,generation after generation of Chinese women had their feet compressed to make them smaller, while their daughters have always been born with normal feet. Though acquired characteristics are not transmitted through biological inheritance, yet these may be transmitted through cultural or social inheritance about which there is nothing inevitable or blind as there is in biological heredity. Thus, if a person has acquired in his life significant intellectual accomplishments and pre-eminence, it is unlikely that his children would inherit the qualities or powers that he acquired through his efforts. But it is more likely that he would help create an environment at home which is conducive to such efforts being made by those who grow up in this atmosphere.

## 3. MEANING OF ENVIRONMENT

Our environment is made up of those things or agencies which, though distinct from us, affect our lives or activities in some way. We may distinguish between three types of environment: physical, social and psychological.

Physical environment may be either natural or artificial. The natural environment is composed of those external material objects or phenomena which are beyond human control, such as the mountains and the seas, the winds and rains, the sun and stars, etc. Though these natural phenomena may be modified by man in some respects, they are, in general, out of human control. The artificial environment refers to those material things that are considerably modified by the actions of men. Examples are vast stretches of land brought under cultivation, the dams and embankments with which rivers are directed to useful purposes,etc.

The social environment is formed by the society of our fellow men in so far as they affect us. Society affects physical and economic life of man, as also the mental and moral development. It is the most pervasive of all the environments inasmuch as the arts, science, and technology would not have been possible in the absence of social interaction : co-operation, competition and conflict.

The psychological environment comprises those habitudes and dispositions which are built around previous experiences. Thus our ideas of right and wrong, moral and immoral, virtue and vice, etc. are influenced (not determined) by it. Sometimes we are inclined towards a certain type of action simply because the society entertains certain values and attitudes.

## 4. HEREDITY,ENVIRONMENT,AND HUMAN PERSONALITY

Since heredity and environment influence man's behaviour, the question is often asked: which of the two factors is the more important? In explaining the variations of human beings and their societies, some people claim that heredity is the more weighty determinant because of the fact that "the blood of the parents flows in the children." and that "like begets like". Some writers argue that certain physical qualities, such as those of health and intelligence, depend mainly on heredity and some other qualities, particularly those social qualities which are expressed in morals, customs and beliefs, are determined by environment.

Many experiments and investigations have been made to ascertain the relative importance of these two factors. We may briefly note three types of studies : (i) Studies in terms of class or occupational categories. (ii) Studies based on intelligence tests. (iii) Studies in terms of family groups.

### Class or Occupational Studies

These studies show "that the groups with the higher social or intellectual ratings have produced more persons of genius or distinction". One such study shows that in the United States besides the families of the clergy and of professional men, the largest proportion of notable men came from the families of businessmen, farmers and skilled labourers. Another study calculated that the chances of sons of different occupational groups to gain eminence were as follows : unskilled labourers, 1 in 48,000; skilled labourers, 1 in 30; farmers 1 in 70; businessmen, 1 in 600, etc.[5]

These studies indicate a superficial analysis of the problem of heredity and environment. What these studies simply indicate is that the sons born in 'higher' classes or occupational groups have a greater chance to develop intellectual or other attainments. These studies do not tell us anything directly about heredity and environment. The persons who conducted these studies came to the conclusion, on the basis of their findings, that heredity was a more potent factor than environment. But one may use the same findings to establish exactly the opposite conclusion, namely, the relative importance of environment as compared to heredity. It may be argued, and not quire unjustifiably, that each social or occupational class has its own distinctive environment. The differences in attainments as between sons of different groups may very well be ascribed to differences in environment. The case for heredity can only be established if we can successfully discount the effect of environment. Secondly, the explanation of these differences in terms of heredity alone is based on the implicit assumption that "the distribution of occupational groups represents the inevitable assortment of the population into levels of 'natural ability". Such an assumption cannot, however, be made because "the occupational distribution of people is a complex social phenomenon, not basically determined by or measured by the biological or any other single factor".

**Studies based on intelligence tests**

Some writers tried to establish the relative importance of heredity by applying "Intelligence Tests' upon different groups of people. They concluded on the basis of their findings that some races are mentally superior to others. In their opinion, the average score of the Negroes is lower than that of the Whites because the Negroes have inherited the mental deficiency of their forefathers, and the Whites the mental excellence of their ancestors. That is, their contention is that mentality is a product of one's heredity.

These studies suffer from certain defects. In the first place, some writers question the assumption that 'Intelligence Tests', which involve "degrees of facility in performing particular operations under particular conditions", measure faithfully the general intelligence of those who are subjected to these tests. These tests "are to a considerable degree simply knowledge tests scored relatively to the achievement of like-age children". Secondly, these tests do not eliminate the factor of differential environment. such as differences in home life, in training facilities and in social opportunities. The Negroes come off worse in these tests as compared to the Whites because of differential environment. That this conclusion is true is corroborated by the findings that in the U.S.A. "Negroes educated in the North do much better on the tests than those in the South".[6] In the absence of similar environmental conditions "intelligence tests are measures of accomplishment ..... but not of innate racial differences in mental ability"[7].

**Studies of selected families**

Some sociologists have studied selected family groups as evidences of good and poor heredity. We may consider here two such family groups—the Jukes and the Edwards[8]. One Mr. Juke was born in New York in 1720. In 1877, 1200 of his descendants were identified. Of these 400 were found to be physically defective or diseased, 310 paupers, and 300 had died in infirmaries. Another 130 had been convicted of crimes; of them 7 were murderers. Perhaps more than half of the women were prostitutes. A further investigation was made in 1915 which unearthed 2,820 descendants. Of these, 600, then living, were mentally defective. A contrast to this dreary picture is found in the bright record of achievement of the descendants of one Mr. Edwards. In 1900 altogether 1,394 of his descendants were identified. Of these, 295 were College graduates and many of them distinguished themselves in professions and business. They included 13 College presidents, a Vice-president of the United States, and no convicted criminals. Some find in such striking contrasts the incontestable evidence that heredity is relatively more important than environment.

These conclusions are unacceptable for various reasons. To begin with, every generation is a fresh admixture. Hence, after three or four generations, very little of the past hereditary traits remain. The surname merely indicates their ancestry, and little or nothing about hereditary traits and qualities. Of the two brothers, one may be a person of saintly character and another a convicted criminal. The son of a genius may be a fool. Does heredity help us in explaining these striking contrasts? Secondly, we cannot ignore the fact that the Jukes had an unfavourable social environment, while the Edwards had a favourable one. Did not environment play an important part in determining their outlook, way of life and accomplishments ?

### Controlled experiments

All the above studies suffer from the fact that the influences of heredity and environment could not be entirely separated. As a consequence, those who want to discount the influence of heredity may look to one side of the picture and emphasise simply the environmental factors, and those who want to discount the influence of environment may emphasise simply the hereditary factors. In view of these difficulties, several 'controlled' studies have been made. These studies keep one factor constant and make studies of variations of the other factors. Thus, several studies have been made of (a) identical twins reared together, (b) identical twins reared apart, and (c) children of different parentage reared together.

None of these studies have, however, been able to disentangle the influences of heredity and environment and ascertain the percentage contributions of each factor in the making of one's personality. These studies, on the other hand, "help us to see more fully that we must always reckon with man's nurture no less than with his nature". We cannot ignore the fact that the environment of our past as well as the environment of the present are written in our lives. Can we ever measure separately the influence of both ?

### Interaction of Heredity and Environment

It is futile, therefore, to pursue the question as to which of the two is more important or more potent. These studies reveal beyond doubt that both are equally necessary for a given result. "Neither can ever be eliminated and neither can ever be isolated.... Both have been operative, to produce every particular situation, through unimaginable time. For these reasons it seems impossible ever to conceive two situations involving precisely the same combination of heredity and environmental factors. Every situation is in this respect unique, just as every human face is in some way different from every other"[9]. Just as it is futile to try to determine as to whether food is more necessary than air for the sustenance of life, so also it is useless to enquire the relative importance of these two factors. Both are necessary for a given result in the same way as both food and air are necessary for life. Every phenomenon of life is the product of both.

A sociologist is interested in the way in which an individual or group reacts to a certain environment, and not in heredity as such which deeply concerns the biologist. A sociologist accepts heredity as given, and enquires which environmental conditions are favourable for the fulfilment of hereditary qualities and which conditions are not. "Heredity.....contains all the potentialities of life, but all its actualities are evoked within and under the conditions of environment"[10]. It follows from this that the higher the potentiality, the greater is the demand made on environment. Instead of seeking to establish the importance of one factor over the other, we should recognise that, "the finer or the greater the heredity, the more does the fitness of the environment matter". For instance, a talented student will more keenly feel the absence of an academic atmosphere at home or in an educational institution than a student of average calibre. A very minor change in the environmental situation may mean little or nothing to most of the people, but such a change may be vastly significant to a person of sensitive nature, say, to an artist. Moreover, we have to take into account the fact that the quality of an environment matters most during the impressionable periods of our lives. It is doubtful if Einstein could grow up into an eminent scientist if he were born in an Indian village with little or no educational facilities. The opportunities available to us in this industrial age have brought to eminence men who would have remained in obscurity in an earlier age.

Psychologists are of the view that it is not possible for anyone to develop and express all his potentialities in full. According to some, not more than then per cent of one's potentialities can be developed and utilised. In the circumstances, it is worthwhile exploring the conditions which enable a person to make a maximum use of his potentialities. On this point, Dr. Shaffer's observations are very pertinent : "Since it is unlikely that anyone ever attains his full capacity it is important that efforts be directed to a better understanding of the environmental encounters most likely to promote intellectual development"[11]. Dr. Shaffer further observes :"There is.....the strong suggestion that since the change in intellectual structures is most rapid during the child's early life the early environment encounters are the most important".

We should, however, be careful not to read too much into these examples. These illustrations indicate simply that favourable environment may give a man of genius the necessary opportunity to reveal his power, and that a person, however talented he might be, will fail to do so in the absence of adequate opportunities. On the other hand, no amount of opportunity would enable a man of mediocre talents to attain the height of a genius. Both heredity and environment are, in fact, essential for our fulfilment. We cannot over-rate one at the cost of the other.

## NOTES

1. Ogburn and Nimkoff : *A Handbook of Sociology*, page 159
2. G.W. Allport : *Personality : A Psychological Interpretation*, page 48
3. H.B.Watson : *Psychology from the standpoint of a Behaviourist*, page 420
4. Ogburn and Nimkoff :*A Handbook of Sociology*, page 161
5. MacIver and Page : *Society*, page 81-82
6. Ogburn and Nimkoff: *A Handbook of Sociology*, page 66
7. MacIver and Page : *Society*, page 85
8. *ibid*, page 88
9. *ibid*, page 15
10. *ibid*, page 95
11. An article entitled Psychology and Society by G. Wilson Shaffer, Ph.D., Professor of Psychology, Director of Psychological Clinic, and Dean of the Faculty, Johns Hopkings University, Baltimore, U.S.A. This article is included in the book, *"The Biological Basis of Pediatric Practice"*. page 53
12. *ibid*, page 53.

# CHAPTER TWELVE

# THE PSYCHOLOGICAL BASIS OF SOCIAL LIFE

## 1. INSTINCT THEORY Vs. NEEDS THEORY

Man is a social animal. He has a "craving for relationship with others, seeking and giving response". In all sociological discussions, the social nature of man is accepted as an axiomatic truth. The reasons which prompt man to associate with his fellowmen should be analysed in depth in order to shed light on the relationship between man and society.

Since the dawn of civilization, there has been a continuing attempt at exploring and analysing the basic urges and propensities of man. The exploration is still continuing. We present here two schools of thought which developed as a part of the aforesaid exploratory attempt. One school has grown around the 'instincts' of man, and the other around the varied 'needs' of man.

According to McDougall, Freud and others, man is born with some instincts. His behaviour is to be explained in terms of these inherited attributes or instincts. McDougall defined instinct "as an innate disposition which determines the organism to perceive (to pay attention to) any object of a certain class and to experience in its presence a certain emotional excitement and an impulse to action which find expression in a specific mode of behaviour in relation to that object"[1]. He enumerated fourteen primary instincts, each with a central emotional core of its own. McDougall identified the following instincts: parental, combating, curiosity, food-seeking, repulsion, escape, gregariousness, self-assertion, submission, sex, acquisitiveness, constructiveness, appeal and laughter. Corresponding to these instincts, he mentioned the following emotions : Love or tender feeling, anger, wonder, appetite, repugnance, fear, loneliness, domination, inferiority, lust, possession, creativeness, helplessness and amusement. He mentioned certain other minor instincts also, such as sneezing, coughing, etc.

According to McDougall, instincts were in-born. At the time of birth, certain instincts manifest themselves. Others emerge and begin to function much later when the physical structure matures. Gregariousness is, therefore, an instinct and the fact of social living has to be explained in terms of this instinct.

Freud also explained the fact of social living in terms of instinct. But his approach was slightly different from that of McDougall. According to him, the driving force of life in all its varied aspects—his thinking as well as his behaviour—was the 'libido' or the sex urge. The use of the word 'sex', it should be noted, is not the same as the use of the word in our day-to-day conversation. To Freud, sex was the tendency to seek sensuous gratification of any kind and thus it had a broader significance than mere 'sex' as such. The sex instinct was considered to be in-born and the new-born child was said to bring with it the germs of sexual feelings. Freud explained the inherent tendency of man to associate with the fellow-men in terms of libido.

Morris Ginsberg interpreted Freud's point of view thus : "Upon the whole, it would seem to be Freud's real intention to urge that all tenderness to others is diffused and aim-inhibited sexuality. This is the root of the family, but also of wider groups; theoretically indeed Eros is capable of binding into a unity the whole of manind"[2].

During the twenties of the 20th century, the attempt to explain all social behaviour in terms of inherited propensities or instincts has been subjected to criticism from more than one point of view. To begin with, it has been held that there is no universal inherited propensity or instinct in man. Various ethnological research findings are put forward in support of this point of view. There are tribes which exhibit very pronounced combative impulses. There are, on the other hand, tribes among whom such combative impulses are comparatively weaker. Such differences are noticed in respect of all impulses. It is, therefore, argued that there is no such thing as universally applicable inherited instict, and that its existence is simply imagined. Besides, it is pointed out that the combative impulses among Red Indians and Maoris have virtually disappeared in the course of a few generations. This could not have happened if combative impulse were an inherited propensity. Explanation of human behaviour in terms of instinct would be subject to so many exceptions that the explanatory theory itself would appear to be naïve and unrealistic. Such exception would be readily available from a study of cross-cultural behaviour-patterns of peoples and tribes in different parts of the world. Hence study of human behaviour in terms of instinct eludes scientific analysis.

In view of these difficulties, among others, the study of human behaviour in terms of instinct has been abandoned. Instead, human behaviour is sought to be interpreted in terms of varied needs of man. The importance of needs was recognised by Hamley as early as 1936 when he emphasised the importance of needs in the following words: "We begin with the analysis of the child's nature—not in terms of 'instincts', a concept of limited value to the child psychologist, but in terms of the child's physical and psychological needs. It is......important for him (the teacher) to realsie that the child has real and fundamental needs; the need, for example, of security, of recognition, affection, independence, freedom and adventure"[3]. Man has various kinds of needs which he seeks to fulfil in and through society. There are, of course, differences among psychologists about the kinds and nature of these needs. We may, however, draw up a list indicating broadly these needs.

It is to be particularly borne in mind that each individual combines communality with individuality. Poet Tagore emphasised this aspect in his book, Religion of Man. He said that it is the nature of man to receive as well as to give. Man is both a self-seeker and a self-loser. Even when he loses and makes sacrifices, he fulfils himself. The need to receive tenderness, affection and appreciation is as basic as the need to display tenderness, to give love and to admire and appreciate. On the one hand, he is selfish and pugnacious, and, on the other, he longs for others' company, feels for them and is even prepared to make sacrifices to make others happy. This mingling of opposities was expressed vividly by Kant in the phrase "the unsocial sociableness of man". He cannot live at peace with his fellow-men and yet cannot live at all without them.

The following chart shows the fund^mental physiological and psychological needs of human beings :

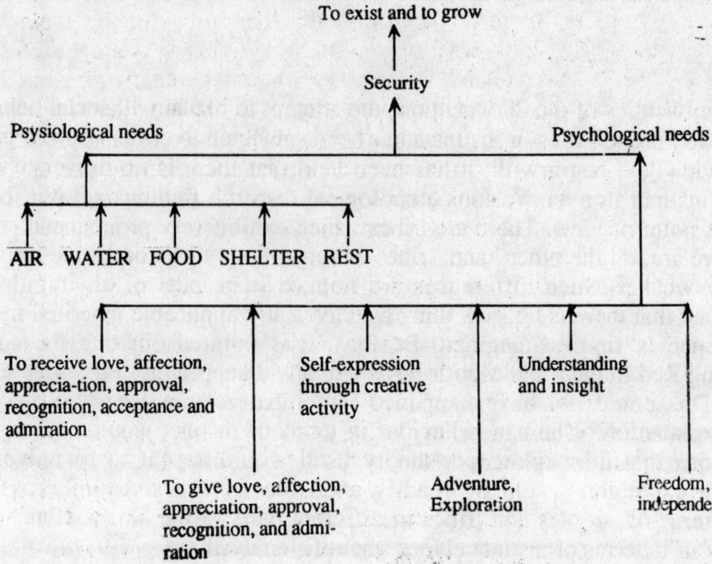


It is to be noted that man can fulfil these needs only as a member of society, in company with his fellow-men, and not in isolation. No man can ever grow into an accomplished musician in the absence of critical appreciation and moral support from those around him. In other words, man fulfils himself only in the company of men. The "needs" theory seeks an explanation of social living in these pragmatic terms.

## 2. ATTITUDES AND INTERESTS

It follows from the aforesaid discussion that man lives in society in company with his fellow-men for the purpose of fulfilling his various needs. But 'needs' do not explain the nature of relationship that grows among different members of society. Such an explanation is to be sought in the attitudes that an individual has toward others. Attitudes develop during infancy. The presence of some gives joy to a child The presence of some other makes him unhappy. With advancing years his attitude acquires other dimensions. He holds some people in respect. He is sympathetic to some, and apathetic toward others. He may even be hostile toward some. The subjective reaction of a person toward others is called attitude in psychology.

For sociological purposes two classes of attitudes may be distinguished. There are some attitudes that tend to unite those affected by them. Some examples will be illuminating. "Love seeks to approach, fear or disgust to avoid. Hate separates, socially if not physically, and sympathy unites. Distrust and envy may unite those who share such attitudes, but in common resistance of those toward whom they are distrustful".

It is to be noted that attitudes and interest are correlative. Attitude is a subjective reaction in relation to an object. When X has an affectionate attitude toward Y, Y becomes the object or interest. Objects or interests may be both material and external facts or non-material and internal facts."Man's interests are those items to which he devotes his attention. They range from such material phenomena as tools and soil and climate to immaterial beliefs, mythologies, and scientific theories"[5].

For sociological purposes interests are divided into two classes. One is called common interest and the other like interest. The following illustrations of these two classes of interest may be cited. "The like is what we have distributively, privately, each to himself. The common is what we have collectively, what we share without dividing up. The credits we receive at college represent like interests; the college life in which we participate we share in common"[6]. The two businessmen may have like interest in making profit. This very like interest may persuade them to enter into a partnership deal. After the partnership agreement is signed, they have a common interest of augmenting profit. Likewise, when a group of people campaign for a common cause, they are said to have a common interest.

Such a distinction is of much sociological significance. Like interest is exclusive and narrow while common interest is inclusive and wide in scope. Social cohesion is strengthened to the extent that the area of common interest is broadened in relation to like interest. In all human activities both common and like interests are combined. It is inevitable that man will seek to further his private interests. It is equally inevitable that he will consider it worthwhile to pursue impersonal goals that are oriented towards furtherance of interests of the group to which he belongs. This is as it should be. If all were bent upon furthering private interest exclusively, the society would have fallen apart. The society endures because individuals, on some occasions at least, subordinate their ego-centric interest to socio-centric interests. Both ego-centric and socio-centric elements are inextricably fused in man. He lives for himself and, at the same time, he also lives for the group. This quality of human nature has to be taken into account in any analysis of society.

## 3. MOTIVATIONS AND SOCIAL BEHAVIOUR

All human behaviour involves attitudes and interests. But adequate explanation of overt behaviour of human beings is not possible simply in terms of these two elements. A question of deeper significance remains unanswered. Why should a particular individual have an attitude of hostility or friendlines toward, say, one of his neighbours ? This brings us to the question of motive. That is, it is exceedingly important to know what exactly motivates people to act or behave in the way they do. For instance, there may be variety of reasons which prompted a murderer to commit the crime. It may be the lure of money, or it may be consideration of self-defence, or it may be the desire to wreak vengeance. It is obviously not enough to record that a murder has been committed. It is necessary, in the interest of social stability, to delve into the motives which prompted the murderer to commit the crime. The attitude of the murderer towards his victim may be partly, if not wholly, responsible for the crime.The desire to wreak vengeance falls under this category. Or, the interest of the murderer might have been primarily responsible. The lure of financial gain falls under this category. It is necessary to disentangle, as far as possible, one from the other and ascertain the true 'motive' behind the murder. In seeking to do so, we may have to go deeper into "various levels of the conscious, sub-conscious or unconscious".

In sociology we are not interested in a discussion on the entire gamut of psychological exploration and analysis. A sociologist is rather interested in finding out how far and in what manner social conditions " are the effective incitements to action that lie behind our acts, behind the show of things".

We have already noticed in the first section of this chapter that 'motives' cannot be explained in terms of instincts. Sometimes attempt is made to explain 'motive or 'motivation' of man in terms of hedonistic principle, i.e., the pursuit of pleasure and avoidance of pain. The basic assumption of such an exercise is that man is selfish and that he seeks to maximise his gain and minimise his loss. Talcott Parsons has characterised this line of thinking as 'self-interested' or 'egoistic' theory. In his opinion, the theory is fallacious. The theory assumes that man is guided by rational considerations of gain and loss. Such an assumption is unacceptable. To begin with, many of our actions are dictated by customs and rituals. The hoary past beckons to us, as it were, and we respond to the call. Max Weber characterised such action as traditional action. Secondly, we live in a normative society. As such, various norms in the form of values, beliefs, maxims, etc. exercise a profound influence in all we do, in the way we behave. In other words, many of our actions are culturally determined, and not always in terms of rational calculation of gain and loss. Thirdly, even some economic activities defy explanation in terms of economic rationality, i.e., the desire to maximise gain and minimise loss, the desire to maximise productivity and minimise cost. Economic motivation is one among many others which have a bearing on economic pursuits. The observations of Talcott Parsons on this aspect are very pertinent. "Economic motivation is not a category of motivation on the deeper level at all, but is rather a point at which many different motives may be brought to bear on a certain type of situation. Its remarkable constancy and generality is not a result of a corresponding uniformity in 'human nature' such as egoism or hedonism, but of certain features of the structure of social systems of action which, however, are not entirely constant but subject to institutional variation"[7]. That economic motivation is not entirely autonomous, and that it is subject to various other cultural factors will be evident from the following illustration. Both a medical practitioner and a businessman aim at earning as much as they can. But a medical practitioner cannot flaunt such an economic objective openly in the way a businessman does. The reason is not far to seek. The society expects a doctor to be altruistic in his aim and not make economic gain the summum bonum of his life. There is no such cultural inhibition upon a businessman. The only inhibition upon him is that he must conduct business in a legitimate fashion. A powerful society can enforce these norms very strictly.

The issue can be examined from another angle. Since childhood, we are exposed to various prescriptive and proscriptive social norms through process of socialisation, and our thinking and conduct are conditioned accordingly. Even if the society fails, for some reason or other, to enforce its norms, the members of society follow some of those norms, more or less, as a matter of habit. In our example a doctor will feel the pricks of his conscience to say, even in his close circle, that earning, and not service, is his primary goal. Similar is the case with teachers. We may quote Talcott Parsons again on this point : "We should bear in mind that economic activity takes place within the 'institutional' framework of a society, and that economic behaviour is therefore a phase of institutional behaviour. Deeper moral sentiments are inculcated in early childhood and are deeply built into the structure of personality itself. They are, in the deeper senses, beyond the range of conscious decision and control, except perhaps, in certain critical situations, and even when consciously repudiated, still continue to exert their influence through repressed guilt feelings and the like. In situations of strain these may well come to be in radical opposition to the self-interested impulses of the actor, he is the victim of difficult conflicts and problems of conscience. But there is evidence of a strong tendency, the more that people are integrated with an institutional system, for these normal sentiments to be closely integrated with the self-interested elements"[8].

We may refer, in passing, to the attempt made by Vilfredo Pareto to deal with the problem of human motivation with a view to emphasising the complexities involved in an analysis of human motives. Pareto observed that the actual motivations are sometimes "obscured by all sorts of unsound reasonings and misleading explanations". That is, human beings tend to give logical explanation of all sorts of non-logical actions. Pareto names such explanations 'derivations'. The idea of Pareto's 'derivations' has often been compared with Freud's rationalizations. "As social beings, we are disposed to select socially esteemed reasons for our conduct and present them to others, and also to ourselves, as grounds for our action. We form habits of concealing petty and self-seeking motives under high names, like duty and honour and principle and patriotism. We want to stand well in the sight of others and in our own eyes"[9].

We shall, therefore, not be far wrong in concluding that of all quests, none is more complex than the adequate understanding of motivation. The quest must, nevertheless, continue in order to shed light on the nature of social behaviour of man.

## NOTES

1. McDougall, *An Outline of Psychology*, 1923, page 110
2. M. Ginsberg, *Sociology, 1961*, page 104
3. H.R. Hamley, *The Place of Psychology in Training of Teachers*. The British Journal of Educational Psychology, Feb 1936. Part I, vol. vi, page 2
4. MacIver and Page, *Society*, page 25
5. *ibid*, page 24
6. *ibid*, page 32
7. Talcott Parsons, *Essays in Sociological Theory*, 1964, page 53
8. *ibid*, page 539.
9. MacIver and Page, *Society*, page 39

# CHAPTER THIRTEEN

# RACE

## Human Types

The term 'race' is often used loosely to indicate groups of men differing in appearance, language or colour. We shall use the term here solely to the biological grouping of human types. On account of the lack of sharp lines of demarcation the attempts at classification, based on varying characteristics, have not led to a generally accepted system. The unscrupulous power-seekers, however, at different times in history seized upon the concept of race as a means of glorifying some groups and of scapegoating or even destroying others.

The term 'race" is scientifically defined as a group of people possessing the same biological inheritance, identified primarily on the basis of external physical characteristics. Thus, shape of the head, colour of the hair, eyes, skin, contours of nose and jaw, height and body build are some of the physical characteristics that are taken into account in determining race. Hooton defined 'race' thus : "A race is a great division of mankind, the members of which, though individually varying, are characterised as a group by a certain combination of morphological and metrical features, principally non-adaptive, which have been derived from their common descent."

Some authropologists adopt the scheme suggested by Huxley in 1870 giving five principal types, vis : (i) Negroid (ii) Australoid (iii) Xanthochroid and (v) Melanochroid. Some others use a four-fold division into (i) Caucasian, (ii) Mongol, (iii) Negro, (iv) Australian and sub-divide the Caucasian into Nordic, Alpine, Mediterranean and Hindus.

But attempts to classify mankind in a specific number of well-defined races invariably fail. In the first place, the great mixed populations defy attempts to fit all their members into any definite race.No one can draw boundaries within which all whites, all negroids, or all mongoloids fall. Classifications based on colour are vitiated by the predominance of intermediate colours. If hair be used as a standard, the colour groups are broken up. For example, skin colour puts the aboriginal Australians with the Congo Negroes; but hair puts them with the European Whites. Which is correct ? Secondly, most peoples have mixed racial ancestry. In rich accessible regions no race remains pure. Travel, immigration and invasion effect intermixture. In modern times, isolated pure races are very few. Thirdly, from the biological point of view, all races of men originate from the same trunk. This view has been upheld by the UNESCO Committee of experts on race problems (UNESCO Courier, July-August, 1950. Page 8). It is argued that prior to the invention of the steamship, railway, motor car and aeroplane, small local populations often experienced long period of isolation from the outer world. "These groups naturally inbred. Contrary to popular superstition, inbreeding does not necessarily result in inferior off-spring. In domesticated animals, for example, inbreeding fixes a type and may improve it. This happened among isolated human groups. In this way there developed tribes of common descent whose members manifested similar physical characteristics. These were true races".[1]

Despite scientific inaccuracy, convenience has led to a rough division of mankind into three major stocks and several minor groups. These are : (i) The *Caucasoids* include the light-skinned, highly variable Europeans and their discendants in America, South Africa and Australia and also the dark-skinned Hindus. (ii) The term *Mongoloid* denotes the Chinese. Mongols, Japanese and aboriginal Americans plus several variable minor stocks. (iii) The *Negroids* include the many dark-skinned people of Africa and Oceania.

## Racial differences and intelligence

Racial differences are often used to prove the mental superiority or inferiority of certain races. Psychologists and sociologists have attacked such claims as entirely baseless by giving mental tests to members of different races. Some of the results of these tests are as follows. The average score of the Chinese and Japanese is 99, as compared with 100 for Whites while the American Red Indians (who belong to the race of Mongoloids like the Chinese) have an average score of only 75. If these tests really measured racial differences, we should not expect the average scores of the Chinese and the American Red Indians, who belong to the same racial stock, to vary so greatly. These differences, therefore, reflect in all probability variations in cultural development rather than inherited racial ability. This conclusion is corroborated by the sharp contrasts in scores obtained by American Negroes of the North and of the South. It has been found that those American Negroes who have been in the Northern States only for a short time got about the same rating as Negroes of the Southern States, while a positive correlation has been found between increase in I.Q. and the number of years of schooling of the Negroes in the North.[2] Brigham found that "among groups of Europeans who had immigrated at various times and had been subjected to intelligence tests those who had stayed longest in the United States gave the best results. While originally he ascribed this to the immigration of more poorly equipped stock in later years, subsequently he withdrew this conclusion. It seems more probable that the improvement is due to a gradual assimilation to American speech and customs. Klineberg found this to be the case among Negroes migrating from rural districts to cities. The evidence in regard to mental differences between races has been assembled by Garth who reaches the conclusion that no essential differences have been proved."[3]

D.G. Haring of Syracuse University, therefore, concludes : "Any racial group, however defined, includes all sorts of personalities. Both geniuses and idiots occur in all races. Always there are the clever and the stupid, the honest and the deceitful, the arrogant and the meek, the pious and the godless, the alert and the lethargic. No so-called race monopolises any of these qualities. The practical question about any individual is not, what is his physical type, but what sort of person is he ? Opportunity and taste for learning, not bodily features, play the leading role in the development of personalities."[4]

## Race and Culture

Biological factors cannot obviously explain adequately the growth of cultural patterns. There are many aspects of cultural life of a community which cannot be easily related to biological facts, such as bodily adornment, decorative art, dancing, hair styles, etc. These cannot be explained in terms of biological needs.

Some writers have tried to explain diversities in cultural patterns in terms of race. They assume that the external physical characteristics--such as, the shape of the head, colour of the hair, eyes and skin, height and body build, etc.--have a definite relationship to the kind of behaviour people will exhibit and the kind of culture they will possess. According to them, the Negroes, Caucasians and the Mongoloids are expected to possess different cultures by virtue of their different biological features.

This theory is unacceptable for various reasons. In the first place, from the biological point of view, all races of men originate from the same trunk. This view has been upheld by the UNESCO Committee of Experts on Race Problems (UNESCO Courier, July-August, 1950, page 8). Secondly, most peoples have mixed racial ancestry. This makes the concept of race of dubious reliability for social science. Thirdly, the irrelevance of heredity to the kind of culture an individual acquires is confirmed by a number of studies that have been made in this field. The following report of an American reared in a Chinese family illustrates this point :"A few years ago a young man of American parentage but who had been reared in a Chinese family from infancy on, paid his first visit to America. Reporters commented not only upon his apparently complete bewilderment in the American way of life, but also upon the fact that his walk, arm and hand movements, and facial expression were 'Chinese—not American'. They insisted that one had to fix one's attention upon his blond hair and blue eyes to convince oneself that he was of white stock at all. Here the point is that an individual's acts and attitudes not only failed to resemble those of his own close relatives in this country but that they resembled those of all members of an alien physical group and contrasted with those of all members of his own physical group."[5] Fourthly, there is overwhelming evidence that similar cultures can be found among peoples with very different physical characteristics, that different cultures can be found among peoples with similar characteristics, and that culture may change quickly without any corresponding change in racial composition of the people.

## Race Prejudice

We have seen that the term 'race' refers to distinct human stocks characterised by physiological differences which owe their origin "to a remote separation of ancestry". Race as such is, therefore, a biological phenomenon which does not concern the sociologists. A sociologist is, however, concerned with social reaction to racial differences, i..e. race consciousness.

Some races, because of their physiological differences from other races, lay claim to superior mental or intellectual ability. In other words, they become conscious of their own racial superiority, and look down upon other races as intellectually and mentally deficient. We have discussed in the foregoing paragraphs that these claims cannot be scientifically sustained. But, however unjustified, race feelings persist which find expression in race riots, racial segregation, and various other discriminations against a race based upon rights, opportunities and status. The emotions and feelings involved in these relationships are commonly called race prejudice. Race prejudice is nothing but prejudice applied against a race. Such prejudices are also applied against people of different religious groups. As a matter of fact, number of religious wars fought in different periods of history have probably been much greater than those of racial wars. Prejudice is, therefore, a general attitude which may be harboured by a group against another group. Race prejudice is widely prevalent because "race carries a label that is visible and can be inherited", such as colour, hair or any other physical features.

There is an extensive literature dealing with prejudice as a social phenomenon. On the individual level, prejudices may owe their origin to the images about a group that a person may carry from childhood. These images may be derived from such sources as family, school, peer groups, mass media, folk-lore, tales, proverbs, etc. On the social level, prejudice is mainly a cultural phenomenon. Prejudice, which is embodied in a culture, is conveyed to children through their parents, teachers, peers, etc. Scientists agree today that the individual is not born with prejudices. The anthropological, sociological, and psychological researches have established that prejudice "is at bottom the result of social indoctrination, in both its direct and indirect forms, indoctrination that inculcates beliefs and attitudes, which easily take firm hold in his life through the processes of habituation".[6]

But how does prejudice get embedded in a culture? Various theories have been advanced to explain this process. Some of these theories are the following:

(i) **Ethnocentrism** : The growth of prejudice is explained in terms of ethnocentrism which is "conceived as an ideological system pertaining to groups and group relations". The members of the in-group have a somewhat exalted opinion of themselves, and display towards members of an out-group a selfish, callous attitude or one of hostility. Thus the members of the in-group are prejudiced against the members of the out-group. If the members of the two groups are of different races, the prejudice is called race prejudice.

(ii) **Economic Advantage** : Sometimes race prejudice is practised in the hope of economic gain. In the Southern states of the U.S.A., for example, the Negroes supplied cheap labour which was of immense benefit to the agricultural economy of those states. Hence, race prejudice was used as a pretext for keeping the Negroes in "the bottom rungs of the prestige ladder" and withholding from them equal pay for equal work and equal schooling, so that they might be available for less remunerative and more arduous jobs.

(iii) **The scapegoat function** : Several investigations and experiments with small children have shown that they are often afraid of anxiety. The child may manifest several possible reactions to this situation and find ways of coping with the new situation or he may react in an unconstructive manner which results usually in a negative effect in the form of fear. Later on, in the course of his development, the child may learn to project his fear on the members of various groups.

The mechanism of projection, as described by Freud, is an important concept in the explanation of prejudice. One's own fears, failures and deficiencies may be "projected" upon others. When one is not able to cope with others because they are richer or more intelligent, one may, instead of constructively directing one's energies towards removing the deficiencies, project destructive tendencies upon others. This is the so-called scapegoat theory of prejudice. The Jews are attacked or discriminated against in certain European countries because "many individual Jewish persons have attained higher social and economic status than that gained by members of other minority groups." It has been aptly remarked by a writer that "those whom we consider below us, we may despise or pity, but we neither love nor hate them as we do our equals."

(iv) **Ignorance** : The most prolific source of prejudice is ignorance. Often we make mental images of other people which are not based on facts. Where ignorance is widespread, emotion reinforces our prejudice against a group, because conclusions based on emotion are difficult to change. "Prejudice means to prejudge. We prejudge readily when emotion forces us to a conclusion without much thought. Indeed, strong emotion can at times block thought and blind us to observation. Once prejudice takes root, even familiarity with the facts may not eradicate it."[7]

**Some lines of attack against race prejudice and/or conflict.**

It is not possible to suggest any short-cut device to eliminate race prejudice.

We may, however, note, in the first place, that race conflict is of comparatively recent origin which became a serious problem since improvements in transportation threw the races into close contact. Long periods of enforced isolation have bred in man prejudices about others whom he does not know well enough to appreciate the differences in features, habits of mind or body language and even dress. Hans Kohn says : "At the root of race prejudice is an aversion to strange appearances and ways of life which are often held to be proof of inferior standards ......"[8]. It has been aptly remarked by Delisle Burns that "if man had no history then we could begin without difficulty to arrange the world upon the best plan conceivable; for then all men would be made according to one excellent definition, all turned out according to one pattern and each easily to be understood by studying the other. But each of us individually and each group of us collectively is a result of the past. We are burdened or we are benefited by our descent."[9] Ogburn and Nimkoff emphasise the role which transportation plays into forcing races into relations with each other in these words: "In almost all cases, the contacts which bring out the friction are due to the transportation inventions which have thrown the races into close contact. Technology changes first, and the adaptation of the races to these changes occurs much later."[10] From this point of view, race prejudice may be viewed as a kind of cultural lag. The only lasting solution of this deep—seated malady seems to lie in proper education of children from an early age so that they may grow up with the conviction that all men are created equal, and that the rights of every man are diminished when the rights of one man are threatened. It is a moral question, a question of conscience, and not merely a legal or legislative issue. laws are necessary, no doubt, but law cannot make man see right. "Race prejudice is a matter of attitudes, which are often thought to be amenable to education; and the usual approach to the question concerns changing attitudes." Hans Kohn says : "Unless decisive changes are made in the attitudes and practices of dominant toward backward races - and such changes are not now in prospect outside of the Soviet Union — wars and revolts must inevitably result."

We have to note, in the second place, that in so far as race prejudice is mainly concerned with motives of economic or political gain, other effective measures, besides legislation should be undertaken to supplement and strengthen the efforts of pedagogic agencies. Conditions favouring economic or political gains to be derived from race prejudice or race conflict should be gradually removed. This point of view has been very forcefully expressed by Father Bruckberger while referring to the controversy between Carey[13] and Abraham Lincoln regarding the question of emancipation of Negroes. Lincoln thought primarily in terms of politics; his chief concern was with the Rights of Man........... Carey saw little use in giving the Negro political freedom, only to have him engulfed in the still more horrible slavery of the economic proletariat. In Carey's view, the solution was to hasten the industrialisation of the south. If the south were industrialised, it would no longer depend on the English market or on buying England's manufactured goods. The resulting prosperity would bring continually increased economic benefits to both planter and Negro, and would therefore very soon make possible the emancipation of the slaves. Before the Civil War began, and even while it was going on, Carey kept pressing Lincoln to construct a great highway across the whole South, linking it to the North and thereby establishing closer economic relations between the two regions. If one can resist the seductions of political romanticism and look at the situation objectively, it is impossible not to see how right Carey was. Of course, this does not mean that Lincoln was wrong. Yet the Civil War did not solve the Negro problem, it undoubtedly could not have solved it, and it is only today and because of the advance of industrialisation in the south and throughout the nation, that the condition of the American Negro is now rapidly improving with the greater diversity of economic choices opened up to him by industrialisation. Emerging at last from his proletarian servitude, the Negro is better able than ever before to defend and exercise his rights"[14].

Thirdly, Hans Kohn argues that a peaceful and durable solution of racial conflicts "demands equal opportunites for all races in all occupations and professions and equal rights in the exercise of citizenship. It cannot be attained without vastly increased facilities for the backward races in education, in capital equipment and in the development of resources in their interest"[15].

None of these measures can, however, be expected to resolve race conflicts or to remove race prejudice within a short period of time. The problem is too deep-seated to be resolved quickly. Since emotion and deeply entrenched traditions are involved, the process of change will be slow and gradual, and sometimes even painful. But patient and determined efforts, coupled with more frequent contacts between groups of men belonging to different races, will certainly help to cut into the darkness of mistrust, hostility, bigotry and hatred.

## Races in India [16]

In considering race and race movements in India, we should bear in mind that there are both *primary* and *secondary* races in India. Primary races are "differentiated by early geographical and genetic isolation, by the loss of some genes and fixation of others, by mutations, by inbreeding, and by selection". Secondary races are formed "by the stabilization of blends of two or more primary races". We should also bear in mind that terminologies which are generally used in order to refer to racial elements are sometimes confusing. Thus the terms "Aryan" and "Dravidian" refer to linguistic groups, but these terms have often been used, and are still being used, in the ethnic sense. Some authropologists, for example, call all the peoples of North India as belonging to the *Hindu* race—a term which has only a religious connotation, Similarly, the term *Proto-Australoid* has been used in Indian authropology without a proper perspective. The term was applied to mean the primary race of Inida. In this sense the proper term would be 'veddid' or Australoid'. The term *Proto-Australoid* literally means a race living before the Australoids.

All these confusions are due to lack of proper data regarding race and race movements in India. During a long stretch of a few thousand years, there have been immigration on a fairly large scale during different periods. As a result, there have occurred inter-mixture of various races on a fairly extensive scale. Yet attempts have been made to explain the differentiation of the population of India into racial types in terms of immigration only without taking into account the fact that India has bred her own races. It is difficult to accept the assumption that this vast sub-continent was once a vacuum. In *The Cambridge History of India* a question is asked: "Is there any evidence to show whence they (i.e. the Dravidians) came to India?"[17]. But the most relevant question which has been ignored is this: Could not the Dravidians have evolved on Indian soil? Keith is inclined to regard the Dravidian type as having evolved from the Veddids.

Similarly, the ethnic difference between the peoples speaking Mundari and Dravidian has also been ignored. The district of Santal Parganas in Bihar sheds light on this. Here the Dravidian-speaking Māle reside on the slopes of the Rajmahal Hills, while the Mundari-speaking Santals occupy the valleys between the hills. The two differ in physical features, language and culture. The differences are too obvious to be ignored. The Māle represents the northern extension of the Veddids of the South, while the Santals are habitual migrants. "Each village has its quota, and as soon as it is full, a band of pioneers goes out, seeking to establish another suitable village. The Santals are said to restrict their migration along the lateritic soil. Their population is also fast increasing, and this pressure of population has caused the people to migrate far and wide."

The Mundas also exhibit the same physical traits and migratory habits. They have always inhabited the eastern coastland of India, and have not penetrated deep into the hinterland which was already occupied by the Veddis. The Mundas have given rise to some peculiar hybrid combinations which are not found in the case of any other aboriginal tribe in India. These hybrids are known as (i) Khangar-Munda, (ii) Kharia-Munda, (iii) Konkpat-Munda, (iv) Karanga-Munda, (v) Mahili-Munda, (vi) Nagbansi-Munda, (vii) Oraon-Munda,

(viii) Sad-Munda, (ix) Savar-Munda, (x) Munda-Bhuiya and (xi) Munda-Chamar. There is a theory that the Mundas entered India without women. H. H. Risley was of the view that these hybrids are descended from intermarriages between Munda men and women of other tribes.

The greatest immigrant group into India from outside has been the Aryans or the Indo-Aryans. They caused a considerable change in the ethnic and cultural history of India. Though sporadic infiltrations might have begun earlier, the largest influx occurred about 1200 B.C. from the Aral-Caspian basin. These people are represented by the eneolithic skulls found from the archaeological excavations at Tepe Hissar, Period I and II, near Damghan in Persia. In period III we find another mesocephalic (medium-headed) people, besides the dolichocephalic (long-headed) Aryans. On the West, at Alishar in Anatolia, the same type of long-headed skulls has been discovered in Period IV. The people of this race extended along the banks of the Indus, and are now found in the populations of the Punjab, Rajasthan, and Kashmir. They entered the adjacent regions of Tibet, as is evident from the physical features of the Ladakhis. They spread far into eastern India along the Ganga and also migrated into South India. The Todas of the Nilgiris constitute, in their ethnic composition, a branch of this race. The Namputiri Brahmanas migrated from North India during the fifth century A.D.

The mesocephalic (medium-headed) people form another immigrant population in India from the Iranian plateau. They are known as Scythians. They appear to have followed the Indo-Aryans not only in India but also elsewhere. At present, Iran shows a predominantly mesocephalic population. Since some affinity seems to exist between the Iranians and the Scythians, these people may be called Irano-Scythians.

The dolichocephals and the mesocephals kept the north-western frontier of India so much occupied that little brachycephaly (broad-headed) people could infiltrate through them. Whatever brachycephaly has entered into India is probably due to the 'brachycephalic hordes' of the pre-historic period. They have not probably influenced appreciably the head-form of the peoples of Western India.

Population pressure appears to be the main cause of migration. In this connection, reference may be made to the "expulsion and attraction' theory of Haddon *(The Wanderings of Peoples*, Cambridge, 1911).

It appears, therefore, that India is a predominantly dolichocephalic country. The following people have this form of head :

(i) The aboriginal peoples of India. They show a basic Veddid strain in almost all of them in varying degrees. this strain owes its origin to the Veddas of Ceylon. Because of their similarity with the Australian aborigines, this ethnic element is also known as Australoid.

(ii) The Dravidians, as represented by the Tamils, Telugus, etc. of South India. They appear to have evolved out of the Veddids through various ecological changes. Their physical features have been changed by the varied environmental conditions.

(iii) The Caucasians or the Indo-Aryans. They entered India across the north-western frontier about 1200 B.C. with a different language and culture, and occupied the plains of the Indus and the Ganga upto the borders of Bengal. They overran the whole country and crossed over to Ceylon during the early centuries of the pre-Christian era. They also intermixed with other racial types, thereby bringing about many changes in physical features.

As already pointed out, the mesocephalic (medium-headed) people appear to have followed the Indo-Aryans into India. Much of their ethnic strain is due to the Irano-Scythians.

The brachycephalic (broad-headed) population of India has its origin in four different sources : (a) The Irano-Scythian element contained some brachycephaly. (b) The brachycephalic hordes of Central Asia (Pamirs) who entered India during the pre-historic times, (c) The Malayan, found in the coastal regions of the Chittagong Hill Tracts and Tirunelveli. (d) Mongolian.

Another immigrant population in India are the dolichocephalic Mundas. They got highly mixed up with the Veddids. They appear to have reached India along the eastern border.

The North-East Frontier of India is inhabited by a large number of tribes who appear to belong to different racial strains. Thus, the Naga tribes exhibit in them a strong Indonesian strain both in race and culture. Haddon tentatively suggested a strong ancient Australoid strain among the Khasi, Kuki, Manipuri, Miri, Kachari, etc. and in a weaker form among the Nagas. Assam and the north-east region of India have been occupied by the immigrants comparatively recently. The Ahom invasion of Assam took place during the thirteenth century. The Indonesian movements appear to be much earlier. Possibly, it began with the Polynesian movements during the first century B.C. A mongoloid strain is obvious among all the people of north-eastern region—their straight lank hair, high cheek bones, yellowish colour of skin and, above all, the short thickset build.

According to Sir Herbert Risley, India has seven racial types : (i) pre-Dravidian type surviving among primitive tribes of the hills and jungles. (ii) The Dravidian type living in the southern peninsula upto the Gangetic valley. (iii) The Indo-Aryan type of Kashmir, Punjab and Rajputana. (iv) The Aryo-Dravidian type in the Gangetic valley. (v) The Cytho-Dravidian type running east of Indus. (vi) The Mongoloid type found in Assam and the foothills of the eastern Himalayas. (vii) The Mongolo-Dravidian type.

## NOTES

1. D.G. Haring, *Contemporary Human Types,* Quoted in *Readings in Sociology,* edited by A.M.Lee, page 192
2. Ogburn and Nimkoff, *A Hand book of Sociology*, page 66
3. An article entitled *Race* by Franz Boas in Encyclopaedia of the Social Sciences, Volume XIII
4. D.G. Haring, op. cit., page 194
5. Clyde Kluckhohn and W.H.Kelly, *The Concept of Culture,* in *The Science of Man in the World Crisis,* quoted by Ely Chinoy in the book *Sociological Perspective*, page 14
6. MacIver and Page, *Society*, Page 407
7. Ogburn and Nimkoff, *A Hand book of Sociology,* page 68
8. An article entitled *Race Conflict* by Hans Kohn in Encyclopaedia of the Social Sciences, Volume XIII
9. Delisle Burns, *Political Ideals,* pages 175-176
10. Ogburn and Nimkoff, op. cit., page 545
11. *ibid,* page 545-546

12. An article entitled *Race Coflict* by Hans Kohn in Encyclopaedia of the Social Sciences, Volume XIII.
13. Carey was a contemporary of Abraham Lincoln. He was a successful businessman, a philosopher and a writer. Marx considered Carey " the only American economist of importance.
14. R.L. Bruckberger, *Image of America*, pages 171-172
15. An article entitled *Race Conflict* by Hans Kohn in Encyclopaedia of the Social Sciences, Volume XIII.
16. This section is based on material contained in an article entitled *Race and Race Movements in India* by Sasanka Sekhar Sarkar, D. Sc., in The Cultural Heritage of India, Vol.I, published by The Ramakrishna Mission Institute of Culture, Calcutta
17. Vol. I (Indian reprint, 1955), page 37

# CHAPTER FOURTEEN

# SOCIAL SYSTEM

The perspective of society as a system is found in the writings of Spencer and a few other writers. They gained this perspective from their experience of a biological organism. If anyone is interested in knowing how an organism functions. it is not enough for him to study separately the various parts of the organism, such as the brain, heart, lungs, liver, etc. He has to study and examine the parts in relation to one another for the simple reason that no part exists or functions in isolation. They all work together to maintain the organism. This means that the organism has to be viewed as a whole. Those who look upon society as a system has a similar perspective. It is not possible to gain an insight into the nature and functioning of a part of society, such as the family, the economic or religious institution, unless the various parts of society are seen to be inter-related and taken together, as a complete system. Just as a biologist studies a particular part of the body in terms of its contribution to the maintenance of the organism, so also, it is argued, a part of the society should be studied in terms of its contribution to the maintenance of the social system. Before we proceed further, it will be appropriate to define social system and a few other related terms.

## 1. WHAT IS A SOCIAL SYSTEM ?

The concept of system got currency in modern sociology only a few decades ago. Previously, the sociologists dealt with every social phenomenon as a phase of social organisation. In their analysis they did not make much use of the word 'system'. The reason which prompted sociologists to give up the previous approach and adopt a systems approach is that there was the need for a term which would "put the emphasis on the arrangement and interaction of parts". Talcott Parsons, more than anyone else in recent years, has given the concept of system currency in modern sociology . He defined social system thus: ".....a social system consists in a plurality of individual actors interacting with each other in a situation which at least has a physical or environmental aspect, actors who are motivated in terms of a tendency to the 'optimisation of gratification' and whose relation to their situations, including each other, is defined and mediated in terms of a system of culturally structured and shared symbols", (The Social System). Ogburn and Nimkoff have given a simplified version of this definition of Parsons: "A social system may be defined as a plurality of individuals interacting with each other according to shared cultural norms and meanings".[1]

A careful analysis of the above definition would show that the emphasis has been placed on interrelationship or interaction among individuals within the framework of a normative pattern. That is, individuals do not behave with one another erratically or in a haphazard manner. On the contrary, their mutual interaction is very much patterned. They play their roles in terms of the statuses they occupy in the society. The relationship among individuals is thus structured. Likewise, social groups function within the normative pattern of the society. Here also haphazard or erratic functioning of social groups is ruled out.

A system presupposes a structure that is designed to perform certain functions. A watch, for instance, may be considered to be a system because it has a structure consisting of different parts which are interrelated with one another in such a way as to perform its function, which in this case is to indicate correct time. If any part gets detached or if the balance existing among the parts is disturbed, the watch fails to fulfil its function, viz. of indicating the time correctly. If society is looked upon as a system, it also must have a structure consisting of various parts which are designed to perform certain functions of the system.

What are then the parts of the social structure ? From what has been discussed above, it follows that individuals and groups in a society may be considered to be parts of the social structure.We also noted that individuals and groups have patterned roles in terms of the prevailing social norms. Again, these social norms reflect the dominant values of society. Following Durkheim, we may consider social norms and values as 'things' and hence parts of the social structure. Radcliffe-Brown has defined social structure thus: "The components of social structure are human beings, the structure itself being an arrangement of persons in relationship institutionally defined and regulated".

We have seen that a system presupposes not only a structure but also certain functions which its structure is supposed to perform. What are the functions of the social system? Talcott Parsons has given a four-function paradigm. This paradigm posits that every social system must continually confront and solve the four sets of organisational problems indicated below. In abbreviated form, the four-function paradigm is referred to as AGIL.

1. Adaptation : The problems of adapting the social system to its physical and social environments. The most important problems in this respect are procuring resources needed for its activities, providing for protection against physical and social threats, and developing information relating to these.

2. Goal attainment : The organisational problem of effecting co-ordination in any collective tasks directed outside the system itself.

3. Integration : The internal problem of maintaining satisfying relations among the interacting members and avoiding disrupting conflicts. For small groups, this concerns inter-personal relations. For larger organisation, it concerns inter-group relations.

4. Latent pattern maintenance : The internal organisational problem of ordering activity patterns of the system, and also of adjusting the role demands on members, so that these are compatible with their other role commitments.

It is evident that the first two organisational problems concern the external relations of the social system with its environment, including its physical habitat, the bodily needs of its members, and other social systems with which it comes in contact. The second pair of problems concern the internal organisation of the social system as a human group of socialised and interacting persons with cultural commitments.

How does a social system ensure that these important functions are properly performed ? The society sets up various institutions which are "a constellation of socially significant customs collected around some function or set of functions, such as ruling, fighting and worshipping......"[2] We may identify five of these great social institutions—namely, family, economic, political, educational, and religious institutions —which are found in all societies in all eras and in all parts of the world. These institutions" centre upon getting food and other items of wealth, procreation, worship,and ruling. Getting a living, begetting and rearing children, believing in higher powers, and enforcing order are repetitive activites found in Babylon and in New York, among the Australian aborigines and among the Australian whites"[3]. The social institutions are all closely interrelated and they form a complex whole. That is why institutions are referred to as "a cluster of institutions", one impinging upon the others.

The social system, the social structure with its interrelated parts, the basic functions of the system together with corresponding institutions designed to fulfil these functions are set out in diagrammatic form below :

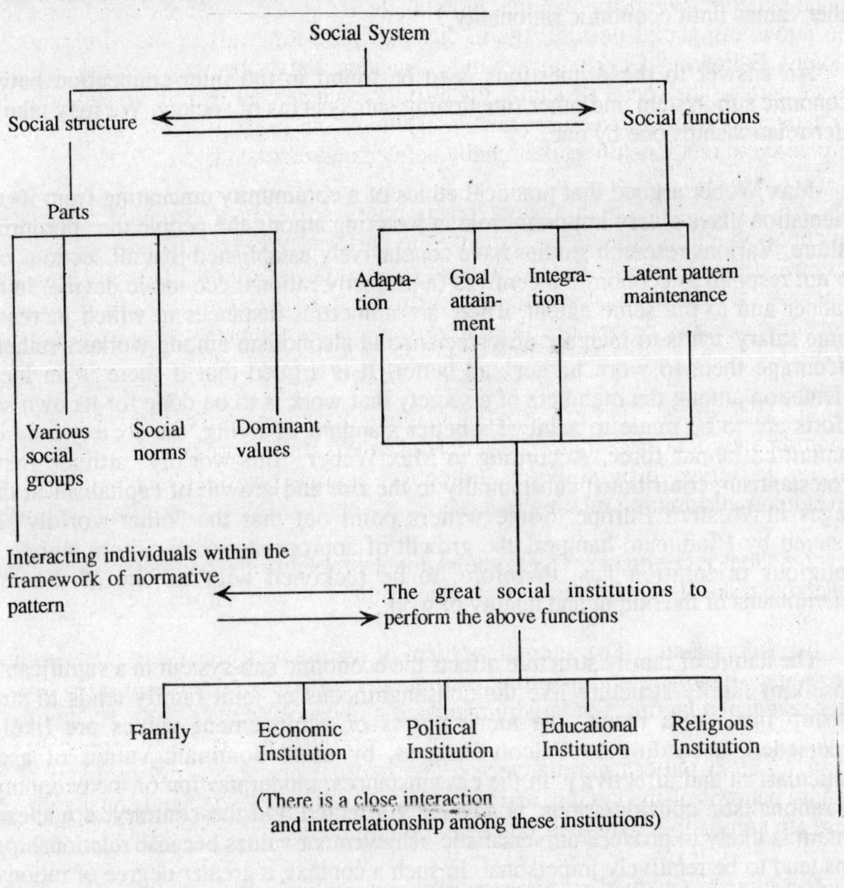


## 2. INTER-RELATIONSHIP OF INSTITUTIONS

The inter-relationship and interaction among various social institutions may be discussed with reference to an example.

An economic institution, for instance, is a system in which goods and services are produced and provided for the community. The production and distribution of these goods and services are, *ideally speaking*, governed by *rational economic motives*, viz., the motive of maximising productivity and minimising cost. This implies that the factors of production are put to the best use at a minimum cost. This is the picture of an *ideal* economy.

In actual practice, however, this is far from true. Since the economic institution is part of the social system, it should be deemed to be a sub-system that is tied to other sub-systems of the society, such as, religious, familial, educational and political sub-systems. For obvious reasons, therefore, the economic sub-system is very much affected by the activities of other sub-systems.

In this context, two questions may be raised. First, one of the important sociological questions about any economy is the *degree to which economic rationality is limited by values* nurtured in other sub-systems. Second, another related question is : *In what ways* do other values limit economic rationality ?

An answer to these questions is to be found in the inter-connection between the economic sub-system and other functioning sub-systems of society. We may take up these inter-relationships one by one.

Max Weber argued that practical ethics of a community emanating from its religious orientation plays a very important role in fostering among the people the appropriate work culture. Various research studies have conclusively established that all sections of people do not respond to economic incentives (a perfectly rational economic device) in the same manner and to the same extent. There are numerous instances in which increased 'take home salary' tends to increase absenteeism and alcoholism among workers rather than to encourage them to work harder and better. It is argued that if there is an ideological orientation among the members of a society that work is to be done for its own sake, that efforts are to be made to achieve a better standard of living, the society may expect a committed labour force. According to Max Weber, "this-worldly" attitude fostered by Protestantism, contributed substantially to the rise and growth of capitalism in the initial stages in Western Europe. Some writers point out that the "other-worldly" attitude, fostered by Hinduism, hampers the growth of appropriate work culture among Hindus. Religious orientation has, therefore, to be reckoned with as one of the important determinants of the output and quality of work.

The nature of family structure affects the economic sub-system in a significant way. A close-knit family structure like the consanguineous or joint family tends to strengthen kinship ties. As a result, the merit norms or achievement values are likely to be superseded, according to Talcott Parsons, by more dominant values of ascription, particularism and affectivity. In the circumstances, modernisation of the economy, based on rationalistic considerations, is adversely affected. On the contrary, a nuclear family pattern is likely to produce universalistic-achievement values because relationships among kins tend to be relatively impersonal. In such a context, a greater degree of rationalisation to likely is pervade the entire society, including the economy.

Political sub-system affects the economy in various ways. In the first place, an enviornment conducive to hard and honest labour can be created and sustained only by the political authority. Gunnar Myrdal characterised the governments of the Third World as "soft" governments, meaning thereby that these governments are unable or unwilling to take hard decisions affecting the society as a whole, and the economy in particular. Vices of corruption, nepotism, unwholesome industrial relations, unhealthy and inequitable distribution of wealth and income—which have a very close bearing on the efficient functioning of the economy—can be tackled by a government which has the political will to do so. In most of the developing societies such political will is unfortunately missing, with the result that the economy stagnates. Secondly, the ideology which informs political institutions also affects the economy. For instance, some of the countries of the developing world uphold the ideal of socialism as the guiding principle for moulding the economic system. The result is that the pitfalls of socialistic economy in terms of diminished productivity and efficiency are overlooked. Pragmatic considerations are superseded by ideological commitment to socialism, even when socialistic patterning of the economy proves to be economically wasteful. Economic sub-system is, therefore, very much affected by the nature of political institution prevalent in a society.

The importance of the educational institution *vis-a-vis* the economy cannot be over-emphasised, particularly in the modern world. History of industrial advance since the eighteenth century is marked by use of various kinds of energy one after the other. vis., steam power, electrical power and electronic power. The latest innovation is the use of robots in industrial production. Obviously, educational system has a very important role to play in producing skilled man-power to run industrial establishments on modern lines. Further, various management strategies have been developed in order to achieve optimum utilisation of the factors of production. The prospective managers have to be taught the necessary skills in this field also. As Daniel Bell has argued, we are gradually moving towards a new knowledge society. Knowledge has, of course, been necessary in the functioning of any society. What is distinctive of the present-day society is the change in the character of knowledge itself. There is greater emphasis now-a-days on theoretical knowledge as opposed to empirical knowledge. Every modern society has to carry on continuous research on various experiments and innovation in the field of production and management. Those who will fail to do so run the risk of being thrown out of the race for economic advance. The educational system has, therefore, to be geared to meet these challenges.

The above discussion throws into focus the inter-relationship among various institutions. It is clear that no institution can be isolated from other institutions and treated as an exclusive category. That is why the five great social institutions are referred to as a 'cluster' of institutions.

## 3. STRUCTURAL FUNCTIONAL ANALYSIS

In modern social sciences few concepts have generated so much discussion and controversy as those of structure and function and the various analyses associated with them. At the outset, it should be made clear that structural-functional analysis is not at all new either in the social or in the natural sciences. If there is anything new in the analysis, it is its formidable name.

There are variations among structural-functionalists in emphasis and in the extent of their acceptance of an organic analogy of society. The basic perspective of the structural-functional point of view is to be found in its main emphasis upon society and upon the inter-relations of its institutions, rather than on the individual or groups or an isolated institution. The basic question with which the theory is concerned is this : How is social life maintained over time in spite of the fact that membership of society changes completely from generation to generation ? The explanation which the theory offers is this: "Social life persists because societies find means (structures) whereby they fulfil the needs (functions) which are either pre-conditions or consequences of organised social life". Thus, if a society is to survive and continue, it must find new members to take the place of those who are dead. In all known societies, this requirement is met by some form of family system. The family is an institution which acts 'for' the society by ensuring that the functions of sexual reproduction, of early care of the dependent baby and of his initiation into the ways of society in which he will live his entire life or a considerable period of his life are undertaken with ease in the socially approved manner. The significance of other institutions in the maintenance of social life over time may be similarly explained.

Another basic question (though related to the first) with which the theory is concerned is this : How is the *unity* of social life maintained ? The structural-functionalist theory deals "with the way in which the different structures are co-ordinated and integrated to preserve the unity of society as a complete system (or organism)". The theory does not take up for analysis any institution or structure in isolation from other institutions or structures. In other words, the structural functionalists take a total view of society.

We should note, however, that 'social structure' is an abstract concept which is useful as an analytical tool. In a society human beings are connected by a complex network of social relations. The term 'social structure' is used to denote this network of actually existing relations. Since it is a conceptual tool, we can understand social structure only in terms of the functions or roles of its component units. Classification of a particular phenomenon as a function or as a structure depends on the point of view from which the phenomenon concerned is discussed. What is a function from one point of view is a structure from another. For example, the politeness of small children may be considered as a structure of their behaviour or as a function of operation in terms of the structures (that is, patterns) of discipline enforced by their parents.

Confusion, however, arises because of the variety of meanings in which these two terms are used. The difficulty is much greater with the concept of function than with the associated concept of structure. Most of the general discussions in the literature have been largely pre-occupied with the concept of function. The concept of structure has largely been left undiscussed. To prevent confusion, the most general form of the concepts "structure" and "function" must be defined in such a manner that the other uses of the terms represent sub-categories. The term 'function" may be defined as any condition or any state of affairs which result from the operation (mere persistence is also included in the term 'operation') of a unit of the type under consideration in terms of a structure. In the case of the biological sciences that unit is usually an organism or a sub-system of an organism. In the case of the social sciences the unit is usually a system of action involving a set of one or more persons (actors). The term 'structure' may be defined as a pattern, as an observable uniformity, in terms of which action or operation takes place.

The contribution of structural- functional point of view to sociological thought and research may be summarised as follows :

(i) Many features of society which appear, on the surface, to be devoid of any significance to social life become meaningful when we relate these features to their functions—that is, the contributions of these features "to the flow of social life". Reference may be made to "the significance of public ceremonials as a way of increasing social solidarity (vide Durkheim, Elementary Forms of Religious Life). Similarly, the practice of offering ceremonial gifts, which is widely prevalent in all societies, becomes meaningful when seen in this light.

(ii) The emphasis of the structural—functionalist approach on the inter-relatedness of several parts of society makes us aware of the fact that a change in one part of society, whether intended or unintended, affects other parts of society. This perspective is particularly valuable to social planners. Structural-functionalists have taught us to see society as a "whole".

(iii) The structural-functional theory has been of great help in making comparative studies of societies in various stages of development. For example, in primitive societies there may not exist a government in the sense in which we use the term. There may not also exist the complex economic structure of the type we are familiar with. But even such societies must have some arrangement to regulate the use of force or to provide for the flow of goods and services. Otherwise, such societies could not exist. In our study of a primitive or strange society we shall naturally look for the institutions which meet these and similar other urgent requirements of society. The structural—functional theory, therefore, widens our perspective and broadens our horizon "concerning the possibilities for variation in the forms of social life".

The structural-functional theory has, however, been subjected to various criticisms.

In the first place, reference has already been made to the varied uses of the term 'function' by the advocates of the theory. Most often, the term 'function' is used in the sense of 'eufunction'. ("With respect to a given unit 'eufunction' may be defined as any function that increases or maintains adaptation or adjustment of the unit to the unit's setting, thus making for the persistence of the unit as defined in its setting"). The critics point out that what may be 'functional' from the point of view of the structure or unit may not be 'functional' for the individual or for a section of the people. Aristotle justified the institution of slavery, saying that it was not only necessary but also desirable. If we accept Aristotle's contention as valid, we have to answer the question : Was it equally 'functional' for the slaves ? It is, therefore, held that "the functionalist point of view easily leads one to under-emphasise the importance of the individual and his needs relative to those of the group".

Secondly, the structural-functional approach is criticised on the ground that it is teleological. "Function seems only another word for purpose, and it is often argued that a person can have purpose but that a collectivity cannot".

In reply to this criticism, it is held that "many groups act so effectively in unision that it seems "as if they were a single organism possessed of only a single will or purpose". It must also be pointed out, in fairness to the exponents of the theory, that the leading advocates of the theory use 'function' only to mean 'as a consequence of', thus avoiding value-judgments and teleological implications altogether.

Thirdly, the structural-functionalist approach is criticised on the ground that it is concerned with the *status quo* and that the possibilities of social change are virtually ruled out. It is an equilibrium model based on assumptions of consensus. Conflict situations have been neglected. The theory, therefore, tends to produce an impression that everything which exists in a society at any given time is easily assumed to be there because it is 'functional'. "Worse still, the theory produces an apprehension that no social institution, because it is considered to be 'functional', can be changed or abolished without endangering the system. On these grounds, the critics conclude that the structural-functional approach "serves as a politically conservative influence in sociological thinking".

The aforesaid criticisms appear to be based on a totally wrong interpretation of the theory. One should not ignore the fact that the theory is only a model, a paradigm. The structural-functional approach involves "a more limited time perspective", as compared to an evolutionary perspective of society in which "time, stages of development, and change" are of central interest. "The structural-functional approach stops the motions of the system at a fixed point in time in order to understand how, at that moment, it works as a system"4. If one remembers that the structural-functional theory is simply an analytical tool to find out how the system actually works, many of the criticisms levelled against it would appear to be misplaced. Stability assumptions of the theory are quite in order when it is interpreted and understood as a model for analysing society. Part of the blame for misinterpreting the theory has to be shared by some of the proponents who looked upon the structural-functional approach as a master key to sociology. Some of the advocates of the theory even tend ' to invent functions for everything in sight".

## Functional and Structural Requisites

The stability assumptions of the theory may be further examined with reference to the concepts of functional and structural requisites. A functional requisite may be defined as a condition which is necessary for the maintenance of the type of unit under consideration, given the general setting of such a unit. In seeking to discover the functional requisites of a unit, one asks the question : What must be done to maintain the system concerned in its setting on the level under consideration ? A given condition is a functional requisite if its removal (or absence ) would result in (a) the total dissolution of the unit, or (b) the change of one of the structural elements of the unit (i.e., one of the structural requisites). A structural requisite may be defined as a pattern of action (or operation) which is necessary for the continued existence of the type of unit under consideration, given the general setting of such a unit. Briefly speaking, functional requisites are answers to the question : What must be done ? Structural requisites are answers to the question : How must what must be done be done ? Both the questions invlolve the qualifying phrase : If the unit is to persist in its setting without change (i.e., alteration of structures) on the level under consideration.

Most of the misunderstanding with regard to the stability assumption of structural functional theory has been associated with this question of persistence. It should be borne in mind that on the basis of an assumption of stability one gets at a list of requisites. This does not mean that any unit which is analysed on the basis of such an assumption must, in fact, be stable. To make such units stable by definition is to reduce most discussions of this sort to trivia. To use a stability assumption as an element in a model (i.e., paradigm) does not.

There is nothing new about requisite analysis. There has never been a time in which people failed to ask questions as to whether given conditions or patterns were not in some sense necessary for the continued existence of certain types of units.

## Functional and structural pre-requisites

The requisite concepts are not obviously concerned with questions of change. The pre-requisite concepts are, on the contrary, oriented towards questions of change. All questions of change involve comparisons between at least two of at least three possible stages. These are : an initial stage, a transitional stage and a resultant stage. Systematic knowledge about any two of these stages makes possible systematic derivation (prediction or postdiction) or knowledge about the third stage.

A functional pre-requisite may be defined as a function that must pre-exist if a given unit is to come into being in a particular setting. Correspondingly, a structural prerequisite may be defined as a structure that must pre-exist if a given unit is to come into being in a particular setting.

The closer that two states of a given unit under consideration are in point of time, the greater is the probability that the requisites and the pre-requisities of a given unit will be identical. If, however, the two stages of a given unit under consideration are separated by a long time-gap, the probability is that the requisites and pre-requisites of a given unit will be different. The following illustrations may be cited. In trying to understand the problems of development in 'developing' countries, it is sometimes erroneously assumed that the requisites and pre-requisites of a 'developed' country must or do coincide. Thus, it is supposed that all the structural requisites of the present-day American society which may enable it to continue as a highly modernised society are identical with the structures that must pre-exist if India or any other 'developing' country is to develop as a highly modernised society. Similarly, the structural pre-requisities which enabled the United States to embark upon industrialisation in the nineteenth century are not identical with the structural pre-requisites which would enable an 'under-developed' or a 'developing' country in the late twentieth century to embark upon modernisation and industrialisation.

### Varieties of functional analysis

For the past few decades functional analysis has been a major approach to understand and explain the organisation of society. But the term 'functional analysis' or 'structural—functionalism' has been applied to a great variety of approaches which share only one common element or feature, namely, relating one part of a society or social system to another part or to some aspect of the whole. Within this variety, sharing the aforesaid common element, three types of functionalism can be distinguished.

#### (i) Postulate of the Functional Unity of Society

The first type is based on the concepts and assumptions of sociology. It stresses sociological analysis, as opposed to psychological or historical analysis. The basic assumption of this type of analysis is that a pattern or an ordered relationship among various social institutions is discernible. This basic assumption is also accompanied by an implicit consensus among the proponents on the important elements of social structure which consist of social groups and various social institutions.

Radcliffe-Brown puts this postulate of functional unity in explicit terms : "The function of a particular social usage is the contribution it makes to the *total social life* as the functioning of the *total social system*. Such a view implies that a social system.........has a certain kind of unity, which we may speak of as a functional unity. We may define it as a condition in which all parts of the social system work together with a sufficient degree of harmony or internal consistency, i.e., without producting presistent conflicts which can neither be resolved nor regulated"[5].

#### (ii) Postulate of Universal Functionalism

This type of functional analysis may be called traditional functional analysis because it is most widely used. It is based on the assumption that the elements of the social structure assist in the integration and adaptation of the larger social system. There are two other distinguishing features of this type of functional analysis. First, a social pattern is explained by the effects or consequences of the pattern. Second, these consequences must be beneficial and necessary to the proper functioning of society. The functionalists, who belong to this group, take up a few aspects of society at a time and link one pattern or social institution with one need and thus attempt to 'explain' the pattern.

Malinowski advances this point of view in its most extreme form : 'The functional view of culture *insists* therefore upon the principle that in every type of civilization, every custom, material object, idea and belief fulfills some *vital function....". Kluckhohn in Navaho Witchcraft* joins Malinowski in postulating functional value for all surviving forms of culture : "My basic postulate.... is that no culture forms survive unless they constitute responses which are adjustive or adaptive, in some sense ....."[6].

Another postulate, called the postulate of indispensability, follows from the postulate of universal functionalism. If is is assumed that social institutions perform vital functions, it is only the next step to conclude that these institutions are indispensable[7].

(iii) **Formal functionalism**

The third type of functional analysis may be called formal functionalism. "This approach is concerned with homeostatic or equilibrating systems, and so with feedback and self-regulation". It abandons the basic assumption of traditional functionalism that the consequences or effects of a pattern must always be beneficial or necessary. According to this type of functional analysis, the consequences or effects may or may not be beneficial or necessary to society. This approach is called 'formal' because it is not based on a substantive hypothesis about empirical events. Formal functionalism consists in the attempt to construct models that describe how the units of a system are inter-related so as to maintain each other or some other state of the system.

R.K.Merton, whose views fall broadly in line with formal functionalism, observes "that the motive and the function vary idependently and that the failure to register this fact.... has contributed to the unwitting tendency among sociologists to confuse the subjective categories of motivation with the objective categories of function"8. Merton observes further that ' in functional theory, stripped of those traditional postulates which have fenced it in and often made it little more than a latter-day rationalisation of existing practices, sociology has one beginning of a systematic and empirically relevant mode of analysis"[9].

## NOTES

1. Ogburn and Nimkoff, *A Handbook of Sociology*, page 331
2. *ibid*, page 334
3. *ibid*, page 334
4. Alex Inkeles, *What is Sociology ?* page 35
5. R.K. Merton, *Social Theory and Social Structure*, pages 79-80
6. *ibid*, pages 84-85
7. *ibid*, page 86
8. *ibid*, pages 114-115
9. *ibid*, page 136

# CHAPTER FIFTEEN

# MARRIAGE AND THE FAMILY

Society is a conglomeration of families.It is necessary, therefore, that the problems of family ought to be studied in order to study the problems of society. In no other social institution is it easier to detect influences of the rapid social and economic changes that are overtaking society in every country as a result of industrial revolution. Family has, therefore, been studied from different standpoints by different scholars, social scientists, psychologists, psychiatrists, and all serious students of human behaviour.

An objective unbiased study of family is, however, beset with innumerable difficulties, sometimes almost insurmountable.The family is, in the first place. "a relationship charged with emotion". It is almost impossible to view without bias one's own home situation. Secondly, the family also"hides itself behind a privacy not shared by any other institution".In most cases, family members are unwilling to express in perfect frankness their most intimate experiences, particularly when these disclosures are likely to affect their self-respect.

## 1.. DEFINITION OF FAMILY

A human child needs care and protection for its survival for a longer period than is necessary for the survival of other animal babies.The relationship that develops around reproduction and care of off-spring between father, mother and children is thus lengthened, enlarged and refined. The term family is used to refer to that portion of human experience which results from the behaviour of men and women in connection with reproduction and care of off-spring. Both these activities, related to reproduction and care of the offspring, have the biological purpose of the survival of the species. This distinguishes the family from all other associations that grow out of the needs of the individual organism so as to fulfil them. The family came into being to satisfy three primary needs. There is, in the first place, the sex urge which has driven man and woman to seek an established basis for its satisfaction.Secondly, there is the reproductive urge, particularly strong among women, which finds its fulfilment in the family. Thirdly, in its attempt to perform a biological and social function, the family is necessarily forced to assume economic responsibilities and, as a consequence, becomes an economic unit.

"The family", according to MacIver and Page, "is a group defined by a sex relationship sufficiently precise and enduring to provide for the procreation and upbringing of children". Having defined family in this manner, they bring out its characteristic features as follows : (i) It is a mating relationship which is determined and maintained by some form of marriage. (ii) It provides a system of reckoning descent. (iii) The family must have some economic provision to meet "the economic needs associated with child bearing and child rearing". (iv) The family must have a habitation, home or household which it may either enjoy exclusively or share with others.

### Distinction between domestic group and family

The word 'family' has its origin in a Latin word which could be roughly equated with 'domestic group'. But for sociological purposes the two must be sharply distinguished.

A 'domestic group may be defined as a group of people who habitually share a common dwelling and a common food supply. These minimal activities of domestic groups may be greatly extended, and, as a result, domestic groups may vary in size and stability. Thus domestic groups may be made up of individuals between whom no kinship ties exist. Conversely, members of one family may be distributed over two or more domestic groups.

The term 'household' may be used interchangeably with 'domestic group'.

**Distinction between 'pater' and 'genitor'**

In the case of the father-child relationship., the disjunction between biological and social paternity has led to a distinction between 'pater' and 'genitor'. The former term is used to refer to a child's legally recognised father and the latter to his supposed biological father. In come societies a child's father (pater) may be a woman or a dead man. Among the Nuer of East Africa, the kin of a man killed in war before he had married would sometimes marry a woman to "his name". After payment of the bride price the woman cohabited with a lover, but any children born to her were the legal offspring of the dead "husband", inheriting from him and sacrificing to him as their ancestor. Cases such as this make clear the differences between biological and social links.'[1]

## 2. FUNCTIONS OF THE FAMILY

It is evident from the definition of family, as given by Maclver and Page, that family fulfils certain functions that are vital to community life. It meets emotional and sexual needs, it ensures the reproduction of children; it acts as basic economic unit; and it provides for the care and training of children. Societies vary enormously in the importance they attach to each of these functions.

We may analyse the functions of the family in greater details, dividing for analytical purposes, the importance of these functions to the individual and to the society. It should however, be borne in mind that the functions of the family for society are inseparable from its functions for its individual members. It serves both at one and the same time and in much the same way. The analysis of functions, as given in the following paragraphs, provides examples of this.

**Importance to the individual**

"The family is the only social institution charged with transforming a biological organism into a human being"[2]. What is the nature of this biological organism ? Like many other animals, man is helpless at birth and would die quickly without care. Unlike most other animals, however, man cannot become self-reliant until several years have passed after birth. There are a few other traits which are unique to man as compared to other animals. Man matures much later than any other animal. At what age man reaches enough maturity so as to be self-reliant is a matter of speculation, because maturity does not simply mean physical maturity. Even if he develops physically, he cannot protect himself or collect his food simply on the basis of physical strength.This is because of the fact that, unlike lower animals, he is not endowed with instinct which may simplify his adjustment to the environment. "No instincts impel him to build a shelter, to kill other animals, to grow plants, or to create tools"[3]. His reflexes are very limited in scope and do not seem sufficient to enable him to survive alone. His lack of instinct is, however, compensated by his possession of the most complex brain among all animals. The last-named trait enabled man to build several cultural aids to protect himself, to collect food, to build shelter, etc. Among many other cultural aids, the family is one which he builds in order "to be fed,protected and taught what nature has not provided"[4]. Family thus transforms a biological organism into a human being introducing him to several cultural aids by way of compensating, as it were, nature's failure to teach him the instinctive art of survival.

Secondly, family enables adults of both sexes—husband and wife—to maintain a socially approved sexual relationship. Besides, the family shapes, channelises and restricts the sex drive of man in all societies in terms of social norms. "Some people who might be physically attractive and geographically available—for example, sisters and brothers—come to be viewed as impossible sex partners, who arouse no conscious sex desire at all"[5].This is because "our complex neural mechanism permits a rich conditioning to occur, by which only certain familial behavioural patterns seem right or desirable"[6].

Thirdly, the family helps an individual develop an integrated personality. Man is a cultural being and, as such, he has both emotional and physical needs. He needs food, protection and care for his survival. He also needs love, affection, understanding and sympathy for satisfaction of his emotional needs. In their absence, he would fail to develop a well-rounded personality. The family creates the necessary environment in which his personality may blossom basked by the warmth of family affection. Family is, therefore, described by Talcott Parsons as a 'factory' which produces human personality.

Fourthly, since an individual is born in a family, he acquires a social status at birth—the son or daughter of a particular family, the membership of a particular class or caste, etc. This kind of social status which we acquire at birth through our family fulfils our sense of security. We become conscious at a very early age in life what we should or should not expect from others and what others may expect from us.

**Importance to the society**

The importance of family to the society may be discussed from the following points of view.

To begin with, the family provides opportunity for the sexual gratification for the spouses. At the same time, the sexual function of the family helps to stabilise society. The prescriptive and proscriptive rules which contain sexual activity between the spouses within the family prevent the probable disruptive effects on social order that would result if the sex drive were allowed 'free play'. A family thus provides both 'control and expression' of sexual drives and in doing so performs important functions for its individual members, for the family as an institution and for society as a whole.

Secondly, the reproductive functions of the family helps the human species to survive. We have already noted the helpless condition of a human baby at birth and for several years thereafter. For his survival it is necessary that the family must feed and protect him and, at the same time, teach him various cultural aids. If the family does not make adequate provision for the biological needs of man and teach him all other cultural aids that are required for his survival, he would die and obviously society also would die.

Thirdly, Talcott Parsons refers to two "basic and irreducible functions" which the family performs in all societies. These are the 'primary socialisation of children" and the "stabilisation of the adult personalities of the population of the society".

By 'primary socialisation' Talcott Parsons refers to socialisation during the early years of childhood which takes place within the narrow circle of the family. This is to be distinguished from 'secondary socialisation' which takes place in later years when the family is less involved and the other agencies like the peer group and the school exert increasing influence. Parsons points out that two basic processes are involved in primary socialisation : First, the internalization of society's culture; second, the structuring of the personality in terms of society's culture. The internalization of society's culture is essential for the existence of society, because society cannot exist in the absence of shared norms and values. Likewise, if the child's personality is not moulded in terms of the central values of society's culture he would be a misfit in society in later life. Talcott Parsons believes that family is essential for producing 'socialised' personalities. Primary socialization requires a context which provides warmth, security and mutual support. He can conceive of no institution other than family which could provide this context.

Parsons argues that it is not enough to produce the personality. Once produced, the personality must be kept stable This is the second important function of family to which Parsons refers. Family creates a situation in which the spouses provide emotional security and affectionate sympathy for each other. This enables the couple to stand the strains and stresses of everyday life which tend to make the personality unstable Besides, the family relationship allows the adult members to act out 'childish' elements of their own personalities which they have retained from childhood but which cannot be given expression in an adult company. For example, the father plays with his son's toy train and indulges in many other childish pranks in his child's company. This is as necessary for father as for his son. The family, therefore, provides a situation in which 'husband and wife can express their childish whims, give and receive emotional support, recharge their childish whims, give and receive emotional support, recharge their batteries and so stabilise their personalities".

Fourthly, "the family is the fundamental instrumental foundation of the larger social structure........ The role behaviour that is learned within the family becomes the model or prototype for role behaviour required in other segments of the society. The content of the socialization process is the cultural traditions of the society; by passing them to the next generation the family acts as a conduit or transmission belt by which the culture is kept alive"[8].

**Family and the larger society**

While considering the functions of the family, it will be appropriate to consider also the relationship between the family on the one hand and the larger society on the other. The family, as we have seen in the previous chapter, is a part, a sub-system of the larger social system. While the family indoctrinates the child into certain values and in various other ways teaches the child to adapt to the social norms and grow up to be a 'fit' member of the society, the family acts merely as an agent of the larger society. "The family transmits values which are determined elsewhere; it is an agent, not a principal"[9].

We have to consider, in the second place, the impact of the changes which take place in the larger society on the family. In no other social institution is it easier to detect the impact of rapid social and economic changes that are overtaking society in every country as a result of technological revolution and industrialisation. Various kinds of household gadgets have relieved women of the drudgery involved in pursuing day-to-day domestic chores, making it possible for them to participate in activities outside the home. Similarly, industrialisation has shattered agrarian family structure and helped to usher in family patterns suited to demands of factory life and urban living which, by the way, is itself a consequence of industialisation. In the words of Bottomore : "..... Social change originates in other institutions, not in the family; the family changes in response"[10].

Thirdly, "the family is the keystone of the stratification system, the social mechanism by which it is maintained"[11]. It is the family, not merely the individual, that is ranked in the class structure. Thus, one is a Brahmin or a Sudra by being born into a Brahmin or a Sudra family. An individual gets the class ranking from the position of his family in the class hierarchy. It is very interesting to consider one common experience. An individual belonging to a class ranked high in the class hierarchy may invite a person who enjoys a comparatively lower social ranking to join him at a dinner in some hotel or restaurant. But he would hesitate to invite him to a family dinner. This is to be found not only in Indian society in which caste and religion prevent commensal relationships from growing among individuals belonging to different castes or religions, but also in Western stratified societies. In the interaction of families one can notice both distance and equality on caste or class lines. Moreover, ".......homogamy ........... bolsters the existing class structure"[12]. There is a tendency in all stratified societies to marry into a family equal in ranking to one's social class. It is thus evident that family not only maintains but also strengthens the existing class division.

## 3. VARIATION IN FAMILY PATTERNS

Though the conditions which are responsible for the growth of the institution of family are almost universal. yet different societies have met these conditions differently. Hence the family has varied greatly in different cultures. We may consider some of these variations as follows.

### (i) Variation based on family circle

The family may grow up around the nucleus of husband, wife and children. This type of family is called conjugal or nuclear family.

*Distinction between conjugal and nuclear family*

Though these two terms are used interchangeably, there is a subtle distinction between the two. Either term may be used interchangeably when reference is made to the family unit itself. But the term 'conjugal' is preferable when reference is made to the family system as a whole. By 'family system' we mean that the members of the nuclear family maintain relations with their more extended kin. All contemporary studies in the industrialised Western countries, including U.K. and U.S.A., indicate that 'visiting the relatives' during week-ends is the largest single category of 'recreation' for the members of nuclear families. In this sense, no nuclear family system exists. When we use the term 'nuclear,' greater emphasis is placed on the structural form of the nuclear family. When, on the other hand, we use the term 'conjugal'. greater emphasis is placed upon the social aspects of the conjugal tie[13].

*Consanguineous or joint family*

We have another type of family "where the central core is the relations of blood kin, of brothers and sisters, or of parents and off-spring". The bonds between these blood kins seem stronger than these spouses. Hence, such a family is depicted as "a nucleus of blood relatives surrounded by a fringe of spouses". This type of family is called 'consanguineous family', since the family group is organised around blood ties rather than around marital ties between husband and wife, as in a conjugal or nuclear family. The consanguineous family is also known as joint or extended family.

*Distinction between a joint family and an extended family*

Some anthropologists, however, make a distinction between a joint family and an extended family. According to the handbook " Notes and Queries on Anthropology", a joint family exists when "two or more lineally related kinsfolk of the same sex, their spouses and off-spring, occupy a single homestead and are jointly subject to the same authority or single head". An example would be a group consisting of a man and his wife with their married sons and their wives and children. It would be wrong to think of such a group as being a mere mechanical aggregate of nuclear families. Joint families generally arise, exist and persist because they carry out activities more extensive than would be possible for a nuclear family group. An extended family, on the other hand, is a dispersed version of the joint family. The members of the constituent groups of an extended family do not all live together in one dwelling. They usually live close together and engage in common activities.

The concept of extended family exhausts the usefulness of the word 'family' for this kind of empirical classification, since an extended family is a short lineage (for the meaning of the word 'lineage' consult the Chapter on Kinship) and can be discussed in terms of lineage theory. Or, it is a kindred and may be analysed as such. Since birth is the criterion of membership in lineages and kindreds, they tend to develop considerable interest in the birth, training and ultimate loyalties of their recruits, so that there is a close 'fit' between these formations and the 'families' which provide and train the recruits.

*Compound family*

When a concrete group is formed through the amalgamation of nuclear-family units or parts of them, it is known as 'compound family". A polygynous household consisting of one man, his wives, and their respective children would constitute a compound family A family group consisting of re-married widow or divorcee with children from a previous marriage would also constitute a compound family. A compound family need not constitute a co-residential group.

*Famille-souche or stem family*

In the 19th century, Le Play constructed a typology of European family structures ranging from the patriarchal systems of the semi-feudal Eastern European areas, which resulted in the development of extended families, through the famille-souche, or stem family, of the semi-industrial areas to what he considered to be the unstable and disorganised systems of the urban industrial areas.

Le Play considered famille-souche, or stem family, as preserving familial continuity while adapting to the demands of industrialism. While many of the younger members of the family migrated or went to work in industrial centres, the main family, or stem, continued and was generally located on its own land or in its own house[15].

**(ii) Variation based on post-marital residence**

When the newly-wed couples establish independent domestic units after marriage, it is known as 'neolocal residence'. This practice is in vogue in Western societies.

When marriage takes place in a consanguineous family, one of the partners joins the family of the other partner. When a husband joins the family of his wife, the system is known as 'matrilocal residence'. We have such a practice among the Khasis in Meghalaya. When a wife joins the family of her husband, the system is known as 'patrilocal residence'. This practice is in vogue all throughout India with a very small number of exceptions.

Residence is characterised as virilocal when the couple joins a domestic group in which the husband resided prior to marriage and in which he rather than the wife has proprietory or other claims.

Residence is called uxorilocal when the couple joins the domestic group to which the wife was attached prior to her marriage and in which the wife rather than the husband has proprietory or other claims.

The above terms may be compounded with others to describe more precisely the nature of the domestic group joined by the couple. Thus, 'viriparilocal residence' refers to domicile in a domestic group whose core includes the groom's father. 'Uxorimatrilocal residence' refers to domicile in a group whose core includes the bride's mother.

The term avunculocal is used to describe residence in a group whose core includes the groom's mother's brother.

### (iii) Variation based on the principle of descent

The mode of inheritance of family name and property, of reckoning of descent and succession to rank and office lead to a four-fold classification of (a) patrilineal in which property inheritance and reckoning of descent take place along the male line, (b) matrilineal in which property inheritance and reckoning of descent take place along the female line, (c) patronymic in which the off-spring inherit the father's name, and (d) matronymic in which the off-spring inherit the mother's name.

### (iv) Variation based on authority

From the point of view of exercise of authority, a family may be classified as (a) partriarchal or patripotestal in which authority lies with the father, (b) matriarchal or matripotestal in which authority lies with the mother, and (c) avuncu potestal in which authority lies with groom's mother's brother.

(v) A distinction is also made between the family of origin or orientation in which one is born and the family of procreation which one helps to set up after one's marriage.

## 4. THE AGRARIAN FAMILY

A major theme in sociological studies of the family is the relationship between the structure of the family and the process of industrialisation. Under the impact of industrialisation, the family has undergone tremendous changes in the Western societies. Similar changes have just started appearing on the Indian scene as a consequence of rapid industrial growth and spread of technology. These changes may be understood better with reference to the features of the traditional agrarian family. As a staring point, we may examine the family in pre-industrial societies in order to establish a standard for comparison.

An agrarian family is, for obvious reasons, closely associated with landed property, a permanent homestead, livestock, poultry and, sometimes handicrafts. Such a family generally exhibits the following characteristics.

To begin with, family\ life is built around economic activities and functions related to housekeeping. All elders, including women, are engaged either in agricultural production or in handicrafts, such as weaving, sewing, making of furniture, making or repairing the dwelling shed, etc. In such a family, the men usually work outside the home, while the women are expected to look after the home. Her role may be described as that of the manager of the household.

Secondly, the importance of wife in the economic life of the family determines the criteria of choosing one's mate. Thus, a man considers the work habits and skills of the prospective mate while contracting a marriage. A woman, on the other hand, looks for a good 'provider'. In either case, affection or love has a subordinate role in the choice of a mate.

Thirdly, an agrarian family is generally large-sized. Farming is, by nature, labour-intensive. A large labour force is needed for efficient management of a farm. A large number of children is the most natural way to achieve this result, for every new born child is an addition to the labour force of the family.

Fourthly, this very factor also explains the popularity of joint or extended families in agrarian societies. The labour force of the family "may also be augmented by keeping the married sons at home and bringing in daughers-in-law." The family may, thus, expand vertically, as in the case of a family in which three or four generations live under the same roof—grand-parents, parents, children, grand-children, etc.Sometimes the family may expand laterally, as in China, where relatives are invited to stay with the family.

Fifthly, since an agrarian family is "attached to so stable a property as land", the reputation of the family largely determines the status of an individual. A person, whatever might be his individual worth, may enjoy a superior status in the community by virtue of the reputation of the family to which he belongs. Similarly, a person may suffer in prestige for no fault of his own but for some bad reputation of the family. There is, thus, a complete subordination of the individual to the family. As Ogburn and Nimkoff say : "the status of the family may become so important that it overshadows the individual who tends to be identified as one family's son or daughter, not as a personality in his or her own right".[16]

Finally, an agrarian family may be called a miniature community which is the centre of various kinds of activities : educational, religious, protective and even recreational. Since the members of an agrarian family do not stay away from their homes for a long period, a child grows up under their direct influence. They help him discover what is good or bad, just or unjust, moral or immoral; they help him imbide family tradition, as also the tradition of the larger community. Since mobility is very restricted in an agrarian community, the social control is pretty rigorous with the result that deviations from social norms are few and far between. An agrarian family performs different kinds of protective functions, such as the care of the sick, the aged and the unemployed. Recreation facilities are also generally confined to the family circle in an agrarian community. This may be explained by\ the fact than an agrarian family is large-sized and that the members spend their leisure-hours together.Another important factor is, of course, the absence of cheap, commercial entertainment in rural areas. It is interesting to note that even when there is some community ceremony - say, a community worship - the participation in the function is on a family basis, rather than on an individual basis.

## 5. THE EMERGENCE OF MODERN URBAN FAMILY

The family is not an establishment as is the house, but a group of activities that gather around reproduction and care of offspring. It is not just people, but people who live together and make a home.Family life may, therefore, be described as a type of social conduct. Naturally, therefore, family life is affected by the behaviour of men, women and children in their other social relationships. Moreover, a family will fail to fulfil its purposes if it "settles into a self-satisfied stiffness". It must remain sensitive to varying conditions of society and make appropriate adaptations,

### Influences affecting famil-

"The family has not so much changed as it has had change forced upon it. It is in transition because civilisation itself is in transition".[17]

We may consider, in the first place, the effects of applied science. Science has brought about revolutionary economic changes in the field of industrial organisation."The factory, instead of the homestead, became the unit of production", because "the steam boiler was too big for the home and the power generated required more space for the machinery"[18]. The transference of production from the family to capitalistic organisations is of tremendous significance to the modern family. The productive functions tended to forge links of unity in a rural agrarian family. Contrasted with this is the urban family which is confined largely, in so far as the economic activities are concerned, to the function of "justly dealing out an income earned by the members of the family who work outside".

Among the important changes affecting family that have occurred in the wake of industrialisation, the new status of women is perhaps the most important.This is true not only of Western society but also of Indian society.

Another influence of applied science upon the family has been the improvement and the dissemination of the techniques of birth control. It is true that birth control is not new in the sense that there has been in the past efforts to discover some satisfactory method of birth control. It is, however, new from the point of view of its high degree of efficiency and its wide appeal. It is also being widely talked about, propagated and widely advertised. Small family norm is held up before the members of the public in persuasive language.

A social change of major importance in its effect on the family is the dominance of urban culture. Among various aspects of city life which influence family, we may discuss here two important aspects of urbanisation. On the one hand, the concentration of population gives rise to the necessity and opportunity of providing certain services on a community basis, such as common recreational facilities, health services, etc. On the other hand, the male members of an urban family stay away from home in connection with their work for a greater part of the day. As a consequence, a father plays a comparatively negiligible role in the education of his children as compared to the role of a father in an agrarian economy. Sometimes even mothers work outside. In the circumstances, the city dwellers have developed various pre-school agencies, such as creches, nurseries, kindergartens, etc. to take care of young children.

The influence of the city is not, however, confined to those who live within its geographical limits. Its influence is more pervasive and permeates almost all strata of society.

We have, finally, to take note of the fact that complexities of modern life have forced upon the state various social and economic responsibilities which were previously the exclusive concern of the family. As illustrations, we may refer to various social security measures adopted by modern states.

As a consequence of these various influences, every feature of modern family reveals the breaking down of long-established fundamental patterns of thought associated with agrarian or household family.

## Structure of modern family

To begin with, the nuclear family has largely replaced the consanguineous family, particularly in Western societies. Such changes are also increasingly taking place in urban areas in India. The decline of the economic significance of the family as a producing unit has impaired the old-time unity of the family group. When a man gets a job in a factory and earns his pay independently of the efforts of his parents and brothers, he is not so prone to turn over his earnings to the common family fund, as was the case when he and his brothers worked on the soil together.

Secondly, we have to take note of change in husband-wife relationship. This economic independence of a woman has affected her whole attitude towards marriage. She does not have to look so much for a "provider". Her choice of mate is generally determined by considerations of love, affection and similarity of interest or temperament. Since the modern family is no longer a producing unit, a man also usually chooses his bride on similar considerations and not on the basis of her skill or capacity for work. Moreover, economic independence of both men and women have freed them from "parental control and other forms of social pressure concerning whom and when they shall marry".

Husband-wife relationship in modern family may be looked at from a different angle. The agrarian family being an economic organisation, there was the need for some sort of leadership. Generally, the men-folk used to fill this role. But in a modern urban family, the necessity for leadership and control is not so great. Hence both husband and wife confront each other on terms of equality. They discuss the problems of the family together and arrive at decisions which meet with the approval of both.

We may consider, thirdly, the comparative instability of modern family. The possibilities of conflict between a husband and his wife are, therefore, greater in modern urban families than those in agrarian families of old in which roles of husbands and wives were clearly determined. These role conflicts are further reinforced by various other factors, such as disappearance or decline of the economic and protective functions of the family. The increased rates of divorce among urban families, not only in the West but also in India, indicate the strains and stresses to which these families are subjected.

Fourthly, modern families tend to be smaller in size than agrarian families. Two reasons are primarily responsible for this trend. On the one hand, with the transference of production from the family, the raison d'etre for a large-sized family, which supplied additional labour force for the farm, disappeared. The advances in the techniques of birth control, on the other hand, made it possible for deliberate planning of parenthood.

**Functions of modern family**

The modern family has parted with many of the traditional functions of the agrarian family. We have already seen that production functions have been transferred from the family to economic organisations away from home.

Education has similarly been moved outside the home. The schools provide various kinds of education which no family in the past could ever provide for children. With the increased use of nursery schools and kindergartens much of the early training of the child has been taken over by the specialists. Moreover, small houses in cities with little or no playground have also tended to put the children on the streets or on public parks or playgrounds during their leisure time, thereby further removing them from the influence of their parents, brothers cr sisters. The fact that the father, and in some the influence of their parents brothers or sisters. The fact that the father, and in some cases also the mother, work outside the home has necessarily limited their contributions to the education of their children.

The protective functions of the family such as the care of the sick, the aged and the unemployed have been taken over either by the hospitals, nursing homes and clinics or by the state which provides for social security for its citizens in the form of old age pensions, unemployment relief, etc.

Recreational facilities are now largely sought outside the family circle. The smallness of the living quarters, the smaller number of the members of the family, the difficulty of getting them together, lack of recreational facilities at home, the development of relatively cheap commercial entertainment in the form of theatres, movies, etc., comparative ease of modern transportation—all these make the members of the family seek recreational opportunities outside the home circle. Moreover, the organisation of these outside entertainments on age lines hinders the participation in these programmes of the family as a unit.

Having been thus stripped of most of its traditional functions, the modern family performs mainly the following three functions which MacIver and Page characterise as essential functions of the family: The procreation and rearing of children. Even here some of the responsibilities of the family have been taken over by outside agencies, such as maternity homes, ante-natal clinics, etc. (ii) Providing a stable basis for statisfaction of the sex needs of the partners. The institution of marriage provides the partners with an opportunity not merely to seek release for their physical appetite but also to deepen their mutual love and elevate it to a level higher than the physical. (iii) Providing a home for its members who share, not simply a house, but , in addition, intimacy, affection, and a warm relationship which no other association can provide.

## 6. TRADITIONAL INDIAN FAMILY

The traditional pattern of the family in India is that of the joint family. Just how great an antiquity may be ascribed to the joint family system in India is not known. In Vedic times, sons did not acquire co-ownership in family property at birth. The Vedas, however, spoke of several families of the same stock residing together in the same house. By the time of Chandragupta, about 300 B.C., some form of the joint family was common.

When the codes of Manu were being written about two or three centuries later, the joint family became quite common. The legal framework of the joint family was crystallised about the 11th century A.D. in the Mitakshara, a commentary on earlier sacred writings. We presume that the author of the Mitakshara only formulated practices that must then have been long and well established, having been in operation for centuries. Since then, for some nine centuries the rights and duties of family members towards each other, the general structure of the Hindu family, etc. have followed without great deviation the prescriptions of the Mitakshara.

The traditional Indian joint family consists of a number of married couples and their children who live together in the same household. All the men are related by blood—as a man and his sons and his grandsons, or a set of brothers and their sons and grandsons; the women of the household as their wives, unmarried daughters and perhaps the widow of a deceased kinsman. After marriage, a girl leaves her ancestral family and becomes a part of the joint family of her husband. Even now in rural areas there are households in which three or four generations are to be found living under one roof, and the number of members of the family group may approach one hundred. The characterisitcs of such a family are the same as are found in all agrarian families. There is, in the first place, a common kitchen in which food is prepared for the whole household. Secondly, all property is held in common. There is a common purse into which all the members of the family contribute their gains and earnings and from which the expenses of all the members, earners and non-earners alike, are paid. The eldest male member of the household generally handles this common family fund. Thirdly, the joint family is not only a single consumer unit, but typically a single producer unit as well. Among the agricultural population, all the members of the family cultivate the family fields and work the harvest together. Among the artisan castes too, it is the family that is the producing unit, since the members of the family co-operate in the output of handicraft goods. Fourthly, like agrarian families in other parts of the world, Indian joint family also performs educational and protective functions. Fifthly, the traditional Indian family is, barring a few exceptions, patrilineal and patrilocal in form. Sixthly, the family group is bound together by *sraddha,* which is a rite of commemorating the ancestors at which balls of rice called *pinda* are offered to the dead. It is believed that three generations of the dead are beneficiaries of the benefits of the ceremony. Sons, grandsons and great grandsons of the deceased join together in sraddha. "Thus the dead and the living are linked together by this rite, which, like the ancestor worship of the Chinese, was a most potent force in consolidating the family"[19]. The family group is defined by *sraddha.* Those who are entitled to participate in the ceremony are called sapinda members of the family group. Finally, the traditional Hindu marriage practice exhibits elements of both endogamy and exogamy. Both the partners must belong to the same caste. The caste of the prospective mate is, therefore, to be considered first. The second thing to be considered is the *gotra* of the prospective mate. Gotra may be defined as "a patrilineal clan which reckons descent from some common and usually mythical ancestor"[20]. Basham explains the origin of gotra thus : "The original meaning of gotra is a 'cowshed', or 'a herd of cows'; in the Atharva Veda, the word first appears with the meaning of 'clan', which it has retained with a special connotation. Some ancient Indo-European peoples, such as the Romans, had exogamous clans, as well as generally endogamous tribes. It may well be that the gotra-system is a survival of Indo-European origin which had developed specially Indian features". The marriage partner must not come from a family having the same gotra. Here is the element of exogamy exhibited by Hindu marriage practice. There is another element of exogamy. Among many of the upper castes of Northern India, marriage is prohibited among partners who are connected with one another within certain degrees of relationship, called *sapinda.* It means that a man's wife may not be a sixth cousin as reckoned through the male line or a fourth cousin as reckoned through the female line. Another interesting feature is that before marriage is settled, the horoscopes of both the bride and the groom are compared. If the astrologers agree that the comparison is favourable, only then the wedding can take place. If not, the negotiations are cancelled. Another unique feature of traditional Indian family is that divorce is not sanctioned by the sacred writings. Marriage is for eternity, irrespective of whether the marriage proves happy or unhappy, fecund or barren . This has, of course, been superseded by Hindu Marriage Act which permits divorce.

We have seen that the traditional Indian joint family is based on the relations among adults rather than on the conjugal bonds between spouses. The chances of break-up of such a family into nuclear households because of intense conjugal bond are lessened by a few other arrangements. One is the system of arranged marriages in which the guardians on both sides play important roles. Segregation of the sexes for most part of the day after marriage further lowers the possibility. There are certain norms which still further lessen the chances of break-up of joint family into nuclear households. Husband and wife are not expected to show much affection toward each other in the presence of others. A father is not expected to express tenderness and affection towards his children and take care of them to the exclusion of all other children in the family. These and many other rules "block the normal tendency of the nuclear family to break away and to form a separate household".

There are, however strong pressures in the opposite direction also. Wives come from outside and they cannot be expected to share the weakness of their husbands toward other members of the joint household . If the husband earns more than his other brothers and nephews, his contribution towards the common pool of the family would naturally be high. This may be resented by his wife. Such tensions and simmering discontent would grow when there are lazy members whose families have to be fed, protected and taken care of by more diligent members of the family. In an agrarian society, such problems did not exist because the expenses of the joint household were met out of income drawn from common ancestral property. In an industrialised society, all the brothers, far instance, may not be at the same level in terms of income. Such disparities in income have the potential of breaking up the joint family household into a number of nuclear households.

We have briefly indicated the nature of centripetal and centrifugal forces which operate in respect of joint family households. It is difficult to make a generalised statement this way or that for a vast country like India. The picture that comes out from a survey of a particular region may not agree with the picture which emerges from another survey in another region. Contradictory statements about the state of joint family households in India are, therefore, made by sociologists. Goode, for instance, observes: " ... it is not surprising, then, that surveys over the past decade show that a majority of Indian families live in nuclear households..."[14] William Kapp, on the other hand, makes an exactly opposite observation : "It is often believed that the number of joint families in relation to nuclear families is declining especially under the impact of urbanisation. However, such limited data as are available on this subject seem to refute this belief. Thus, it has been found that the joint family structure is not disintegrating and that there are almost as many joint families in urban areas as in rural areas"[21]

The fact is, however, undeniable that the centrifugal forces are more powerful and are increasingly being strengthened by urbanisation, industrialisation and many other modernising influences. During the transitional period, Indian family system is exhibiting diverse forms and features and will defy all attempts at neat categorisation One such form which stands out very prominently in so far as rural families are concerned is the stem family pattern in which the main trunk of the family is located in its own ancestral house while most of the members, particularly those belonging to comparatively younger age-group, live most of the time in urban centres and work there. It is, however, interesting to note that the bonds of the joint family are rarely severed completely. The members of the joint family who work and live in cities generally remit something to their village homes towards the expenses of the joint family because some members, usually the elderly ones and women, remain in the ancestral village and maintain the old family patterns. Those who stay in urban centres sometimes have a feeling that their real home is not in urban centres or towns but in their joint household of the village. They generally visit their village homes in connection with some religious festivals and social functions. The most important such occasion is, of course, a wedding which is usually a common family enterprise. The members of the family who may have stayed away from ancestral village home for a long period come back to participate in the preparation and celebration of the wedding ceremony. Such deep attachment to the ancestral village household explains the migratory character of Indian labour.

## 7. MARRIAGE

It is only through the establishment of culturally controlled and sanctioned marital relations that a family comes into being. The institutionalised form of these sex relations is called marriage. Marriage may, therefore, be regarded as a part of the institution of family. Marriage and the family are two aspects of the same social reality, viz. the bio-psychical-cum-social drives of man. Without the family there could be no preservation of the species and culture and without marriage there could be no family.

### Reasons for marriage

Marriage ensures a biological satisfaction (that of sex) and a psychological satisfaction (that of having children) on the individual plane.

On the wider collective plane, it ensures a survival of the species (or of the group) and a survival of its culture. This aspect may be discussed from three points of view.

To begin with, a human baby requires a considerable period of time to be mature or self-reliant. It has, therefore, to be fed, protected and nursed during early years of childhood. The obligation to feed and protect the child must be clearly assigned to some one. Otherwise, there is the possibility that the responsibility may not at all be carried out with disastrous consequences upon the child. The institution of marriage prescribes that sexual activity be confined to the married partners only so that the responsibility of rearing up a child, born of a particular married pair, may vest on that married pair alone. No society, therefore, approves of illegitimacy, i.e., the birth of a child to an unwed mother.

Secondly, at birth a human baby is no more than a biological organism. Through persistent efforts, it has to be transformed into a social being. Here also the responsibility for introducing the child into the culture of the group must be assigned specifically to someone during the first few years of childhood. The institution of marriage enables the society to assign this responsibility of socialising a child to the parents. The problems of socialising an illegitimate child are pointed out by Goode in these words : "The child whose parents are not married does not belong to the father's family, and neither the father nor his family needs to meet more than minimal legal obligations to the child. The child's position is ambiguous, and its socialisation experience is likely to be inadequate"[22].

Thirdly, in the interest of social stability it is necessary to assign a social status to a child during the early years of childhood, so that he knows clearly about his role-obligations and his relationship with other members of society. Assignment of social status also gives him a sense of security. He feels secure in the thought that like others he has a place in society. This is possible only in the case of children who are born of duly married parents. Malinowski's observations on the need for legitimacy from this point of view are very pertinent : "No child should be brought into the world without a man—and one man at that —assuming the role of sociological father, that is,guardian and protector, the male link between the child and the rest of the community"[23]. The rule of legitimacy, which is "as universal and fundamental as the familial institution itself", ordains that "a father is indispensable for the full status of the child and its mother. Otherwise the child is illegitimate and the mother disesteemed"[23]. The principle of legitimacy implies obviously the control of sex relations. If there is any case of conception outside marriage, "it is likely to be eliminated with abortion or the resulting offspring may be eliminated through infanticide"[23] These two courses could be avoided if the concerned man and woman decide to marry. Davis has therefore pointed out that liberty of sexual intercourse is not identical with liberty of parenthood. Malinowski observed that "Marriage cannot be defined as the licensing of sexual intercourse, but rather as the licensing of parenthood[24].

In matrilineal society in which descent is traced through the mother,there would be less concern about the exact identity of the biological father so long as the mother were married. But even in such a society, an illegimate child is as much a problem as in a patrilineal society. "The rules of marriage—i.e., who is permitted to marry whom—determine the social placement of the child, guarantee its socialization, and thus define both illegitimacy and legitimacy. The illegitimate child is a burden, with no benefit to its mother's kin since his lack of a secure place in the kinship line means that his obligations to them are not firm or definite. They receive no gifts from the other kinship line, since there has been no marriage. The child represents, in some societies, a violation of the elders' power to decide and execute the marriage itself. Usually, there is no father to assume the social and economic care of the child, and the child is not an extension of the kinship line"[25].

We thus see that marriage is as much significant to an individual as to society. In order to impress upon all the new roles that the newly-wed couples would play as husband and wife, a ceremony is generally arranged in which relatives, kinsmen and friends are invited to witness the wedding. Anderson and Parker bring out the significance of wedding ceremony in these words : "The wedding is the recognition of the significance of marriage to societies and to individuals through the public ceremony usually accompanying it. Such a ceremony indicates the society's control. The pageantry impresses upon the couple the importance of the commitment they are undertaking"[26].

**Marriage as a tie between two kin groups**

In a lineage system marriage is regarded not so much as a relationship between two individuals as a relationship between two kin groups. The way of assessing its importance in a particular society is to examine the wedding ceremony and the pattern of gift-giving that accompanies it.

In our society, the couple generally get presents from their respective families and friends. But in many small-sized societies, very little is given to the couple themselves. It is the two sets of relatives who exchange gifts. Our type of gift-giving emphasises the individual aspect of marriage—i.e., the marital relationship of husband and wife. The exchange of gifts between two sets of relatives, on the other hand, marks the marriage as a contract between two kin groups.

Some societies have the custom of the dowry. Apart from being a form of inheritance for the daughter and the daughter's children, it also gives the girl's relative a way of providing for her and her children after her marriage.

Some societies, on the other hand, have the custom of paying bride wealth. It is particularly common in societies with patrilineal lineages, though it does occur in some matrilineal societies. According to this practice, the husband's family is required to give cattle or other goods to the bride's family. The bridewealth is often so great that a man has to take the help of other men in his lineage in order to pay for his bride. Among the Nuer, for instance, 20 to 40 cattle must be paid to the father of the bride by the bridegroom's lineage. The bride's father then distributes the cattle according to strict rules among his daughter's relatives.

One common misconception should, however, be dispelled. Although the bride is paid for, she is not a chattel. She cannot be resold. Her social status remains high after marriage. It is said that there are two ideas behind the practice. First, the bride's lineage should be compensated for the loss of a working member. Second, the payment of bridewealth transfers control of the woman's offspring from her father's to her husband's lineage. That is, it is the children rather than the wife whom the husband's family buys.

## 8. FORMS OF MARRIAGE

There are several types of marriage. If we make a cross-cultural study of marriage practices in different societies, we shall come across rules laying down preferences, prescriptions as well as proscriptions in deciding the form of marriage.

Before we take up different forms of marriage, we may refer to universal taboo on sexual relations between closely related kin like parents and children and between siblings. This is known as incest taboo.

We may consider below some of the classifications of marriage.

(a) On the basis of the number of mates, marriage is classified into two broad types: Monogamy and Polygamy.

The practice of having only one partner in marriage ( i.e. a husband having one wife only and a wife having one husband only) is called monogamy.

The practice of having only one partner in marriage ( i.e., a husband having one wife only\ and a wife having one husband only ) is called monogamy.

The practice of having more than one partner in marriage is called polygamy. Polygamy may be of two types: polygyny and polyandry. When one man has two or more wives at a time, the practice is known as polygyny. When a man marries several sisters, the practice is known as sororal polygyny.

When one woman marries more than one man at the same time, the practice is known as polyandry. Polyandry may be of two types: fraternal or adelphic polyandry and non-fraternal polyandry. When one woman marries sevaral brothers at the same time, the practice is known as fraternal or adelphic polyandry (reminiscent of Draupadi of Mahabharata ). The practice is prevalent among Todas. When a woman has several husbands none of whom are necessarily brothers, the practice is known as non-fraternal polyandry.

We may consider, in this connection, two types of polygamous marriages, namely levirate and sororate.

Marriage of a man with the childless widow of his deceased brother is known as levirate. Where the 'true' levirate prevails, upon the death of a husband, it is the duty of one of his brothers to marry the widow, and any children born to the union are counted as the progeny of the deceased man.

Where the 'true' sororate prevails, the husband of a barren woman marries her sister, and at least some of the children born to the union are counted as children of the childless wife. The term sororate is also used with reference to the custom whereby, upon the death of a wife, her kin supply a sister as wife for the widower. In this case, however, any children born to the woman are recognised as her own.

Levirate and sororate emphasise the acceptance of inter-familial obligations and the recognition of marriage as a tie between two families and not simply between two individuals.

We may consider another kind of polygamy called 'group marriage'. When two or more grooms are married simultaneously to two or more brides, it is called group marriage. It is a combination of polyandrous and polygynous marriages. It occurs infrequently among the Kaingang of Brazil and also infrequently among the Marquesans.

(b) Classification based on mate-choice.

When the marriage partners are chosen by the partners themselves, the practice is known as romantic marriage or love marriage. When the marriage partners are chosen by the guardians or relatives or even by friends, the practice is known as arranged marriage.

When marriage is prescribed only among partners who belong to the same group, the practice is known as endogamy or endogamous marriage. In endogamy marriage outside one 's group is prohibited. We may think of various kinds of endogamous marriages, such as tribal endogamy, caste endogamy, class endogamy, race endogamy, etc.Due to the universal fear of the strange, the novel and the unknown, almost all the Indian tribes are endogamous.

In certain cases there is a prescription or preference for marriage to a particular kin. Thus, a Gond is required to marry his/her cross-cousin. If one would like to have this prescription waived in one's case, a compensation has to be paid to the losing party. Fiftyfour per cent of Gond marriages were found by Grigson to be of this type. The Kharia and Oraon practise cross-cousin marriage. So does the Khasi. But a Khasi male can have such a marriage only after the death of his father with his paternal aunt's daughter.[27]

When marriage is prohibited among partners who belong to the same group, the practice is known as exogamy or exogamous marriage. We have among the Hindus 'gotra' exogamy and 'pravara' exogamy in terms of which marriage is not permissible among partners having the same gotra or pravara. There is also 'pinda' exogamy. In Hindu society marriage within the 'pinda' is prohibited. 'Pinda' means common parentage. Offspring from five maternal generations and seven paternal generations are 'sapinda' and they cannot intermarry. There is also among some Indian tribes village exogamy. This restriction is prevalent among the Munda and other tribes of Chhotanagpur in Bihar. The Naga tribe in Nagaland is divided into Khels. Khel is the name given to the residents of a particular place and the people of one Khel cannot inter-marry.[28]

(c) Classification based on status of married partners.

The marriage between partners who exhibit parity in terms of age, education, temperament, economic condition, social status, etc. is known as homogamy. On the other hand, the marriage between partners who differ widely in terms of these criteria is known as heterogamy.

Classification is also made in terms of marriage between partners of unequal social status. When a man marries a woman belonging to a comparatively lower social stratum, the marriage is known as hypergamy or 'anuloma'. The man does not generally suffer any loss of social standing because of his marrying a woman of lower social status. When a woman belonging to a higher social stratum marries a man of a comparatively lower social status, the marriage is known as hypogamy or 'pratiloma'. In such a case, the woman attracts social scorn and in some societies even ostracism because of her marrying a man of lower social ranking. Such differential evaluation in the cases of men and women is to be found in all societies. Basham points out : "This distinction is to be found in other societies; for instance, in Victorian England the peer who married an actress rarely incurred the same scorn and ostracism as the lady who married her groom".[29]

(d) A distinction is made between closed marriage system and open marriage system:-

Societies which prescribe that a spouse be chosen from among one or more designated categories of persons have been said to possess closed marriage systems.Those societies in which such prescriptions do not exist have been characterised as having open marriage systems.In open marriage systems, the only group of persons unequivocally proscribed as marriage partners are those to whom the incest taboo is extended.

In addition to the aforesaid dichotomous forms of marriage, there are various other types which may be noted.

There is, for instance, companionship marriage which is " the marriage of two persons on the understanding that as long as there are no children the marriage may be dissolved simply by mutual consent".

Reference may also be made to concubinage which is a state of living together as husband and wife without being married.

Under the system of experimental marriage, a man and a woman may be allowed to lead matrimonial life temporarily in order to find out if they can settle down permanently in matrimonial relationship.

## 9. MARRIAGE AMONG HINDUS AND MUSLIMS

Among Hindus, marriage is a sacrament. It is necessary in the life of a Hindu, because a Hindu male cannot enter the "Grihasthaasrama', i.e., the stage of a householder without a wife. This is the second of the four stages of life (asrama) ordained by the holy law-givers. Marriage is also required for another reason. An offspring, in particular a son, is necessary to seek release from the chain of birth, death and re-birth. This is based on the Hindu conception of immortality and transmigration of soul.

Hindu law-givers have designated marriage as one of the 'samskaras', i.e. as one of those taken sanctifying rituals which every Hindu has to be associated with. These rituals are meant to emancipate an individual from various limitations, shortcomings and weaknesses which constitute a part and parcel of the body of flesh and blood. One cannot escape from or ignore these limitations and weaknesses. What one can and should do is to try to transcend these limitations as far as possible. Observance of 'samskaras' or sanctifying rituals is designed to achieve this end. Manu, the Hindu law-giver, has described the purpose of 'samskara' thus: *brāhmiam kriyate tanuh*. That is, one should cleanse one's body ,mind and spirit in such a manner that passion and detachment, enjoyment and renunciation, self-assertion and self-abnegation may blend harmoniously in one's life, so as to enable him to emancipate himself from the bondage of life and death. Marriage is a 'samskara' inasmuch as the newly-wed couple are advised to use the nuptial tie in order to untie the bondage of flesh and passion.

It is, therefore, not surprising that there is a religious sanction behind the Hindu conception of marriage. The marriage ceremony consists of a series of ritual performances.'Kanyadan' or the gift of his daughter by the father to the bridegroom, the lighting of sacrificial fire as divine witness and sanctifier of the ceremony (vivāha-homa), the holding of the bride's hands by the bridegroom (pāni-grahana), and the walking of the bride and bridegroom over seven steps around the sacrificial fire, the bridegroom leading the bride ('sapta-padi) are important rituals associated with marriage ceremony. After these rituals are over, the bride is carried away. 'Vivaha', the Sanskrit word for marriage, means 'carrying away'.

Marriage must take place within one's caste (varna) but in practice it takes place within one's sub-caste. In seeking a spouse one must move beyond five degrees on the mother's side ( beyond sapinda) and beyond seven degrees on the father's side ( beyond gotra and pravara ).

Various forms of marriage have been recognised in Hindu Law books. When a father gifts his daughter to a man of good character and learning it is called *brāhma* marriage. If it is a priest to whom the daughter is gifted, it is called *daiva* marriage. When a prospective son-in-law makes the gift of a bull and a cow to the girl's father before receiving her as gift, it is called *ārsha* marriage. This form of marriage should not, however, be confused with marriage by purchase which is called *āsura* marriage and has been condemned in the cases of Brahmins and Kshatriyas but commended in the cases of Vaishyas and Sudras by Manu.When a father gifts his daughter to a man after duly honouring him and exhorts the couple to perform their *dharma* together, it is called *prājapatya* marriage. Marriage based on mutual love and contract is called *gandharva*. Abduction is called *rākshasa* and regarded as lawful. But the seduction of a girl who is asleep, intoxicated or of unsound mind is called *pāisacha* marriage and is condemned as transgressing the rules of civilised life.

It is to be noted that the Hindu law-givers succeeded in meeting many urgent social problems by giving recognition to various kinds of marriage. India has been invaded from the north-west many times in the past. There has also been within the country a large number of non-Aryans with whom the Aryans came in contact. At the instance of the succeeding waves of immigrants and indigenous non-Aryans, there have been cases of illicit sexual intercourse and, as a result, children were born of unwed women. The problems posed by the presence of a large number of illegitimate children were solved by recognising cases of abduction, elopement, etc. as some forms of marriage, though these were not commended as desirable. Commenting on this aspect, A.L. Basham has this to say : "It would seem that, with surprising realism, the jurists recognised a wide range of relationships, so that the girl seduced by her lover's promises or carried off by raiders would have some legal claim to wifely status, and her child some degree of legitimacy".

### Marriage among Muslims

Muslim marriage is not a religious sacrament, but a secular bond. Prohibited degrees of alliance are few and limited. Thus, marriage between even half-siblings and first parallel cousins can take place. Muslim men can be polygynous under the condition that two sisters or an aunt and niece cannot be taken as co-wives and one cannot have more that four wives at a time. A Muslim can marry his deceased wife's sister and also the parent-in-law of his/her children. A Muslim man can marry a non-Muslim but only a non-idolatrous woman like a Jew or a Christian. A Muslim woman, however, does not enjoy a similar right.

Marriage is solemnised by signing a legal document and can be dissolved. But divorce is the privilege of the husband. He can have it even without assigning a cause. Divorce can be obtained by merely repeating three times the formula of repudiation called *talaq* in the presence of at least two witnesses. But a husband was to pay "dower" which is a settlement made on the wife out of her husband's property, to compensate her in the event of death and divorce. A wife can obtain *khula* or release from her marriage by giving consideration to the husband whose consent in essential. If wife and husband separate by mutual consent, it is called *mubarat*. Under certain circumstances, Islamic law does give a wife the permission of unilateral action. Widow remarriage is commonly practised by Indian Muslim women.

## 10. IS NUCLEAR FAMILY THE PRODUCT OF INDUSTRIALISM ?

We may consider three conflicting views on the above question.

In the first place, there is the widely held view that in pre-industrial society of Europe the joint or extended family was in vogue. Such a family fulfilled the various needs of its members—economic, educational, recreational, ensuring social security, etc. But with the advent of industrialisation, the modern family was stripped of these functions and "reduced to a pale shadow of its former ample self". Modern family is viewed, in its ideal form, " as a nuclear-family group living in its own house independently of other kin and subsisting upon the wages or salary of the husband-father". It is further pointed out that "falling birth rates, an increase in the incidence of divorce, a decline in home food-processing, clothes making, and so on" signify "a decline in family living and a shift toward increasing individualism and material values".

Secondly, Talcott Parsons and others have argued that the family system of the urban U.S. is not a denuded form of a more 'normal" or 'natural' family system but is itself a highly specialised form that fits in more satisfactorily with a highly differentiated economic and political system and with institutionalised values that stress achievement rather than ascription. Parsons views the emergence of the isolated nuclear family in terms of his theory of social evolution. The evolution of society involves a process of 'structural differentation'. This means that during the process of evolution social institutions evolve which specialise in fewer functions. It is, therefore, nothing surprising that the family and kinship groups no longer perform a wide rage of functions. Instead specialist institutions, such as schools, hospitals, business firms, factories, etc. take over many of the functions of the family. Parsons further argues that there is a functional relationship between the isolated nuclear family and the economic system in industrial society. The isolated nuclear family is required to make suitable adaptations in response to the requirements of industrial society. It is argued that the smallness and relative isolation of the family from other kinship ties is an adaptation that makes possible the spatial and status mobility of its members which is required by the modern industrial system. Individuals with specialised skills are required to move to places where those skills are in demand. Parsons gives another instance to establish his thesis. In an industrial society, status is achieved rather than ascribed. That is, individuals are judged in terms of the status they achieve. Such judgments are based on what Parsons calls 'universalistic values", i.e. values that are universally applicable to all members of society. Within the family, however, status is ascribed. Such ascription is based on what Parsons calls 'particularistic values', i.e. values that are applicable to particular individuals only. (For universalistic and particularistic values, see the section on Social Action Approach in the Second Chapter). Parsons argues that in an extended family these two kinds of values may be a source of conflict within the family. Thus, if the father is a factory mechanic and the son a doctor or an engineer, the particularistic values of family life would give the father a higher status and a more dominant position in the family. The universalistic values, on the other hand, would give the son a higher social status which might tend to undermine the authority of the father. Conflict may thus arise and threaten the solidarity of the family. The isolated nuclear family largely prevents such conflicts of values from arising. In other words, the nuclear family is an adaptation to the requirements of industrial society.

Thirdly, the functional interpretation of the importance of nuclear family, as given by Parsons, is considerably weakened by the work of Peter Laslett, the Cambridge historian (The World we have lost, London, Methuen, 1965). The work of Laslett indicates that the pre-industrial family system in England did not have large extended families occupying single dwellings. On the contrary, the nuclear-family household seems to have been the normal type of dwelling group. Laslett found that from 1564 to 1821 only about 10 p.c. of households contained kin beyond the nuclear family. The percentage is the same for England in 1966. One explanation for this surprisingly low figure is that people in pre-industrial England married rather late in life and that life expectancy was short, with the result that within a few years of the marriage of a couple, their parents died. Whatever be the explanation, Laslett found no evidence that extended family was widespread in pre-industrial England that gave way to the small nuclear household of modern industrial society. It is, therefore, suggested that it was not industrialisation that produced the nuclear family. On the contrary, the nuclear family may have been one of the factors encouraging the development of the industrial revolution in England. That is, if the nuclear family has been the major form of European family structure for many centuries, pre-dating the industrial revolution, and if this family form was the product of social values rather than of demographic or other constraints, then the modern family forms may be simply the continuation of culturally preferred form.

## 11. IS THE NUCLEAR FAMILY A UNIVERSAL FORM OF FAMILY RELATIONSHIP ?

Murdock suggested that the nuclear family is the universal form of family relations and that it performs "distinctive and vital functions—sexual, economic, reproductive and educational"[30]. He elaborates his thesis further : "The nuclear family is a universal human grouping. Either as the sole prevailing form of the family or as the basic unit from which more complex familial forms are compounded, it exists as a distinct and strongly functional group in every human society"[31].

Murdock's thesis has been criticised from different points of view.

To begin with, it has been pointed out that Murdock's picture of the family is rather "like the multi-faceted, indispensable boy scout knife". Since it is multi-functional, it has been considered to be indispensable and hence universal. It is held that in his enthusiasm Murdock failed to identify other alternative ways of getting, at least, some of those functions performed[32].

Morgan notes in his criticism that Murdock does not answer "to what extent these basic functions are inevitably linked with the institution of the nuclear family"[33].

The evidence for Murdock conclusion about the inevitability and universality of nuclear family is far from conclusive. He may have arrived at this conclusion because of the fact that he collected his data from Euro-American societies. It has been pointed out that the cases such as those of the Nayar in India and the Ashanti of Central Ghana tend to disprove his assertion.

In the large Ashanti villages of Central Ghana the children may carry pots of food from their mother's house to the house of their father. The may eat with their father. Thereafter they may go home to sleep at the house where their mother lives. The mother may visit her husband for the night. This pattern of divided residence and visiting back and forth seems to exist because the Ashanti traditional social system is based on matrilineal descent for important social purposes, such as inheritance of land, succession to office and political status. Women often value the tie to their brother as highly as, or higher than, the relationship to their husband, since it is from the brother that their children will inherit. Because the child's place in society is mainly determined through its relationship to its mother and her matrilineal kin, the breaking of a marital tie is of little consequence either for the spouses or for the children.

Another factor inducing women to remain in their own homes even after marriage is the very close relationship between mother and children, and particularly between mothers and daughters. This case demonstrates the way in which interests and relationships can cut right across the solidarity of the nuclear family. And it would be very difficult to demonstrate that the nuclear family is either a normal or a necessary co-residential unit among the Ashanti. The Ashanti concept of family is quite different from the concept of family with which the people of Europe or America or Asia are familiar.

The most extreme and best known example of the effect of matrilineal descent upon familial relationships was to be found among the Nayar caste of Southern India in the period before the effects of British rule were felt. Among the Nayar, it appears that the marital relationship was reduced to a merely symbolic level, being contracted around the time that the girl reached puberty and shortly thereafter being ritually broken. Afterward, the women were allowed to have informal love affairs with men who visited them at night. The households consisted of a group of brothers and their sisters and the sisters' children, and any children born to the woman of the household became members of the matrilineal joint family. The children were discouraged from developing any strong attachments to either their *pater or genitor*. While it would be impossible to argue that the role of father was completely absent from this social system, it was obviously diminished in favour of the solidarity of the property-owning matrilineal group. It seems likely that many of the functions that are normally performed by fathers in relation to socialisation and personality development were carried out by male members of the matrilineage.

Cases such as these have led some writers, including Radcliffe-Brown, to suggest that the basic structural unit of kinship systems is the unit of mother and children and to separate the nuclear family into a number of paired relationships or dyads, and to see how, in different societies, they fit in relation to each other and to other groups. This is toward loosening the categories involved in the nuclear-family complex and exploring more fully their independent connections. Even in societies with pronounced patriarchal authority we find that the mother-children unit often forms an idependent sub-group, and is given special recognition and marked by close emotional ties among its members. Talcott Parsons has suggested that the father role is always an "instrumental" one as opposed to the more emotional or "expressive" quality of the mother role.

In tribal societies where kinship determines both social relationships and social roles, the family has to keep in touch with descent groups and "becomes a mechanism for the continuous generation of new kinship ties"[33].

In more differentiated social systems with an increased division of labour, a literary tradition, and a well-developed class or caste system, such as those of India or China, it is still true that families may be large, multi-functional units—a far cry from a nuclear household. The absence of a sufficient property base leads the grown-up mature sons to go out of the family and set up idependent households. "Large joint families are found mainly among landowning and merchant groups, where sons have a continuing material interest in the patrimony to re-inforce and sustain filial piety. Such large 'families' are really lineages or descent groups (for lineages see the next chapter) which constitute perpetual corporations managing a common enterprise"[34]

## 12. THE FAMILY : A MARXIAN PERSPECTIVE

Lewis H. Morgan's work "Ancient Society" was published in 1877. Marx read this work and made extensive notes on it. But it was Engels who published in 1884 an extensive commentary on it after Marx's death under the title of "The Origin of the Family, Private Property and the State". In this work, Marx's general theories of social and economic history are combined with Morgan's speculative history of kinship institutions.

Engels argued in this work that during the early stages of human evolution the forces of production were owned by the community and the family in its present-day form did not exist. He further posited that promiscuity of sexual relationships characterised the period of primitive communism. There were no prescribed rules regulating sexual relationships. In effect, the society was the family.

Engels has been criticised to indulge in this kind of speculation because it implied, according to some, that Engels was opposed to any sort of family relationships and that the family should be abolished in socialist societies. The anthropologist Kathieen Gough argues that the picture drawn by Engels may not be far from the truth. She bases her arguments on the type of sex life prevalent among man's nearest relatives, the chimpanzees, who live in 'promiscuous hordes'. She believes that this may have been the pattern of early man.

The other criticism of Engels that he advocated, indirectly though, the abolition of family is also misplaced. Engels went out of his way to point out that the emotional and sexual elements involved in family relations can only be paramount when considerations of property do not vitiate the relationships. He argued that the proletariat makes and breaks marital unions only upon the basis of mutual attraction, whereas in bourgeois societies the conjugal pair are united in marriage even when they have no love for each other and may even engage in adultery with other available partners.

The most general conclusion of the book is that a stable monogamous family system, dominated by male authority and prescribed and supported by law, has really developed as a device for the perpetuation of the private ownership of property. In Engel's words "It is based on the supremacy of the man, the express purpose being to produce children of undisputed paternity, such paternity is demanded because these children are later to come into their father's property as his natural heirs".

Engel's scheme of the evolution of family is much more detailed than what has been sketched above. Modern anthropological researches have, however found many of its details to be incorrect. For example, many hunting and gathering bands have been found to have monogamous marriage and nuclear family. It is argued that man lived in hunting and gathering bands for 99.9 p.c. of his existence. Hence, the evolution of monogamous, and nuclear family, as sketched by Engels, may be nothing more than figments of his imagination. It is further pointed out that although nuclear families and monogamous marriages exist in small-scale societies, they form a part of a larger kinship group. When individuals marry, they take upon themselves various obligations to their spouse's kin. The result is something like a large extended family.

It is interesting to note that Marxian analysis of the family in capitalistic society developed mainly in the late 1960s as a part of the feminist movement. The feminist writers attacked the male-dominated family system by employing Marxian concepts. It was argued that the male-dominated family served the purposes of a capitalist society from more than one point of view. To begin with, the family produces one of the basic commodities of capitalism very cheaply, namely, labour. The production is cheap because the capitalists do not pay anything for the production and rearing of children. Secondly, the wife is not paid anything for bearing and rearing of children. It is pointed out that the amount of labour given by women in the course of their household duties is quite large and very profitable to those who own the means of production. The wife serves the husband who happens to be a wage-earner under a capitalist system. The capitalist, therefore, gets the services of two individuals by paying only for one. This is, it is held, no more than exploitation. Thirdly, the husband is committed, under the existing family system, to support his wife and children. This acts as a brake upon him when he has genuine grounds for revolting against his capitalist employer and withdrawing his labour. Margaret Benston, one of the feminist writers, therefore, argues : "As an economic unit, the nuclear family is a valuable stabilising force in capitalist society". Fourthly, Fran Ansley, another feminist writer, puts the view of Talcott Parsons that the family tends to stabilise adult personalities into a Marxist framework. She looks upon the emotional and affectional support given by the wife to her husband as a safety valve for the frustration from which the husband suffers by working in a capitalist system. The wife absorbs her husband's frustration by being soft, sympathetic, comforting and affectionate towards him. In the words of Ansley : "With every worker provided with a sponge to soak up his possibly revolutionary ire, the bosses rest more secure." Finally, some of the feminist writers point to male dominance in the family and relate it to the stability of the capitalist system. "The petty dictatorship which most men exercise over their wives and families enables them to vent their anger and frustration in a way which poses no challenge to the system"[35].

As noted in the first few paragraphs of this section, Engels saw female subordination as a result of the emergence of private property, particularly the private ownership of the forces of production. It is interesting to note that both Marx and Engels saw in the increasing demand for female wage labour in nineteenth-century capitalist society the beginnings of women's liberation. They argued that female employment would largely emancipate women from economic dependence upon their husbands and thereby from male dominance within the family.

Marx and Engels believed that true equality between the sexes would be established only in a socialist society, because the onerous duties of house work and motherhood would no longer be performed by individual women. All work would be the responsibility of the community. In the words of Engel, "Private housekeeping is transformed into a social industry. The care and production of the children becomes a public matter".

In capitalist societies there has been a large-scale entry of women in the labour market. But the women have not yet been emancipated from male dominance, as will be evident from the writings of feminist writers which we noted earlier in this section. The comparative studies of' working wives' and 'full-time housewife' have shown that power relationship within the family have not changed much even in cases where wives work outside the home. Some feminist writers even go so far as to say that female wage labour in a capitalist society has the effect of strengthening the capitalist system because entry of female workers in large numbers tends to keep wages down and profits up.

In socialist societies also things have not moved in the way Marx and Engels predicted more than a hundred years ago. Women in USSR have definitely improved their position in the labour market. In 1922 they constituted 22% of the labour force. In 1973 the figure has gone upto 51%. Despite the fact that over half the labour force is female, women are still primarily responsible for housework and child care it has been reported by David Lane that women in USSR find it difficult to combine their domestic and occupational roles, and that traditional attitudes about a women's place in family still linger, particularly in rural areas[36]. David Lane concludes that collective ownership of the forces of production is "a necessary but not a sufficient condition for female liberation", and that cultural attitudes are only partly, and not in their entirety, shaped by economic conditions. Lane observes: "Thousands of years of history of the subjection of women influence attitudes which men learn, and while communist governments may significantly alter the institutional arrangements of society, it is much more difficult to change attitudes to get women accepted in authority roles on the same basis as men"[37]. Hilda Scott, who lived in Czechoslovakia from 1948 to 1973, after having surveyed the position of women in families in Eastern Europe, reported that working women's domestic responsibilities are similar to those in USSR. Her concluding observations are very significant. "The early proponents of Marxism evidently did not realise that a lag in consciousness is involved which is more difficult to overcome than it is to win recognition for the rights of labour or the rights of Blacks or other minorities or oppressed nations, because belief in women's inferiority is old and more deeply ingrained, and involves the total population, since woman sees herself in the mirror man holds up"[38].

In the face of these facts, may feminist writers agree that Marxian theory fails to provide an adequate explanation for the inequality between sexes. They consider the promise that socialism would ultimately liberate women too naive to accept. Shulasmith Firestone argues that sexual inequality is rooted in biological differences, that men and women are born different. Women bear children and, as such, they become dependent on men. This dependence produces unequal power relationships within the family. Thus, inequality between man and woman began, according to her, not with private property, as was argued by Engels, but with the reproductive functions of men and women.

It is argued that women would be truly freed when they cease to be slaves to their biology. The answer lies not simply in reliable birth control techniques but in artificial reproduction. Women will only be free when babies are conceived and developed outside the womb[39].

## 13. THE FUTURE OF FAMILY

George Peter Murdock claimed on the basis of a sample of 250 societies ranging from hunting and gathering bands to large-scale industrial societies that some form of family existed in every society and that the family is universal. Similarly, Talcott Parsons could conceive of no institution other than the family which could produce and keep stable human personalities.

Both Murdock and Parsons have been criticised on the ground that they have failed to explore functional alternatives to the family. Some functions are not necessarily tied to the family. It is argued that the views of sociologists, such as those of Murdock and Parsons,owe more to their beliefs about what the family ought to be. Barrington Moore observes : "Among social scientists today it is almost axiomatic that the family is a universally necessary social institution and will remain such through any foreseeable future... I have the uncomfortable feeling that the authors, despite all their elaborate theories and technical research devices, are doing little more than projecting certain middle-class hopes and ideals onto a refractory reality."

In his book entitled 'The Coming World Transformation', Ferdinand Lundberg expressed the apprehension: "The family is near the point of complete extinction." The psychologist William Wolf commented : "The family is dead except for the first year or two of child raising. This will be its only function." Alvin Toffler named one of the chapters "The Fractured Family' in his book entitled The Future Shock. In this chapter he sketched the picture of a streamlined family that might develop in an age of super-industrialism. He described a streamlined family thus : "Industrialism demanded masses of workers ready and able to move off the land in pursuit of jobs and to move again whenever necessary.Thus the extended family gradually shed its excess weight and the so-called 'nuclear' family emerged - a stripped down, portable family unit consisting only of parents and a small set of children. This new style family, far more mobile than the traditional extended family, became the standard model in all the industrial countries. Super-industrialism, however, the next stage of eco-technological development, requires even higher mobility.Thus we may expect many among the people of the future to carry the streamlining process a step further by remaining childless, cutting the family down to its most elemental components, a man and a woman"[40]. The noted anthropologist Margaret Mead hinted at a similar possibility when she said that "parenthood would be limited to a smaller number of families whose principal functions would be childbearing", and that the rest of the population would be "free to function for the first time in history - as individuals". These possibilities are not utopian. About a year or two ago, advertisements appeared in newspapers in England on behalf of a voluntary organisation for 'lending a womb'. Surrogate motherhood is no longer a matter of speculation. There are already limited number of cases of surrogate motherhood. Who knows that in future such cases would not multiply ?

The family in the Israeli Kibbutz presents another alternative to the present-day nuclear family.About 4 p.c. of Israel"s population live in some 240 Kibbutzim settlements. Although there are differences between one Kibbutzim and another, the general pattern of family life in a Kibbutzim may be described as follows. Marriage is monogamous. The married couple share a single bedroom cum living room. Children live in communal dormitories where they are brought up by child caretakers or educators. They eat, live and sleep in the dormitories away from their parents. They have an oppourtunity of seeing their parents for an hour or two each day. The parents do not use these visits for teaching the children. Such visits are considered as a time for 'fun'. Thus, the parents have transferred their role obligations to the community. All children are viewed and cared for as children of the Kibbutz. Kibbutz thus represents a rejection of the family, particularly in so far as parental roles are concerned.

Kibbutz has other aspects which also represent a rejection of the traditional family pattern. There is no economic co-operation or sharing of household duties between the married couple. They work for the Kibbutz, not for the family. They get all they need from the Kibbutz. They eat in the communal dining room.Food is cooked in common. All other necessary services, such as laundering, are provided for the entire kibbutz, the married couple having no responsibility in this regard.

Thus, family in the sense of multi-functional unit does not exist in Israeli Kibbutz. It is, however, contended by\ some that Kibbutz may be looked upon as a large extended family because Kibbutz is a unit of production, a unit of child rearing,a unit of socialising the child in the culture of the Kibbutz as well as a unit of consumption and recreation."

The Hungarian Marxist writers Vajda and Heller propose a commune or 'collective family' as an alternative to present-day nuclear family pattern. According to them, all adults in a commune are responsible for the care of children within the commune. Relationships among adults may range from monogamy to promiscuity since 'the commune does not have value references concerning sexual relationships'. The family commune, however, differs from Israeli Kibbutz in that the activities of the commune are confined to domestic and child care relationships only and do not embrace the field of production which involves the organization of occupational roles.

We have given in the foregoing paragraphs the suggested modifications and alternatives to the family. The world is changing pretty fast. It is not possible to indicate, at this stage, fairly firmly the shape of things to come. One can, however, make a safe prediction that the family will not remain the same. Some sociologists are of the view that mankind is entering a golden age in so far as family relationships are concerned. "Entrance into marriage primarily on an affectional basis, the reduction of economic pressures, and the voluntary bearing and rearing of children would appear in the long run to provide the soundest foundation for an enduring family"[41].

## NOTES

1. Article on Family by Ramond T. Smith in *International Encyclopaedia of Social Sciences,* Volumes v and vi, Reprint Edition, 1972, pages 302-303
2. Willam J. Goode, *The Family,* page 8
3. *ibid,* Page 12
4. *ibid,* Page 13
5. *ibid,* Page 13
6. *ibid,* page 13
7. Haralambos, Sociology—*Themes and Perspectives,* Page 333
8. Goode, *The Family,* Page 5
9. Bottomore, *Sociology,* Page 175
10. *ibid,* page 175
11. Goode, *The Family,* page 80

12. *ibid*, page 81
13. *ibid*, pages 51-52
14. *ibid*, Page 50
15. An article by Raymond T. Smith in ***International Encyclopaedia of Social Sciences***, **Volumes v and vi, pages 306-310**
16. Ogburn and Nimkoff, *A Handbook of Sociology*, **page 450**
17. Groves, *American Family*, pages 124-125
18. Ogburn and Nimkoff, *A Handbook of Sociology*, **page 451**
19. Basham, *The Wonder that was India*, page 153
20. *ibid*, page 153
21. K. William Kapp, ***Hindu Culture, Economic Development and Economic Planning in India***, page 28
22. William J. Goode, *The Family*, page 20
23. Malinowski, *Parenthood*—the ***Basis of Social Structure***, **quoted by Kingsley Davis in** *Human Society*, page 400.
24. *ibid*, Page 401
25. William J. Goode, *The Family*, page 21
26. Anderson and Parker, *Society :Its Organisation and Operation*, **(1966), page 150**
27. D.N. Majumder and T. N. Madan, ***An Introduction to Social Anthropology***, **(Asia** Publishing House), page 82
28. *ibid*, page 83
29. A.L.Basham, *The Wonder that was India*, **page 148.**
30. Murdock, *Social Structure*, 1949 edition, page 3
31. *ibid*, Page 2
32. Haralambos,*Sociology—Themes and Perspectives*, **page 332**
33. *ibid*, page 332
34. Taken with suitable adaptations from an article entitled *Family—Comparative Structure* by Raymond T. Smith in *International Encyclopaedia of the Social Sciences*. **Vols. v and vi.** Reprint Edition, 1972
35. Haralambos, *Sociology—Themes and Perspectives*, **Page 341**
36. *ibid*, page 393
37. *ibid*, page 394.
38. *ibid*, page 395
39. *ibid*, pages 397-398
40. Alvin Toffler, *The Future Shock*, page 242
41. Anderson and Parker, *Society—Its Organisation and Operation*, **pages 176-177.**

# CHAPTER SIXTEEN

# KINSHIP

## 1. KINSHIP SYSTEM

The bond of blood or marriage which binds people together in group is called kinship. In order to understand kinship, we may start with a familiar biological fact : men and women have sexual intercourse and, as a result, women bear children. We may also consider a second fact : given the nature of human memory and language, blood ties are held in mind and recognised by special terms of relationship : mother, child, father, mother's brother, etc. The relationship based on blood ties is called consanguineous kinship, and the relatives of this kind are called consanguineous kin.

The desire for reproduction gives rise to another kind of binding relationship : the bond between spouses and their relatives on either side. This kind of bond, which arises out of a socially or legally defined marital relationship, is called affinal kinship, and the relatives so related are called affinal kin. The affinal kins are not related to one another through blood.

## 2. RULE OF DESCENT

The principle or set of principles by which one's relatives are determined is known technically as the rule of descent. There are three basic rules of descent :patrilineal, matrilineal and bi-lateral or bi-lineal.

In patrilineal descent, each individual automatically becomes a member of any consanguineal kin group to which his father belongs, but not of those to which his mother belongs.

In matrilineal descent, an individual joins the consanguineal kin group of his mother but not those of his father.

In bi-lateral descent, an individual inherits some but not all of his father's consanguineal relatives and also the corresponding consanguineal relatives of his mother.

Strictly speaking, probably no society is perfectly bi-lateral. No society is perfectly unilineal either, if that term implies total neglect of one side in favour of the other.

If a common ancestor binds a group of people together, they are called *cognates*. If their common ancestor is a male, they are called *agnates* or agnatic kin or patrilineal kin. The descendants of common female ancestress, on the other hand, are called *uterine kin* or matrilineal kin

Those kin who are related to one another directly through descent are called lineal kin and those who branch out from the main group, like uncles and cousins, are called collateral kin.

On the basis of nearness or distance, kins are classified into (i) Primary Kins, (ii) Secondary Kins, and (iii) Tertiary Kins.

There are eight primary kins : Husbarid-wife, father-son, mother-son, father-daughter, mother-daughter, younger brother-elder brother, younger sister-elder sister, sister-brother .

Our Secondary kins are primary kins of our primary kins. For example, father's brother, sister's husband, brother's wife, are our secondary kins. Anthropologists have identified altogether thirty-three secondary kins.

Our tertiary kins are secondary kins of our primary kins. For example, brother of sister's husband is our tertiary kin. Anthropologists have identified 151 tertiary kins.

In every society, the rule of descent is important for at least two reasons :

(i) It automatically establishes for every individual a network of social positions in which he participates with specific obligations and rights. Apart from mutual aid of various kinds among members of the kin group, these rights and obligations ascribed on the basis of descent always include some rules regulating marriage relationships among them.

(ii) By law or well-established custom, the rule of descent automatically defines some rights of inheritance : rights established by birth— either the eldest son or the youngest son or all the sons or all the sons and daughters inheriting the property of the deceased—as well as rights established by marriage—the wife inheriting the property of the deceased husband.

**Bilineal/Bilateral Group and Unilineal/Unilateral Group**

The family is based on the integrative bond of kinship, and this integration extends universally in two directions, viz. the direction of the father's family of origin and the direction of the mother's family of origin. For some reason or the other, stress may be laid on either of these directions. For example, we have the modern practice of ignoring the surname of the mother's family of origin. Not only do her children not take this name, but she also gives it up after her marriage and takes the surname of her husband's family. However, a family never ignores either of the two contributory sides in any considerable degree or manner. The family is, therefore, called a bilateral or bilineal group.

There are other types of groups with kinship as their basis of integration which differ from bilateral group in so far as they ignore one of the contributory sides completely. These are called unilateral or unilineal groupings.

**Lineage**

The simplest type of unilateral grouping is the lineage which consists of all the probable blood relations of one line of descent exclusively. A lineage consists of descendants in one line, either partilineal or matrilineal, who know their exact genealogical relationship and who recognise obligations to one another. A lineage is thus smaller, more localised and more function-laden that the broad kinship grouping.

**Clan or Sib**

When the simplest type of unilateral group (called lineage) is extended to include all those believed to be related through common descent, then we have a sib or clan. Thus, a sib or clan is often the combination of a few lineages and descent may be ultimately traced to a mythical ancestor who may be human, human-like, animal, plant or even inanimate The *gotra* of the Hindus is an example of clan. Obviously, the terms clan or sib describe larger, more geographically dispersed, near-functionless unilineal groups.

Sibs are often bound together by a common totemic name and by a common ritual taboo against eating the flesh of the totem animal. The fiction is solemnly maintained that the sib members are all descended somehow from a common ancestor of the totemic species.

**Phratry**

A kinship group is called a broad-range or a narrow-range one according to the number of persons it includes. The modern kinship system is a narrow-range system, whereas the primitive clan or sib is a broad-range system which includes people scattered over relatively large areas among whom it is not possible to trace relationship without bringing in a mythical common ancestor.

## 3. KINSHIP USAGES

Kinship usages or the rules of kinship accomplish two major tasks.

First, they create groups, special groupings of kin. Thus, the social invention of marriage assigns each mother a husband,. and makes her children his children, thereby creating special group of father, mother and children which we call family. By use of additional rules and social conventions, larger kin groups are created, such as extended families or lineages or sibs or clans.

The second major function of kinship rules is to govern the role relationships among kins. Kinship provides a sort of social grid. In a society people are joined to one another by genealogical ties and by common kin-group membership. Kinship usage assigns guidelines for interactions among persons in these social groupings. It defines proper, acceptable role relationships, say, between father and daughter, between brother and sister, between young son-in-law and mother-in-law, etc. Kinship usage thus acts as a regulator of social life.

The importance of kinship as a regulator of social life depends on three things : (i) The extent to which a person is surrounded by kinsmen. Kinship usage would have a limited role when the kinsmen are dispersed over a wider geographical area. (ii) The degree of development of 'patterned' kin behaviour. Certain kin relationships in certain societies are so highly 'patterned' that little leeway is allowed for spontaneity. In some societies kin relationships have little 'patterning' which leaves much room for individualised behaviour.(iii) The degree of development of alternative basis for assigning people to roles. In urban areas, our own behaviour is not affected by kinship rules inasmuch as we do not ordinarily interact with kinsmen. This is in marked contrast to the usual peasant village in which practically everyone in'the community is related to one another. As a result, almost everything that a person does is in the presence of his kinsmen. In very small societies with little or no geographical mobility, kinship usage practically governs social behaviour.

Patterned kin behaviour might be divided into two categories : (i) Rules governing rights and obligations and (ii) Rules of comportment or 'manners".

## Rules governing rights and obligations

These rules apply where one kinsman owes another certain services or duties or privileges. For example, a general hospitality ethic generally prevails among kin. If a relative expresses a desire to pay a visit to any of his kins, he may rightly expect free meals, a place to sleep, and other tokens of hospitality. His expectation or claim is considered to be legitimate on the ground that he is a kinsman. Rules of inheritance provide another example. These rules may prescribe that a deceased father's property would go over to his wife or to his eldest son or that the property would be divided among the children. A further example of kinship usage is the manifold obligations that go with parenthood: namely, obligations to feed and provide shelter to one's child, to train him up properly for life, and, in some societies as in India, even to pay dowry at the time of daughter's marriage. Even the division of responsibilities between husband and wife is largely determined by kinship usage prevalent in a particular society.

In some societies these rights and obligations are balanced fairly equally. In some other societies, these are quite unbalanced : one party gives and the other receives; one has rights and the other has obligations. This state of affairs characterises husband-wife relationship as well as parent-child relationship in our country. According to the tradition prevalent in Indian society for a long time, a husband is not expected to help his wife in domestic chores. On the other hand, a wife is expected to serve her husband as best as she can. Similarly, an Indian child, as soon as he reaches working age, is expected to assume heavy return obligations toward his parents and continue to shoulder this responsibility till the death of parents.

## Rules of comportment or manners

These rules may be sub-divided into several sub-categories :

### (i) Rules of deference

Deference customs are a ritual expression of social inequality. For example, in Indian society a child is expected to touch the feet of his father or mother or anyone considered to be of higher status than his own. Deference customs also forbid a young boy or girl to say certain things in the presence of adult members of the family or kin group. There are sections of Indian society in which smoking and even betel chewing by young people are not allowed in the presence of elders by deference rules.

### (ii) Rules of avoidance

These rules are designed to curtail intimacy, and usually apply to cross-sex relationships. In almost all societies avoidance rules prescribe that both men and women must maintain a certain amount of modesty in dress, speech, gait and gesture in a mixed company. There are more strict avoidance customs which restrict kin relationships in certain societies. For example, in many societies spouses are not supposed to touch each other or show affection in the presence of others. The personal name taboo may apply between them—the wife calling her husband 'Husband" and the husband calling his wife 'mother of so and so'. In all societies, avidance of one kind or another is observed in the relations between a daughter-in-law and her parents-in law.

There are three common avoidance relationships : brother and sister, a man and his mother-in- law, and a woman and her father-in-law. These extreme avoidance relationships are 'focal' because they appear to determine other and less common avoidance relationships. If a man must avoid his sister, he will often avoid various female cousins. If a man must avoid his mother-in-law, he usually avoids other female relatives of his wife—most typically, the mother-in-law's sisters. Similarly, if a bride must avoid her father-in-law, she will often avoid her father-in-law's or mother-in-law's brothers.

The aforesaid three 'focal' avoidance rules tend to be associated with one another. As a result, the societies fall under two polar extremes : (i) avoiding societies with many extreme avoidance relationships, and (ii) non-avoiding societies with little, if any, avoidance beyond the bare minimum of 'modesty' between the sexes.

Nothing much is known about the origin of these rules of avoidance. There are two functionalist explanations for kin avoidance. First, avoidance rule serves to forestall further and more serious trouble. Radcliffe-Brown has argued that the respect implied in avoidance practices and the formalised disrespect demonstrated by joking relationships (discussed below) are expressions of alliance or consociation. The actors in roles characterised by avoidance or by joking have divergent interests which could generate conflict between them and thereby undermine the bases of their common interests. The institutionalisation of avoidance and joking serves to minimise the chance of the development of openly hostile relations between the parties. According to the second functionalist explanation, advanced by G.P. Murdock, avoidances exist because they re-inforce incest taboos. According to him, if sufficient self-control is instilled during the socialisation process, then the extreme avoidances are unnecessary. In societies whose members lack the necessary internalised inhibitions , the avoidances arise as an added safeguard against incest.

### (iii) Rules of joking

Many societies provide for joking relationships among particular kin relatives, generally of opposite sexes but not always so. By way of illustration, we may refer to the joking relationships between a grandson or grand-daughter on the one hand and his or her grand -father or grand-mother on the other, or between a man and his older brother's wife, or between the husband of an elder sister and his wife's younger sister. There are many such joking relationships.

The origins and causes of joking relationships are utterly obscure. Some anthropologists refer to the possibility that these joking relationships might permit a sort of 'safety valve' for giving expression or release to the pent up feelings and emotions.

### (iv) Teknonymy

According to this usage, a kin is not referred to directly, but he is referred to through another kin. For example, all over rural India, and among some tribal groups, a wife does not utter the name of her husband but refers to him as the father of so and so. The husband also refers to his wife or calls her in the presence of others as the mother of so and so.

(v) **Avunculate ( Avunciate )**

If the maternal uncle enjoys, as a matter of convention, a pre-eminent place among his nephews and nieces, if he has special obligations towards them which exceed those of their father, if he transmits according to convention his property to his nephew, if the nephew works for him rather than for his own father, then this kinship usage is called avunculate or avunciate. This is a common usage among patrilineal people.

(vi) **Amitate**

When a special role is given to the father's sister, the usage is known as amitate. This usage is more common among patrilineal people.

(vii) **Couvade**

This kinship usage involves only husband and wife. Anthropologists have reported the prevalence of this usage among the Khasis and the Todas, and also among some people from outside India[2]. According to this usage, the husband is made to lead the life of an invalid along with his wife whenever she gives birth to a child. He refrains from active work, takes sick diet, and observes certain taboos.

This kinship usage involving wife and husband has been variously explained. Malinowski, for example, considered couvade to be a cementing bond of married life and a social mechanism designed to secure paternal affection. Some writers have sought to give a psycho-analytical explanation. They have attributed this usage to the husband's desire to lighten the wife's discomforts by a process of participation through identification.

## 4. KINSHIP IN INDIAN CULTURE

Kinship system is essentially a 'cultural system.' There is no universal kinship pattern in the world. It varies according to varying cultural systems. By way of illustration, we may refer to differences in kinship patterns obtaining in European and Indian societies. In the former a very clear-cut distinction is drawn between consanguineous kin and affinal kin—the two are poles apart. Kinship terminologies used in these societies bring out the distinction very boldly. A married man and a married woman refer to the relatives of their spouses as in-laws. Usage determines the relationships with in-laws. The very use of the term "in-law" sets them apart from blood kins. Again, in Western society a married woman has the status of an affinal kin in her husband's family. In Indian society, on the other hand, the distinction between blood kins and affinal kins is not so sharply drawn. Sometimes the distinction is so blurred that it is difficult to tell one from the other. After marriage, the wife enjoys the status of a blood kin in her husband's family, enjoying all the rights and discharging all the obligations of her husband's blood kins. In Indian society, apart from blood kins and affinal kins, even the fictive kins are looked upon as one's own people . That is, among one's own people are included persons related by blood, by marriage, by living together in the same house, neighbourhood and village, by being members of the same class in school, by working together in the same office, by being initiated by the same Guru , and so forth. Inden and Nicholas have brought out the basic difference in cultural values in this regard among Westerners and Indians by saying that "because of the dualistic assumption" in Western culture, they "emphasise the distinction within the larger class" between persons related by natural substance and the others who are 'merely' related by a code for conduct". "Under the monistic postulate" of Indian culture, by contrast, " all of one's own people are seen as related both by substance and by a code for conduct"[3].

The difference in kinship patterns obtaining in Western society and Indian society owes its origin to a deep and basic difference in the underlying principles of social organisation in these two types of societies. Our society extends beyond family only to the limits of a village, and no farther. The defining characteristics of such a narrow society, including rights and obligations of all groups of people in such a society, are shaped by the demands of the collective life of the family and the village. Naturally, a very close-kint relationship among members of a village develop. On the other hand, a Western society extends far beyond family and village. As a result, formal ties replace informal ties of relationship, and a sharp distinction between blood kins and affinal kins is the natural off-shoot[4].

We cannot also speak of a uniform kinship pattern for the whole of India so long as different social conditions continue to persist in different parts of the country and influence norms and institutions in those regions. But we may broadly delineate a picture of kinship pattern which prevails all over India with minor variations from region to region.

**Wider ties of kinship in India**

Outside his family, a villager spends much of his time with his other kinsmen. In the village a family depends on them in an emergency or on ritual or festive occasions or in connection with work in the field and sometimes even in settlement of disputes. We may take into account various classes of kinsmen outside his immediate family with whom he interacts.

We may, in the first place, consider those families which are closest to him in terms of residence as well as in terms of patrilineal descent. Such a group has been characterised by Mandelbaum as a *localized lineage* . These men are brothers who have set up separate households or the sons of brothers or patrilateral cousins. All the persons who reside in such households, including wives, adopted children and resident sons-in-law, are considered to be part of the lineage even though they are of different partrilineal descent .

The families who belong to one lineage usually perform formal ritual functions together, particularly observance of mourning rites. Such joint observance helps to define the boundaries of the group. They also participate jointly in many other activities. The lineage is regarded as an extension of the family and, as such, it is an exogamous unit.

Secondly, a larger exogamous category is known in many jatis, though not in all. It is called *gotra* or *clan*.. "It is usually a grouping rather than a group, a taxonomic category rather than the basis for joint action." Each person inherits the *gotra* of his father. Marriage within the *gotra* is forbidden because persons bearing the same *gotra* are considered to be descended from the same progenitor. The members having the same *gotra* tend to be too dispersed and their kin ties too remote to be able to share much in the way of common interests or joint action. Gotra grouping is, however, mainly used " to classify jati fellows into eligible and ineligible spouses."

Thirdly, there is a class of kinsmen who provide a basis for some joint action. In this category are the families of the *jati group*, i.e. those belonging to the same jati, who live in one village. They are looked upon as kinsmen in the sense that they are "either actual or potential relatives with the added bond of village residence".

Finally, there is a class of fictive kin. Since villagers consider kinship bonds to be the best basis for reciprocity and allegiance, people who are not actually related by blood or marriage can establish *fictional bonds of kinship* with one another. " In this way a person can secure for himself the benefits of a wider circle of kin than biology can provide for him"[5].

**Kinship Bonds in North and in South India**

Marriage alliances are the principal means by which new kinship bonds can be forged. There is, however, a fundamental difference in this regard between North and South India.

In the first place, broadly speaking, in the South a family tries to strengthen existing kin ties through marriage. In the North, on the other hand, a family tends to affiliate with a separate set of people to whom it is not already linked.

The system of kinship terms used by most Dravidian-speaking people of South India is connected with closer marriage. All descent lines are divided into two categories : those with whom one may marry and those with whom one may not. According to Mandelbaum, the structure of Dravidian kinship terminology " can be derived from a few postulates, a principal one being that the children of brother and sister should marry. The term used for cross-cousin of the opposite sex (a man's mother's brother's daughter and usually also his father's sister's daughter) has the connotation of prospective or possible spouse. By extension all potential mates are called cross-cousin"[6]. Co-operation among kins is periodically strengthened by marriages within that circle. In his analysis of South Indian kinship, Nur Yalman says : "Brother and sister must be separated but their off-spring must also be united"[7].

In view of this, Mandelbaum observes : "In most of North India, by contrast, there is a centrifugal rather than a centripetal tendency in making marriage alliances. A prospective match is seen more as an opportunity to ally two different sets of kin than as a way of strengthening an existing set"[8].

Secondly, in Northern India "unilineal kin are often linked to a particular locality either in fact or by implication, so that village exogamy is common. In the Southern usage, the emphasis is more on bi-lateral connections, and there is little or no territorial exogamy"[9].

Thirdly, " affines in the south may co-operate and are involved in each other's affairs in a way that is not tolerated in northern jatis"[10].

## NOTES

1. Most of the materials in this chapter are taken from (i) *An Introduction to Social Anthropology* by D.N. Majumdar and T.N. Madan and (ii) An article on *Family* and *Kinship* by William N. Stephens included in the book *Sociology* edited by Smelser.
2. D.N. Majumdar & T. N. Madan : *An Introduction to Social Anthropology*, page 107

3. Ronald B. Inden and Ralph W. Nicholas : Kinship in Bengali Culture. University of Chicago Press. 1977. P 89
4. *Complete Works of Rabindranath Tagore* (in Bengali). Centenary Edition.Vol X, Pages 934-935.
5. David G. Mandelbaum : *Society in India.* Popular Prakashan. Bombay. Chapter VIII.
6. *ibid,* Pages 156-157
7. Nur Yalman : Under the Bo tree : studies in caste, kinship and marriage in the interior of Ceylon. University of California press 1967. Pages 374-375. Quoted by Mandelbaum in his book *Society in India,* page 157
8. Mandelbaum, *ibid,* page 157
9. *ibid,* pages 157-158
10. *ibid,* page 158

# CHAPTER SEVENTEEN

# ECONOMIC INSTITUTIONS

## 1. ORIGIN AND DEVELOPMENT OF ECONOMIC INSTITUTIONS

Economic activities have been the major activities of mankind all throughout history. Even in the modern technological age, we spend a greater portion of our working hours to economic pursuits. The concern of the sociologist with economic institutions arises from the fact that economic and other aspects of social life are closely inter-related. Sociology, therefore, studies economic institutions as a part of society.

The complex economic organisation of ours had its humble beginning in the food-gathering and hunting cultures of old. There was simple division of labour between men and women. Men, and not women, were generally the hunters; women were the gatherers of fruits. The family was generally the producing and consuming unit. The wife prepared the food which was brought in by the men, and sometimes also by the women of the family. Occasionally, hunting was undertaken by the members of the entire community, as is the case with hunting of big games like buffallo, walrus, etc. In cases like this, the entire community was the consuming unit. These hunting communities were economically self-sufficient. Hence, trade did not exist. There were, in addition, serious practical difficulties in the way of exchange. For instance, the distances between settlements were great, and the means of transportation undeveloped. In these circumstances, exchange between settlements was not obviously possible. Another obstacle to trade was the absence of a common medium of exchange. Sometimes there existed barter between neighbouring tribal settlements.

Within a particular settlement, however, exchange was effected by hospitality or by gifts. Services were rendered or goods given without payment, but with the expectation of a return in kind at a later date. Hospitality was not wholly one-sided; it was reciprocal in the long run. Hospitality and gifts, therefore, rendered functions which money renders to us at present. In the words of Ogburn and Nimkoff: "A gift is a social substitute for money among moneyless cultures".

Both private ownership and common use prevailed among these hunting tribes. All personal effects, such as clothing, utensils, etc., including dwelling huts, were privately owned. Land was used in common. And the reason is obvious. Since hunting was their main occupation and since animals moved from place to place, private ownership of land was out of the question. A tribe used to extend its sphere of influence over particular areas of the forest.

Gradually, hunting as a means of making one's living was replaced by agriculture, and, with it, a number of changes were introduced. In the first place, land was assigned in plots to different families for use. In other words, private ownership of land was introduced. Secondly, food supply became more certain and substantial, and an element of stability was introduced in the community. Thirdly, with stability came specialisation and development of skills in different lines, viz., weaving of cotton, wool, etc., pottery-making, and similar other handicrafts. Specialisation, in turn, led to trade and other kinds of exchange against payment. Another offshoot of agriculture that is particularly significant from the sociological point of view is the development of the social institutions that came in its wake. Private ownership of land that became the rule in an agricultural community meant individual family ownership. In course of time, land came to be identified with wealth. So large land holdings came into being "by purchase, by marriage, or by force, where enough labour could be had to do the work". The community, thus, came to be divided into classes, namely, landed aristocracy and peasantry. Again, the family became an important economic unit with the advent of cultivation, domestication of animals, and development of the various handicrafts. All these activities demanded leadership; and the role of the husband became quite important in the family economy.

## 2. FEATURES OF PRIMITIVE ECONOMIES

In the context of the above resume of the growth and development of economic organisation over the years, we may pinpoint certain prominent features of primitive economies.

### (i) Shifting cultivation

Primitive economic organisations were of the subsistence type. That is, they fall into the broad category of production-consumption economies. One important reason for this is the absence of technological aids in their attempts to exploit nature, as is illustrated by shifting cultivation. Shifting cultivation means that the same plots of land are not cultivated for long and that cultivators move from one plot to another. The reasons for doing so are understandable. The decreasing yield of land as a result of continuous cultivation can be counteracted through proper manuring. But manuring represents a rather advanced scientific level of cultivation. The primitive people were not aware of the various ways of conserving the fertility of soil through manuring. Shifting cultivation was thus the only alternative open to them. This was facilitated by the fact that the primitive people did not experience the problem of pressure of population on soil. They could, therefore, easily explore and exploit virgin lands. Obviously, such cultivation is wasteful, inefficient and uneconomic.

### (ii) Exchange

In the absence of money as a store and measurement of value and a medium of exchange, economic transactions were always based on exchange. There were various forms of exchange prevalent in a primitive society. Some of these forms are noted below :

#### Barter

Barter is a direct form of exchange. It involves bargaining and haggling unless it is regulated by customs or norms. Barter is an exchange of (a) service for service, (b) goods for service and (c) goods for goods. Money does not figure in the barter transactions.

#### Silent trade/exchange

There is another type of exchange called silent trade or silent exchange. There are societies in which goods are placed for exchange without the individual concerned being personally present. If the goods are found to be of unequal value, these are not picked up. The person who had placed them understands the problem and adds more to balance the bargain. Such a practice is known as silent trade or silent exchange. According to

Herskovits : "Similar means of effectuating 'silent' exchanges occur today, or did occur until recent times, between the Chuckchee of Siberia and the inhabitants of Alaska".

**Jajmani system**

Jajmani system is another type of exchange. It is akin to barter system. The unique character of Jajmani system lies in the fact that exchange of service for goods may occur in a deferred manner. The word 'jajmani' is derived from the Vedic term for a patron who employs a Brahmin to perform a sacrifice for the community. In its original meaning, therefore, jajmani economic relations involved the exchange of gifts for service rendered or to be rendered in future. This meaning has not changed even today. But its ambit has been widened in course of time. Jajmani has come to mean all the basic reciprocal relations of patronage. It was a privilege and a responsibility for a family to patronise not only the family priest, but also all other specialists in the village. The system ensures the services of specialists like cobblers, washermen, barbers, potters, blacksmiths, etc. to the patrons on the one hand, and, on the other, it also ensures subsistence for the specialists who render the service. In exchange for the services rendered, the specialists receive annual gifts of products from the soil - a fixed portion of the crops - as well as cloth and sometimes even money. Such rewards or gifts are given in accordance with hierarchical status and not related in any manner to the 'economic' value of services rendered. According to Lannoy : "The intrinsically religious nature of the system is dramatised during the occasions when it combines exchange of services and of gifts with family rites, festivals and, above all, marriages."

The jajmani links are between families rather than between jatis. Thus, a farmer's family gets its metal agricultural tools from a particular blacksmith family and, in return, the latter gets a share of the farmer's crop at harvest.

The jajmani relationship is supposed to be - and often is - *durable, exclusive* and *multiple.*

The relationship is *durable* in the sense that the link may be inherited on both sides. Thus, a blacksmith serves the same farmer family that his father and grandfathers served. In the same manner, the farmer family gets its tools made and repaired by the descendants of the blacksmith family whose members made tools for their forefathers. If a member of a family dies without any issue, another of its lineage may take its place in the relationship. Again, if a blacksmith family (and, for the matter of that, any specialist family) has more sons than its clientele can support, some seek other associates in places where there is a shortage of smiths. Some may even take up other employment, often in farming, since traditionally men of any jati may work on the land.

Jajmani relationships are *exclusive* in the sense that the farmer family is supposed to carry on such transactions with a particular blacksmith family only. Reciprocally, these blacksmiths should make tools for their own families only. They are free to make some tools for sale in the market. But they are not allowed to poach jajmani associates from other blacksmiths.

Jajmani relationships are *multiple* in the sense that more than economic exchange is involved. Economic exchange is only one facet of jajmani relations. Thus, "a family of cultivators expects help on its ceremonial occasions from most of the associated families. There is also an expectation of mutual personal support in family emergencies or factional quarrels. Sometimes the specialist families are pressured to support the jati of their patrons when that whole jati is embattled ." (Mandelbaum P 165)

According to Dr. D. N. Majumdar, such reciprocal services are often *formally* prescribed, particularly for life-cycle rites. He notes : In a village of Lucknow district, a marriage in a family of Thakurs, the dominant landowners, involves the formal participation of families from ten of the fourteen jatis represented in the village. (D. N. Majumdar *et al*, Inter-caste relations in Gohanakallan, a village near Lucknow. The Eastern Anthropologist, 1955). Mandelbaum cites an interesting example in this regard : "A principal ceremonial role is taken by the associated family of the barber jati. The barber's wife cleans and refurbishes the house; she massages the bride, helps her bathe and dress. She joins in the wedding songs and in the stylized derisions with which the groom's party is met. The barber himself accompanies the marriage party in the ceremonial round, doing for the members of the wedding whatever tasks need to be done. He is present through all the ritual, helping the priest, performing such bits as the formal tying of the groom's shirt to the corner of the bride's dress. In return, the barber and his wife are given a sum of money .......... when they perform some special service in the course of the rite." These examples clearly indicate that more than economic exchange is involved in jajmani relationships.

**Coercion and consensus in jajmani relationships**

Some writers (for instance, Beidelman) condemn jajmani relationships "as the means by which the rich and powerful exploit the poor and coerce the workers into sustaining the power of those who have the upper hand and the higher rank".

Some students of Indian village life argue, on the other hand, that in spite of coercive element in jajmani relations, there is no doubt that such exchanges "bring solidarity and mutual benefits." It is also totally wrong, they argue, to conclude that service workers, such as, artisans, blacksmiths, etc., are totally helpless against the landowners. Each jati tries to maximise its gain and exercise as much power as it can in the matter of jajmani transactions. Condemnation of jajmani transactions "as brutally exploitative is too sweeping and obfuscating a generalization" (M.S.A. Rao, The jajmani system. The Economic weekly, 1961.)

**Decline of jajmani system**

At present, not much of the village economy is carried on through jajmani arrangements. By now, the jajmani relationship has been largely supplanted in many villages, although in relatively few villages it has completely disappeared. In this connection, we may note the findings of Gould (H. A. Gould, The jajmani system of North India : its structure, magnitude and meaning. Ethnology 1964) relating to his study of contemporary jajmani relations in Sherurpur - Naktipur in a densely populated area south of Faizabad city in U.P. According to his study, families of six specialist jatis maintain regular jajmani relationships with other villagers. Of them, washermen have the largest proportion of their clientele, about 77 per cent, on a fixed grain-payment basis. Carpenters and blacksmiths are next highest in jajmani clientele with 69 per cent and 67 per cent respectively of their customers. The barbers have 62 per cent of their clientele on a jajmani basis in spite of the easy availability of commercial barbering and its financial attraction for barbers. Thakurs and Brahmins have 70 per cent of jajmani relationships. Gould concludes that jajmani relationships tend to be maintained on a comparatively larger scale "because of the ritual importance" of the specialists, such as barbers, washermen, etc. Gould argues that carpenters and blacksmiths were able to maintain a considerable proportion of their jajmani clientele because "the capacity to retain traditional ties with carpenters and blacksmiths marks a household as socially important."

Mandelbaum points out that the above figures of jajmani transactions should not give the impression that such transactions are of great importance in the village economy under reference. The real state of affairs is contrary to this, as will be evident from the following facts. "The most valuable and productive crop is sugarcane and this cash crop does not enter into jajmani. The harvest of grain and peas in 1960 for the 70 households that engage in jajmani relations came to 221 tons. Of this production, a little over three tons was disbursed as fixed payments to jajmani specialists."

It appears that jajmani relationships were and, to a large extent, are still important for the ritual and social order. Jajmani interchange in Sherurpur - Naktipur and many other villages, "provides a measure of economic credit and stability; even more, it helps to define the local social order by defining those who can secure ample ritual services." Gould says that jajmani system "arises from a religious dichotomy between pure and impure whose implications work themselves out as a complex system of religious and economic relationships embracing, and indeed in large part defining the dimensions of a locality." We may further note that jajmani relationship is now increasingly being supplanted mainly because more money is now used in village economy and also because modern transport makes market transactions more feasible.

**Ceremonial exchange**

Yet another type of exchange is known as ceremonial exchange. It is a form of social exchange, as distinguished from an economic exchange. It implies giving of goods or money on an auspicious or a festive occasion to a relation, friend or a neighbour without expecting immediate reciprocity. The return is expected to follow in course of time on an appropriate future occasion. For example, birthday gifts, gifts on the occasion of marriage, diwali, etc.

The features of ceremonial exchange are the following :

(a) Value or quality of the gifts is not a consideration. That it matters in certain cases cannot be denied. Gifts of low value or of inferior quality may raise frowns or cause anger. The relationships may also be adversely affected. But, usually, the reciprocity is regulated by customs.

(b) Ceremonial exchange symbolises goodwill, trust and mutuality. It stimulates social relations.

(c) The form of goods given or the amount of money given as gift is indicative of the closeness of the relationship.

(d) Ceremonial exchange does not involve discussion or bargaining. It "involves the principle that one person does another a favour, and where there is a general expectation of some future return, its exact nature is definitely not stipulated in advance." With reference to the Kula a Western Pacific Community) ceremonial exchange, Malinowski states that "the bestowing of a ceremonial gift has to be repaid by an equivalent counter-gift after a lapse of time .... The second very important principle is that the equivalence of the counter-gift is left to the givers, and it cannot be enforced by any kind of coercion .... If the article given as a counter-gift is not equivalent, the recipient will be disappointed and angry, but he has no direct means of redress, no means of coercing his partner."

**(iii) Absence of profit motive**

The profit motive that is generally associated with economic transactions is generally absent in a primitive economy. A sense of mutual obligation, sharing and solidarity provide the necessary incentive in all economic pursuits.

**(iv) Virtual absence of innovation**

The rate of innovation in simple societies is very low, giving the appearance of an unchanging social structure over a period of time. Stability and uniformity of social structure are also the outcome of simple and uniform techniques of production used in these societies.

**(v) Communal nature of economy**

Primitive societies show strongly developed features of communal economies. All activities starting from construction of shelters to production of primary consumption goods are carried on through co-operative and collective efforts of the members of the community.

**(vi) Absence of division of labour**

There is virtually no division of labour except specialisation based on sex. While men generally participate in activities outside home, women take care of the infants and of preparation of food. These activities naturally force women to stay longer at home.

**(vii) Concept and nature of property rights**

It will be wrong to apply to primitive society modern conceptions of property. Thus, in a food-gathering society, there can be no property or any type of an economic surplus like cattle wealth. Among herdsmen, there is no ownership of land. Pastures are held jointly. Similarly, cultivators may own their lands jointly. Cases of individual ownership of land also sometimes exist. A very interesting variation is that of *multiple possessory rights* as reported from New Zealand, Melanesia and West Africa. Under this practice, several possessors use the same thing, say land, for different purposes. Thus, in Melanesia and West Africa, a person can own trees on another's land whereon the latter cultivates crops. In whatever form property may be recognised, its recognition entails the existence of some rules of inheritance. Inheritance acquires particular importance when individuals possess property. In case of communal ownership, the group as a whole never ceases to exist suddenly as an individual does, and is replenished through fresh recruitment from time to time.

## 3. FEATURES OF MODERN COMPLEX ECONOMIC ORDER

The economic life was radically changed with the development of power, specially the development of steam, later augmented by electrical power and industrial chemistry, and further augmented in recent years by electronics and computer technology.

The application of power to production brought into being a new economic order called capitalistic order. The following are some of the implications of this economic order :

(i) Capitalistic order is based on the idea of profit. A manufacturer or a trader is expected to sell his products for more than costs, the difference going to him as profit. The notion of profit was unknown when exchange was effected by barter or by various forms of gifts

(ii) The ideal of profit beings out clearly the anti-thesis between group-interest and social function. The specific function of this economic order is to maximise production so as to lead to maximisation of profit. There is no guarantee, however, that profit will correspond to service, that these economic activities will automatically further the interests of the community.

(iii) If follows, therefore, that "there is no safeguard against a gross discrepancy between service and return, except in so far as vigilant scrutiny and regulation are maintained by constituted authority".

(iv) Capitalistic order brings into being large joint stock business. Mass production requires large capital which can be collected through the sale of shares among innumerable shareholders. Joint stock business enterprise has the following features : (a) It enjoys a legal personality with definite rights and responsibilities. (b) The liability of the shareholders is limited to the value of the shares one owns. (c) Under it ownership is diffused and there is separation between ownership and management. "This process accentuates the separation of the financial from the industrial administration, of the pecuniary interest from the technological interest". At present, the large companies which dominate the major branches of industry are managed and directed by individuals who do not own them. The owners are the thousands of small and medium shareholders who have little interest except in the profitability of the company and may not even know what the Company produces. Some writers have characterised this development as the 'managerial revolution' and emphasised the transformation of capitalistic order. This view is, however, criticised by some others who point out that those who are on the Board of Directors have an important share holding, and that they are wealthy in their own right. In cases like these, ownership and control are not separated. C. Wright Mills in his book *'The Power Elite'* has shown how ownership and control are interwoven in American industries. Mills observes further that "the chief executive and the very rich are not two distinct and clearly segregated groups".

(v) Capitalism brought in factories which employed thousands of workers whom the employers do not know. "A factory is seen as a mechanistic arrangement and not as a society of human beings". Again, under capitalism labour has become a free contractual good; it is bought and sold freely under terms mutually agreed upon between the employers and the employees. Labour has, therefore, "passed from a condition of status to one of contract". Labour unions are natural offshoots of this system since these unions help them to wrest better terms from their employers.

(vi) This brings us to another aspect of capitalistic order. "It is always an arena of contending forces, for it rests on two premises, competition and bargain". Competition refers to simultaneous offer of similar or alternative services for acceptance by the buyer. Bargaining, on the other hand, refers to the process by which the opposite interest of buyers and sellers, employers and employees, are sought to be settled or adjusted.

(vii) Because of these tensions within the economic system, the state has to pass laws "to safeguard the life and health of workers, to prevent employment of children and to provide a measure of security in case of accidents, unemployment, sickness and old age". Another interesting development has been that the services of sociologists and other social scientists have been commissioned to improve the relations between employers and management, with the goals of preventing work-stoppages and increasing efficiency. Sociologists look upon the factory as a social system, and, on this assumption, they have developed a science relating to interaction of individuals within the factory, known as Industrial Sociology.

(viii) Minute division of labour, which is both a cause and consequence of modern technological method of production, is an important feature of all modern economies. Its social and psychological consequences and implications have been examined by many scholars. We shall discuss these consequences and implications in the following sections under appropriate heads.

## 4. THE DIVISION OF LABOUR

One of the striking features of modern industrial economy is the complex division of labour. The complex nature of division of labour was brought out very dramatically by Adam Smith as late as 1776 when he described the production of a very simple product like 'pin': "one man draws out the wire; another straights it; a third cuts it; a fourth points it; a fifth grinds it at the top for receiving the head; to make the head requires two or three distinct operations; to put it on is a peculiar business; to whiten the pins is another; it is even a trade by itself to put them into the paper; and the important business of making a pin is, in this manner, divided into about eighteen distinct operations ....." The description of the complex nature of division of labour as given by Adam Smith does not, however, throw any light on the social and psychological implications of complex division of labour. Both Marx and Durkheim have examined these aspects from their respective points of view.

### Marxian perspective : alienated labour

To Marx, work provides "the most important and vital means for man to fulfil his basic needs, his individuality and his humanity"[1]. Man gets satisfaction when he applies his creative powers in the production of certain commodity. It is his creation and, as such, he takes pride in and feels joy over the outcome of his effort. Another source of his happiness opens up when his product is appreciated by others. At this stage, his work becomes a fully satisfying activity, encompassing both himself and the community of fellow human beings. Work, though an individual activity, thus becomes a social activity as well. In Marx's words, 'each of us would in his production have doubly affirmed himself and his fellow men'. That is, work becomes a fully satisfying activity when an individual works both for meeting his needs as well as the needs of others. Marx observes that apart from possibly the dawn of history, this ideal relationship of work to man has never been established. On the contrary, work has been "destructive both to the human spirit and to human relationships" all throughout history.

Marx sought to focus attention to this state of affairs by developing the idea of 'alienated labour'. Marx meant by alienated labour the state of a man being cut off from his work. This means that he no longer finds work satisfying to him. He is no longer creative. He works simply because he has to. Being thus unable to express his creative faculties, he actually alienates himself from his true self. Further, since work is a social activity, alienation from work also involves alienation from others. Alienation is thus complete. He is alienated from his work, from his true self and from his fellow workers.

Why and how does this happen ? Marx argued that the source of alienation is to be sought in man's distorted view of the nature of a commodity or an object. A commodity or object is meant for consumption, and not for accumulation. That is, a commodity is a means, and not an end in itself. When, however, man makes commodity the end, it is only a short step to the idea of private ownership. The idea of private ownership finds a dramatic expression in a capitalist economy in which the ownership of the means of production is concentrated in the hands of a very small number of individuals. They engage workers who simply carry out the biddings of their employers. The workers do not follow their own creative urges. Goods are thus no longer a proud possession of those who produce them. In this way "the worker is related to the product of his labour as to an alien object"[2]. In course of time, alienation is further increased by the complex division of labour and the introduction of machine. Marx gives us a step-by-step analysis of the accentuation of alienation in a capitalist economy. This fascinating story is narrated in the following paragraphs.[3]

The first phase in the development of the productive forces within the capitalist mode of production was described by Marx as 'simple co-operation'. Simple co-operation prevails during that period in which capital operates on a large scale, but division of labour and machinery play a subordinate part.

Co-operation of this kind takes place mainly in hand production. Production in these early stages is distinguished from handicraft production in the guilds only by the greater number of workers simultaneously employed by one and the same capitalist. Here the emphasis is on the *socially productive force* that comes into being by bringing many men together to work side by side and to co-operate with one another. The capitalist pays each individual worker for his individual labour. The amount so paid is much less than the value of the product which the workers help to produce. As a result, the capitalist gets more than he bargained for.

At this stage, the existence of large outlays of capital becomes a pre-condition for the co-operation of many workers. The co-operation among workers is not possible unless they are employed simultaneously by the same capitalist. During this phase, capitalists with adequate means of production and money engage workers who do not own either of these, viz., means of production and money. Thus, the 'productive forces' do not come into conflict with 'relations of production.'

The later phase of hand production is based on a more complex division of labour, each worker doing only a part of what he did before. Manufacture naturally involves the union of the formerly independent craftsmen, forging them into one productive organisation whose parts are human beings. This is a new phase in the growth of productive forces. This phase, however, retains the character of handicraft because each operation is still performed by hand, and is, therefore, dependent on the skill and dexterity of the individual worker in handling his tools.

Since he is now engaged in one simple operation, the worker is "alienated from some of the creative prerogatives he exercised before". What he loses in creativity, he gains in efficiency. This is because of the fact that he now takes less time in performing the specific operation than the craftsman who performs the entire series of operations in succession. The division of labour among many workers, each doing a specialised operation, is the basis of the productive system called manufacture.

Such a division of labour enables the manufacturer to make necessary changes in the tools employed in production. Unlike the craftsman who used a number of tools for different operations, the workers now use only a specialised tool designed for each specialised operation.

To Marx, this development is important for a number of reasons. First, it brings about radical changes in the personality of the worker. The increasingly complex division of labour alienates the worker from his creative powers and thus diminishes him as a human being. Second, what is taken away from the individual worker in artistic skill, creativity and reflective powers is given to the organisation in terms of higher productivity. The deficiences of the former become the virtues of the latter. The organisation as a whole is enriched by alienating the worker from his individual powers. Third, manufacture develops a heirarchy of labour. At the very bottom of the hierarchy are those who perform the simplest operations of which anyone is capable. Hence, in contrast to guild production, manufacture brings into being a class of unskilled labourers, a class unknown in handicraft production. The separation of the workers into skilled and unskilled is thus brought into being. According to Marx, therefore, the main tendencies of the capitalist system appear during this phase of production.

The next phase was the introduction of machine. In manufacture the revolution in production began with the organisation of labour power. In modern industry it begins with the introduction of machine. According to Marx, the employment of machinery in the modern industry is the most important phase in the development of the capitalist mode of production.

The changes brought about by machine were far-reaching in their effect on the worker. In manufacture, the productive process was adapted to the skills of the worker, the machine system compelled the worker to adapt himself to it. "The lifelong speciality of handling one and the same tool now becomes the life-long speciality of serving one and the same machine". In manufacture, the worker used the tool; in the factory the machine uses him. In this way, the worker's dependence upon the factory, and hence on the capitalist, is rendered complete. Under these circumstances, the intellectual powers of the worker become redundant and completely disappear in the face of the gigantic physical set-up of the total factory organisation and the mind hidden behind it all. Hence the Marxian concept of alienation which emphasises the growing de-humanisation of man in a capitalist society.

What is the Marxian answer to this problem? His solution to the problem of alienated labour is a communist society in which the forces of production are communally owned. According to Marx, the concentration of alienated labour in large industrial establishments would encourage awareness of exploitation and oppression. They would sooner or later find these conditions intolerable and wrest all capital and power from their oppressors. This would lead to the eventual abolition of classes and class conflicts. In such a society workmen would at one and the same time produce goods for themselves and the community and thereby satisfy both individual and collective needs.

Marx gives little indication of how the specialised division of labour can be dispensed with in a socialist or communist society. Marx simply states: "In a communist society, where nobody has one exclusive sphere of activity but each can become accomplished in any branch he wishes, society regulates the general production and thus makes it possible for me to do one thing today and another tomorrow, to hunt in the morning, fish in the afternoon, rear cattle in the evening, criticise after dinner, just as I have a mind, without ever becoming hunter, fisherman, shepherd, or critic". Marx thus conjures up the vision of a society in which each individual is free to choose his occupation in terms of his inclinations and to move from one occupation to the other in terms of his changing moods.

Marxian view that alienated labour would not exist in a socialist or communist society is criticised as being too simplistic and naive. "In his analysis of East European Communism. Milovan Djilas argues that though the forces of production are communally owned, they are controlled by and for the benefit of a ruling elite"[4]. Djilas, therefore, concludes : "labour cannot be free in a society where all material goods are monopolised by one group"[5]. It is also pointed out by critics that the picture of a society in which a worker would not be tied down to one job against his mood is too unrealistic and exceeds the bounds of practical possibility. We can also assume that in socialist societies technology would be increasingly used in production in future on a scale comparable to that in capitalist societies. This needs must be done in order to give the people goods of better quality and of adequate quantity. Increasing use of technology demands greater and more complex division of labour. It is not clear as to how a socialist society can avoid the problem of alienated labour when a worker would be reduced to an appendage of the machine as a result of mechanisation of the processes of production. That machine tends to de-humanise the worker has been recognised by many philosophers, social scientists and writers. The crucial questions are : Can machine be dispensed with ? Can complex division of labour in a highly technological society be eliminated ? The answers to both the questions will probably be in the negative. What is, then, the remedy ?

If machined and division of labour cannot be dispensed with, the solution, though partial and inadequate, probably lies in giving the workers more free time, so that they can pursue their leisure-time activities according to their inclinations and changing moods. It will be quite pertinent to consider that when Marx outlined his views on alienated labour in 1844, the working hours in a factory varied between 12 and 16 hours a day. Naturally, he had little time for anything else except what Marx described as "animal functions" - i.e., eating, sleeping and procreating. The situation has radically changed today in advanced industrial societies. There has been a significant reduction in working hours and a steady rise in the living standards and income of the population as a whole.

Writers of leftist persuasion, such as the French sociologist and journalist Andrè Gorz and Herbert Marcuse. however, argue that the leisure-time activities of workers are also planned and channelised by big business. There is little or no scope of self-directed and creative leisure. Marcuse argues that : "The people recognise themselves in their commodities; they find their soul in their automobile, hi-fi set, split-level home, kitchen equipment". It is pointed out that "relative affluences and the extension of leisure have simply changed chains of iron into chains of gold"[6]. These observations seem to be an implied call for restoration of pristine values and making people aware of those values. A herculean task indeed which only a handful of brave souls can undertake. The old maxim that man does not live by bread alone seems to acquire a new dimension and urgency in modern affluent societies. it is a challenge for which adequate response has to be found in the coming years.

In this context, it will be illuminating to consider the views of Marx and Rousseau on the question of alienation. There are some striking similarities in their views. In the first place, both the philosophers have faith in the inherent goodness, strength of character and power of discrimination of the people. Secondly, both the philosophers agree that man was initially in possession of his self. According to Rousseau, that initial condition was the state of nature and, according to Marx, it was primitive communism. Thirdly, both the philosophers agree that the origin of private ownership of property and the institutions which developed around 'property' distorted values and introduced aberrations in the natural flow of life. Fourthly, both the philosophers agree that class divisions with accent on inequality bring to the fore the oppressive and distorted view of society. Class divisions keep people apart and artificial barriers to spontaneous social relationships are created. Man becomes the greatest enemy of man. Fifthly, both agree that man was born free and that gradually with the unfolding of civilisation this freedom has been restricted. According to Rousseau, the norms prescribed by society imposed these restrictions. Marx pointed his accusing finger at the growth and development of capitalism which tend to dwarf human personality and stifle the spontaneity of his thinking and action.

## Emile Durkheim : A functionalist perspective on the Division of Labour in society

While Marx was pessimistic about the division of labour in society, Durkheim was cautiously optimistic. "Marx saw the specialised division of labour trapping the worker in his occupational role and dividing society into antagonistic social classes, Durkheim saw a number of problems arising from specialisation in industrial society but believed the promise of the division of labour outweighed the problems"[7].

The theme of Durkheimian thought, as expressed in his book *The Division of labour in Society* (first published in 1983), is the relation between individuals and the collectivity. He posed the problem thus : How can a multiplicity of individuals make up a society ? How can individuals achieve a consensus which is the condition of social existence ?

In answer to this central question, Durkheim kept in view a fundamental difference between pre-industrial and industrial societies, and made a distinction between two forms of social solidarity, namely, mechanical solidarity and organic solidarity.

Mechanical solidarity is, to use Durkheim's language, a solidarity of resemblance. The chief characteristic of a society in which mechanical solidarity prevails is that the individuals differ from one another as little as possible. They resemble each other because they feel the same emotions, cherish the same values and hold sacred the same things. The society is harmonious and coherent because there is little social differentiation and division of labour is unspecialised.

The other form of solidarity, namely, organic solidarity, is one in which consensus or the harmonious and coherent unity of the collectivity results from differentiation. The individuals, who are members of the same collectivity, are not similar, but different. In such a situation, the consensus is achieved precisely because the individuals are different. Their interdependence brings them closer, and social solidarity is established. Whey does he refer to this form of unity as "organic solidarity"? The reason for this terminology is probably this. The parts of a living organism do not resemble one another. Each of the organs of a living creature (for example, the heart, liver, brain, etc.) performs a function. Each such organ is, however, indispensable to life. There is thus a unity or interdependence of these different parts or organs.

In Durkheim's thought, these two forms of solidarity correspond to two extreme forms of social organisation. The pre-industrial society or the society which was called primitive in Durkheim's day is characterised by the predominance of mechanical solidarity. The individuals of a clan are, so to speak, interchangeable. It follows from this - and this idea is central to Durkheim's conception - that the individual does not come first historically. The individual, the awareness of oneself as an individual, is born of the development of society itself. In primitive societies, each man is the same as the others. In the consciousness of each, collective feelings - i.e., feelings common to all - predominate in number and intensity.

As social organisation becomes more differentiated, characterised by multiplication of industrial activities, the 'sameness' among the members in terms of ideas and outlook is missing. There are differences amongst the members by virtue of variety of experience, upbringing and training - in short, by the division of labour. It is to be noted that the division of labour which Durkheim refers to is not to be confused with the one envisaged by economists. According to his use of the term, division of labour refers to social differentiation which is associated with differentiation of occupations and multiplication of industrial activities. The division of labour Durkheim speaks about concerns the structure of the society as a whole of which economic division of labour is merely an expression. Durkheim raises the question : If an industrial society is marked by so much of social differentiation, how is it that such a society coheres ? Why is there not more social disruption and more social disorganisation, leading to a breakdown of relationships and hence of social order ? Durkheim argues that it is the very function of the division of labour to provide this cohesive factor.

Durkheim also discusses other characteristics of these two types of society. In societies marked by mechanical solidarity, law is repressive because in such a society an offence against the community is met with collective reaction of a punitive and repressive kind. On the other hand, in societies marked by organic solidarity, there is a greater preponderance of restitutive law — i.e., a law which endeavours after a breach to restore the status quo ante. In such a society law is also differentiated in the sense that some portions of law apply to merchants only, some portions to employers, to professional men and so forth. In a society marked by organic solidarity, there is also repressive law. But it is only a small part of the total, and it is resorted to only after other measures have failed. Durkheim further points out that in the primitive society most offences are public while in modern societies they are private, civil rather than criminal, calling for adjustments rather than strong and violent reactions.

Durkheim classifies division of labour into two categories : normal division of labour and abnormal division of labour. The division of labour which strengthens social solidarity is characterised by him as normal division of labour. The division of labour which weakens social solidarity is called abnormal division of labour.

He further classified abnormal division of labour into two categories : anomic division of labour and forced division of labour. When division of labour is pushed to such an extreme limit that the workers are divorced completely from the entire production process and there is a permanent estrangement between the employers on the one hand and the workers on the other, such a division of labour is called by Durkheim as anomic division of labour. R.A. Nisbet explains the nature of anomic division of labour thus : "In his division of labour Durkheim had noted the virtually inverse relation between the development of culture and human happiness. States of boredom, anxiety, and despair are relatively unknown in primitive or simple society ...... In civilisation they mount and, with them, endemic unhappiness".

When workers are forced to take up some employment against their will in the absence of an alternative occupation, such division of labour is characterised by Durkheim as forced division of labour. In his view, absence of co-ordination or adjustment between job requirements and professional competence gives rises to this kind of problem.

In order to meet the problem of anomic division of labour, Durkheim advocates the setting up of professional associations and corporations with a view to facilitating regular contacts among workers. He also advocates the setting up of an agency for the purpose of reconciling disputes between the workers on the one hand and the employers on the other.

Whereas Marx suggests a radical solution to the problem of alienation, viz., the abolition of capitalism and its replacement by socialism, Durkheim suggests that the solution to the problem of anomie can be provided within the existing framework of industrial society. According to him, self-interest which dominates business and commerce should be replaced by a code of eithics which emphasises the needs of society as a whole. He looks upon occupational associations as the means to subject economic activity to moral regulation. Such associations would solve the problem of anomie in two ways. First, professional or occupational associations would check individualistic inclinations by re-integrating individuals into a social group within the membership of these associations which would re-enforce social controls. Second, these associations would lay down a code of conduct for their members, their rights as well as their obligations to the community as a whole. Durkheim is obviously influenced by his view of professional associations, such as those of doctors and lawyers, which lay down a code of conduct that is binding on their members. Through control of training and education, the professional associations establish both professional competence and professional ethics. Thus, the lawyer is the guardian of the law in the interests of society as a whole. The doctor, directed by his Hippocratic oath, is concerned primarily in his occupation with the health of the community. These features are lacking in commerce and industry. In his view, professional ethics must permeate all spheres of economic activities, and that is "the key to a future moral order in industrial society".

In order to meet the problems arising out of forced division of labour he advocates the expansion of opportunities for the spread of general education and technical training among workers.

In modern industrialised societies, the above proposals of Durkheim are being seriously considered and put into effect. The branch of sociology which is concerned with these problems is known as Occupational Sociology.

In will, however, be quite in order to consider also the anti-professional perspectives. According to one view, professional or occupational groups deliberately control entry into respective professions in order to restrict competition and obtain high rewards for the services rendered by the professional group. It is argued that "professional ethics, and in particular the emphasis on altruism, care and community service, are simply a smokescreen which serves to disguise professional self-interest"[8].

The second anti-professional view is presented from the Marxian perspective. It is argued that professionals are servants of ruling classes and ruling elites. Their services are requisitioned by the state and private industry. It is particularly so in the case of lawyers, accountants and engineers. They serve the interests of those who can pay their high fees and not the interests of the large number of people who cannot do so. It is doubtful as to whether doctors and teachers may be excluded from this charmed circle.

**A note on anomie : Views of Durkheim and Merton**

With a particular meaning of the word 'anomie' in mind, Durkheim used the term 'anomic division of labour', and elsewhere the term 'anomic suicide'. In what sense does Durkheim use the term 'anomic'?

The word 'anomia' is Greek. It simply means lawlessness—worse than anarchy because anarchy means a society in which there is no ruler but in which, the anarchists hope, the natural order prevails. It appears in English dictionaries as anomic because it came into English language from French or German which transform the Greek final 'a' into a final 'e'. Durkheim uses the word 'anomie' in the sense that the people have a sense of 'normlessness'. The term has been applied to the state of mind of individuals regardless of the state of society. Anomie is not the same thing as the absence of norms. In the condition called anomie, norms are present. They are clear enough, and the actors in the social system are, to some extent, oriented to them. But this orientation, on the part of many, is ambivalent. It either leads toward conformity, but with misgivings, or leans toward deviation, but with misgivings.

It is interesting to note that R. K. Merton uses the word 'anomic' in a different sense. According to him, "anomie may be conceived as breakdown in the cultural structure occurring particularly when there is an acute disjunction between cultural norms and goals and the socially structured capacities of members of the group to act in accord with them". According to him, in American social structure there is a "strain towards anomie". The accepted goal of the American society is to achieve material success, to be affluent. But a large number of people do not have the means to achieve this goal. This kind of incongruence between ends and means places pressure upon people to use other than the approved means in pursuit of success. Thus, according to Merton, anomie arises out of the "seeming contradictions between cultural goals and socially restricted access to these goals".

## 5. WORK ETHICS : SOCIAL DETERMINANTS OF WORK CULTURE

Work is given a pride of place in all economic activities. We cannot produce anything in the field or on the floor of a factory without contributing our humble mite. Even in a highly technological society, a man behind the plough is as important as a man behind the machine. We do not know of any society where it has been possible to replace man altogether from the production process. Even where highly sophisticated electronic device like 'computer' is widely in use, the computer's 'hardware' (the electronic elements and the various peripheral devices constitute the hardware of the computer) can do nothing by itself. It requires 'software' which consists of an array of programmes or instructions. The core of the 'software' is an 'operating system' that controls the operations of the computer and manages the flow of information. The 'operating system' mediates between the machine and the human operator and between the machine and an 'application' programme that enables the computer to perform a specific task. Human factor cannot, therefore, be eliminated from a computerised system. The importance of human factor can easily be guessed in other less sophisticated fields.

Thus the quality and the output of work turned out by a man are of crucial significance in the production process. It will not be an exaggeration to say that a society is richer to the extent that it has a work force which is technically qualified and psychologically committed to do his assigned task with dedication. On the contrary, a society lacking in these qualities among its work force would definitely be poorer.

Has society anything to do with the development of these qualities ? Or, are these to be considered simply as individual accomplishments having little or nothing to do with social environment ?

As we all know, the competence of a work force depends on two factors : first, the capacity to do a work, and, second, the willingness to do a work.

The capacity to do a work is again a function of two factors : first, the health and physical fitness of the workers and, second, the technical qualification of the workers. Both these factors are, barring a few exceptions, socially determined. If there is provision for good and nutritive food, good housing, adequate recreational facilities as well as provision for health care, the physical fitness of the workforce is, more or less, assured. Likewise, opportunities for general and technical education would tend to contribute to the improved capacity of the workers. In the absence of technical know-how and training, a worker would suffer from insurmountable handicap in spite of his best efforts. It is particularly so in modern technological societies.

The crucial question is : If a society creates the necessary conditions for improving the capacity of its work force, does it automatically assure improved performance or dedicated service ? The answer is in the negative. If the workers lack the desire or willingness to work or a sense of commitment to their assigned tasks, mere improvement in capacity would yield no result. It is, therefore, necessary to take account of the motivational aspect.

How can the workers be motivated to work harder and contribute their very best ? There are two lines of thinking on the subject.

There are some who prescribe economic incentives to make the work-force work harder and with greater dedication. In many societies the 'incentive' is sought to be built into the system, so as to bring out the best from the work-force. The basic assumption of this line of approach is that profit motive exists among all men. Greed and the desire for gain are, more or less, universal. In the circumstances, 'incentive' in the sense of extra reward for greater productivity would stimulate the workers to work harder and produce more.

There are, however, some sociologists who do not share these views. They emphasise the role of ideological factor, i.e., the role of ideas and value systems, in instilling among the people the appropriate work culture. The most impressive theory of this kind is associated with the name of Max Weber. According to this school of thinkers, the psychological factors like greed, profit motive, etc. are universal and, as such, not specific to any particular culture. But why is it that all societies do not respond to 'incentives' in the same manner and to the same extent ? There are instances in which increased ' take home salary' tends to increase absenteeism or widespread alcoholism among workers. If human nature is taken to be universal, how can one explain phenomena like these ? In this context, work ethics is emphasised by some as providing a clue to explain this puzzle. It is argued that if there is an ideological orientation among the members of a society that work is something to be done for its own sake, that too much leisure is not desirable and, as such, not to be encouraged, the society may expect a committed labour force. According to Max Weber, such an attitude to work, inculcated by Protestantism, contributed to the growth and development of capitalism. Some writers point out that the spirit of "other worldliness" fostered by, say, Hinduism is not at all favourable for the growth of an appropriate work ethics. Ideological factor has, therefore, to be reckoned with as one of the important determinants of the output and quality of work.

The problem of work ethics may be viewed from another perspective which adds another dimension to the theme. Some American sociologists, for instance, Harold Wilensky and C. Wright Mills, have noted among typical wage or salary earners a trend which may be characterised as a retreat from work to leisure. is it a consequence of the mass media producing the image of a leisure-oriented society ? Or, is it a predictable reaction to automation and highly mechanised production technology ? There are some sections of the working population among whom work is a central life interest. There are, again, some among whom leisure is a central life interest. Are leisure activities conditioned by the variǒus factors associated with the way people work ? Is the way people work conditioned by their leisure activities ? At this stage, sociologists do not have definite answers to these questions.. 'Work and leiśure' would constitute a theme for stimulating investigation in the years to come.

## 6. PROPERTY

While we discussed division of labour or work ethics, we confined our attention to the productive system. But equally important as a productive system is a distributive system. This is concerned with the allocation of rights and obligations with regard to the fruits of productive efforts, irrespective of whether it is simple agriculture or a highly sophisticated technological method of production. Man does not produce all that he needs. There is, therefore, the necessity for exchange. An individual parts with what he has in excess of his requirements and receives in exchange what he does not have or what he has falls short of his requirements. This kind of exchange leads to the social phenomenon of some having more and some having less. It is on the distributive level that conflict of interest arises. Both productive and distributive systems constitute what is broadly called economic institutions. Property, which is described by Kingsley Davis as "essentially the distributive system in its static aspect"[9], is one of the most important economic institutions. It is also universally institutionalised.

### Defining property

Morris Ginsberg defines property thus : "property may be described as the set of rights and obligations which define the relations between individuals or groups in respect of their control over material things (or persons treated as things). The essential point in the notion of property is that there is a recognised right of control over things vested in a particular person or persons, and within various limits, excluding interference by others. By saying that there is a recognised right, we mean that there are regular sanctions attached to it, that is, approved methods of dealing with infringements. The amount and nature of the control with which owners are endowed varies considerably in different legal systems, and there is not always precise correspondence between legal theory and economic usage"[10]. According to Kigsley Davis, property "consists of the rights and duties of one person or group (the owner) as against all other persons and groups with respect to some scarce good. It is thus exclusive, for it sets off what is mine from what is thine; but it is also social, being rooted in custom and protected by law"[11].

It appears from these two definitions that 'property' refers to the whole pattern of rights and obligations with respect to the possession, use, acquisition and disposal of scarce valuable things. It is to be noted that the term 'property' is used both for rights and for the things in which rights are held. The context should always make it clear which reference is intended.

Understood in terms of rights, the following are the characteristics of property rights.

(i) Property can be transferred by its owner by way of sale, exchange or gift.

(ii) The things in which an individual may hold property rights may be both tangible and intangible. Examples of the latter are copyrights of books or goodwill of a business.

(iii) Property rights do not necessarily imply actual use and enjoyment of the relevant things by the owner. Law makes a distinction between ownership and possession. The many kinds of property right may be summarised as *possession, use, alteration ,using up, usufruct, income* and *disposition.*[12] These are explained *ad seriatim.*

A tenant has the right of possession or occupation. The right of possession leads to various *rights of use,* depending on the nature of the object. Thus, the borrower of a book from a public library may use the book for his study. But rights of use do not include all *rights of alteration.* For example, the book-borrower may not make marginal notes. Likewise, a tenant may not pull down a portion of the building in his occupation without prior permission of the owner. The *right to use up* is illustrated by the right of an oil company to take the oil from ground belonging to another. The owner may, of course, get some compensation in return. The *right of usufruct* may be discussed with reference to the following example. The right to the produce of land may be distinguished from ownership itself, and also from rights of use. The owner of a mango garden may lease out the fruits of trees in a particular season to another. The lessee in this case has rights to the produce of mange trees without any rights whatsoever to the use of the land for other purposes. Such rights are called *rights of usufruct.* The *rights to income* may be explained with reference to royalties received by the author of a book from his publisher who publishes the book for profit. *Rights of disposition* include the right to destroy as well as the right to alienate—that is, the right of alienation by gift, sale or lease.

(iv) The possession of property may mean possession of power over others. Money and such other tangibles as well as intangibles like one's good reputation may be bases of power. "The possession of exclusive rights to something that is scarce and valuable necessarily implies the possession of power over others who also desire the scarce and valuable things ... The amount of power which property gives to the owner depends not only upon the definition of his rights but also on the intensity of others' needs for that which is owned"[13].

(v) The institution of property is, like all other institutions, a normative patterning of the relations between individuals and/or groups. Thus, property owners are under the obligation to use property according to social norms. Similarly, those who do not possess a particular property right are under the general obligation not to infringe upon the right of the possessor.

**Stages in the development of the property system**

The development of the property system has been a subject of speculation for a long time. Different writers have indicated the stages differently. We may consider some of these views.

Vinogradoff appears to distinguish four principal phases : First, the formation of property in tribal and communal surroundings. Second, the application to landed property of the notion of tenure. Third, the growth of individual appropriation. Fourth, the restrictions which are being imposed upon such appropriation by collectivist tendencies in modern times.[14]

Hobhouse speaks of three phases in the growth of property system. During the first phase, there is little social differentiation, little inequality. Economic resources are owned in common, or are strictly controlled by the community. During the second phase, wealth increases, great inequalities appear and individual or collective ownership escapes from community control. During the third phase, a conscious attempt is made to diminish inequality and to restore community control.

This scheme of Hobhouse has some resemblances to the Marxist distinction into three stages : that of primitive classless society, followed by class differentiation and the growth of inequality, and the final stage of a classless society at a higher level.

Many recent writers (for instance, R.H.Lowie and N.J. Herskovits) have emphasised the complexity of property systems and have rejected the notion of a unilinear evolution. There have been a number of comparative studies of property in primitive societies which illustrate the difficulty of determining the character and extent of property rights.

Recent sociological studies of property in industrial societies have been largely concerned with two aspects : first, the distribution of property and its social effects; second, the separation between the ownership and the control of industrial enterprises in modern capitalist societies.

Studies on distribution of property (R.H. Tawney, Equality, 1952; C. Wright Mills, The Power Elite, 1956, F. Lundberg, The Rich and the Super-Rich, 1968) indicate that there has been some movement towards greater equality in many of the advanced industrialised societies since the beginning of the twentieth century, though it has been more marked in respect of incomes than in respect of property. The equalisation of incomes has proceeded more rapidly as a result of high progressive taxation and the expansion of social services.[15]

The separation of ownership and control in industrial enterprises is a phenomenon which has attracted much attention from sociologists concerned with the development of modern capitalism. It has resulted from the extension of the joint stock principle. The industrial capitalists of the early nineteenth century were both owners and managers of their enterprises. But as the enterprises grew larger, more and more capital had to be drawn from outside. This was made possible by the sale of shares among innumerable shareholders. The social implications of this development have been briefly indicated in the section on Features of Modern Complex Economic Order in this Chapter.

## Psychological and Social Aspects of Property

It is still not conclusively proved as to whether the desire to acquire and amass property has anything to do with the instinct of man. Some say that it is instinctive. Some dispute this contention and hold that it is a craze conditioned by circumstances.

Morris Ginsberg argues that the interest in ownership of property is very complex and that it has its roots in several fundamental needs. To us, a commodity acquires value for two different reasons. When a commodity directly satisfies our need, it is naturally valuable to us. Our consumption articles and even consumer durables fall within this category. There are, however, some commodities which do not satisfy our needs either directly or indirectly, but these are, nevertheless, considered to be valuable. For example, gold, diamond and many such stones are considered to be very precious and people are prepared to offer fancy prices in order to acquire these metals or stones. Apparently, these have nothing to do with the satisfaction of our needs, either directly or indirectly. Why, then, are these considered to be so valuable? These have come to acquire value "through a process of conditioning or assimilation". Since these are scarce, those who acquire possession of these scarce commodities to the exclusion of many others find pleasure in, and feel proud of, such possessions. Disappointment sets in when we fail to acquire them, and we feel happy and proud when we have them. "In this way, habits of attachment may be formed in relation to objects which may have no intrinsic or *prima facie* attractiveness"[16]. Such objects "gather around them groups of emotional dispositions, including especially the prospective and retrospective emotions of desire, hope, fear, anxiety, disappointment, as well as pleasure in attainment, and joy in mastery"[17]. Ginsberg argues that all these primary needs, which "may serve as nuclei for the sentiments of property", are "aided by the tendency to confuse means and ends"[18]. That which is essentially a means to an end is accepted uncritically as an end in itself. In *One Dimensional Man* Herbert Marcuse points to this kind of distortion in perspective and says that an individual feels gratified by the satisfaction of 'false needs' which are largely imposed by the mass media. A feverish attempt to acquire various types of electronic gadgets even at a great personal sacrifice of many other essential goods is an example of pursuit of 'false needs'. It is, thus, obvious that "interest in ownership is very complex and has its roots in several fundamental needs".

Comparative jurisprudence teaches us that there are three original forms of acquiring property. First, goods may be taken directly from nature. Second, goods may obtained by the sweat of one's brow. Third, possession of goods may be obtained by the assertion of power over other people.

"In all these forms of acquisition, but especially in the last, the self-assertive tendencies of man come into play. Men come to love things because they have put their energy into them, and because they are instruments of general satisfaction, but especially because they give them power over nature and other human beings. It is not so much the direct use of things, as the exercise of power, which they at once embody and facilitate, that gives to property its tremendous drive, and makes it one of the roots of ambition"[19]. If, therefore, we look at the subject from a psychological point of view, property arises, not from a direct need to acquire and possess, but from the interweaving of myriad basic interests with self-regard and self-assertion.

We may also look at property ownership from another angle. "Ethically, the function of property is to provide the material conditions of a free, secure, and purposeful life". In actual practice, however, this object remains unfulfilled in the case of a large majority of the population in all societies. The reasons for this failure of the economic system to ensure carefree and meaningful life lie deep in the history and psychology of property. It is clear from the brief outline of the evolution of property (sketched in the preceding section) that ownership of property has gradually passed on in the hands of a limited number of people, resulting in deprivation of the bulk of the population from ownership rights. Another parallel development has been the gradual institutionalisation of the rights of property. Several consequences flow from this. The owners of property have come to enjoy their property rights without any interference from others. They have also been able to exercise power and domination over those bereft of property. To make matters worse still, the bulk of the population are denied the opportunities, in the context of minute division of labour calling for specialisation, for making work a vehicle for "self-expression and self-fulfilment". Ginsberg, therefore, concludes that "as far as the masses of workers are concerned, property cannot be said to have fulfilled its primary social functions of providing security and permanence, a basis of freedom and initiative, and an opportunity for the active expression of faculty"[20].

The solution to this intricate problem lies in devising appropriate methods for curbing and restricting within prescribed limits the opportunities of a few to establish domination over others. At the same time, conditions must be created so as to enable the vast majority of the population to release their creative talents and make their lives joyous and meaningful. Obviously, the institution of property must be suitably modified, so as to serve these twin purposes.

## Principal forms of the institution of property

Broadly, we may distinguish common, collective and individual property. Common property is that over which several individuals have rights. They, however, hold this property collectively as against the rest of the community. The rights of sharing this property are defined by customary rules of distribution and supervised by the community. There are numerous forms of collective property, the variation being based on the type of collective entity : that is, whether it is a private corporation, or a quasi-public corporation, or a public corporation. Finally, in private property the control of property is vested in an individual, subject, of course, to varying types of control imposed by the society in respect of its enjoyment, alienation and bequest.

It is difficult to make a reliable assessment as to when and among whom a particular ownership right was prevalent. However, the picture which emerges as a result of investigations conducted by social anthropologists among primitive people may be briefly indicated. Among primitive peoples, private properly is recognised in such things as clothing, implements, dwelling huts or divisions within these huts. In respect of these sharing is governed by customary rules and by exchange of gifts. With regard to land, there are great variations. Common property prevails among hunters, pastorals and early agriculturists. With development and expansion of agriculture, the principle of common property is gradually given up. But the abandonment of common property does not, as can be generally expected, lead directly to the acceptance of the principle of private ownership. On the contrary, "the gainers are the chiefs and the nobles, and we find more and more cases in which the mass of the people become dependent cultivators : slaves, serfs, or tenants of a landed class". It should, however, be remembered that alongside the emergence of individual ownership, common property also exists in a modified form. "The principle of private property is seen more closely at work among the pastoral people where communal restrictions are probably less effective and the chances for individual accumulation of property greater. At the stage in which 'barbarism' is beginning to pass into 'civilization', the different principles are found interwoven, and the signorial and the communal principles are still fairly balanced. Thereafter, the tendency is for the preponderance of power to pass to the nobles, leaving the commoners in an increasingly dependent position". Gradually, feudalism appears. There are varieties of feudal tenure which appear in different places according as circumstances demand. Eventually, industrial revolution demolishes the foundation of feudalism, paving the way for the establishment of the capitalistic order.

Explanations about the nature and characteristic features of capitalism vary. Capitalism has also, like all other social institutions, undergone changes in response to environmental changes and historical conditions. Keeping this in view, we may consider a few definitions in order to find out the sociological significance of capitalism. Sidney Webb defines capitalism as "that particular stage in the development of industry and legal institutions, in which the bulk of the workers find themselves divorced from the ownership of the instruments of production, in such a way as to pass into the position of wage-earners whose subsistence, security and personal freedom seem dependent on a relatively small proportion of the nation; namely, those who own, and through their ownership, control the organisation of the land, the machinery and labour force of the community, and do so with the object of making for themselves individual and private gains". Hobhouse defines it as "the employment in the production of goods for sale of those who have not the means of production by some who have or can command this means". From a sociological point of view, the essence of capitalism lies in the relationship that develops between those who own the means of production and those who do not, between those who enrich themselves at the cost of the bulk of the population. In course of time, the people press for removal of the inequities of the system by extending communal control over capitalist enterprises through legislative and administrative regulations. As a consequence, there has been an extension of the collective types of property in the forms of the co-operative systems and of public ownership, an increase in the public control of quasi-public bodies, and public ownership of 'natural monopolies'. At the same time, the workers have organised themselves into trade unions and they seek thereby to check the attempts of owners to exploit the workers. Their attempts are, generally speaking, considerably successful.

It may also be noted that socialism as an ideal and as a programme of work has emerged as a reaction to the inequities of the capitalist system. Opinions differ as regards the meaning of socialism. Some socialists advocate social ownership of the means of production while some advocate merely social control and regulation of enterprises in private ownership. The form and extent of social control "belongs to the bitterest controversies of today". Various alternative proposals are suggested, debated and even tried with an eye to the attainment of the twin objectives of distributive justice and economic growth.

## 7. "PROPERTY IS THEFT" — PIERRE JOSEPH PROUDHON (1809 - 1865)

Proudhon is one of the few French socialists of genuinely plebeian origin. Through a scholarship from a local fund, he was able to continue his studies after graduating from the *lycée*. While accepting this aid, he vowed that he would remain faithful to the cause of those whom he called his brothers and comrades.

His pamphlet entitled *Qu'est-ce que la propriété?*, which was published in Paris in 1840, created a sensation. It was here that he declared that "property is theft". He believed that justice was the law of nature. He concluded from this conviction that man should have complete control over things acquired by dint of his labour. The reasons which prompted him to characterise property as 'theft' may be discussed briefly.

It appears from his writings that in condemning property he had in mind chiefly that form of property which is made up of accumulations from profits, interest and rent[21]. It seems from his specific economic proposals that he intended only to eliminate the monopolistic and exploitative features from private property. He did not advocate abolition of other types of property.

He declared himself to be an anarchist. As such, his "most specific complaint against the state was that it had evolved out of the system of private property and had sustained the inequitable incidents of that institution"[22]. "What Proudhon feared above all was any meddling on the part of the state, even on the part of a democratic state; he was fundamentally antipathetic to the principle of authority"[23].

His ideas on property would be further clarified if one takes into account his specific proposals to render financial assistance to workers. He proposed the setting up of a 'Bank of the People'. Those workers who are able to work and are prepared to give an undertaking that they would do so would be permitted to draw in advance Bank Notes without interest on the basis of their undertaking. The amount of their withdrawal from the Bank would be determined in terms of the hours of work they would put in. He characterised this arrangement as *mutualism*. The idea is that the workers would gain as a result of co-operation among themselves. He visualised a definite advantage in the arrangement for the common people in that the moneylenders would be forced to wind up their usurious practices. Thus, the workers themselves, according to him, would be in a position to eliminate exploitation. There would no more be any need for "coercive social organisation".

If follows from the aforesaid discussion that he characterised as 'theft' only that kind of property which originated from exploitation of labour. On the other hand, the property that would accumulate under the ownership and control of the society would not be exploitative in nature. That explains the reason which prompted him to lay stress on co-operative banking associations. Since his proposals would make redundant any kind of "coercive social organisation" he called himself a *positive anarchist.*

To Proudhon, communism was repulsive. He sought to find a middle course between the socialist theories and the theories of classical economics. He sought the road to his *utopia* through the organization of free credit and equitable exchange. When the Revolution of 1848 broke out, he was chosen deputy and he tried to start a 'people's bank' as a way of realizing his scheme of free credit.

Proudhon was very much devoted to the rearing of just and honest citizens, who would in turn be able to organise equitable relations of exchange between groups of producers"[24].

C. Bonglé points out that his individualistic trend is "surprisingly enough linked up with a sociological approach. He lists among his discoveries what he calls 'the metaphysics of the group' which involves the idea that collective force is something more than the sum of the individual forces"[25].He sums up Proudhon's paradoxical position in the history of sociology thus : "he forced collective reason to consecrate personal rights and assigned to the community the goal of protecting individual equality."[26]

## 8. ECONOMICS AND SOCIOLOGY

An economic system is a system in which goods and services are produced and distributed for purposes of further productive use and consumption. The system is assumed to be governed by *rational* economic motives, i.e., the motive of maximising productivity as well as the motive of minimising costs. In other words, the factors of production are sought to be put to *best* use at a *minimum* cost.

This is the picture of an ideal economy. This would have been true if the economic system (or sub-system) were not tied to other sub-systems. In reality, however, all the social sub-systems are so closely linked together that it is well-nigh impossible to de-link one sub-system and treat the same in isolation from all the other sub-systems. Economy is not an exception to this rule.

One of the important sociological questions about any economy is the *degree* to which economic rationality is limited by other values and institutions that prevail in the larger society. Another related question is also equally important. *in what ways* do other values limit economic rationality ?

An answer to these questions is to be found in the inter-connection between the economic sub-system and other functional sub-systems. The subject merits detailed discussion. But in view of the paucity of space in a work like this, only the broad linkages are indicated.

Let us first consider the bearing of family pattern on the economy. Being highly streamlined and small-sized, a nuclear family adapts itself much better to the demands of industrialisation than a large extended family. Kinship ties, for instance, are comparatively weaker in the former than in the latter. As a consequence, in a society dominated by nuclear family pattern 'universalistic' values supersede 'particularistic' values and merit norms replace ascribed norms. Obviously, these changes are conducive to modern industrialisation. On the contrary, extended families provide various kinds of constraints to the adoption and expansion of modern industrial practices. Extended family is also not at all suitable for spatial and status mobility which is required by the modern industrial system. These aspects have been discussed exhaustively in the Chapter on Marriage and Family.

Political institution has also a close bearing on the growth and nature of the economy. Economic growth can take place only in an environment that is conducive to hard and honest labour. If the political institution fails to enforce its legal imperatives, so as to relate reward to productivity, maintain discipline in work sites, curb corrupt practices and improve industrial relations, economic growth would be slowed down. Gunnar Myrdal, while analysing the nature of economy in Asian countries, commented that the 'soft' governments in these countries blocked industrial advance to a considerable extent. The bearing of political institution upon economy may be analysed from another angle. Political ideology has an important impact on the economic pattern of society. Thus, a government, wedded to the principles and ideology of socialism, would encourage expansion and proliferation of state undertakings at the expense of what is called private sector. A government, wedded to a *laissez faire* ideology, would produce the contrary pattern. It follows, therefore, that economy is very much affected by the nature of political sub-system.

In a highly technological society like ours, the importance of education cannot be overlooked. Daniel Bell has characterised the post-industrial society as a 'knowledge society'. The characterisation is undoubtedly very apt. The gradual progress in technology prompted successively by steam power, electrical power, electronic power and, finally, the use of robot, the machine man, demands education of a high order. A society, which is deficient in terms of quality of teaching and learning, can never aspire to be a reasonably advanced industrial society. Thus, economic sub-system and educational sub-system are very closely linked together.

Even religion, which is primarily concerned with the world-view of man, cannot be de-linked from the economic sub-system. It is now, more or less, well established that financial incentive alone cannot motivate people to work. The 'will to work' is influenced by the values which a particular group of people cherish. Max Weber, for instance, in his penetrating study on the growth of capitalism indicated as to how the ethic of Calvinism paved the way for the rise and growth of capitalism in its early phases. His conclusion that "there is a direct relation between the practical ethics of community and the character of the economic system" cannot be ignored as irrelevant by a student of history of economic growth. There are instances which lend support to this conclusion. We may consider the case of other-worldly religions like Hinduism. "In fact, by placing a premium on acceptance of one's *Dharma*, on sacrifice and contemplation, and by inducing its devotees to view the course of events within a scheme of cosmological causation, Hindusim tends to lower the level of human aspirations. It leaves man in a more helpless position than he would be if his world outlook and his social institutions were such as to encourage an attitude more in harmony with the scientific temper and the use of existing scientific and technological knowledge."[27]

Thus, economic rationality is a characteristic feature of an *ideal* economy. The *actual* economy is, however, tied with other functioning sub-systems. As a result, economic rationality is modified by the values and institutions associated with other sub-systems. Moreover, economic rationality is itself a value which must be inculcated among the members of a society.

## Social Determinants of Economic Development

While seeking to identify the social determinants of economic development, we should bear in mind that the causes of under-development vary from country to country. It follows, therefore, that the remedies must also vary. Rostow spoke of the stages of economic growth and suggested that each country must take up remedial steps by taking into account the specific requirements of that country. A quotation from Galbraith would be illuminating: "...... we must recognise that economic development is a process — one that extends in range from new nations of Africa but slightly removed from their tribal structure to the elaborate economic and social apparatus of Western nations. At each stage along this continuum there is an appropriate policy for further advance. What is appropriate at one stage is wrong at another."[28] An example may be cited in order to bring home the truth of the statement. It is often assumed that capital is the greatest stumbling block to economic development. This is a wrong assumption in so far as the statement is accepted as relevant to all countries, irrespective of the stage of economic growth of each particular country. The truth is that in one case capital may be a stumbling block, in another it may not be so. We may consider Galbraith's pertinent observation on the point: "The ability to use capital in any considerable volume is itself the result of development. If it is available before the conditions for its use are available it will be ineffectively employed or possibly wasted."[29] This illustration underscores the important point that employment of a factor of production is not simply a matter of choice but is very much conditioned by cultural and social factors. The people must have the ability, experience and knowledge to make the best use of the facilities that are made available. The response ratio of people to the availability of facilities and resources varies in terms of its ability to use properly the avenues that are opened up. Economic development is, therefore, not a function of economic resources alone, but of social and cultural factors as well.

In the previous two sections on Work Ethics and Economics and Sociology, we indicated that both work culture and economic rationality are moulded by cultural and social factors. Obviously, the social determinants of work ethics as well as cultural and social factors which have a close bearing on economic rationality are to be taken into account while we seek to identify the social determinants of economic development. In addition, some other social determinants of economic development may be discussed briefly.

To begin with, adoption of technology is not governed by simple mechanical considerations. Technology can yield results only when appropriate social conditions are present. A technology which is eufunctional in one society may prove to be dysfunctional in another. It is, therefore, not proper to speak simply of technological development. Technological development becomes meaningful only under appropriate social conditions. Hence, the use of the term 'socio-technological' development is more apt. Galbraith's note of warning as regards adoption of appropriate technology is very pertinent. He observes as follows : "The borrowing of technology is .... a subtle matter. In principle, it is highly desirable .... One must know, however, why the thing was worked out. Was it a step forward in process or product of universal application ? Or, was it an adaptation to the requirements of advanced economic development itself ? .... They (the first type) are as appropriate and important for the less as for the more developed country. But much of the technology of the more advanced countries represents an accommodation to labour shortages or reflects the other special requirements of the more advanced economy.'[30] The observations of R.T. Gill are equally illuminating. "Ideally, the under-developed countries would employ a technology which is neither the Western technology (which is adapted to a different kind of economic context) but a *third* technology which consists of an adaptation of modern methods to the special conditions of the under-developed world. Despite some efforts in this direction, however, this third technology does not really exist. Lacking it, the modern under-developed country typically tries to import the "latest' Western methods, with the consequence that it faces acute shortages in certain areas (capital and trained personnel) while it has idle surpluses in others (large numbers of unemployed, unskilled workers)."

We may next take up the requirement of innovative personality for economic development. The formation of creative and innovative personality is largely a function of early socialisation and the nature and contents of education to which the child is exposed from primary stage onwards. In some societies, a child is taught to solve problems independently and encouraged to be creative. In some other societies, particularly the traditional ones, there is more emphasis on conformity and children are encouraged to accept uncritically the lore and practices handed down from previous generations. Obviously, innovative personality cannot grow in circumstances obtaining in such traditional societies. Economic development in these societies would naturally be slow and halting.

We noted that technology requires a favourable cultural support in order to yield desirable results. This means that there is a preparatory stage to the adoption of technology in a meaningful manner. Obviously, a time lag between preparation and adoption must exist. In Western societies such a time lag actually existed. For several decades the cultural traits and social conditions appropriate to technology were developed prior to the actual discovery and adoption of sophisticated technology. In underdeveloped countries, however, the problem is "to accomplish simultaneously both the industrial revolution and the preparation for such a revolution". (R.T. Gill) The mass media of communication carry advertisements of products turned out by advanced technology of the West. The end result is what is called "a revolution in expectations of the people" in under-developed societies. The democratic political process cannot ignore the rising expectations of the people and the government is obliged to go in for sophisticated technology in the absence of appropriate cultural and social support. This creates complications for smooth economic development.

We have also to take into account the explosive growth of population in the Third World countries. The dysfunctional aspect of explosive population growth in relation to economic growth is brought out by Professor Gill in these words : "... population growth is not a stimulant to development ... but a depressant. Because of the lack of industrial capital the growing labour force cannot find jobs in the city and therefore adds itself to the already congested rural areas. Rapid population growth in such 'labour surplus' economies may mean that despite the attempts to increase industrial employment, the absorption rate is insufficient, and that open and disguised unemployment increases as a percentage of the labour force—the reverse of successful development"[32].

In the preceding section on Economics and Sociology, we referred to the role of values and religion in influencing economic rationality and discussed the subject at some length. In economic development one has, therefore, to reckon with religion and values. Particular values stimulate the process of development. There are also values which retard the process. For instance, acceptance and obedience constitute the only meaningful and appropriate attitude towards life among the eastern people. They have a tendency to be fatalistic and to resign themselves to their fate. The powerful role of astrology and even palmistry in the daily life of contemporary India needs no documentation. While commenting on the attitude to life of the eastern people, Dr. Radhakrishnan observes : "Eastern civilizations are interested not so much in improving the actual conditions as in making the best of this imperfect world, in developing the qualities of cheerfulness and contentment, patience and endurance. They are not happy in the prospect of combat. To desire little, to quench the eternal fires, has been their aim"[33]. Obviously, this kind of attitude is not at all conducive to economic development.

## NOTES

1. M. Haralambus, *Sociology—Themes and Perspectives*, page 229
2. *ibid*, page 229
3. The description and analysis of alienated labour is based on Irving M. Zeitin's analysis of the subject in his book, *Ideology and the Development of Sociological Theory*.
4. Haralambos, page 231
5. Quoted by Haralambos, page 231
6. *ibid*, page 236
7. *ibid*, page 237
8. *ibid*, page 241
9. Kingsley Davis, *Human Society*, page 452
10. Morris Ginsberg, *Sociology*, pages 181-182
11. Kingsley Davis, *Human Society*, page 452
12. Harry M. Johnson, *Society*, page 225
13. Kingsley Davis, *Human Society*, page 454
14. Morris Ginsberg, *Sociology*, Page 190
15. T.B. Bottomore, *Sociology*, page 140
16. Morris Ginsberg, *Sociology*, page 192
17. *ibid*, page 192
18. *ibid*, page 192
19. *ibid*, page 193
20. *ibid*, page 194
21. Coker, *Recent Political Thengat*, page 195
22. *ibid*, page 195
23. Article on Proudhon by C. Bongle' in *Encyclopaedia of the Social Sciences*, Vol. XII
24. *ibid*,
25. *ibid*,
26. *ibid*,
27. K. William Kapp, *Hindu Culture, Economic Development and Economic Planning in India*, page 43
28. J.K. Galbraith, *Economic Development in Perspective*. The United States Information Service. page 1
29. *ibid*, page 2

30. *ibid*, page 22
31. T.N. Gill, ***Economic Development : Past and Present, Second Edition, 1970, Page 86***
32. *ibid*, page 88
33. Dr. S. Radhakrishnan, ***Eastern Religions and Western Thought***, Oxford University Press, 1939, page 257

# CHAPTER EIGHTEEN

# POLITICAL INSTITUTIONS

## 1. THE STATE AND SOCIETY

No study of society is complete without a study of the state or the governing institutions of society, because the government is an important factor in our lives from the cradle to the grave. As soon as a baby is born its birth is registered with the government; when it grows into a child, the government often takes care of its education. A citizen is also protected by various social security measures undertaken at the instance of government. In this way a person comes in close contact with the government in different spheres all throughout his life. Even when he dies, his death is registered with the government.

In view of its importance in the life of a man, we may study the state from the point of view of (a) its sphere of activities, (b) its relation to the broad society of which it is a part, and (c) its relation to the international community.

### Sphere of State Action

Various questions relating to the end or purpose of the state have been asked in different epochs almost in all countries. Why does the state exist ? Is it an end in itself or is it only a means ? Can we not do without the state ? These questions have been asked and debated in different ages by different people with particular premises at the back of their mind. Naturally, answers to these questions often varied. There were, for instance, the anarchists who advocated the abolition of the state. The Greeks, on the other hand, regarded the state as the highest fulfilment of human life and as an end in itself. This view has been revived by philosophers who belong to the Idealistic School. The names of Fichte, Hegel and Dr. Bosanquet are associated with this conception of the state. Some writers proceed to the other extreme and think somewhat lightly of the state, and value rather the liberty of the individual. They look upon the state merely as a means or mechanism for securing this. One of the most popular of these lines of thinking is the individualistic view.

The general consensus of opinion today is that if we consider the question of end to the exclusion of means or of means to the exclusion of the end, we shall misunderstand the nature of both terms. As a matter of fact, the state is both an end and a means. If we look at the state purely from the point of view of an individual, it is only a means, a mechanism through which the highest individual development is obtained. If, however, the state is considered to be an institution, distinct and apart from the citizens who compose it, it is an end in itself. In this capacity, the state represents the collective good of the community.

Related to the question of the purpose of the state is the question of the proper sphere of state action. These questions did not concern the Greeks, because they identified the good of the individual with the good of the state. According to them, the state embraced everything which was concerned with the life and the highest development of the individual.

In the seventeenth century there was, however, a new movement in favour of limited state action. Gradually, this movement became powerful and the ideas underlying the movement formed the philosophical background of the *laissez faire* theory of the nineteenth century. The guiding principle of this philosophy is maximum possible individual freedom and minimum possible state action. The legitimate functions of the state, according to this school, are to protect the individual against external and internal enemies as well as to enforce contracts that are lawfully made. The phrase " Man *versus* the State" sums up the attitude of mind of those who advocated this doctrine in earlier times. Since group is considered essential for the growth of individual personality in modern times, the present-day advocates of this doctrine emphasise group autonomy. Their idea is best represented by the phrase "Group *versus* the State".

As a reaction to the evils and deficiencies of the system of free enterprise, there grew up a school of thought known popularly as socialism. There are different strands of socialistic thinking. Some advocate state ownership of the means of production; some advocate equal distribution; and some equitable distribution. The advocates of socialism also differ in terms of the methods suggested by them for the achievement of socialism. Some believe in the violent overthrow of the capitalist class and establishment of a socialistic society. Some others, on the other hand, believe that socialism can be achieved through evolutionary processes without recourse to violence.

The truth, however, lies in a balance between the two lines of thinking. The individualists are right when they emphasise that too much of interference by the state would kill individual spontaneity and initiative. But they are wrong in considering an individual an independent entity apart from society . The socialists are right in emphasising the social nature of man. But they are wrong in overlooking the reality of individual personality. Delisle Burns, therefore, rightly observes : "If we could imagine an ideal at once individualistic and socialistic, such would be the effective ideal for most thinking men".

It is, therefore, more helpful to think concretely in terms of this broad question : What, in general, are the tasks of government ? According to Professor W. W. Rostow, governments must exercise power in three major directions : (i) to protect the territorial integrity of society; (ii) to provide for the general welfare; and (ii) to preserve the constitutional order, that is, "to maintain public order, orderly change, and legitimate succession by some enforceable balance between public constraint and individual freedom of action and expression of opinion".

The heart of politics and of political debate, emphasises Professor Rostow, lies in these fundamental questions, from ancient times down to the contemporary world, from simple tribes to elaborate industrial societies, from advanced democracies to totalitarian dictatorships. Every society strikes a balance between these tasks in terms of "that society's history and cultural heritage, the state of education of its citizens, and the nature of the problems it confronts as a domestic community and the world scene".

## The State as a Unique Association

The relation between the state and other associations has been a subject-matter of controversy between two schools of writers, viz., the monistic writers who advocate absolute powers for the state and the pluralistic writers who look upon the state as merely an association among many having limited competence and restricted authority.

According to the monists, the state is the supreme social institution and all other associations owe their origin to its initiative, acquiescence, and support. They exist because the state allows them to exist. The monists recognise other forms of association as essential to the existence of men, but they regard the position of the state in relation to the other associations as unique. These associations, according to these writers, function in a certain way and on certain terms laid down by the state.

The pluralists do not accept this position. They recognise the special role of the state as a regulator of social life. But they see no reason as to why the regulator is to be identified with that which is regulated.They charge the monists "with the error of regarding all non-political associations created by the state as dependent for their continued existence upon the will of the state and as exercising only powers conceded by the state"[1]. They further hold that "other associations arise naturally and spontaneously and in their peculiar spheres act independently of state control",[2] These other associations are as necessary for the growth of individual personality as the state itself. We have various social needs which cannot be met by the state alone. Because of their select membership, those other associations are better adapted than the state for serving these needs. Laski has, therefore, argued that the state "does not exhaust the associative impulses of men". In his opinion the society "should be regarded as essentially federal in its nature". The other associations are real in the sense that the state is real. Hence, the state must compete with churches, trade unions, etc. for winning the loyalty of men and women. "No association," says Laski, " can legislate for the whole of myself". The pluralists, therefore, conclude that "the state can not in any important sense be said to be sovereign in its relation to these independently originating and functioning associations"[3]. The other associations are as native to the soil of society as the state itself.

The pluralistic doctrine is, thus, a welcome reaction against the glorification of the state. It rightly emphasises the moral limitations upon the unfettered authority of the state. We should recognise limitations of the state" to sponsor the more intimate or more personal interests, those which admit a variety of spontaneous and variant expressions."But one should not carry the idea of group autonomy too far. There are certain functions which the state alone can perform. If the state fails to discharge its responsibilities in the three areas of social life, as emphasised by Professor Rostow, no individual citizen can attain full growth and stature. From this point of view, the state may be viewed as a "community agency," charged with the responsibility of coordinating and adjusting the claims and activities of various associations. This distinctive function gives the state its unique character.

**The State and International Community**

The interests of humanity likewise demand the limitation of sovereignty. The concept of an absolute and sovereign state implies the right of a state to deal with other states in any way it likes. This right involves the right of a nation to wage war in order to settle differences and conflicts of interest.

In the context of the modern world, however, this right can no longer be conceded. In the first place, the scientific advances and tecnological developments have annihilated distances and increased "the range and degree of the interdependence of nations", We have long left behind the days when nations could afford to remain in isolation, if they had chosen to do so. On the contrary, we live virtually in "one world" in which an economic depression in one country may affect the economic well-being of the rest of the world. Even a change in fashion, say,in dress in one country becomes popular in other parts of the world in an unbelievably short period of time. It follows from these economic and social realities that we have to develop a global outlook and plan for the whole of humanity, and not for a part of it. There is much that we can achieve through co-operative efforts; there is comparatively little that we can gain through division and conflict in this progressively shrinking world. Secondly, unlimited exercise of sovereign power by\ a state has become, in the context of modern weapons of mass destruction, a matter of the greatest menace to the security of the world. War can no longer serve to settle disputes. It can no longer be regarded as a rational alternative."It makes no sense in an age when the deadly poisons produced by a nuclear exchange would be carried by the wind and water and soil and seed to the far corners of the globe and to generations yet unborn"[5]. A nuclear disaster may engulf the great and the small, the rich and the poor, the committed and the uncommitted, the victors and the vanquished alike. In terms of military realities of today, no nation can, therefore, be truly secure." In a spiralling arms race, a nation"s security may well be shrinking even as its arms increase"[6]. The interests of a nation-state have, therefore, to be subordinated to the interests of humanity. In the words of Laski: "Our problem is not to reconcile the interest of humanity with the interest of England; our problem is so to act that the policy of England naturally implies the well-being of humanity"[7]. In other words, we should recognise the existence of an international community of nations of which every nation-state is a part. It is a reality which we shall overlook only at our peril.

## 2. POLITICAL INSTITUTIONS IN PRIMITIVE AND MODERN SOCIETIES

Being disturbed by the existence of a government which denies the just rights and liberties of citizens, many people have dreamed of abolishing political institutions altogether. They assumed that since the government was not a natural institution but was created by man and rested on the willing consent of the people, it was easy to eliminate the institution altogether, so that people could pursue their natural inclinations and find their true happiness. Such anarchistic arguments appealed to countless people in all ages. But the idea has ever remained an aspiration. There is an overwhelming opinion now that the idea is merely a utopian dream.

The idea of a stateless society was strengthened by what some people considered to be an almost complete absence of differentiated political institutions in some primitive societies. The statement is not, however, accurate. It is true that in primitive societies, there is no law, no court, no legislature and no executive in the form in which we find them in a complex society like ours. Nevertheless, no discerning observer of a primitive society failed to notice that in such societies, there was a need for political control and that institutions of a non-political nature were made to serve such a need.

Why is the need for political control a universal feature of social living ? Are not non-political agencies of social control adequate enough to keep occasional violence of social norms in line?The answer is obviously in the negative. There are in all societies persons who are persistent violators of social norms and are not amenable to social pressures. In their case, social norms have to be enforced. Political control, thus, becomes indispensable, because political control involves not simply authority but *ultimate* authority, backed whenever necessary by the use of force. No society can dispense with the use of force in extreme cases. Hence, the need and indispensability of political institution.

Apart from this functional explanation of the emergence of the state, there are two other explanations. Political institution, it is argued, is the consequence of the increasing size and complexity of societies in which warfare was a major factor. Oppenheimer,, for example, discussed the origin of the state in terms of the conquest of one tribe by another with the sole object of subjecting them to a tribute...." Marxist theory, on the other hand, accounts for the emergence of the state in terms of differentiation into social classes within the community following the growth of productive forces and of wealth.

Whatever be the explanation, one distinctive feature of primitive and early societies was that where a separate political authority existed, it was closely bound up with kinship, religion and other institutions.

In terms of the nature of political institutions, primitive societies fall under two categories : (i) those without a distinct and permanent political structure, and (ii) those with a distinct and permanent political structure, but strongly influenced by kinship and religion.

## Political Institutions of Modern Times

Bottomore has identified three types of political situation in the contemporary world[8].

First, there are tribal societies, mainly in African countries, which are being modernised under Western influence on the lines of Western political institutions. It is difficult to say how far this kind of modernisation process would help to keep in check the tribal feuds and establish national unity and cohesion on a firm foundation. Africa was parcelled out among colonial powers according to their needs and convenience. As a consequence, a particular tribe had been distributed among three or four neighbouring colonies under different European powers. This created tension and produced instability both within a nation-state and among newly independent neighbouring nation-states. Thus, these African societies faced, in addition to the challenge of bringing about rapid economic advance and ensuring economic well-being to the vast majority of the population, the uphill task "of consolidating a national community formed out of tribal groups whose existence within their frontiers is in some measure the result of the arbitrary division of Africa among the colonial powers".

Second, another type of political situation obtains in those developing countries of ancient civilisation which are attempting to modernise their societies after emancipation from foreign rule. Apart from the newly independent states of Africa which have already been discussed above, the Arab States of the Middle East and North Africa, the Asian states and the Latin American States fall under this category.

There are some political conditions and problems which are common to most, if not all, of these developing countries. Some of these problems are : (i) the problems of establishing altogether a new political system based principally on Western political institutions, (ii) devising appropriate governmental machinery for the purpose of bringing about rapid economic growth, and (iii) effecting, as rapidly as possible, general improvement in the levels of living of the common people.

These developing countries face a number of difficulties in implementing the aforesaid programmes of work. In most of these countries, the political institutions which have been set up on the Western model are not working as well as is expected because the people of these countries have not been able to develop the appropriate political culture. Social institutions in the form of kinship system, patterns of familial ties, class divisions, and, above all, traditional outlook on life do not favour smooth functioning of a modern political system. These factors are also not very conducive to the growth of 'work culture'. As a consequence thereof, economic growth is halting. Failures of the government in meeting the aspirations of the people encourage army generals or ambitious political leaders in some of these countries to assume dictatorial power and do away with democratic political institutions. Bangladesh, Pakistan, Burma and a host of countries in Africa and Latin America bear testimony to this type of development.

In the third category are included industrially advanced countries of Europe, North America, Australia, Japan, etc. Here a distinction should be made between two types of political systems obtaining in countries under this category : the democratic-capitalist or democratic-socialist countries on the one hand and communist countries on the other.

The general political characteristics of the modern industrial societies of the first type are : (i) the existence of a nation-state as the political community, (ii) the existence of political parties, pressure groups and political movements, (iii) the election of the political executive by universal adult suffrage, and (iv) the administration of public affairs by a large bureaucracy.

The most important characteristic feature of the industrial societies of the second type is the existence of single party which monopolises political power. "This situation is justified in terms of Marxist theory as the expression of social unity resulting from the elimination of antagonistic social classes. The dictatorship of the party is equated with the dictatorship of the proletariat in a transitional period during which the foundations of the ultimate classless society are being laid". It is argued on the basis of Marxist theory that after the establishment of the classless society, the state will 'wither away'. The theory and practice of communism have, however, been criticised. It is pointed out that the coercive apparatus of the state does not show any sign of 'withering away'. On the contrary, the coercive power of the state in communist societies has vastly increased, jeopardising in the process the liberty of the individual and unfettered freedom of expression. The suppression of dissident opinion in the Soviet Union and countries of Eastern Europe is an evidence of this development. Voices are raised, not infrequently, against too much concentration of power, particularly in countries of Eastern Europe. In Yugoslavia, there was an attempt to decentralise political authority. "The major sociological criticism of most orthodox Marxism is that it asserts, against the evidence, that political power is always based upon, and can only be based upon, economic power, and fails to analyse in a scientific and exact way, the notion of 'economic power'... The assertion of a one to one causal relationship between economic power and political power goes back to the eighteenth century distinction between 'civil society' and the state, and to the impression made upon social theorists by the rapid emancipation of economic life from political regulation in the early stages of industrial capitalism. But in a broader historical perspective, while recognising the important influence of economic structure upon other social institutions, we must also admit the relative autonomy of politics"[9]. A development of far-reaching importance in communist societies is the experiment launched in China in terms of giving private enterprise a pivotal role in the economic field, both in agriculture and in industry.

The events which have taken place in the Soviet Union and in the countries of Eastern Europe in the year 1989 clearly prove that concentration of power in the hands of the office-bearers of the Communist Party does not ensure the end of exploitation and the promise of freedom for the vast majority of the population.

## 3. POLITICAL SOCIOLOGY

In the first section of this chapter, we referred to the debate over the analytic primacy of *society* or the *state*. Various social philosophers argued for the legitimacy and primacy of state authority, while others questioned the claim entirely, arguing that the interest of society and of citizens were superior to those of the state, that the state must serve rather than control its citizens, and that the state should be weakened rather than strengthened. The conflict arose from the fact that the two concepts, viz., state and society, were all-encompassing. Political scientists pointed to the fact that the state has sovereignty, i.e., legitimate supreme authority over all persons and institutions within its boundaries. The notion of society was equally all-embracing. It was claimed by those who argued for society that all that came within the province of a society was part of it. Much of what concerned the sociologist seemed to many early political scientists to be a part of political science, while the sociologists took the opposite position.

The controversy is, at present, almost hushed to silence. It is now broady agreed that the two disciplines deal with behaviour of men and women within the social system, each having its distinct *focus*. Thus, a political scientist is primarily concerned with the dimension of power and the factors and influences that affect its distribution. The state is the only authority which exercises ultimate power in a legitimate manner. This gives the state its unique character. The sociologist, on the other hand, "is more concerned with social control, with the way in which the values and norms of a society pattern relationships among different units of the larger system[10]. That is, sociologist is more concerned with social ties, rather than with "formal structures and legal definitions".

Since the two disciplines are concerned with human behaviour within the larger social system, it can be assumed that there are areas of overlap between social structures and political institutions, between values and culture of a group and the political institutions which they develop. On its part, political institutions also affect social values and culture. Political sociology does not, therefore, study simply the social factors that condition the political order, but also the way political institutions affect non-political social structures. It is important to note that the domain of political sociology, as defined above, does not assign causal priority to society over polity or to polity over society.

In this context, reference may be made to the thinking of Montesquieu (1689-1755). He was the first philosopher to initiate discussion on the relationship between political structure and institutions on the one hand and the various socio-cultural variables on the other. By analysing social and economic events, he sought to find out the linkages between the two types of events.

He classified political institutions into a few *ideal types*, such as, republic, aristocracy, monarchy and autocracy. In his view, these political institutions did not arise by accident. On the contrary, social factors were responsible for their emergence during different historical periods. One cannot, therefore, understand the true nature of political institutions without taking into account the socio-economic variables which have a bearing on them. When Montesquieu speaks of monarchy or aristocracy, he has in view the entire social system of which political institutions form a part.

He did not arrive at his conclusion by following the deductive method. His conclusions were based on analysis of historical events, comparative studies of various social systems, both past and present, travelogues of different people, and his own experience gathered from travels, far and wide.

He sought to find out the essence of republican form of government by analysing the political institutions which were prevalent in the city states of Athens, Sparta and Rome. On the basis of such comparative studies, he laid down the following pre-conditions for the success of a republican form of government, viz., limited population, economic equality among the citizens and the willingness of citizens to discharge their social obligations. In his view, if population exceeds an optimum number, social cohesion would be considerably weakened. Likewise, excessive disparity in the distribution of wealth and income among the citizens would be equally prejudicial to social solidarity. Such economic inequality would pave the way for the emergence of aristocracy in place of a republican form of government.

By making a comparative study of the contemporary monarchical systems of Europe, he came to the conclusion that moderate size of population and spontaneous respect and loyalty of the subjects towards their monarch contributed to the stability of monarchical form of government. While analysing the social background of monarchy, he pointed out that expansion of agriculture, industry, trade and commerce gave rise to social stratification of a complex nature. According to Montesquieu, conflict of interest among various classes prevented any one class from gaining upper hand in society. As a result, the citizens are able to enjoy maximum political freedom. But the total well-being of the people suffers inasmuch as each class pursues its sectarian interest to the complete neglect of the larger interest of society. People are encouraged to abide by their social obligations and commitments simply in expectation of enjoying royal favour and not in response to a genuine concern for the good of society.

He accepted Eastern autocracy as an ideal type instead of European autocracy. The attitude of the Eastern people towards the autocrat, at once fearful and reverential, as well as a large population favoured the emergence and stability of autocracy in eastern regions. The disunity among different classes and communities prevented united action against the autocratic ruler.

Today we do not exactly follow the line pursued by Montesquieu in classifying political systems into ideal types or in identifying the social environment favourable to particular types of political systems. But his main thesis regarding linkages between social and political systems is equally relevant even today. He discussed exhaustively with reference to actual case studies how a change in social or economic system affects political system and vice versa. He also made it abundantly clear that an understanding of the nature and implications of political system is not possible without a perception of the play of social and economic forces in society. Montesquieu can, therefore, be regarded as a pioneer in initiating studies on political sociology.

Another pioneer in the field of political sociology was Tocqueville. He pursued the line of inquiry initiated by Montesquieu in exploring the mutual relationship between social and political systems. But he confined his investigation into the United States alone and did not go in for comparative studies. In his book *The Democracy in America*, he sought to identify the reasons which were responsible for the success of democratic institutions in that country. While doing so, he referred to some non-political factors which, in his view, had a bearing on the political life of the country, such as, tradition, environmental situation as well as the character, behaviour-pattern and ethical ideals of the American people. Analysing the bearing of these non-political variables upon the political system, he emphatically states that institutional safeguards alone cannot contribute to the success of democracy. In the ultimate analysis, democracy will succeed to the extent that the people have been able to inbibe democratic values and to inform all social institutions with appropriate democratic spirit. He goes further to emphasise that those institutional arrangements. which have contributed to the success of democracy in the United States may not facilitate the success of democratic institutions in other societies in which people lack appropriate qualities conducive to the working of democracy. He also points out that institutions cannot simply be transferred from one society to the other in the hope that they will function satisfactorily. Norms of conduct and values conducive to the success of democracy or of any other form of government must grow from within. In other words, there must take place transformation of society on appropriate lines before we can expect a particular form of government to succeed. Tocqueville expressed this basic premise of political sociology in the most unambiguous terms.

Two distinct but converging intellectual traditions are to be found in the theoretical and empirical writings on political sociology.

On the one hand, political sociology is very broadly conceived with emphasis on the social basis of power in all institutional sectors of society. In this tradition, political sociology deals with patterns of social stratification and their consequences in organised politics. This is a particular approach to the study of social organisation and societal change. This pervasive view has been derived from the formulations of Marx that class conflict and social stratification originate from economic factors, i.e., from the relations of production generated by the forces of production. Marx made the study of political sociology equivalent to the study of societal structure or macro-sociology. His view that the political system reflects the pattern or social stratification has been a dominant theme in the development of an empirical anlysis of politics.

Marxian view has been criticised both by political scientists and by sociologists on two main grounds : that it reduces political events to a social by-product, and that it fails to consider the consequences of differing types of political institutions on societal change.

By contrast, political sociology is also conceived in narrower terms. According to this conception, political sociology focuses on the organisational analysis of political groups and political leadership. In this perspective, the core of political sociology, for example, involves the study of both formal and informal party organisation with its linkages to the governmental bureaucracy, the legal system, interest groups and the electorate at large. This approach is an expression of an institutional or organisational point of view.

It is from the writings of Max Weber that political sociologists received their intellectual orientation for a more autonomous and more institutional view of politics. As a sociologist, Weber adopted a line of thinking which converged with that of Marx in that he held a comprehensive view of social structure as a basis for analysing politics. However, he differed from Marx in that he viewed social stratification as encompassing both economic relations and social status—prestige and honour. (For details consult the Chapter on Social Stratification). Furthermore, in his essay 'Class, Status and Party' Weber indicated that the emergence of modern society implied a historical process of separation of political institutions from economic and social structure. Political institution, therefore, emerge as worthy of direct sociological inquiry because they are an independent source of societal change.

## 4. ORGANISATION AND BUREAUCRACY—A WEBERIAN PERSPECTIVE

All contemporary societies are essentially organisational societies in the sense that almost all our needs are met in organisational settings. If we look at any urban area in India, either large or small, we can see how true is the above statement. Our babies in cities and towns are born in hospitals, educated in schools, subsequently employed in governmental or private organisations, enrolled as members of professional or recreational organisations and myriad other associations. In course of time, rural areas in India will also fall in line, as is the case in all advanced societies. It is to be noted that organisations differ from 'social units'. such as the family, friendship or kin groups or the community, in that these are designed to realise clearly defined goals.

As there is more specialised division of labour in society, organisations also increase in number and variety, each organisation performing one or a few specialised functions. In the interest of efficiency, these organisations must develop a hierarchy of authority and devise a system of rules designed toward the pursuit of a specific goal. Thus, a particular form of organisation, known as bureaucracy, emerges. Bureaucratic organisation is increasingly becoming the defining characteristic of modern industrial society. Max Weber's analysis of bureaucracy is a pioneering study in this particular field in sociology.

Weber's views on bureaucracy should be seen in the context of his general theory of social action ( for details consult chapter 2). It is Weber's thesis that every man gives some meaning to his conduct. Human action can, therefore, be understood and appreciated in terms of the meanings and motives which lie behind it. Weber identified four types of social action. These include (i) rational action in relation to a goal, (ii) rational action in relation to a value, (iii) affective or emotional action and (iv) traditional action.

The classification of types of action governs, to a certain extent, the Weberian interpretation of the contemporary era. According to him, the chief characteristic of the world we live in is *rationalisation*. For example, economic enterprise is rational, because it entails precise calculation of costs and careful weighing of the advantages and disadvantages of the various factors involved in the enterprise. So also is the control of the state by bureaucracy. In fact, society as a whole tends towards goal-oriented organisation. "Bureaucratisation is the prime example of this process. A bureaucratic organisation has a clearly defined goal. It involves precise calculation of the means to attain this goal and systematically eliminates those factors which stand in the way of the achievement of its objectives. Bureaucracy is, therefore, *rational action in an institutional form*"[11]. (Italics added).

Bureaucracy is also a form of *control*. It implies a hierarchical organisation in which there are superiors and subordinates with clearly defined responsibilities and powers. Some are required to issue orders, and some others to carry out those orders. In a large-sized organisation there is also the need for co-ordination of activities of the organisation. All these imply control of those in the lower ranks of the hierarchy by those in the higher. Such controls become effective as well as smooth if there is a minimum of voluntary submission to higher authority. People voluntarily submit to authority when it is regarded as legitimate. Max Weber identified three forms of legitimacy which derive from three kinds of social action. Thus, it can derive from traditional meanings. Legitimacy of this kind, which we may call *traditional legitimacy*, depends on belief in the sanctity of immemorial traditions and the right of those established on the strength of tradition in positions of authority to exercise it. Similarly, legitimacy can derive from rational meanings. Such legitimacy may be called *rational legitimacy* which reflects belief in the legality of patterns of normative rules and the right of those people designated by the rules to exercise authority to command. There is another type of legitimacy, called *charismatic legitimacy* (so termed after the Greek word for grace), which depends on the devotion of followers to an individual who, according to their perception, is endowed by exceptional sanctity, heroism or other personal qualities. Charismatic legitimacy, therefore, derives from affective or emotional action.

The organisational structure derives its form from the type of legitimacy on which it is based. While emphasising this aspect, Max Weber observes as follows : "According to the kind of legitimacy which is claimed, the type of obedience, the type of administrative staff developed to guarantee it and the mode of exercising authority, will all differ fundamentally". In order to understand bureaucracy, it is, therefore, necessary to take into account the type of legitimacy on which bureaucratic control is based.

The corresponding type of authority which emerges from his typology is as follows: traditional authority, rational-legal authority and charismatic authority. Weber, however, points out that none of these ideal types are to be found in a pure form in any historical instance. But any case can be seen to approximate to any of these types.

While analysing types of administrative organisation, Max Weber selects the *ideal-type of bureaucracy* (for Weber's conception of the Ideal Type consult the section on Max Weber in the concluding chapter) for special attention. It is based on rational-legal authority which is the source of its legitimacy.

Weber brings out the following characteristics of a bureaucratic organisation :

(i) As an organisation, bureaucracy implies a continuous performance of official functions according to rules.

(ii) Complex tasks of an organisation are broken down into manageable parts with each official specialising in a particular area. For example, governmental functions are divided into various departments, such as health, education, agriculture, defence, etc. Within each department, every official has a clearly defined sphere of competence and responsibility. They are given the necessary authority to enable them to fulfil their duties.

(iii) This authority is differentially distributed so that a hierarchy of official positions is formed, some officials having controlling and supervisory duties with respect to others.

(iv) "Bureaucratic administration", says Weber, "means fundamentally the exercise of control on the basis of knowledge. This is the feature of it which makes it specifically rational". Certain specified qualifications are required of those who are to exercise authority. They are appointed according to their possession of formal qualifications, usually based on examinations.

(v) The bureaucrats do not own the means of production or of administration. They are also not allowed to make use of their official position for private purposes. Official quarters or other perquisites which are occupied or enjoyed by the persons while in service can not be appropriated by them after superannuation or termination of service.

(vi) Acts of an administrative kind are recorded in writing, thereby ensuring continuity and consistency of the administrative process.

(vii) The officials are personally free agents. But they are required to act impersonally according to rules which define their specific spheres of competence. The activities of the bureaucrat are governed by the rules, not by personal considerations, such as his feelings towards colleagues or clients. His actions are, therefore, rational rather than affective.

(viii) The bureaucrats are paid a salary, although this may be on a scale of pay, increments being given according to age and experience, and they are paid a pension after a fixed number of years of employment and at a given age.

(ix) Normally, bureaucrats have no other employment and at all times during their service career the officials are subject to rules governing their conduct in so far as it is related to their official duties.

Max Weber's portrayal of a rational-legal bureaucratic organisation may be contrasted with administrative organisation associated with the traditional form of authority. In the latter case "obedience is not owed to enacted rules, but to the person who occupies a position of authority by tradition". The tradition may either determine the way a chief acts and the contents of the commands he issues. Or, the tradition may leave him free to act arbitrarily. In making use of his followers, he may recruit from among those who are bound to him by particular traditional ties of loyalty, or he may choose favourites who owe a purely personal loyalty.

Although Weber was aware of the positive contribution, and even indispensability, of bureaucracy to the operation of large-scale industrial societies, he was equally aware of its limitations. He pointed out that specialisation, which is the essence of bureaucratic set-up, may contribute to efficiency in the performance of specialised tasks, but too much of specialisation may rob the bureaucrats of their spontaneity, creativity and individual initiative. The impersonality of official conduct and meticulous observance of rules may tend to produce 'specialists without spirit'. Being trained to observe carefully, and almost blindly, the enacted rules of the organisation, particularly governmental organisation, and enjoying, as they do, security of service, the bureaucrats tend to forget that rules are meant for men and not men for rules. To Weber, therefore, "the process of rationalisation, of which bureaucracy is the prime expression, is basically irrational. It is ultimately aimless since it tends to destroy the traditional values which give meaning and purpose to life"[12].

Weber also pointed to two inherent dangers of bureaucratic set-up in governmental organisation. According to him, the bureaucrats in government offices represent the most complete and effective institutionalisation of power so far created". Such power, if left unchecked and uncontrolled, is undesirable from two points of view. To begin with, bureaucracy is unsuitable during periods of crisis . The civil servants are trained to observe procedure and apply rules to particular cases and not to take decisions. Crisis situation demands innovation and improvisation, and if situation so requires, even scrapping of routine procedures. In terms of training and orientation, they are ill-equipped for the task. Secondly, " in capitalist society, top bureaucrats may be swayed by the pressure of capitalist interests and tailor their administrative practices to fit the demands of capital"[13].

According to Max Weber, these two dangers "could only be avoided by strong parliamentary control of the state bureaucracy. In particular, professional politicians must hold the top positions in the various departments of state. This will encourage strong and effective leadership since politicians are trained to take decisions"[14]. If the political executive is placed in charge of a department, "it will help to open the bureaucracy to public view and reveal any behind the scenes wheeling and dealing between bureaucrats and powerful interests. Politicians are public figures, open to public scrutiny and the criticism of opposition parties. They are therefore accountable for their actions"[15].

It may be pointed out that Weber was not oblivious of the fact that politicians are amateurs, and lack technical knowledge in many fields. In the circumstances, the bureaucrats, who possess both technical expertise and experience, may guide, and even control, their political bosses. In the words of Max Weber : "The political master always finds himself vis-a-vis the trained official, in the position of a dilettante facing the expert".

### Merton's views on dysfunctions of bureaucracy

In an article entitled, *Bureaucratic Structure and Personality,* Merton observes that "the very elements which conduce towards efficiency in general produce inefficiency in specific instance," and that bureaucratic procedure may inhibit the realisation of organisational goals. Against the backdrop of these general observations, we may refer to specific weaknesses of bureaucracy as seen by Merton. First, the bureaucrats are taught to conform and to obey, not to improvise and explore alternative ways. This way of thinking is further strengthened by the tendency of bureaucrats to play safe, because " disciplined action and conformity to official regulations" are rewarded by promotions. This kind of self-interest prompts them not to deviate and make slight adjustments even when such actions are called for in terms of realisation of organisational goals. Second, the bureaucrats tend to follow scrupulously the formal procedure, however time-consuming it might be. In a hierarchical organisation, files and papers move from one official to another at a snail's pace because observance of formal procedure involves delay. This is called bureaucratic 'red-tape' which stands in the way of providing efficient service to the clients of the organisation. Third, the emphasis on impersonal approach may lead to misunderstanding, and even friction, between the bureaucrats on the one hand and the clients on the other. It is so particularly in an organisation, whether public or private, which is primarily concerned with rendering some form of service to its clients. The businesslike and impersonal manner of carrying out their duties might give a wrong impression about the bureaucrats. They will be seen by their clients as cold, unsympathetic and even arrogant. The organisational goal of establishing rapport with their clientele is thwarted thereby.

### Bureaucracy—a Marxian perspective

According to Max Weber, bureaucracy is a defining feature of an industrial society, irrespective of whether it is capitalistic or socialistic. The question as to who owns the means of production is not relevant. Marx, however, looks upon bureaucracy as an essential feature of a capitalist society. In such a society, a small minority owns the forces of production. Bureaucracy is a tool in the hands of this small minority to serve the interest of the ruling group. A socialist society, in which the forces of production are communally owned, can, therefore, dispense with bureaucracy in the form in which it prevails in a capitalist society. "Lenin believed that after the dictatorship of the proletariat was established in the USSR in 1917, there would be a steady decline in state bureaucracy"[16]. He was conscious of the fact that some form of bureaucracy was essential. But he wanted it to be remodelled on the lines suggested by Marx and Engels. One such proposal was that administrators would be directly appointed and subject to recall at any time. The second proposal was that the salary of the administrators would be at par with that of an ordinary worker. The third proposal was to simplify the work to a point "where basic literacy and numeracy were sufficient for their performance". Lenin visualised a state of affairs in which there might be a mass participation in administration, since all would possess the necessary skills to participate in the administrative process. Since every one could be a bureaucrat for a time, none would develop the bureaucratic style of functioning or the bureaucratic attitude.

Marx, Engels, or Lenin did not, however, give a detailed blue-print of how this system would work, how the democratisation of bureaucracy would actually take place. It is to be noted that the Russian Revolution of 1917 was not followed by dismantling of the bureaucratic structure. On the contrary, there was expansion of bureaucracy. The observers of the Russian scene have not reported the existence of any evidence of the weakening or shrinking of the bureaucratic set-up. There are some who justify the expansion and strengthening of the bureaucratic structure on the ground that central economic planning, which is directed toward the economic wellbeing of the entire population, requires for its successful implementation a well-knit bureaucracy. They are also of the view that since the forces of production are communally owned, the functioning of bureaucracy would be different from that in a capitalist society.

During the period of 'cultural revolution' in China, attempt was made under the leadership of Mao Tse-Tung to modify bureaucracy of the ideal type provided by Max Weber. The re-organisation, that was attempted, may be pictured as follows : "The rigid hierarchy of officials will be abolished ...... Leaders will remain but they will lead rather than command. The specialised division of labour and the fragmentation of tasks are rejected in favour of a system whereby everyone should 'take care of everything' within the organisation. The expert will become a figure of the past since his technical knowledge and expertise will be spread among the masses. The full-time professional administrator will disappear. All administrative leaders must spend some of their time involved in actual production in the fields and factories. Finally, the fixed rules and regulations which characterise the typical bureaucracy are seen as instruments to repress the masses. They should therefore be changed as the masses see fit"[17].

The aforesaid changes were sought to be enforced (a) by 'role-shifting system' in terms of which the leaders would periodically be moved to the base of the organisation in order to acquaint themselves with problems at the grass-roots level, and (b) by means of 'group-based decision-making systems' in order to enable workers to participate directly in the decision-making process of the factory.

It appears that China's recent moves towards modernisation have halted the process of democratisation on the above lines. It has been suggested that "Mao's intervention was a kind of charismatic breakthrough from the bureaucratic routinisation". If, as inidicated by Max Weber, charismatic authority is routinised into traditional or rational-legal authority, then the experiments of the cultural revolution were bound to be short-lived. Some have even commented that "Marxian predictions of the disappearance of bureaucracy in a classless society owe much to a commitment to a utopian vision"[18].

## Mechanistic and Organic types of Organisations

Max Weber presented an ideal type bureaucracy and argued that actual organisations in modern industrial societies approximated to that model. The suggestion is, therefore, implicit that there might be variations from the ideal type. Weber did not throw any light on why and how such variations take place. A number of researches have been undertaken in recent years in England and U.S.A. on this particular theme. The broad conclusions of such research studies is that bureaucracy of the Weberian ideal type was particularly suited to the administration of routine tasks and to the tackling of predictable and familiar situations, i.e., to stable situations. On the other hand, this type of bureaucratic organisations are not at all suited to those sectors of modern industry in which the technical and commercial situation is practically unpredictable because of rapid changes in technology, i.e. to changing situations. We may consider, for instance, the electronics industry in which newer sophistications are introduced so quickly that no one in the production or marketing fields can foresee what tomorrow would bring, In such a situation rule-oriented and hierarchical bureaucratic organisation of the Weberian ideal type would be unsuited.

The two ideal types of organisations suited to these two types of situations are termed respectively 'mechanistic' and 'organic'. The mechanistic organisation is, in many respects, similar to the ideal type of Max Weber. "It includes a specialised division of labour with the rights and duties of each employee being precisely defined. Specialised tasks are co-ordinated by a management hierarchy which directs operations and takes major decisions. Communication is mainly vertical : instructions flow downward through a chain of command, information flows upward and is processed by various levels in the hierarchy before it reaches the top. Each individual in the organisation is responsible for discharging his particular responsibility and no more"[19].

On the other hand,"areas of responsibility are not clearly defined in organic organisation. The rigid hierarchies and specialised divisions of labour of mechanistic systems tend to disappear. The individual's job is to employ his skills to further the goals of the organisation rather than simply carry out a pre-determined operation. When a problem arises, all those who have knowledge and expertise to contribute to its solution meet and discuss. Tasks are shaped by the nature of the problem rather than being pre-defined. Communication consists of consultation rather than command, of information and advice rather than instructions and decisions. Although a hierarchy exists, it tends to become blurred as communication travels in all directions and top management no longer has the sole prerogative over important decisions nor is it seen to monopolise the knowledge necessary to make them"[20].

As already indicated, mechanistic types of organisations are best suited to stable conditions, organic types of organisations to changing conditions. This type of research tends to introduce refinements and clarifications into the Weberian model. The relevance of this type of analysis lies in the fact that we are now passing through times which are changing pretty fast. Hence, these and similar refinements are called for.

## 5. ROBERT MICHELS : DEMOCRATIC ORGANISATION AND IRON LAW OF OLIGARCHY

The Italian sociologist Robert Michels (1876-1936) published in 1911 a book entitled *Political Parties.* This is a study of European socialist parties and trade unions with particular reference to the German Socialist Party. These organisations were ostensibly anti-capitalist and pro-socialist in their aims. Their activities were directed towards abolition of capitalism and establishment of socialist societies in their respective countries. These organisations also claimed to be democratic inasmuch as they represented the interests and wishes of their members. In this book Michels analysed the activities, and in particular the ways in which these organisations functioned, and concluded that democratic ideals bore little resemblance to the actual situation.

Michels begins his analysis with reference to a paradox. In large-sized and populous nation-states of today, the masses of people are completely helpless in making their wishes felt at the centre of power till they are able to organise themselves. According to Michels, therefore, organisation is essential to democracy. The masses cannot participate directly in the decision-making process for obvious difficulties. Numbers stand in the way. What is possible for one or the few is not possible for the 'many', particularly when 'many' means hundreds, thousands or hundreds of thousands. The only way out is to adopt the representative system whereby 'delegates represent the mass and carry out its will'. Theoretically, this system meets the demands of democracy. Michels, however, argues that, in practice, the picture is entirely different. Organisation, which is indispensable for ensuring the participation of the masses in the democratic process, sounds the death knell of democracy. Power tends to be concentrated in the hands of those who are at the helm of affairs of the organisation. This is a paradox and a tragedy which constitute the theme of

Michel's book. Michels gives us a step-by-step analysis of the way in which an oligrachy actually monopolises power under the facade of a democratic set-up.

In the early stages of the development of an organisation, the various functions and positions are all equal in the sense that "differential amounts of wealth or power are not associated with the various positions". The social honour which is accorded to the head of the organisation and other top functionaries does not enable them to transform that honour into special perquisites and privileges. In Michels' words : "Originally, the chief is merely the servant of the mass". The democratic and equalitarian character of the organisation is assured, in the early stages, by the strong commitment of its members to the principles of democracy and equality. "Functions are rotated, delegates and representatives are totally subject to the will of the collectivity, and in general a high degree of camaraderie prevails"[21].

This state of affairs is possible as long as (i) the organisation is relatively small in size and (ii) functions of the organisation do not call for specialised knowledge and skill. Things begin to change, however, when the growing scale of the organisation leads to complex division of labour, so much so that certain tasks and duties require training, skill of a special kind, and a considerable amount of expert knowledge. Expertise becomes a 'foot in the door'. "The experts increasingly resemble not servants but masters and the organisation becomes increasingly hierarchical and bureaucratic"[22]. With the growing scale of the organisation, administrative duties and tasks proliferate, with the result that "it is no longer possible to take them in at a glance". In course of time, these tasks and duties become incomprehensible to those who do not possess expert knowledge. "Faced with this complexity, rank and file members of trade unions and political parties tend to leave matters to their leaders. Decisions are increasingly taken by executive committees within the bureaucracy rather than by assemblies of the rank and file. Thus the very organisation which was created to represent its members ends up by largely excluding them from participation and decision-making"[23]. There is another parallel development. The men who were originally appointed to serve the interests of the collectivity soon develop interests of their own which are often opposed to that of collectivity. Michels, therefore, concludes that organisations, which are set up to preserve democracy, inevitably produce oligarchy, that is, rule by a small elite. This is the 'iron law of oligarchy'.

Given the oligarchical nature of bureaucratic structures, may not the interest of the rank and file be attended to ? Michels is very pessimistic. He argues that those, who enjoy various perquisites and privileges by virtue of their occupying certain positions in the organisation, gradually develop vested interests of their own. Naturally, such vested interests take priority over the stated goals of the organisation. This clearly involves a displacement of organisational goals whereby preservation of the organisation becomes an end in itself rather than a means to an end. The leaders of the organisation naturally refrain from doing anything which may eventually endanger their own positions, even though realisation of organisational goals demands such actions.

Leaders are able to maintain power for a variety of reasons of which three are important. In the first place, the leaders harp on 'experience', 'expertise' and 'indispensability' in order to legitimise their positions of power. They assiduously create an impression among the rank and file that the organisation would suffer if they cease to be at the helm of affairs of the company. Second, the rank and file are apathetic. they are actually quite content to have others attend to their affairs. their indifference is evident from the 'slackness of attendance at ordinary meetings". Third, the masses are incompetent. Michels characterises this frailty as "perennial incompetence of the masses".

According to Michels the weakest link in the Marxian view of the new socialist society is the problem of administration. In large organisations, there will necessarily be concentration of power in the hands of a few. Human nature being what it is, this small minority would, in course of time, develop interests of their own which may be in conflict with those of the collectivity. Moreover, they would try by all means to retain their privileges. Michels, therefore, concludes that conflicts of interests emerge between leaders and led, not unlike the class conflicts of old society. This process is characterised by Michels as an absolute social law. He says : "By a universally applicable social law, every organ of the collectivity, brought into existence through the need for the division of labour, creates for itself, as soon as it becomes consolidated, interests peculiar to itself. The existence of these special interests involves a necessary conflict with the interests of the collectivity. Nay, more, social strata fulfilling peculiar functions tend to become isolated, to produce organs fitted for the defense of their own peculiar interests. In the long run they tend to undergo transformation into distinct classes"[24]. Michels, it should be particularly borne in mind, does no intend this as a refutation of Marxian theory of class struggle, but of his vision of a classless society. He made a very significant comment long before a single socialist regime had taken power anywhere : The socialists might conquer, but not socialism, which would perish in the moment of its adherents' 'triumph'. Zeitlin observes in this context that "the victory of the bureaucratic organisation over the socialist soul, had already become evident in the violation of a fundamental socialist principle: international solidarity"[25].

The views of Robert Michels, particularly his views about the Iron Law of Oligarchy as an absolute social law, have been criticised from different points of view. To begin with, the suggestion that the iron law of oligarchy will inevitably operate in all largesized organisations is not acceptable. Various cross-cultural and even intra-cultural studies of political parties indicate that the internal organisations of political parties do not exhibit a uniform pattern and that oligarchical rule may develop in some while in some others it may not. S.M. Lipset says that the internal organisational structures of the Democratic and Republican parties are decentralised, so much so that there is no central leadership in either of the parties which can dictate and impose its views on party members or local chapters of the party. The party members at the local level exercise considerable influence and power. But no oligarchical rule at the local level can develop. for the simple reason that the members themselves are divided into various factions.

Secondly, Michels' treatment of the subject has been one-sided. He emphasised only the possibilities of misuse of power, and not have a word to say about the efforts made by party bosses to realise the goals of the organisation. This they needs must do in their own interest. The accumulated grievances of the members of the organisation may eventually endanger the position of the party bosses. Possibililties of revolt among the rank and file may act as a brake upon them to misuse power beyond a certain limit and ignore the wishes of rank and file.

Thirdly, in all demoractic organisations, commitment to democratic ideals and norms is, more or less, all-pervasive among the members. In such a situation, party bosses cannot act undemocratically with immunity.There are pockets of resistance at all levels of the democratic organisations to the attempts of party bosses to utilise power solely in furtherance of their selfish interests. In the words of Talcott Parsons, power is only one of several cognate factors in the determination of social events". As pointed out by Lipset, rivalry among party bosses themselves may serve as a check to absuse of power and consequent subversion of the goals of the organisation.

## 6. ANALYSIS OF SOCIAL POWER: POWER, AUTHORITY AND FORCE

It is difficult to anaslyse the nature of social power for the simple reason that it cannot be perceived by senses. Indeed, we feel the existence of this power at all levels. The consequences that flow from the application of power are also evident. But it is not possible to define in precise terms the meaning of social power. In this respect, it is comparable to electricity. There is no definition which can adequately bring out the essence of electricity. It has been described as 'a fundamental entity of nature'. Its outward expression can be seen in the form of light, heat and motion.We are familiar with these outward manifestations, but not with electricity. Likewise, social power is an immanent feature of society. We can experience its outward manifestations in the form of order, force and authority, but not the phenomenon itself. In all walks of life, such as educational institutions, family relationships, playfields, social groups and associations, power is expressed in one of these three forms. In fact, it is difficult to find any social relationships which are not in some way influenced by social power.The only exception we can think of relates to what Simmel characterised as 'polite acquaintance". When, for instance, we meet somebody in a wedding reception for a very brief period, the social encounter does not apparently bear any trace of power. It will, therefore, not be an exaggeration to say that social power is a fundamental entity of society.

### Max Weber's views on power : A constant-sum view

Max Weber defined power as "the chance of a man or a number of men to realize their own will in a communal action even against the resistance of others who are participating in the action". Defined thus, power is, therefore, power over others and, as such, power is an aspect of social relationships. Nobody can hold power in isolation."This is a very broad definition of power since it enters into every aspect of social life. It extends from parents assigning domestic chores to their children to teachers enforcing discipline in the classroom, from a manager organising his workforce to a political party enacting legislation. In each case, an individual or group have power to the degree to which others comply with their will. Many sociologists argue that 'political sociology' is the study of power in its broadest sense"[26].

Weber's definition of power represents a view which is sometimes known as a 'constant-sum' concept of power. The reason is that according to Weber's definition those who hold power do so at the expense of others. If some hold power, others do not. The underlying assumption is that the amount of power is constant.

### Views of Talcott Parsons: A variable-sum approach to power

Talcott Parsons, on the other hand, rejects the 'constant-sum' view of power. In his view, power does not belong to an individual or a group but to the society as as whole. This social power is utilised or employed for the attainment of goals of the society, for the furtherance of collective interests. The power of the society is, thus, contingent upon the efficiency of the society in achieving its goals. The greater the efficiency, the greater is the power and vice versa. This view is sometimes known as a 'variable-sum' concept of power inasmuch as power is not constant or fixed, but variable in the sense that it may increase or decrease.

Parsons' views on power are developed from his general theory of society. He assumes that consensus among members of society with regard to values is essential for social stability. The next step is to have common goals which they all share. The power of the social system lies in the extent to which the society is able to realise these goals. The more able a society is to realise these goals, the greater is the power that resides in the social system. Parsons also assumes that snice goals are shared by the collectivity, the power of the society will be used toward the furtherance of the interest of the collectivity and not toward the furtherance of sectional interests.

Parsons' analysis of the basis of political power in Western democracies provides a typical illustration of his views on the nature of power."Political support", he says, "should be conceived of as a generalised grant of power which, if it leads to electoral success, puts elected leadership in a position analogous to a banker.The 'deposits' of power made by constituents are revocable, if not at will, at the next election". Just as money is deposited in the bank, members of society deposit power in political leaders. Just as the depositor can withdraw his money from the bank, so the electorate can withdraw its grant of power from political leaders at the next election. In this sense power resides ultimately with members of society as a whole. Finally, just as money generates interest for the depositor, so grants of power generate benefits for the electorate since they are used primarily to further collective goals. In this way power in society can increase[27].

Parson's views on the nature and application of power have been criticised. First, Parsons simply translates into sociological jargon the arguments which the holders of power in society advance by way of justifying their use and enjoyment of power. Second, Parsons has failed to appreciate that power may not always be applied in furtherance of collective interest. That power is not infrequently used in furtherance of sectional interest is common knowledge. Marxiasn analysis of power, to which we shall turn in the next paragraph, emphasises this aspect.

## A Marxian perspective on power

The view that power is a social resource held in trust and applied by those in authority is rejected by Marxist writers. They argue that power is held by a particular group to the exclusion of all others, and applied by this group in furtherance of their class or sectional interest which may conflict with the interests of those who are subject to power. Marxian concept of power is, thus, a 'constant-sum' concept of power in the sense that net accretion of power in the hands of the dominant group means a net loss of power for the rest. "This is very different from the picture presented by Parsons in which rulers and ruled pull together for the benefit of society as a whole, undivided by any fundamental conflicts of interest"[28]. From a Marxian point of view, the source of power lies in the economic infra-structure. Forces of production determine the relations of production. Those who emerge as economically dominant are able to grab power which they use in furtherance of their interest. According to Marxist theory, power of the ruling class extends beyond specific economic relationships, and pervades the entire super-structure.

## Various facets of power

In the foregoing paragraphs, we tried to understand and analyse the essence of power from three perspectives, viz., Weberian perspective, functionalist perspective of Talcott Parsons and Marxian perspective. In this section, different dimensions of power are briefly described. Various meanings are often attributed to the term 'social power'. Francis Bacon, for instance, said that 'knowledge is power'. The term is also variously identified with prestige, influence, dominance, authority and even force.

E.A. Ross, the American sociologist, referred to the close association between power and prestige when he made the following observations. "The immediate cause of the location of power is prestige". "The class that has the most prestige will have the most power". Undoubtedly, prestige is sometimes related to power in the sense that powerful groups tend to be prestigious and prestigious groups powerful. But the two phenomena are not identical. The teachers enjoy considerable amount of prestige in society. They do not, however, enjoy power in the sense that they can impose their will on others. A police constable, on the other hand, enjoys power in the sense that, within limits, he can impose his will on others., It follows, therefore, that prestige does not suffice to create power, and that the two phenomena, both sociologically important, are not identical and may or may not appear together.

Similarly, there is a very intimate connection between power and influence. But a line of distinction should be drawn between the two for the simple reason that the way an influential person uses his influence is different from the way a powerful person uses his power. A writer may be very influential in the sense that he influences the thinking of those who read his works. He does not certainly impose his opinions on others against their will. Marx, for example, was very influential. But he did not wield any power. Stalin, on the other hand, was very powerful in the sense that he was in a position to impose his will on others, often against their wishes. It is doubtful if he ever enjoyed influence in the sense that Marx did. It is, therefore, necessary to distinguish the two phenomena because power is coercive while influence is persuasive. An eloquent speaker may be very influential because he is able to persuade his audience to his line of thinking by his oratory or reasoned arguments. Yet he is not in a position to make them accept his views against their wishes. He is influential, but not powerful.

The term 'dominance' is sometimes used to mean 'power'. It is, however, relatively easy to distinguish power from dominance. Power is a sociological phenomenon, dominance a psychological. Power vests in an individual and also in groups. most often in the latter. Power is a function of various factors which are mostly social. Dominance, on the other hand, is a function of personality or of temperament. It is a personal quality. "A timid robber, who flaunts his gun, has more power than his unarmed victim, however dominant or aggressive the latter may be in his normal social relationships. Furthermore, and one of the most interesting facets of this distinction, dominant individuals play roles in powerless groups and submissive individuals play roles in powerful ones"[29]. It follows, therefore, that dominance is a problem in social psychology, power a problem in sociology.

We have distinguished power from prestige, from influence and from dominance. Two other distinctions are called for in order to make the meaning of power free from ambiguity. These are the distinctions between power and force and between power and authority.

Force may be defined as 'manifest power'. When a robber armed with a revolver holds out a threat to his victim "Your money or your life", he is apparently applying coercion or force and offers only two options to the victim. A robber armed with a revolver is certainly a powerful man. His power manifests itself in the force which he applies against his victim. In this sense, force is a manifest power. We may look at the same thing from another perspective. Power may be viewed as a 'latent force'. The robber in question has at his command force which he may apply if he wants to or if circumstances so require. Power and force are, thus, inextricably mixed.

While discussing the relationship between authority and power, it should be recognised that authority is by no means a purely political phenomenon in the narrow sense of the word. Authority appears, not only in the political organisation of society, but in every association in society, no matter how small or how temporary it may be.

Before discussing the nature of authority, it will be convenient if we distinguish it from two other phenomena with which it is sometimes confused. The first of these is competence. Sometimes we describe a person as an authority on a certain subject when we actually refer to his competence in the subject. We voluntarily respect the competence of others, but authority requires submission. That is, competence exerts influence; authority exacts obedience.

The second phenomenon with which authority is sometimes confused is the phenomenon of leadership. In the opinion of some sociologists, Max Weber was mainly responsible for this confusion. He spoke of three types of authority: the traditional, the rational-legal and the charismatic. The first two may be regarded as genuine authority inasmuch as the decision-making power is *conferred* by the group or society. In the case of the third, the essential attribute is leadership. "A charismatic leader is believed to be different from other men; he rises above them because he is touched with divinity; there is something of the celestial afflatus about him, and an almost tangible magnetism. He operates beyond the boundaries of legitimacy. He needs no extant organisation in society because he creates his own, a new and sometimes revolutionary one"[30]. Thus, Gandhiji and Lenin were charismatic leaders. But leadership, even charismatic leadership, is not authority. As in the case of a competent person, no one is required to follow involuntarily a leader's directive or to satisfy his wishes. The situation with regard to authority is quite different. "A leader can only request, an authority can require". In the case of leadership, personal qualities of the leader are of crucial importance. In the case of authority, however, relationship ceases to be personal. One individual or a group, entrusted and recognised by the society to issue commands of a binding character, may be designated as authroity. "In a leadership relation the person is basic; in an authority relation personal identity is irrelevant". Like competence, leadership is a species of influence. Authority, on the contrary, is a function of power.

After having distinguished authority from competence and from leadership, we may proceed to discuss the locus of authority. Authority is always a property of social organization. Where there is no organization, there is no authority. Moreover, "the exercise of authority never extends beyond the limits of the organisation or association in which it is institutionalised and which gives it support and sanction".

Besides, authority is always attached to statuses and never to individuals. An individual, for instance, exercises the authority of a Principal of a college only so long as he occupies that status and ceases to exercise it when he resigns, or when he is removed, or when his term of office expires. "The exercise of authority is wholly and indeed exclusively a function of associational status".

It will be illuninating for an understanding of authority to examine the process in which an unorganised group is transformed into an organised one. First, informal procedures and patterns of interaction come to be standardised as statuses. The institutionalisation of procedures into norms and of roles into statuses results in the formal organisation of the association. Such institutionalisation is necessary "in order that the stability of the association may be assured and its continuity guaranteed".

We have now to answer a question : What sustains the authority exercised by some people over others ? The answer is that the person who exercises authority is recognised as an agent of the group. He acts not in his own but in the group's name. It is apparent that any disinclination to obey authority is "a threat not to a personal relationship but to the continued existence of the group".

The next question is as to whether authority is a phenomenon exercised by coercion or by consent. That is, does a person who obey the command of a superior authority do so because he has to or because he wants to ? The answer is both yes and no, depending on the type of association we are concerned with. In a voluntary association, membership is a matter of consent, and people voluntarily give their allegiance to it. In involuntary associations, on the other hand, voluntary withdrawal of membership is not possible and coercion is very much present in the exercise of authority in such associations. It is, therefore, said that in voluntary associations authority is 'institutionalised leadership' and that in involuntary associations it is 'institutionalised power'.

The solution is not very happy. In voluntary associations, an individual is free to join. If, however, he refuses to carry out the obligations of the association, he is simply asked to resign. Element of consent applies to the fact of membership and not to the acceptance of authority. From this point of view, power phenomenon is not absent from institutionalised leadership. It seems desirable, therefore, to assert that authority is always a power phenomenon and to define authority as institutionalised power.

## 7. ELITE THEORY

Elite theory was first developed by two Italian sociologists, Vilfredo Pareto (1848-1923) and Gaetano Mosca (1858-1941). Elite theory developed as a reaction to Marxist theory. The Marxist dream of a classless society was rejected by it as an illusion. All societies, according to Elite theory, are divided into two main groups—the ruling minority and the majority of the ruled. This kind of division is accepted as inevitable, irrespective of whether society is capitalist or socialist. Even a proletarian revolution will mean replacement of one ruling elite by another.

According to Pareto and Mosca, the elite owe their position to the superiority of their personal characteristics or attributes. Pareto and Mosca, however, differ with regard to the nature of these personal characteristics. While Pareto emphasised personal qualities of cunning and intelligence of a high order as important prerequisites of power, Mosca emphasised personal qualities of considerable organisational ability as pre-requisites of leadership, and hence of power.

Later versions of elite theory do not emphasise the personal qualities of those who happen to enjoy power, but the institutional framework of society. It is held that the hierarchical organisation of social institutions allows a minority to monopolise power.

### Vilfredo Pareto : The Circulation of Elites

For centuries attempts have been made to explain the behaviour of men by attributing it to 'human nature'. Perhaps the most famous attempt by a sociologist to deal with the problem of human motivation is that of Vilfredo Pareto. He views human conduct as inspired by certain constant ingredients of human nature which he terms "residues". He classifies the residues under six main groups :residues of combinations ( the faculty of associating things or thinking them together ), of group persistence or persistence of aggregates (the conservative tendency), of self-expression, of sociability, of individual integrity, and of sex. According to Pareto, these are the actual motivations of human conduct. But these are obscured by all sorts of unsound reasonings and misleading explanations which he names "derivations". According to his interpretation, "derivations" are nothing but logical explanatior of non-logical actions. Pareto refers to the human tendency to 'rationalise' motives, "to form habits of concealing petty and self-seeking motives under high names, like duty and honor and principle and patriotism", and "to stand well in the sight of others and in our own eyes"[31].

Having made a detailed analysis of the 'theories' of action, distinguishing between logical and non-logical action, residues and derivations, Pareto discusses the place of various elements of action in the equilibrium of the social system. Here, for purposes of detailed discussion, he confines himself to two of his six classes of residues — the 'residues of combinations' and the 'persistence of aggregates'. Very broadly, the former consists of the commitments or propensities in social groups to *adapt flexibly* to environmental or situational exigencies, while the latter consists of the propensities in social groups to maintain patterns of commitment once they have become institutionalised.

Pareto makes one of his most important empirical generalisations by combining this analytical distinction with a conception of the elite element in social stratification systems. He confines himself to the simplest level of analysis of such systems, distinguishing only between elite groups which combine control of great political power with the enjoyment of high prestige in various other respects, and the other groups which constitute the mass of the society and which have relatively little power, prestige or wealth.

Pareto makes psychological characteristics the basis of elite rule. In his view, there are two main types of governing elite which, following Machiavelli, he calls 'lions' and 'foxes'. 'Lions' are those who are more actuated by 'the persistence of aggregates'. Pareto shows that in a political context, the commitment of the lions to belief systems and values is connected with a readiness to resort to force and to rule by force. Military dictatorships provide an example of this type of governing elite. 'Foxes' are those who are more actuated by 'the residues of combinations'. In a political context, the flexibility and adaptability of the foxes mean that they are not likely to be very much concerned about the stability of the political system in which they operate. Foxes rule by cunning, guile and manipulation. In his view`, European democracies provide an example of this type of elite. Thus, Pareto argues that members of a governing elite owe their positions primarily to their personal qualities either to their lion-like or fox- like characterisitics.

He, then, develops the idea that the composition of the elites alternates cyclically, a process which Pareto calls the 'circulation of elites'. All elites tend to decay in quality and lose their vigour. Being used to easy life. they may become soft and ineffective. The privileges of office may make them set in their ways and too inflexible to changing circumstances. Moreover, an elite may lack the qualities of their counterpart, qualities which, in the long run, are essential to maintain power. "An elite of lions lacks the imagination and cunning necessary to maintain its rule and will have to admit foxes from the masses to make up for this deficiency. Gradually foxes infiltrate the entire elite and so transform its character. Foxes, however, lack the ability to take forceful and decisive action which at various times is essential to retain power. An organised minority of lions committed to the restoration of strong government develops and eventually overthrows the elite of foxes"[32].

The differences of views of Marxists and Pareto with regard to the transformation of class systems may be noted. Pareto maintains that the fall of elites is due to their decline in relative numbers and to their decay in quality. The Marxists insist that the material conditions of a social order inevitably bring about the transformation of class power. Further, to Marx history ultimately leads to and ends with the communist utopia; to Pareto, history is a never-ending circulation of elites. According to Pareto, nothing ever really changes and history is, and always will be "a graveyard of aristocracies".

Pareto's analysis of circulation of elites led to a set of empirical generalisations. In modern terms, Pareto's analysis throws light on "an important rhythm in the processes of change in dynamic societies (like that of the West, both ancient and modern), consisting of successive phases in which leadership is primarily in the hands of adaptive-innovative and then of conservative-regressive groups".

## C. Wright Mills : The Power Elite

C. Wright Mills published a book entitled *The Power Elite* in 1956. In this book Mills does not provide a general theory to explain the nature and distribution of power in all societies in the manner Pareto has done. On the contrary, he limits his study to the analysis of American society. Unlike Pareto, he does not believe in the inevitability of elite rule. Nor does he accept it as something as something inescapable. In so many words he condemns it.

Unlike Pareto, again, Mills does not explain elite rule in psychological terms, in terms of personal qualities of the rulers. He does not believe that the elite groups find themselves in positions of authority by virtue of their superior fox-like or lion-like qualities which distinguish them from the rest of the population.

Mills seeks to explain elite rule in institutional terms : He identifies three key institutions in the U.S.A. (i) the major business corporations, (ii) the military and (iii) the federal government. These institutions occupy 'pivotal positions' in society. Those who occupy 'command posts' in these three key institutions constitute the elite. Mills argues that the holders of those 'command posts', though apparently distinguishable from one another in terms of their association with three key institutions, are sufficiently similar in their values, interests and ideals and are interconnected to form a single ruling minority. He names this ruling minority ' the power elite'. He argues that economic, military and political interest which these three groups represent are promoted to the extent that there is co-operation and sharing among them. Thus, as armaments pour out of factories in huge quantities, the interests of both economic and military elites are served. Likewise, business and government "cannot now be seen as two distinct worlds". Economic pressure groups influence governmental decisions on economic matters, particularly those pertaining to giant corporations. Moreover, those who are in government have substantial interest in these corporations. "The net result of the coincidence of economic, military and political power is a power elite which dominates American society and takes all decisions of major national and international importance"[33].

Another cementing bond which further strengthens the cohesiveness and unity of the power elite is the similarity of the social background of its members and the interchange and overlapping of personnel of the three components of the power elite. They share similar educational background, similar values as well as similar life-styles. There is, as is to be expected in such circumstances, mutual trust, understanding and co-operation among them. The Director of a giant corporation may be associated with the government, either directly or indirectly, for some time. Similarly, an army general may be on the Board of

Directors of a business corporation. Mills argues that there are many such cases of interchange and over-lapping of personnel among the three elite groups which tends to strengthen the power-elite further.

Mills posits the view that American society is dominated by a power elite of "unprecedented power and unaccountability". By way of illustrating his statement, he refers to the dropping of atom bomb over Hiroshima. Such a decision of stupendous importance to the world at large and to the people of the United States in particular was taken by the power elite. Another disquieting feature is that the power elite is not accountable for its actions either directly to the public or to any body which represents public interest. Mills sounds a note of warning that the rise of the power elite has led to "the decline of politics as a genuine and public debate of alternative decisions".

Mills points out that the power elite has at its disposal the media of mass communication which he describes as "instruments of psychic management and manipulation". With a great deal of subtlety and cleverness, the power elite uses the mass media to persuade the men in the street to think, act and behave in certain ways. Ideas of consumerism, recreation and leisure grip the minds of the common people. They are occupied with their respective worlds of work, and outside working hours they spend their time with their families and passively participate in entertainment programmes presented by the mass media, such as the T.V. and the Cinema. They do not, therefore, bother at all with the activities of the power elite. Free from popular control, the latter pursues its own concerns —power and self-aggrandisement.

Robert A. Dahl has criticised Mills on the ground that his evidence is suggestive rather than conclusive. Even if it is granted that the power elite has the 'potential for control', we should recognise that 'potential for control' is not 'equivalent to actual control'. A series of concrete cases, particularly those pertaining to matters of public concern, such as taxation, social welfare programmes, etc., must be taken into account in order to establish the thesis that the power elite has the power to decide such issues. Dahl argues that since Mills has not investigated a range of such key decisions, the thesis that 'actual control' lies with the power elite remains unestablished.

## Elite Theory and Communist Societies

Though elite theory does not fit in with the Marxian vision of a classless society, a number of scholars have argued that the nature and distribution of power in communist societies can be best explained in terms of elite theory. T. B. Bottomore, for instance, observes as follows : "The political system of Communist countries seems to me to approach the pure type of 'power elite', that is, a group which, having come to power with the support or acquiescence of particular classes in the population, maintains itself in power chiefly by virtue of being an organised minority confronting the unorganised majority".

Raymond Aron argues in the same vein that power in communist societies can be best interpreted in terms of an elite model. He argues that in the U.S.S.R.a 'unified elite' monopolises political, economic and military powers which are 'absolute and unbounded". This small minority of ruling elite takes all crucial economic decisions pertaining to production, investment, wage differentials and pricing. The entire military establishment is under the control and direction of this ruling elite. All political decisions, both national and international, are also taken by the same group. To cap it all, the constitution recognises the existence of one political party. Pointing to this aspect, Aron observes: "Politicians, trade union leaders, public officials, generals and managers all belong to one party and are part of an authoritarian organisation". Aron proceeds further to say that the common people are left "without any means of defence against the elite"[34]. Bottomore emphasises this aspect thus": 'Contrary to the orthodox Marxist view, popular control may well be greater in some of the capitalist countries, where independent trade unions can bring pressure to bear upon managements, and where the competition among political groups prevents the emergence of a single, omnipotent elite"[35]. It has also been argued by some, Milovan Djilas is one of them, that the members of the ruling elite are self-seekers who pursue self-interest at the cost of the interest of the society as a whole.

## NOTES

1. F.W. Coker, *Recent Political Thought*, page 504
2. *ibid*, page 504
3. *ibid*, page 504
4. Mac Iver and Page, *Society*, page 461
5. John F. Kennedy, *Toward a Strategy of Peace*, a lecture delivered on June 10, 1963
6. John F. Kennedy's address to the United Nations, September 25, 1961
7. Laski, *A Grammer of Politics*, page 64
8. Bottomore, Sociology, pages 156-162
9. *ibid*, page 160
10. An article on Political Sociology by S.M. Lipset included in Sociology—An Introduction edited by Smelser, page 440
11. Haralambos, *Sociology—Themes and* Perspectives , page 280
12. *ibid, page 284*
13. *ibid*, page 284
14. *ibid*, pages 284-285
15. *ibid*, pages 284-285
16. *ibid*, page 286
17. *ibid*, page 288
18. *ibid*, page 322
19. *ibid*, page 302
20. *ibid*, page 302
21. Irving M. Zeitlin, *Ideology and the Development of Sociological Theory*, page 222
22. *ibid*, page 223
23. Haralambos, op. cit page 289
24. Zeitlin, op. cit, page 232. Quotation from Michels' *Political Parties*, page 389
25. *ibid*, page 232
26. Haralambos, op. cit, page 98
27. *ibid*, pages 100-101
28. *ibid*, page 101
29. Bierstedt, *Social Order*, page 345
30. *ibid*, page 331
31. Mac Iver and Page, *Society*, page 39
32. Haralambos, op. cit, pate 108
33. *ibid*, page 110
34. *ibid* page 113
35. Bottomore, Sociology, page 143.

# CHAPTER NINETEEN

# EDUCATION AND SOCIETY

## 1. MEANING OF EDUCATION

The term 'education' may be interpreted either in a broad or in a narrow sense. In a broad sense, education refers to a process which continues all throughout life, and which is promoted by almost every experience in life. In this sense, educational materials are to be found in all walks of life. No single item of experience may be left out. According to this interpretation, therefore, to live is to learn. If we closely explore our past, we shall invariably find that the greatest experiences of our lives have been derived from the most unexpected quarters. We may further notice that this type of education comes to us unconsciously. That is, we have not made any effort to derive such educational experience. "It comes from the problems of life with which we have to deal, from the influences and suggestions of nature, from intercourse with our follow-men, often from our failures and sufferings"[1]. This concept of education emphasises chiefly the process by which personality is developed, and by which we realise the relationships of man to man, and of man to the universe.

In a narrow sense. 'education' refers to a consciously directed activity or effort "to develop and cultivate our powers". The instructions that we receive in schools and colleges fall under this category. The teachers place before their pupils ideas and images with a view to directing their mental or psychological growth in a certain direction. The students also join educational institutions with the express purpose of 'receiving' instructions. Professor Dewey, in his book 'Democracy and Education', used the expression *intentional* education to mark the distinction between education which comes to us unconsciously and that which implies a definite purpose.

We generally use the term 'education' in this narrow sense, i.e., as "a process consciously organised by the state or the family or some other authority for the development of young people towards some end regarded as important by the authority in question—an end which may or may not involve a general cultivation of personality"[2].

Having accepted this narrow interpretation of education, we may discuss its social significance by considering the part played by some of the important educational agencies of our time.

## 2. IMPORTANT EDUCATIONAL AGENCIES OF OUR TIME

The primary function of the school is to help a child unfold his personality and develop good habits, and to initiate him into the life of the larger community. In every society, therefore, a child is first initiated into what is simplest and best in the tradition of his community. With this end in view, Aristotle emphasised the use of music and fairy tales as media of instruction in early education of a child. Good music, according to him, mirrors, in itself, the goodness of the world. This is what links the hearers of music to contemplation of the world's purpose. Of all the fine arts, music is the most effective in producing a clear image of virtue. In modern times music is used as a medium of instruction in kindergarten and nursery schools. Other very effective media of instruction in early education of a child are rhymes, poetry and fairy tales. "A fine thought or a deep experience enshrined in a beautiful story, or embodied in an immortal phrase, sinks readily into the heart, lingers long in the memory, is stored up as a joy for ever, and becomes an inspiration throughout the whole of life"[3]. Seen in this light, music, poetry, and fairy tales prepare the ground for the enforcement of laws. Laws give definiteness and permanence to the best traditions of a people. But their efficacy depends upon the extent to which the traditions of the community are engraven on the souls and minds of the people.

Among the subjects of study in the early education of the child, the most important one is the study of language of his people "in which the knowledge, the insight, the purposes and ideals—unhappily also the prejudices and the limitations—of the community are largely embodied". There is, at the same time, the study of nature; that is, the relations of the child to his actual surroundings. Tagore emphasised such a study because it was, according to him, one of the most effective and fascinating methods of opening up the mind. "It begins as observation, but soon involves reflection; and it leads on easily to the study of human life in its more obvious features"[4]. When a child grows old enough to develop analytical thinking, he is initiated into the subtleties of grammar, arithmetic, geometry, and eventually into the simpler conceptions of morals and some insight into the religious ideas by which men have sought to interpret the universe and their relation to it, as well as the ultimate questions of life and death.

The most important function of schools is therefore to socialise the new generations, to indoctrinate them with the values and ideals, traditions and thoughts of the community. But this process of socialisation does not follow a uniform pattern. It assumes different forms in different societies. Thus, in ancient India, formal instruction was provided by the Brahmins "who were the repositories of learning and the directors of Hindu life". According to ancient Indian tradition, a child should commence his studies at the age of five by learning the alphabets. The emphasis of this educational system was on life than on learning or instruction. After his initiation, a student had to undergo a two-fold course of discipline, physical and spiritual. The tols, vidyalayas, and *chatuspathis* served as agencies for the transmission of religious and cultural traditions to succeeding generations. In almost all societies, the early education of a child followed roughly the same pattern, with this difference that "the predominance of religious education was greater in India than in Western or Islamic societies, or in China"[5].

So far we have considered education as a specialised social activity. In the simplest societies, however, education was not organised as a separate activity. It was provided by the family and other primary groups, and, broadly, by the society as a whole through participation in the "everyday routines of living".

The school prepares the child for the general duties of good citizenship. Hence, the type of education that we have sketched above is, more or less, common for all citizens of the age-group ranging between, five and, say, eighteen. Those who are intellectually or mentally competent enough to follow up this basic education and pursue courses leading to advancement of knowledge, the application of knowledge to actual problems, such as law, medicine, engineering, etc. would need the type of training that is provided in colleges and universities. A college seeks to make accessible to students all the knowledge and skill that is available in particular departments, and to prepare the way for further advance. The chief function of a college is to provide a form of liberal education of a higher kind than that given in schools. Though collegiate studies are somewhat more specialised than is commonly the case in schools, but still these studies are designed to promote general cultivation rather than specialised knowledge and skill. In a university, on the other hand, the studies are definitely specialised, and are designed to qualify the students for some specific work for which the students have expressed their preference. The universities also aim at the promotion of research in particular departments. Besides colleges and universities, there are technical institutions which offer special training of a more technical kind, preparing a student for a particular function for which he is found to be fitted by natural ability and circumstances.

In ancient societies, before the rise of modern science and industry, technical skills were imparted chiefly through the family and the occupational group in informal and practical ways. There was then no special institution, as is the case at present, to offer such training. For example, a child born in the family of a carpenter or a blacksmith used to learn the skills of the trade informally from the members of his family. This is till the case with a vast majority of technical hands in our country, particularly in rural areas.

## 3. FUNCTIONS OF EDUCATION FOR SOCIETY AS A WHOLE

According to Emile Durkheim, the major function of education is the transmission of society's norms and values. "Society can survive", he says, "only if there exists among its members a sufficient degree of homogeneity; education perpetuates and reinforces this homogeneity by fixing in the child from the beginning the essential similarites which collective life demands". A vitally important task for all societies is to bring close together a mass of individuals into a united whole. The individuals must have a sense of belonging to society. Durkheim holds that education provides the necessary link between individuals and society by indoctrinating them with the values and ideals, traditions and thoughts of the community.

Second, Durkheim argues that the formal education imparted by schools cannot be provided either by the family or the peer groups. The family is a group of kins knit together by ties of blood. Family relationships are, therefore coloured by love and affection, emotions and sentiments. One cannot, in the nature of things, look beyond one's family and get acquainted with the promise and problems of living in the larger society. Peers are one's personal choice. Naturally, membership of a peer group cannot prepare one for the larger society. The school system, on the other hand , is a miniature society in which a pupil interacts with other members of the school community in terms of a fixed set of rules. In the words of Durkheim : "It is by respecting the school rules that the child learns to respect rules in general, that he develops the habit of self-control and restraint simply because he should control and restrain himself. It is a first initiation into the austerity of duty. Serious life has now begun". In the words of Talcott Parsons, a family or a peer group upholds 'particularistic" standards whereas a school upholds 'universalistic' standards. Thus, the school prepares young people for their adult roles.

Third, Durkheim argues that formal educational institutions, apart from transmitting general values which provide the 'necessary homogeneity for social survival', also transmit specific skills which provide the 'necessary diversity for social co-operation'. In pre-industrial societies, technical skills were imparted chiefly through the family and the occupational group in informal and practical ways. Thus, a child born in the family of a carpenter used to learn the skills of the trade informally from the members of his family. Industrial societies have become highly specialised and complex, calling for skills of a very high order. Complex division of labour, which is the defining feature of an industrial society, tends to strengthen social cohesion. This he calls organic solidarity. Industrial society is thus knit together by value consensus and a specialised division of labour which makes interdependence a condition for survival.

Fourth, the object of education, as defined by Durkheim, is "to awaken and develop in the child those physical, intellectual and moral states which are required of him by the milieu for which he is specially destined". By way of elaborating this statement of Durkheim, Bottomore observes that "the function of education in preparing the child for a particular milieu in society..... has traditionally meant preparing him for membership of a particular group in the social hierarchy"[6]. Social divisions exist in almost all societies. Wherever there is a system of social stratification, there is a corresponding differentiation within the educational system. Class divisions are reflected in the educational system. In fact, education is used as an agency for preserving class privileges and interests and thereby maintaining class distinctions. Thus, in ancient India, the education of children belonging to higher castes was quite distinct from the education that was available for the great majority of the population. The education of the former was conducted by a hereditary priesthood, and it largely excluded secular instruction and was chiefly concerned with the transmission of religious doctrines and knowledge of the scriptures. With the establishment of British rule in India, the ancient educational system declined. But the introduction of English education tended to re-inforce the separation of those who received English education from the rest of the society. Even after four decades of India's independence, class distinctions are maintained by the existence of different types of schools for the various social groups. This kind of educational differentiation exists in all modern societies, however much they may be committed to egalitarian policies.

Fifth, the importance of education as an agency of social control cannot be ignored. The major function of education, according to Durkheim, is the transmission of society's norms and values by\ the older generations among those who are not yet ready for social life. Once a child internalises through intellectual exposure the distinctive traits of this culture, his actions and behaviour -patterns are moulded by his intellectual orientation. Conformity to social norms and values becomes easy and spontaneous. Links are firmly established between the society on the one hand and individuals on the other. Seen in this perspective, education appears to be a powerful and very effective agency of social control. The question of applying social sanctions arises only when there are deviations or tendencies toward deviations from socially prescribed norms of behaviour. The application of social sanctions becomes unnecessary if educational agencies can transmit effectively society's norms and values to individuals during impressionable periods of their lives.

We should note, however, that the effectiveness of formal education as a means of social control is diminished by certain factors in modern times. In earlier societies, for example, literacy was highly valued so much so that it was the basis of prestige and power. The teachers also naturally enjoyed great respect and honour. Hence it was not difficult for teachers to communicate to their pupils social traditions and values and to regulate their conduct in a manner consistent with the recognised code of the community. With the establishment of industrialised order, the scale of values has changed. Wealth, and not education, is the main determinant of one's status in modern industralised societies. This has undermined the prestige of teachers to some extent. Moreover, the expansion of mass literacy in the modern world has also contributed to the decline of the prestige of teachers, for he is "no longer set apart as the literate man". There is yet another factor contributing towards the same end. Now-a-days the values professed by a teacher are no longer authoritative. They have "to compete with the values presented to the child by his family, peer group, and the media of mass communication". There is, therefore, the possibility of a conflict between "different codes of behaviour and different agencies of social control in contemporary societies". For instance, India being wedded to the ideal of secularism, Indian schools do not provide for any religious instruction. In these circumstances, a boy or a girl who comes from a very conservative family with religious tradition, is likely to face conflicts between "secular character of state education as contrasted with the religious values of the family". We may conceive of innumerable cases of such conflicts among different agencies of social control.

## 4. MODERNISATION AND EDUCATION

The aforesaid changes and conflicts are reflected in the changes that the contents of instruction in modern educational institutions have undergone. Modern schools, colleges, and universities do not give as much emphasis upon transmitting a way of life to the students as was given by earlier forms of education. This is due to the fact that traditional education was meant for an unchanging and static society, a society not marked by rapid changes associated with industrialisation. Modern society is, on the other hand, characterised by very rapid and extensive changes. Hence in such a changing society, education aims at communicating empirical knowledge, that is , knowledge about science, techonology, and other types of such specialised knowledge. In other words, in keeping with the demands of a changing society, there has been a corresponding transformation in the contents and methods of instruction.

Some consequences of far-reaching importance follow the transformation in the contents and methods of instruction. To begin with, inclusion of heavy study materials on modern science and technology into the syllabus makes it imperative that courses of study on classical language and literature should be abridged or altogether dropped. This means a break of the learners with the past traditions and cultural heritage of the community. It is argued that in such circumstances an individual would be cut off from his 'roots' and his creative faculties, particularly his emotional and spiritual talents, would languish for want of nourishment. This poses a dilemma for a modern man. He needs knowledge of science and technology to move about and eke out a living. But importance attached to acquisition of technical knowledge and skill in the course of study would tend to deprive him of easy access to the rich treasures of past traditions. It is not easy to suggest a way out of this dilemma. Secondly, under the impact of modern science and technology many of the cherished values of the past have lost their previous importance. The people are no longer persuaded to accept them without question. Unfortunately, no new set of values have yet taken the place of the old. This poses two kinds of dangers : one to the society and the other to the individuals. The danger to society stems from the fact that the society may fall apart in the absence of a consensus about some basic questions as to what is right and what is wrong, what is proper and what is not, and what is desirable and what is not desirable. The danger to individuals arises from the fact that 'even surrounded and served by intricate and marvellous machines man may be little more than a cruel and clever ape unless he constantly thinks about what is truly good and strives to attain it"[7]. Thirdly, this brings us to an aspect of science and technology which we can ignore only at our peril. All throughout the nineteenth century, man was over-awed by discoveries in the field of natural sicence. Bacon echoed the views of many when he said "knowledge is power". But today many eminent scientists have reluctantly come to the view that "knowledge is unfortunately power". Commenting on this other side of science, Robert Jungk in his famous book *Brighter Than a Thousand Suns* made the following observations : "The age which culminated in the development of absolute weapons identified progress, almost unanimously, with progress in science and technology. But today the outstanding physicist Heisenberg declares: "The space in which man had developed as intellectual being has more dimensions than that of the single direction in which he has moved during the last few centuries'.... This new modesty, like the inhuman and superhuman weapons, has grown from the tree of atomic research.... The atom bomb, whose power is the clearest expression of the lack of moderation in modern man, comes from the same root as the new philosophy of moderation, inspired by the experience of nuclear research"[8]. This calls for rethinking and re-appraisal in the field of educational planning as part of modernisation.

## 5 CULTURAL DEPRIVATION AND COMPENSATORY EDUCATION

In an age when we swear by democracy, the ideal of providing equality of educational opportunity for all is accepted as a part of the democratic process. All societies, barring a few exceptions to the contrary, are characterised by a steady and slow decline of inequality of educational opportunity. But experience suggests that one cannot expect equality of results as a follow-up of equality of educational opportunity. Among various factors which stand in the way of achieving equal results is the cultural deprivation of a section of the population. Let us consider, for example, the cases of children of backward classes, scheduled castes and scheduled tribes in India. There may, of course, be many other groups who may be placed in this category. The characteristic of a culturally deprived child is that his environment is not only poverty-stricken in economic terms but also in cultural terms."He may have come to school without ever having had his mother sing him the traditional lullabies, and with no knowledge of nursery rhymes, fairy stories, or the folklore of his country".In other words, a culturally deprived child does not come to the school with a mind sufficiently enriched by long exposure to intellectual resources in his home and surroundings to respond meaningfully to suggestions.

The cases of culturally deprived children pose problems for the democratic ideal of equality of opportunity in education. The underlying principle of the ideal of equality of educational opportunity is that the provision of similar educational opportunities for all would give every student an equality of opportunity to fulfil his talents. But it has become increasingly apparent that " a uniform state educational system would not provide everyone with an equal chance since many would enter and travel through the system with the millstone of cultural deprivation hanging round their necks"[9].

This realisation changed the notion of equality of educational opportunity. Previously, it was held that the requirements of the ideal of equality of educational opportunity were fulfilled when access to all spheres of education was made freely available to all. Now it is argued that equality of educational opportunity may be said to exist when the levels of attainment of all social groups are similar. That is, emphasis has now shifted from equality of opportunity to equality of results.

The next question is : How to ensure equality of results ? It has been suggested that this can be done by compensating for the deprivations and deficiencies of those who are stricken both in economic and cultural terms. It is assumed that such compensatory measures would enable the culturally deprived to take advantage of the opportunities that are freely made available to all. That is, those who are lagging behind must be given a helping hand in order to enable them to compete on equal terms with those who are not so disadvantageously placed. This is the theory behind the idea of positive or protective discrimination in favour of culturally deprived children. This means additional educational provision for the culturally deprived.

Compensatory educational programmes were undertaken in a big way in the U.S.A. as a part of President Johnson's war on poverty. Billions of dollars were poured into "Operation Head Start', a massive programme of pre-school education in low-income areas across the entire country, This programme aimed at providing a stimulating educational environment to the culturally deprived children and at motivating them for making full use of educational opportunities. It is reported that the results have not been encouraging. In England compensatory education began in the late 1960s in selected areas known as Educational Priorities Areas (EPAs). Programmes of compensatory education were introduced in these areas. Haralambos observes : "Though it is difficult to evaluate the results, reports from the EPAs are generally disappointing"[10]. What are the reasons for the failure of compensatory education programmes in the U.S.A. and in England ? It is doubtful as to whether protective discriminatory measures have achieved the expected results in India also. How to account for this ?

It has been argued that instead of concentrating solely on the child inside the educational institution, efforts must be directed toward an improvement of the environment, so that the entire community and families therein may be deeply involved. "No matter how much you do inside the school, you can make virtually no impact at all without the informed support of the home". It is suggested that a community school with strong links between the school and the community as a whole should be set up. It is further suggested that parents should be educated to help their children. It may be mentioned, in this context, that the National Adult Education Programme (NAEP), which was launched by the Government of India in the year 1978, aimed at, among other things, educating the adult members of the community in the age-group 15-35, so that they could serve as catalytic agents in stimulating the young to make the best use of educational opportunities made available to them.

Though the idea of compensatory education has its adherents, there are also critics who question the idea and its theoretical basis. The theory of cultural deprivation, the critics argue, is only a smokescreen which conceals the cruel fact of economic deprivation and social inequality. It is held that basically the problem is economic and social and the problem has to be tackled on the economic and social planes. Compensatory education does not provide any solution to this basic problem. Critics go so far as to say that compensatory education serves as a "diversion from the pursuit of a genuine egalitarian policy", and that it can never succeed as long as there exists social inequality and economic deprivation. In other words, piecemeal approach must be replaced by a total approach, embracing different aspects of social life.

## NOTES

1. J.S. Mackenzie, *Outlines of Social Philosophy,* page 94
2. *ibid,* page 95
3. *ibid,* page 97
4. *ibid,* page 97
5. T.B.Bottomore, *Sociology,* page 247
6. *ibid,* page 266
7. Gilbert Highet, *The Immortal Profession,* page 33
8. Robert Jungk,*Brighter Than a Thousand Suns,*A Personal History of the Atomic Scientists, Penguin Books, page 304-305
9. Haralambos, *Sociology,* page 202
10. *ibid,* page 204
11. *ibid,* page 204

# CHAPTER TWENTY

# RELIGIOUS INSTITUTIONS

## 1. HOW DID RELIGION EVOLVE

There are mysteries and perplexities of life for which adequate explanation cannot always be found. The elements of nature —sunshine, wind, storm and rain—affect man in diverse ways. But these are, to a large extent, beyond his control. Then there is the mystery of birth and death. By way of response to such mysteries, man in all ages has thought of some super-natural and super-sensory power. Religion is the expression of the manner and type of adjustment effected by a people in terms of their conception of the super-natural. James G. Frazer in his book *The Golden Bough* defined religion as a belief in "powers superior to man which are believed to direct and control the course of nature and of human life". According to Ogburn and Nimkoff: "Religion is attitude towards super-human powers". Such attitudes gave rise to a coherent system of beliefs and practices concerning the supernatural order. Malinowski emphasised this aspect in his definition: "Religion is a mode of action as well as a system of belief, and a sociological phenomenon as well as a personal experience". Some writers, however, look upon religion as a belief in the immortality of the soul. They define religion in terms of a belief in God.

In the nineteenth century the sociology of religion was concerned with two main questions : How did religion begin ? and How did religion evolve ? This evolutionary approach was influenced by Darwinian Theory of Evolution. Two main theories. animism and naturism, were advanced to account for its origin.

### Animism

According to animism, the idea of the soul (anima) is central to religion. Hence the name animism. According to E.B. Tylor, primitive man hit upon the idea of soul because of an error. In his dreams, he walked about various places, engaged in various types of activities and met his dead ancestors even while his body remained in one place. He deduced from this experience that each individual has a double, another self, which has the power of leaving the body and travelling to distant place. This double is distinguished from the person in several respects. "It is more malleable and plastic; for, to leave the body, it must pass out by its apertures, especially the mouth and nose. It is represented as made of matter, but of a matter much more subtile and ethereal than any which we know empirically. This double is the soul"[1].

Conceived thus, how did the soul attain the status of a disembodied spirit ? An answer to this question is provided by another error supposed to have been made by primitive men. They thought of death as a prolonged sleep as a result of which the body disintegrated and ceased walking. The soul consequently became disembodied and free and roamed around those who were living. Gradually, the population of spirit souls grew. It was thought that these spirits had the needs, passions, and interests of living men and were inclined either to aid or to injure their erstwhile living companions. Being ethereal and fluid, these spirits could enter into the bodies of living beings and cause either all sorts of disorders or increase the strength and vitality of the bodies. It was assumed that an evil spirit caused the disorders while benign spirit increased the strength and vitality of the body and brought about other wholesome changes. Primitive men thus found an explanation for all kinds of happenings that varied from the ordinary in terms of the activities of spirits. Illness or some such misfortune was ascribed to the work of evil spirits while good things of life were attributed to the work of benign spirits . The next step was, therefore, an attempt to conciliate and appease the spirits in order to ensure that they did not harm the living beings. The modus of appeasement took the form of prayers, offerings, sacrifices and other practices. Thus was deity created from a simple conception of a 'double' in a human body. Since death brought about this apotheosis, "it was to the dead, to the souls of the ancestors, that the first cult known to humanity was addressed. Thus the first rites were funeral rights; the first sacrifices were food offerings destined to satisfy the needs of the departed; the first altars were tombs"[2].

Tylor explained animism by formulating the theory that early men could not distinguish animate from inanimate objects. He endowed all things, even inanimate objects, with human characteristics and hence with souls. It was held that the souls of men governed the affairs of men. Likewise, it was also held that the soul of other things, including those of trees and animals, governed the external world—"the flow of rivers, the movement of stars, the germination of plants, the reproduction of animals, etc".[3] Early men were more attracted by these cosmic spirits than by those of his ancestors, because the external things inhabited by spirits were more real to them than the ancestors who existed only in their imagination. They, therefore, implored the assistance of these spirits with offerings and prayers. Thus came into being a completely animistic view of the world. The ancestor cult was supplemented by a nature-worshipping cult.

## Naturism

The theory of naturism is associated with the name of Max Muller. He accepted Tylor's theory of the origin of the conception of soul with the exception that he placed greater emphasis on death as the source rather than on dreams. This development was, however, considered by Max Muller as secondary in importance. The source of religious inspiration was to be sought, according to him, in the deep influence exercised by nature in all its varied aspects upon the mind of early man. He actually deified nature. In the words of Max Muller : "At first sight, nothing seemed less natural than nature. Nature was the greatest surprise, a terror, a marvel, a standing miracle, and was only on account of their permanence, constancy, and regular recurrence that certain features of that standing miracle were called natural, in the sense of foreseen, common, intelligible... It was that vast domain of surprise, of terror, of marvel, of miracle, the unknown, as distinguished from the known, or as I like to express it, the infinite, as distinct from the finite, which supplied from the earliest times the impulse to religious thought and language". Max Muller maintained that an attitude of awe or love and reverence towards objects of nature was born as a result of a 'diseased' mind which invested lifeless things with life and all the power that is associated with life. This was brought about by early man's stupidity again—this time his linguistic confusion. Such linguistic errors as the sun rises and sets, or thunder sends rain, or that trees bear flowers and fruit, gave rise to belief in some power inherent in the sun, thunder, trees, etc. "Hence a spirit had to be attributed to the objects in order to account for the acts which were confounded with them in their names. Language thus superimposed upon the material world as revealed to the senses, a new world composed of spiritual beings created out of nothing and felt to be the causes of physical events. Once invented, the vocabulary representing this spirit world was capable of indefinite expansion, so that a pantheon, a hierarchy of deities could be created. The idea of man's own soul was a secondary growth, and the religion of ancestor worship was a reflection of the more important nature worship"[5].

### Animatism and Manaism

The assumption that the people have a conception of the soul has been criticised by some anthropologists. According to them, the entire religious life of the primitive people was born out of their belief in the existence of a certain supernatural power or spirit in all objects, animate and inanimate. They did not distinguish between the animate and inanimate objects, because, in their view, such distinctions were a later development. It is therefore, wrong to assume that the primitive people became aware in the first instance of a soul in man and subsequently conceived of soul in lower animals and in inanimate objects. Marett characterised such idea of spirit or supernatural power among primitive people as 'non-personalised concept of spirit', and he called such a set of beliefs animatism or manaism after the term 'mana' used by Melanesians to designate this force. Some North American tribes called this power orenda or maniton.

Reference is made to child psychology in support of this point of view. It is argued that a baby fails to distinguish between an animate and an inanimate object, as is displayed by his attitude to dolls. He caresses the doll and talks to it as if it were a living being. Similar must have been the psychology of the primitive people who ascribed the qualities of human beings to all non-human beings and inanimate objects.

## 2. MAGIC

There are two ways of tiding over various crises of life. One is the religious approach which means worshipping and offering prayers to the Higher Power in order to earn Divine grace. The other is the magical approach which is a system of manipulation by which some superior power or powers are sought to be coerced into service. Such manipulative action is not obviously validated by scientific knowledge.

In *Golden Bough* Frazer made a detailed study of magical practices on the basis of evidence collected from different parts of the world. He found that magical formulae are based on two principles : (i) Like produces like, (ii) once in contact always in contact. He reduced these two principles into laws.

The first one is the law of similarity. The magic based on it is called homoeopathic or imitative or mimetic magic. Some examples may be cited. In Chota Nagpur (in Bihar) some tribal groups believe that thunder with its rumbling noise is the direct cause of rain. Because of this belief, when they want rains, they go to a hill top, sacrifice a hen or a pig, and then start flinging down stones, rocks and boulders down the hill, expecting rain to follow the rumbling noises created by their action. just as it follows thunder. Burning of effigies is yet another common form of imitative magic. To get rid of an enemy, an image of him may be made and then burnt or nails driven into it. It is believed that its original will also suffer likewise.

The second law is the law of contact or contagion. The magic that is based on it is called contagious magic. The law of contact or contagion is based on the assumption that a part is always associated with the whole to which it belongs or belonged—that is, once a part, always a part. This association is extended to clothing, nail and hair trimmings, excreta, utensils, personal effects and so on. It is because of such belief that the personal effects of the dead are not made use of by many primitive groups but are instead buried or cremated along with the dead body. Contagious magic operates on the principle that whatever is in contact with the supernatural power would be affected by it. Thus, many people wear a mascot or talisman to ward off evil spirit. The magical practice of neutralising the effects of the evil eye by the application of black mark on the foreheads is found both among tribals and non-tribals.

**Fetishism**

Magic is often associated with fetishism. According to this belief, certain objects are supposed to be possessed of powers to help man out of various difficulties or in achieving his desires. Such objects are called fetishes. Such an object may be a feather, a skull or an amulet. Its test is its efficacy.

**Totemism**

According to Goldenweiser, when we refer to totemism, we mean that a tribe has a social organisation, usually of the sib pattern, which is associated with a form of supernaturalism, consisting of certain typical attitudes towards species of animals or plants or classes of natural objects. This attitude manifests itself in several different ways. Thus, descent may be traced from the totemic animal or plant (a totem is generally an animal, rarely a plant). The killing and/or eating of the totemic species may be taboo, but may be permissible on ceremonial occasions. The death of a totemic animal may be ceremonially mourned. The totemic animal may be looked upon as a sort of guardian-angel of the totemite.

**Taboo**

The word 'taboo' has been derived from the Polynesian *tabu* meaning 'to forbid' and 'forbidden'. Taboo is used to characterise all the restrictions, communicated through verbal Don'ts and Do's, and generally associated with ritualistic behaviour which a member of a primitive society has to submit to. Taboo has been called the unwritten law of savage society. But society does not deal with cases of violation. The culprit himself becomes the chastiser. He fears a calamity. Taboo may, therefore, be said to have a supernatural or magical sanction behind it. The aim of taboo appears to be to limit an individual to the norms of his society. It is society which is vitally affected by the observance or non-observance of taboo. Yet the initiative for enforcement of taboo always rests with the individual.

It has been very well said that the woof and warp of magical beliefs and practices is made up of positive and negative strands. Taboo represents the latter. Its purpose is three-fold : productive, protective and prohibitive. Taboos associated with the process of cultivation are designed to be productive. There are taboos which keep, for example, women and children away from certain places or actions. These are protective in nature. The prohibitive taboos are those which seclude a person or limit contact with him or her. These are designed to be prohibitive in the sense that they prohibit the persons tabooed from doing harm to others. Protective and prohibitive taboos are the same.

**Relation between religion and magic**

It is held that both religion and magic are very close to each other inasmuch as both are resorted to as tools of adaptation when common skills and capabilities are of no avail. Malinowski noted that the Trobriand Islanders had a very good knowledge about how to make a boat, how to make it float and what to do in order to ensure that the boat does not sink. But they were completely in the dark as to why a storm breaks out and how to meet it. So they relied on both magic and religion to meet the challenge for which they had no explanation. Magic and religion are concerned with the mystery of the world. This is the only feature common to both.

Magic and religion, however, differ sharply in many respects. In the first place, magical practices are resorted to with definite ends in view. Religious practices, on the other hand, are not result-oriented. The devotees seek the grace of Good through prayers and offerings. Prayers and offerings are often ends in themselves. Secondly, an air of secrecy surrounds the magician and his practices. Religion, on the contrary, is public and communal. It has a congregational aspect. Thirdly, though both the magician and the priest mediate between the world we know and the world we do not, the former is feared, the latter commands respect, the former is malevolent and the latter benevolent.

In spite of these differences the veil of separation between the two appears to be very thin. The techniques followed in magic and religion are ritualistic. A great deal of importance is attached to traditional observance of rituals. A slight departure is supposed to destroy the efficacy of both. A slight change in the formulation of words may convert a magical formula into a religious prayer. As a matter of fact, in every religion, there are magical practices and rites which cannot be completely isolated. That is why the roles of magician and priest are sometimes combined in one person.

## 3. RELIGION VERSUS SCIENCE

The basic question about science and religion is this : Is there any inherent conflict between the two ? The answer is both 'yes' and 'no', depending on how one views it.

Religion is concerned with a world beyond the senses. Belief is its essence. Such beliefs can neither be proved nor disproved. Science, on the other hand, is concerned with a world known to us in terms of our sense-perception. A scientist refuses to accept anything which can not be tested. There is thus an apparent conflict between religion and science.

This apparent conflict does not concern those who look at science and religion from a different perspective. If one holds the view that religion deals with first causes and science with immediate causes, there is no possibility of any conflict between the two . Seen from this point of view, a scientist can be a devoutly religious man, and, at the same time, a good scientist. Thus, a biologist may see the facts and principles of biology as so many manifestations of God's handiwork. He may meticulously pursue scientific investigations in the laboratory and, at the same time, marvel at the grand design of creation in the manner of a devotee. There is apparently no feeling of inconsistency or incongruity in an individual who deals with facts in the laboratory and behaves in a totally different manner outside the laboratory. Many eminent scientists, including Nobel Prize winners,, belong to this category.

Conflicts between religion and science, however, arise when religion seeks to explain natural or physical phenomenon and such explanations are proved to be devoid of any meaning and without any basis whatsoever. Science insists that a theory can survive only if it passes rigorous tests of its simplicity and predictive powers. Thus, as science expands there will be conflict between religion and science. An illustration would be illuminating. "Only a short while ago, the origin of man on the earth was unknown to the human intellect. Religious belief filled in the gap by giving a very precise account of man's origin. The account was believed because it was thought to be divinely revealed . Eventually, however, scientific investigation began to bring the earthly origin of man into the factual domain. Here, then, there was serious conflict. The scientist could not accept the religious account as literally true and still be true to his science"[6]. The conflict may also be illustrated by theories about planetary movement. In the past, it was thought that each planet was guarded and propelled by its own God or 'guardian angel'. The people were not, therefore, able to predict the behaviour of planets in terms of such religious explanation. Eventually, such religious explanation was replaced by a less complex scientific theory based on the action of a small number of inanimate forces obeying simple uniform laws. Thus, the scientific theory provides us with much greater powers of prediction.

Thus, as science and technology advances, there is a decline in the worship of God as *explanations* of and as *instruments* to control natural forces. In simple societies, people use religion as an instrument primarily in situations where they feel they are at the mercy of the environment or other outside forces. Often, the result of any given activity of a society remains uncertain even when the people's skills have been used to the utmost. For example, such a simple operation as deep-sea fishing requires great skill in order to yield results. But even where such skill is available, some natural calamity like storm may bring disaster. Similarly, in the event of disease, famine or drought, a simple community is quite powerless to affect the outcome. But with the growth of technology and advance of scientific knowledge comes an ability to control at least some natural forces. The importance of religion as *explanations* of and as *instruments* to control natural forces has naturally declined in modern times.

So religion becomes concerned with other, less wordly matters, matters concerning the meaning of life. "The religious ideology grows more and more vague, more and more philosophical, and less and less anthropomorphic. It changes from fundamentalist to liberal, from dogma to philosophy"[7]. Commenting on this aspect, Kingsley Davis states that as religion loses its battle with science, it retreats to higher level. Obviously, the question of conflict with science recedes into the background. In the past there have been conflicts of eminent scientists with the institutionalised religious order. The roots of such conflicts lay in the fact that scientific investigations unravelled the mysteries of the universe and found explanations in empirical terms which were different from those prevailing in the then prevailing religions. That chapter is now virtually closed. People turn to religion today not for explanation of worldly matters, but as a source of love and emotional security. Science has taken over the role of religion to explain and influence events. But science cannot become a substitute for religion in its role of providing emotional support to people who need it.

## 4. THE INSTITUTIONALISATION OF RELIGION

All religious organisations evolve out of the specific religious experiences of particular founders and their disciples. Centering around such experiences, a form of religious association develops. In course of time, such an association grows into a permanent institutionalised religious organisation. It has been very aptly said that the religious experience marks a breakthrough from the ordinary in the sense that it is a 'charismatic experience'. The evolution of a stable organisation based on such a charismatic experience is an example of what Max Weber called "the routinization of charisma"[8].

The character of the religious organisation changes radically upon the demise of the charismatic figure who founded the organisation. According to Max Weber, if charisma is not "to remain a purely transitory phenomenon, but to take on the character of a permanent relationship forming a stable community of disciples or band of followers", its character must undergo a radical change. Pure charisma is important and vitally necessary at the time of origin. For continuity of the organisation, the charismatic experience of the founder has to be kept alive and the authority of explaining and/or interpreting the experience must be created. "This crisis of continuity", says O'dea, "is also a crisis of succession—who shall constitute the authority in the group to replace the charismatic founder"?[9] The way this crisis is met is of crucial importance for the character of the subsequent social relationships.

Religious institutions evolve (i) as patterns of worship, i.e., as a cult; (ii) as patterns of ideas and definitions, i.e., as beliefs; (iii) as forms of association or organisation. In other words, religious institutionalisation occurs on the cultic level, on the intellectual level and on the organisational level. These three aspects develop simultaneously as parts of the same developmental process. How do these three aspects develop ? From the preaching of the message of the Founder develop creeds and theology; from the cult, elaborate symbolic liturgies; from the brotherhood of followers the ecclesiastical organization.

What is cult ? The cult is "that complex of gesture, word, and symbolic vehicle which is the central religious phenomenon". The cult is explained in terms of *acting out* of feelings, attitudes, and relationships. "The relationships acted out in the cult are first of all relationships with the sacred object......They are only secondarily relationships among the members and between members and leaders......"[10]. Cultic act is the root of the division that we find in almost all institutionalised religions between clergy and laity.

The patterns of ideas and definitions which evolve alongside the institutionalisation of religion fall under two heads : the mythical and the rational. Myth is the primitive form of the intellectual expression of religious beliefs and attitudes. Through it, men not only 'explain' their world but symbolically represent it. It involves another way of seeing the world, a way which expresses its coherence together with human emotional involvement and participation in it.[11] Besides myth, other forms of thought and other modes of explanation of the world develop with growing experience of men. This is called the process of rationalisation. Human thought becomes progressively rationalised in terms of its consistency and its systematic character and also in terms of the elimination of fantasy and mythic elements. Rational theology develops as part of the rationalisation of thought. It is to be found in one form or another in all the world religions. Theology is concerned with a rational explanation of "what is" and "what ought to be done". These are brought to bear upon the education of the priestly class, a highly professional group which is differentiated from the rank-and-file members of the religious organisation.

All religious groups are originally diffuse in nature. With the gradual emergence of cult and rational theology, religion establishes a new community of believers and a new pattern of life to the members. They differ from other groups in the society by virtue of its rituals, its beliefs, and its type of organisation. There is a high degree of fraternal equality among the members of the religious group. At the same time, the distinction between the clergy and the laity is accompanied by a hierarchical pattern of authority among the clergy who can interpret the message of the Founder and the intellectual contents of the world-view represented by that particular religion in an authoritative manner.

## 5. RELIGION AND SOCIETY

Different sociologists have defined religion and described its role in society differently in terms of their ideological commitments. In terms of their value judgments, they have commended some aspects of religion as worthy of study and dismissed some other aspects as irrelevant and devoid of worth. Some of these perspectives are presented here separately. The strength and weakness, the functions and dysfunctions of institutionalised religion will be brought out in this mosaic of differing sociological perspectives.

### Emile Durkheim on religion

The sociological theory of religion, which Durkheim developed in his book *The Elementary Forms of Religious Life,* was inspired by Marx's celebrated idea that the social existence of men determines their social consciousness. Durkheim does not, however, keep himself limited to socio-economic relationships. He goes beyond socio-economic relationships to include other social relations. In this book Durkheim presented what is probably the most influential interpretation of religion from a functionalist perspective. Durkheim argues that all societies divide the world into two categories: 'the sacred' and 'the profane'. More simply, this means the distinction between the sacred and the non-sacred. Religion, according to him, is based on this distinction. It is " a unified system of beliefs and practices related to sacred things, that is to say, things set apart and forbidden". He insists that 'sacred things' do not simply mean those personal things which are called gods or spirits. Anything can be 'sacred', such as a pebble, a piece of wood, a rock etc. This is not the particular quality of the pebble or the wood which makes it sacred. Sacred things are considered to be sacred simply because they are symbols of something. Durkheim, therefore, says that to understand the role of religion in society, the relationship between these symbols and that which they represent must be established. He argues that if one can study the most rudimentary forms of social existence and the thought forms which accompany them, then perhaps one can understand the relationship or connection between the symbol (i.e., collective existence) and that which the symbol represents (i.e., collective representations).It is for this reason that the various primitive groups of Australia and North America form the basis of his study.

Durkheim considers the religion of Australian aborigines, which he calls totemism, as the simplest and most basic form of religion. The totemic object among these people is connected not only with religion but also with clan membership. Aboriginal society is divided into several clans. A clan is like a large extended family with its members sharing certain duties and obligations. Each clan has a totem, usually an animal or a plant. The totem is a symbol. It is the emblem of the clan. "It is its flag; it is the sign by which each clan distinguishes itself from all others". The totem is , however, more than this . It is a *sacred* symbol. The totem is the outward expression of the totemic principle or god. The totem, being thus a religious or sacred object, inspires respect and awe. Specially is this true when the otherwise scattered parts of the clan come together periodically on a ceremonial occasion. It is then that an excitement is bred which lifts the individual out of himself. It is a minor case of creative synthesis. The totem is only an object; yet it is symbolic of a reality unseen. The 'images of the totemic beings are more sacred than the beings themselves". This fact makes it evident that the totem has a special symbolic significance. Because it symbolises the moral unity of the clan as a whole, it is sacred and eventually transforms itself into a divinity. Durkheim argues that if the totem "is at once the symbol of the god and of the society, is that not because the god and the society are only one"? Thus, he suggests that in worshipping god, men are in fact worshipping society. Society is the real object of religious veneration.

How does man come to worship society ? Durkheim argues : "Primitive man comes to view society as something sacred because he is utterly dependent on it". Society is more important and powerful than the individual. But why does man not simply worship society itself ? Why does he invent a sacred symbol like a totem ? By way of explanation, Durkheim argues: " it is easier for him to visualise and direct his feelings of awe toward a symbol than towards so complex a thing as a clan". He sees this as a situation in which religion " ceases to be an inexplicable hallucination and takes a foothold in reality. In fact, we can say that the believer is not deceived when he believes in the existence of a moral power upon which he depends and from which he received all that is best in himself: this power exists, it is society".

In the Australian tribes studied by Durkheim, the totem is represented in various ways. Each totem has its emblem or blazon. In almost all clans, there are objects, such as pieces of wood, stones, etc. which bear a figurative representation of the totem. Ordinary objects, which are referred to as *churinga*, are transfigured once they bear the emblem of the totem. They share the sacred quality that is associated with the totem, a phenomenon which we can easily understand by observing ourselves. In modern societies, the flag may be regarded as the equivalent of the *churinga* of Australian aborigines. The flag of a collectivity shares the sacred quality which we attribute to the native land. Totemic objects, bearing the emblem of the totem, give rise to behaviour typical of the religious order, i.e., either prescriptive or proscriptive practices. The members of the clan must abstain from eating or touching the totem or the objects which share the sacred quality of the totem. Or, they must display with regard to the totem some explicit form of respect. In this way, there is formed in the Australian societies a division into two fundamental categories of the whole of reality: the sacred and the profane.

For Durkheim, the "sacred and the profane have always and everywhere been conceived by the human mind as two distinct classes, as two worlds between which there is nothing in common". There is a logical chasm between the two domains, and it is precisely the totality of sacred beliefs and practices which constitutes a religion. Religion is a group phenomenon, for it is a group which gives a religion its specific character and unity. Moreover, the religion unifies the group; literally, it binds men together. In this way, Durkheim emphasises his general thesis that religious ideas are derived from society and serve to bind the members of a society together. This essential and positive function of religion—viz., solidifying a society—explains why it is a ubiquitous and permanent institution.

Durkheim's ideas on religion are influential. These have, however, been subjected to several criticisms. It is argued that he was wrong in accepting totemism as a religion. He is also criticised on the ground that religion does not imply worship of society. It is pointed out that Durkheim's ideas are more relevant to pre-literate, simple societies in which "there is a close integration of culture and social institutions", and in which "work, leisure, education and family life tend to merge, and where members share a common belief and value system". Durkheim's ideas are not wholly applicable to modern societies "which have many sub-cultures, social and ethnic groups, specialised organisations and a range of religious beliefs, practices and institutions". He ignores the fact that in more complex societies religious beliefs and practices vary from one stratum to another and that these strata have conflicting conceptions of the "same " religious doctrine. It is also striking that he fails to see the negative, alienating consequences of religion.

## Bronislaw Malinowski on religion

There are striking similarities in approach to religion between Durkheim and Malinowski. To begin with, Malinowski bases his thesis on religion on data collected from small-sized non-literate societies in the Trobriand Islands off the coast of New Guinea in the same way as Durkheim draws on the activities of the Australian aborigines for his thesis on religion. Second, like Durkheim, Malinowski sees religion as re-inforcing social norms and values and promoting social solidarity. There is, however, one difference of a basic nature between the two. Unlike Durkheim, Malinowski "does not see religion reflecting society as a whole, nor does he see religious ritual as the worship of society itself". On the contrary, Malinowski identifies specific areas of social life with which religion is concerned. These areas are situations of emotional stress which threaten social solidarity.

In his handling of science, magic and religion, Malinowski accepted essentially the traditional Western conception of the dual reality—namely, the reality of the natural world, grounded in observation and rational procedures that lead to mastery over nature, and supernatural reality, grounded in emotional needs that give rise to faith. For example, Malinowski derived science not from magic but from man's capacity to organise knowledge, as demonstrated by Trobriand Islanders' technical skills in gardening, ship-building, etc. In contrast, he treated magic, which co-existed with these skills, as an organised response to a sense of limitation and impotence in the face of danger, difficulty and frustration. Again, he differentiated between magic and religion by defining magical systems as essentially pragmatic in their aims and by defining religious systems as self-fulfilling rituals organised, for example, around life crises. It is also significant that he differentiated between the individual character of religious experience and the social character of religious ritual.

Anxiety and tension tend to disrupt social life. Situations which produce these emotions include 'crises of life' such as birth, puberty, marriage and death. Malinowski notes that in all societies these life crises are surrounded with religious ritual. He looks upon death as the most disruptive of these events and observes: "The existence of strong personal attachments and the fact of death, which of all human events is the most upsetting and disorganizing to man's calculations, are perhaps the main sources of religious beliefs". Religion deals with the problem of death in the following manner. "A funeral ceremony expresses the belief in immortality, which denies the fact of death, and so comforts the bereaved. Other mourners support the bereaved by their presence at the ceremony. This comfort and support checks the emotions which death produces, and controls the stress and anxiety which might disrupt society. Death is 'socially disruptive' since it removes a member from society. At a funeral ceremony the social group unites to support the bereaved. This expression of social solidarity re-integrates society"[12].

In addition to the above, there are also events which produce emotional stress and strain, tension and anxiety. Emotional disturbances occur because these events are not amenable to human control or manipulation. For example, fishing in the high seas by Trobriand Islanders is open to danger and uncertainty. It is dangerous because a storm may result in loss of life. It is uncertain because the catch is dependent on the presence of a shoal of fish which cannot be predicted. Hence, fishing in the open sea is preceded by rituals to ensure a good catch and protect the fishermen from storm. Although Malinowski refers to these rituals as magic, it is argued by some that these rituals should be regarded as religious practices. Here is an example of a ritual associated with a specific situation which tends to produce anxiety. Rituals reduce anxiety by providing confidence and a feeling of control. Fishing rituals, like funeral ceremonies, are also social events. The group unites to deal with situations of strees, and the unity of the group is thereby strengthened.

The distinctive contribution of Malinowski to the sociology of religion lies in the fact that he emphasised the role of religion in promoting social solidarity by dealing with situations of emotional stress that tend to threaten the stability of society.

## Karl Marx on religion

Karl Marx looks upon religion as an illusion which is necessary for the alleviation of sufferings of the people in a capitalist society. In the words of Marx: "Religion is the sigh of the oppressed creature; the sentiment of a heartless world and the soul of soulless conditions. It is the opium of the people". Obviously, therefore, religion would completely disappear in a communist society where there would no more be division of people into classes, the oppressor and the oppressed, the exploiter and the exploited. In other words, communism would usher in a situation in which the social conditions which produce religion would disappear. Religion has therefore, no place in a communist society.

The ways in which religion can mitigate the pain of oppression may be briefly noted. First, it promises a life of eternal bliss in the afterlife, i.e., life after death. Pain becomes bearable when people have something better to look forward to. Second, there are religions which extol the virtues of poverty and even of suffering produced by oppression. The well-known biblical quotation brings this out dramatically": It is easier for a camel to pass through the eye of a needle than for a rich man to enter the Kingdom of Heaven". The implication is clear. Those who would bear the deprivations of life with dignity and humility will be rewarded for their virtue. Third, religious teachings persuade men to hope for supernatural intervention to solve the problems on earth. Fourth, religion often teaches man to bear with injustice and accept the social order, however inequitous it may be. In Hinduism and in many other religions, the social order is represented as a handiwork of the Creator and, as such, social stratification is inevitable with all its inequitable concomitants. Interpreted thus, the social order is immutable and unchangeable. The people have, therefore, no other alternative but to accept stoically their position in the social order.

From a Marxian point of view, religion not only serves to create a series of myths which justify and even rationalise the social order based on injustice and exploitation, but it also serves as an instrument of that oppression. Historically, all organised religions have received patronage from the ruling class and in exchange these religious leaders have diverted attention of their followers from the real source of their oppression and thereby have helped the ruling class to remain in positions of power.

There is ample evidence to establish many of the charges levelled by the Marxists against organised religion. But will religion completely disappear in a situation where there would be no exploitation of one class by another ? There are many aspects of life which are unpredictable and uncertain. Death, for example, creates void which no amount of logic can close. In situations such as this one, people naturally raise questions about the meaning of life. Religion gives them the required emotional support and security. During the Second World War, Russian men and women in thousands thronged in and around the churches to say prayers for the well-being of near and dear ones who were in the thick of the battle. "One estimate places the number of baptized Orthodox Christians in the period 1947-57 at ninety million which is roughly the same as in 1914. Religion in Russia is not simply a hangover from pre-communist days. Despite official disapproval a number of small religious movements such as the Baptists and Evangelical Christians continue to spiring up"[13]. It has, therefore, been very aptly said that "these examples suggest that there is more to religion than a set of beliefs and practices which develop in societies based on the private ownership of the forces of production"[14].

## Religion and Secularisation

It should be borne in mind, however, that the dysfunctional aspects of religion relate to institutionalised religion. Instead of strengthening social solidarity, organized religions have served all throughout historical period as divisive forces, encouraging directly and indirectly religious feuds of varying dimensions.

The functions and dysfunctions of religion with respect both to society and to individuals may be examined with reference to the most outstanding social and cultural development of the last several centuries: namely, the *secularisation of culture*. In primitive and traditional societies, religion was all pervasive in the sense that religion ordained everything from birth to cremation or burial, including even mundane matters, such as occupational groupings. In short, religion determined the world-view of the believers. These characteristics are applicable to religious people in modern societies also. But a subtle difference has crept in. With regard to theology, people are gradually moving away from mythical interpretation to a more rational one. The "rationalisation of religious thought is part of a general process of the rationalisation of thinking in general". Secularisation of culture involved not simply an increase in rationality in the thinking of men, but also "a diminution of the sacred" which is often characterised as "desacralisation" (some sociologists term it as "desacrilisation") of the attitude toward persons and things. Desacralisation (or desacrilisation) actually means "the withdrawal of the kind of emotional involvement which is to be found in the religious response, in the response to the sacred". Thus, "the secularisation of culture, combining both desacralisation and rationalisation, means that a religious world-view is no longer the basic frame of reference for thought. Another view of the world as no longer sacred and composed of things to be manipulated comes into existence. This view more and more crowds the religious world-view into the sphere of 'private' experience and becomes the mode of thought in the 'public' sphere'"[15].

Max Weber's interpretation of industrial society provides one of the earliest statements of the desacralisation theme. According to him, the industrial society is characterised by rationalisation and intellectualisation and, above all, by the "desenchantment of the world". The world is no longer charged with mystery and magic; the supernatural has been banished from society. The meanings and motives which direct action are now rational[16]. A number of sociologists have accepted Weber's interpretation of the basis of action in industrial society. In his book *Religion in a Secular Society*, Bryan Wilson observes : "Religious *thinking* is perhaps the area which evidences most conspicuous change. Men act less and less in response to religious motivation : they assess the world in empirical and rational terms". Wilson identifies the following factors which were mainly responsible for the development of rational thinking and a rational world-view. First, 'worldly asceticism' of Protestantism 'created an ethic which was pragmatic, rational, controlled and anti-emotional'. Second, in an industrial society men are involved in organisations which are based on rational principles. Examples are firms, public service, educational institutions, government, etc. Naturally, these organisations impose rational behaviour upon them. Third, modern knowledge is based on reason rather than on faith. "Science", says Wilson, "not only explained many facets of life and the material environment in a way more satisfactory (than religion ), but it also provided confirmation of its explanation in practical results". Fourth, the development of ideologies such as communism and organisations such as trade unions offer practical solutions to problems. By comparison, religious solutions, such as the promise of justice and reward in the afterlife, do not produce practical and observable results[17]

It is obvious that a rational world-view is opposed to religion because the latter is based on faith and as such is non-rational. People no longer interpret the world around them in religious terms. There has, therefore, developed what is called 'secularisation of consciousness'. It must, however, be conceded that this represents one side of the picture. We have already seen that there are several 'life crises' which are unpredictable and uncontrolled and which leave people completely bewildered, helpless and forlon. During such periods they seek comfort and security in religion. This may be non-rational and non-logical, and not at all consistent with their rational behaviour in other walks of life. Such ambiguities and conflicts involved in secularisation of culture are inevitable.

## 6. RELIGION AND MORALITY

Morality is ascribed to universal principles of right conduct endemic to mankind. Right is the differentia of the moral. The character of the enforcing agency decides the classification of the conduct involved. If the enforcing agency be political, the *right* thing is a matter of law; if ecclesiastical, a matter of religion; if public opinion, a matter of convention. *Right* conduct is only occasionally the same for all institutions. There are often conflicts as regards *right* conduct in various fields. Thus, people are described as morally bound and legally free, morally guiltless and legally responsible, moral victors and actual losers, and vice versa. Morals are very often identified with sexual habits, 'moral' and 'immoral' being so much identified with sex conduct that bad citizens and unscrupulous businessmen are condoned as "good husbands and fathers".

The patterns and principles of conduct that come under the scope of moral are so diverse that it is not possible to analyse the subject matter scientifically on the basis of a single formula. Explanation of morals in terms of the biological instinct of self-preservation or in terms of use appear to be artificial and without any basis. Huxley said : "the notion that the doctrine of evolution could furnish a foundation for morals, seems an illusion". In all societies birth, wealth and position modify the obligatoriness of the code.

The subject becomes further complicated by the fact that one group's virtue or moral code of conduct may be a type of conduct forbidden or prohibited for another group. Thus, the code for females is stricter than the code for males. The woman known to live like a man is condemned while a man who consorts with prostitutes is accepted everywhere. Likewise, racial factor introduces variations in moral codes among different racial groups. In countries where colour bar exists, *right* conduct for whites is not the *right* conduct for negroes and vice versa. In fact, the code of right conduct or moral code is not universally followed. Sometimes variations are allowed, sometimes variations assert themselves, and sometimes variations operate in secret. In other words, variations always exist.

Every moral code depends for its due observance on the socialisation of children from their infancy. The values and ideals of society are indoctrinated into children by the family and other socialising agencies. The children are made to develop some emotional attachments and loyalty to these values and ideals. "The emotions soon become so overladen with habitual rules that the rules themselves seem intuitive and inevitable, when they are only familiar"[18]. Where this is not the case, the moral codes "receive protective elaboration and are reenforced with secondary agencies created *ad hoc*. Such elaborations and agencies are the courses in 'character building' now in vogue in American school and in some other countries, the rise of the discipline called 'social ethics' and the curious 'citizenship' courses. Others are the extra-governmental censors; 'patriotic' societies ........... and the new creations of the churches. All endeavour to validate codes recognised though not admitted to be shaky" [19]. In India also we have many such character-building associations.

But the most pervasive sanction for any complex of morals, irrespective of whether these are codified or not, is religion. "Its sanctions, involving supernatural rewards and punishments, enter early into the consciousness of the young. In the child's experience the God invoked to enforce right conduct consists of the word "God" and the feeling and attitude of the person speaking........ By its use the code is readily made momentous...... The same practice keeps atheism reprehensible and obscene and sustains the widespread delusion that disbelieving in God and possessing a criminal disposition are synonymous, that without religious sanctions morals must decay"[20].

The close link between religion and moral code is gradually being snapped in recent times. Two developments are responsible for this. Institutionalised religion is gradually losing its sway over the minds of people. Religion is increasingly becoming more individualised. The most outstanding social and cultural development of the last few centuries has been in the direction of *secularisation of culture*. In traditional societies, religion was all-pervasive in the sense that religion ordained everything from birth to cremation or burial, including even mundane matters. These characteristics are also applicable to religious people in modern societies. But a very subtle difference has crept in. With regard to theology, people are gradually moving away from mythical interpretation to a more rational one. Secularisation of culture involves not simply an increase in rationality in the thinking of men, but also" a diminution of the sacred" which is often characterised as ' desacralisation' (or desacrilisation) of the attitude toward persons and things. Desacralisation actually means "the withdrawal of the kind of emotional involvement which is to be found in the religious response, in the response to the sacred". Hence the religious world-view is no longer the basic frame of reference for thought. People no longer interpret the world around them in religious terms. "The separation between morality and religion is one prominent feature in the cultural changes of the past century, both in the sense that a clear distintion has been made between ritual and moral rules, and in the sense that, with the decline of religious belief, it has been necessary to find a new basis and content for the moral rules"[21].

Paradoxically, this separation between religion and morality brings the two closer on another level. As Bottomore points out : "religion has become more an individual and private matter .......... while morality has become more social, in that it is increasingly concerned with social justice rather than individual virtue. This change of emphasis is apparent even in the moral doctrines of religious organizations, which are much more concerned with social relations and social problems than ever in the past"[22]. In India a discerning observer of various religious organisations will not fail to notice that "there is a disposition to tone down the doctrinal and religious aspects of religion, and emphasise above all the utility of religion in solving social problems and creating fellowship"[23]

In recent years there has been another important development. Moral codes are increasingly becoming closely associated with political doctrines. "Moral disagreements are now very frequently political disagreements, and moral beliefs are largely incorporated in political ideologies"[24].

## NOTES

1. Kingsley Davis, *Human Society*, page 511
2. *ibid*, pages 510 -511
3. *ibid*, page 512

4. *ibid*, page 513
5. *ibid*, page 513
6. *ibid*, page 535
7. *ibid*, page 536
8. Thomas F.O'dea, *The Sociology of Religion*, page 37
9. *ibid*, page 37
10. *ibid*, page 39
11. *ibid*, page 42
12. Haralambos, *Sociology*, page 457
13. *ibid*, page 463
14. *ibid*, page 463
15. Thomas F. O'dea, *The Sociology of Religion*, page 81
16. Haralambos, *Sociology*, *Page 484*
17. *ibid*, page 485
18. An article on *Morals* by Horace M. Kallen in *The Encyclopaedia of the Social Sciences,Vol. X*
19. *ibid*,
20. *ibid*,
21. Bottomore, *Sociology*, pages 247-248
22. *ibid*, page 248
23. *ibid*, page 248
24. *ibid*, page 248

# CHAPTER TWENTY ONE

# SOCIAL PROCESS

In the Chapter on Society, we have seen that society is viewed by sociologists both as a structure and as a process. The first represents a static view of society and the second a dynamic view. An understanding of society requires consideration of both aspects just as an understanding of a human body requires consideration of both anatomy and physiology.

That society is a process needs no explanation. A moment's reflection would bring home to everyone that society is in a state of flux. Just as chemical changes in an organic body (known as metabolism) take place without any cessation or stop, so also changes in social relationships (which may be called social metabolism) take place in an uninterrupted manner. This process may be explained thus: Interaction is the basis of all social relationships. And interaction, as the word itself suggests, is not a momentary occurrence, not a single response to a single stimulus. On the contrary, it is a persisting process of action and reaction. It is to be noted further that such actions and reactions are not mechanical. These are, on the contrary, meaningful or communicative interactions. The physical gestures or the spoken words carry some meaning to the concerned person and he reacts according to his perception of the comunication conveyed to him by the particular gesture or spoken word. It is obvious that similar gesture or the same spoken word may be interpreted differently on different occasions, depending on the attitude or the interests of the person on each such occasion.

In terms of their intrinsic nature and effect on social relationships, the interactions are broadly classified into (a) associative or conjunctive and (b) dissociative or disjunctive. The former tends to strengthen social ties and the latter tends to weaken them. Co-operation, accommodation and assimilation belong to the first category while competition and conflict belong to the second category.

## Co-operation

"Co-operation is a form of social interaction wherein two or more persons work together to gain a common end". The need for co-operative effort in human life cannot be over-emphasised. It is both a psychological and social necessity. Modes of co-operation in social life may be divided into two principal types : (i) Direct co-operation and (ii) Indirect co-operation. Under direct co-operation may be included all those activities in which people do *like* things together. The essential character of such activities is that people do in company the things which they can not do separately or in isolation. When two or three people carry a load together which would be very irksome for one of them to carry alone, such co-operative activities may be characterised as direct co-operation. Under indirect co-operation may be included all those activities in which people do *unlike* tasks towards a common end. The principle of division of labour. that is imbedded in the nature of social life,exemplifies indirect co-operation. This mode of co-operation is revealed wherever people combine their differences for mutual satisfaction or for a common end[1].

It is interesting to note that the process of transition from preindustrial to industrial society is marked by replacement of direct by indirect co-operation. This is because advanced technology demands specialisation of skills and functions. Some sociologists, however, express the view that in terms of human needs this development is not all gain. Direct co-operation tends to bring people closer and in more intimate contact with one another. This is psychologically satisfying. In indirect co-operation, such intimacy and warmth of relationships are lacking. Bereft of the close ties of intimate community life, the people tend to develop highly individualised 'neurotic' characteristics[2].

## Accommodation

Accommodation is essentially a process of adjustment, a sort of working arrangement among persons or groups who are not favourably disposed towards one another. Just as adaptation is a biological process, so also is accommodation a social process. The question of accommodation arises only in conflict situations. Had there been no conflict, there would have been no necessary for adjustment, and hence no need for accommodation. The compromise reached by conflicting parties has been termed 'accommodation' by sociologists.

## Assimilation

Assimilation refers to a process whereby a group of people having lived among another group of people for a considerable period of time, adopts the way of life of the latter in such a way as to be completely indistinguishable from the latter. Assimilation is both psychological and social process. The following definitions would bring out the significant features of the process of assimilation. "Assimilation is the process whereby individuals or groups, once dissimilar, become similar, and identified in their interests and outlook". (Nimkoff). "Assimilation is a word used to designate a process of mutual adjustment through which culturally different groups gradually obliterate their differences to the point where they are no longer regarded as socially significant or observable".(Lundberg).

## Distinction between accommodation and assimilation

The chief points of distinction between accommodation and assimilation may be stated thus : When people belonging to two or more cultures, for some reason, happen to live together, there may be in the beginning a deliberate attempt at adjustment in order to avoid conflict or lesser degrees of unpleasantness. During this phase, the different cultural configurations or patterns can be identified. This process is accommodation. Gradually, however, adjustment leads, without anyone noticing it, to fusion and inter-penetration. In course of time, distinct cultural configurations get obliterated and one group is completely merged in another, sharing the same sentiments, outlook and goals. Such merger is effortless and unconscious. This process is termed assimilation.

## Competition

Kingsley Davis has defined competition thus : "Competition simply aims to out-do the competitor in achieving some mutually desired goal"[3]. The question of 'out-doing' arises only when the 'desired goal' is in scarce supply. Competition is an impersonal, unconscious, continuous struggle between individuals or groups for possession of goods which, because of their limited supply, all may not have. Competition is actually the most fundamental form of social struggle. It is also considered to be very healthy and a necessary social process. For this reason, competitive spirit is deliberately inculcated in order to produce a result which is considered to be socially desirable. For example, the practice of awarding prizes and scholarships to those who occupy the few top positions on the merit list is designed to foster creativity and promote striving for excellence.

## Conflict

Conflict is the anit-thesis of co-operation. When a competitive endeavour turns into a violent or a potentially violent strife among the concerned persons or groups to attain the same goal, the competitive situation gives way to a conflict situation. "Conflict expresses itself in numerous ways and in various degrees and over every range of human conduct. Its modes are always changing with changing social and cultural conditions. Some types disappear..... and new types emerge"[4].

MacIver has distinguished between two types of conflict : direct and indirect conflict. "When individuals or groups thwart or impede or restrain or injure or destroy one another in the effort to attain some goal, direct conflict occurs"[5]. On the other hand, "when individuals or groups do not actually impede the efforts of one another but nevertheless seek to attain their ends in ways which obstruct the attainment of the same ends by others, indirect conflict occurs"[6]. According to MacIver, bargaining and competition in all their varieties come within this class. Competition, as such, does not directly interfere with the efforts of another to attain such goals, but only indirctly with the other person's success.

It should, however, be noted that "not all struggle in which man is engaged is *social* conflict of either type. We are struggling to master difficulties, to overcome obstacles, to achieve ends in other ways than through conflict with our fellows. Man's 'battle' with the physical enviornment is a case in point, Social conflict, man against man or group against group, reveals itself wherever there is society"[7].

Thus, conflict is an ever-present process in human relations. Kingsley Davis has explained the persistent nature of the process of conflict in human society thus: ""Conflict is a part of human society because of the kind of thing human society is. There is no social mind, but only the minds of particular individuals; no social end, but only the ends of concrete persons. In so far as harmony is attained, it is through the agreement of individual minds, and this agreement thrives best when there is an external danger"[8]. Kingsley Davis observes further : "As a matter of fact, society itself engenders conflict situations and cannot avoid doing so. By allotting different statuses to different people, it lays the basis for envy and resentment. By giving authority to one person over another, it sets the stage for the abuse of authority and for retaliation by force. By instilling ends that are competitive, it makes it possible for competition to spill over into violence"[9].

## The combination of co-operation and conflict in social life

We have seen that co-operation and conflict are universal elements in human life. Over a vast range of activities they are present together. It is not conceivable in society that there is only co-operation and no trace of conflict or that there is only conflict and no trace of co-operation of some sort. Even in the most friendly relations and in the most intimate associations, there is some point where interests diverge or where attitudes differ. The persons concerned cannot, therefore, co-operate beyond that point and conflict becomes inevitable. Even the closest co-operation within the family does not prevent the occurrence of quarrels. In the physical world, there are forces of attraction and repulsion which operate simultaneously and determine the position of bodies in space. Likewise, in the social world, there is a combination of co-operation and conflict which is revealed in the relations of men and of groups. C.H.Cooley observes: "The more one thinks of it, the more he will see that conflict and co-operation are not separable things, but phases of one process which always involves something of both"[10]. Cooley observes further : "It seems that there must always be an element of conflict in our relations with others, as well as one of mutual aid; the whole plan of life calls for it; our very physiognomy reflects it, and love and strife sit side by side upon the brow of man"[11].

It should, however, be noted that when we speak of conflict, we have in mind that type of conflict which is limited in its scope and method by conditions which involve some sort of co-operation among the contending parties. We are here concerned with 'social conflict'. The qualifying adjective 'social' implies the assumption of social living which involves, in its turn, co-operative activity. We may think of one kind of conflict which does not involve any kind of co-operative activity. On the contrary, it implies unmitigated violence which is not tempered or limited by any kind of social norms or values. Besides this solitary case, all types of social conflict are subject to social rules. According to MacIver, "Co-operation crossed by conflict marks society wherever it is revealed"[12], be it a tribal society or a highly developed industrial society. Unless "Co-operation penetrated deeper than conflict, society could not endure"[13].

We have seen that co-operation, accommodation, assimilation, competition and conflict are the basic processes of social life. we have also to recognise the dynamic quality inherent in these processes which are imbedded in social organisation. It is, therefore, no wonder that society is always in a state of flux. Seen in this perspective, social process may be compared to a flow of river which is an ever-changing phenomenon. Pointing to this aspect, Heraclitus said : "It is impossible for a man to step into the same river twice. It is impossible for two reasons : the second time it is not the same river, and the second time it is not the same man. In the interval between the first and the second stepping, no matter how short, both the river and the man have changed". Contrasted with this is the statement of Parmenides: "Change is an illusion, everything remains the same, the only reality is being". Permanence and change, being and becoming —each of these has been emphasised by different philosophers as more important and more pervasive than the other. The task of sociology is not concluded when it exhibits the structure, the anatomy of society. The order that is society is, after all, a changing order, a moving equilibrium. Ever since Comte, sociologists have encountered two large questions, the question of social statics and the question of social dynamics, what society is and how it changes. While emphasising the dynamic nature of social order, arising out of basic social processes, MacIver observes : "Society exists only as a time-sequence. It is a becoming, not a being; a process, not a product. In other words, as soon as the process ceases, the product disappears.....If people no longer observe a custom, the custom no longer exists on the face of the earth . It has no body that remains after it dies. It exists only as a mode of activity, patterned in the minds of those who follow it...... A social structure cannot be placed in a museum to save it from the ravages of time".[14]

## NOTES

1. MacIver and Page, *Society*, page 63
2. *ibid*, page 63
3. Kingsley Davis, *Human Society*, page 162
4. MacIver and Page, Op.*cit*., page 64
5. *ibid*, page 64

6. *ibid*, page 64
7. *ibid*, page 64
8. Kingsley Davis, Op. *cit.*, page 162
9. *ibid*, page 161
10. C.H.Cooley, *Social Process*, page 39. Quoted by MacIver and Page in their book, *Society*, pages 64-65
11. C.H.Cooley, *Social Process*, page 56. Quoted by MacIver and Page, page 65
12. MacIver and Page, *Society*, page 65
13. *ibid*, page 64
14. *ibid*, page11

# CHAPTER TWENTY TWO

# SOCIAL CHANGE

## 1. TOWARD A DEFINITION OF SOCIAL CHANGE

The dynamic quality inherent in the basic social processes leads us to the investigation of the problems of social change. We have seen that the basic social processes are imbedded in social organisation. But social change itself is so complex and so significant in the life of individual and of society that we have to explore the 'why' and 'how' of social change in all its ramifications.

When we speak of social change, we do not mean what is generally known as social process. The kind of change that is associated with basic social processes does not come under the category of 'social change'. More appropriately, these changes may be characterised as social metabolism. In an animal body, chemical changes take place constantly. This is known as metabolism. Likewise, the changes which take place in society constantly may be called social metabolism. In course of time, however, these changes accumulate and become significant. We need, therefore, to introduce *time dimension* into our discussion on social change.

Against this background, we may explore the definition of social change. Morris Ginsberg has defined social change thus: "by social change I understand a change in social structure, e.g. the size of a society, the composition or balance of its parts or the type of its organisation. The term social change must also include changes in attitudes or beliefs, in so far as they sustain institutions and change with them".[1] In this definition, Ginsberg emphasises two types of changes, e.g., (i) changes in the structure of society and (ii) changes in the values and social norms which bind the people together and help to maintain social order. These two types of changes should not, however, be treated separately because a change in one induces changes in the other. For example, a change in the attitude of the people may bring about changes in the social structure. Towards the close of the nineteenth century, there was a tendency in the countries of Western Europe for families to grow smaller in size. "There is a general agreement that this has been brought about in the main by voluntary restriction of births"[2]. In this case, a change in the attitude of the people is mainly responsible for change in the social structure. On the other hand, a change in the social structure may bring about attitudinal change among the members of the society. Transformation of rural society into urban is not simply a change in the structure of society but it also introduces changes in the attitude and mentality of the people. Differences in objective situations that obtain in the country and the city impress themselves on the mentality of the countrymen and of the city people. Hence, these two types of changes should be treated as two facets of the same social phenomenon.

Some sociologists lump together these two types of changes under the category of cultural change'. Kingsley Davis, for example, defines social change thus: "By 'social change' is meant only such alterations as occur in social organisation that is, the structure and functions of society. Social change thus forms only a part of what is essentially a broader category called 'cultural change'. The latter embraces all changes occurring in any branch of culture, including art, science, technology, philosophy, etc. as well as changes in the forms and rules of social organisation".[3] Having defined social change, he goes further to say : "Cultural change is thus much broader than social change"[4]. It is doubtful if a clear-cut distinction between social change and cultural change can be maintained. Davis himself concedes that " no part of culture is totally unrelated to the social order...."[5]. If that be so, there is obviously no justification for treating social change and cultural change as two separate social phenomena. Davis observes : "Sociologically, therefore, we are interested in cultural change only to the extent that it arises from or has an effect on social organisation"[6]. Does not all types of cultural changes, in the ultimate analysis, affect social organisation ? Davis refers to phonetic change as an example of cultural change which does not, however, "noticeably affect the social system". He considers phonetic change as "purely a linguistic phenomenon, a cultural rather than a social change".[7] A phonetic change does not occur autonomously in a vacuum. It arises from changes in social organisation. For example, quick means of transportation in the 20th century have made it possible for people to come closer in meaningful contact. As a consequence, phonetic changes occur in almost all languages in recent years. Do not such phonetic changes make communication among different groups easier ? So, from whatever angle we may analyse the thesis of Kingsley Davis, it appears that a distinction between cultural change and social change cannot be maintained. Social change should, therefore, be interpreted to mean both a change in social structure and a change in any branch of culture.

We have already referred to the fact that social change ought to be distinguished from social process, and that it can be done by introducing the dimension of time in an analysis of social change. A specific *period* of time is to be taken into account in order to determine as to whether any social change has actually occurred during that period. That is, a base year has to be chosen and with reference to this base year one has to asses the type, nature and extent of change that may have taken place during the intervening period between the base year and the year of comparison. There will, therefore, be no scope for confusion between social process and social change.

We have to grapple with a few other methodological issues. In the first place, what will be the unit of change ? Should it be analysis of change in the society as a whole ? Or, should it be analysis of change in the parts of society ? Some sociologists have tried to delineate types of societies on the basis of certain characteristic features and "to interpret social change as the successive shifting from one type to another". For example, in his book, *Social and Cultural Dynamics,* Sorokin classified societies into two types : Ideational and Sensate. The ideational culture emphasises the spiritual and non-material; the sensate stresses materialism and agnostic concepts of value and reality. According to Sorokin, Taoist China, Buddhistic India and mediaeval Christian Europe represent ideational cultures, and the Western culture of today represents the sensate system. This kind of typology, and for the matter of that any other kind of typology, "seems rough and vague", because societies differ in myriad ways. Different scholars "looking at the same society are apt to characterise it differently, according to which particular traits they emphasise". In the circumstances, contradictory characterisations of the same society cannot be ruled out. In view of these difficulties, it is broadly agreed that "the analysis of change in the parts of society may throw light on changes in the whole". Secondly, in any discussion on social change, one should identify clearly the parts of society in which change has occurred and also the type and nature of change that has affected those parts. It is not enough to say that social change has occurred because such a vague statement does not indicate anything beyond what is inevitable. To be meaningful, one should be very specific about the areas in which changes have occurred and also about the nature of changes that have taken place. Thirdly, there are difficulties in measuring the rate of change and in indicating the *direction* of change. There are some changes which are easily amenable to measurement. For example, one can easily assess the *rate* and *direction* of changes in the field of literacy by comparing the enrolment figures in elementary schools prevailing in the base year and the year of comparison. There are, however, areas which defy all attempts at such measurement. If, for example, one tries to find out as to whether people of a particular society have become more pragmatic and rationalistic during the last fifty years, the attempt is bound to be a failure, because there is no way of assessing in quantitative terms changes that take place in the mind and attitude of people. Fourthly, there is another issue to be taken up — namely, whether change is cyclical or linear. "An extreme statement of the cyclical hypothesis would be that social phenomena of whatever sort (whether specific traits or whole civilisations) recur again and again, exactly as they were before. An equally extreme statement of the linear hypothesis would be that all aspects of society change continually in a certain direction, never faltering, never repeating themselves".[8] Neither of these two statements can be accepted as valid. We can only know and analyse the social change that is observable. Any claim that a pattern and sequence of change have always persisted and will always persist in future clearly goes beyond empirical knowledge. The linear hypothesis can also be subjected to the same kind of criticism. "The question of what is the ultimate nature of social change is therefore simply a philosophical puzzle that has no place in social science. When we confine ourselves to what is knowable, we find both trends and fluctuations. Indeed, whether a given change is cyclical or linear depends largely on the span of time under consideration. A decline in business appears as a trend if only a few years are taken, whereas in a larger time context it appears as merely one phase of the business cycle"[9]. Finally, we have to consider the central issue, e.g., the question of causation—what brings social change and what retards it. In the following sections we shall discuss the various explanations of social change offered by different sociologists from their respective perspectives.

## 2. MARXIAN EXPLANATION OF SOCIAL CHANGE

According to Marx, social change occurs as a sequel to class struggle. The seeds of class struggle which generate change are found in the economic infra-structure of society. At the dawn of human history, when man used to live, in the words of Marx, in a state of primitive communism, those contradictions or conflicts of interest among classes did not exist. Both the forces of production and the products of labour were communally owned. As such, class distinctions did not exist. With the emergence of the private ownership of the forces of production, however, the fundamental contradictions or class distinctions were created. In other words, the forces of production give rise to particular relations of production. Through its ownership of the forces of production, a minority is able to control, command and enjoy the fruits of the labour of the majority. This dominant group also determines the superstructure in keeping with the interest of the group. Law, literature, philosophy, etc. are all created accordingly. In other words, the impact or influence of the dominant group is discernible in all areas of social life.

The forces of production do not, however, remain unchanged. Whenever the forces of production undergo a change, there is a corresponding change in the relations of production also. A new class emerges as dominant and seeks to control, command and enjoy the fruits of the labour of the majority. A conflict naturally ensues between the emerging dominant group on the one hand and the group which had hitherto enjoyed all the privileges. The emerging dominant group endeavours to determine the superstructure in terms of its own interest. The society, as a whole, thus undergoes a change.

Marx seeks to explain all social changes in terms of the contradictions which are found in the economic infrastructure of society. "The history of all hitherto existing society", says Marx, "is the history of class struggle". In his view, class struggle will continue till class distinctions are completely obliterated and a classless society comes into being.

Marxian theory of social change has been criticised from various points of view.

To begin with, it has been argued that the forces of production do not uniquely determine the relations of production. Thus, the same mode of production may be applied in situations that differ radically from one another in terms of social and economic systems. The technological bases of the American and the Soviet economy are not as different as are the relations of production obtaining in these countries. Moreover, the influence of science and technology is very widespread and far-reaching, in so far as thinking, behaviour-pattern and value-systems are concerned. In this context, it is not unrealistic to assume that the people of two different societies may share similar thinking, behaviour-pattern and value-systems despite and fact that the economic systems in these countries are different. Another important factor should not also be overlooked. The terms "socialism' and 'communism' do not convey today the same meaning as they did a few decades ago. Both the systems are undergoing transformation in response to the demands of technology. The new economic experiment that is being tried in the Republic of China, Soviet Russia and socialist countries of Eastern Europe, dramatically illustrates this point. Marx recorded his observations at the dawn of industrial revolution. It was not, therefore, possible for him to anticipate the far-reaching and all-embraching developments in the sphere of science and technology.

Secondly, the Marxist thesis that those who are economically dominant become, by virtue of their economic power, dominant in society is not fully supported by historical facts. Thus, the organised religion, such as the Church in Europe, the Brahmin priesthood in India, etc., established its domination in almost all societies in the past through non-economic influence. It is true that economic power helps one to gain other forms of power. But it is equality true that other forms of power help one to gain economic power. The conclusion of the Marxist doctrine that economic power is primary and that other forms of power are consequential cannot, therefore, be accepted.

Thirdly, the Marxist thesis that politics and culture of a particular epoch are explained by the fact that they subserve the interest of the economically dominant class in that epoch is also open to several objections. All human actions cannot always be explained in terms of economic motivations. Religious pursuits, for example, cannot be explained in economic terms. The prayerful attitude of a true devotee has nothing to do with considerations of economic gain or loss. The motives which impel a poet to write a poem are, in most cases, non-economic. Again, the pursuits of eminent scientists are inspired by non-economic motives. It is also wrong to assume that those who exercise political power are always influenced by economic motives. If we try to analyse closely the motives of some of the well-known figures of history, we shall find that sometimes purely non-economic motives, such as the desire for distinction or personal glory or a desire for doing good to people, deeply influenced their thoughts and actions. King Ashoka, for example, decided to give up warfare as a means of winning other kingdoms from motives that were decidedly non-economic. Hitler was probably more influenced by the lure of personal glory than by the balanced calculations of probable material gain. A consideration of the motives that inspire art, culture, music, painting, and sometimes even politics of a country will show that human nature is too complex to be explained simply in terms of economic motives. It is, of course, true that sometimes art and culture are made to subserve the interests of the economically dominant class in society. But such cultural products cannot permeate the whole of society because they lack the qualities, such as spontaneity of expression, strength and vitality, which characterise genuine works of art.

Fourthly, all the aspects of social dynamics, barring economic forces, are ignored in Marxian analysis. For example, can disputes between two religions or racial groups be explained simply in economic terms ? Economic reasons may or may not generate such conflicts. Even when economic reasons are responsible, there may be many other non-economic reasons which are no less responsible for fanning the fire of dispute. If we view the genesis of such disputes from this angle, it is apparent that emphasis on economic reasons, to the exclusion of all others, makes the study biased and partial.

Fifthly, the assumption of Marxism that the establishment of classless society would bring to an end the exploitation of man by man is too simple to be accepted. As MacIver and Page have pointed out : "the power of man over man has deeper roots than economic advantage and that it can be at least as formidable and as tyrannical under a socialist economy as under any other kind of regime"[10].

In conclusion, we may say that it is undeniable that the economic factors exert a very important influence on politics and social philosophy of a given society. But to regard the economic system as the sole determinant of legal codes, political and cultural systems, is evidently wrong. There are other aspects of human life, besides economic, which are equally significant.

It should, however, be borne in mind that Marx was not a determinist. According to him, class struggle will not ensue automatically when the objective situation seems to be favourable for the same. Till the people become class-conscious and consciously work for the struggle, no revolution will take place, even if the objective situation may be ripe for the same. It may be said that Marx anticipated what Talcott Parsons developed much later as the voluntaristic theory of social action. The observations of Hoselitz, the noted economist, will be in order: ".... he (Marx) was perhaps the first scholar to anticipate what Talcott Parsons calls the voluntaristic theory of social action. Marx's conception that revolution, although in an ultimate sense inevitable, occurs only when people are motivated to carry it out (when they have become 'class conscious') implies that deterministic social forces exist, but that they become operative only through affecting voluntary action —an important insight made explicit and elaborated by Max Weber"[11].

## 3. THE WEBERIAN ANALYSIS : PROTESTANT ETHIC AND CAPITALISM

Max Weber did not agree with Marx that economic forces alone bring about social change. "Weber saw that there is a direct relation between the practical ethics of a community and the character of its economic system, but he refused to accept the position that the latter determines the former"[12] He developed his views in this regard with reference to his thesis on the origin and growth of capitalism in Western Europe in the eighteenth century.

Max Weber aimed at bringing out clearly the distinctive features of modern Western capitalism, because he looked upon it as a unique historical event. He recognised that Capitalism had appeared at various times in the history of the world and in various places. But he asked himself this question: What made the modern Western Capitalism unique ?

As seen by Weber, this kind of capitalism represented a complexity of institutions and institutionalised forms of behaviour. It was founded on the establishment of the Joint Stock Company, stock exchange machinery and introduction of a certain kind of currency and means for making currency exchanges. Certain political developments were also associated with the evolution of modern capitalism. But, above all, he recognised the necessity for what he called the Spirit (*Geist*) of Capitalism. According to him, what distinguishes modern Western Capitalism is not acquisitiveness nor a strong desire to engage in economic adventures. These are undoubtedly present. But these are ubiquitous and may be found in many kinds of economic activity which obtained in other ages and other places. "What Weber laid his finger on was the set of ethical *desiderata* associated with the modern form of capitalism, it was a moral outlook, a set of attitudes to life"[13]. This is what he called the Spirit of Capitalism. He emphasised the indispensability of this spirit for modern Western Capitalism. "In the last resort, the factor which produced capitalism is the rational permanent enterprise, rational accounting, rational technology, and rational law, but again not these alone. Necessary complementary factors were rational spirit, the rationalisation of the conduct of life in general, and a rationalistic economic ethic".

His views are expressed in the celebrated book on *The Protestant Ethic and the Spirit of Capitalism.* In this book he endeavoured to identify some, if not all, of the origins of capitalism. By the term *Spirit of Capitalism,* Weber meant a set of attitudes, a belief "in maximising wealth without much consideration of the means as long as the means are efficacious"[14].

How did this capitalist spirit originate ? Weber argued that it was not difficult to see how a well-developed economic and social system could generate such attitudes and thereby enabled them to persist. But how could they develop initially out of a situation in which the values of people and their habits were so vastly different? He was of opinion that there must have been some particular factor favourable to the emergence of the Spirit of Capitalism. He discovered it in the rise of the Protestant movement. "Protestantism propagated the traditional Christian virtues of selflessness, humility, and charity"[15]. There were certain elements in the Protestant ethic which were consistent with the Capitalist Spirit.

The Protestant ethic in which Max Weber was interested was essentially Calvinist. He summarised the Calvinist conception in five points : (i) There exists an absolute, transcendent God who created the world and rules it. But he is incomprehensible, inaccessible to the finite minds of men. (ii) This all-powerful and mysterious God has pre-destined each of us to salvation or damnation, so that we cannot by our works alter a divine decree which was made before we were born. (iii) God created the world for his own glory. (iv) Irrespective of whether he is to be saved or damned, man is obliged to work for the glory of God and to create the kingdom of God on earth. (v) Earthly things, human nature, and flesh belong to the order of sin and death, and salvation can come to man only through divine grace[16].

According to Max Weber, all these elements exist separately in other religious conceptions. But their combination in Calvinism is original and unique and entails important consequences.

First, a vision of this order excludes all mysticism, since the communication between the finite mind of the creature on the one hand and infinite mind of God on the other is, by definition, impossible.

By the same token, such a conception is anti-ritualist. The natural order, conceived by such a philosophy, can only be explored by science and not by rituals. Such a religious philosophy is thus contrary to all forms of idolatry and ritualism and is indirectly favourable to the development of scientific research.

Second, what can the Calvinist do in a world which is so interpreted? Apparently, he must do God's work. In different periods Calvinists have given different interpretations of what it means to work for the glory of god. (a) On the basis of the Calvinist vision, one can try, like Calvin himself, to build a republic true to the law of God, a kind of Kingdom of God. (b) Another interpretation is also conceivable. The Calvinist cannot know whether we will be saved or damned. This may eventually prove to be intolerable. He will, therefore, be prompted to seek psychological satisfaction by achieving worldly success, including economic success, as a sign of his salvation. The individual is thus driven towards work in order to overcome the anxiety which inevitably results from his uncertainty about his eternal destiny. Work comes to be interpreted as obedience to a commandment of God.

Third, the Protestant ethic calls upon the believer to consider flesh as guilty and to pursue asceticism as an ideal in life. This means that a believer is to work hard and use all rational means in order to maximise his profit for his comfort and for seeking the pleasures of life. This type of attitude and the conduct which follows from this attitude are necessary to the development of capitalism. Capitalism implies that work is to be rationally organised with a view to maximising productivity and profit and that the greater part of this profit is to be saved to permit capital accumulation for further economic advance. Thus, a spiritual affinity between the Protestant ethic and capitalist attitude can be clearly established.

Weber's arguments have been expressed in a very brief compass. Some warning is, however, necessary, so that his view-point is not misunderstood. As Talcott Parsons points out : "It is not Weber's thesis that Protestantism influenced capitalism through religious *approval* of acquisitive activities, expressed by preachers or otherwise, but because the religious interests of the believing individual directed his action in that direction"[17]. To this may be added another warning. Weber did not argue that Protestantism caused capitalism. In fact, he explicitly denied anything so crude. He also did not present an idealistic interpretation of history to counter Marx's materialistic one. Weber's last words in his essay on the subject are : "It is, of course, not my aim to substitute for a one-sided materialistic an equally one-sided spiritualistic causal interpretation of culture and of history"[18].

What Max Weber had in mind was to analyse the extent and nature of the impact of religion upon other aspects of human social structure, particularly upon the economy. His analysis clearly brings out that some religious beliefs, or at least some aspects of them, are seen to facilitate economic activity and that there are also religious beliefs which place obstacles in the way of economic development. In this connection, reference may be made to the difficulties in under-developed countries where traditional beliefs, often indirectly, but sometimes directly, prevent technological innovations from taking root, and thus hinder a new and more economically viable system to be established. In Weber's thought, there are two aspects of this problem. First, he was concerned with beliefs of an ethical and religious kind which had a bearing upon economic values. Second, he was interested in the way in which beliefs conditioned the growth of social groups and the ways in which these groups facilitated or hindered economic development. This kind of enquiry led him to embark on his studies in the sociology of religion.

## 4. ALTERNATIVE THEORIES OF THE RISE OF CAPITALISM

R. H. Tawney points out that Weber's approach to the problem of growth of capitalism seems to lay too exclusive an emphasis upon intellectual and ethical forces. But his analysis of those forces themselves requires to be supplemented. There are other forces which have a very close bearing on the rise and growth of capitalism. If all these forces are not taken into account, the discussion remains incomplete and is apt to produce an erroneous impression that capitalism owes its origin to one factor only, viz. the religious orientation of the people. Brentano's criticism to the effect that the political thought of the Renaissance was as powerful in breaking conventional restraints as the teaching of Calvin merits serious consideration.

Tawney also refers to the favourable environment which contributed to the rise of capitalism. "The rise of new forms of economic enterprise was the result of changes in the character of the economic environment. It was due to the influx of the precious metals from America in the sixteenth century, to the capital accumulated in extra-European commerce, to the reaction of expanding markets on industrial organisation, to the growth of population, to technological improvements made possible by the progress of natural science."He further remarks: " Why insist that causation can work in only one direction ? Is it not a little artificial to suggest that capitalist enterprise had to wait, as Weber appears to imply, till religious changes had produced a capitalist spirit ? Would it not be equally plausible, and equally one-sided, to argue that the religious changes were themselves merely the result of economic movements ? Weber pursued a single line of enquiry with masterly ingenuity. His conclusions are illuminating; but they are susceptible, it may perhaps be held, of more than one interpretation. There was action and reaction, and, while puritanism helped to mould the social order, it was, in its turn, moulded by it. ( R. H. Tawney, Foreword in Max Weber's *The Protestant Ethic and the Spirit of Capitalism, pp 8-10)*

Loomis and Loomis point out that the teachings of Calvinism did not inspire the businessmen to follow the profit motive and other ascetic ethics. On the contrary, the businessmen adopted the teachings because it suited their purpose. By way of explanation, they observe as follows : "The earlier teachings... had put severe restrictions on the businessman. Calvin and the church in general preached unceasingly against unjust money lenders and avarice. The Council of Geneva, a body made up of businessmen, heard the ministers on thrift and simplicity....... They were glad to invoke the sanction of religion on traits which their secular activity found valuable—honesty, industry, sobriety, as well as the dynamic interpretation of predestination." (C.P. Loomis and Z.K. Loomis (eds), *Socio-Economic Change and the Religious Factor in India — An Indian Symposium of Views on Max Weber* , Affiliated East-West Press, New Delhi, 1969. pp 16-18). That the businessmen did not consider the teachings of Calvin in their entirety but accepted only those of his teachings which suited their purpose is corroborated by the fact that Calvin also taught his followers to take to meditation—a far cry from vigorous worldly activity. Calvin writes :"With whatever kind of tribulation we may be afflicted, we should always keep this end in view, to habituate ourselves to a contempt of the present life that we may thereby be excited to meditation on that which is to come."

## 5. THE VEBLENIAN ANALYSIS

Veblen is regarded as a technological determinist, because, according to him, men's habits and mental discipline are moulded by the kind of work by which men live and particularly by the kind of technique which that work involves. These are the influences "which shape men's thoughts, their relations with one another, their culture and institutions of control". Once they are habituated to a particular method of work, their minds are moulded accordingly. The following two statements of Veblen bring out his point of view. One such statements is : "The way of habit is the way of thought". The second one: As he (man) acts, so he feels and thinks"[19].

Veblen tried to explain social change from this point of view. He observes: "The evolution of society is substantially a process of mental adaptation on the part of individuals under the stress of circumstances which will no longer tolerate habits of thought formed under and conforming to a different set of circumstances in the past"[20].

If, however, a particular section of the population is, for some reason,outside the influence of these circumstances, that section would hinder the process of social change. In the words of Veblen : " If any portion or class of society is sheltered from the action of the environment in any essential respect ...... it will ...... tend to retard the process of social transformation". He considered the wealthy leisure class as belonging to this category. "The wealthy leisure class in such a sheltered position with respect to the economic forces that make for change and readjustment"[21]. He gave an illustration in support of his thesis.

Under a feudal order, production was largely dependent on man-power. The large number of workers had, therefore, to do hard manual work under the direction of a very small number of people. In the words of Veblen: "it represents a system of trained manpower organised on a plan of subordination of man to man". He observes further : "it prescribed diligent unremitting toil and obedience to the superiors ...." It is not surprising, therefore, that the state of "subordination of man to man" in the sphere of production was reflected in the social life in terms of a stratified society.

However, the replacement of man-power by mechanical power initiated far-reaching social changes. Under a feudal order, it was necessary, in the interest of production , to keep the large number of workers under subordination and subject them to "diligent unremitting toil". The introduction of mechanical power obviated the necessity of subordinating man to man. The thinking pattern of the feudal order also yielded place to new lines of thinking called for by the new economic order based on mechanical power. According to Veblen, only those who were associated directly with the processes of production experienced this transformation, but not those, such as the wealthy leisure class, who were not directly related to the processes of production. Hence, there developed within society two different cultures instead of one. But the power of regulating social order in terms of prescribed social norms rests in the hands of the wealthy leisure class. The prescribed social norms, for obvious reasons, are designed to promote their sectional interests rather than the interests of production or the interests of the large number of workers connected with the processes of production. The prescribed norms thus represent " at best a wearisome tribulation". They represent feudal values and ideals and are entirely inconsistent with the demands of economic order based on mechanical power.

According to Veblen, the establishment of "industrial-democratic regime" would change the scenario altogether. Under it, "the influence of technique is more pervasive, and all behaviour is more closely related to the same work-day generalisations. Social attitudes and speculative thought conform more directly to the lessons and impressions derived from the industrial arts. All alike tend to think in terms of mechanism, of geometrical relations, of standardised patterns, of inexorable law".[22]

For Veblen it is the habit of work of everyday life, be it pastoral, agricultural, industrial or any other form, which is of decisive importance. These habits are embodied in institutions. These institutions intervene "between the material exigencies of life and the speculative scheme of things". Veblen points out that "the speculative scheme" may not always correspond to "the material exigencies", because in times of transition men work in new ways while they still think in terms of the old. In course of time, however, a correspondence between the two is established. Veblen, therefore, concludes that "social systems reflect technological advance". He further points out that there would be continuous improvement in the industrial arts toward greater efficiency and that, as a consequence, the evolutionary process would also continue.

In this connection, the views of Veblen may be contrasted with those of Marx. "He (Marx) projects a goal or consummation of social evolution which ... will bring about a great liberation of the human spirit and a new social harmony. It is a form of revelation. Veblen ..... offers no revelation, no goal".[23]

## 6. SOCIAL CHANGE: A FUNCTIONALIST PERSPECTIVE

All living beings have three basic biological needs which must be met if they are to stay alive as individuals and as species. These are the need for food, reproduction and protection. Most mammals are equipped by heredity with special talents, skills, and instincts which enable them to meet their basic needs, and to adapt themselves to their environment. All animals except man which lacked the requisite capacity perished from this earth long also. Man is neither particularly strong physically, nor are his senses particularly acute. He cannot reproduce himself rapidly, for it takes a long time to create a human child and a longer time to bring it up to the point where it can take care of itself independently. But man has survived the challenge of nature because of the fact that he has "the capacity to invent and learn language, which in turn enables him to build a culture and to organise society". Man has not to adapt himself to his environment. On the contrary, he changes his environment to suit himself. It has been very aptly said that "he cannot grow fur to keep himself warm, but he can and does weave cloth to make clothing".

It follows, therefore, that the primary function of culture and of social organisation is the meeting of man's basic needs. Man has also needs other than basic ones. These needs are derived from the way he meets his basic needs. So these needs are called *derived needs* of man. For example, the needs for school, writing materials, etc. are derived from the use of language which is utilised by man for the purpose of meeting his basic needs. Hence, another function of culture and of social organisation is the meeting of derived human needs.

The foregoing discussion will make clear that social change is likely to occur under three situations :

1. *Social institutions change when human needs change*. The basic biological needs of man are by their very nature unchanging. As long as human beings are animals, they will need food and protection, and they will also need to procreate. The derived needs of men do, however, change. For instance, there are changes in the nature and form of good that a particular group of men may prefer at a particular time. The techniques of protecting oneself from nature and from enemies also change from time to time. Again, the individuals who make up society are constantly changing through birth, growth, death, and migration. All these naturally produce new problems and new needs. Another reason

for change in our needs lies in the fact that institutional changes that have already taken place may create new derived needs. For example, introduction of automobile in place of horse-drawn carriage has created the need in our society for broader streets, traffic regulations, and traffic police.

So our needs may change for a number of reasons, and their change contributes to the necessity of change in our social institutions.

2. *Social institutions change when they fail to meet existing human needs.* The failure of social institutions to meet needs even when the specific need in question has not changed is due primarily to two reasons. In the first place, "some human needs are at times more compelling than others and sometimes we sacrifice the meeting of one group of needs in order to meet another". Thus, when a country is involved in a war, the needs for national defence become so pressing that we consciously restrict the satisfaction of many of our individual needs. The mechanism of price .control and rationing, which generally replaces the normal economic system of distribution in times of war, becomes necessary because of the fact that the needs of the majority of the people for food and other necessaries cannot be met by the system of free competition.

Another reason why social institutions sometimes fail to meet some of the existing needs lies in the fact that social institutions have manifest and latent functions. Manifest functions are those objective consequences for society which are intended and recognised by the persons who are involved. Latent functions are those consequences which are neither intended nor recognised. The manifest functions(purpose) and latent functions (result) do not always completely coincide. For example, the express purpose of the competitive economic system is to promote efficiency both in the field of production and distribution. But in actual working, the system gives rise to problems of unequal distribution of wealth and income, of unemployment and of social injustice. In other words, the competitive economic system fails to meet our psychological need for a feeling of security. Hence, there arises the need for the Government to regulate the competitive economic system in order to meet the demand for social security.

3. *Social institutions change when new materials suggest better ways of meeting needs.* This may be illustrated by the fact that introduction of automobile in place of slow-going methods of transportation has made people increasingly dependent upon large centres of trade and commerce and much less dependent upon services which are available in small communities. Likewise, introduction of technology and industrial methods of production have changed the economic activities of families considerably.

Man's culture and social organisation are, therefore, in a constant state of flux as both major and minor adjustments are made in order to meet the various needs as they arise and decline in importance. Hence we may look upon the institutional structure of society " as a dynamic imperfect equilibrium subject to constant change". Social change is a process which, once begun, tends to continue for a very long time inasmuch as change in one segment of our social structure gives rise to dysfunctions in another, creating the need for further change and so on.

It will, however, be wrong to assume that changes in institutional structure occur easily in response to some stimuli. All social institutions are, by their very nature, resistant to change. Folkways and mores are grounded in the habits of human beings, and they find it difficult to change their habits. There is another reason way people resist change All of us plan our lives on the assumption that the social organisation and the social institutions will remain essentially stable. We, therefore, resist change out of sheer self-interest when any change is suggested to us. We fear that changes in social structure will "leave us stranded among our old, useless plans and preparations". We may conclude then that social change is more likely to begin in those areas of our institutional structure which we hold least sacred, and that 'the process of change is likely to be least rapid and most convulsive in those areas which we hold most sacred".

## 7. FACTORS OF SOCIAL CHANGE

Social change cannot be explained in terms of a particular theory. A theory is no more than looking at a phenomenon from a particular perspective. That particular perspective may single out those conditions which are, so to say, decisive. Which conditions are taken as decisive depends to a large extent on the perspective of the inquiry. Obviously, many conditions are not specified. All theories of social change are, therefore, partial. In order to appreciate the complex nature of the phenomena, it is worth considering various factors which generally bring about social change. In one particular case, a particular factor may prove to be decisive in the sense that social change can be adequately explained in terms of that factor. In another case, social change may have to be explained in terms of other factor or factors. In short, there is not a single master key with which we can unlock all the doors leading to an unravelling of predisposing causes of social change.

With these general considerations in mind, we may bring out, following Morris Ginsberg, the sort of factors to which causal agency has been attributed by competent authorities.[24]

(i) There are cases in which social changes may be attributed "mainly to desires and decisions of individuals". As an illustrative case, Ginsberg refers "to the rise of the small family system in Western countries in the latter part of the nineteenth century". The decline in birth rate is to be accounted for, in the main, by voluntary restriction of births. The people practised birth control in increasing numbers and the end-result was a rise in the number of small families.

A question may be raised : Why did people in increasing numbers practise birth control during the last part of the nineteenth century, and not earlier ? The answer is found in a number of interlocking changes in the social and economic structure during this period. Among these mention may be made of introduction of compulsory education which virtually removed children from the labour market. This meant an additional burden upon parents of rearing large families. The opportunities for employment of women outside the home were considerably widened, and , as a result, they did not want to be encumbered by a large number of children. The women's liberation movement which gained strength and popularity during this period further strengthened the desire of women to have small families. To all these must be added changes of moral and religious outlook as well as the availability of effective contraceptive devices.

(ii) Circumstances favourable to a change constitute an important *sine qua non* for change to take place. Some individuals and groups may be motivated to bring about a particular change and even appropriate steps toward that end may be taken. But the entire effort might prove futile because circumstances do not favour the change. Pandit Iswar Chandra Vidyasagar initiated a movement for the re-marriage of Hindu widows. At the instance of Vidyasagar and a few others, the Hindu Widow's Re-marriage Act was passed in 1856. But the passing of the Act or the ceaseless efforts of social reformers like Vidyasagar could not create much impact on the Hindu community for over a century simply because the people were not prepared to accept the change. Ginsberg emphasises this aspect thus : "The causes are the motivated acts, but the motives are shaped by the change in the conditions"[25].

(iii) In a society there may occur structural changes, i.e., changes in the parts of a structure due to changes in other parts or to a change in the balance of forces. As a consequence, tensions may be set up by a lack of equilibrium between its parts. These strains set up disturbances, latent or overt, which sooner or later find expression in movements for change. Ginsberg gives the following illustration. "Thus the domain economy was made impossible in Europe in the eleventh and twelfth centuries by the rise of the towns. The urban population could not feed itself and had therefore to obtain the means of subsistence by purchase from the rural areas. This meant that the domains no longer restricted their production to meet their own needs. As production became remunerative, the idea of working for profit began to exercise people's minds. On the other hand, the landowners, restricted to customary revenues, found it difficult to satisfy their growing needs. In this way the moral and economic foundations of the domainal system were shaken by the growth of cities and the change in the relations between town and country".[26] We may take another familiar example from India. The process of urbanisation has set up pressures which tend to weaken the foundations of the traditional joint family pattern.

According to Ginsberg, "The major sources of social change are conditions generating these strains or 'contradictions', and the efforts made to overcome them. The Marxists have concentrated on the contradictions that arise between the forces of production and the relations of production. But it seems clear that the sources of strain are many and varied,and indeed hardly reducible to a system"[27].

(iv) Changes of social structure can be brought about by external influences due to contact with other societies, peaceful or warlike. According to Toynbee, civilisation grow and develop in either of the three ways.[28] (a) *Original creation.* Creation and innovation are realities. If they were not realities, no changes could ever have occurred. And if creation and innovation are realities, every act of creation and innovation must have been achieved by some agent at some point of space-time. (b) *Mimesis.*This means the reception and adoption of elements of culture that have been created elsewhere and have reached the recipients by a process of diffusion. If the only possible form of human action were original creation, a human being's whole energies would have to be taken up, from birth to death, in willing each pulsation of his heart and each inflation of his lungs. Far from this being characteristic of human nature, one of its distinctively human features is its capacity for learning and for translating what it learns into habits organised in those patterns of relations between people that we call 'institutions'. Besides the psycho-physical heritage that Man, like all other living creatures, transmits to his off-spring automatically and involuntarily, he transmits a cultural heritage by the social process of teaching and learning and it is this second capacity that makes and keeps Man human. (c) *Stimulus Diffusion.* A.L. Kroeber has shown that an anti-thesis between two terms—originality and mimesis —does not cover all the phenomena. There is at least one more alternative which Kroeber calls 'stimulus diffusion'. "Stimulus diffusion might be defined as new pattern growth initiated by precedent in a foreign culture... A goal or objective was set by something previously existing in another culture; the originality was limited to achieving the mechanisms by which its goal could be reached"[29]. Kroeber demonstrates his case by bringing forward illustrations from the most diverse fields of human activity. Since then, this new concept has been employed to account for the genesis of the Egyptiac Civilization as a creative response to a stimulus received from the Sumeric Civilization. The observations of Frankfort are quite pertinent. "We observe the Egypt, in a period of intensified creativity became acquainted with the achievements of Mesopotamia; that it was stimulated; and that it adapted to its own rapid development such elements as seemed compatible with its efforts. It mostly, transformed what it borrowed and after a time rejected even these modified derivations".[30] It will be seen that the role of Sumeric influence in the genesis of the Egyptiac Civilization, as described by Frankfort in the above passage, is a classic illustration of Kroeber's concept of 'stimulus diffusion'.

(v) The contribution of outstanding individuals or groups of individuals to social change cannot be ignored.Their importance has been exaggerated as frequently as it has been underestimated. Spencer argued that the great man had first to be made before he could remake society. There are others who argue that, however made, he is rarely the arbiter of events. Bismarck, who exercised an enormous influence on the political events of the nineteenth century, said : "The statesman can do nothing for himself. He can only lie in wait and listen until amid the march of events he can hear the footsteps of God. Then he leaps forward and grasps the hem of His garment. That is all he can do".

So little is known as yet of the genetic basis of genius or exceptional ability. In sociology we are not concerned with that question or the question as to whether a great man is a product of his age. Any answer to these questions will raise other questions. But the fact remains that in all epoches men of exceptional ability leave a deep impress of their personality on the society. In contemporary India, the influence of Gandhiji, Nehruji or Netaji cannot be overlooked by any means. Can anyone ignore the contribution of Lenin to the success of Russian revolution ? Can anyone underestimate the contribution of Henry Ford to the expansion of automobile industry ? It seems "foolish to deny the great importance of men of genius whether as innovators or as the vehicles of large and massive forces"[31].

(vi) Social changes are often due to a confluence or collocation of elements derived from different sources but converging at a given point. Ginsberg refers to the occurrence and eventual success of the Russian Revolution as an example of this factor. In his view, there was a very complicated combination of circumstances which prepared the ground for Russian Revolution. "There were first the prolongation of the war of 1914 and the inability of the Czarist regime to sustain a large-scale war. There were the land-hunger of the peasantry and the presence together of a depressed peasantry with a relatively advanced proletariat. There was the fact that in Russia capitalist industry had developed as a result of foreign pressure and under the patronage of the state, with the result that a proletariat had been created without an independent class of bourgeois entrepreneurs. There was the further fact that the Russian intelligentsia did not possess social roots in the commercial bourgeoisie and was not committed to any deep -seated bourgeois allegiance. To all this must be added the existence of a small and determined group of men, able to seize power and, above all, the 'accident' of the great personality of Lenin"[32].

(vii) Sometimes fortuitous or accidental causes are responsible for bringing about social change of considerable significance. Ginsberg illustrates this point by referring to Black Death, a name given to the epidemic of plague in Europe in the 14th century, which changed the history of the entire Jewish people. Among the various consequences of this epidemic was the letting loose of a wave of superstitious terror. "This expressed itself in many German towns......in barbarous attacks on Jews in the belief that the plague was a malignant device for the confusion of Catholics. The savage attack led to an exodus to Poland where.... the Jews found protection. In this way a series of events originating in the Far East was an important factor in the formation of an East European Jewry, which in the centuries to come was to develop distinctive characteristics of its own and to play an important role in the history of the entire Jewish people"[33]. The partition of India is another accidental factor (the decision was so sudden that the people, including the leaders, were not prepared for the same) which has changed the entire course of history of the sub-continent. More far-reaching repercussions are likely to follow in the years to come.

Ginsberg has analysed the phenomenon of social change in a historical background indicating how in myriad ways the society may undergo changes. Some of these changes may be of little significance and some may be of far-reaching importance. The analysis is particularly important for two reasons. In the first place, it has been made abundantly clear that social change cannot be explained in terms of one or two factors only and that various factors actually combine and become the 'cause' of the change. Ginsberg observes: "A cause is an assemblage of factors which, in interaction with each other, undergo a change of character in combination in the manner of a chemical substance and are continued into the effect.. In practical life and in the scientific studies arising out of practical needs we are always in search of such continuities. We assume that one difference implies another and that changes do not occur in isolation, but are linked without gaps in time or space with other changes"34. Thus, causal relationship has much the same significance in the social sciences as in the natural sciences. Secondly, there are important differences between social and physical causation. Social facts are more variable and less likely to be repeated in identical fashion than physical events. "Because of this, and the ensuing difficulty of isolating cause-factors, causal relationships in the social sciences cannot be stated in the form of uniform sequences or connexions between specific events, but in the form of changes of pattern within a series of interlinked events"[35]. There is another important difference between social and physical causation. Social causation involves mental factors which obviously mark off social causation from physical causation. Unlike physical objects, individuals 'respond' rather than react to their environment, and they do so selectively.

While analysing social change, we are to take a macro-view, keeping in mind the similarity and differences between the social universe and the physical universe. Micro view of a particular social event in the manner of analysing a physical event cannot adequately bring out the causes responsible for the social event. The analysis of Ginsberg is particularly important, in so far as it draws attention to this aspect.

In the aforesaid analysis of Ginsberg, two important factors are not considered at all. These are demographic factors and technological factors both of which are of crucial significance in terms of their bearing on social change in the contemporary world.

## 8. DEMOGRAPHY AND SOCIAL CHANGE

The following four areas fall within the domain of the study of demography : (i) To ascertain the total population within a prescribed geographical area. (ii) To ascertain as to whether the population in particular period or year has increased or declined as compared to a base period or year. (iii) To analyse the probable reasons for the increase or decline of population. (iv) To indicate, in the context of the aforesaid data, the future trend of population.

### Social demography

A change in population of any area depends on three factors or variables : (a) birth, (b) death, (c) migration. This may be put in the form of an equation:

$P_2 = P_1 \pm$ (Net increase/decrease) $\pm$ Net migration.

(In this equation, $P_1$ = Population of the base year. $P_2$ = Population of the year of comparison. Net increase/decrease = Birth rate - Death rate. Net migration = Immigration Emigration).

Birth rate is a function of fertility, i.e., the *actual* reproduction of women. Demographers distinguish fertility from fecundity. The latter means the biological capacity to conceive and bear children. Usually, it covers women of the age-group 14-50 years.

Kingsley Davis observed that "fertility, mortality and migration are all to a great extent socially determined and socially determining"[36]. We may, therefore, take note of the social factors which bear on fertility, mortality and migration. We may thereafter take up the impact of demographic changes on society.

## Social factors determining fertility

Human fertility involves the physiological capacity of women and men to reproduce, subject to individual choice and social control. Both individual choice and social control are, however, considerably affected by cultural factors, either negatively or positively. We may note briefly some of these factors.

(i) A society in which a couple is not supposed to marry until the husband is able to support a wife and family is likely to experience a lower birth rate and vice versa.

(ii) Birth rate depends on whether law of the land lays down the minimum age at which men and women are permitted to marry. Birth rate goes down if the prescribed minimum age is comparatively high.

(iii) Birth rate depends on whether the community adopts family planning as a way of life. If the community upholds values conducive to family planning, the birth rate is likely to be low and vice versa.

(iv) Birth rate depends on whether abortion or temporary termination of pregnancy is or is not legally permissible.

(v) Fertility depends on whether society permits widow re-marriage. Kingsley Davis has shown that this is one of the main cultural factors responsible for lesser fertility among Hindus than among Muslims in India.[37]

(vi) A number of recent investigations have confirmed the fertility- reducing effect of breast feeding. Prolonged breastfeeding reduces the chances of pregnancy by delaying the return of menstruation as well as the return of ovulation in women after childbirth. It is interesting to note that demographers estimate that, at least, upto 1974, the aggregate contraceptive protection provided by breastfeeding in developing countries has probably been greater than that achieved through family planning programmes. Hence a decline in the practice of breastfeeding can increase fertility, if it is not controlled by other means.[38]

(vii) Education affects fertility. This may be discussed from different points of view. Several studies of differential fertility at both individual and aggregate levels have shown that education, particularly female education, is more influential than any other factor in decreasing fertility. Among the major states in India, Kerala has currently the lowest birth rate and the highest literacy rate; Uttar Pradesh, which has the highest birth rate, ranks lowest in literacy rate — with the exception of Bihar.[39] The relationship between educational level and fertility may be discussed in terms of use of contraceptive. According to an all-India sample survey conducted in 1970 by Operations Research Group, only 13 per cent of reproductive age couples with illiterate wives ever used any contraceptive method and the corresponding percentages were 29, 43 and 72 among couples with primary—, secondary—, and college-educated wives respectively.[40]

Apart from acceptance of family planning, delayed age at marriage is another way by which education can be instrumental in fertility decline. Several surveys have confirmed that educated girls tend to be married at a later average age, some of them late enough to have fewer children. For example, the 1961-62 National Sample Survey data show that among couples living in urban areas, the average age of illiterate wives was 16 years while that of college graduates was 22 years.[41]

(viii) The theories linking economic development and fertility recognise that one main reason for high fertility in less developed countries is parents' expectations of support from their surviving children, especially sons, in their old age. The decline in such expectations is presumed to be one of the ways in which economic development reduces fertility.[42]

(ix) The fertility level of a society may be related to its mortality level. A decline in mortality eventually produces a decline in fertility. So far as decline in fertility is concerned, reduction of infant and child mortality seems to be more pertinent than other components of mortality. Many parents in developing countries depend heavily on children for old age security and as insurance against various kinds of potential risks. Since the degree of uncertainty regarding survival of children is high in many developing countries, "the most plausible response of parents is toward over-compensation for the loss of children. An actual reduction in infant and child mortality, accompanied by a perception of reduction in the degree of uncertainty, is expected to reduce fertility ......".[43]

The social and cultural factors affecting fertility, which are listed above, are only illustrative and not exhaustive. what is the implication of such a study ? Fertility behaviour of couples in every society is undoubtedly a matter of individual choice. But individual choice is influenced considerably by values and social institutions. In recent years, state intervention in fertility regulation in the form of state-sponsored family planning programmes appears to be a very powerful agency whose influence will be felt in the years to come.

**Social determinants of mortality**

Like fertility, mortality is also determined by social factors some of which are noted below.

(i) A high income at aggregate and individual levels is expected to cause decline in mortality because it facilitates increased consumption of items favourable to health, such as food and nutrition, medical and public health services, education, housing and leisure.

(ii) Provision of public health services is another important factor affecting mortality. "In developed countries the validation of the germ theory of disease in the late 19th century and its impact on public health practices and technology had a significant impact on subsequent mortality decline"[44]. Demeny, the demographer, is of the view that the application of modern techniques of public health control in less developed countries, independent of income level and distribution, is the main reason for the uniform trend in post-war mortality decline.[45] A comparative study of mortality in Kerala and West Bengal shows that greater accessibility of health services in the rural areas of Kerala is one of the main reasons for lower mortality in that state.[46]

(iii) Education has an important role in affecting mortality. The link between education and mortality may be stated thus. The education of mother is of crucial significance. "One possible mechanism is greater awareness among literate women about the need to use modern health facilities and, consequently, higher utilisation of the facilities by them than by illiterate women. Other mechanisms through which education affects mortality are perhaps by generating modern attitudes regarding health, disease, nutrition, personal hygiene and sanitation"[47].

As in the case of fertility, so also in the case of mortality the factors effecting it, as listed above, are only illustrative and, by no means, exhaustive.

## Social determinants of migration

Migration is a function of two kinds of factors : (i) Push factor which pushes people out of the country, resulting in what is generally known as emigration. (ii) Pul factor which attracts people into the country, resulting in what is called immigration.

Some of the factors which exercise either of these two kinds of influences are summarised as follows : (i) The prospect of better jobs or working conditions outside the country may push people out of the country while similar prospect in the home country may attract people from outside. (ii) Climate may be a factor influencing decisions of people either to go out or to come in. (iii) Religious or political persecution/freedom in a country may be a factor which influences the decisions of people either to go out of the country or to attract people of another country to come in. (iv) Law may influence migration directly. The host country may have immigration laws which may either encourage immigration or may serve as a deterrent.

## Impact of demographic changes on society

Impact of demographic changes on society may be examined from three points view : (i) Size of population; (ii) age composition of population; (iii) economic development.

### *Size of population*

Demographic changes may lead to either increase or decrease in the size of population. Apart from its impact on the economic life of society, the size of population affects social attitudes and social relationships. The observations of MacIver and Page on this aspect are very revealing. "For example, countries with growing populations and relatively limited resources have, under appropriate conditions, an incentive to imperialism and to militarism, while these attitudes in turn encourage a further increase of population. Thus, in Italy, which is both populous and relatively poor in resources, Mussolini constantly proclaimed that empires cannot be won or defended except by "fecund peoples". On the other hand, increase of population threatens the standard of living and thus inspires a change of attitude. At a certain stage in the unprecedented growth of population in the nineteenth century the practice of birth control took a new development. This practice in turn had many repercussions on family relationships and even on attitudes toward marriage."[48]

*Age composition and society*

With a change in population, there is a change in the age-composition of the population. The proportion of elderly people may either go up or go down in relation to total population, or the proportion of young people may either go up or go down in relation to total population. Such changes have far-reaching social consequences.

In the first place, a very important economic consequence of differences in age structure is the effect of age structure on the *dependency ratio*. The dependency ratio is defined as "the ratio of persons in dependent ages to persons in economically productive age-groups."[49] The lower dependency ratio makes it easier for persons in the economically productive ages to support those in the dependent age-group. The dependent ages refer to ages 'under 15 years' and '65 years and over'. The remaining age groups are economically productive.

The second important economic consequence of differences in age structure is in respect to the average age of the labour. In the rapidly sloping age distribution caused by high fertility, the average age of persons within the broad age group 15 to 64 years will be relatively low. In the gently sloping age structure caused by low fertility, the average age will be relatively high. The average age of the labour force may produce several social consequences. A younger labour force has this advantage that they are likely to be more flexible and more receptive to new ideas and they are thus likely to learn new skills more readily. An older labour force, on the other hand, are likely to be more responsible and experienced and, at the same time, less receptive to new ideas and less adaptable to new innovations.

The third economic consequences of differences in age structure are in terms of pattern of consumption. Societies having large proportions of children are required to spend relatively larger amounts of money on food and education. On the other hand, societies with larger proportions of elderly people have to spend relatively more on medical care. There will be many other changes in patterns of consumption consequent upon changes in age composition of a population.

Fourthly, variation in age structure will also have demographic consequences. Thus, a young population will tend to have a much lower crude death-rate (the number of deaths per thousand population per annum) than an old population. This is obviously due to the fact that mortality rate is comparatively higher among aged people.

*Population growth and economic development*

We may approach this theme from two points of view :

First, theoretically speaking, population growth may have two contradictory effects on costs of production. There is one possibility that growth of population may expand the market for goods and thus may prepare the ground for increasing the scale of production. If this happens, the economies of scale would accrue. Thus, an increase in population may lead to a lowering of production costs. There is also a second possibility. The growth of population may strain the existing resources so much that "the law of deminishing marginal returns" may begin to operate resulting in lower rate of productivity for every additional application of in-put. If what is visualised as the first possibility actually happens, living standards are bound to improve. If, on the other hand, the second possibility becomes a reality, living conditions are bound to decline.

Second, changes in the rate of growth of population produce differences in the dependency ratio. This will affect the average living conditions of most of the families. In their book, *Population Growth and Economic Development in Low-Income Countries*, Ansley Coale and Edgar M. Hoover prepared projections in order to indicate how changes in fertility and mortality might affect the ratio of non-earning dependents to earners in India. According to their projection, which was based on the assumption of declining mortality and unchanged fertility, the ratio of dependents to wage-earners would rise during the period from 1956 to 1986. On the other hand, according to the projection based on the assumption of the same declining mortality but also a 50 per cent decline in fertility by 1981, the ratio of dependents to wage-earners would have declined by 1986. It is clear from these projections that the level of living in the average Indian family would be greatly improved by a reduction in fertility. On the other hand, continued decline in mortality might threaten existing levels of living merely by increasing the number of persons dependent on each wage-earner.

*Theory of the demographic transition*

The theory of the demographic transition was popularised just after the end of World War II This theory has been advanced as a comprehensive explanation of the effects of economic development both on mortality and fertility decline. The theory is as follows :

It is held that there are four stages of demographic transition. In the initial stage prior to economic development both birth and death rates are high. Because the birth rate is only approximately equal to the death rate, the natural increase in population is just about nil. During the second stage when there is simultaneous occurrence of economic development, industrialisation and urbanisation, birth rate is high and death rate declines. The rise in birth rate may be attributed to the comparative affluence of the people and their lack of motivation in the initial stages of economic development for practising family planning. The fall in mortality may be explained by the fact that economic development leads to a rise in the standard of living, including a higher level of nutrition, better sanitary facilities, and improved medical care. The second stage is, therefore, marked by an explosive population growth. This stage is characterised as pre-transitional stage. During the third stage (called transitional stage), birth rate begins to decline with the result that the rate of population growth is positive but of lesser magnitude than in the second stage. In terms of population growth, there is approximately a levelling off at this stage. The fourth stage (called post-transitional stage) is characterised by small or negative growth of population, since a low birth-rate approximates in magnitude a low death rate[50].

## 9. TECHNOLOGY AND SOCIAL CHANGE

Economic activities occupy a major importance in the culture of every social group. Apart from the time spent in eating and sleeping , most of the people devote the greater part of their lives to earn a living. As a consequence, the patterns of their daily activity are greatly influenced by their technology, i.e., by the kinds of goods which they are able to produce, by the ways in which they use them, and by the methods which they employ to produce them. In primitive societies, production was carried on with the aid of simple hand tools, and men spent most of their waking hours hunting, fishing, or tilling the soil. In modern industrial societies, on the other hand, technology is very much a part of our lives. We travel long distances by automobile, bus or train to reach our places of work, and spend a considerable portion of each day in offices, factories or laboratories. In our day to day living, we take the help of various technological aids. It will not be wrong to say that technology provides the basis of the material aspects of modern culture.

## Relationship between values and technology

The term 'technology' should be understood in sociology in a much wider sense than the meaning usually attributed to it. The term does not simply mean machines and scientific instruments. It also implies an appropriate attitude, habits of thought and action. The reason is obvious. In the absence of the latter, mere installation of machine does not yield the desirable result. Machine does not work on its own. It has to be worked by man. The effectiveness of the machine, therefore, depends on the way it is worked. If we make a comparative study of the working of the same type of machinery in different societies, we shall find to our surprise that in one society eighty to ninety percent of the productive capacity of the machinery might have been obtained while in another society the percentage might be forty or fifty or even less. The differences in the utilisation of the productive capacity of the machinery have to be attributed to the differences in the personnel behind the machine. In one case the men who work the machine may have the right attitude and the right motivation whereas in another case they may not have similar attitude and motivation. The observations of G.M. Foster are very pertinent : "Technological development is, indeed, a complex process. It does not simply mean the overt acceptance of material and technical improvements. It implies a cultural, social and psychological process as well. Some writers, therefore, prefer to use the term socio-technological development"[51].

Max Weber in his classic book, *The Protestant Ethic and the Spirit of Capitalism,* discussed at length the relation between the dominant values and the entrepreneurial role of those who share those values. The same analysis applies to the use of machinery as well. The observations of Kingsley Davis are very illuminating. "One common feature of the fixed society is what might be called diffuse other -worldliness —the tendency to fix attention on transcendental world and to view the material world primarily as symbolic of transcendental realities. Since technology and science deal with the intrinsic relations between phenomena, the insistence upon a supernatural interpretation in every detail is a serious obstacle"[52]. Professor D.P. Mukherjee brings out this point very forcefully thus : "The ideal pattern of Hindu values was woven round 'wantlessness'. How could technology and machines geared to the production of goods for the satisfaction of wants, which created more wants, joint wants, derived wants, the infinite hyperbola of wants, be consonant with the pattern of Hindu norms ? How could such norms square, for that matter, with economics, ground as it was on wants and their satisfaction ? If absolute separation of the soul from the body be the utter sum of existence, then Gandhiji, and with him every Hindu,... would raise the eternal query : Why this craze for machinery ? Why machine civilisation at all ?[53]

The same theme may be discussed from another perspective. The full utilisation of machine demands a flexible attitude and receptivity to new ideas and new methods. "Some cultures value positively novelty and change for their own sake. The fact that something is new and different is sufficient reason to examine it and perhaps to try it".[54] There are some cultures, on the other hand, which are not favourably disposed towards novelty and change and discourage all attempts toward introducing novelty and change. Technology does not yield the best results in the hands of those who are not open to the pragmatic test, more hedonistically rational and experimental.

The foregoing discussion establishes beyond doubt the close relationship between values and technology. When we discuss the type of changes which technology brings about, we should bear in mind that technology is both a promise and a demand. When the demands of technology are fully met, only then can we expect the promise of technology to be fulfilled in large measure.

### How technology causes social change

Ogburn has made an extensive study of the patterns of change in material culture. He refers to two basic patterns. First, mechanical inventions tend to accumulate, and, as a result, the material culture becomes enlarged. Ogburn illustrates this process as follows : "The use of bone is added to the use of stone. The use of bronze is added to the use of copper and the use of iron is added to the use of bronze. So that the stream of material culture grows bigger"[55]. Ogburn, however, notes that all material culture does not accumulate. As the use of some objects declines, the knowledge of making them is gradually lost. "For instance, we no longer chip flints to make stone implements for the chase". Hence, the process of accumulation of material culture can be described as selective accumulation. Second, mechanical inventions become increasingly diversified and elaborated over the years. Such diversification and elaboration becomes possible because "a basic invention makes possible may various applications of its principle". For example, the development of the internal combustion engine has made possible many mechanisms driven by such power plants.

Ogburn has studied the *process* of social change that takes place under the impact of technology from three angles : (i) *Dispersion* or the multiple effects of a major material invention. (ii) *Convergence* or the coming together of several influences of different inventions. (iii) *Spiral* or the circular cumulative accelerating process.

(i) Dispersion: Any mechanical invention may have both *direct* and *derivative* social effects. Ogburn noted one hundred and fifty social effects of the radio : effects ranging all the way from entertainment, education, diffusion of culture to morning exercises. No invention is limited to a single social effect; its influence extends over a very wide range covering almost all aspects of society.

Besides these direct effects, a mechanical invention has some *derivative* effects as well. "When an invention has an influence on some institution or custom, the influence does not stop there but continues on and on, each influence succeeding the preceding one like links in a chain". For instance, generation of hydel power has led in many cases directly to the spread of electric power in rural areas. Availability of power, in its turn, is followed by gradual growth of cottage and small scale industries in the countryside. This might eventually lead to a change in the modes of life, attitudes, and beliefs of the people of these areas. In this way, various social changes may be linked to the spread of electricity in the countryside.

(ii) Convergence: It should, however, be noted that the spread of electric power is not the sole determining cause of the growth of industrial units in rural areas. The industrial policy of the Government of India relating to the establishment and growth of 'big' industries also contributes to the emergence of rural industries as ancillary units of big industries. Thus, "the primary result of an invention is itself only one of many factors producing the secondary derivative influence and so on". This brings us to the concept of *convergence* or the combination of several influences of different inventions. For example, the facilities of telephone, quick transport and of less expensive accommodation have led people to live far away from their place of work in the heart of the city. This leads to the size of a city or town getting bigger and bigger and to the development of suburban areas. It is, therefore, clear that group of inventions may converge together and may jointly have a derivative effect in the same way as a single invention has a derivative effect.

(iii) Spiral : So long we have been discussing only the derivative effects, that is, one social change leading to a number of social changes. But sometimes one social change leads to another which, in turn, reinforces the former change. Ogburn characterises this as 'spiral'. Gunnar Myrdal calls this process "a circular cumulative accelerating process" because the effects of a change accumulate and the social changes are accelerated. The following example may be cited to illustrate this process. The industrial development of India is hampered by lack of capital. The government tries to meet this problem by stimulating and mobilising peoples' savings and, at the same time, by drawing upon foreign aid. The industrial development, which is an offshoot of added capital investment, leads to additional employment, greater income and, finally, to greater accumulation of savings and capital. Thus, the derivative effect of additional capital investment is turned back to stimulate the growth of capital. It is interesting to consider in this connection the view of Myrdal "that the social systems of developed countries are spiralling more rapidly than those of unaided underdeveloped countries and that hence the gap is widening between the developed and the underdeveloped countries".

## Social Effects of Technology

That technology plays an increasingly dominant role in shaping our present day way of life is beyond question. Our modes of life and of thought and all our social institutions are influenced profoundly by mechanisation. Modern civilisation could not have developed in the absence of its technological base.? Though technological and scientific advance has conferred great benefits on man, it has also created for him many problems. For example, when the industrial revolution first took place in England, it greatly accelerated the tempo of production, but, at the same time, it forced men and women, particularly men, to stay away from home for long hours and thereby created problems not known before. Similarly, the development of nuclear power has given man the power to abolish all forms of human poverty and, simultaneously, also the power to destroy all forms of human life. In fact, technological changes are followed by far-reaching social changes. We may discuss these effects from different angles.

The increasing use and constant improvement of machines have raised tremendously the productivity of labour, that is, output per man-hour. It is true both of industrial worker and of farm labour. Greater quantities of goods are thus available. Most technological inventions have either of two purposes : either they are intended to create entirely new products for the direct satisfaction of human desires and needs or else their purpose is to produce familiar products more efficiently. Thus, technology raises our standards of living by providing for our enjoyment both new kinds of goods and greater quantities of goods. Technological advance has improved conditions of life for the average man in at least two other ways also. First, it has given him more leisure. Second, it has greatly improved the quality of many of the goods which he buys.

Modern technology has brought into existence quite a number of jobs that require specialised skill and knowledge. Thus, "there are engineers who plan and design machines and factories, skilled construction workers, plumbers, electricians, and a great variety of machinists and mechanics who are engaged in making, operating and repairing machines". There are also people who are specially trained in the organisation and administration of industrial enterprises, in advertising and selling, in keeping accounts and records, etc. In other words, technology has brought into being new occupational classes and an open-class structure replacing the closed social system of old.

Modern technology has in many ways accelerated the tempo of human life. As illustrations, we may consider the following factors which contribute to the acceleration of the general tempo of living :

"The absence of adequate artificial light forced many projects to be confined to daylight hours; now they are carried on into the night.

The slowness of transportation gave much more leisure in travelling, though there was less comfort.

The slow rate of communication forced transactions to be spread over a longer period of time.

The dearth of professional entertainment—stage, screen, radio, and others—left time for meditation and thought.

The dispersal of a smaller population over rural districts provided fewer social contacts than are necessitated by today's urban crowding"[56].

By destroying the domestic system of production, modern industrialism has radically changed the family organisation. Technology has placed man's work, except in agriculture, wholly away from the homestead and has removed nearly all woman's economic duties, except cooking, house-cleaning, sewing and laundering. It has, therefore, been possible for women to come away from home to the factory and the office and have their independent earnings. The women have thus a new social life in this new environment.

Technology has affected man's ideas, attitudes, beliefs, and philosophies. Scientific discoveries and inventions have changed the attitude of men and women towards many rituals, creeds, and religious practices. Space explorations may change these ideas more radically in the near future. It is held that modern men and women are less serious, more inclined towards superficial excitements, and that wealth is esteemed more than cultural or intellectual attainments. The qualities that assure quick material success in life are prized highly. Men have grown pragmatic in their philosophies. They refuse to accept anything on trust. Every idea, concept or belief is tested by reason and experience before it is found acceptable. In other words, functional utility, rather than abstract value, dominates man's thinking in the modern world.

The government has also been affected by technology. By changing the family and the social organisation, technology has forced upon the government new functions and responsibilities in the form of social security measures and welfare activities. Another by-product of modern technology and industrialism has been a great expansion of government controls over business. Machine technology has brought into being large industrial enterprises which carry on production on a large scale. These mammoth enterprises have a great deal of economic power. If they are left to themselves, they are likely to engage in unfair competitive practices or to combine with one another in order to create unhealthy monopolies. The government has, therefore, to take action in order to protect the public against these abuses and dangers.

Besides, there are various other changes that follow from technological changes. Some of these changes can be identified. Improvements in transportation have led to the disintegration of the neighbourhood and to the growth of towns and cities. There is, moreover, the undermining of local folkways and the increasing dominance of urban ways over those of the country. Technology has also indirectly facilitated the growth of democratic ideas by transforming the position of labour from one of status to one of contract, and by bringing into existence the challenge of organised industrial groups, particularly the organisations of labour, to the older forms of authority.

## 10. THE CONCEPT OF CULTURAL LAG

The concept of cultural lag was first introduced by W.F. Ogburn in his book *Social Change* which was published in 1922. Since that date 'cultural lag' has been discussed from different angles by sociologists. Thus, Mac Iver has spoken of technological lag, technological restraint, culture clash and cultural ambivalence.

According to this theory, the culture of any society consists of a pattern of interrelated elements. We can easily see that all aspects of a culture will not change at the same rate at the same time. Hence, a change in any one part of the cultural pattern may create strains and disturbances in the other closely related parts. Adjustments between these parts will have to be made eventually to restore harmony. But there will naturally be a time lag before harmony is restored. This is known as cultural lag.

In modern societies, it is technological change that sets the pace. According to Ogburn, "technological progress produces rapid changes in the material aspects of our culture, but the non-material aspects fail to adjust or they do so only after an excessive time lag. As a result, many troublesome social problems are created". For example, automobile was introduced long before we could sufficiently broaden our streets, which were suitable for horse-drawn carriages, and enforce strictly traffic rules in order to avoid motor accidents. There is, thus, a gap between the material aspects of a culture, represented by the automobile, and the non-material aspects, represented by broader streets and appropriate traffic rules. Similarly, when we make a statement that man's wisdom is lagging behind his power to make weapons of mass destruction, we actually refer to a kind of cultural lag. In this atomic change, such a lag is steadily increasing. "In atomic cultural lag, the leading variable is the maximum area within which, at any given date, people could be killed from a given base. The lagging variable is the ability to prevent this accelerating power from damaging or destroying the kind of civilisation which is valued within the accepted frame of values"[57].

The above illustrations indicate that cultural lag appears when technological innovations move faster than social innovations. But many instances may be cited in which the leading factor of social change, which leads to cultural lag, has been political or social-psychological. Thus, a country may adopt parliamentary form of democracy as an instrument of political action. But, in the initial stages, this form of government may not be very effective because of the failure of the people to develop habits of thought, attitudes, and temperaments that are so necessary for making the best use of this machinery. The initial failure of democracy in some of the newly independent countries of Asia and Africa is partly due to this reason.

We may also think of some striking forms of cultural lag which emerge from the development of non-technological innovations. For instance, the progressive income tax, that is, income tax assessed at a progressive rate, may be regarded as a definite social innovation that is non-technological in character. Since the amounts of money involved are often quite large in the case of some persons, the inducement to find some dishonest method of escaping from part or all of the payment becomes great. The higher the rates of taxation, the greater is the inducement to evasion of taxes. The cultural lag in this case is the time interval between the innovation of progressive income taxation and the development (which is not yet completely achieved) of adequate social controls to prevent tax evasion and to maintain honest tax payments.

### Limitations of the concept

Some sociologists hold that the concept of cultural lag may be accepted with important qualifications.

To begin with, we must not assume that changes in the material aspects of culture always precede changes in the non-material aspects. There is a constant interaction between the two . In the long run, technological progress itself is largely dependent on certain non-material factors, such as social attitudes. For instance, most , if not all, of the material products of culture originate in the minds of men, and their application and use are dependent upon a favourable social and cultural atmosphere. Thus a desire to improve the standard of living has to be kindled first in a community before it can accept technology and industrialised way of life. The rapid material progress, which is characteristic of present-day society, is itself the result of earlier changes in our thinking and other non-material aspects of culture.

A second qualification of the theory arises out of the difficulty of determining just what kind of adjustment to change is desirable. For example, the technological advances in transportation and communication have annihilated distances between countries, so that what happens in one part of the world immediately affects other parts. It may, therefore, be argued that, as a logical corollary of this technological development, small nations should now be abolished and combined into larger political units, that tariff barriers should be abolished and marketing area enlarged in order to derive the economic gains of international division of labour. But doubts may be raised as to whether the creation of these large political units would be socially desirable. According to E.F. Hunt, by destroying the homogeneity of small nations, we would sacrifice non-material social values which are no less important to the welfare of the people than are higher standards of living[58].

Another objection raised against the cultural lag concept is that it inherently involves valuation. A question naturally arises : Can the value judgement implied in the term *lag* be reduced to objective and verifiable facts ? In other words, we must have a standard of measurement by which to identify the pacemaker and the laggard. Where no such standard is available, we can not speak of a lag. "Wherever one part or aspect of a productive system fails to measure up in efficiency to another part or aspect, the term *lag* is relevant. But wherever the question at issue is not one of comparative efficiency, the use of this term becomes dubious and may convey erroneous implications"[59].

Some critics of the cultural lag theory have expressed doubts as to whether the concept has any usefulness in helping us to understand social change. They argue that social change is always disturbing because it disrupts the patterns of life to which we have become accustomed, and also because such a change affects different people differently. Though it may benefit some groups, it is almost sure to injure others. According to Professor F.H.Knight, "what the culture lag theory really amounts to is the assertion that some social changes of which the theorist approves have taken place, while others of which he thinks he would approve have not, or "wrong" changes have occurred instead; the word 'lag' has no proper application"[60].

Cultural lag theory is also criticised on the ground that the 'reasons' for the lag are not given the importance which they deserve. In two cases of cultural lag, the reasons for the lag may be not only different but these differences may be socially significant. For example, we may acquire the necessary skill and expertise to make the best use of the resources of the forest, but there may be a time lag before we acquire the necessary know-how of preserving forest resources. In another case, there may be a time lag in broadening the streets necessitated by the introduction of automobile because of the opposition of some vested interests. The 'reasons' for the lag in the two cases are different and should be brought out, because the two reasons are qualitatively distinct and sociologically significant. Such distinctions are not, however, brought out in the theory of cultural lag, as enunciated by Ogburn.

MacIver is, therefore, of the view that more refined analysis is necessary. "The complexity of modern social organization gives peculiar significance to the various ways in which the inter-dependent parts of the inclusive system fail to function harmoniously together..."[61]. Hence, MacIver gives distinctive names "to the very different phenomena with which we have to deal within this broad area of lack of coordination amongst the various part of the social system.

### Technological Lag

What is generally known as 'industrial bottleneck' illustrates the concept of technological lag. This lag appears when any one aspect of an inclusive system of technology fails to keep in step with other aspects, resulting in impairment of productivity of the whole system. There may be many kinds of technological lag. This may occur when the management of a company fails to maintain over-all efficiency when it expands its scale of operations, particularly when it becomes a part of a combine or trust. The example we gave in the preceding paragraph of a lag between our knowledge of exploitation of forest resources and that of preservation of forest resources illustrates the concept of technological gap.

### Technological restraint

There is no guarantee that discovery of efficient technological device will be easily adopted. Its adoption or application may be opposed by various interest groups. This state of affairs is characterised by MacIver as technological restraint. Some examples may be cited.

One reason for opposition may be that its adoption would affect adversely the vested interest involved in the pursuit of the existing method or procedure. In all countries, innovations in administrative procedure receive stiff opposition from the entrenched civil service. Such opposition may stem from the apprehension that honour, power or pecuniary benefit may be affected adversely by the adoption of new procedure or a new technological device. Computer, for example, is undoubtedly of immense help in any kind of work situation. But the introduction of computer has not been easy in any work place, be it a government department or a semi-government or private enterprise. Trade unions oppose its introduction on the ground that it would restrict employment opportunities. Sometimes opposition may stem from cultural consideration. For example, when tube well was introduced in India about seven or eight decades ago, many conservative Hindu families did not use or drink water from tube wells on the ground that water came in contact with leather (in the form of washer) and thereby became 'impure'. Many innovations and discoveries have been opposed in the past on religious grounds, on the ground that those discoveries contradicted the statements in the scriptures. The case of Galileo is well known. Even Darwinian theory of evolution received opposition from the Established Church on the same ground. MacIver observes that in its resistance to technological advance, culture fights a losing battle. "It has become increasingly clear that culture cannot successfully oppose the advance of civilisation, but that instead its task is to accept and to direct that advance, controlling it to serve cultural ends. Only thus can the maladjustments of culture and civilisation, which must constantly arise in the course of technological advance, be progressively reconciled"[62].

## Culture Clash

MacIver defines culture clash thus : "We do not include under culture clash the conflicts of creeds and ideologies so frequent in every modern society. We refer only to conflicts between two entire culture patterns, each of which embraces a whole way of life. Such clashes arise pre-eminently from the coming together within a single community of groups that have been bred in separation before they become thus conjoined. Usually one of the cultures concerned is an imported culture. while the other is indigenous or at least has long been established in its present home. The two are brought rather abruptly into contact, and under these conditions one of them appears to be a threat to the very existence of the other, especially if the former is associated with a dominant group"[63]. When Islam came to India about one thousand years ago with an entirely different cultural pattern, the indigenous population embracing Hindu way of life could not absorb it, as it had done in respect of earlier immigrant groups such as Sakas, Huns, etc. The natural outcome was culture clash which has, unfortunately, gone on for the past several centuries. It appears that such culture clash would have considerably abated in the course of sharing joys and sufferings of common living for centuries, had there been no intervention of economic and political forces. Vested interests of both economic and political nature have grown around this division between the two communities and tend to fan the fire of separatism under the facade of culture clash.

## Cultural Ambivalence

The phenomenon of cultural ambivalence is a socio-psychological phenomenon which arises in the cases of individuals who are subjected to contradictory pulls, each representing a particular normative pattern. In a society there is usually a 'trend to consistency" (in Sumner's words) in respect of the prevailing mores, and an individual does not generally find any difficulty in accommodating to the mores of society, thanks to the processes of indoctrination and habituation to which he has been exposed since his early childhood. "But when the individual is subjected, especially in the formative stage of life, to the counter demands of clashing culture patterns, he may fail to achieve an adequate *personal* accommodation. He undergoes a process of cultural denudation or, seeking vainly to reconcile in his behaviour the opposing demand, he becomes more or less schizophrenic. We have then the phenomenon of cultural ambivalence"[64]. While discussing the causes of maladjusted behaviour among young people today, a UNESCO Report contains the following analysis which emphasises that conflicting cultural values leave a young person in an ambivalent state of mind with regard to the role he must play in society : "This generation has grown up in an ever more swiftly changing world. Social relationships are conditioned and characterised by the large-scale organisation of industrial economy, by technical development, automation and bureaucracy, by the strict laws of supply and demand, and by the functioning of depersonalised mass units. In contrast to non-industrialised society, where moral principles and customs are sometimes pre-determined and understood to which everyone is expected to conform, the great social changes introduced by industrialised society bring in their train the breaking up of these norms. In this urban civilisation with its new freedom for the individual, each person must find and create his own way of life. Freedom from old feudal and class distinctions has presented man today with the problem of freedom to establish a new standard of morals and values.

The relationship of young people to God and the Church is typical of this process today"[65].

## 11. SOCIAL CHANGE, SOCIAL EVOLUTION, SOCIAL DEVELOPMENT AND SOCIAL PROGRESS

During its early phase, sociological inquiry was mainly directed toward an interpretation of the rapid and violent changes that had overtaken European societies in the eighteenth and nineteenth centuries. The approach was connected with the philosophy of history. Early sociologists were all concerned to explain or interpret the social and political revolutions of their age within the framework of a general theory of history. The writings of Saint-Simon, Comte, Marx and Spencer bear witness to this. Though Max Weber did not present a theory of universal history, he was inspired by a historical concern with the origins and significance of modern Western Capitalism and with the increasing rationalistion of social life over the years. Even Durkheim, who rejected Comte's evolutionary approach, classified societies in terms of an evolutionary scheme.

In these earlier sociological theories, social change, social evolution, social development and social progress have been often treated as synonymous terms. Even when treated differently, these were treated as logically related terms. We have to examine how far this contention is correct.

That society changes is a demonstrable certainty. The notion of social evolution, which was adopted in order to describe social change,"was taken directly from the theories of biological evolution which, in the nineteenth century, powerfully reinforced the influence of the philosophy of history upon sociology. "The term 'evolution' is used to describe any form of orderly change. In biology, it stands for a particular type of orderly change, namely, that whereby new specific forms have arisen by a process of differentiation from the old. In other words, biological evolution refers to 'descent with modifications'. This means the diversification of species from a common genus.

In the social field, however, the notion of evolution in the sense of the diversification of species cannot be appropriately applied. The term 'evolution' could be used in sociology in a sense analogous to that given to it in biology, if new elements of culture can be shown to arise from the old by a process of diversification.

According to Morris Ginsberg, the notion of evolution in the sense of the diversification of species can be fruitfully applied in, at least, two realms of culture, namely, in the field of language and of tools[67]. Languages have been classified into families or stock s and their similarities and differences have been studied with the aid of a theory which can be appropriately described as 'descent with modifications'. Comparative philosophy is concerned with establishing connections between linguistic stocks which had formerly been regarded as remote from each other in order to explain their derivation from a common source.

In the case of tools, a similar approach has also proved fruitful. As Tylor pointed out: "The geographical distribution of these things and their transmission from region to region have to be studied as the naturalist studies the geography of his botanical and Zoological species". Marx made a similar point when he called for a history of tools which would be to social progress what Drawinism was to organs of animal species, and he thought that such a history of human technology ought to be easier to write than the history of 'natural technology"[68].

The idea of evolution in the sense of diversification of species may prove to be valuable in certain elements of culture. But in many cases the idea of evolution may not be applicable at all. According to Ginsberg, this is due to the difficulty in arriving at a workable social morphology.

The concept of social evolution which holds that each society passes through the same stages of development has been almost entirely abandoned. That is, the crude application to society of such concepts of biological evolution as natural selection, adaptation, and survival of the fittest has been thoroughly discredited. While rejecting the concept of social evolution, V. Gordon Childe observes: "... it is essential not to lose sight of the significant distinctions between historical progress and organic evolution, between human culture and the animal's bodily equipment, between the social heritage and the biological inheritance. Figurative language, based on the admitted analogy, is liable to mislead the unwary...Man's equipment and defences are external to his body; he can lay them aside and don them at will. Their use is not inherited, but learned, rather slowly, from the social group to which each individual belongs. Man's social heritage is not transmitted in the germ-cells from which he springs, but in a tradition which he begins to acquire only after he has emerged from his mother's womb. Changes in culture and tradition can be initiated, controlled, or delayed by the conscious and deliberate choice of their human authors and executors. An invention is not an accidental mutation of the germ-plasma, but a new synthesis of the accumulated experience to which the inventor is heir by tradition only. It is well to be as clear as possible as to the sort of differences subsisting between the processes here compared."[69].

In view of the difficulties associated with the use of the term 'evolution', some sociologists have used the term 'development' to denote the change of society from one stage to the other. Thus, Hobhouse held the view that in the historical development of society from the primitive stage to the advanced one, four characteristic features gradually emerged, namely, expansion, increase in efficiency, mutuality and co-operativeness, and extension of individual freedom.[70]

The question is : Whether such an advance can be characterised as 'development'? In its application to social phenomena, the term 'development' is no more precise than the term 'evolution'. Development is a process whereby that which exists 'potentially' becomes actual.[71] In this sense, we speak of the development of a child or of a disease. It is not clear if we can speak of social development in the same way by referring a particular social phenomenon to its germ. In the case of an organic body, we can speak not only of its development but also of its decay. Can we speak in the same way of the development and decay of the whole society ?

The theories of social development may be expressed in the form that human development consists in the unfolding of man's powers, individual and collective, and the use of such powers in dealing with nature and with himself. Bottomore elaborates this point thus : "There are only two (related) social processes to which it seems possible to apply the term 'development' with any accuracy, namely, the growth of knowledge and the growth of human control over the natural environment as shown by technological and economic efficiency. It is, indeed, these two processes which have figured most prominently in developmental or evolutionary accounts of human society."[72] It is clear, therefore, that the term 'development' can be applied to particular aspects or features of society, and not to the society and a whole. That is, we cannot speak in terms of 'development' of the society.

There is another difficulty in speaking in terms of 'development'. Nagel points out that the term has not only a backward reference in the suggestion that something latent or hidden is progressively made manifest, but also a prospective one; "it possesses a strong teleological flavour."[73] This is apparent from the fact that the development of a child is related to some known characteristics of the adult human being. In the case of particular social phenomena, we can relate the development of knowledge to a condition of more extensive and exact knowledge, and the development of control over nature to such things as survival and population size. But the development of society as such can hardly be related to any prospective condition of society except in terms of a moral ideal. In that case development becomes synonymous with progress.[74]

We have examined the difficulties in using the terms 'social evolution' or 'social development' with reference to changes that take place in society. That society changes in course of time is an undoubted fact. But is there any specific direction in which the process is moving ? Can we say with any amount of certainty that all these changes had led to social progress ? An answer to these questions involves a definition of the concept of progress. Progress is development or evolution in a direction which satisfies rational criteria of value.[75]

All throughout the nineteenth century, the idea persisted that all social change marked successive stages toward social progress. A few quotations would be revealing. Tocqueville, for whom progress consisted in the movement towards equality, urged that it was a providential fact, possessing all the characteristics of a divine decree : "it is universal, it is durable, it eludes all human interference". From a totally different point of view, Spencer concluded that : "The ultimate development of the ideal man is logically certain — as certain as any conclusion in which we place the most implicit faith".

The popularity of the idea of progress was due in great measure to two factors : (i) The buoyant hopefulness inspired by the triumphs of applied science. (ii) The idea was given powerful impetus by its association with the biological theory of evolution. With reference to these two developments, Marris Ginsberg observes : "The culminating point in the history of the belief in progress was reached towards the end of the nineteenth century. Its high priests and incense bearers were .... all rationalists. It owed its wide prevalence to the optimism inspired by the triumphs of applied science, made visible in the striking advances made in the technical conveniences of life, and, on the theoretical side, by the deeply ramified influences exerted by the ideas of development and evolution on all branches of thought and inquiry".[76]

Though the culminating point of the idea was reached toward the end of the nineteenth century, no law of progress had, in fact, been scientifically established. But the general idea of progress harmonised with notions of development that had become current during the period in science and philosophy. It also provided an inspiring justification for movements of social and political reform. In spite of the fact that the concept of progress was vague and imprecise, it became "part of the general mental outlook and for many it provided the basis for a working faith of great value".

In the twentieth century, the mood is more cautious. The concept of unilinear or automatic progress is subjected to searching criticism. The devastation of World War I shattered to pieces the confident optimism of the inevitability of progress. "In more recent times the belief in progress has been further weakened by the growing recognition that advances in technical knowledge are by no means sufficient to ensure social and moral progress, and the fear that the use of scientific knowledge for destructive purposes may outpace and arrest the growth of its powers for good".[77]

The idea of progress is not popular with social scientists in this century for some other reasons also. In the first place, there is no universal agreement on the standards of value and, as such, we cannot tell from the mere fact that a thing has changed whether it has progressed or not. Evolution or change is an objective condition. Progress, on the contrary, means change for the better, and hence implies a value judgment. Secondly, since the components of society are interdependent, change at any point is likely to precipitate changes elsewhere. Some of these changes may be unwanted. A social change is never received as an unmixed blessing. In the words of MacIver : "Every achievement has its costs, and men often differ as to whether the costs outweight the values accrued."[78] Thirdly, values change over time. What is universally hailed as a progressive measure at one period of history may be condemned with equal or even greater force as a retrograde measure at some other period of time.

Faced with the difficulties involved in giving clear-cut connotation to the term progress, attempts are sometimes made to settle the matter by proclaiming a set of social values that are sufficiently general to be accepted by everybody. Some of these generalised social values are : "Thou shalt not kill", 'Do not tell a lie'; 'The greatest good of the greatest number', etc. It is true that opinions will not clash on this level of abstraction. They will clash, however, when it comes to a specification of these values. For example, there might be a general consensus on the goal of social policy that it should strive to secure the greatest good of the greatest number. But controversies will arise as to what actions are to be taken to secure these ends. People have different ideas of what is good for them, Similarly, the commandment prohibiting 'killing' is accepted by almost all cultures. But while some people look upon both war and legal hanging as necessary, even though each results in loss of life, there are some others who want both the practices to be abolished unconditionally. It is, therefore, obvious that "while it may be possible to formulate conceptions of progress or valuations of change which apply to all time, the statements are too general to afford definite and sure guidance in specific situations at different times and in different cultures".

Sometimes attempts are made to avoid these difficulties by adding a qualifying adjective to the word 'progress', such as 'agricultural', 'industrial', 'economic', etc. It is true that progress in these specific fields can be measured. What cannot, however, be measured is the degree in which these measurable advances in specific fields 'contributes to the ill-defined and unmeasured end, which is progress itself.'

Despite these limitations and many-sided attacks, the idea of progress has not lost its vitality. It is so deeply rooted in the modern mind that its critics never reject it entirely. Some examples may be given. Professor Toynbee, who strongly upholds a cyclic theory of civilisations, ends by suggesting that "the breakdowns and disintegrations of civilisations might be the stepping stones to higher things on the religious plane" and even goes so far as to say that the next stage in this advane may lead to a new species of society "embodied in a single world-wide and enduring representative in the shape of the Christian Church"[79]. Even the Marxists, who reject the 'bourgeois' concept of progress, retain the belief of the early rationalists that man can make himself. They look forward confidently to an age when the 'true realm of freedom will blossom out of the realm of necessity in the fully developed Communist Society of the future'[80].

The concept of progress is as old as mankind. In all ages, people had a concept of that which would be most desirable. These concepts may and do vary from age to age. Even when everything seems lost, people look forward to a better future. In all that we do, there is a consciousness that we are working to usher in a brighter and happier future. It rings through the speeches of religious preachers, social reformers, and even politicians. The faith in progress sustains us through all vicissitudes and trials and gives us the necessary strength to face the hard and cruel realities of life. Emphasising that faith in progress is ineradicable from the life of man, MacIver observes : "To live is to act, and to act is to choose, and to choose is to evaluate. Hence as human beings we cannot get rid of the *concept* of progress, though we are of course entitled to deny the reality of progress. The fact that men ininevitably differ about it, that we cannot demonstrate the validity of our concept as against theirs, only makes it indubitably ours. If one can prove it none can refute it. At the least it is a vital myth, ineradicable from the creative strivings of life"[81].

## 12. SOCIAL MOVEMENT AND SOCIO-CULTURAL DRIFT

When social interaction is specifically directed towards the accomplishment of change, such organised efforts to bring about social change are called social movements. In the beginning, such movements are amorphous, poorly organised, and without any clear-cut form. They have their origin, on the one hand, in dissatisfaction of a group of people with the prevailing state of affairs, and, on the other, in the hopes of the group that a new and a better social order would eventually emerge. As a social movement develops, it takes a definite form, an organisation under an established leadership and clear-cut social philosophy.

Much social change, however, results from human interaction which is directed towards ends other than change itself. Thus, industrial production was organised with a view to increasing production. But it had the important effect of changing radically the structure of family. This kind of social change is called *sociocultural drift*. Changes in education, in laws, in administrative patterns, in business practices, and in most other areas of life take place in such an unplanned manner. As a matter of fact, sociocultural drift accounts for much of the social change that takes place in a society.

## NOTES

1. Morris Ginsberg, *Essays in Sociology and Social Philosophy*, Peregrine Book, 1968, page 129
2. *ibid*, page 138
3. Kingsley Davis, *Human Society*, page 622
4. *ibid*, page 622
5. *ibid*, pages 622-623
6. *ibid*, page 623
7. *ibid*, page 622
8. *ibid*, page 628
9. *ibid*, page 629
10. Maciver and Page, *Society*, page 565
11. B.F. Hoselitz (ed), *A Reader's Guide to the Social Sciences*, The Free Press, Glencoe, Illinois, 1960,page167
12. MacIver and Page, *Society*, page 582
13. G. Duncan Mitchell, *A Hundred Years of Sociology*, page 95
14. *ibid*, page 96
15. *ibid*, page 96
16. Raymond Aron, *Main currents in Sociological Thought, Volume* 2, Pelican Edition, pages 221-222

17. Talcott Parsons, *The Structure of Social Action,* page 531. Quoted by Mitchell, page 97
18. Quoted by Mitchell, page 97
19. MacIver and Page, *Society,* 566
20. The theory of the Leisure class by Veblen, pages 192-193. Quoted by MacIver and Page, *Society,* page 567
21. *ibid,* page 567
22. *ibid,* page 569
23. *ibid,* page 569
24. Morris Ginsberg, *Essays in Sociology and Social Philosophy,* Peregrine Book, pages 138-149
25. *ibid,* page 140
26. *ibid,* pages 140-141
27. *ibid,* pages 141-142
28. Toynbee,*A study of History,* Vol.XII (Reconsideration), Oxford University Press, 1961, pages 343-348
29. A.L. Kroeber, *'Stimulus Diffusion', in The American Anthropologist, New Series,* Vol.42, No.1 (January - March, 1940), quoted by Toynbee, op. cit.
30. Frankfort, *The Birth of Civilizations in the Near East,* page 110. Quoted by Toynbee, op. cit.
31. Morris Ginsberg, op. cit., page 144
32. *ibid,* page 146
33. *ibid,* page 148
34. *ibid,* page 150
35. *ibid,* page 150
36. Kingsley Davis, *Human Society,* page 552
37. Kingsley Davis, *The Population of India and Pakistan,* 1951
38. Moni Nag, *Modernisation and its Impact on Fertility — The Indian Scene.* Article published in Indian International Quarterly Journal, Vol.8, Nos.3 and 4, 1981, page 241
39. *ibid,* page 236
40. *ibid,* page 236
41. *ibid,* page 237
42 Moni Nag, *Article entitled Modernisation affects fertility,* published in Populi, Vol.10. No.1, 1983, page 57
43. *ibid,* page 62
44. *ibid,* page 62
45. P.Demeny, *Investment Allocation and Population Growth. Demography* 2 : 203- 232, 1965. Referred to by Dr. Moni Nag in his paper, ibid, page 62
46. M.Nag, *Impact of social development and economic development on mortality* : A comparative study of Kerala and West Bengal. Center for Policy Studies (Population Council). Working paper No. 78. New York, Population Council.
47. M.Nag, *Article entitled Modernisation affects fertility, published in Populi,* Vol.10,No.1,1983, page 63
48. MacIver and Page, *Society* page 537
49. David M. Heer,*Society and Population,* page 83.
50. *ibid,* page 10
51. G.M.Foster, *Traditional Cultures and the Impact of Technological Change,* Harper and Brothers, N.Y., page 2.
52. Kingsley Davis, *Human Society,* pages 446-447
53. D.P.Mukherjee, *Mahatma Gandhi's view on Machinery and Technology.* International Social Science Bulletin. Vol.6, No.3, UNESCO, Paris, 1954.
54. G.M.Foster, op. cit., page 64-65
55. Ogburn, Social change, page 73
56. E.F.Hunt, Social Science, page 119
57. Allen, Hart, Miller, Ogburn, Nimkoff, *Technology and Social Change,* edited by J.F. Cuber, page 432.
58. E.F.Hunt, *Social Science,* page 103
59. MacIver and Page, *Society,* page 575.
60. Frank H.Knight, *Freedom and Reform,* page 39. Quoted by E.F. Hunt in his book *Social Science,* page 104.

61. MacIver and Page, *Society*, page 575
62. *ibid*, page 579
63. *ibid*, pages 579-580
64. *ibid*, page 580
65. Report of International Expert Meeting on *"The Maladjusted Behaviour of young people in Present Day Society"*, Bulletin of UNESCO Youth Institute, June 1958, Number Two , Page 36.
66. Bottomore, *Sociology*, pages 283- 284
67. Morris Ginsberg, op. cit., page 101
68. *ibid*, page 101
69. V.Gordon Childe, *Man Makes Himself* (3rd Edition), London, 1956, pages 16-17. Quoted by Bottomore in his book, *Sociology, page 284*
70. Bottomore, Sociology, page 285
71. Morris Ginsberg, op. cit., page 100
72. Bottomore, op. cit., pages 285 - 286
73. *ibid*, page 286(Footnote)
74. *ibid*, page 286
75. Morris ginsberg, op. cit., page 101
76. *ibid*, page 78
77. *ibid*, page 79.
78. MacIver and Page, *Society*, page 613
79. Morris Ginsberg, Op. cit., page 80
80. *ibid*, page 80
81. MacIver and Page, Op. cit., page 619

# CHAPTER TWENTYTHREE

# TRADITIONAL SOCIETY AND MODERNISATION

## 1. TRADITIONAL SOCIETY : ITS CHARACTERISTIC FEATURES

From an economic point of view, societies are distinguished between developed and developing or under-developed societies. A few definitions would make the distinction clear. According to one definition: "An economically underdeveloped country is one which on the average affords its inhabitants an end product of consumption and material well-being appreciably inferior to that provided by the economies of the development countries. Poor is a relative term. To designate a country as underdeveloped also implies that its present economic performance—as evidenced by the average of consumption and material well-being could be improved by means which are known and understood[1]. Another definition runs as follows: "A country characterised by mass poverty which is chronic and not the result of some temporary misfortune, and by obsolete methods of production and social organisation, which means that the poverty is not entirely due to poor natural resources and hence could presumably be lessened by methods already proved in other countries"[2]. Jacob Viner gives yet another definition: ".... an underdeveloped country... is a country which has good potential prospects for using more capital or more labour or more available natural resources, or all of these to support its present population in a higher level of living, or if its *per capital* income level is already fairly high, to support a larger population on a not lower level of living"[3].

An analysis of the aforesaid three definitions would bring out the following points of distinction between developed and underdeveloped economies. First, the standard of living of the inhabitants of underdeveloped countries is much lower than that of developed economies. Second, the comparative poverty of the underdeveloped economies is not due to lack of natural resources. Third, such poverty is to be attributed mainly to use of obsolete method of production and consequent underutilisation of natural resources. Fourth, in developed economies the social organisation has been adapted to the requirements of the economy. In an underdeveloped economy, on the other hand, the traditional social organisation has been adapted to the requirements of the economy. In an underdeveloped economy, on the other hand, the traditional social organisation impedes the full utilisation of the capacity of machines and resources. In the Chapter on Economic Institutions this aspect has been discussed at length.

When we speak of a traditional or backward society, we have to take into account, besides the aspect of poverty, other aspects of social organisation also. As a matter of fact, the economy of a society cannot be kept separate and distinct from other aspects of social life. All are inter-related, so much so that any one aspect cannot be treated in isolation from the rest. Having made these general observations, we may note some of the characteristic features of a traditional society.

(i) "A society is traditional if behaviour is governed by custom and if ways of behaviour continue with little change from generation to generation"[4]. Such a society is averse to all sorts of innovation because of its abiding faith in the time-worn, traditional methods of dealing with problems confronting the society. Loyalty to the past makes it blind to the scope and promise of non-traditional ways of dealing with the problems of society.

(ii) A traditional society is marked, in the words of Talcott Parsons, by 'particularistic' values as opposed to 'universalistic' values which characterise a modern society. Family and kinship ties are very strong. Inadequate development of transport facilities tends to limit spatial mobility which, in its turn, restricts marriage and all other kinds of social relationships within a narrow circle.

(iii) It follows from the above that social status in a traditional society is ascribed rather than achieved, as is the case in a modern society. In the words of Hagen : "In a traditional society the social classes form a pyramid, from the peasants and labourers at the bottom to the small group of powerful individuals at the top. The individual's position in the society is normally inherited rather than achieved, except that a group sometimes gains political control of the country by force"[5].

(iv) A traditional society is basically agricultural in nature. Agriculture, as has been pointed out earlier in the chapter on society, is a way of life. Agriculture, therefore, determines the thinking, patterns of living and behaviour of the inhabitants of a traditional society. Gemeinschaft relationships predominate over gesellschaft relationships.

(v) Social mobility, like spatial mobility, is very much restricted in a traditional society. There is a clear cleavage between the elite and the masses. It is particularly so in countries which were under colonial rule. In the particular situation of underdeveloped countries, intellectuals often represent modern Western culture and find themselves separated from, and in conflict with, the traditional cultural values of the mass of their fellow countrymen.

(vi) One can discern differences in the political activities of traditional and modern societies. Mass participation in politics, not simply in terms of voting periodically during elections but in terms of building powerful lobbies or pressure groups to influence political decision-making, is a very recent phenomenon in traditional societies. Discerning observers of the Indian political scene have noted that "intellectuals, in a broad sense,have dominated political life in India since independence and that active participation in politics of the mass of the population such as occurred in the independence movement has only recently begun to revive, on a limited scale, with the emergence of peasant movements. .....Students are the principal source of recruitment to active political work, and this fact accounts in part for the prevalence of factionalism in the major parties"[6].

(vii) All the characteristic features of a traditional society are, for obvious reasons, reflected in the education system. Stagnant economy, absence of diversification in occupational patterns and allegiance to tradition—all these have a bearing on the system of education prevailing in these societies. Literacy is low as compared to advanced societies. Enrolment in general stream is far greater than that in specialised fields. The reason is obvious. Agriculture and industry are not developed to the extent that they can absorb technical hands beyond a certain limit.

## 2. MEANING OF MODERNIZATION

It has been very aptly said that "modernisation is the current term for an old process—the process of social change whereby less developed societies acquire characteristics common to more developed societies"[7]. This process is facilitated, sometimes hastened, by international, or intersocietal, communication. The developed societies transmit 'images' of their developed states to traditional societies. Such transmission has become very frequent and efficacious since world War II , thanks to the expansion of mass media. The mass media have been called the "mobility multiplier", because these 'images' of developed societies arouse among people of traditional societies a hankering for a 'better' or 'higher' standard of living. The mechanism by which such expectations are aroused is known as *empathy*. "Empathy is the psychic mechanism that enables a person to put himself in another person's situation—to identify himself with a role, time, or place different from his own. Among the range of psychic mechanisms that supply imagination, empathy is distinctively the one that nourishes 'upward mobility'.... The mechanism may or may not be innate, but it can certainly be trained to operate more efficiently in people with a desire to better themselves. Since World War II such training has been supplied by the mass media of print, film and radio"[8]. Karl Marx noted over a century ago in the preface to *Das Kapital* : "The country that is more developed industrially only shows, to the less developed, the image of its own future".

**Criteria of Modernity**

If modernisation is the process whereby less developed societies acquire characteristics common to more developed societies, the next important task is to identify the characteristics which are common to more developed societies—that is, to identify the criteria of modernity.

Sociologists have not yet arrived at a consensus about the criteria of modernity. But there has been a broad agreement among scholars on certain key points concerning modernisation. These key points are (i) a degree of self-sustaining growth in the economy—or at least growth sufficient to increase both production and consumption regularly; (ii) a measure of public participation in the polity—or at least democratic representation in defining and choosing policy alternatives; (iii) a diffusion of secular-rational norms in the culture—understood approximately in Weberian-Parsonian terms; (iv) an increment of mobility in the society, understood in terms of urbanisation, spread of literacy and media participation; and (v) a corresponding transformation in the modal personality that equips individuals to function effectively in a social order that operates according to the foregoing characteristics.[9] While discussing the criteria of modernity, Daniel Lerner observes: "According to this typology, the modern person is an urban literate who participates fully in the public forum, market place, political arena"[10].

## 3. COMPLEXITIES OF MODERNISATION

We have already noted that every nation that is undeveloped or less developed, but regards itself as developing, constantly receives pictures of modernity transmitted by more developed societies, and embarks on social planning in the direction of modernization. The experiences of such planning have been varied, happy in a few cases and unhappy in the case of most nations. It is one thing to define in detail the criteria of modernity and an altogether different thing "to plan the rational transfer of these 'items' from more developed to less developed societies". To be successful and efficacious, modernisation process should involve not simply a mechanical 'transfer' of a few chosen items, but a complete 'transformation' of the society in question. Transfer of 'items' can only be meaningfully accomplished by the transformation of individuals. We may discuss some of the complexities involved in the planning process toward modernisation.

To begin with, the planning policy is often ambivalent. As a result, the planning works, not infrequently, at cross purposes. Dr. S.C. Dube refers to the ambivalent attitude of Indian planners in this respect. "The small modernising elite continues to have a dominant voice, but the forces of tradition and conservatism are by no means dead or even insignificantly weak. When plans for progress fail, appeals of obscurantism become attractive. But whatever the lip-service rendered to traditional ideas and forms, the goal of modernisation appears to have been generally accepted. There is, however, no consensus on the elements of tradition to be preserved and no assessment of the social costs of economic development and technological change : thinking on these themes continues to be hazy and wishful. It would be desirable not to approach the "take off" stage with a divided mind on these seminal issues"[11]. Dr. Dube highlights the failure of the Indian planning process directed toward modernisation in these words :"The main failures have been on the educational and communicational fronts. Efforts in these fields lack direction : they are weak, poorly organised, and not quite in harmony with the national effort on the agricultural and industrial fronts. Their major failures are : (i) they have not effectively projected a positive image of the New India—of what the country wants to be, and of what it should be. (ii) They have not seriously tried to inculcate the attitudes and values that are conducive to modernisation. (iii) A new system of rewards and sanctions necessary for economic development and social change,has not received imaginative and careful handling on their part"[12].

Secondly, modernisation is the process of social change in which economic development is the principal component. Naturally, economic development is a high priority objective of every modernising society. But in most cases this objective remains unfulfilled. The cause of failure lies in lack of proper appreciation and understanding of the dynamics of modernising process. The attainment of 'selfsustaining' economic growth involves more than purely economic processes of production and consumption. It involves, in particular, the transformation of human resources. "For an economy to sustain growth by its own autonomous operation, it must be effectively geared to the skills and values of the people who make it work. On this view. a society capable of operating an economy of 'self-sustaining growth' is *ipso facto* a modernised society"[13].

Thirdly, modernisation does not involve a mechanical transfer of institutions of the advanced societies to those which are not so advanced. "Modernisation operates rather through a transformation of institutions that can only be accomplished by the transformation of individuals"[14]. It is, therefore, required of modernising societies that they 'must learn how transferred institutions may be transformed, how adopted life-ways may be adapted"[15].

Fourthly, the developed and modernised societies of today experienced low rates of change over long periods of time. Today, on the other hand, the modernising societies experience high (and usually accelerating) rates of change over short (and usually decreasing) periods of time. This poses problems for the latter. There is hardly enough time for slow adaptation to new ways of life and transformation of individuals which are the essential pre-conditions for successful modernisation.

Fifthly, in the case of those societies which are developed and modernised, the impulse for modernisation came from within whereas in the case of the present-day modernising societies the impulse comes from without. S.N.Eisenstadt explains the point thus : "It was in these European countries (Western Europe, England, the Netherlands, the Scandinavian countries, the United States, and in the English-speaking Dominions) that the first historical processes of modernisation developed, mostly through the transformation and working of various internal forces in these societies, and only to a small extent through the impact of external events"[16]. The conclusion at which the social scientists have arrived on the basis of this experience is this: "Traditional societies can respond effectively to internally generated demands for institutional change articulated over a relatively long period, but they are typically incapable of rapid institutional changes to meet externally induced demands.[17]" Since the start of international development programmes in 1949 (with President Truman's point IV programme), the traditional societies of Asia and Africa receive pictures or images of their own future from a more developed society. Experience of the few decades suggests that the transmission of such images is likely to constitute an intrusion into the less developed, traditional society, and that such intrusions prove to be disruptive to traditional societies.

This point merits detailed discussion. The images of developed societies arouse the expectations of the people of traditional societies. These societies "manifest an urgent will-to-change but are unable to incorporate rapidly an efficacious way-to-change. The disruptive effect, which is produced by the imbalance between the will and the way to modernise, emerges as a key problem of induced and accelerated social change."[18] The result is that a 'revolution of rising expectations', which is an outcome of externally induced stimulus, is giving way to a 'revolution of rising frustration'.

The distruption that is caused to traditional societies as a result of externally induced stimulus and accelerated (high rates of change over short periods of time) social change may be discussed with reference to some illustrations.

To begin with, let us consider the case of urbanisation which is a criterion of modernity. In Western societies urbanisation proceeded slowly over a long period of time accompanied by, and in response to, other social changes, the most important of which was industrialisation. Empolyment opportunities expanded and people were naturally attracted by the prospect of employment in urban centres. Those who came were absorbed and they became truly urbanite. Urban amenities developed simultaneously. It is not so with urbanisation in modernising sodieties of today. "This is an urbanisation of very high density, of individuals living under conditions that may be even worse than the rural areas from which they have come, of not having available the kinds of work or the means of support which will permit them to do more than merely survive." [19] Lerner observes: "The great cities of the transitional world often have become massive impediments to orderly social change rather than productive centres of modernisation. In much of Latin America, vast lands are deserted while the people are crushed into the megapolis - for example, half of all Cubans live in and around Havana, half of all Uruguayans live around Montevideo and about 80 per cent of the Venezuelan population lives on the 10 per cent of land located between Caracas and Maracaibo. In the transitional societies of Asia, which produce far less wealth than those of Latin America, the consequences of over-urbanisation are even more disruptive." [20]

We may next consider literacy as a criterion of modernity vis-a-vis new modernising societies.Eradication of illiteracy constitutes an important component of planning process for modernisation. But this may also prove to be disruptive. In these societies literacy is often a status symbol. Those who are introduced to alphabets or to 3 R's are sometimes alienated from their ancestral occupation, and at the same time they cannot fit themselves well with the requirements of an industrial society because of their limited capability. The result is frustration. That is why literacy is now-a-days conceived of as functional literacy having three inter-connected components: literacy, functionality and awareness.[21] That is,literacy is linked to the occupation of the learner so that he may be more competent in his calling than before. At the same time, through literacy he is exposed to the environment around him, acquainting him broadly with the environmental problems and the ways to tackle them. It will be prudent to heed the warning of Bernard Shaw : "How can you dare to teach a man how to read before you have taught him everything else?" The experience of Western societies in this particular field is narrated by Lerner thus: ......"The growth of free public education was functionally related to industrial society, with its evergrowing need for literates to perform the skilled and semi-skilled functions of industrial production, distribution and even consumption. In the modern West, literacy developed intitially as a skill with a ready pay-off to the ambitious individuals who acquired it. Only later, and at a much higher level, did it become a personal and cultural adornment".[22]

Even in the field of higher education, the modernising societies do not appear to have designed their courses of study to effect 'behavioural transformations' of individuals.On the contrary, education that is imparted proves to be not only disruptive but often dysfunctional for societal modernisation. Teaching is also equally defective. Not only does it fail to arouse curiousity, it also discourages, and sometimes even dampens,curiosity of students. Sir Ivor Jennings, who was for sometime the Vice-Chancellor of Colombo University, recorded the conversation between a student and his teacher of English literature thus :

"Teacher : 'O daffodil wer weep to see you fade away so soon'.

Pupil : What is a daffodil ?

Teacher : Just an English flower, but the examiners will not ask questions on that. Take this note : The imagery in this poem......"[23]

The experience recorded by Dr. Jennings is, by no means, unique to Sri Lanka. One may derive similar experience in India, and for the matter of that in all traditional societies which are going through the process of modernisation. Can such education develop among pupils adaptive capacity which is the most distinctive feature of societies that are genuinely modernised ?

Let us take up political participation vis-a-vis the modernising societies of today.Even here the effect has been disruptive. Political participation has brought about "the relatively quick development of the political aspiration of the wider social groups and their overall political modernisation before a concomitant extent of economic, professional, and often even educational development. The high level of modernisation of political demands, in its turn, usually gave rise to a quicker development of educational facilities and aspirations - especially of the more generalised and humanistic ones which often outstripped the economic facilities".[24] Establishment of many schools, colleges and Universities in various states in India was dictated more by political expediency than by considerations of promoting the cause of modernisation.

Media participation has also proved to be dysfunctional. The attractive advertisements of various consumer items, including consumer durables, in the mass media, tend to arouse expectations of having those attractive items. There is no corresponding increment of ability to fulfil those expectations. "The disruptive imblance that weighs most heavily on traditional societies in our time is the imblance between what people have been taught to want and what they have learned to get."[25] The result is frustration which "is accelerating in transitional societies because articulated wants are increasing, diversifying and spreading at very rapid and erratic rates."[26]

## Conclusion

From the brief resume of the various pitfalls that a traditional society may experience in the course of its modernising efforts, we may draw certain lessons. It should be borne in mind that problems of a disruptive nature arise from the eagerness to introduce changes at an accelerating rate within a short period of time. Institutions are transferred from the highly modernised societies to traditional ones without any apparent attempt at adaptation or transformation of those institutions. There is little or no indication at all of any attempt being made to transform individuals of traditional societies, in the sense of instilling into them new values in place of traditional ones. No enduring change can be expected when people think and act in old ways. It is not certainly desirable that life in a traditional society should be disrupted in the name of modernisation. But this is exactly what is being done. This is attributed to the series of 'explosions' that take place in 'transitional' societies - population, urbanisation, literacy - "that consume all gains in production as soon as they are made , and often more rapidly than they are made". Gunnar Myrdal pointed out that it is the worsening situation of the poor countries as compared to those which are rich that defeats the planning of modernisation in our time. The reason is to be sought in the fact that these transitional societies have not been able to incorporate the individual and institutional mechanisms that make growth self-sustaining.

Another crucial factor has to be borne in mind. Rostow spoke of stages of economic growth, culminating in an 'take-off' stage. In the case of modernisation also, we have to think in terms of modernisation in stages. Just as an individual cannot absorb large quantities of food and information within a short period of time, so also a society cannot assimilate changes of a far-reaching nature within a short span of time. All traditional societies are not in the same stage of development. Response ratio to development facilities varies from society to society. What is beneficial for one society may not be so for another. This recognition imposes obligations both upon the 'modernised' and 'traditional' societies. The former should take note of the response ratio of a traditional society and accordingly transfer institutions in such a fashion that these can be 'transformed' by the modernising societies. The modernising societies should, on their part, learn how transferred institutions may be transformed, how adopted life-ways may be adapted. "As the modernised succeed in learning their own lesson, they will be better equipped to teach the lesson to the modernising. For, the lesson, they will be better equipped to teach the lesson to the modernising. For, the contemporary world has become interactive in the sense that all nations and people now are continuously exposed to each other"[27]. If these elementary precautions are not taken, indiscriminate transfer of institutions from the modernised to the modernising countries would open up a pandora's box, and more harm that good would follow. Any attempt to jump the queue in this case, as in all others, creates chaos and disorder. Modernisation of traditional societies, therefore, calls for very careful social planning.

## 4. THE CONCEPT OF WESTERNIZATION

M.N. Srinivas criticises Lerner's concept of modernisation on the ground that it is a value-loaded term. According to him, "modernisation is normally used in the sense that it is good"[28]. He, therefore, prefers using the term *'Westernization'* "to characterise the changes brought about in Indian society and culture as a result of over 150 years of British rule"[29]. He further observes that "the term subsumes changes occurring at different levels—technology, institutions, ideology, values"[30]. By way of developing his concept, he says that westernisation not only introduces new institutions but also results "in fundamental changes in the old institutions"[31]. Westernisation also implies, according to him, "certain value preference"—an important value being humanitarianism "by which is meant an active concern for the welfare of all human beings irrespective of caste, economic position, religion, age, and sex'[32]. He observes further that *equalitarianism* and *secularisation* "are both included in humanitarianism" and that as British rule progressed "rationality and humanitarianism became broader, deeper and more powerful, and the years since the achievment of independence have seen a remarkable increase—a genuine leap forward—in the extension of both"[33].

He considers it necessary "to distinguish conceptually between westernisation and two other processes usually concomitant with it—industrialization and urbanization"[34]. He advances the following reasons for doing so : (i) "Urbanization is not a simple function of industrialization" and "there were cities in the pre-industrial world" also. (ii) "There are cases of rural people who are more urbanised than urban people".

Daniel Lirner has raised the following objections to the use of the term 'Westernisation' as conceived by Srinivas[35]. (i) It is too local a label and the model which is imitated may not be a western country but Russia. (ii) Anti-colonial feeling prompts some societies to ignore certain behavioural and institutional compulsions common to all countries (Europe, America and Russia) which have achieved modernisation and to try "instead new routes and risky by-passes". (iii) "One of the results..... of prolonged contact with the West is the rise of an elite class whose attitude to the West is ambivalent." In this context, Lerner refers to the appeal of communism in non-Western Countries. (iv) "While there are certain common elements in Westernization, each European country along with the United States, Canada, Australia and New Zealand represents a particular variant of a common culture and significant differences exist between one country and another". (v) Westernization in one area or level of behaviour does not result in westernization in another related area or level. The two remain 'discrete'.

Besides, the concept of westernization is not really "ethically neutral"[36], as claimed by Srinivas. He himself says that it implies " certain value preferences", such as humanitarianism, equalitarianism, secularisation, and a degree of rationalism. Does not reference to these values carry the implication that westernization is, in general, good and desirable ?

Moreover, does not the Western model sometimes convey values contrary to these ? What about race prejudice, colour segregation and exploitative nature of the Western economy ? Do not these facts contradict humanitarian ideals or rational outlook on life?

Further, if the contents of Westernization are not clearly spelled out in specific terms, the concept will be of little use in explaining the nature of social change taking place in post-independent India. Professor Srinivas is aware of this limitation when he says : "I am using it deliberately in spite of its vagueness and omnibus character"[37].

## NOTES

1. N.S. Buchanan and H.S. Ellis—*Approaches to Economic Development*, N.Y. The Twentieth Century Fund, 1955, pages 3-4
2. Eugene Staley, *The Future of Underdeveloped Countries*, N.Y.Harper and Brothers, 1954, page 13.
3. Jacob Viner, *International Trade and Economic Development*, Glencoe. The Free Press, 1952, page 125
4. E.E. Hagen, *On The Theory of Social change*, page 21

5. *ibid,* page 21
6. Bottomore, *Sociology, pages 165-166*
7. Daniel Lerner, *Modernisation :* Social Aspects, International Encyclopaedia of the Social Sciences, volumes 9-10, pages 386
8. *ibid,* page 391
9. *ibid,* page 387
10. An article by Daniel Lerner entitled *The Transformation of Institutions, included in the book. The Transfer of Institutions,* edited by William B. Hamilton, Published for the Duke University Commonwealth Studies Center, Duke University Press Durham. N.C. Cambridge University Press, London, 1964, page 19
11. *Some Aspects of Social Change in India,* Edited by Kuppuswamy and Prayag Mehta. An article entitled Formulating the goals of Change by Dr. S.C. Dube, page 55
12. *ibid,* page 55
13. Daniel Lerner, *Modernisation : Social Aspects, International Encyclopaedia of the Social Sciences* ,Volumes 9-10, page 388
14. *ibid,* page 388
15. *ibid,* page 394
16. S.N.Eisenstadt, *Modernisation — Protest and Change.* Prentice-Hall of India Pvt. Ltd., New Delhi. 1969, page 55
17. Daniel Lerner, *Modernisation : Social Aspects,* page 390
18. *ibid,* page 390
19. Gerald Breese, *Urbanisation in Newly Developing Countries,* page 5
20. Op. cit., page 390
21. Reference may be made to NAEP or National Adult Education Programme of the Government of India.
22. Daniel Lerner, *The Transformation of Institutions,* page 16-17
23. *An article on Universities in the Colonies by* Sir W. Ivor Jennings. Published in The Political Quarterly. Vol.17. No.3, 1946, page 228-224.
24. Eisenstadt, *Modernisation — Protest and change, pages* 117-118
23. *An article on Universities in the Colonies by* Sir W.Ivor Jennings. Published in The Political Quarterly. Vol.17. No.3, 1946, page 228-244.
24. Eisenstadt, *Modernisation—Protest and change,* pages 117-118
25. *Daniel Lerner, Modernisation : Social Aspects in International Encyclopaedia of Social Science,* page 392
26. *ibid,* page 392
27. *ibid,* page 394
28. M.N. Srinivas, *Social Change in Modern India,* page 51
29. *ibid,* page 47
30. *ibid,* page 47
31. *ibid,* page 48
32. *ibid,* page 48
33. *ibid,* page 49
34. *ibid,* pages 51
35. *ibid,* page 51-54
36. *ibid,* page 51
37. *ibid,* page 47

# CHAPTER TWENTYFOUR

# PIONEERING CONTRIBUTIONS IN SOCIOLOGY

In this chapter, an attempt will be made to present briefly the seminal ideas of a few sociologists and social anthropologists who contributed 'a sense of the structure of society, a sense of society as a unique phenomenon, and of sociology as a challenging subject for intellectual inquiry'. In a work like this, names of many pioneers have to be left out, though their contributions have been acknowledged in appropriate places in the preceding chapters. Proper justice cannot also be done to those whose names appear in this chapter.

## 1. POSITIVISM OF AUGUSTE COMTE (1798—1857)

August Comte's important contribution to sociology was the positivist legacy which he left behind him. In his *Course de philosophie positive,* he propounded his positivist philosophy. It embraced five methodological precepts : (i) *le réel,* (ii) *la certitude,* (iii) *le precis* (iv) *I'utile* and (v) *le relative.*

*Le réel* meant that the scientific status of knowledge had to be guaranteed by the direct experience of an immediate reality. This required a particular conception of causality in which causal relations amounted to regular associations between phenomena. Comte claimed that a causal relation 'discovered between any two phenomena enables us both to explain them and foresee them, each by means of the other'. The limitation of the terms of scientific explanation to the phenomenal level, therefore, meant that the positivist could not have recourse to any supernatural or abstract forces which were by definition outside his direct experience. Comte traced three fundamental stages of knowledge : from a 'theological' state in which the world was explained in terms of supernatural forces, to a 'metaphysical' state in which the world was explained in terms of abstract forces, and finally to a 'positive' state in which the world was explained in terms of regular connections between empirically observable phenomena.

This rule of phenomenalism has to be complemented by *la certitude* which meant that the scientific status of knowledge had to be guaranteed by the common experience of reality, a mode of apprehension which was accessible to all scientists and which ensured the replicability of their observations—in other words, the unity of the scientific method. If followed from this that disciplines were to be distinguished by their object of study, and not by their method.

This, in turn, required *le précis,* which defined the scientific method as the formal construction of theories whose consequences could be tested in some way. Value-judgements were immediately excluded from scientific inquiry because they were ethical assertions rather than empirical predictions, incapable of verification.

*L'utile* confirmed this by regarding all scientific knowledge as technically utilisable, concerned with 'means' not 'ends and although in one sense this could be interpreted as nothing more than instrumentalism, its main function in the Comtean scheme was to rule value-judgements out of the scientific court.

Comte conjoined *le précis* and *l'utile* in a distinctive way. His scientific method was intended to reveal the laws of co-existence and succession which governed society, and he maintained that these allowed no variation. Once man realised this, then the battalions and barricades would be removed from the map of Europe. As Comte put it himself, "there is no chance of order and agreement but in subjecting social phenomena, like all others, to invariable laws, which shall as a whole prescribe for each period, with entire certainty, the limits and character of political action". If the scientist was obliged, however, to accept society as these laws dictated it to be, *he did not have to accept society as it was,* particularly when he looked out on a continent disrupted and corrupted by politicians who evidently did not recognise the inexorable force of these social laws. While excluding value-judgments, which were not in accordance with these laws, Comte's positivism was also distinguished by an affirmative impulse of critical enlightenment, in the sense of seeking to remove the misery which resulted from misguided attempts to force society down paths which were necessarily closed to it. This impulse was regarded as non-ideological in so far as the positivist was not required to assume any ethical position in order to demonstrate the truth of his statements or the invincibility of the social laws which they embodied.

Finally, *le relative* depicted scientific knowledge as unfinished and relative, progressing by the gradual unification of theories which would consolidate man's awareness of the social laws. It followed from this that scientific progress was paralleled by social progress, and Comte tied his three stages of knowledge to three modes of action' : the theological to the military, the metaphysical to the defensive, and the positive to the industrial. From this fundamental correlation there also results the general explanation of the three natural ages of humanity. Its long infancy, which fills the whole of antiquity, had to be essentially theological and military; its adolescence, in the Middle Ages, was metaphysical and feudal; finally, its maturity, which has only begun to be appreciated in the last few centuries, is necessarily positive and industrial.

Comte was neither the first nor the last to devise a tripartite history of civilisation, but his proposals show that he saw positivism very much as a child of the nineteenth century[1].

## 2. KARL MARX (1818-1883)

In its present state of development, sociology is an attempt to describe impartially, to measure exactly, and to connect by means of scientific generalisations the diverse phenomena of social life. Seen in this perspective, Marxism is more than a system of sociology. It is, on the contrary, a philosophy of man and society as well as political doctrine. "The originality of Marx's thought", says Maxmilien Rubel, "lies in his immense efforts to synthesise, in a critical way, the entire legacy of social knowledge since Aristotle. His purpose was to achieve a better understanding of the conditions of human development and with this understanding to accelerate the actual process by which mankind was moving toward an 'association in which the free development of each is the condition for the free development of all'. The desired system would be a communist society based on rational planning, co-operative production, and equality of distribution and, most important, liberated from all forms of political and bureaucratic hierarchy"[2]. Rubel points out, however, that this dual commitment—to scholarly understanding and to political action—created constant difficulty for Marx.

Marx's ideas on division of labour, alienation, class and class struggle have been discussed in appropriate places in the preceding chapters. Many other topics, such as religion, family, bureaucracy, etc. have also been examined from a Marxian perspective. In this section, we propose not to go over those themes again, but to concentrate exclusively on Dialectic Materialism or Materialistic Interpretation of History.

Dialectic Materialism is the philosophy sketched out in the philosophical writings of Marx and Engels. The leading principles of the doctrine may be expounded as follows:

(i) The principle of realism. The existence of any object does not depend upon its being perceived or experienced in any way. Although some characters of existence may depend upon the mode in which it is experienced, existence itself cannot be deduced from psychological or logical considerations alone.

(ii) The principle of Dialectic. Dialectic Materialism took over the dialectical interpretation of reality developed by Hegel. The term dialectic, as originally used in Greece, meant the process of getting at the truth through a debate carried on by opposing sides. For Hegel, the movement of experience itself represents a sort of logical debate carried on by reality, with a logical thesis being opposed by logical antithesis and yielding thereby an endless movement toward higher synthesis. The extent of the debt of dialectical materialism to the Hegelian philosophy and its divergence from it may best be indicated in Marx's own words . In the preface of the second edition of *Das Kapital* he writes : "My dialectic method is not only different from the Hegelian, but is its direct opposite. To Hegel, the life-process of the human brain, i.e., the process of thinking, which, under the name of the 'Idea' he even transforms into an independent subject, is the demiurgus of the real world, and the real world is only the external, phenomenal form of 'the Idea'. With me, on the contrary, the ideal is nothing else than the material world reflected by the human mind, and translated into forms of thought".

(iii) The principle of causality (determinism). Although there are chance elements in the world, the methodological assumption of science presupposes that all objects of enquiry in different fields are subject to law. There can be no dispute about this, and where there is dispute the real problem is whether some subject matter can be treated scientifically. Dialectic Materialism holds that no limits can be drawn to the progress of science and although many things will probably remain unknown, none of them is inherently unknowable. Engels repeats Hegel's argument that the nature of a thing is not some mysterious X but the sum total of all its qualities or the synoptic formula which unifies its appearances from all possible points of view.

(iv) The principle of historical materialism. Dialectic materialism, applied to the realm of culture, i.e., to the field delimited by the common activity of men as members of society, gives us the principle of historical materialism. The hypothesis of historical materialism is that "the causes of all social changes and political revolutions are to be sought, not in men's brains, not in man's better insight into eternal truth and justice, but in changes in the modes of production and exchange. They are to be sought not in the philosophy, but in the economics of each particular epoch". Historical materialism is the doctrine that "the mode of production determines the character of the social, political, and intellectual life generally".

As its name suggests, historical materialism differs from all other materialistic interpretation of history on the ground that it does not explain the rise and fall of social systems in terms of factors which are non-social. While admitting that climate, topography, soil, race, etc. are genuine conditioning factors of social and historical activity, it denies that they determine the general character of a culture or its development. The reason is two-fold: first, in any given area these factors are relatively constant while social life is more variable; second, there can be no intelligible reduction of the specific qualities of human behaviour—exhibited in a social context—to categories of physics and biology. Not the slightest evidence has been produced, for example, to show that the climate of Greece from the 6th century B.C., to the first —a period of tremendous social change—varied in any appreciable way.

The positive principles underlying the theory of historical materialism may be summed up as follows: (a) Every existing culture is a structurally inter-related whole. Consequently, any aspect of that whole—its legal code, educational practices, religion, art or the like—cannot be understood by itself. (b) Culture is not only an inter-related whole but a developing whole. The independent variable in the developing social whole will be the explanatory key not only to the causes of change from one society to another but to the dominant culture pattern existing at any time. According to historical materialism, the independent variable is the mode of economic production. Hegel had maintained that "political history, forms of government, art, religion and philosophy—one and all have the same common root, *the spirit of the time*". On the other hand, Marx contended that all of these cultural phenomena are "rooted in the material conditions of life..........".

The view that the independent variable is the mode of economic production does not deny that the cultural products of economic development react upon that development. Engels writes: "The political, legal, philosophical, literary and artistic development rest on the economic. But they all react upon one another and upon the economic base. It is not the case that the economic situation is the *sole active cause* and everything else is merely a passive effect. rather there is a reciprocity within a field of economic necessity which *in the last instance* always asserts itself".

Similarly, historical materialism does not deny the role played by social tradition in modifying the rate of change in the non-material aspects of culture. "The tradition of all dead generations", Marx writes in the 18th Brumaire, "weighs like a nightmare on the brain of the living". Family relationships, religion, art and philosophy, although they reflect the new social equilibrium produced by changes in the economic order, lag behind both in time and structural form. From the vantage point of a long time perspective, the phenomenon of cultural lag may not appear significant; but from the point of view of short-term political operation they are of great importance.

(c) By the economic structure of society historical materialists mean "the sum total of the relations of production". By the 'relations of production" Marx means not the mechanical agencies used in manufacture or the technical organisation of the factory but the social relations into which human beings enter or, better still, find themselves whenever they participate in the economic life of society. Property relations are the formal expressions or signs of these social relations of production. These, in turn, constitute a whole of which technique is only one of the parts. Marx argues: "Machinery is no more an economic category than is the ox which draws the plough. Machinery is only a productive force". Indeed, it is possible to find societies with different social relations but certain identical productive fores : techniques of tilling the soil were sometimes the same in feudal economies as in slave economies: the use of machinery in the Soviet Union parallels that in the United States. Mote important still is the assertion of the historical materialist that the very development of techniques is not independent but is guided by the needs of a larger social productive whole, of which it is a part.

(d) The mode of economic production is expressed in certain social relationships which are independent of any individual. Man is born into a society in which property relations have already taken form. These property relations define the different social classes, such as feudal lord and serf, employer and employee. The conflicting interests of these classes flow not merely from the consciousness or lack of it of individual antagonisms but from the different objective roles played by them n the processes of production. The absence of class conflicts, which may often be the consequence of the activity of professional social pacifiers, no more eliminates the real opposition of class interests than the willingness of Negro slaves to serve their masters proves that they were not enslaved:

(e) The division of society into classes gives rise to different ideologies—political, ethical, religious and philosophical—which express existing class relationships and tend either to consolidate or to undermine the power and authority of the dominant class. A struggle for survival goes on in the realm of ideas. Since those who control the means of production also control, directly or indirectly, the means of publication, the prevailing ideology is a support to the existing order. Marx, therefore, observes: "In every epoch the ruling ideas have been the ideas of the ruling class".

(f) In every social order there is a continuous change in the material forces of production. Sometimes, as in early societies, this change is produced by some natural phenomenon, such as the drying up of rivers or exhaustion of the soil. Usually, however, this change is produced by a development in the instruments of production. At a certain point in their development, the changed relations in the forces of production come into conflict with existing property relations. It no longer becomes possible on the basis of the existing methods of distribution of income to permit the productive processes to function to full capacity. Property relations are now recognised as a fetter upon further social development. The class that stands to gain by the modification of property relations becomes revolutionary. It asserts itself as a political force and develops revolutionary ideology to aid it in its struggle for state power. Marx, however, observes: "No social order ever disappears before all the productive forces for which there is room in it have been developed; and new, higher relations of production never appear before the material conditions of their existence have matured in the womb of the old society"[3].

(g) Viewed in this perspective, all history since the disappearance of primitive communism may be regarded as a history of class struggles. Every class struggle is a political struggle, because the state is an organ of class repression and is never really neutral in class conflict.

(h) The struggle between capitalist and proletariat represents the last historic form of social opposition, because in that struggle it is no longer a question of which class should enjoy ownership of the instruments of production, but of the very existence of private ownership. The abolition of private property in the means of production actually means the abolition of all classes. This can be accomplised only by a victory of the proletariat. Political power is to be consolidated in a transitional period of revolutionary dictatorship after which the state dies out . That is, its repressive functions disappear and its administrative functions become part and parcel of the productive process[4]. "For the creation on a mass scale of this communist consciousness, as well as for the success of the cause itself, it is necessary for men themselves to be changed on a large scale, and this change can only occur in a practical movement, in a *revolution*. Revolution is necessary not only because the *ruling* class cannot be overthrown in any other way, but also because only in a revolution can *the class which overthrows it* rid itself of the accumulated rubbish of the past and become capable of reconstructing society"[5].

The theory of historical materialism raises certain questions of a basic nature. We may take up these questions in the following paragraphs.

To begin with, what are the specific mechanisms by which economic conditions influence the habits and motives of classes, granted that individual are actuated by motives that are not always a function of the individual self-interest ? Since classes are composed of individuals, how are class interests furthered by the non-economic motives of individuals ? For example, the workers, who fulfil the objective conditions of a class in the Marxian sense, may be actuated by narrow ethnic or religious interests and get involved among themselves in ethnic or religious disputes. Such disputes do not obviously further their economic interests nor can such disputes be explained in economic terms.

Secondly, the statement that economic conditions "in the last instance" determine social life or that they are "the real foundations" of society implies a theory of measurement. So far, however, no theory of measurement for the social discipline has been evolved.

Thirdly, if it is true, as Marx states in *Das Kapital,* that in changing his external environment man changes his own nature, then human nature under ancient slavery must have been different in some respects from human nature under modern capitalism. If this is so, how is it possible to understand past historical experience in the same way as we understand present experience, since understanding presupposes an unvarying explanatory pattern? This is a problem which is not peculiar to historical materialism. Such a problem confronts all philosophies of history. This is, however, no valid reason for avoiding it.

Fourthly, to what extent are chance events to be admitted as operating forces in history? Most historical materialists have contended that "to appeal to chance in history is to exhibit a certificate of poverty", Marx and Engels were more cautious. In a letter to Kugelmann on the Paris Commune (April 17, 1871) Marx goes so far as to claim that for some specific and local issues chance may be a decisive factor. Engels with his eye on long-range tendencies admits the presence of chance phenomena, but holds that their influence is compensatory with the result that in the final account they cancel one another.

It is instructive, in this connection, to compare the views of H.A.L. Fisher who writes in *History of Europe* : "One intellectual excitement has, however, been denied me.Men wiser and more learned than I have discerned history, a plot, a rhythm, a pre-determined pattern. These harmonies are concealed from me. I can see only one emergency following upon another as wave follows wave, only one great fact with respect to which, since it is unique, there can be no generalizations, only one safe rule for the historian : that he should recognize in the development of human destinies the play of the contingent and the unforeseen. This is not a doctrine of cynicism and despair. The fact of progress is written plain and large on the page of history; but progress is not a law of nature. The ground gained by one generation may be lost by the next. The thoughts of men may flow into channels which lead to disaster and barbarism".

Fifthly, is the truth of historical materialism itself historically determined ? Or, is it valid for all history, past and present ? Both Marx and Engels declared that its truth was relevant only for class societies and that consciousness of the conditions of its truth would lead to action which would abolish class society. Does this mean that "the leap from the kingdom of necessity to that of freedom", the phrase with which Engles describes communism in *anti-Dühring*, implies a condition in which man escapes the limitations of his earthly fate? There is no warrant for the belief that historical materialism justifies any such historical apocalypse.

Sixthly, although the theoretical scheme of historical materialism was intended to have a universal character, Marx actually employed it in a partial manner. His own researches were limited almost entirely to the nineteenth century capitalist societies and he gave only fragmentary accounts of the other types of society. Furthermore, some of his most important theoretical ideas were derived immediately from the observation of modern societies, and they fit closely those particular societies. His theory of social classes applies, in the main, to the formation and development of the modern bourgeoisie and proletariat; it is not so helpful when applied to the phenomenon of a caste system. Clearly, the theory of social conflict originated in an interpretation of the French Revolution, the materials for which had been prepared by earlier historians and it was developed further by observation of the class struggle which accompanied the growth of the labour movement in Western Europe.

Seventhly, Raymond Aron, C. Wright Mills and Ralf Dahrendorf reject, as inconsistent with the evidence, the constant association between economic ownership and political power which is a basic postulate of Marx's theory. They draw attention, in particular, to the alternative bases of political power in societies where private ownership of industrial wealth is non-existent.

In this context, the views of Polish sociologist, Stanislaw Ossowski, may be considered. He makes a profound re-appraisal of Marxian theory of class and he comes to the conclusions which do not differ widely from those reached by sociologists elsewhere. Ossowski recognises that substantial changes have occurred in the class structure of capitalist countries. He observes that in all the modern industrial societies the political authorities increasingly determine the system of social stratification, rather than being determined by it, as a rigorous Marxist view would maintain. He also criticises the arguments, which have been put forward, on opposite sides, for regarding both the United States and the Soviet union as 'classless societies'[6].

Bottomore emphasises two points while dealing with Marx's contribution to sociological thinking. In the first place, Marx adopted and maintained very consistently in his work a view of human societies as wholes or systems in which social groups, institutions, beliefs, and doctrines are interrelated, so that these have to be studied in their inter-relations rather than treated in isolation. Secondly, he viewed societies as inherently mutuable systems in which changes are produced largely by internal contradictions and conflicts.

The questions which have been raised with regard to historical materialism are no doubt very important and deserve serious consideration. These questions will agitate the minds of men for years to come. Herein lies the importance of the contribution made by Marx. Except physical sciences, there is no discipline which has not been affected by this debate between the Marxists on the one hand and the non-Marxists on the other. In his preface to Ideology and the Development of Sociological Theory, Zeitlin has made an assessment of Marx's contribution in these words: "Marx's contribution to sociological thinking..... is one of the most important of the late nineteenth century—perhaps the most important. This is true, I believe, not only because of the immensely rich ideas he himself advanced but also becuase his work provoked a response that accounts, in a large measure, for the character of Western sociology".

It will be quite in order to point to the various Marxist schools which have come into being since Marx. There are different versions of Marxist doctrine—the Soviet version, the Chinese version, the Western version, "whose most perfect form is probably Swedish society where there is a mixture of private and public institutions, and a very extensive equalization of income"[7]. There is no way of knowing how Marx would have reacted to this development, had he been with us today. Raymond Aron observes: "In all probability, Marx, who had a rebel's temperament, would not be enthusiastic about any of the versions, any of the modalities of society which call themselves Marxist. But which would he prefer? An answer seems to me impossible and, in the last analysis, pointless"[8].

Those who claim to be Marxists hold the view "that the true lineage of Marx is Soviet society"[9]. If that be so, how has Marxist sociology developed in Soviet Russia? Stanislaw Ossowski notes that in the sphere of theoretical sociology, the contributions from communist countries have been few and this brings out the difficulty of maintaining the Marxist system in tact[10]. Maxmilien Rubel has this to say on this aspect: "The process of incorporating Marx's ideas into the social sciences in western countries contrasts vivdly with the unsure attempts by Marxist regimes to invent and decree a 'Marxist 'sociology. The efforts of these regimes unwittingly confirm one of Marx's major hypothesis that the dominant ideas of a society are those of its ruling class"[11].

## 3. EMILE DURKHEIM (1858—1917)

Durkheim was a professor of the French University. In his age, sciences seemed to professors 'to provide the model for precise thinking, successful thinking, one might even say the only model for valid thinking."

At the end of the nineteenth century, Durkheim noted with other intellectuals of his age the erosion of religious beliefs under the impact of science. He could clearly see that traditinal religion was being exhausted. This was a matter of deep concern for him. As a sociologist, he was inclined to believe that society could retain its cohesion and unity only by a common faith which would bind together the members of the collectivity. The crisis of modern society seemed to him to have been created by the non-replacement of traditional moralities based on religions by a morality based on science. His intellectual problems may be stated thus : He was for a precise and methodical study of society. At the same time, he was convinced that science could not unite men. In his view the coherence and stability of society depended largely on beliefs and values cherished by the people. As a sociologist, he, therefore, set before himself the task of finding out how sociology could help establish such a morality— "a morality inspired by the scientific spirit." As a spiritual disciple of Auguste Comte, he emphasised the necessity for social consensus.

Durkheim wrote four great books which mark his intellectual itinerary and which represent variations on the fundamental theme of consensus.

The first, *The Division of Labour,* is concerned with the following theme. Modern society exhibits an extreme differentiation of jobs and professions. How are we to ensure that a society divided among innumerable specialists will retain the necessary intellectual and moral coherence? How can individuals achieve a consensus which, incidentally, is the condition of social existence? Durkheim's answer to this central question is to set up a distinction between two forms of solidarity, viz., mechanical solidarity and organic solidarity. Durkheim's views on division of labour in society and the distinction between mechanical and organic solidarity have been discussed at length in the chapter on Economic Institutions.

The purpose of his long and interesting contrast of the two types of society is to discern what Durkheim calls the 'social factor'. What led him to undertake this quest was his criticism of the prevailing individualist and utilitarian philosophy which argued that society is composed of individuals who act in such a manner as to satisfy their individual wants, and that in doing so they enter into contractual relationships which thus form the basis of social order. Durkheim set out to destroy this false view of human society. To do so, the true science of sociology had to be established, because, he thought, sociology must be able to account for the social factor. Durkheim was convinced that other sciences could not answer the question posed. Gabriel Tarde, for instance, had attempted to explain social phenomena in terms of the characteristics of individuals when he emphasised the psychological process of imitation. Durkheim rejected this kind of explanation because it failed to account precisely for the social factor.

His alternative approach was to look for social phenomena (a) which were exterior to the individual and could not be attributed to internal psychic states, and (b) which stood over the individual in some compelling way. For Durkheim, these are law and custom and the whole range of obligations which morally compel the individual and which exercise constraint on him. These he called 'social facts'. According to him, it is the task of sociology to study these social facts and herein lies the peculiar subject matter of this social science. In his words, "....... society is not an aggregate of individuals but a reality *sui generis*". The concept of the 'social fact' received lengthy treatment in the *Rules of Sociological Method* which was written after *The Division of Labour*.

While analysing the nature of 'social fact', Durkheim introduces the concept of *conscience collective,* In French, the terms *conscience collective* mean both common consciousness and common conscience. According to him, there are certain values in every society which are engraven on the minds of its members. This explains common approach and attitude among mrmbers of a society to social events. For example, if an act is considered by the society to be wrong, then that act is adjudged to be wrong. Such evaluations vary from society to society according to *conscience collective of* each society. This explains as to why what is considered to be wrong in one society may not be considered as such in another society.

According to Durkheim, *conscience collective* falls under two categories, namely, *collective representations and individual representations.* Collective representation is simply 'the body of beliefs and sentiments common to the average of the members of a society'. Durkheim adds that the system of these beliefs and sentiments has a life of its own. Individual representation, on the other hand, refers to preferences or values cherished by an individual. When an individual expresses his preference for fish as compared to, say, meat or when he has abhorrence for some food, such preference or abhorrence may be taken to be examples of individual representation. When, however, the Hindus consider beef to be forbidden food, this is an example of collective representation. In this case, individual preferences have no place whatsoever. Judged from this view, collective representation is objective, and not subjective. This is in the nature of a commandment of the community.

According to Durkheim, collective representation, whose existence depends on the sentiments and beliefs present in individual consciousness, is nevertheless separable, at least analytically, from individual consciousness. It evolves according to its own laws. It is not merely the expression or effect of individual consciousness, but something more than that.

How does *conscience collective grow ?* According to Durkheim, intense debate and sharing of ideas give rise to new values and new sentiments which acquire an enduring quality. "The essence of social life is the interaction of people's minds. Sometimes, indeed, there is a peculiar intensity in the interaction which brings forth new sentiments, sentiments which possess a stronger power than purely individual sentiments possess, for these are group ones and represent a collective ferment of intense social communion out of which something new may emerge, something creative, indeed a new ideal. Thus are values created"[12]. Durkheim cites a number of historical instances. The growth of scholasticism in the 12th and 13th centuries in Europe sprang from the meeting and intense interaction of scholars gathered together in Paris. The Renaissane and the Reformation were other instances. So also the French Revolution in the 18th century and the rise of socialist movements in the 19th century. He argues that all these were cases of creative syntheses. In such times new ideals are born, sectional interests are subdued and forgotten for a while and the ideal becomes real. Of course, the occasion passes and life becomes humdrum again. So men wish to revive the memory, because faith in the new ideal has to be repeatedly restored, and the experience has to be re-lived. Hence, ceremonies, religious events and feasts, public occasions and speeches, plays and pageantry are utilised. They are "minor versions of the great creative movement". Durkheim further observes: "Through the very awareness of itself society forces the individual to transcend himself and to participate in a higher form of life. A society cannot be constituted without creating ideals"[13].

In his book, *The Rules of the Sociological Method,* his first rule is : "Consider social facts as things". He emphasises that "far from being a product of the will, social facts determine it from without; they are like moulds in which our actions are inevitably shaped"[14]. The conceptions of time, space, numerals and even religion are derived, according to him, from social experience. Thus, "time is the collective representation of the rhythm of social life". In other words, "the categories of thought are not *a priori* but derived from the structure of social existence'; once implanated in men's minds the categories do indeed appear *as if* they were immanent"[15].

Social facts, as defined by Durkheim, have two objective criteria: (i) the criterion of exteriority and (ii) the criterion of constraint. Durkheim says that if individuals are constrained by external social facts like laws, they are also constrained by some social facts which are not so clearly perceived and identified, and here Durkheim argues that the sociologist must discover statistical rates which reflect these social facts. It is the rate of crime, the suicide rate, the birth rate, the divorce rate and incidence of drunkenness which provide the empirical referents for an analysis of social currents and trends.

## Le Suicide

His third great book, *Le Suicide,* is an analysis of a phenomenon regarded as pathological, intended to shed light on the evil which threatens modern or industrial societies : *anomie.*

Durkheim's study of suicide begins with a definition of the phenomenon. He then proceeds to refute the earlier interpretations of suicide. Finally, he develops general theory of the phenomenon.

Durkheim defines suicide as "every case of death resulting directly or indirectly from a positive or negative death performed by the victim himself and which strives to produce this result". A 'positive act' would be to shoot oneself in the temple or to hang oneself. A "negative act" would be to remain in a burning building or to refuse all nourishment to the point of starvation. Thus, a hunger strike carried out until death is a case of suicide according to Durkheim's definition. The distinction between 'directly' and 'indirectly' is the one between 'positive' and 'negative' acts of committing suicide.

Having defined the phenomenon, Durkheim refutes the psychological explanations of suicide. He criticises those who say "that the majority of people who take their own lives are in a pathological state when they commit the act, and that they are predisposed to it by the pathological state of their sensibility or of their psyche". According to Durkheim, "the force which determines the suicide is not psychological but social"[17]. In support of his thesis, he remarks that the proportion of neurotic or insane persons among Jews is particularly high, while the frequency of suicide in these populations is specially low. Similarly, he tries to show that there is no correlation between hereditary tendencies and the suicide rate. The percentage of suicides increases with age. This, according to Durkheim, is hardly compatible with the hypothesis that the efficient cause of suicide is transmitted by heredity[18].

Having dismissed explanations of a psychological nature, he proceeds to analyse the types of suicide cases. He takes into account the three types of suicide : *egoist suicide, altruist suicide and anomic suicide*.

Men and women commit suicide more often than others when they are egoists, when they are not properly integrated into a social group and when they think primarily of themselves. Such individuals experience infinite desires which are not tempered or limited by their obligations to the group to which they happen to belong. The gap between expectations and fulfilment produces a sense of frustration which forces them to commit suicide.

While egoistic suicide takes place as a result of excess of individualism, altruistic suicide takes place when an individual completely effaces himself through merger in the group. Durkheim gives two types of examples of altruistic suicide. Sometimes an individual chooses death in conformity with social imperatives. This is illustrated by the case of a Hindu widow (the practice of sati) who agrees to take her place on the pyre on which the body of her dead husband is to be burned.Another example is that of the captain of a ship who chooses to go down with the sinking ship. In both cases, the instinct of self-preservation is stiffled by the values or social imperatives internalised by the concerned individuals.

The third type of suicide, vis., anomic suicide is characterised "by a state of irritation or disgust, irritation resulting from the many occasions of disappointment afforded by modern existence", and disgust resulting from a disproportionate gap between aspirations and satisfactions.

Having analysed the three types of suicide, Durkheim concludes that "suicide is an individual phenomenon whose causes are essentially social",

His fourth great book, *The Elementary Forms of Religious Life*, is concerned with the essential characteristics of religious order at the dawn of human history. He undertook this study "not out of curiosity about what might have happened thousands of years ago, but in order to rediscover in the simplest societies the essential secret of all human societies — in order to understand what the reform of modern societies requires in the light of primitive experience". In this book Durkheim tried to derive a general sociologial theory of religion from what he believed to be its simplest form : totemism. He justified this approach on the ground that religion does not require communion with a God. Religion involves, on the contrary, "a classification of all things known to men as either *sacred or profane*.The theme has been discussed at length in the chapter on religion.

While making an assessment of Durkheim's contribution to sociological thinking, we are to note, in the first place, his conscious attempt to keep sociology separate and distinct from other social sciences. He was aware of the need for devising a distinct method for pursuing sociological studies, and emphasised the value of comparative approach to the study of society. His analysis of division of labour, suicide, education and religion paved the way for subsequent investigation and study of various social problems.

The second point to be noted in this connection is that Durkheim belonged to what Pitirim Sorokin described as Bio-sociological or Sociologistic School. Those who belong to this school "interpret social and psychical phenomena as a derivative of various forms of interaction"[19]. They are right in their contention that "the factor of social interaction is to be taken into consideration in an explanation of the growth of the mind and the psychology of human beings"[20]. They are also right in their attempt "to establish the correlation between social processes of interaction and psychological processes, and in insisting on the social origin of language, science, concepts, logical categories, morals and religion and other social values"[21]. As Sorokin rightly points out, if such an approach were suggested as one among many possible approaches, there would have been no valid reason for opposing it. But the sociologistic school pretends to be exclusive and declares all other approaches to be wrong. This line of thinking is, therefore, one-sided, and hence unacceptable. Their main criticism against Durkheim stems from this one-sided approach.

Thirdly, in terms of the interpretation of the sociologistic theory, we should reasonably expect that the 'mentality' of species living in societies and continually interacting would be higher than that of animals who are not living in societies. "Facts do not corroborate this expectation. L. Morgan is right in declaring that we do not have any reason for saying that the non-social wasps are inferior psychologically to the social wasps, or that a non-social tiger is inferior to the social jackals, or that many non-social birds are more stupid than social birds". These examples indicate that "the factor of interaction is not sufficient to explain the miracle of the origin and growth of mind"[22].

Despite these weaknesses of his approach, the real contributions of Durkheim consist not so much in his general statements "as in his factual studies and in the series of correlations which he tried to establish to support his fundamental principles"[23]. Sorokin discusses the eminence of Durkheim as a sociologist in these words: "He fortunately combined the ability of broad, logical, and philosophical thought with the scrupulous and careful method of a scientist. Every hypothesis formed by him is formulated on the basis of patient study of the corresponding facts. After the formulation he carefully tries to verify it again through an inductive study of the factual data. This has made his works quite superior to the purely speculative philosophizing in social sciences, as well as to the narrow, matter-of-fact descriptions of a definite phenomenon. Hence the eminence of Durkheim"[24].

## 4. MAX WEBER (1864—1920)

During the last quarter of the nineteenth century, intellectual discussion in Germany was dominated by historical studies. Historical researches of an eminently high quality were carried out. Almost all subjects were examined from historical angle. For example, economic studies were made from historical perspective. Karl Marx was the foremost among those who studied economic issues from this perspective. As a matter of fact, the social and economic thinking of the period was deeply influenced by Marxian philosophy. No one could escape this influence, not even Max Weber. But Weber could not accept in toto Marxian analysis of contemporary European society. He, therefore, attempted a new approach and adopted a new angle to interpret contemporary European society. One of the critics of Max Weber, Albert Salomon, very aptly observed: "Max Weber became a sociologist in a long and intense dialogue with the ghost of Karl Marx". His differences with Marx provoked him to explore and analyse the origin and growth of capitalism in Western Europe. In the course of this exploration, Weber initiated studies on various aspects of society. Sociology has been considerably enriched by these studies. We noted in preceding chapters Weber's critical views on the Marxian analysis of social stratification, his delineation of status groups, his analysis of bureaucratic organisation, his typology of social action and his thesis on protestant ethics and the growth of capitalism. His views on these subjects are of abiding value and interest to sociologists even today. In this section we propose to take up those subjects of his study which were not covered in earlier chapters. Of these two are important : One is his concept of the Ideal-Type and the other is his views on rationality which, according to him, is the distinguishing mark of present-day industrial society.

## Ideal Type

In the last quarter of the nineteenth century philosophical discussion in Germany was dominated by the question of the place of science in human studies. According to the then prevailing idealist philosophy, there was no possibility of the application of scientific method to cultural subjects, on the ground that the facts of human life were unique. The general categories which science utilises were, therefore, inappropriate in so far as cultural subjects or human studies were concerned. The core of this argument was that social phenomena are unique and do not, therefore, allow generalisation.

Weber did not agree with this view. He claimed that scientific categories could be used in the field of human studies or cultural subjects. But he hastened to add that they must be used with care. Weber's belief that scientific method was relevant to social studies encouraged him to offer a set of operational definitions and to construct concepts which could be used. He classified and described types of social pehnomena. He argued that if the types were rigorously defined and the elements of each type were consistent with each other, then it should be possible to compare existing cases to the type. He called the latter an *ideal-type*. "An ideal-type is formed by the one-sided *accentuation* of one or more points of view and by the synthesis of a great many diffuse, discrete, more or less present and occasionally absent *concrete individual* phenomena, which are arranged according to those one-sidedly emphasised viewpoints into a unified *analytical construct*. In its conceptual purity, this mental construct cannot be found empirically anywhere in reality. It is a utopia"[25].

Max Weber cautions that the ideal-type is to be constructed and used with care. To begin with, the ideal-type is not a hypothesis, nor an 'average', nor a faithful description of reality. Nor is it a model of what 'ought to be'. It is rather an accentuation of what the researcher considered to be the essential characteristics and tendencies of the phenomenon in question.

The possible pitfalls that accompany the use of this device are (i) that one might confuse the 'construct' with 'actual reality'; (ii) that one might regard the 'construct' as a procrustean bed into which to force the data; (iii) that one might hypostasize the ideas so that they may assume the character of real forces. If these dangers are averted, the ideal-type can become an extremely useful instrument with which to confront reality[26].

His classification of four types of social action is an example of ideal-type construct. Weber did not regard human beings as mechanically responding in set ways to stimuli. On the contrary, they endeavoured in their behaviour to conform to some ideal conception of action. In other words, Weber conceived of action as being normatively oriented. Thus, a man performing quite simple social tasks like buying a commodity in a shop or playing a game with a child has some standard by which he measures his behaviour. There is, therefore, an ideal-type of shopping or playing with children. Actual instances approximate to it. It may not be ideal in the sense of being the best conceivable way, but at least the elements are selected in terms of the ends and values of the actors. As he put it, the ideal-type describes "objectively possible action"[27].

Weber believed that the most fruitful use of the ideal-type 'constructs' was exemplified in the work of Marx. He regarded Marx's method of abstraction, particularly his *two-class model* (the bourgeoisie and the proletariat), as one that had yielded important insights into the nature of the modern economic system. Just as Marx had attached great importance to the locus of control over the material means of production, so also Weber, in his analysis of political, military and scientific institutions, centred his attention on the locus of control over the means of administration, violence and research. Marx observed the increasing concentration of the means of production and the consequent separation of the worker from those means, so that a clear dichotomy emerged between those who owned and controlled the means of production and those who did not. Weber used it as an ideal-type and called attention to the increasing concentration of the means of administration, means of violence, means of research, etc. In this way, Weber argued that the tendency which Marx dramatised as a special case in the sphere of production could be seen as part of a much more general process[28].

Max Weber used the ideal-type concept in order to explain the impact of religion on economic activities. While analysing the growth and development of capitalism in Western Europe under the influence of Protestantism, he considered, for purposes of his analysis, one dominant aspect (according to his perception) of both Capitalism and Protestantism and ignored all other aspects. Thus, he considered 'rationality' to be the essence of capitalism and 'work ethics' to be the most important teaching of Protestantism. Taking help of this ideal-type 'construct', he established with reference to case studies that Protestantism with its accent on 'work ethics' encouraged rational economic activity culminating in the growth of capitalism in Western Europe. He analysed the religions of India and China and with the help of his ideal-type tried to explain as to why rational capitalism, as he defined it, did not emerge in India and China because religions of these countries did not emphasise 'work ethics' to the same extent and in the same manner as did Protestantism.

It will be interesting to relate briefly his anlysis of the religions of China and India vis-a-vis development of rational capitalistic system on the lines of Western Europe. Weber noted that rationality was prominent in many aspects of Indian cultural life ; the rational number system, arithmetic, algebra, rational science, and, in general, a rational consistency in many spheres, together with a high degree of tolerance toward philosophical in many spheres, together with a high degree of tolerance toward philosophical and religious doctrines. The prevailing judicial forms appeared compatible with capitalist development. There existed an autonomous stratum of merchants. Handicrafts as well as occupational specialization were developed. Finally, the high degree of acquisitiveness and high evaluation of wealth were a notable aspect of Indian social life. Yet, Weber points out, modern capitalism did not develop indigenously before or during the English rule. By way of explanation, Weber refers to the absence of Protestant ethic in Indian religion. Despite the rational, scientific elements in the East, and the existence of economic strata and forms seemingly conducive to the emergence of a modern rational economy, the 'East remained an enchanted garden." This meant that all aspects and institutions of Oriental Civilization were permeated and even dominated by the magical mentality which became a brake on economic developments in particular and on rationalization of the culture as a whole. For Weber, one criterion of rationalisation of religion is the degree to which it has rid itself of magic[29].

It is also to be noted that Weber's studies of the world religions embrace much more than religious phenomena and institutions. He takes the entire social structure of the society in question into his purview. In the case of India, the caste system was of fundamental importance.

Speaking of China, Weber observes that the Chinese city dweller never became a citizen in the Western sense. He retained his relations to the native place of his sib, its ancestral land and temple. Hence, all ritually and personally important relations with the native village were maintained. Thus, "the fetters of the sib were never shattered."This was the opposite of the West where Christianity, according to Weber, played an important role, at least initially, in developing an ethic which transcended kinship obligations[30].

### Rationality in Law and Administration

According to Max Weber, the quality, which marks off Western civilisation from other civilisations, is its rational quality. It is expressed in its economic system—the capitalist system governed by rational economic considerations. The peculiarly rational character of modern Western civilisation is also seen in its type of law and administration, particularly when we contrast the type of administrative organisation associated with it to other types, such as that of feudal England and France.

In modern Western Civilisation, he argued, there is always a conception of authority, because in a corporate group some individual member or members give orders and others obey. Moreover, those who give the order expect to be obeyed. The reason for this is that both those who give orders and those who obey commands share certain beliefs about the rightness of the process. In other words, authority is held to be legitimate. The bases of this legitimacy may, however, differ from one instance to another. He said that there are three ideal-types of authority which derive legitimacy from three distinct sources:

(i) **Rational legitimacy** reflects belief in the legality of patterns of normative rules and the right of those people designated by the rules to exercise authority to command.

(ii) **Traditional legitimacy** depends on belief in the sanctity of immemorial traditions and the right of those established on the strength of tradition in positions of authority to exercise it.

(iii) **Charismatic legitimacy** depends on the devotion of followers to an individual who, according to their perception, is endowed by exceptional sanctity, heroism or other personal qualities.

Weber points out that in the first case obedience is owed to the legally established impersonal order whereas in the second and third cases it is owed to a person. In this typology, Weber's emphasis is on rational legitimacy. The corresponding type of authority which emerges from this typology is as follows : rational-legal authority, traditional authority and charismatic authority.

Weber, however, points out that none of these ideal-types are to be found in a pure form in any historical instance. But any case can be seen to approximate to any of these types[31].

In the second part of his book, *Wirtschaft und Gesellschaft* (Economy and Society), Weber engages in a long disquisition on law. His main purpose is to trace, in various civilisations over the centuries of history, the broad changes in the character of legal systems, picking out specially the relationships between legal and economic system, and showing how there has been a progressive development in the rationality of law. (Max Weber's use of the term *law* is a precise one: "An order will be called law when conformity with it is upheld by the probability that deviant action will be met by physical or psychic sanctions aimed at compelling conformity or at punishing disobedience, and applied by a group of men especially empowered to carry out this function." The Theory of Social and Economic Organisation, 1947).

When he speaks of rationality, Weber refers to two things: *formal rationality and substantive* rationality.

When men are engaged in legislating, or in discovering what the law is, their activities are *substantively rational*, provided they consciously follow a set of principles. Such principles may be vastly different in different systems. Thus, there may be religious principles (laws based on shariat or religious scriptures in Islamic countries), or ethical ones (laws based on principles of equity, justice and fair play), or political principles (in USSR "law is an instrument of politics", according to Andrei Vyshinski, which means that law is a means for supporting the Communist ideology"[32].

In contrast to this, there is irrationality in law which we find in Moslem kadi justice. Here the Kadi, traditionally sitting in the market place, adjudicates on an *ad hoc* basis, freely considering the merits of each case as he sees them[33].

*Formal rationality*, as distinct from substantive rationality, refers to the processes of legislating and law discerning. In this case what is held to be important is the set of formal rules governing procedures.[34]

Formal rationality itself may be of two kinds. In one case, law is *extrinsically* formal. This is so when a contract is held to have been validly entered into on the ground that it was written down and signed or sealed or concluded in some prescribed manner[35].

The other case is where law is *logically* formal. This is so when the rules employed in drawing up the law are themselves made up of abstract concepts of a legal nature and are employed systematically. This stands in contrast to procedures based on oracles or some other similarly irrational means[36].

In this analysis of law, Weber stresses the fact that formally rational law is a relatively new phenomenon in the history of the world, and that its advent coincided largely with the rise of modern capitalism. Like modern capitalism, formally rational law is a product of modern Western civilization. What is the link between the two—that is, between capitalism and formally rational law—if there be a link at all ? Weber had no doubt that there was a connection and he found it in the development of what he called bureaucratic administration[37].

What were the main contributions of Max Weber to the development of sociological thinking ? The general consensus among sociologists is that Weber made a lasting contribution to sociology. He attempted an exploration of the origin and growth of capitalism in the Western societies. While doing so, he initiated studies on various aspects of society from his distinctive angle. His original thinking on bureaucracy, religion, law, authority, social stratification and economic sociology enriched the discipline considerably. He discerned correctly the subtle change taking place in the nature of stratification in terms of growth of status groups in industrial societies. His views on work ethics are very helpful in understanding the nature of problems connected with economic development of under-developed countries. His ideal-type concept laid the basis for the present use of sociological models. "He introduced rigour into sociological analysis as well as providing it with such breadth of vision that it must remain an inspiration to social scientists.... Above all, he was intellectually bold, politically committed and thoroughly professional in his outlook and habits. These are qualities indispensable to the growth of sociological studies"[38].

## 5. A.R. RADCLIFFE-BROWN (1881—1955)

Alfred Reginald Radcliffe-Brown was one of the most eminent anthropologists of the first half of the twentieth century. He helped to develop and establish modern 'social' anthropology as a generalising, theoretical discipline. The most notable of his many important contributions was his application to primitive societies of some of the ideas of systems theory, which led to a revolution in the analysis and interpretation of social relations.

Radcliffe-Brown formed his theoretical approach as early as 1908 when, as a post-graduate student, he stated the requirements of a science of human society. He considered them to be three-fold : (i) to treat social phenomena as natural facts and thus subject to discoverable necessary conditions and laws; (ii) to adhere to the methodology of the natural sciences; (iii) to entertain only generalisations that can be tested and verified. He never departed from these rules, although his conceptual thought developed steadily.

Instead of explaining social phenomena in historical or psychological terms, which he believed to be impossible, Radcliffe-Brown explained them as persistent systems of adaptation, coaptation, and integration. His main working hypothesis was that the life of a society can be conceived of as a dynamic fiduciary system of inter-dependent elements, functionally consistent with one another. He had used the notion of "social structure" as early as 1914, though not in a well-defined sense, as almost a doublet of 'organisation'. But gradually his ideas of 'social structure' underwent changes. In his final formulation, structure refers to an arrangement of persons and organisation, to an arrangement of activities. At the same time, he substituted the concept of 'social system' for that of 'culture'. All these changes were connected.

Radcliffe-Brown's social anthropology is best described by separating two main elements : a general theory and a central theory.

The general theory produced three connected sets of questions. The first set deals with *static or morphological* problems : What kinds of societies are there ? What are their similarities and differences ? How are they to be classified and compared ? The second set deals with *dynamic* problems :How do societies function ? How do they persist ? The third deals with *developmental* problems : How do societies change their types ? How do new types come into existence ? What general laws relate to the changes ? The general theory dealing with these problems was borrowed from biology and bore the stamp of Spencer in its emphasis on three aspects of adaptation : ecological adaptation to the physical environment; social adaptation, i.e., the institutional arrangements by which social order is maintained; and the socialisation or 'cultural adaptation' of persons.

The central theory dealt with the determinants of social relations of all kinds. Radcliffe-Brown phrased it in terms of the coaptation or fitting together or harmonisation of individual interests or values that makes possible "relations of association", i.e., socially established norms or patterns of behaviour, and 'social values'.

The two theories—the general theory and the central theory—are based on the idea that the life of a society can be conceived and studied as a system of relations of association and that a particular social structure is an arrangement of relations in which the interests or values of different individuals and groups are coapted within fiduciary 'social values' expressed as institutional norms.

The idea of coaptation is fundamental to Radcliffe-Brown's whole outlook. But the logical and conceptual implications of the idea are not fully worked out, nor are the static and dynamic aspects of the coaptative process. What he did write is probably best viewed as only a sketch for a 'pure' theory dealing with all classes of relations of association and all classes of functioning systems or social structures.

While Radcliffe-Brown did not regard the study of social structure as the whole of anthropology, he did consider it to be its most important branch. But he asserted that "the study of social structure leads immediately to the study of interests or values as the determinant of social relations", and that a "social system can be conceived and studied as a system of values"[39].

Important works by Radcliffe-Brown

1. The Andaman Islanders (First publication, 1922)
2. The Social Organisation of Australian Tribes (First publication, 1931)

## 6. BRONISLAW KASPAR MALINOWSKI (1884—1942)

B.K. Malinowski was a Polish-born social anthropologist whose professional training and career, beginning in 1910, were based in England. Through his scientific activities, specially his methodological innovations, he was a major contributor to the transformation of nineteenth century speculative anthropology into a modern science of man. As a field worker, a scholar, a theorist, and, above all, a brilliant and controversial teacher and lecturer, he played a decisive part in the formation of the contemporary British school of social anthropology. He viewed anthropology as a field-oriented science in which theory and the search for general laws must be based on intensive empirical research involving systematic observation and detailed analyses of actual behaviour in living, on-going societies. His principal field-work was carried out among the Papuo-Melanesian people of the Trobriand Islands, located off the coast of New Guinea. Malinowski regarded residence among the people under study, competent use of the native language, observation of the small events of daily life as well as the large events affecting the community, sensitivity to conflict and shades of opinion, and a consideration of each aspect within the context of the whole culture as indispensable conditions to ethnographic work and, indirectly, to the sound development of theory.

Malinowski's primary scientific interest was in the study of culture as a universal phenomenon. At the same time, he was interested in the development of a methodological framework that would permit the systematic study of specific cultures and open the way to systematic cross-cultural comparison. For purposes of research and exposition, he treated each culture as a closed system and all countries as essentially comparable. In other words, he treated the empirical study of a specific culture as a contribution to the understanding of the universal phenomenon of culture.

Malinowski presented two axioms which must underlie every scientific theory of culture. First, every culture must satisfy man's biological needs, such as nutrition, procreation, protection against damaging forces of climate, dangerous animals and men. But culture must also provide for occasional relaxation and the regulation of growth. Second, every cultural achievement is an instrumental enhancement of human physiology contributing directly or indirectly to the satisfaction of a bodily need.

Malinowski was also the originator of the functionalist approach to the study of culture. Although the idea of 'function' is a key concept throughout his work, the use of this term was open-ended, exploratory, and subject to continued modification.

Until very recently, theoretical codification of the functional approach had not been developed except by Malinowski. As propounded by Malinowski, the functional theory is applicable to the study of social structure and cultural diversity. The outline of this theory may be stated as follows: The maintenance and the possible extension of a group and its social system as well as the persistence and the possible improvement of the group's culture are defined, at least implicitly, as the group's objectives or goals. Empirical study should reveal the functional requisites of a given system, that is, the conditions under which these objectives can be achieved. It can then be shown that specific parts of the social structure and culture of the group operate as mechanisms that satisfy (or do not satisfy) the functional requisites. The following aspects may be considered in this connection.

First, universal functional needs can be met in different ways, as is evidenced by social and cultural variation. In individual societies, particular procedures from a wide range of cultural possibilities are 'selected'.

Second, the number of such 'choices' is always limited, limited by the biological characteristics of man and by his social and psychic needs. Hence the prevalence of independent and parallel inventions in different societies.

Third, the range of 'choice' for a specific society is further limited by the interrelationship and, in some measure, the interdependence of the choices themselves. For example, modern industrial growth in traditionally agrarian societies no doubt limits, but does not determine, the number and type of possible political and other institutional developments. A major task of functional analysis is to discover the number and type of cultural possibilities under diverse social conditions which exist in different societies, so as to determine the functionalism of the societal organisation. This is the essence of Malinowski's functional theory.

In addition to his study of culture and functionalist approach, reference must also be made to his observations on magic, science and religion. In his handling of science, magic and religion, he accepted essentially the traditional Western conception of a dual reality, viz., the reality of the natural world, grounded in observation and rational procedures that lead to mastery over nature, and supernatural reality, grounded in emotional needs that give rise to faith. For example, Malinowski derived science not from magic but from man's capacity to organise knowledge, as demonstrated by Trobriand technical skills in gardening, ship-building, etc. In contrast, he treated magic, which co-existed with these skills, as an organised response to a sense of limitation and impotence in the face of danger, difficulty and frustration. Again, he differentiated between magic and religion by defining magical systems as essentially pragmatic in their aims and by defining religious systems as self-fulfilling rituals organised, for example, around life's crisis. It is also significant that he differentiated between the individual character of religious experience and the social character of religious ritual. Particularly illuminating is his discussion of the use of public magic among the Trobriand Islanders as an initiating act in the organisation of stages of work. His book *The Foundations of Faith and Morals* represents an attempt to apply hypotheses based on primitive cultures to the problems of European societies.

**Assessment of Malinowski**

It is exceedingly difficult to assess Malinowski's place in Anthropology. In the subsequent year since his death, much of his theoretical work has been bypassed. Some of his ideas that made him a storm centre in the 1920s have been so fully incorporated into anthropological thinking that his exposition now appears unnecessarily didactic.

The stress on precision and solid empirical evidence in present-day anthropological researches is mainly due to Malinowski's breadth of vision which made this advance possible.

His method of institutional analysis made it possible for him to express, through a model, certain core ideas of his theory, viz., the integrity of each culture; the complex interrelationship of the society, the culture and the individual; the grounding of culture in the human organism (in man's needs and the individual; the grounding of culture in the human organism(in man's needs and capacities and in the individual as the carrier of culture); and the systematic nature of culture as a phenomenon.

Malinowski's theoretical framework is a major contribution. Today no anthropologist is, however, prepared to make the dizzying leap from the particular to the universal that characterised his attempt to create an effective methodology. There are essential intermediate steps. For example, these involve intensive studies of process within and across cultures and over time. We also require fine-grained systematic comparison of intensively studied cultures and cultural process. Today the required tools have been devised and these tools make feasible more delicate and systematic research. Malinowski's search for an adequate methodology was a step toward broadening the base of empirical research. For this, collaboration among all the relevant sciences will be necessary. The study of culture is crucial to, but not in itself sufficient for, the development of a science of man.

Important works by Malinowski :

1. The Dynamics of Culture Change
2. A Scientific Theory of Culture
3. Argonauts of the Western Pacific

4. The Family Among the Australian Aborigines
5. The Sexual Life of Savages in North-Western Melanesia
6. Magic, Science and Religion
7. Crime and Custom in Savage Society
8. Myth in Primitive Psychology
9. The Foundation of Faith and Morals.

## 7. TALLCOTT PARSONS (1920—1979)

In contrast to a fascination with the techniques of sociological inquiry, applied to small-scale, and sometimes trivial, problems, there developed during the 1940s and 1950s a pre-occupation with the construction of elaborate conceptual schemes. This is exemplified most fully in the work of Talcott Parsons and his followers.

In his first book, *The Structure of Social Action,* Parsons expresses the view that action is the basic unit which sociologists have to observe and consider. He attempts to postulate a general theory of action. In his view, such a theory would provide a solution to "the Hobbesian problem of social order by locating the springs and orientations of action in reference to the *normative* aspects of social life".

The Theory of action, as developed by Parsons, has been discussed in detail in the Second Chapter (pages 22-25). It was noted in the course of discussion that pattern-variable scheme is one of the main innovations of Talcott Parsons.

Max Weber, who discerned for the first time the growing importance of rationalisation in the modern era, feared that rationalisation could pervade the entire modern social fabric and threaten all spontaneous human relations with destruction. Parsons, however, argued that rationality as a principle had limits just as kinship values have. He contended that kinship and personal relations will be maintained, cherished and protected in the private sphere.

We may mention two main points about this approach which remains central to Parsons' subsequent development of his theory. In the first place, despite their many differences, it is argued that all stable societies have certain basic values in common, indicated by the pattern-variables. In exterme contrast to cultural relativism, Parsons believed in the cultural unity of man, and the pattern-variables give a starting point for identifying important universals. Second, the major differences between cultures are matters of degree, to be seen in the priorities and nuances given to the same basic concerns. While differences of degree are by no means unimportant, he argued that doctrines of unique cultural spirits mislead by only identifying the dominant values and beliefs of a culture, ignoring its lower priority values and over-particularising their meanings.

Apart from the theory of social action, Parsons contributed substantially to the structural—functional school of sociology. Mention may be made, in particular, to his four-function paradigm. These ideas of Parsons have been elaborately discussed earlier in the chapter on social system. Besides, many other themes have also been discussed in earlier chapters from a Parsonian perspective.

Some criticisms have been levelled against the sociological theories of Talcott Parsons. To begin with, it is argued that in his sociological theories, the element of physical coercion in social relationships is almost entirely neglected. He emphasises an 'equilibrium model' of society whereas a 'conflict model' would be more realistic. Secondly, it is pointed out that "Parsons has been largely concerned with elucidating the conceptual structure in the thought of the classical sociologists, and with elaborating new concepts within the framework of his notion of 'social action'. He has not, however, developed any comprehensive explanatory theory and his work has not given rise to a school of sociology characterised by new kinds of explanation of social events"[40].

## 8. ROBERT K. MERTON (1910— )

Robert K. Merton, the American Sociologist, with his customary perspicacity, has developed the theories of the middle range. By way of illustrating his concept, he referred to certain social phenomena the significance of which was not brought out or emphasised in earlier theories.

Merton defines 'theories of the middle range' as "theories that lie between the minor but necessary working hypotheses that evolve in abundance during day-to-day research and the all-inclusive systematic efforts to develop a unified theory that will explain all the observed uniformities of social behaviour, social organisation and social change"[41]. By way of elaboration of his thesis, he further observes : "Middle-range theory is principally used in sociology to guide empirical inquiry. It is intermediate to general theories of social systems which are too remote from particular classes of social behaviour, organisation and change to account for what is observed and to those detailed orderly descriptions of particulars that are not generalised at all. Middle-range theory involves abstractions, of course, but they are close enough to observed data to be incorporated in propositions that permit empirical testing. Middle-range theories deal with delimited aspects of social phenomena as is indicated by their labels"[42]. He speaks of, by way of illustration, a theory of reference groups and relative deprivation, a theory of role-conflict, etc.

The seminal ideas in such theories are characteristically simple. The theory of reference groups and relative deprivation starts with the simple idea that people take the standards of significant others as a basis for self-appraisal and evaluation. Some of the inferences drawn from this simple idea are not consistent with common sense expectations based upon an unexamined set of 'self-evident' assumptions. For example, common sense suggests that a family or a group would suffer from a sense of deprivation to the extent of the loss sustained by it in a mass disaster. This is based on an unexamined assumption that the magnitude of objective loss is related directly and lineally to the subjective appraisal of the loss. But the theory of relative deprivation leads to an altogether different conclusion. According to this theory, self-appraisal is not confined to one's own experience only. On the contrary, it depends upon people's comparison of their own situation with that of other people perceived as being comparable to themselves. The theory, therefore, suggests that a group or a family may actually suffer heavy losses. But it will *feel* less deprived if those, who are considered to be comparable, suffer more severe losses. It is clear therefore, that this theory has not been logically derived from a single all-embracing theory of social systems. Similar is the case with the theory of reference group or the theory of role-set. These theories start with very simple observable social phenomena and draw inferences which shed light on the nature of the phenomena.

Merton's concepts of manifest and latent functions, of anomie as related to social structure and of role-set have been discussed in earlier chapters.

## NOTES

1. Adapted with suitable modifications from the chapter on 'The positivist legacy and geography' in Derek Gregary's book *Ideology, Science and Geography.*
2. Article on Karl Marx, by Maxmilien Rubel in The International Encyclopaedia of Social Sciences, Volumes 9 and 10, page 35.
3. Marx in Preface to a Contribution to the Critique of Political Economy.
4. Adapted from an article on Materialism by Sidney Hook, *Encyclopaedia of the Social Sciences,* Vol.X, paged 209-220
5. German Ideology. Marx-Engles Gesamtausgabe Sec.I. Vol.5 pages 59-60. Quoted by Bottomore and Rubel in their book on *Karl Marx,* page 80
6. International Encyclopaedia of Social Sciences, Volumes 9 and 10. *Article on Marxist Sociology* by T. B. Bottomore, page 51
7. Raymond Aron, *Main Currents in Sociological Thought,* Vol.I, Pelican Edition, page 181.
8. *ibid,* page 182
9. *ibid,* page 182
10. International Encyclopaedia of Social Sciences, volumes 9 and 10, page 51
11. *ibid,* page 37
12. *G. Duncan Mitchell,* A Hundred years of sociology, page 81
13. *ibid,* page 81
14. Irving M. Zeitlin, *Ideology and the development of Sociological Theory,* page 268
15. *ibid,* page 277
16. Raymond Aron, Main Currents in Sociological Thought, Volume 2, Pelican Edition, pages 35-36
17. *ibid,* page 37
18. *ibid,* page 37
19. Pitirim Sorokin, Contemporary Sociological Theories, page 434
20. *ibid, page 452*
21. *ibid, page 452*
22. *ibid, page 455*
23. *ibid, page 467*
24. *ibid, page 464*
25. Mitchell, *A Hundred Years of Sociology,* page 89
26. Zeitlin, Op. cit., page 120
27. Mitchell, Op. cit., page 88
28. Zeitlin, Op. cit., page 121
29. *ibid,* pages 144-145
30. *ibid,* pages 138-144
31. Mitchell, Op. cit., pages 91-93
32. *ibid,* page 93
33. *ibid,* page 93
34. *ibid,* page 93
35. *ibid,* page 93
36. *ibid,* page 93
37. *ibid,* page 93
38. *ibid,* page 100-101
39. Adapted from an article by W.E.H.Stanner in *International Encyclopaedia of the Social Sciences,* Volumes 13 and 14
40. Bottomore, *Sociology,* pages 44-45
41. R.K. Metron, Social Theory and Social Structure, 1968 Enlarged Edition, page 39
42. *ibid,* pages 39-40










